A Classless Society

N W. TURNER is an acclaimed writer on post-war Britain. He is the
r of *Crisis? What Crisis? Britain in the 1970s* and *Rejoice! Rejoice! Britain in the*
both published by Aurum. His other books include *The Biba Experience*,
Rock: Dandies in the Underworld, *Halfway to Paradise: The Birth of British Rock* and
Nation: The Man Who Invented the Daleks. www.alwynwturner.com

SE FOR ALWYN W. TURNER

ssless Society: Britain in the 1990s

'Th eld of instant history now attracts some of this country's liveliest and
mos ntelligent writers ... Alwyn W. Turner ranks high among them ...
H. earch is phenomenal. There seems to be no haystack through which
he h. not rummaged in search of every needle ... Turner has a talent for
zoon ig in and out from the general to the particular and back again. This
mea he is able at one and the same time to see both the wood and the
trees *A Year In Provence*, Squidgygate, the Chippendales, Cool Britannia,
Black Wednesday, Swampy, Robert Maxwell, "Something of the Night";
Alw W. Turner conjures them all up, as vivid and eerie as a dream'
Crai Brown, *Mail on Sunday* 'Book of the Week'

'Lik iis previous histories of the seventies and eighties, *A Classless Society* is
an e traordinarily comprehensive work. Turner writes brilliantly, creating
a cc pelling narrative of the decade, weaving contrasting elements
tog her with a natural storyteller's aplomb'
Irv e Welsh, author of *Trainspotting* and *Skagboys*, *Daily Telegraph*

'S rb. I was a journalist throughout the 1990s, but did not notice a tenth
or what Turner has seen or write about it half as well'
Nick Cohen, author of *What's Left?*

'John Major may have struggled to create a country at ease with itself,
but Alwyn Turner's sedu   reportage
and cultura'   aders'
David Kyna

'Isn't it too soon for a history of the nineties – their recentness carrying an inherent danger of not seeing the wood for the trees? Turner's solution is to anchor his narrative firmly in the era's politics, splitting the decade into the Major and Blair years – resulting in a very credible first draft'
Andrew Neather, *London Evening Standard*

'It was refreshing to dip into *A Classless Society*, the third volume of Alwyn Turner's history of Britain since the 1970s ... I enjoyed it a great deal'
Toby Young, *Spectator*

'He is amusing, perceptive and reminds the reader of the TV programmes and musical artists they have loved and then forgotten'
David Aaronovitch, *The Times* 'Critics Choice'

'Excellent ... this trilogy is about the most authoritative account of the late 20th century as you are likely to get'
Choice Magazine

'I was captivated, almost smothered, by the incessant flow of facts, opinion and conclusion. Turner, as he proved in the other two books, can sew events together seamlessly ... This is a wonderful panorama of the 1990s, as fluid as a mountain stream with encyclopaedic ripples, a strict adherence to the facts, and all 600 pages as readable as a letter from your mother'
Illtyd Harrington, *Camden New Journal*

Crisis? What Crisis? Britain in the 1970s

'Turner has certainly hit upon a rich and fascinating subject, and his intertwining of political and cultural history is brilliantly done ...
This is a masterful work of social history and cultural commentary, told with much wit. It almost makes you feel as if you were there'
Roger Lewis, *Mail on Sunday*

'Turner appears to have spent much of the decade watching television, and his knowledge of old soap operas, sitcoms and TV dramas is deployed to great effect throughout this vivid, brilliantly researched chronicle ...
Turner may be an anorak, but he is an acutely intelligent anorak'
Francis Wheen, *New Statesman*

'An ambitious, entertaining alternative history of the 1970s which judges the decade not just by its political turbulence but by the leg-up it gave popular culture'
Time Out

'Entertaining and splendidly researched ... He has delved into episodes of soap operas and half-forgotten novels to produce an account that displays wit, colour and detail'
Brian Groom, *Financial Times*

'Fascinating ... an affectionate but unflinching portrait of the era'
Nicholas Foulkes, *Independent on Sunday*

Rejoice! Rejoice! Britain in the 1980s

'Put[s] into cold perspective what at the time we were too befuddled with emotion to understand ... Turner has produced a masterly mix of shrewd analysis, historical detail and telling quotes ... Indispensable'
James Delingpole, *Mail on Sunday*

'This kaleidoscopic history ... provides a vivid and enjoyable guide to these turbulent years. Ranging broadly across popular culture as well as high politics ... Turner brings the period alive and offers insights into both sides of a polarised nation'
BBC History Magazine, 'Pick of the Month'

'One of the pleasures of Alwyn Turner's breathless romp through the 1980s is that it overflows with unusual juxtapositions and surprising insights ... The tone is that of a wildly enthusiastic guide leading us on a breakneck tour through politics, sport and culture'
Dominic Sandbrook, *Sunday Times*

'Dazzling ... Turner's account of the 1980s is as wide-ranging as that fractured, multi-faceted decade demands ... deft at picking out devilish details and damning quotes from history that is less recent than you think'
Victoria Segal, *MOJO*

A CLASSLESS
SOCIETY
BRITAIN IN
THE 1990S

Alwyn W. Turner

Aurum
Press

First published in Great Britain
2013 by Aurum Press Ltd
74–77 White Lion Street
Islington
London N1 9PF
www.aurumpress.co.uk

This paperback edition first published in 2014 by Aurum Press Ltd

A catalogue record for this book is available from the British Library.

ISBN 978 1 78131 237 7

10 9 8 7 6 5 4 3 2 1
2018 2017 2016 2015 2014

Typeset in Spectrum MT by SX Composing DTP, Rayleigh, Essex
Printed by CPI Group (UK) Ltd, Croydon, CR0 4YY

These should be the best days of my life.
The Wonder Stuff, 'The Size of a Cow' (1991)

GUS: After all, this is the caring nineties.
DAVE: Hang on, this is 1991. So who decided the nineties
would be caring?
HENRY: Lots of heartless shits who work in advertising.
Andy Hamilton & Guy Jenkin, *Drop the Dead Donkey* (1991)

ANTHONY: If you and your New Labour Party sound any more
like the Tories, they'll sue you for plagiarism.
Peter Flannery, *Our Friends in the North* (1996)

Contents

Foreword

When I first began working on *Crisis? What Crisis? Britain in the 1970s* it was the autumn of 2005. Tony Blair had recently won his third election victory, the economy had been growing for thirteen consecutive years, and England had just been beaten 1–0 by Northern Ireland in a World Cup qualifying match. Now, as I come towards the end of *A Classless Society*, the third – and last – book in this series, Britain has its first coalition government since the Second World War, the talk is of a triple-dip recession, and England have been held to a 1–1 draw by the mighty Macedonia. It would be hard to see all these things as steps forward.

This was never intended as a trilogy. It started as an attempt to reclaim the memory of the 1970s, the decade in which I spent most of my teenage years and which was not then as well chronicled as it has been since. The project has been extended, into *Rejoice! Rejoice! Britain in the 1980s* and then into the present volume, because the story refused to reach a satisfactory conclusion. The crises that racked this country during the 1970s remained unresolved. By the time some episodes had been wrapped up – with the defeat of the trade union movement in 1984, for example – others were already under way.

To some extent, of course, this is simply because the division of history by dates is a necessarily arbitrary affair. Decades and centuries are artificial, crude concepts that seldom fit the objective facts. They do, however, have an impact on the subjective experience of time, the turning of the years affecting how people see the evolution of their societies. And the current book approaches its conclusion with the biggest of all such markers: the end of the second Christian millennium. Except that even that isn't quite the right place to stop. It was not until the re-election of the Labour Party in 2001, and the second decisive defeat of the Conservatives, that things seem to have been settled in Britain.

And there is, I think, a settlement to be recorded. The social upheavals of the 1960s, when a cultural revolution began to challenge the legitimacy of the established order, were followed by the economic and industrial travails of the 1970s. Between them, they destroyed the post-war consensus, which had always been a typically British muddled compromise of a mixed economy and a shared Christian heritage, held together by the fantasy of growing prosperity. That came to an end in September 1976, with James Callaghan's speech to the Labour Party conference. 'The cosy world we were told would go on for ever, where full employment would be guaranteed by a stroke of the chancellor's pen,' he said; 'that cosy world is gone.'

The story of these three volumes is essentially the tale of the building of a new consensus. It's not as cosy. A sizeable minority of the population has been effectively excluded from mainstream society, historically terrifying levels of unemployment – however the figures are disguised – have become entrenched, and the concept of a job for life has long since vanished. On the other hand, sizeable minorities who were previously excluded are now welcomed. The economic fantasy remains, this time built on a massive increase in personal debt.

The new consensus may not be sustainable. All things change, and this may not last as long as the previous settlement – at the time of writing, it is still unclear what impact the financial crisis that began in 2008 will have. But it is at least the end of a cycle that began with the right-wing backlash against the 1960s and culminated with the victory of liberalism, in all its economic, social and cultural forms.

Alwyn W. Turner
May 2013

Intro
Nineties
'From despair to where'

Margaret Thatcher cast a long shadow. Her enforced departure from office in November 1990, deposed as prime minister by her own colleagues in the Parliamentary Conservative Party, was the biggest political earthquake that Westminster had experienced since the defeat of Winston Churchill in the election of 1945. The key difference, of course, was that Churchill had been removed by the will of the people in a vote that had been delayed due to hostilities; ten years and a world war had passed since the last time the British electorate had been consulted about the future of the nation. Thatcher's exit, on the other hand, came after a hat-trick of election victories, and was brought about by the actions of the 152 Tory MPs who cast their vote against her in a leadership challenge.

The consequences of that contest were to colour Conservative politics well into the next century, many in the party believing that there was still unfinished business, that the Thatcherite revolution had yet to be completed. More widely, though, the new decade was to find it hard to escape the influence and impact of her political philosophy. Even in her heyday, she had never carried the whole country with her, but so powerful and all-pervasive was her presence that she had become the dominant symbol of Britain, whether one supported or opposed her.

In particular she bequeathed the culture a single phrase that echoed through the 1990s. 'There's no such thing as society,' quoted a character in an episode of the television drama *Our Friends in the North*. 'Remember that?' Much of what was to come in the political and cultural developments of the following years was an attempt to overturn that perception, to insist that there was indeed such a thing as society.

The use of the line in *Our Friends in the North* was slightly anachronistic, since the episode in question was set in 1987, the year that Thatcher actually made the comment in an interview with the magazine *Woman's Own*, but the fact that it was still being cited in a television show screened nearly ten years on was tribute to its resonance. As normal with such quotes, it gained something from being seen in its original context. 'There is no such thing as society,' Thatcher had said, in a passage about how looking after one's own was not the same as greed, and she went on to add: 'There is a living tapestry of men and women and people and the beauty of that tapestry and the quality of our lives will depend upon how much each of us is prepared to take responsibility for ourselves and each of us is prepared to turn around and help by our own efforts those who are unfortunate.'

That explanation of her moral faith in Christian charity, however, made less impact than the denial of society, largely because it failed to describe the Britain of popular perception. Many believed that the precise opposite held true, that Thatcherism had unlocked a spirit of greed and selfishness, had played to the baser instincts of humanity. The rhetoric about civic responsibility was not seen to be matched by practice and – however much it infuriated some on the right of the Conservative Party – there remained a widespread belief not only that society did exist, but that it was inextricably tied up with the actions of the state, and specifically with the welfare state.

Thatcher won an economic argument, but not the moral one. While few still thought, by the end of her term in office, that the state should have a role in owning and running car manufacturers or telecommunications companies, most continued to believe that provision for 'those who are unfortunate' should be made by the state, rather than by charity. In 1991 the British Social Attitudes Survey showed that 65 per cent of the population agreed with the statement that the government should 'increase taxes and spend more on health, education and social services'.

The fact that the electorate failed to extend that logic into the general election the following year by voting in sufficiently large numbers for the Labour Party – which was promising to put up taxes in order to raise money for precisely these causes – was a source of considerable discomfort in some quarters. There were those who attributed the gap between professed belief and practical expression to hypocrisy, others who saw the problem as being a lack of credibility on the part of the Labour leader, Neil Kinnock. But surprisingly few were prepared to give much credit to John Major, the successor to Thatcher, who had softened the harsher edges of her policies and, in the process, ushered in a new era for the country.

When, in 1990, Major set out his stall in a bid for the leadership of the Conservative Party, he promised to 'make changes that will produce across the whole of this country a genuinely classless society, in which people can rise to whatever level their own abilities and their own good fortune may take them from wherever they started'. Six and a half years later, in his last press conference as prime minister, he returned to the same theme, saying that he wanted 'the chance to take forward my belief in a classless society, where more of the have-nots are able to join the haves'.

This was, in his mind at least, the defining philosophy of his premiership: the pursuit of an inclusive Britain that didn't leave large swathes of its population trapped in hopelessness and underachievement. 'I want to see us build a country that is at ease with itself,' he urged in his first speech as prime minister, 'a country that is confident and a country that is prepared and willing to make the changes necessary to provide a better quality of life for all our citizens.' In his memoirs, he went on to explain what he meant by a classless society: 'not a society without difference, but one without barriers.'

From another perspective, this wasn't classlessness at all, but rather a restatement — in warmer, more comforting tones — of the same meritocracy promised by Thatcher, and by previous prime ministers; a Britain in which social and financial background should be no bar to mobility, and where the power of vested interests should no longer hold sway. In 1994 a memo written by John Maples, deputy chairman of the Conservative Party, was leaked to the press, implicitly acknowledging the continuity, whilst also reporting on the failure to realise the objective thus far: 'Although in the 1980s the Conservatives seemed to promise a classless society of opportunity, the reality is now that the rich are getting richer on the backs of the rest, who are getting poorer.'

By that stage Major was already past the peak of his popularity, but in the first couple of years of his premiership, his message of a less ideologically driven Thatcherism chimed with the mood of the nation. As Thatcher left office, the country was entering a recession that was to last for nearly two years, longer even than the recession at the start of the 1980s, and there was a growing suspicion that Conservative assurances of economic rejuvenation had proved false. Worse, many felt that something valuable had been lost over the course of the Thatcher decade, as private profit took precedence over public service; that Britain was in danger of throwing away an intangible but powerful cohesion, something that might well be termed 'society'.

The Tories had become widely distrusted, perceived to be – in a phrase that would shortly gain currency – the 'nasty party', but it was Major's unique achievement at the beginning of the 1990s to distance himself in the public mind from this image. Aided by the fact that he was virtually unknown when he became prime minister, he benefited hugely from being not-Thatcher. And to a country that seemed somehow a colder place than it had once been, he offered the reassurance that a sense of community could be rebuilt, healing the divisions of the previous decade.

When his premiership was blown off course and fell into disrepute, Major was seen to have failed to deliver on that undertaking. By then the country was emerging from recession and commencing a period of uninterrupted growth that would last well into the new century, fuelled by growing productivity, an expansion of credit and – with manufacturing starting to move to the Far East – the falling cost of consumer goods. But Major was given little praise for that long boom, nor for the social progress that was made possible as a result of such increased prosperity. Instead the beneficiary would be Tony Blair, the future Labour leader.

In the later years of the long Conservative government, the dividing line in British politics was drawn very sharply between the Tories on one side and most of the rest of the country on the other. Blair, while seldom defining himself as a product of the Labour Party, and deliberately eschewing the tag of socialism, was very insistent on where he stood in terms of that fault line. 'I am not a Tory,' he would say repeatedly. Nonetheless, his achievement was to sell a repackaged version of Conservatism at a time when the brand seemed irredeemably tainted; he articulated Major's dream more convincingly than could Major himself.

It remained, however, the same dream, as Blair's most powerful colleague, and rival, Gordon Brown, was to make clear when talking about his wish to create 'a truly classless society to promote opportunity'. That echoing of language across the parties was one of the most striking features of the decade. Equally notable was the way in which Westminster politics was no longer in the vanguard. Britain changed substantially in the course of the 1990s, but very little of that change came from Westminster. Rather it was the product of cultural initiatives, from Cool Britannia and the new lads to television soaps and the internet. 'It's the people's will,' Jim Hacker had said in a 1981 episode of the comedy *Yes, Minister*. 'I am their leader. I must follow them.' That turned out to be a central part of the story of the 1990s. Politicians were no longer leading, but following, trying to catch up with the nation's aspirations and wishes. The growing obsession in political circles with focus groups, targeted marketing and private polling was a symptom of this development. Mistaking effect for cause, however, Tony Blair attributed the transformation of society to his own adoption of Tory policies in relation to the economy, defence and crime, concluding that it was only then that: 'The zeitgeist was free to turn less deferential, more liberal on social issues, less class-bound, more meritocratic.'

Blair was correct in his identification of the nation's mood, but ultimately it was neither his creation nor that of Major. Rather it was the outcome of two political forces born in the 1960s that reached maturity in the 1980s: first, the anti-establishment tendencies embodied in Thatcherism, and second, the liberalising identity politics that were particularly associated with Ken Livingstone and what had once been known as the 'loony left'. Between them, they brought into being a new Britain, characterised by a tolerance for diversity and a democratisation in social and cultural – if not political – arenas.

The popular icons of the age were those who most convincingly conveyed the impression of normality, reaching a new level when the Manchester United footballer David Beckham married Victoria Adams of the Spice Girls; despite their extreme wealth, the couple's appeal was that they were so essentially ordinary. Blair's determination to play down his privileged background, especially when contrasted with Major's much more humble origins, was a recognition of that tendency, as was his habit of slipping a hint of the now ubiquitous Estuary English into his public-school accent.

It was noticeable too that Blair's inner circle seemed more inclined towards swearing than politicians had hitherto been. When John Major was overheard describing members of his own cabinet as 'bastards', there was a certain sense of shock, since it felt so out of kilter with his public persona; by the end of the decade, such language was par for the course in Downing Street. As, indeed, it was more widely. It became normal to see demonstrators against the government displaying placards that proclaimed the prime minister a 'wanker' or a 'cunt', while literature joined in the Gadarene rush towards profanity with ever more provocative marketing ploys. The novel *Martin and John* (1993) by the gay American writer Dale Peck was retitled for British publication as *Fucking Martin* and spent two months on the best-seller lists – it was hard to believe that it would have done so well under its original moniker. Similarly Mark Ravenhill's play *Shopping and Fucking* (1995) started in the artistic ghetto of the Royal Court Upstairs in London, but went on to enjoy a national and then international tour, its success helped greatly by the attention-grabbing title.

The decade started with no consensus about the identity of the nation, and politicians and commentators expended much energy in trying to find common ground, starting from a position of fracture and confusion. In the immediate aftermath of the 1992 general election, the novelist Michael Dobbs, formerly an advertising executive and a political adviser, acknowledged that things hadn't gone as smoothly as they might for any of the parties. 'The campaign never really caught the mood of the voters,' he admitted. 'But the trouble for the admen was that there was no real mood to catch.'

The search for an identity, for a shared set of values, was largely prompted by the supposed Thatcherite repudiation of society, but was made more acute by the growing influence of the European Union and by the looming inevitability of devolution within the United Kingdom. The political shape of the nation was being redefined, and with that came a need to redefine what constituted Britishness. Gradually a new consensus emerged, less homogenous than that of the post-war period, but discovering, slightly to its surprise, that homogeneity was not absolutely necessary for social cohesion; in modern Britain variety was tolerable, diversity was desirable. The task for politicians was to recognise that new mood, to develop a politics that could reflect it, in content as well as in appearance.

In terms of their own methods, it was a challenge that they singularly failed to meet. The experience of factionalism within Labour in the 1980s and the Conservatives in the 1990s prompted the leaderships of both parties to change their constitutions, accumulating more power at the centre, exerting control over MPs and the choice of parliamentary candidates, and trying to ensure that the correct line, whatever it might happen to be that week or that day, was parroted by all representatives. Dissent and debate was stifled, conformity enforced, and the numbers of those actually involved in decision-making reduced. Even being a member of a cabinet or shadow cabinet was no longer a guarantee of power, when compared to the influence of spin doctors and unelected officials. By the end of the decade, the coming stars on both sides – many of them still serving their time as political advisers, but destined to inherit their parties – managed to look and sound almost indistinguishable from one another, a monoculture that was increasingly remote from the rest of the population. The consequences included a sharp decline in the numbers of those choosing to use their vote in elections.

The same disinclination to participate was not evident elsewhere. The great buzzword of the second half of the 1990s was interactivity, whether in advertising, computer games, reality television or – the biggest, most unpredictable development of all – the internet. If politicians were unable to lead, it was also true that the public were less inclined to follow. Some commentators began to talk about the growing redundancy of representative democracy and the dawning of a new era of participatory democracy. Such developments were at this stage to be found only in cultural form, but then these were still very early days of what was still known as the information superhighway.

With the democratisation of culture came an atomisation of society and therefore, in reaction, a need for shared experience, a wish to be seen to be part of a recognisable community. As the Conservative heritage secretary Virginia Bottomley put it, when the plans for the Millennium Dome were first announced, 'people want the sense of congregation, of coming together'. In August 1996 Oasis played two gigs at Knebworth to a quarter of a million people; had everyone who applied for tickets been successful, it would have been a three-week residency. That was not simply a tribute to the populism of the group's music; it also expressed a deep desire to be present in a mass moment. The same phenomenon of seeking comfort in the anonymous democracy of the crowd could be seen everywhere, from the excited fever that greeted the arrival of the National Lottery, through the proliferation of replica football shirts and the rise of festival culture, to the very public enthusiasms for figures as diverse as Harry Potter, Tim Henman and Mr Blobby.

Most obviously there was the public grieving for Diana, Princess of Wales, in 1997, in the week leading up to her funeral. 'Never have I, and millions of others, felt such a sense of community,' remarked the journalist and critic Anthony Holden. 'It finally gave the lie to Mrs Thatcher's cold, hollow dictum that there was no such thing as society.' Even more extraordinarily, the same phenomenon was to be seen in the behaviour of the public the day after the funeral; no events had been arranged for that Sunday, there was nothing to do or to see, but still three million people found their way to the royal parks in London, seemingly responding to a deep-seated desire to be part of a collective.

That week, just four months after his entry into Downing Street, was the high point of Tony Blair's popularity, the moment when he transcended political allegiance and came close to embodying the spirit of the nation. Significantly, however, he showed no sign of knowing what to do with that position, having achieved it. There was no great transformation of Britain in the wake of Diana's death, largely because Blair had no real agenda for reform. He responded to the public, offering it a mirror, rather than becoming an architect of change. For all his talk of the future, he did as little to shape it as had Major.

Indeed, Diana herself could plausibly claim to have been more influential in creating a new country. Since the 1930s, the royal family, under the influence of Queen Elizabeth, wife of George VI, had established a façade of middle-class normality in opposition to the celebrity glamour of the Duke and Duchess of Windsor. The appeal of that image was acknowledged by Edward VIII in his address to the nation on his abdication in 1936, saying of his younger brother: 'He has one matchless blessing, enjoyed by so many of you and not bestowed on me – a happy home with his wife and children.' Diana found a way of bridging that gap; she was both more glamorous than Wallis Simpson and more in touch with the people than her mother-in-law's family. The Queen Mother, previously the most popular royal, had maintained her position by saying nothing at all in public, but Diana learnt early on how to use the media; treated like a film star, she responded by behaving like one, appealing directly to the public and claiming a democratic legitimacy as measured in column inches.

Yet it was a flawed glamour so that, despite being the daughter of the 8th Earl Spencer, she remained seemingly accessible, scarred by self-harming and eating disorders. Like Blair after her, the assumption of speaking for the people was achieved despite the accident of her birth, but unlike him, she used her authority to address issues that were unfashionable and sometimes unpopular; her charity work came with a distinctly un-royal element of campaigning on leprosy, AIDS, homelessness, domestic violence and landmines. (Noticeably excluded were animal charities, normally the first refuge of celebrities.)

The shift in the royal popularity stakes also reflected the passing of a generation. The Queen Mother's reputation rested ultimately on her public profile during the Second World War. That conflict remained central to Britain's self-image, but with fewer and fewer alive who actually remembered the time, the need arose for a new source of mythology. Thatcher was the last prime minister to have memories of the war, and her replacement by Major seemed to offer the possibility that the late 1950s might become a substitute, a time of relative stability and prosperity, of Harold Macmillan's reassurance that the country had 'never had it so good'. But that era was too indeterminate, too transitional, too colourless a period in the public perception to serve convincingly as a rallying point. Instead, as the recession came to an end, it was the 1960s that seized the nation's attention and Blair, eleven years old when the Beatles swept all before them in 1964, who was perfectly placed to claim this as his heritage.

Again the phenomenon was initially cultural, but it swiftly acquired a social and political dimension. For if Major's talk of society, however classless, could be seen as a repudiation of Thatcherism, this public embrace of the 1960s was even more so. In one of her last speeches as prime minister, Thatcher had talked of 'the waning fashions of the permissive 1960s', but she spoke too soon. Even at the height of her popularity, she had been unable to convince the nation of her perspective; a Gallup poll conducted in 1986 found that 70 per cent of the population thought the 1960s were the best decade of the century, and much of the 1990s would see coming to fruition seeds that had been planted a quarter of a century earlier.

One issue in particular symbolised the change. The question of homosexuality had been chosen in the 1980s as the battleground on which the war against 1960s social liberalism was to be waged, but despite some temporary triumphs, that offensive proved unsuccessful. By the turn of the century, even the Conservative Party was ceding the ground, so that when, in 2001, the Labour MP Jane Griffiths introduced a Parliamentary Bill testing the waters for the concept of civil partnerships for lesbian and gay couples, only one MP spoke against the resolution: the Labour member Stuart Bell. Fifty Tories voted against, but none of them ventured to speak up in the debate and, more significantly, no member of the Conservative shadow cabinet entered the lobbies, a decision having been taken that it was too controversial a subject to address.

In this process of liberalising society, it was not always acknowledged that Britain was forging a distinct and unique identity as a nation. Despite much talk that British politics was following an American model, there was no replication of the culture wars that animated so much debate in the United States. The opposition to secular liberalism came not from politicians but from church leaders. In 1996 Cardinal Thomas Winning, the Catholic Archbishop of Glasgow, attacked Tony Blair's argument that abortion shouldn't be a matter for the criminal law, and suggested that his professed Christianity was therefore 'a sham'. Three years later, Winning again criticised Blair, this time over his position on the Act of Succession, leading the prime minister to denounce 'fucking prelates getting involved in politics and pretending it was nothing to do with politics'. Blair was quite clear about his own faith, as were John Major and the Liberal Democrat leader, Paddy Ashdown ('I pray every night,' noted the latter; 'I believe in a Christian God'), but he tended to follow the advice of his press officer. 'Never talk about God,' commented Alastair Campbell, adding that both he and Gordon Brown, the son of a minister, had agreed that 'God was a disaster area'. Without political expression, the voice of religion faded still further into the background noise of society.

Indeed, as the new millennium approached, it was abundantly clear that Christianity no longer had a serious role to play in the cultural and social life of the country, save as a suitable setting for sitcoms: *The Vicar of Dibley* and *Father Ted* were hugely popular. In 1992 Waddingtons announced that the character of Reverend Green was to be dropped from the game of *Cluedo*, on the grounds that having a clergyman involved was 'no longer appropriate in the Nineties'; he was to be replaced by 'a contemporary City entrepreneur'. Public pressure, according to the company, forced a rethink and the traditional characters survived, but then *Cluedo* had long been a deeply nostalgic game, rooted in the English detective novels of the 1930s and '40s.

Much of popular culture, of course, continued to be informed by America, but even here there was an assertion of independence with the sounds of Britpop, trip-hop and jungle, and the discovery that British movies could be successful even when they weren't costume dramas. While the structure of politics increasingly came to resemble that of America, with two parties converging on the centre ground, there could be no doubt that social and cultural attitudes were somewhat different.

Nor was Britain always in tune with its neighbours on the Continent. The relationship with Europe was to be the most divisive and significant political issue of the decade. Many would-be constitutional reformers looked across the Channel for inspiration on how to modernise what were said to be the anachronistic, crumbling institutions of British public life, but, taking an opposite position, it was not only Conservative Eurosceptics who wished to preserve differences. It was possible, for example, to celebrate Britain's continuing, and thus far mostly successful, transition to a multiracial society without the serious political reaction evident in some European neighbours. In the 2001 general election, the leading far right group, the British National Party, received just 0.2 per cent on a historically low turnout, and was outpolled by three fringe organisations on the left: the Scottish Socialists, the Socialist Alliance and the Socialist Labour Party. In the French presidential election the following year, by contrast, Jean-Marie Le Pen of the National Front got a hundred times as many votes as the BNP had managed from a comparably sized electorate.

Nonetheless, Europe did exert some cultural influence, most apparent, perhaps, in food. On the one hand, there was the arrival of European supermarket chains – notably Lidl and Aldi – and on the other, a rise in the standard of British cuisine, and in the status of celebrity restaurants. Amongst the latter was Granita in Islington, North London, which in 1993 was named Best New Restaurant in the *Time Out* Eating and Drinking Awards.

Granita was a product of its time, a narrow, almost colourless space with concrete walls. Steel chairs gathered around square, uncovered tables made of unbleached pine set closely together. It was not necessarily a place to be seen but, on a good night, it was a place to observe some of the rich and famous customers, who might range from the Conservative cabinet minister Peter Lilley to the *Monty Python* star Terry Jones.

Minimalist to a fault, it was, said journalist John Walsh, 'the most stripped-down eating-house I know'. The food was similarly typical of the day, a severely restricted selection of dishes that drew primarily on Italian cuisine, made a point of ingredients rather than of treatment, and fitted the newly health-conscious mood of fashionable London. 'The menu offers a range of food ideal for keeping the healthy ideologue under nine stone,' wrote Giles Coren in *The Times*, though his fellow restaurant critic, Jonathan Meades, was not overly impressed. 'The cooking is pleasant,' he noted, 'but well this side of exciting.' Nonetheless, booking was essential.

It was here, on the last day of May 1994, that Tony Blair and Gordon Brown, the two brightest young stars of the Labour Party, met for an early supper to finalise their response to the death of the party's leader, John Smith. The most important element of the agreement had already been settled: that Brown, the older, more senior and more experienced man would stand aside from the contest to find Smith's successor, and allow his friend and colleague to run as the candidate for their faction within the party. What else was agreed – whether a deal was done that would allow Brown to succeed to the leadership in due course, and would in the meantime give him not only the post of chancellor in a future Blair-led government, but also wide-ranging control over domestic policy – was to be the subject of dispute for years to come, provoking a protracted feud in Labour circles for that generation and the next. Probably the most famous dinner in modern British politics, it inspired books, articles and documentaries as well as, in Peter Morgan's *The Deal* (2003), a television drama with Michael Sheen and David Morrissey in the lead roles.

Brown and Blair ate at the back of the restaurant and, at the time, their presence attracted little interest. Instead the media's attention that evening was focused on a table at the front, where the paparazzi were flocking around the actress Susan Tully, formerly of *Grange Hill* and now starring as Michelle Fowler in *EastEnders*, in which role she had recently been shot and wounded by a psychotic veteran of the Falklands War. The overwrought storyline was characteristic of the increasingly melodramatic developments in modern soap operas, and was being used to introduce viewers to a regular third weekly episode of the show.

Like its predecessors – *Crisis? What Crisis?* and *Rejoice! Rejoice!* – this book addresses what happened in the front and at the back of Granita, exploring both the high politics and the low culture of the era, in the belief that the latter not only reflects but often pre-empts the former. It is also concerned with the world beyond, with the very different realities that existed in the country, and that were even evident in the London Borough of Islington itself.

Because, despite its reputation as an enclave for the fashion-conscious left, Islington was a diverse place. Plenty of politicians lived there, and it was too a media haven, with residents including Charles Moore, Paul Dacre and Ian Jack, editors of the *Sunday Telegraph*, *Daily Mail* and *Independent on Sunday* respectively. But it was also riddled with inner-city poverty: 60 per cent of the borough's inhabitants lived in council housing, half didn't have a car, and a quarter were not working. When Tony Blair contributed his Granita-esque recipe to *The Islington Cookbook* in 1993 (fettuccine with sundried tomatoes and capers), he was culturally out of touch with many of his neighbours, let alone with the country at large. Which is perhaps why he claimed elsewhere that his favourite food was fish and chips – also said to be the staple diet of John Major.

PART ONE

THE BUDDHA OF SUBURBIA
1990–1997

We are not slaying dragons any more, just cleaning up the shit they leave behind.
Edwina Currie (1991)

It's a great responsibility bringing a child into the world. You get all those embarrassing questions, like: What's a Labour government?
Helen Lederer (1991)

CHARLES FOX: Do you enjoy anything, Mr Pitt?
WILLIAM PITT: A balance sheet, Mr Fox. I enjoy a good balance sheet.
Alan Bennett, *The Madness of King George* (1994)

1
Enter John Major

'The devil you know'

NORMAN ORMAL: I spotted the potential of John Major way
before we realised he didn't have any.
Craig Brown, *Norman Ormal* (1998)

ALAN PARTRIDGE: People forget that on the Titanic's maiden
voyage, there were over a thousand miles of uneventful,
very pleasurable cruising, before it hit the iceberg.
Patrick Marber, Steve Coogan & Armando Iannucci,
Knowing Me, Knowing You with Alan Partridge (1994)

'I've always voted Labour,' I said. 'But . . .' I hesitated. Suddenly
the stakes had become very high. 'But what?'
'But I felt secretly relieved when the Tories won.'
David Lodge, *Therapy* (1995)

John Major was a very young prime minister. In this, as in so little else, he
was part of a trend, for the fashion, as the twentieth century progressed,
was very definitely away from the older premier. In the decades either side
of the Second World War, the average age of a prime minister was sixty-
seven; in the years after 1960, it fell to fifty-eight before, in the 1990s, a
further ten years were shaved off the figure. Much of that latter reduction
was due to Tony Blair, who was often cited as the youngest prime minister
of the century, being just shy of his forty-third birthday when elected in
1997. Less well remembered is the fact that the record he broke was that of
his predecessor.

And perhaps it isn't surprising that Major's youth is so easily forgotten.
He made far less play of that dubious merit than did Blair, giving the
appearance of someone who had been middle-aged for some considerable
time. There was too, when he became prime minister in November 1990,
a higher cultural premium placed on experience than was to become

the norm, and it was more important for him to emphasise his record in government, in contrast to that of the two opposition leaders – Neil Kinnock and Paddy Ashdown – though both were older than he was.

That record, however, was so compressed that it resembled a crash course in statesmanship. Major had never been in opposition, having entered Parliament in the 1979 general election that brought Margaret Thatcher to power. He had served as foreign secretary and then as chancellor of the exchequer, but these had been only brief appointments. Most of his three and a half years in the cabinet had been spent in the backroom job of chief secretary to the Treasury. Little known outside Westminster, he was far from an obvious choice to become leader of the Conservative Party.

His standing was illustrated by the media coverage that followed the political demise of Margaret Thatcher in 1990. Having been challenged in an election for the leadership of the party by her former defence secretary, Michael Heseltine, Thatcher had failed to secure sufficient votes to win on the first ballot. She was then informed by her cabinet colleagues that she stood little chance of prevailing in the next round, and announced her resignation on the morning of Thursday 22 November, thereby freeing cabinet ministers to enter the race – an opportunity immediately picked up by the chancellor, John Major, and foreign secretary Douglas Hurd. That evening, the BBC and ITV news bulletins produced graphics to illustrate how the electoral process worked; both followed the conventional wisdom of the day and showed Major coming last and being knocked out, leading to a final third-ballot showdown between the flamboyant self-made millionaire Heseltine and the patrician Old Etonian Hurd.

In the real world, to the surprise of the media, it took just four days for Major to move into Number 10, having seen off both rivals with no need for that final ballot. His opening words to his first cabinet as prime minister summed up the mood of a perplexed public: 'Well, who'd have thought it?'

The implausibility of his rise helped create an image of accidental premiership that he never quite threw off. As prime minister, he served for longer than, say, Clement Attlee, David Lloyd George or Edward Heath, longer than James Callaghan and Neville Chamberlain put together, and just a few months shy of Harold Macmillan, yet he made less impression than any of those figures even at the time. In retrospect his premiership is remembered by many as being little more than a brief interregnum. Indeed that was the view of the *Independent*'s editor, Andrew Marr, even as Major was leaving office: 'he was what happened after Margaret Thatcher and before Tony Blair.' Others were less certain of his role. 'I simply find myself asking: Does he really exist?' commented the veteran MP Enoch Powell in 1991, and if that was unnecessarily cruel, it reflected a widespread perception. Satirists, used to the raw red meat of anti-Thatcher savagery, were at a loss to know how to caricature this mild, affable but seemingly bland embodiment of suburban man. Guy Jenkin, the co-creator of Channel 4's topical sitcom *Drop the Dead Donkey*, recalled that 'Trying to write jokes about John Major was like trying to write jokes about grass growing,' and his writing partner, Andy Hamilton, agreed: 'They were dull days for comedy writers.' Their best joke in those early days came with the concept of a John Major-o-gram: 'They send round a bloke in a suit. He stands here for ten minutes, no one notices him and he goes away again.'

The satirical puppet series *Spitting Image* reached much the same conclusion. On air at the time of the change in leadership, the programme's first attempt to depict Major showed him with a radio antenna on his head, so that Thatcher could operate him by remote control, but when the show returned for its next series in 1991, it had devised a more enduring incarnation: a puppet sprayed all over with grey paint who had an unhealthy obsession with peas and starred in a new feature, 'The Life of John Major – the most boring story ever told'. The greyness became the defining public image of the man so that when, in 1992, someone drew a Hitler moustache on a portrait of Thatcher in the House of Commons, Neil Kinnock could joke on *Have I Got News for You*: 'Next week they're going to colour in John Major.' He was by common consensus dull, boring and lacking in glamour; in 1996 readers of the BBC's *Clothes Show Magazine* voted him 'the person they would least like to see in his underpants'.

Major's voice, too, with its slightly strangled, expressionless tone and its tendency to pronounce the word 'want' as 'wunt', came in for mockery. 'He doesn't speak English,' raged the irascible newsreader Henry Davenport in *Drop the Dead Donkey*, 'he speaks Croydonian, an incomprehensible suburban dialect,' while the comedian Jo Brand concluded that he 'talks like a minor Dickens character on acid'. The view from abroad was no more encouraging. The French newspaper *Le Figaro* nicknamed him 'Monsieur Ordinaire', while even the Belgians – not universally renowned as the most vibrant and colourful people in Europe – were unimpressed: 'In his grey Marks and Spencer suit, he is hardly a charismatic figure,' sniffed the Brussels-based daily *Le Soir*.

Yet this allegedly grey man had risen to become prime minister, leader of the most successful political party in the history of democracy. Not for nothing was one of his early biographies titled *The Major Enigma*; there had to be more here than met the casual eye. And behind the demure demeanour, it transpired, there lurked a shrewd and effective political operator. His closest friend in the Commons, Chris Patten, was later to describe him as 'very, very competent – the best of our political generation', while the BBC's political editor John Cole wrote: 'he was more politically astute than his critics, and had run rings around them.' Nor was his appeal confined to Westminster: in the 1992 general election Major secured for the Conservatives the largest popular vote ever recorded by a British political party, despite the supposedly widespread opinion that he was deeply uninspiring. Even with all the derision directed at him, he was, for a while, genuinely popular. 'The public liked him,' wrote Michael Heseltine with a truthful simplicity.

And in person he was clearly very likeable, displaying a generosity of spirit that is not always evident in politics. In January 1991 the veteran socialist Eric Heffer, now riddled with cancer, made what was clearly going to be his last ever appearance in the House of Commons to vote against Britain's involvement in the war against Saddam Hussein. Before the debate began, Major crossed the floor of the chamber, knelt beside the dying man and had a private conversation, an emotionally charged gesture that provoked an outbreak of applause from MPs of both sides. Tony Benn, in tears at the condition of the man who was probably his closest friend at Westminster, noted in his diary: 'I have never, in forty years, heard anyone clapping in the House of Commons. Eric was overwhelmed.'

Major was also very tactile, offering men a two-handed handshake and flirting with women to great effect, so that even political opponents were disarmed. John Prescott's wife, Pauline, was said to have been 'bowled over by how witty and charming he was', while the hardened Eurosceptic Teresa Gorman was almost persuaded to abandon her rebellious inclinations and vote with her own government, as Major sat holding her hand and talking gently to her: 'It was very seductive; I could feel myself tingling all over.' At a dinner thrown by the Speaker of the House of Commons, Paddy Ashdown saw the prime minister chatting up Labour's former deputy leader Margaret Beckett with a line worthy of a *Carry On* script: 'Would you like a nibble of my mace?' As Ashdown remarked, 'He is a terrible flirt!'

Major had too a gift for personal communication when meeting the electorate that hadn't been noted in his predecessor, though his empathy was less evident in the heated environment of the House of Commons or when delivering platform speeches. In an age that was, we were repeatedly told, dominated by television, he was adjudged by many to be a poor performer on the small screen, though some of his charm evidently came through. The journalist John Diamond attended a dinner party in 1991 at which a woman 'listed for the amazed assembly the things she would gladly do with John Major between a pair of satin sheets'. It was, noted Diamond, the men, not the women, who were puzzled by this declaration and who demanded clarification of the prime minister's inexplicable sex appeal.

Perhaps the issue did ultimately come down to gender. The commentators, critics and comedians of the time were predominantly male, while Major's air of quiet self-assurance and mild coquettishness played best with female voters, many of whom had deserted the Conservative Party during Thatcher's incumbency. 'His polling figures, especially among women, are amazing,' marvelled Chris Patten in 1991. The very ordinariness of the man, his decency and honesty, however mocked, was an appealing attribute and was deliberately played up. Major himself was clear that he wanted 'to be prime minister without changing, without losing the interests that every other Briton had, without having no time for holidays, no time for sport, no time for anything but the higher things of life'. The restoration of normality was, to use a phrase often associated with him, most agreeable.

Much of this was only to emerge as Major's premiership wore on. Certainly it was of less significance over those few days in November 1990, as Tory MPs considered who was to succeed Thatcher as their leader. Then there was just one overriding question: which of the candidates was most Thatcherite and could best protect the legacy? Loyalists, outraged at her defenestration, wished to keep the flame alive, while even some of the regicides were troubled by feelings of guilt over what they had done and sought to make amends. Their verdict rapidly became clear. 'Most Tory backbenchers regard Mr Major as the most Thatcherite of the three contenders,' reported *The Times*, 'although it is something of a mystery why he should have acquired this reputation.'

Major's privately expressed position was clear – 'I'm not a Thatcherite, never have been' – but in public that mystery remained unsolved and, for the moment at least, largely unaddressed. His campaign team for the leadership election included most of the leading right-wingers, the likes of Norman Lamont, Michael Howard, Peter Lilley and Norman Tebbit, while his victory was greeted rapturously by Thatcher herself. 'It's everything I've dreamt of for such a long time,' she said, as she embraced Major's wife, Norma, on the night of his triumph; 'the future is assured.' Within a year, Thatcher was telling her friend, the journalist Woodrow Wyatt, that 'I think he has deceived me,' and although the truth was rather that she had deceived herself, her sense of betrayal was shared by many on the right of the party, contributing heavily to the disloyalty that became increasingly prevalent amongst Conservative MPs in the 1990s.

As chancellor, Major had taken Britain into the European Exchange Rate Mechanism (ERM), tying the value of sterling to that of the deutschmark. Given that record, how could the Eurosceptic supporters of Thatcher have persuaded themselves that he was on their side? Part of the answer was his demonstrable dryness in economic matters. His espousal of the ERM was based on counter-inflationary concerns, rather than any great enthusiasm for the European project, and his one well-known quote as chancellor, as the country slid into recession, was to urge resolution in the fight against inflation: 'If it isn't hurting, it isn't working.' Beyond that, there was a studied refusal to reveal anything much about his own political beliefs. He was associated with no particular faction in the party, had written no influential papers for think tanks, delivered no speeches that anyone had noticed, appeared at not a single press conference during the 1987 election campaign.

Many years later, when he was in opposition, Major was asked by a colleague, Michael Spicer, where he had really stood on the great European questions that had dominated his premiership. 'He smiles and makes no audible response,' wrote Spicer in his diary. 'I suppose that is how he became prime minister in the first place.' Others had spotted this characteristic earlier. 'His whole life,' noted the Tory MP Edwina Currie, his former lover who knew him better than most, 'has the waft of an opportunistic silence reflecting tremendous self-discipline.'

Equally important to his image as a Thatcherite, however, was a simple cultural perception of his humble origins. His father was a trapeze artist in the music halls, who had moved with some success into the garden ornaments business, before the bottom dropped out of the gnome market on the outbreak of the Second World War. By the time John Major was born in 1943, the family had suffered a severe fall in living standards, and he grew up in straitened circumstances in South London, leaving school with just three O-levels. The fact that he subsequently rose so high was entirely due to his involvement in the Conservative Party, and was seen as a fine illustration of a new meritocracy. 'What does the Conservative Party offer a working class kid from Brixton?' asked a Tory election poster in 1992. 'They made him prime minister.' In all the tribulations that were to come, he clung on to this. 'I love my party,' he explained in later years, contrasting himself with his predecessor. 'She never loved the party. That was the difference.'

Major was clearly not cast in the same mould as, say, Douglas Hurd — the former Eton head boy turned diplomat, whose father and grandfather had both been MPs — rather his story seemed the living embodiment of

Thatcher's promises to those who aspired to better themselves. It was widely assumed therefore that he bought into her ideology. Certainly that was her feeling. 'I don't want old style, old Etonian Tories of the old school to succeed me,' she observed. 'John Major is someone who has fought his way up from the bottom and is far more in tune with the skilled and ambitious and worthwhile working classes than Douglas Hurd is.'

There was at least some truth in this perception. As prime minister, Major's evocation of a classless society echoed Thatcher's mindset, even as it pointed the way forward to Tony Blair and New Labour. 'I want to bring into being a different kind of country,' he said in 1991, 'to bury forever old divisions in Britain between North and South, blue-collar and white-collar, polytechnic and university. They're old style, old hat.' The one-nation theme and the emphasis on newness was to become very familiar with Blair, but that specific proposal – of removing divisions in further education – was reminiscent of Thatcher's assault on the pillars of the establishment.

It also, of course, came from a man who had left school at the age of sixteen, and it revealed an insecurity that he mostly kept hidden. Sitting at a cabinet table still dominated by ex-public schoolboys, he was in a small minority of those who had been state educated, and he was entirely alone as a non-graduate. The subject of his restricted education was eagerly seized upon by a press desperately trying to find an angle on the man. 'Never has so much been written about so little,' he commented, in one of his best lines, but it was clearly an important part of his make-up. 'He is terribly lacking in confidence in himself, especially all the social things,' observed Chris Patten. That awkwardness was to play an important role in Major's premiership, amplified by the sheer bloody-mindedness that had been required to take him from Brixton to Downing Street. For the immediate future, however, the momentum of the leadership election was sufficient to give him a chance to establish a new style.

Even so, his first cabinet demonstrated a strong continuity with Thatcher. Many of her ministers remained in place, while those who were introduced or promoted were mostly acceptable to the right wing; Norman Lamont became chancellor and places were found for Michael Howard and for a returning Kenneth Baker. The one controversial decision was to bring Michael Heseltine back into the fold after five years on the back benches.

As the man who had ended Thatcher's premiership, Heseltine was loathed by many of her supporters, but it would have been perverse if his talents had not been utilised. Regardless of ideology, he was one of the few genuine stars that the party had at its disposal, as he demonstrated on his return to the conference platform in 1991. Reviving his celebrated line in knockabout humour, he mocked the Labour Party's attempts to rebrand itself by launching into songs from *Oliver!* – 'Who will buy my sweet red roses?' and 'You've got to pick a pocket or two' – while suggesting that the opposition leader, Neil Kinnock, was a dead ringer for the Artful Dodger. It was rare for a report of a Heseltine speech not to use the word 'bravura', and there were few senior Tories of whom that could be said. 'He is very like an ancient matinée idol in an MGM movie,' noted the television personality Gyles Brandreth; 'the performance is stagey and the colour isn't quite true, but there's still something rather compelling about it.'

Displaying a shrewd sense of politics, Major appointed his former rival to be environment secretary, charged in the first instance with finding a replacement for what was now known almost universally as 'the hated poll tax', the abolition of which had been the cornerstone of Heseltine's challenge for the leadership. The result was the creation of a new charge on property to fund local authorities, the council tax, and, as an interim measure, while that was being introduced, a reduction in the level of the poll tax by £140 per person, funded by a rise in VAT from 15 to 17.5 per cent. (To no one's great surprise, the temporary VAT increase was never rescinded.) Further popular moves by the government came with a rise in child benefit – which had been frozen for three years – and a long-overdue award of compensation to haemophiliacs infected with HIV as a result of their treatment by the NHS, though of course this came too late for the many who had already died. Clear signals were being sent that this was a new, more compassionate Conservatism, and the Tories enjoyed an immediate boost in their opinion poll ratings.

There were other items outstanding on Major's desk as he took office. Chief amongst them was the imminent war against Iraq, a nation then ruled by Saddam Hussein, whose troops had invaded the neighbouring country of Kuwait in August 1990. Margaret Thatcher had led the international response to the invasion, pushing the American president, George Bush, into committing his country to military action, and already some 14,000 British troops were in position in the region as part of a United Nations-approved coalition.

Although the change in prime minister on the very brink of hostilities was far from ideal ('It distracted us from the business of facing up to Saddam Hussein and created a damaging sense of uncertainty,' noted General Peter de la Billière, commander of the British forces), there was never any doubt that Major would follow through on his predecessor's resolve. What was at question was how effective a war leader he would be, and for some the answer came as a surprise. Displaying neither bellicosity during the conflict nor triumphalism afterwards, Major proved to be popular amongst the troops, while his homely style – he ended his television broadcast on the eve of war with the words 'God bless' – helped distance him from the confrontational legacy of Thatcher. Similarly the shots of him, in casual trousers and a jumper, addressing the soldiers, making no pretence at being anything other than a civilian, played very well back home.

Overshadowed in popular memory by the invasion of Iraq twelve years later, the 1991 Kuwaiti War was, in military terms, an unqualified success. Five weeks of bombing was followed by a ground war that was shorter than anyone had dared hope. Within four days of the tanks rolling into Kuwait, the Iraqi army had been routed and the operation completed, despite Saddam's dire warnings that the coalition would face 'the mother of all battles'. (That was one of the phrases from the hostilities that entered the language, alongside 'friendly fire' and 'collateral damage'.) British and American casualties were remarkably few in number, and if Saddam remained in power, that was what had always been intended; the UN resolution authorising military action had talked of the removal of the occupying force from the sovereign territory of Kuwait, but said nothing of regime change in Iraq. Nonetheless, some were later to regret the decision not to press onwards to Baghdad, believing that it merely stored up future problems.

There was some opposition at home to Britain's involvement in the war, though nowhere near the level that was to be seen in subsequent conflicts. A couple of peripheral figures, Clare Short and Tony Banks, resigned from the Labour front bench in protest, but few noticed or cared; in any event, both had already resigned on previous occasions and a law of diminishing returns operates in such circumstances. There was, however, some disquiet about the media treatment of the hostilities. On the one hand, the new cable news station CNN showed what amounted to a nightly firework display as bombs rained down on Baghdad, and on the other, the American propaganda footage purported to show 'smart missiles' pinpointing their targets with unerring accuracy. In the midst of this, huge numbers of civilians were being killed and wounded in Iraq, though one would have been hard pushed to detect that fact from the coverage. Instead the most memorable images came from BBC Two's *Newsnight* programme where, in the words of comedian Mark Steel: 'each night Peter Snow clambered around in a sandpit, surrounded by toy helicopters like a spoilt child, adding to the impression that the whole episode was an elaborate computer game.'

Elsewhere the BBC exercised a degree of self-censorship bordering on parody. The comedies *'Allo 'Allo* and *M*A*S*H*, together with a planned screening of *Carry On Up the Khyber*, all set during previous conflicts, were withdrawn from the television schedules, while the BBC banned a bewildering variety of records, lest they give offence: not only obvious suspects like John Lennon's 'Give Peace a Chance', Edwin Starr's 'War' and Frankie Goes to Hollywood's 'Two Tribes', but also, in an impressive display of lateral thinking, Roberta Flack's 'Killing Me Softly with His Song', the Bangles' 'Walk Like an Egyptian' and Lulu's 'Boom Bang a Bang'. A BBC spokesperson explained that 'Radio 1 realises it's got a lot of servicemen's families among its listeners and it's very sensitive to what it plays because of that,' but it was hard to believe that army wives, after two decades of seeing their loved ones depart for tours of Northern Ireland, were so fragile that they would be notably upset by an old Eurovision hit.

There was little to choose between the real Radio 1 and the version parodied in the radio comedy *On the Hour*, which included a disc jockey named Wayne Kerr explaining that he couldn't play 'Puff the Magic Dragon' in a time of war 'because it reminds everyone of flame throwers'. Meanwhile the Bristol trip-hop band Massive Attack were prevailed upon to change their name, so that their best-known single, 'Unfinished Sympathy', was released under the name Massive and, more reasonably, the new Rolling Stones single, 'Highwire', which explicitly addressed the West's sale of weaponry to Iraq and the experience of soldiers involved in the conflict, was deemed unsuitable for broadcast.

John Major came out of the Kuwaiti War with his reputation and his poll ratings much enhanced, the most popular war leader since Winston Churchill. The other outstanding issue from the Thatcher years, however – the state of the British economy – was less easily resolved. The country was suffering a severe slowdown in economic activity that turned officially into a recession in the second half of 1990; GDP fell for seven consecutive quarters, and then simply refused to recover. We were, said Major, 'languishing in the no-man's land of negligible growth', though the more common expression at the time was 'bumping along the bottom'. Unemployment and business bankruptcies rose steadily, interest rates remained stubbornly high, and retail sales fell.

It was the second serious recession since the Conservatives had taken office in 1979 and, unlike that of the early 1980s, its impact was felt nationally, with London and the South-East hit as badly as the North. This time it was not just manufacturing that took the brunt of the slump, but commercial construction and the financial services industry, as the boom of the late

1980s juddered to a halt. Some forty million square feet of office space were said to be lying unoccupied in London, and even estate agents – those great symbols of the Thatcherite high noon – were suffering. The huge rises in house prices in affluent parts of the South went into reverse, provoking a wave of repossessions by mortgage companies and leaving many mired in a hitherto unknown state called negative equity, whereby the amount they owed exceeded their homes' market valuations.

'The politics of the property-owning democracy had come temporarily unstuck,' admitted Michael Heseltine in later years, and for many who had bought into the dream, the comedown was especially bitter. Disillusion was everywhere apparent, as Major, a longstanding fan of Chelsea Football Club, discovered in late 1991 when he met Vinnie Jones, the club's hard-man midfielder who also happened to be a Tory supporter. 'Sort out the fucking interest rates, will you?' said Jones, and Major could only reply: 'I'm trying, I'm trying.'

Little of this, though, attached itself personally to Major. He had been chancellor of the exchequer when the recession started, but his tenure had been so fleeting, so much in the shadow of his predecessors in the job, Geoffrey Howe and Nigel Lawson, that he escaped much of the blame. When asked in a 1992 Gallup opinion poll who was responsible for the recession, the answers split fairly evenly between 'the worldwide economic recession' and 'the Thatcher government'; just 4 per cent answered 'the Major government'.

Instead the flak was aimed at the new chancellor, Norman Lamont, largely because he projected none of Major's essential niceness ('unpleasant and untalented', thought Edwina Currie) and because he seemed such a lightweight figure to be in so senior a position. It was a perception shared by his colleagues: 'I never believed that he was the right choice for chancellor of the exchequer,' revealed Douglas Hurd in his memoirs. The image was all wrong too; with his badger-streaked hair and his cherubic face, Lamont looked, said Labour MP Giles Radice, 'like a discontented squirrel', though the most disarming comment was that of comedian Linda Smith: 'It is nice to see that little boy from the Addams Family doing so well.'

The public were deeply unimpressed by Lamont, both personally and as a steward of the economy. He never quite recovered from an ill-advised speech in 1991, responding to the biggest April rise in unemployment ever recorded. 'Rising unemployment and the recession have been the price that we have had to pay to get inflation down,' he said, before handing the opposition a phrase that they didn't let him forget: 'That price is well worth paying.' In retrospect, he was quick to lay the blame on others. 'This recession has its origins in the boom of 1988 and 1989,' he was to insist. 'That boom made the recession inevitable.' He was perfectly correct, but the observation did him little good, and he was widely seen as an unconvincing, if over-promoted, politician.

It was an impression confirmed when, in April 1991, the *News of the World* revealed that Lamont was making £15,000 a year from renting out his furnished house to a woman who called herself a 'sex therapist'. The tenant in question specialised in sadomasochist services (a Miss Whiplash, in tabloid shorthand), though it was clear that Lamont knew nothing about her profession and had never even met her. Much fun was had at his expense, some of which ceased on the revelation that the cost of evicting the woman was partially to be borne by the taxpayer. Though it was not yet apparent, this was merely a foretaste of tabloid scandals to come.

That moment of gaiety aside, the news in the first eighteen months of Major's premiership was relentlessly downbeat, dominated by economic gloom. As 1991 drew to a close, with a general election due the following year, it appeared that little progress had been made in the twelve years of Conservative government, whether judged by unemployment, interest rates or inflation. By any normal standards the opposition should have been in an unassailable position. But although opinion polls frequently gave the Labour Party a small lead, it was far from consistent, and while Major's personal ratings were far in advance of those of his party, Labour's leader, Neil Kinnock, continued to underperform his. There was a danger that the public mood for change, inevitable after Thatcher's long period in office, might have been satisfied merely by the arrival of Major, with no requirement for a completely new government.

There were plenty of people within the Labour Party who shared that fear, and who identified Kinnock as the key problem. The party's environment spokesperson, Bryan Gould, noted that 'some of his colleagues could barely conceal their contempt for him', and Paddy Ashdown, leader of the Liberal Democrats, recorded in his diary conversations with senior figures like Michael Meacher ('Kinnock was considered useless') and Austin Mitchell ('Kinnock wouldn't pull it off and it was time the Labour Party realized that'), who had come to the same conclusion.

Much of the criticism was unfair but unavoidable. Kinnock had been Labour leader since 1983 and, although he had fought only one general election, he had already spent longer in the post in opposition than any previous incumbent. Under his leadership, the party had slowly and painfully pulled back from the left-wing policies associated with the heyday of Tony Benn in the early 1980s, but there was a feeling that perhaps Labour required someone new at the helm if it was to make a final break with the past.

Kinnock himself, however much he argued for the abandonment of the old shibboleths, was perceived as being essentially an opportunist, with no real belief in the message he was articulating. Memories of him as a passionate left-wing rebel were kept alive by the Tories and by the media, and the image persisted. As Heseltine pointed out, he may have begun the process of rehabilitating Labour, but he 'personally looked and sounded the old familiar brand: truly a Welsh Valleys boyo, with plenty of form stretching deep into his past'. The racist abuse of Kinnock as 'Valleys boyo' or a 'Welsh windbag' came particularly ill from the Swansea-born Heseltine, but the tactic worked, and by the start of the new decade opinion polls were showing that Kinnock himself was now perceived as a bigger handicap to his party than was the hard left he had spent so much time fighting.

When, for example, the Labour conference in 1990, following the collapse of Soviet communism, voted for a reduction in defence spending to the average of other west European countries, in order to fund the welfare state, Kinnock — fearful of Tory claims that Labour was always soft on defence — immediately disowned the decision, announcing that it would not be in the next manifesto: 'We live in the world of realities not resolutions.' And, of course, he got the worst of both worlds; undecided voters, remembering his former passion for the cause of nuclear disarmament, still didn't trust him, while many of the party activists felt betrayed.

Indeed that was the terminology he used himself, according to his colleague Peter Mandelson, the party's sometime director of communications: 'I would rather get my betrayal in before the election than after.' Mandelson's explanation of that comment was perfectly sound. 'What he meant was this: too often Labour leaders in the past have not faced up to the difficult arguments. Well, Neil Kinnock would rather face up to the practicalities with honesty and conviction before we go into government.' There was reason and history behind that account, but it convinced few, because the transformation from firebrand to mainstream statesman, untouched by office, stretched credulity too far. 'Not one of the major policy positions that Kinnock enthusiastically embraced at the time of his election as leader in 1982,' wrote the former cabinet minister Peter Shore, 'survived to the end of his leadership. Moreover, he made no public attempt to explain why he had changed his mind.'

It was that last remark that pinned down Kinnock's problem. Changing direction as a result of a political conversion might be acceptable; to do so in response to opinion polls looked like weakness.

There was a sense too that Kinnock's moment had passed. His greatest strength had been as a platform orator, by far the best of the 1980s, capable equally of warm humour and of impassioned rhetoric. Though he had become more restrained since he took over the leadership, and though he seldom shone in the Commons, he was still capable of assimilating and articulating the mood of a crowd, particularly when expressing the fury and hatred that had come to be felt for the Conservative Party in large parts of the country. That talent, however, was of dwindling value now that John Major had replaced Margaret Thatcher; virulent anti-Tory sentiments were much less in evidence in 1991, and apocalyptic warnings about the collapse of society needed a more convincing bogeyman than Major could ever be. And so the idea that Labour might fare better under a different leader began to gain ground.

There was, as it happened, a potential alternative waiting in the wings. John Smith, the shadow chancellor, was generally considered to be the heir apparent, whether the succession came before or after an election. A balding, rotund lawyer from Edinburgh, Smith personified respectability and was seen as a reassuring presence for voters, someone who wouldn't frighten the horses in southern England. 'If John Smith could visit every home in Britain,' remarked his parliamentary colleague, Tony Banks, 'every home would have stone cladding, double glazing and a full set of encyclopaedias.' Or, as another colleague, Tony Wright, was to put it, he had 'the great gift of making ideological declarations sound like a request to call and read the gas meter'.

Smith was also one of the few survivors of the last Labour cabinet, having spent six months as trade secretary in the dying days of James Callaghan's government, and – which was more important – he had some of the bearing of an experienced politician. Like John Major, he had come through his political career with little sign of ideological positioning. He was always seen as being on the right of the Labour Party, but during the internecine warfare of the early 1980s, he had avoided taking a lead in the fight against the left, while never looking as if he might be tempted to defect to the SDP. As the *Sunday Times* pointed out in 1992: 'All the resources of Tory Central Office have failed to find any evidence of his ever having deviated from the most orthodox politics.'

Perhaps for this reason, as well as because he was known to be convivial company, he was popular throughout the party. From the left, Tony Benn observed in November 1991: 'if there was an election for the leadership on a secret ballot tomorrow, Smith would win, with only about five votes going to Kinnock, and our standing would rise in the polls instantly.' Meanwhile, amongst those murmuring in Smith's ear that he should challenge Kinnock for the leadership sooner rather than later was the young right-wing employment spokesperson, Tony Blair, promising his support and that of his friend Gordon Brown if the gauntlet were to be thrown down. In his memoirs, Blair noted: 'Had John moved to replace Neil, it would have been bloody, but in my view he would have succeeded and history would have been very different.' Smith did consider the possibility of a challenge but rejected it. Characteristically, he gave no public indication of disloyalty or even dissatisfaction, though neither he nor anyone else could do anything to silence the backstage whispering that continued to undermine Kinnock's authority.

Throwing himself into his job, Smith set off on what was to become known as the prawn cocktail offensive, a series of meetings with people in the banking and financial sectors aimed at convincing the City that its interests would be safe in Labour's hands. 'Never have so many prawns been sacrificed in vain,' joked Michael Heseltine, and he had a point. In the search for the centre ground of politics, Labour's broad economic policy had become almost indistinguishable from that of the Conservatives. The party had come round to an essentially monetarist position, and had jettisoned its old anti-Europeanism to such an extent that it too believed the future lay in the protective embrace of the ERM. Even Norman Lamont's cheerful endorsement of rising unemployment had been pre-empted by Smith, who had praised the 'counter inflationary discipline' of the ERM, accepting that if the private sector pursued an inflationary course then 'there would be unemployment'.

The only question facing voters was who they believed would best implement the policy. And here, despite the recession, the Tories still had a healthy opinion poll lead. Smith was a far better performer than Lamont, but with the shadow of Thatcher still shaping public perceptions of politics, party leaders were what counted, and Major looked so much more reliable than Kinnock. Back in the early days of Major's leadership, a Tory MP had urged: 'No more ideology, please! Let's just wrap our manifesto around John Major's personality, and ask the people to trust him.' And in essence that was the sum total of the Conservative campaign for the April 1992 election.

By any conventional measure, the omens were not good. In an opinion poll published on the day the election was called, Labour was shown to have a three-point lead over the Tories. No government had ever started a campaign behind in the polls and gone on to win and there was no reason to suppose that the trend would be bucked now. 'It is difficult to imagine circumstances more favourable to the Labour opposition,' noted Peter Shore. A decade earlier there had been a real fear that the SDP/Liberal Alliance might overtake Labour, certainly that its existence would split the anti-Tory vote, but that threat had now receded, and the most charismatic third-party figure, David Owen, was stepping down in defeat from Westminster politics. Above all, the government had failed to engineer an economic recovery in time for the election, and the recession was now officially the longest since the Second World War. House repossessions continued (75,000 of them in the previous year), unemployment was still rising, the amount owed in consumer credit was twice the level of a decade earlier, and 1,200 businesses were going bust every week. All that Kinnock and Labour had to do, it appeared, was to hold their nerve and avoid any serious gaffes.

Nonetheless, Major still put the economy upfront in the campaign, with the promise: 'Vote Conservative on Thursday and the recovery will continue on Friday.' No evidence was offered in support of this claim, but it expressed Major's gut instinct that when it really came down to it, the electorate simply wouldn't trust Kinnock on the economy. (Nor indeed did John Smith, who was of the opinion that 'Kinnock didn't understand economics'.) In the words of Gyles Brandreth, now standing as Conservative candidate for Chester, the hope was that wavering Tory voters would 'come back to us at the last minute, clinging on to nurse for fear of something worse'.

The ammunition that would be needed for that last-ditch stand was supplied right at the beginning of the campaign, when John Smith and the shadow trade secretary Gordon Brown posed on the steps of the Treasury building to launch a 'shadow budget', effectively a pre-announcement of Labour's economic plans should they win the election. At a time when average male earnings were £18,000 a year, Smith promised that everyone on less than £21,000 – 80 per cent of taxpayers – would gain from his proposed rises in thresholds for tax and national insurance: 'we are starting to take back something for the average taxpayer and the average family.' In order to fund these changes, a new top tax rate was to be introduced of 50 per cent on those earning over £40,000. It sounded like a reasonable pitch for the votes of middle England, and was presented with the kind of authority that Norman Lamont was unable to muster, but perhaps warning bells should have sounded when it was greeted with enthusiasm by Tony Benn. 'Very clever,' he noted in his diary, 'attacking the rich and with plans to help the poor. Excellent, good socialist budget.'

Approval by the likes of Benn was not what Kinnock, Smith and Brown had been aiming for, and the impression that they might be working to a socialist agenda was precisely what they were seeking to put behind them; the party manifesto studiously avoided any use at all of the word 'socialism'. But they had got their pitch wrong. The proposed level at which tax rises would kick in was high by the standards of the North-East or Scotland, but well within the dreams of much of the south-eastern middle class, and – as Labour's then health spokesperson Robin Cook was later to point out – was not unknown in the media: 'every sub-editor in Fleet Street or Wapping thought someone on £20,000 a year was poor.' The proposals were seized on by the Tories and portrayed as an attack on success. Furthermore, it was suggested, this was only the first stage of a tax-raising programme. 'Labour's Tax Bombshell,' read one Conservative poster: 'You'd pay £1,250 more tax a year under Labour.' (The message was accompanied by an image of a decidedly retro-looking shell, particularly in the wake of the Kuwaiti War's smart missiles; this was less Baghdad in 1991 than Walmington-on-Sea fifty years earlier.)

Generating even more column inches was a poster showing two red boxing gloves with the slogan 'Labour's Double Whammy' and a claim that both inflation and tax would go up under a Kinnock government. It wasn't an entire success: 'Most of the comment has been "What's a whammy?" and the reaction is bemused or bewildered,' noted Edwina Currie. But while the word may have been new – at least to those who weren't aficionados of the work of blues singer Screamin' Jay Hawkins or novelist Carl Hiaasen – it was instantly memorable, and the discussion it provoked helped push the Tories' core message that you couldn't trust Labour. Less impressive was the fact that, after thirteen years in power, the government had so little to boast about that it was still indulging in such negative tactics.

What positive campaigning there was resolved around Major himself. Determined to appeal directly to the people, he had initially wanted to stage open-access public meetings where he would take questions from all-comers, but this was deemed to be too risky in both political and security terms. Instead, during a walkabout in Bolton, where he was surrounded by a hostile crowd of protestors, he stumbled upon the idea of standing on a box to deliver his message. And thus was born Major's soapbox, without which no subsequent appearance was complete, the single most memorable image of the election. The sight of the prime minister, standing up alone for his beliefs against a shouting mob, many of them bearing

Socialist Workers Party placards, made for fantastic television, even if his words were entirely inaudible.

'You can see them saying: How can we make him look charismatic?' reflected comedian Paul Merton, on *Have I Got News for You*. 'Let's stand him next to a wooden box!' But perhaps Merton was failing to recognise a kindred spirit lurking beneath the grey suit. 'It's pure theatre,' Major said of his campaigning style. He had never been involved in planning an election before, but he took to it with considerable energy and effectiveness. This was a man who had show business in his blood, and he seemed to relish the rough and tumble in a way that should have been understood by a stand-up comic: 'I liked the unpredictability and the dialogue with the crowds. I was invigorated when things went well, and shrugged off the few unpleasant moments.'

He was also prepared to borrow from others. In 1987 the Labour Party had engaged the film director Hugh Hudson to make a party political broadcast known as 'Kinnock – The Movie', which sought to raise the leader's profile. Now the Tories turned to John Schlesinger, director of *Billy Liar*, *Midnight Cowboy* and *Marathon Man* amongst many others, to make 'The Journey', a broadcast that saw John Major revisiting his childhood home in Brixton. 'Is it still there?' Major wondered aloud as the car approached his old house, and then excitedly exclaimed: 'It is, it is, it's still there!' Like his soapbox, it was much mocked by smart young men in the media, but it too helped emphasise the sheer ordinariness of Major.

Against this effective combination of knocking copy and normality, Labour's message was slightly confused. Its campaign theme song was the Farm's 'All Together Now', intended presumably as an anthem of unity and solidarity, though there was also perhaps a pro-European subtext, since the lyrics were about British and German soldiers celebrating together the Christmas of 1914 in the trenches of Flanders. Its uplifting message was hardly matched by the downbeat poem by Adrian Henri, quoting T.S. Eliot's 'The Journey of the Magi', that opened the manifesto:

> 'A cold coming we had of it'
> huddled together in cardboard cities,
> crouched over shared books in leaking classrooms,
> crammed into peeling waiting-rooms.

There appeared some doubt about the balance to be struck between denouncing the distressed state of the nation's fabric under the Tories and the promise of better times to come under Labour. And then there was the notorious Sheffield rally, a whooping American-style extravaganza staged a week before polling day and attended by the entire shadow cabinet. The Sheffield Arena had opened in 1991 as part of an urban redevelopment of land that had previously been the site of a steelworks, the complex also including the Meadowhall shopping centre and the Don Valley stadium. It was thus a symbol of the way that leisure and retail had taken over from industry in the British economy, though whether or why this was a useful association for Labour was not entirely clear.

Nor was the backdrop to the stage quite right on the night. It featured the Union Jack and the flags of the constituent nations of the United Kingdom, but the appeal to patriotism and localism was somewhat spoiled by the fact that the Welsh flag was hung the wrong way round, with its dragon facing to the right. The music was similarly intended to evoke a coalition of cultures: a video of Simply Red's hit 'Something Got Me Started' was followed by performances from violinist Nigel Kennedy, opera singer Elizabeth Brice, the Frickley Colliery Brass Band, a pipe band and a school choir.

All of which was a way of working the 10,000-strong audience up into a frenzy ready for the arrival on stage of Neil Kinnock, just in time for the BBC television news at nine o'clock. And frenzy did indeed seem to be the keynote. Jack Straw, the shadow education spokesperson, thought the atmosphere was 'surreal, unlike any that I've experienced before or since'. Overwhelmed by the enthusiasm of the crowd, Kinnock opened his comments with a repeated shout of 'Well, all right!', though it sounded rather like 'We're all right!' He was, he later explained, simply responding as a rock and roll singer would have done: 'It's what Johnny Cash does. It's what the Everly Brothers used to do.' As seen by television viewers, however, it gave the impression that he and the party were already celebrating a Labour victory at the polls combined with the winning of the Oscar for best actor and the taking of the world heavyweight title. It seemed to confirm all the negative elements of his public image.

When Kinnock finally delivered his speech, it turned out to be a good one. 'The British people want a country with a sense of community,' he urged. 'They want a Britain that is whole and fair and free.' And he promised: 'In nine days' time Britain is going to have a Labour government.' Perhaps unwisely, however, he also drew attention to Major's campaigning: 'What's at issue in this election is not the soapboxes that people stand on. It's the cardboard boxes that people live in.' It was a typically neat oratorical opposition, but not entirely helpful. The contrast between, on the one hand, the man in the marketplace facing down what looked like an SWP mob and, on the other, the man counting his chickens in front of the shrieking faithful at an event that cost £150,000 to stage, was not one that reflected well on Labour.

In retrospect, many blamed the Sheffield rally, in its display of premature triumphalism, for alienating voters. The real problem, however, was not one of tone but of logistics. A coach laid on to transport journalists to East Midlands Airport, where they were booked on a flight to London, became stuck in mud and never made it out of the car park. A replacement bus eventually arrived, but then broke down, and the journalists didn't get back to the capital till 5 a.m. the next day, leaving the media thoroughly grumpy and disinclined to give any favourable coverage. With a week still to go, there was plenty of time for the image of Sheffield to become a story in its own right, particularly since it fed into an established narrative of Kinnock as a boastful braggart. 'There is a fine line between confidence and cockiness,' noted the outgoing home secretary, Kenneth Baker, in a campaign speech, 'and on Wednesday night in Sheffield, Mr Kinnock stepped over it.' Twelve months later, Kinnock reflected on the rally and, recalling the dictum of American politician Adlai Stevenson that adulation is all right as long as you don't inhale, he admitted: 'for just a few seconds, I inhaled.'

Kinnock, as ever, received criticism from both sides. From the left, the French newspaper *Libération* headlined its coverage of the rally RED KINNOCK WATERS DOWN HIS WINE, and Bryan Gould identified the key issue in Labour's position as being its surrender to the economic wisdom of the Tories: 'We were trying to achieve through pzazz what we dared not try to achieve in substance. If we had been braver on policy and on breaking from the monetarist consensus, we would not have needed the Sheffield rally.' Similarly Kim Howells, a former union official and now MP, was later to denounce 'the clique of spin doctors and party managers who foisted on us the anodyne policy statements and gut churning embarrassment of the Sheffield rally'. From another direction entirely came the comments of Sir John Banham, director general of the CBI, who warned a meeting of business executives held in Sheffield the very next day that Labour's tax plans ran the risk of turning the recession into a slump.

With the polls mostly predicting that no party would win an outright majority, much of the talk in that last week concerned the possibility of a hung parliament and of the coalition government that would necessarily result. This caused great excitement amongst the Liberal Democrats, who had been born in 1989 of the merger of the SDP and the Liberal Party and were now emerging as a more targeted and disciplined force under the leadership of Paddy Ashdown. He let it be known that his price for participating in government would be four cabinet seats and a commitment to proportional representation in future elections. The Tories refused to engage in such talk, publicly insisting that they would make no deal, but Labour was less rigid and some leading figures allowed themselves to be drawn into talk about coalitions, while Neil Kinnock floated the idea of inviting other parties into a discussion of electoral reform. The effect was that Labour suddenly looked as if they lacked self-confidence, the precise opposite of the message sent out by the Sheffield rally, but equally damaging.

Nonetheless, the assumption was that Labour were the favourites to win the election. Few shared the eternal optimism of Tony Benn ('it looks to me as if this is going to be a 1945-type breakthrough'), but most were convinced that the government would fall, including most of the members of that government. Social services minister Ann Widdecombe was sufficiently doubtful that she took her pot plants home from the office, not expecting to return, while the Conservative Party chairman, Chris Patten, issued instructions on the day before the poll that no senior ministers should appear on television in the early hours of the election broadcasts; the implication was that he believed a loss of the government's majority was likely and that he didn't want anything said that might scupper negotiations with other parties. It wasn't an encouraging message, as Kenneth Baker noted: 'From the very top of the party the prospect of defeat was being signalled.' If one were looking for a dissident opinion, however, there was always the stock market, which – like bookmaking – is more often right than not in making such calculations: as trading started on the morning of election day, share prices rose in anticipation of a Conservative victory.

As voting closed at 10 p.m., the BBC and ITN unveiled the results of their exit polls, both showing a hung parliament. The BBC predicted that the Conservatives would emerge as the largest party on 301 seats, still twenty-five seats short of an outright majority, with Labour on 298. On this projection, with the Lib Dems achieving just twenty-four seats, there was no easy or obvious coalition to be constructed that could command a majority of the House of Commons, but one thing was certainly clear, as a smiling Gordon Brown was quick to point out: the Tories had 'lost their mandate to govern'.

Unfortunately for Labour, the exit polls were misleading. Not quite as misleading as the opinion polls during the campaign, but still suffering from the same basic flaw; it transpired that many of those who voted Conservative were unwilling to admit the fact to strangers bearing clipboards, either before or after the event. It wasn't a very encouraging message for the Tories. The massive discrepancies between the opinion polls and the actual votes cast suggested that the electors were troubled by feelings of guilt; in the privacy of the polling booths, they opted for a party that promised tax cuts, but they were aware enough of what was expected of them, when asked by pollsters, to protest the opposite, to say they wished to contribute more of their income in order to fund greater investment in public services. They were attracted to the thought that there was such a thing as society, if not necessarily willing to foot the bill.

Those, however, were considerations for the future. At the time, with election night shading into the early hours of the next day, the emerging story was one of Tory success. The key moment came with the declaration in Basildon, a Tory marginal that was considered essential for Labour to win. This was the heartland of 'Essex man', the southern working-class voter who had been won over by Margaret Thatcher and Norman Tebbit in the 1980s. Since Major's appeal was thought to reside in the suburbs rather than in the new towns, hopes were high in Labour circles that Basildon could be taken. It wasn't, and the Conservative candidate David Amess was returned to represent the seat he had held since 1983. There was a swing from Tory to Labour, but too small to offer any real hope for the rest of the night.

As the election results started to mount up, predictions were revised again and again, each time showing a more substantial move towards the Conservative cause. By the end of the night, it had become apparent that it was all over for Labour and for Neil Kinnock. The Conservatives had recorded 14.1 million votes, the largest endorsement ever achieved in Britain and, though their share of the vote was lower than had been attained in any of the previous three victories under Margaret Thatcher, they were still 7.5 percentage points clear of Labour, greater than the margin of victory in 1979. And much of that margin was the result of the female vote; the lead amongst women was more than twice as great as that amongst men.

Most importantly the Conservatives had a reduced, but still workable, majority of twenty-one seats in the Commons. It was an historic victory, the first time that any party had won four consecutive general victories since the days before the Great Reform Act of 1832 had wiped out the rotten boroughs. And it was all the work of John Major, a man untainted by associations with Thatcherism or with anything else. It was hard to believe that any other Tory leader, even Michael Heseltine, could have achieved such a result.

For the millions who had genuinely believed that this was Labour's moment, the election night saw a slow, cruel collapse of hope. Yet again the party had failed to win over 40 per cent of the popular vote, as it had similarly failed in every general election since 1970. If the Tories couldn't be defeated in the depths of a recession caused by their own policies, with all the concessions made by Kinnock, then it was reasonable to ask the question put by Giles Radice: 'Can Labour ever win?'

Much of the talk in political circles concerned the question of whether Britain might have become a one-party state, along the lines of Japan, where the Liberal Democratic Party had been in power since 1955. By removing Thatcher and replacing her with a very different kind of leader, the Tories had shown that they were capable of reinventing themselves sufficiently to satisfy the public need for a new direction. 'We live in a dominant party system, where political changes occur through shifts in the dominant party,' argued Tony Wright, a political lecturer who had just been elected as Labour MP for Cannock and Burntwood. 'Mr Major is the perfect politician for such a system, without ideological baggage and willing to open and close windows of political opportunity as circumstances demand.'

In the depths of a despair-filled night, there were few enough moments for Labour supporters to celebrate. A couple of rising Conservative stars – Lynda Chalker, the overseas development minister, and Francis Maude, financial secretary to the Treasury – lost their seats, but neither was exactly a household name, and neither was on the Thatcherite wing of the party. Nor was Chris Patten, the one major opposition scalp, who lost his seat in Bath to Don Foster of the Liberal Democrats. Indeed the cheers that rang around Labour clubs when Patten's result was announced were far exceeded by the whoops of delight heard at a Conservative gathering in London, where the guest list included Thatcher herself; there the wild applause was accompanied by shouts of 'Tory gain at Bath!'

The absence of Patten from the Commons was a crucial loss, for his was a presence that would have made a considerable difference to Major's cabinet. Conservative historian Robert Shepherd thought he was 'the most able Tory strategist and thinker of his generation', while Major reflected simply: 'I had lost my next chancellor of the exchequer.' More than that, he had lost the one senior Conservative who could persuasively argue a pro-European position with passion and conviction, in a language that was readily understood by the public. In 1994 the cabinet minister William Waldegrave explained that, although Major had the right position on Europe, 'he knows he hasn't yet got the right language. This is where he misses Chris so much. Terribly. He could put the words on it.' Patten was instead appointed as the last ever governor of Hong Kong (a job for which Thatcher had once considered Prince Charles, though it was ultimately decided that he wouldn't be up to negotiating with the Chinese). He was never to return to British politics, much to the relief of the Thatcherite wing, for whom his articulate advocacy of the European cause was always a threat.

For his enemies, Patten's handling of the election campaign had offered, during its course, another excuse for attacking him. The overwhelming consensus at the time was that it had been 'run dreadfully badly', though of course the result retrospectively justified everything. The same could clearly not be said of the Labour Party, though despite the misery of election night, there was some hope for the future. A close analysis of the results showed just how tenuous was Major's grasp on power: it transpired that if just 1,284 voters in eleven marginal constituencies had voted differently, the Conservatives would have been denied a majority in the Commons. All elections are to a greater or lesser extent decided in a handful of swing constituencies, but this was particularly the case in 1992; the swing to Labour in Tory-held marginals was twice that of the national average, for Labour had learnt to target its campaigning, and was actually very well placed for the next election.

But the vagaries of the British electoral system meant that for the next four or five years there was to be a Conservative government. And the significance of that fact was hard to avoid. When Margaret Thatcher was asked, as the result became clear, what she made of her successor's remarkable victory, she was exuberant. 'It is a great night,' she proclaimed. 'It is the end of socialism.' In her memoirs, published the following year, she wrote about James Callaghan's administration as 'the last Labour government and perhaps the last ever', and it seemed all too plausible an analysis.

The Labour leadership's immediate response was more defensive, finding a scapegoat in the shape of the tabloid newspapers. In the wake of the election defeat, Neil Kinnock announced that he was stepping down as Labour leader, and in his resignation speech he drew attention to an article by the Conservative Party's former treasurer Alistair McAlpine which had cited as 'the heroes of this campaign' David English, Nicholas Lloyd and Kelvin MacKenzie, editors of the *Daily Mail*, the *Daily Express* and the *Sun* respectively. 'Never has their attack on the Labour Party been so comprehensive,' wrote McAlpine. 'This was how the election was won and if the politicians, elated in their hour of victory, are tempted to believe otherwise, they are in very real trouble next time.' Those comments inspired one of the *Sun*'s most famous front-page headlines: IT'S THE SUN WOT WON IT, following on from its election-day cover which had shown a crude illustration of a light bulb containing Kinnock's head, accompanied by the message: 'If Kinnock wins today will the last person to leave Britain please turn out the lights.'

Whether McAlpine's analysis, and the *Sun*'s chest-beating, were accurate or not remained debatable. Chris Patten had been sufficiently interested in the influence of the nation's biggest-selling daily to commission some research into the question and discovered that, after more than a decade of Thatcherite cheerleading, 'the majority of its readers throughout the campaign thought it a left-leaning and left-supporting paper'. But truth was less important than perception, and when Tony Blair eventually came to power in the Labour Party, he was clear in his own mind that the *Sun* had played a crucial role in the 1992 election. Consequently, he took great care to court the paper's proprietor, Rupert Murdoch, much to the fury of Neil Kinnock, who was still nursing his wounds years later. 'You imagine what it's like to have your head stuck inside a fucking light bulb, then you tell me how I'm supposed to feel,' he raged at Blair's press secretary, Alastair Campbell.

Kinnock's departure as Labour leader, along with his deputy Roy Hattersley, marked a final break with the 1980s. Over the course of two elections, he had improved the Labour vote by three million from its low point in 1983, had put on nearly seven percentage points in the share of the vote, and had added sixty-two MPs to the parliamentary party. Most importantly, he had kept the party together and ensured that it survived as the principal opposition to the Conservatives, which at times in the early 1980s had been far from certain. In the 1983 election the SDP/Liberal Alliance had come second in 63 per cent of Tory-held seats, in 1992 the Liberal Democrats came second in just 43 per cent of them. Kinnock had achieved everything except power (he never in his career held office in a British government), destined to be the leader who didn't take his people to the promised land.

The weight that came with the leadership of Labour was never more apparent than in the few months after the election, as Kinnock shrugged off the burden and could be seen to relax after years of pressure. Appearances on television – notably on *Have I Got News for You* – and on radio, where he did a stint as a disc jockey on Radio 2, revealed that the humour and the passion that had first made his name had survived. His own verdict on his long period as leader demonstrated a sense of relief that it was all over: 'What a bloody way to spend my forties!' But perhaps the last word on Kinnock's stewardship of the Labour Party should rest with the man who he faced at the despatch box twice a week, and who had no reason to feel any warmth towards him. 'Neil was a more forceful leader than the Tory Party or the press ever acknowledged,' wrote John

Major in 1999. It was a typically generous tribute that reflected rather well on both men.

There was never much doubt about who was going to succeed Kinnock. Even before nominations for the leadership closed, the leaders of the three biggest trade unions – the AEU, the TGWU and the GMBW – had all endorsed the claim of John Smith, and the result was a foregone conclusion. Even so, Tony Blair tried to persuade his closest colleague Gordon Brown to enter the race, not in the hope of winning but with the intention of putting down a marker on behalf of the impatient young faction who were already becoming known as the 'modernisers'.

But Smith was far too experienced an operator to allow himself to be outmanoeuvred by the likes of Blair and had already squared Brown before the election, offering him the shadow chancellorship as a consolation prize on condition that he didn't stand. 'Gordon had not seized the moment,' wrote Blair reprovingly in his memoirs, though his comment at the time was more forthright: 'He chickened out.' Brown's own account was somewhat different. 'I felt I had to be loyal,' he claimed afterwards. 'I never thought for a minute of standing against John Smith.' Blair himself, who Major said was the person he most feared on the Labour front bench, considered running for the deputy leadership, but allowed himself to be talked out of it.

There was one other potential candidate for the top job who didn't materialise. From the left, Ken Livingstone, the former leader of the Greater London Council, announced his intention of standing. He had the support of the *Sun*, the paper that had once described him as 'the most odious man in Britain' and for whom he now wrote a column, but that was about as deep as his backing went. Under the rules then operating, a candidate needed to secure the nominations of a fifth of the parliamentary party, which in 1992 meant fifty-five MPs; Livingstone managed just thirteen.

The absence of Brown and Livingstone meant that the only challenge Smith faced was from Bryan Gould, and it was touch-and-go whether even he could secure enough nominations. Gould had long carved out an alternative viewpoint to that of Kinnock and Smith, putting forward arguments that were to look much wiser in retrospect than many were prepared to credit at the time. He opposed British membership of the ERM and suggested that, rather than simply pushing up interest rates to deal with the effects of a credit boom, a responsible government would 'look at restricting the general level of lending by banks and other institutions in conditions where that lending threatened to become excessive'. He further insisted that the British political establishment was mistaken in its 'belief that monetary measures matter more than the real economy in which ordinary people live and work and that one can take a shortcut, through fiscal policy and the mere assertion that we have a strong currency, to the economic success which we see others enjoying'. Curiously enough, Major in his memoirs seemed partially to come round to this way of thinking, reflecting on his time as chancellor: 'Like Nigel Lawson before me, I had my eye on the wrong ball: the monetary statistics, and not the real economy.'

But Gould's position of a modernising, Eurosceptic left enjoyed little support within the party. Labour had become so demoralised by its failure to defeat the Tories over what was now four elections that it had effectively ceded the economic ground and was looking hopefully towards Europe to deliver some sort of alternative on social policy. Furthermore Gould was not a great faction-builder, lacking a power base within either the parliamentary party or — as was still important at the time — the union movement. Indeed his own expertise in economic matters sometimes had the effect of alienating his colleagues, who were aware of their own limitations and felt that he displayed 'arrogance'. If that were the case, he was far from apologetic. 'It always amazed me that so few MPs knew anything about economics,' he later reflected. 'Almost none found it possible to reach their own independent conclusions.'

Ultimately the leadership election, insofar as there was a debate to be had, came down to something more straightforward than economics and Britain's relationship with Europe. It was a question of comfort. Smith was the steady-as-she-goes candidate, reassuring the party that there would be no more great upheavals on policy, that it was in prime position to take the next election, and that its traditions would be fully respected, for Smith was nothing if not a man of the Labour movement. Opposing that heartening message was the outsider Gould, the New Zealand-born academic who had gone on to work in broadcast journalism, and who insisted that the party was not yet properly prepared for government. 'A "safety first" approach and waiting for the Tories to lose won't produce election victory. We'll have to reach out to those voters who felt unable to trust us,' he argued, adding that in the election: 'Our policies appeared to set a cap on the aspirations of the voters we need to win.'

From another wing of the party, the Europhile social democrat Giles Radice had arrived at the same conclusion. Noting that in the 1992 election Labour had won just three of the 109 seats in the South-East outside London, he called on Labour to recognise and address this regional imbalance. In a series of pamphlets titled 'Southern Discomfort', he analysed the problem that the lower-middle class and skilled working class, those in the socio-economic groups C1 and C2, 'do not trust Labour and think the party is against people "getting on"'. His research discovered 'that the wavering voters came down in favour of the Tories because they feared that Labour would mismanage the economy, put up taxes and be in hock to the unions'. The regional issue was also expressed in personal terms, as one of Chris Patten's advisers had observed during the election campaign: 'We were finding that the reaction against Mr Kinnock was stronger the further south you got.'

But the need to improve the party's position in the South was not apparent to all. John Smith was born, educated and worked in Scotland, he represented a Scottish constituency and, from his vantage point north of the border, there seemed far less pressure for radical reform of the party. In Scotland Labour had been comfortably the most successful party in the 1992 general election, with a lead over the Conservatives of thirteen percentage points, and it seemed less important to win over Essex man than to avoid being outflanked on the left by the Scottish National Party. There was little sense of urgency in Scotland, just a belief that one last push would be sufficient.

Gould was the obvious answer to Labour's southern weakness. Sufficiently cosmopolitan and forward looking that he could hardly be painted as an eccentric, extremist Eurosceptic, he was also an adept television performer. Although he was to the left of John Smith, he lacked the taint of union backing, projecting a less obviously aligned image that could have reached out beyond the party's heartlands. But in the final analysis, none of this counted. Smith took just over 90 per cent of the votes available, winning an overwhelming majority in all three sections of the Labour Party's electoral college: the MPs, the trade unions and the constituency parties.

A simultaneous election for the deputy leadership, to replace Roy Hattersley, ran much the same course. The would-be left candidate, Bernie Grant, failed to get enough nominations to stand, and the result was a convincing win for Margaret Beckett, who Smith had made clear was his personal choice. She beat both Gould — who was standing in both contests and who trailed in a poor third — and John Prescott, whose pitch was a more traditional left message that the party was in danger of losing its identity. 'Playing safe hasn't done us very well, has it?' he reasoned. 'All the individuality, the chance, the difference has been taken out of our politics, and the electorate doesn't trust us.'

Prescott's opportunity to change that was yet to come. The same was not true of Bryan Gould. In the autumn of 1992 he was voted off the party's national executive committee and then resigned from the shadow cabinet, acknowledging that he had lost the argument over Labour's adoption of Tory economic policy. The following year he accepted the offer of a job back in his native New Zealand as the vice-chancellor of Waikato University, and in early 1994 he departed from the House of Commons, another of the best leaders Labour never had. The party he left behind, he believed, had given up on its radical mission and now offered little that was distinctive: 'More compassionate and competent government, yes, but a new vision, a conscious attempt to change society, to project Britain into a new era — that was definitely off the agenda.'

That perceived lack of a crusading spirit was a verdict not far removed from Thatcher's announcement of 'the end of socialism', and nor was it far from John Major's own thoughts on the 1992 election. 'Our victory ensured that our reforms over the previous thirteen years were made permanent,' he wrote in his memoirs. 'Above all, our victory in 1992 killed socialism in Britain. It also, I must conclude, made the world safe for Tony Blair.'

2

Lads

'All I found was cigarettes and alcohol'

> Basically, when all's said and done, I'm just drawn to sluts with
> big tits.
> Frank Skinner (1994)

> The higher up the tree the women climb, the easier it is for the
> men to see up our skirts.
> Reg Gadney, *Just When We Are Safest* (1995)

> GORDON BRITTAS: In a divided and troubled world such as this, it seems
> to me that sport is the one thing that can bring people together.
> Richard Fegen & Andrew Norris, *The Brittas Empire* (1991)

In 1990 the comedian David Baddiel went to a screening of John McNaughton's harrowing, low-budget film *Henry: Portrait of a Serial Killer*, which had been made in 1986 but still hadn't been passed for general release. During a panel discussion that followed the showing, an audience member began railing against the extreme violence in the movie, about which, she said, she had received no warning. At which point another member of the audience interrupted her: 'For fuck's sake, what did you expect?' he called out. 'It's not called *Henry the Elephant*, is it?' Baddiel was convulsed with fits of laughter, and later reflected: 'I think it was at that point that the eighties fell away for me, or at least that *seriousness* fell away for me, seriousness as in that adolescent, or post-adolescent, concern about everything. I was never going to be intense again.'

Seriousness had indeed been the keynote of the 1980s counterculture. The era may have seen the rise of yuppies, power-dressing and the creed of 'greed is good', as articulated by Gordon Gecko in the film *Wall Street*, but for many the experience was very different. It was a decade that started and ended with devastating recessions, and which seemed to lurch from one apocalyptic fear to another: the Cold War rhetoric of Margaret Thatcher and American president Ronald Reagan was matched by dire warnings about environmental destruction – whether centred on acid rain, the depletion of the ozone layer or global warming – while the arrival of AIDS threatened a health crisis of proportions not seen for decades.

For those who came of age in the early Thatcher years, those born in or around 1960, these were not reassuring times. As they emerged from school and college – part of the most numerous generation in British history – into a society scarred by record levels of unemployment and beset by uncertainty, the world felt like an inhospitable place, on both a political and a personal level. Much of this was experienced most keenly in the deindustrialised wastelands, far beyond the prosperous enclaves of the South-East, but there was also a tranche of the population who, in another time, might have expected to be among society's success stories, the should-be middle class who now found themselves, as Jon Savage wrote of the original punks, 'people whose intelligence is surplus to requirements'. Many of these latter drifted to London.

It was, unsurprisingly, a generation that was inclined to the left, defining itself by its opposition to nuclear weapons, apartheid, Israel, racism, sexism, vivisection, hunting with hounds: the list was extensive. To an extent, of course, this was true of almost all post-war youth; there had long been fashionable causes calling on the allegiance of the school-leaver and the student. What was different this time was the additional factor of the early 1980s recession, the absence of a rising tide of prosperity to soak up the protest. The social optimism of the 1950s and 1960s had faded to nothing, and even the more recent rebellion of punk was looking quite positive in retrospect.

On an early punk single, the group Chelsea had demanded the 'Right to Work', but the Clash's better known 'Career Opportunities' had a slightly different take: 'They offered me the office, offered me the shop,' sang Joe Strummer. 'Do you wanna make tea at the BBC? Do you wanna be, do you really wanna be a cop?' Five years on, unemployment had tripled, and that kind of choice sounded little more than a pipe-dream. By the time the economy recovered in the middle of the 1980s, there were a couple of million more young adults entering the job market, and many who had struggled to find work during the recession found themselves leapfrogged or left behind.

Amongst those left behind were substantial numbers eking out an existence on the fringes of the cultural industries. With success having passed by on the other side, and with regular employment in short supply, there developed a celebration of underachievement, as though there were virtue in spurning mass popularity. The concept of not 'selling out', of refusing to compromise artistic vision for commercial gain, was derived from the beatniks and hippies of previous generations, and had been one of the legacies of punk. What had seemed a temporary pose of credibility, a staging-post on the road to success, became in the 1980s a semi-permanent way of life. The mainstream culture of the time was shiny, apolitical and unashamedly driven by money, but running parallel to the booming good times was a fertile alternative that continued to maintain its independence. It was capable of occasional, sporadic eruption into the mainstream of music, as with groups like the Jesus and Mary Chain and the Smiths in the mid-1980s or the Madchester bands at the end of the decade; it could even produce a major commercial success like *Viz* comic; and it channelled a great deal of energy into creating a new incarnation of stand-up comedy. But mostly this end of youth culture was characterised by its defiant refusal to seek a mass market.

It was also known for its right-on attitudes, and in particular its embrace of sexual politics. This was, remarked the comedy writer John O'Farrell, 'the world of the new puritans', where the campaign to drive sexism out of society seemed sometimes to shade into a suspicion of heterosexuality and of sex itself. David Baddiel's account of the discussion about *Henry: Portrait of a Serial Killer* was in part a riposte to this dour current, and was certainly seen as such in some quarters.

Baddiel was far from alone, as the new decade dawned, in seeking a lighter tone to life. Billy Bragg's protest songs and one-man benefit gigs had epitomised the alternative culture of the 1980s. Now, in 1991 – the year he left the Labour Party – he turned up with a cheerfully positive single, 'Sexuality', that came complete with a full band and a happy video, the former featuring guitarist Johnny Marr, and the latter directed by comedian Phill Jupitus. The serious intent was there, with a robust defence of gay equality, but the record became his biggest and best-known hit because it was a feelgood pop song in the great English tradition of the Kinks, Madness and Squeeze, celebrating the joys of physical intimacy in a way that simply wouldn't have seemed appropriate on the left a few years earlier. The opening line – 'I've had relations with girls from many nations' – managed not only to rejoice in multiculturalism, but also to legitimise promiscuity. Coming hard on the heels of a self-emasculating era, when Ben Elton had made his name with a comedy of male humiliation, this was heady stuff.

It was difficult, of course, to see Bragg as any kind of sex symbol, and no one was likely to mistake his music for the erotically charged work of Prince or Madonna, but that seemed part of the point. It was his ordinariness, along with his impeccable political credentials, that made 'Sexuality' a song of liberation. It was a world away from comedian Nigel Planer's novel *The Right Man* (1998), in which the hero, Guy Mullin, estranged from his wife, visits a prostitute and is informed: 'You have to tell me what you like.' He's confused by the comment: 'I have no idea what I like. That never comes into it. I aim to please, I suppose.'

Mullin was to be seen as a product of his time. The impact of feminism had left men, some argued, uncertain of their role, and there was said to be a crisis of masculinity. 'Men are struggling for an identity,' remarked Mick Cooper, editor of the magazine *Achilles Heel*, which was aimed at pro-feminist men, in 1991. 'They want to call themselves something.' The same year, a six-part documentary series on BBC Television, titled *From Wimps to Warriors*, purported to be a study of the modern man, though its chosen subjects – amongst them a nightclub bouncer on trial for GBH and a masochist who liked being dressed in a dog suit and walked on all-fours in the park by his Mistress – did not appear to have been chosen as typical representatives of their gender.

They did, however, have the advantage of reality, unlike the contemporary advertising fantasy of the New Man, typified by a Rover commercial in which a man used the smooth driving capacity of his car to lull a baby to sleep. Around the same time, a flurry of greetings cards featured men showing off their gym-honed torsos as they cradled babies in their arms. The New Man was said to be caring, sharing and emotional, as devoted to home-making as an American housewife of the 1950s. This unattainable, and as far as anyone could tell undesired, vision of masculinity had a very brief shelf life. Against such absurdity, Billy Bragg's larking about on the video of 'Sexuality', kicking a football around with his mates, offered a plausible alternative vision of what it meant to be a man.

But the most enduring contribution to the debate came from the journalist Sean O'Hagan, who – also in 1991 – coined the expression 'new lad' in an article for *Arena* magazine. This construct was intended, he explained, as 'a tentatively positive reaction to three decades of feminism'. While recognising that men's interests in sex, beer and football were unlikely to disappear simply by wishing them away, the new lad was said to blend these traditional pursuits with a more recently acquired sensitivity: boozing and bonding did not have to preclude mature relationships with women.

It took a while for the phrase to catch on beyond the opinion pages of the broadsheets, but in 1992 the new lad found cultural expression in an ITV sitcom and he never looked back. Adapted by Simon Nye from his 1989 novel, *Men Behaving Badly* was sold on the strength of its star Harry Enfield, then riding high with his BBC sketch series and teamed here with the much less well-known Martin Clunes. Respectively they played Dermot and Gary, a pair of socially and sexually inept flatmates whose misbehaviour lay more in their bark than their bite. 'Twenty years ago, when men had no respect for women, they just used to say: You're chucked,' mused Dermot. 'But now we do respect them, we have to lie to them sensitively.' Behind the bravado, however, the truth was that they lost out to women in almost every encounter.

That first series of *Men Behaving Badly* had a slightly different tone from its better known successors, one that suggested a much more middle-class milieu. Gary and Dermot had met as students and were to be seen reminiscing about their time at college, drinking wine with their dinner, and playing chess and squash together. It was, in other words, more faithful to the tone of the original novel, in which Gary doesn't have a television, goes jogging and enjoys Bach organ recitals on Radio 3. He also has a beard. Both men spend much of their time, and all of their energy, trying to get their upstairs neighbour, Deborah, into bed but, in truth, they don't really behave very badly at all – they are merely social underachievers.

If Simon Nye was one writer helping to shape the new lad, the other was Martin Amis, whose appeal lay in the combination of his own celebrity and the amoral depravity of his 1980s novels *Money* and *London Fields*. As the new decade dawned, Amis's depictions of the corrupting power of affluence, and of the hedonism that follows in its wake, began to seem less satire than blueprint. His influence on men a dozen or so years his junior, well beyond the rarefied realms of literary fiction, was not hard to discern. The racing driver Damon Hill cited *Money* as the funniest book he'd ever read, and when his female interviewer ventured to disagree, he had the perfect riposte: 'Well, that's because you're not a man. Amis is a boys' writer.' Indeed he was, and the casual glamour of the slumming intellectual was, for some men, hard to resist. 'He did not invent that combination of blokeishness and cerebrality,' the writer Nick Hornby observed, 'but his emergence seems to have validated it.' Or, as Alex James, bassist in the group Blur, was later to put it: 'We're aspiring yobbos and aspiring thinkers.'

Inevitably, however, the cerebral half of Hornby's formulation proved less durable than did the blokeish. A shift was signalled with the departure of Harry Enfield from the cast of *Men Behaving Badly* and his replacement by Neil Morrissey as the non-student Tony. With his addition, and then with a subsequent transfer to a later timeslot on BBC One, the series became more classless; the references to college, wine and squash faded away in favour of farting, boozing and fantasising about women (though oddly the pair remained completely uninterested in football) – Gary now boasted of having received his education in 'the university of life'.

'The characters are conducting their lives in a way that no child should admire,' huffed the Conservative MP Patrick Cormack, unaware that he was missing the point: these were children. The programme became one of the defining shows of its era partly because it was seen as a retort to the years of right-on comedy and partly because it portrayed young men as gleefully arrested adolescents. From the outset, the reference points were to the popular culture of the characters' teenage years – Showaddywaddy, Linda Lusardi, Barry White – as the boys fled the modern world for the security of their happy place. They were in their early thirties and represented a generation beginning to worry that it had missed out on the fun of youth, tempted onto the path of righteousness by David Baddiel's 'seriousness' and John O'Farrell's 'new puritanism'. It was a reversal of the progress in 1960s youth culture, when a fast-maturing Eric Burdon, formerly of the Animals, had sung about 'all the good time that I wasted having good times', and regretted that 'When I was drinking, I should've been thinking.'

As he evolved, the new lad increasingly wore his emotional immaturity as a badge of honour. 'Like most blokes,' explained Neil Morrissey, 'we resolve all our problems by having a lager in front of the TV and not talking about anything.' Or, in the case of Baddiel himself, having a lager in front of a TV camera and talking about football with his real-life flatmate Frank Skinner in *Fantasy Football League* from 1994.

And there was always the option of invoking the spirit of irony as justification for naughty behaviour. 'I feel we've let ourselves down,' smirked Skinner, after an entirely gratuitous screening of Erica Roe's 1982 streak at Twickenham. When Tony is told in *Men Behaving Badly* that having a topless picture of a woman on his bedroom wall is sexist, he cites the same defence: 'It's ironic,' he argues. It became a common cry, satirised in *Drop the Dead Donkey*, where the veteran newsreader Henry Davenport finds a job as the sidekick to a late-night youth presenter, adjudicating in events like Breast Fight, in which 'women pummel each other with their breasts'. He tries to explain that he knows what he's doing ('That item was ironic'), but his closest friend, Dave, points to the elephant in the studio: 'Knowing it's crap does not stop it being crap.'

The fact that the portraits in *Men Behaving Badly* were drawn from life was demonstrated in 1994 with the launch of *Loaded* magazine, which promoted itself with the slogan: 'For men who should know better.' Its founding editor was James Brown, a veteran of 1980s alternative culture ('Radio 1's Steve Lamacq and I used to run fanzine stalls at all Ken Livingstone's GLC free festivals,' he remembered), and a former features editor at the *New Musical Express*. The editorial in the first issue proclaimed that the magazine was 'dedicated to life, liberty and the pursuit of sex, drink, football and less serious matters'. A desire to change the world was not immediately apparent. 'Post-feminism has forced men to try out many impossible roles,' sighed the television presenter Paul Ross, but 'the idea of being a good bloke is such a low target that you can actually achieve it.'

There was a level of energy, wit and style about *Loaded* in those early days. The deadpan Biscuit of the Month review, for example, was not far removed from the humour of *Viz* comic, and the double-page poster spreads of bikini-clad babes were backed with images of, say, a bacon sandwich. But at root it gained its popularity by revelling in laddish behaviour. This was typified by a 1995 interview with Robbie Fowler, in which the Liverpool footballer revealed that he fancied women 'as long as they've got a fanny and breathe', and that his favourite chat-up line was: 'Do you like jewellery? Well, suck my cock, it's a gem.' Fowler was a fine instinctive striker, and his prowess in the opposition's penalty box was beyond question, but no one ever accused him of being cerebral.

Loaded's cheerful mix of birds, booze and football was instantly and spectacularly successful, inspiring several less stylish imitations, most notably in the shape of *Maxim* and the reinvention of the already established *FHM*. The monthly magazine had previously been seen as primarily a female medium, but in August 1997 the circulation of *FHM* broke through the half-million mark, overtaking *Cosmopolitan*, the leading women's title, for the first time, with *Loaded* lagging not far behind. A year later and *FHM* had added another quarter-million to its circulation and was selling twice as many copies as *Vogue*, *Tatler* and *Harpers & Queen* combined.

So big had this market become that it impacted adversely on more venerable titles. In 1997 the retailers W.H. Smith announced that they were no longer going to stock the pornographic *Penthouse* because its sales had fallen so markedly; the British edition of the magazine toned down its content and attempted to rebrand itself as *PH.UK* ('the adult magazine for grown-ups'), but closed within months, unable to hold its own in this new world. Meanwhile the tabloid newspapers responded to a potential threat by allying themselves as closely as possible; the *Sun* celebrated the fiftieth edition of *Loaded* with a five-day series featuring shots of women from the magazine, and the *Daily Mirror* ran a week-long feature on *FHM*'s '100 Women' issue.

Attempts were also made to hitch the new lad bandwagon to other cultural trends, so that in 1996 *Eat Soup*, a cookery magazine aimed at young men, was launched; given that its first issue included a photograph of a naked woman on all fours, marked up to show cuts of meat, few tears were shed when it closed after a handful of editions. It did, however, last longer than *The Larder Lads*, a series commissioned by the BBC and again aimed at teaching young men to cook, which was to be hosted by Neil Morrissey; that venture failed to get off the ground. The times were not yet right for laddish cuisine.

But the sales of the lads' mags continued to rise. 'There has to be a finite number of readers,' marvelled *FHM* editor Ed Needham, 'but no one knows how big the market is.' In fact, the high point had been reached before the end of the decade, and the figures started to fall away in 1999, though the influence lasted far longer.

The relationship between the magazines and *Men Behaving Badly* was made explicit with the arrival on the news-stands in 1996 of *Stuff*, which billed itself as '*Which?* behaving badly', a compliment reciprocated in the programme itself, with Tony seen reading a copy of the fictitious publication *Bloke*. By this stage, the new lad phenomenon had mutated somewhat. It was less knowing now, and it was significantly younger.

The likes of Simon Nye, David Baddiel, Frank Skinner and James Brown were all born a few years either side of 1960, and the culture of that generation was evident in the choice of cover stars for the first issue of *Loaded*: a picture of the actor Gary Oldman was joined by the names of the footballer Eric Cantona and the musician Paul Weller under the headline SUPERLADS. *Loaded*'s core market, however, was younger: 'Most of our readers are in their early twenties,' admitted Brown in 1994 and, though he insisted that this wasn't relevant, arguing that the magazine was 'about a devil-may-care attitude, not demographics', the disparity in age and outlook became ever more apparent as the decade wore on. In the hands of a new generation, untouched by the gender wars and sexual politics of the 1980s, the subtle nuances of irony melted away.

With that fig-leaf gone, there seemed to be less newness and more laddishness on display, so that the new *FHM* was separated from the old *Penthouse* only by an attitude of irreverence and a thong. That thong, however, was a hugely important dividing line, on the other side of which lay pornography. The fact that the lads' mags didn't stray across it was a significant reversal of what had once appeared to be an inexorable trend towards ever more explicit material in high-street newsagents.

Still, it wasn't to the taste of many of the begetters of the new lad themselves. 'I do feel I've created a monster,' admitted Simon Nye in 1996. 'I despise yob culture.' Sean O'Hagan, who had come up with the phrase in the first place, was also having doubts: '*Loaded* has become a little too laddish, even for an ironic, knowing media type like me.' There was something symbolic about the moment in 1997 when James Brown got married and left *Loaded* to become the editor of the upmarket *GQ*, saying, 'if I didn't move on, there was a danger of me becoming a drug addict and an alcoholic'. A year into his new job, at the age of thirty-three, he seemed anxious to distance himself from the world he had helped create, dismissing his old title and *FHM* with a withering putdown: 'I don't read magazines for teenagers.' The baton had clearly been passed, suggesting that even the most protracted of adolescences had to end sometime.

Many insisted that there was nothing new about any of it. 'I can't help feeling that the re-emergence of the Lads reflects our power politics,' wrote Jon Savage, a cultural commentator who was a significant ten years older than the actors in *Men Behaving Badly*; 'pretending novelty, aspiring, as they might say, to hipness, they ruthlessly reinforce the status quo.' There was a clear risk of releasing a genie that the cultural left had spent several years trying to force into his bottle.

But despite the doubts, the early incarnation of the new lad represented an undoubted cultural change that helped to transform the nation's self-image. He had emerged from the middle-class left, wearied by what was seen as a decade of being lectured, as James Brown made clear at the launch of *Loaded*; the magazine was, he said, for men who 'have accepted what we are and have given up trying to improve ourselves'. There was a rejection of the consciousness-raising feminism of the 1980s, but laddism didn't exactly resemble a triumphalist vision of masculinity. 'It was about self-esteem,' reflected Martin Deeson, a staff writer on *Loaded*, 'for a generation of men who had grown up skint during the recession, stoned during the boom, slagged off by feminists but egalitarian by inclination, and horny as goats.'

That claim to egalitarianism was never going to win much applause on what remained of the left, but there was an element of inclusion that hadn't always been apparent in the 1980s. Even if it hardly constituted a revolution, laddism didn't leave society unchanged. It lent a new middle-class legitimacy to a lifestyle that would once have been considered slovenly and irresponsible, while adding a degree of tolerance; even if there lurked a suspicion that this was all a bit patronising, that the adoption of the term 'lad' implied that working-class men weren't really adults, but merely adolescent minds trapped in grown-up bodies. Within a few years the word 'chav' would gain currency, to describe those who behaved like lads without the income or education to justify their conduct.

Meanwhile, there was less talk by the middle of the decade of sexual politics, though the changes wrought by feminism became ever more entrenched. In 1997 the number of women in the national workforce exceeded that of men for the first time in the country's history, a revolutionary moment that largely passed without notice. This was a relatively recent trend and one that had a profound impact on the male half of the population; in the 1960s there were 15 million men in employment in Britain, thirty years later there were just 11 million. Part of the explanation was the move away from manufacturing to services: a survey in 1999 showed that 77 per cent of those entering service industries were female, as were 67 per cent of those taking up clerical and secretarial jobs. Many of these jobs were, of course, low-paid but they were jobs nonetheless, at a time when male unemployment rates were higher than female in all social classes, particularly amongst the young.

At the other end of the social spectrum, high-profile stories appeared in the media about women taking posts previously considered to be resolutely male. In 1992 Betty Boothroyd became Speaker of the House of Commons, Barbara Mills the Director of Public Prosecutions and Stella Rimington the director general of MI5, while the Church of England voted in favour of the ordination of women. There might still be inequality in society and in the workplace, but the direction of travel was clear.

Yet while there was often resistance from a predominantly male establishment to changes in law or in custom, there was virtually no political pressure for a reversal of those gains that were achieved. The one exception was the recurrence of campaigns to reduce the time limit on abortions, and even here the argument in Britain was always couched in terms of scientific progress, rather than in the talk of fundamental moral principles so familiar from reports of the American culture wars. There were no mass movements calling for the restoration of male supremacy, no riots on the streets, no targeting of businesses that employed disproportionately large numbers of women. Instead, what was arguably the biggest change in British society since the Industrial Revolution proceeded on its way quite peacefully, with no modern equivalent of the Luddites, save perhaps the British National Party, whose election manifestos railed against feminism, alongside comprehensive education, homosexual liberation and free love. Undoubtedly there were many men in politics who shared that perspective and some who articulated it in private, but very few would publicly endorse the BNP's 1992 commitment to 'encourage our womenfolk to regard home- and family-making as the highest vocation for their sex'. Nor did that message have any great resonance with the wider public. Judged by the standards that had governed society for generations, individual men in every social class stood to lose from this revolution, yet it continued to roll forward with a sense of historical inevitability.

Many argued that the emergence of laddish culture at a time of women's advances in the workplace was no coincidence. 'Men will be men,' was the scathing summary of the phenomenon by *Independent* columnist Suzanne Moore, 'which means in other words it is the women's job "to get their tits out". Yet at a time when women are encroaching on male power in several vital areas it is hardly surprising that there is a move to keep them in their properly decorative and passive place.'

Mostly, though, it was the decorative, rather than the passive, element that rang true for the new lads: the women who increasingly adorned the covers of *Loaded* and its rivals were even more unobtainable than those who had graced the pornography of earlier eras. For all its attempted swaggering and show, laddism could be seen – despite its apparently reactionary character – as a slightly muddled, slightly disappointing compromise, a way of helping to negotiate a transitional period, as though the evolution in gender roles was easier to accept for men now that some of the more comforting features of traditional behaviour were back on the agenda. The signalling of an end to 1980s seriousness, the retreat to adolescence, was based in part on the inevitability of a reduction in power. In exchange for a loss of social status, the new lad sought the palliative of being allowed to behave badly on occasion, satisfied when permission was given for drinking to excess with his mates or eating pizza in front of *Match of the Day*, after a hard day lusting after images of semi-naked women.

The fact that such things were permissible was attested by the media's enthusiastic discovery that young women also wished to join the fun. Embodied in media personalities like Zoë Ball, Denise Van Outen and Ulrika Jonsson, a new stereotype emerged, briefly touted as the 'new lass' until the term 'ladette' became the favoured cliché. Her defining characteristics were again a predilection for getting drunk and for promiscuous sex. 'Complete with purple lipstick, pierced lips and a litany of bawdy jokes,' explained *The Times*, 'she parties hard, drinks a lot and dares her partner to wax his chest hair.'

At the beginning of the 1990s there had been a vogue for jokes about Essex girls, which associated their supposedly typical behaviour with vulgar stupidity. The term became part of the cultural lexicon (the Essex girl was defined in the *Shorter Oxford Dictionary* in 1998 as being 'unintelligent, promiscuous and materialistic'), so that when Sally Gunnell won a gold medal in the 400 metres hurdles at the 1992 Olympic Games, her victory was hailed in the *Daily Mirror* with the chortling headline: ESSEX GIRLS DO COME FIRST. By the middle of the decade, however, talking publicly about casual sex was becoming the norm for socialite heiresses and Radio 1 DJs alike.

'Women are choosing to have one-night stands, to have sex with whoever they want,' explained television presenter Sara Cox. 'Women can now talk about shagging and not feel obliged to bring in the romance or the commitment or what he actually thinks or whether there's any love there.' Or, as Anna put it in the television drama *This Life*: 'I don't want a boyfriend. I want a fuck.' Anxious not to be left out, Janet Anderson, Labour's shadow spokesperson for women, announced in a 1996 interview: 'Under Labour, women will become more promiscuous. That's an election promise.' She was later obliged, for the benefit of po-faced commentators, to explain that this was a joke.

Equally keen on a lifestyle of shagging and drinking was the eponymous heroine of Helen Fielding's best-selling novel *Bridget Jones's Diary* (1996), a contemporary of the original new lads. Unlike her male equivalents, however, she was not so much looking back to the wild oats she wished she'd sown, as yearning for the time when she could become a Smug Married. Inadvertently, she gave birth to a new genre, swiftly named chick lit.

The conventions were spelt out in the first chapter of Jane Green's typical example *Straight Talking* (1997). The narrator is a thirty-year-old single woman, working in the media, worried about her public persona and frustrated by the lack of 'commitment' shown by men. ('Bastards. All of them.') Whilst pursuing her perfect match, she finds comfort in the women's magazines' recipe for happiness: 'forget about men, crack open a bottle of wine and sit around with your girlfriends cackling about sex.' Because there is, apparently, a sisterhood of women in a similar position, bound together by white wine and chocolate, clothes and romantic comedies. Addressing the reader directly, she makes clear who the target audience is for these books: 'Maybe I'm wrong, but I'm assuming you're a member of the sisterhood, otherwise we wouldn't be talking.'

Again, as with the creators of laddism and the new lads, there was a generational step to be made to the ladettes, reflected in the alcohol they consumed. Bridget Jones drank New World chardonnay (sales of Australian wine in Britain had grown by 4,000 per cent in the seven years to 1992), while the ladettes were on the less respectable, and more rock and roll, vodka and bourbon.

For the even younger, there was a new range of drinks. Having emerged in the late 1980s in the form of ready-mixed bottles containing a double gin-and-tonic (thereby evading the level of duty normally charged on spirits), these had rapidly evolved into what were now known as alcopops. Intensely sweet products, they looked and tasted like soft drinks, but contained alcohol of unspecified provenance at around 5 per cent proof. There was a strong suspicion that they were being launched by a drinks industry fearful that the next generation of drinkers might be lost to the allure of ecstasy and other party drugs. The brand leader in the field was Hooper's Hooch, an alcoholic lemonade, but there were other entrants, including Two Dogs and Cola Lips, while Whitbread's chocolate-flavoured beer, Fuggles, was a not-too-distant cousin of the phenomenon.

In 1996 the Advertising Standards Authority upheld a complaint that alcopops were being sold with packaging likely to appeal to underage drinkers, and Kenneth Clarke increased the duty payable to 'help meet public concern', though none of this stopped new varieties of Hooch being introduced that year in orange and blackcurrant flavours. The fad for such products fizzled out soon enough, but they were replaced by a more sustainable incarnation of the ready-mixed drink – small bottles of Moscow Mule and Bacardi Breezer – that became the favoured tipple of the young women who wished to drink to excess on a Saturday night.

Beyond the drinks industry, the commercial exploitation of the ladette trend was a little stuttering in the first instance, but that didn't stop the media from trying to cash in. As early as February 1995 *Sky* magazine was featuring Zoë Ball on the cover of what it called 'The Women Behaving Badly Issue' with the headline: 'Shagging in burger bars, boozing with Oasis and loads more hair-raising tales.' In 1996, Emap, the publishers of *FHM*, launched a new magazine, *Minx*, 'for girls with a lust for life', while television schedulers made space for a brace of shows with self-explanatory titles: *The Girlie Show* (in the Friday-night Channel 4 slot formerly occupied by *The Word*) and *Pyjama Party*.

All were hoping to cash in on a perceived new market and although none was as commercially successful as those aimed at lads, the future potential was evident in the sales of magazines such as *Bliss*, *Mizz* and *Sugar*. These were aimed at teenage girls, and frequently read by those younger than the suggested age range so that *Just Seventeen*, for example, was regarded by most girls of that age as being a bit on the childish side. Such publications came in for increasing criticism for their unapologetic coverage of sexual issues: 'Fwoarrrgh! 50 Cute Boys Inside!' promised a typical *Just Seventeen* cover, while *More!* attracted criticism for its 'position of the month' feature.

They contributed, it was said, to what Edwina Currie called a 'generation's heedless flirtation with rampant sexuality', though their defence was that they were merely reflecting the concerns and interests of their readers. Whatever the chain of cause-and-effect, it was in the 1990s that it became clear how great had been the change in the behaviour of teenage girls. Surveys in the 1960s showed that just 2 per cent of fifteen-year-old girls were sexually active; by the 1990s more than a quarter said that they had had sex by that age.

Meanwhile one in ten youngsters aged between nine and fifteen were said to be regular drinkers, consuming on average nearly seven units of alcohol a week, the equivalent of a bottle of brandy a month, and though girls were still in the minority, the numbers were growing. The report *Living in Britain 1996* showed a rise in alcohol consumption, for the first time since this was studied in 1984, and in the percentage of those smoking, for the first time in the survey's history. In both instances it was the young, both male and female, who seemed to be driving up the figures.

Other statistics warned of the dangers faced by young women who followed the example set by the opposite sex. Figures published in 1997 suggested that the most likely person to commit suicide was aged between twenty-five and thirty-four, with men outnumbering women four to one. Suicide rates overall had fallen, but had risen amongst men under the age of forty-five. Meanwhile girls were outperforming boys at school, and a spokesperson for the Department of Education argued that cultural factors were the cause of the discrepancy: 'The most worrying thing is this men behaving badly culture where learning is out and mucking about is in.'

The ladette was a genuinely new phenomenon. Perhaps she was a consequence of the rise of young women in employment, ready to take advantage of the psychological and financial freedoms that resulted from that development, but perhaps there was also a simple recognition that misbehaviour was hugely enjoyable and ought to be indulged in while youth still afforded the opportunity to do so. Despite the dangers of pleasure-seeking, the allure of fun remained.

Simultaneous with the arrival of the ladette was a rise in the profile of women in areas of culture that had previously been seen as predominantly male. The alternative comedy clubs of the 1980s had seen the emergence of a wave of female stand-up comedians, including Helen Lederer, Jenny Eclair and Jo Brand. Most successful of all were Dawn French and Jennifer Saunders, whose television series aired on BBC Two from 1987 onwards, featuring inspired cross-dressing sketches in which the duo appeared as wolf-whistling workmen and as the grotesquely lascivious, beer-swilling characters, the Two Fat Men.

In 1987 the performers Morwenna Banks and Amanda Swift had published *The Joke's On Us*, reclaiming the often neglected legacy of British women comics in the twentieth century. 'We hope we have gone a little way to putting the notion that "women aren't funny" to rest,' they wrote. A decade later – when shows like *Absolutely Fabulous*, *The Vicar of Dibley*, *Dinnerladies* and *The Royle Family* were amongst the most popular offerings on mainstream television – such an aspiration scarcely needed articulating.

In a parallel development there emerged a new generation of female pop stars, initially evident in embryonic form in the short-lived Riot Grrrl movement, which grew out of American punk and found a British voice in the mixed-gender band Huggy Bear. In 1993 the group appeared on *The Word* to perform their new single 'Her Jazz', and then stayed on to heckle the presenter Terry Christian for what they perceived to be his, and the programme's, 'trite, casual sexism'. They were briefly lionised in the weekly music press, though their raucous awkwardness was never likely to make much of a wider impact.

More enduring were the Britpop guitar bands that came out of the indie scene and whose members included female singers and musicians, the likes of Elastica, Echobelly, Sleeper and Linoleum. 'These girls want sex on their terms, and they want it now,' wrote Elizabeth Coldwell in *Forum* magazine in 1995; 'and if you don't cut the mustard, you'll probably end up as the derogatory subject of their next single.' Louise Wener, singer with Sleeper, explained that the image of these women derived from a wish to be taken seriously as musicians rather than seen merely as sex symbols, hence a tendency to adopt established male style: 'We talk just like them, look just like them, behave exactly like them,' she wrote. 'We are boy-boot, androgyny central. Denim and leather and loud: rough and tough enough to kick the indie boys' heads in. We barely own a skirt between us.' Running counter to this tendency was PJ Harvey, initially a critical favourite as the Dr Martens-wearing guitarist and singer in a trio bearing her name, but who had, by the time of Britpop, mutated into a hard-riffing femme fatale, touring the world with her album *To Bring You My Love* (1995) in scarlet dress, high heels and vampish make-up.

The question of women's relationship to rock became a topic of intense debate, with a spate of books on the subject, including *Women, Sex and Rock 'n' Roll*, *Hymn to Her*, *She Bop* and *Never Mind the Bollocks*. In particular, the idea of substantial numbers of women playing instruments in bands was sufficiently novel to require some redefinition of rock and roll clichés. 'My guitar's not a penis extension,' explained Oli, guitarist with the Brighton-based band Tampasm, 'but it makes a damn good vibrator.'

These various acts were, it became clear in retrospect, paving the way for the arrival in mid-1996 of the Spice Girls, whose debut release, 'Wannabe', became the biggest-selling single ever in Britain by a female band. For two and a half years the group enjoyed an extraordinary level of success, dominating British popular culture and exporting successfully to Europe and even to America, where their first album sold ten million copies.

The commercial triumph was based not only on their radio-friendly dance-pop but also on the personalities of the five band members themselves, who turned out to be genuinely funny and intelligent in a manner not always associated with pop stars, capable of holding their own whether being interviewed by Clive James or by *Smash Hits* magazine. Each was given a nickname (Scary Spice, Baby Spice, etc.) to convey their personae as directly as possible, but they came together to articulate what they called 'girl power', a concept derived from Riot Grrrl but stripped of any overtly political content to make it accessible to a mass audience. A political dimension did surface in interviews – as when Geri 'Ginger Spice' Halliwell cited Margaret Thatcher as 'the first Spice Girl, the pioneer of our ideology' – but in essence the message was not far removed from that of Cyndi Lauper's 1984 hit 'Girls Just Want to Have Fun'. There was, though, a crucial generational difference: whereas Lauper had sung 'we're not the fortunate ones', the Spice Girls were very clear that they were indeed fortunate in being born female, and that girl power did not require the approval of boys. ('This is happening without your permission,' in the words of Huggy Bear's best line.)

'Girl power' was an easy slogan to mock, and many did so, while others pointed to the manufactured origins of the group as evidence that girl power was ultimately dependent on a male-dominated industry, 'corporate girlypop' in the words of critic Lucy O'Brien. But for the legions of fans, the message carried real weight. Unlike the women in Britpop, the Spice Girls didn't strive for indie androgyny, but flaunted femininity as a positive force. And it was a surprisingly everyday femininity, a pop shorn of glamour. 'They're the sort of girls who you'd see working in Tesco and think, "Hmm, not bad for someone who's working in Tesco",' observed David Baddiel. 'Men like that, because they can look at their favourite Spice Girl and think, "She's not out of my league. I could have her".' More significantly, of course, the girl who was actually working in Tesco could aspire to being her.

Unlike more conventional female pop stars, the Spice Girls weren't afraid to talk about feminism, even if it wasn't a brand that would have been recognised a decade earlier. 'You can look like a babe and make as much of a point as if you burnt your bra,' insisted Melanie 'Sporty Spice' Chisholm, before adding in horror, as the thought struck her: 'There's no way I'm ever burning my Wonderbra. I couldn't. I'm nothing without it.'

The Wonderbra had stamped its mark on the decade with a 1994 poster campaign showing a picture of the model Eva Herzigova in black underwear, looking down at her breasts with the caption: HELLO BOYS. After it received several complaints, the Advertising Standards Authority ruled that the posters, together with others that bore the line 'or are you just pleased to see me', were decent. A spokeswoman for the ASA pointed out that the posters had initially proved uncontroversial: 'It was only after the media started asking if they represented a new post-feminist aggressive female image or were simply exploiting women that the complaints started flooding in.' That debate about empowerment versus exploitation was heard a great deal during the 1990s.

The rise of the Spice Girls coincided with the arrival of various fantasy characters who provided a new, tougher face of young women in screen fiction. From America came the television series *Xena: Warrior Princess* (1995) and *Buffy the Vampire Slayer* (1997), while Tank Girl, who had made her debut the previous decade in British comics, became the subject of a Hollywood movie in 1995. All three had been created by male writers.

The same was true of Britain's most successful entrant in this field, Lara Croft, the heroine of the computer game *Tomb Raider*, which was released in October 1996 while 'Wannabe' was still in the charts. The character had originally been conceived of as male, a figure in the mould of Indiana Jones, before being recast as an athletic young woman. Clad in shorts, hiking boots and backpack and with a pistol-holster strapped to each thigh, she was intended to convey a cool strength. 'She wasn't a tits-out-for-the-lads type of character,' explained creator Toby Gard. 'She was this unattainable, austere, dangerous sort of person.'

Despite the influence of Indiana Jones, Croft could also be seen in the context of an older British tradition of the aristocratic amateur hero, going back to the Scarlet Pimpernel and to the novels of John Buchan, Edgar Wallace and Sapper. According to the back-story, she was the public school-educated daughter of Lord Richard Croft, and had opted for a life of adventure following a plane crash that left her stranded for two weeks in the Himalayas. There were elements here of 1960s television series such as *The Saint* and *The Champions*, even of Tarzan, reinvented for a new generation.

Even so, Croft represented a major break with the conventions of computer gaming. 'The rules at the time were: if you're going to make a game, make sure the main character is male and make sure he's American, otherwise it won't sell in America,' remembered Gard. *Tomb Raider* happily broke both of those rules and went on to become a huge international hit, selling six million copies and helping to establish Sony's new console, the PlayStation, as the market leader. So successful was the figure of Croft that, as each sequel to the original game was released, she spilled over into comics, movies and amusement park rides, as well as being used to advertise products as diverse as Lucozade and Fiat cars.

It was not only in fiction that women were ringing the changes. 'This seems like a demented extension of equal opportunities,' exclaimed the British Medical Association's science and research adviser in 1997, as the first licensed female boxing match was announced. The fact that the scheduled bout was between two thirteen-year-old girls caused such an outcry that the fight was cancelled, but a few weeks later the Whitland Amateur Boxing Club near Carmarthen did put on a licensed fight between Marie Davies and Marie Leefe, both aged sixteen. 'This is a small local event between two local girls and we are not looking for any publicity,' said a club spokesperson, but there was little hope of that. The media were fascinated, including *Bliss* magazine, which provided sponsorship for the event: 'If there's a meaning to girl power,' enthused the editor, 'this is it.' As the bout of three one-minute rounds finished (with a points victory to Leefe), the press closed in for photographs and the ring collapsed beneath their weight.

By this stage Britain already had two professional world champions – Jane Couch at welterweight and Cheryl Robertson at bantamweight – but they were obliged to fight abroad, just as Barbara Buttrick, Britain's first professional, had gone to America in the 1950s, winning titles at bantam and flyweight. The British Boxing Board of Control refused to grant licences to female boxers, and their stand was supported by most of the sport's establishment, including the leading promoters Mickey Duff, Frank Warren and Barry Hearn. 'Maybe I'm old-fashioned,' said Hearn, 'but I can't come to terms with the idea of women beating seven kettles of shit out of each other.'

In 1998 Jane Couch took the BBBC to an industrial tribunal, alleging that she was facing discrimination on grounds of her sex. The Board defended their policy of rejecting all licence applications from women on the grounds that women were too frail, bruised too easily and became emotionally unstable and accident-prone during menstruation. There was also the suspicion that their inclusion might damage the men's sport: 'Boxing is a high-risk sport which can cause injury and death,' explained the Board's medical adviser. 'Should such a tragedy occur when a woman is boxing, I believe the public adversity would put the whole sport at risk.' Couch won her case, and became the first woman to be given a licence to box professionally in Britain. In November that year she took just 184 seconds to knock out her German opponent in a fight staged at Caesar's nightclub in Streatham, South London.

A further break with convention could be seen in a mini-boom in pornographic magazines aimed at a female market. *For Women* started the ball rolling in 1992, followed swiftly by *Women Only*, *Women on Top*, *Ludus* and a British edition of *Playgirl*, twenty years after its American debut. This was merely aping the worst of men's behaviour, some argued, while others saw it as cynical exploitation, pointing to the fact that *Ludus* ('Women and Sex Today') was published by Galaxy, in which stable were also to be found the thoroughly disreputable *Knave* and *Fiesta*.

More pertinent was a problem with the regulations, developing from the case law in obscenity trials, that governed British pornography. The issue was particularly evident in its relation to the depiction of an erect penis. Such imagery was partially governed by what was known in the world of censorship as the Mull of Kintyre Test. 'It used to be,' explained a Channel 4 executive in 2001, 'that if the angle of the dangle is more than the elevation of the Mull of Kintyre on the west coast of Scotland, then the penis is deemed erect.' With such constraints, the pictorial appeal of women's pornography was somewhat hampered, there clearly being a limit to the hardcore fantasy potential of page after page of limp men.

Also leaving rather too much to the imagination were the Chippendales, a male dance troupe founded in Los Angeles in 1979, who arrived on the West End stage in 1991 and went on to tour the country. The Chippendales were routinely described as male strippers, but that was to promise slightly more than was ever delivered, for even after the last strip of Velcro had been torn away, removing what appeared to be the last piece of flimsy clothing, there remained, below the waxed, gym-honed chests and the six-pack stomachs, a posing pouch to preserve the modesty of the pelvic-thrusting musclemen. Such fig-leaves notwithstanding, it was still too much for some local authorities, including West Lothian Council, who banned scheduled performances in Livingston.

The act was designed for hen parties, for the hordes of, in the words of Lynne Truss, 'mini-skirted women who were willingly pulled up on to the stage in order to take part in the show'. Everyone agreed that it was the audience who made the evening memorable; the performance itself was routinely described as flaccid. For a few short years the Chippendales

— and a succession of other such troupes — sold a lot of tickets and a great many calendars, but their appeal faltered when they ventured beyond posing. A single, 'Give Me Your Body', reached only number twenty-eight in the charts, and they didn't enhance their image when they opened their mouths. 'They say the Chippendales is for the lower class. They say it's very crass. They say it's not very tasteful,' explained one of the boys, Mark Smith. 'Well — hey! — Shakespeare in his time, the same thing was said about him by the established critics!'

The success of such ventures suggested a growing commercial awareness of female sexuality outside the media playground of the ladettes, a trend confirmed by the huge success of French writer Alina Reyes's erotic novella *The Butcher* (published in Britain in 1991), which sold half a million copies worldwide. Indeed, it was to be in fiction that a more sustainable cultural expression would be found, when Virgin Books launched their Black Lace imprint in 1993, to provide 'erotic fiction written by women, for women'. Since these books dealt in words alone, they were able to go much further than the magazines or the stage shows.

The underlying story in many of the titles was familiar enough to readers of the romantic fiction that stretched from the Brontë sisters to the mass-produced novels of Mills & Boon and their imitators: an innocent, sometimes wilful, young woman is drawn into a relationship with a powerful, sometimes mysterious, older man, and finds fulfilment and her true self. The key difference was that in a conventional Mills & Boon title, the sex either happened after the book ended or was only vaguely described, through a gauze of circumlocution, towards the end. In a Black Lace story, on the other hand, it all got going round about page three and didn't let up much for the next eighty thousand words; the guidelines issued to authors suggested there should be a sex scene every ten pages. 'Any normal woman would have died of exhaustion by the end of chapter three,' exclaimed a 27-year-old doctor, recruited by a national newspaper to read and review a Black Lace title.

Not only was it all much more explicit, but the activities described were racier. The most popular Mills & Boon writer, Charlotte Lamb, included sex scenes in her work, but insisted on keeping the focus firmly on romance: 'It's straight sex with the hero and heroine in love,' she said firmly. Black Lace tales, on the other hand, while following the publisher's stipulations of 'no children, no animals, no bloodshed', tended to veer towards sadomasochism. Perhaps this shouldn't have come as a total surprise. Back in the mid-1960s, when Gillian Freeman was researching her classic book *The Undergrowth of Literature* (1967), she reported a conversation overheard in a Soho bookshop. 'Got any straight sex, then?' asked a customer, and the proprietor had to apologise: 'Sorry mate, it's all got a bit of fladge in it.' That British fondness for flagellation, bondage and domination seemed to have survived quite happily into a new era and across gender lines, so that as Virgin prepared its new imprint, 'market research suggested spanking and subjugation would go down well'.

Black Lace was soon nicknamed Mills & Bondage, and was joined in the market by other erotic lists, including a relaunch of Virgin's own Nexus, Little Brown's X-Libris and the independent Silver Moon, all of which upped the ante in the level of fetish described and the severity of the treatment endured by their heroines. 'If you like one of our books, you will probably like them all!' boasted Silver Moon, which perhaps suggested that innovation and originality were not the primary assets of these titles. Rather they were sold as genre fiction, with the authorial identity of little interest to readers, though there were exceptions that stood out from the crowd, notably Stephen Rawlings's *Jane and Her Master* (1996), which retold the story of *Jane Eyre* as a particularly brutal sadomasochistic epic.

Retaining the respectable façade of fiction, Black Lace and its ilk brought pornographic material that had previously been found only in specialist shops onto the high street and even, in some areas, into public libraries. The 'Adults Only' warning on the cover might keep them segregated from more decent novels, but it wasn't long before entire top shelves at W.H. Smith were full of such volumes. In fact the problem of where such material should be stocked was one that exercised the minds of retailers and publishers alike. In the early days, when there weren't enough titles to warrant their own section, they tended to be grouped together just before the A–Z of fiction, on the grounds that pornography was assumed to have been written by anonymous authors, regardless of what it said on the cover. As the volume of material increased, special sections were created for erotica, though as a result of their elevated position publishers received plaintive letters from women complaining that, being unable to reach, they had had to ask a man to get a volume down for them from the top shelf. There were many readers too who preferred not to reveal their taste to local shopkeepers and instead bought their copies in the anonymity of motorway service stations and railway bookstalls, which were consequently very well stocked.

The initial assumption of a sceptical media had been that most of these books were actually written by men under female pseudonyms, which turned out to be true of some imprints (though not of Black Lace), and that they would sell to a predominantly male market, which turned out not to be true at all. When Delta – an erotic imprint of Hodder Headline – surveyed its readers in 1997, it discovered that a quarter were women aged between twenty and forty, while the largest demographic group were women in their forties. Black Lace's own surveys came to much the same conclusion: 83 per cent of readers were women, 'the bulk of them in their twenties and thirties with above-average educations and income'. Quite how many readers there were, however, could not be so easily ascertained. Black Lace claimed total sales of two million in its first four years, with each title averaging 15,000 to 18,000, and between them the various imprints were said to be publishing around 400 titles annually.

The figures suggested a popular genre, and a substantial, hitherto untapped market, but one with a still limited appeal, outshone by its older sister, romantic fiction. When John Boon, the head of Mills & Boon, died in 1996, the obituaries paid tribute not merely to his distinguished war record – he was mentioned in despatches for his service on D-Day – but to the success of the company co-founded by his father; sales were then standing at 15 million books a year in Britain and 200 million worldwide. (Boon believed that the key to his stewardship of the firm was that he had never read a single one of the titles; in many ways Mills & Boon was a very conventional publishing house.)

It was never quite clear what any of this meant in sociological terms. Was it a continuation of the romantic subjugation of women by other, more explicit, means? Or a reflection of the growing social status of women, so that the old cliché of the high court judge who visits a dominatrix was being joined by a new one of the businesswoman who fantasises about being beaten? Or perhaps a new phase of feminism in which, public battles having been won, a division between fantasy and reality could be acknowledged in the personal sphere? The Delta survey found that the newspaper most likely to be taken by its readers was the *Sun*, followed in popularity by the *Daily Telegraph*, a discovery that failed to provide conclusive evidence one way or the other.

It was striking, however, how easily what had once been considered a rigid gender divide was being breached by ladettes, by girl power and by female erotica. Public drinking, recreational drug use, fantasies about promiscuous and anonymous sex – these had previously been thought of as behavioural traits of young men, and the fact that increasing numbers of young women were taking to them with some enthusiasm caused moral distress to traditionalists on both the left and the right. Hedonism for the masses, rather than for the bohemian few, was now firmly on the agenda, as was an awareness that the common ground between the genders was not always particularly elevated. 'A man is still a farting, belching, grunting pig, picking his feet when he's alone,' commented the rock singer Chrissie Hynde, in a *GQ* interview in 1996. Her co-interviewee, the Canadian country singer kd lang, retorted: 'Sounds like me.'

There was even a growing female interest in the hitherto male preserve of football, so that by the end of the decade around 15 per cent of the crowds at club matches (and many more for televised national matches) were women. And partly because of this, football emerged as one of the most significant cultural forces of the decade as the game, following the tragedies at Bradford, Hillsborough and Heysel in the 1980s, began to build a new identity, seeking to disown two decades of stories about hooliganism.

The process of rehabilitation began in 1990, when the ban on English clubs playing in European competition – imposed after Heysel – was lifted, and the England team reached the semi-finals of the World Cup with a side that included some of the most gifted players in the game. In particular, the charismatic Paul 'Gazza' Gascoigne – who shed tears when he received a yellow card during the semi-final and realised that he would be banned for the next match – became a star such as England had not enjoyed since the 1960s, feted and celebrated well beyond the confines of football itself. Gazza-mania swept the country, carrying with it the hopes of an entire industry, desperately praying that he could change the image of the game. He was, as writer Harry Pearson pointed out, one of the very few players who could induce an 'all-consuming, irrational and totally childlike happiness' in those watching.

Not everyone was quite swept up in the fever, however. Gascoigne was born in Gateshead and had made his name playing for Newcastle; in rival parts of the North-East, his cult struggled to catch on, and in 1991 a Gazza lookalike contest in South Shields 'was won by a black teenage girl dressed as a fairy'. Nor was the legal establishment convinced. In October 1990 Gascoigne's lawyer went to court in an attempt to prevent the publication of an unauthorised biography under the title *Gazza*. This name, he argued, was so established as to have become virtually a trademark; to use it on a book jacket would imply that Gascoigne had approved the volume. Mr Justice Harman was unimpressed. On being told that Gascoigne was a footballer, he sought further clarification: 'Rugby or association football?' He also made mention of Rossini's opera *La Gazza Ladra*, and suggested that the Duke of Wellington's dictum – 'publish and be damned' – might have some bearing on the current case. Gascoigne's lawyer pointed out that times had moved on since 1815, society had changed, but the judge had the last word: 'The law, fortunately, doesn't change,' he pronounced, as he refused to grant an injunction. He was wrong, of course; the law does and did change, and twenty years later judges would be happily issuing super-injunctions to professional footballers, seeking to protect their privacy from prying tabloid eyes.

Even more important than Gazza, it turned out, was the launch in 1992 of the FA Premier League, replacing what had been the First Division of the Football League. Initially this looked much the same as the institution it had supplanted. It comprised twenty-two clubs, including such humble names as Oldham Athletic, Notts County and Luton Town, and it still had a relationship with the old League structure, with clubs being relegated and promoted. But there was one critical difference: the new organisation had established the right to negotiate its own television deal, and had promptly signed a five-year contract, worth a then-astonishing £305 million, with the satellite broadcaster BSkyB. From that change flowed the vast sums of money that subsequently poured into the domestic game at the highest level. As the economy entered its long boom, so too did football; the number of Sky subscriptions increased rapidly, aided by the importation from the Far East of ever more affordable televisions with ever bigger screens, and by 2001 the rights to broadcast the Premier League were being sold for £1.6 billion.

Having paid the piper, television was quick to call the tune, and the traditional three o'clock kick-off on a Saturday afternoon soon began to seem the exception rather than the norm; an agreement not to screen live matches at that time meant that the most attractive games were simply moved to accommodate the broadcasters. Chief amongst those eye-catching encounters were the ones featuring Manchester United, whose holding company had recently been floated on the stock market.

Despite its status as one of the most glamorous of English clubs, United had not won a League title since 1967, a failing that their detractors were not shy of pointing out. When Terry Waite, the Archbishop of Canterbury's envoy, was finally released in 1991 from his long years of captivity at the hands of the Islamic Jihad Organisation in the Lebanon, Liverpool fans were seen wearing T-shirts with Waite's face on them and the slogan: 'What, Man Utd *still* haven't won the League?' But the Premiership's debut season saw the club triumphant for the first time in twenty-six years, and the global success of the new format was assured.

The player who caught the public imagination in that victorious Manchester United team was the Frenchman, and *Loaded* cover star, Eric Cantona. In the days before the Champions League (another rebranding exercise that started in 1992), less attention was paid in the British press to foreign players, but even so Cantona arrived in England bearing a reputation both as a player approaching genius and as a wayward and difficult character.

This was the man, nicknamed Le Brat, who'd been fined for punching his own goalkeeper in the face, who'd been suspended from the French national team for calling its coach 'un sac de merde' (quoting, as he explained, Hollywood rebel Mickey Rourke) and who, having been banned for three matches after throwing the ball in the referee's face, managed to get the ban extended to two months by going up to each member of the disciplinary committee individually and telling them they were idiots. He was irresistible. And he was successful; having won the League title with Leeds United, he moved to Manchester and promptly did the same again. As Howard Wilkinson, the manager of Leeds who brought Cantona to the English game, observed: 'Eric likes to do what he likes, when he likes, because he likes it, and then fuck off. We'd all like a bit of that.'

Part of Cantona's appeal was simply that he displayed the preening arrogance of a 1970s rock star. He wore his collar upturned, he didn't celebrate goals by rushing around looking for hugs and kisses, but by puffing his chest out and soaking up the crowd's adulation, and his body language exuded ultimate self-confidence. Even the cultural critic Paul Morley, a lifelong Manchester City fan, admitted to buying a pair of Nike trainers because Cantona endorsed them. But there was also the unpredictable play that enabled him to transform a game with a moment of breathtaking imagination, or alternatively add to his list of misdemeanours; he set a club record by being sent off in two consecutive matches, and on another occasion received a red card after the final whistle in a Champions League match.

His most controversial moment, however, came in January 1995 after he was sent off in a match at Crystal Palace. As he left the field, he reacted to a torrent of racist abuse coming from a home fan, 21-year-old Matthew Simmons, by leaping with both feet at the man's chest. He then began punching his tormentor until he was physically restrained from continuing. Simmons was subsequently charged and found guilty of using threatening words and behaviour (and got a seven-day sentence for contempt of court, having tried to attack the prosecuting counsel), but it was for Cantona that the true opprobrium was reserved. He was fined and suspended for four months by Manchester United, but that wasn't enough to preclude a disciplinary hearing at the Football Association, where he appeared contrite enough, apologising to everyone involved, until he could contain his contempt no longer and concluded: 'And I want to apologise to the prostitute who shared my bed last evening.'

The FA doubled his club ban to eight months. He was then tried in the criminal courts, found guilty of assault and given a two-week jail sentence (OOH AHH PRISONA, as the *Sun* put it, in parody of a popular terrace chant), though this was reduced on appeal to two weeks of community service. To cap it all, he held one of the briefest ever press conferences, where he delivered a single sentence before getting up and leaving: 'When the seagulls follow the trawler, it is because they think sardines will be thrown into the sea.'

This wasn't the behaviour expected of a footballer, and it seemed to puzzle even his fellow countrymen. 'The British have succeeded in eliminating football violence to the point where the hideous metal fences supposed to protect the players have disappeared from their grounds,' commented *Le Monde*. 'Now they have to acknowledge that the hooligans are on the pitch, threatening the public.' Which seemed a little unfair, given that Cantona was a French hooligan.

Cantona was the first foreigner to become Britain's favourite sporting bad boy, a role normally reserved for working-class drinkers and womanisers, not for French existentialists. Arguably, his rapid elevation to this status reflected the dearth of home-grown rebels, as sport became ever more professional and media-aware. The likes of Paul Gascoigne and Stan Collymore looked the part initially, but it soon became clear that their errant behaviour was born not of maverick trouble-making but of serious psychological problems, even if football itself was yet to recognise this possibility. When Collymore spoke publicly of his clinical depression, his manager at Aston Villa, John Gregory, was not exactly sympathetic: 'I'm gobsmacked by the whole issue,' he said. 'I find it difficult to understand how anyone in Stan's position, with the talent and money he has, is stressed.'

Moreover, the great sporting lads of the past were starting to look tarnished in retrospect. The alcoholism of George Best and Alex Higgins seemed merely sad as their lives petered out, along with the career of Brian Clough, while the most controversial characters in recent cricket history found themselves in court: Ian Botham sued Imran Khan over allegations of racism, ball-tampering and loutishness and lost; Geoffrey Boycott was found guilty of assaulting a former lover. When reports about Paul Gascoigne beating his wife made his place in the England squad a controversial issue, Best didn't distinguish himself with his response: 'I think we all give the wife a smack once in a while.'

In their place came a wave of domestic sporting heroes who were the dullest of conformists: Formula One driver Nigel Mansell, triple jumper Jonathan Edwards, rower Steve Redgrave, footballer Alan Shearer. Similarly, some of the most impressive performances by national teams were purely defensive: England's 0–0 draw with Italy in Rome that secured qualification for the 1998 World Cup, or Michael Atherton's extraordinary innings in the second Test against South Africa in Johannesburg in December 1995, when he spent nearly eleven hours at the crease, scoring 185 runs to save the match. There were plenty of great sporting achievements, but it took a nonconformist Frenchman to spark the rebel imagination.

Cantona's other achievement, in apparent contradiction to the first, was that he was the harbinger of the revolution that would sweep through much of English football. His greatest virtue, as far as his manager Alex Ferguson was concerned, was his professionalism, his obsession with practising longer and harder than anyone, inspiring the younger Manchester United players – Ryan Giggs, Paul Scholes, David Beckham – to follow his example. He received less credit for this attitude than was perhaps his due, however, the plaudits going instead to his fellow countryman Arsène Wenger, who arrived in Islington as manager of Arsenal in 1996.

The North London club was then still living in the shadow of former manager George Graham, who had guided the team to six major trophies but had been sacked in 1995 for taking a payment of £425,000 (a 'bung', as the sporting press liked to say) from an agent representing two players that he had signed; he was also banned from management for a year by the FA. The contrast between Graham and Wenger could not have been more acute. The former was the son of a Glasgow steelworker who believed that the best form of attack was defence, the latter had a master's degree in economics from Strasbourg University and was as articulate – though seldom as witty – as Cantona. 'I like real, modern football,' he explained at his first press conference in North London. 'Football made of compact lines, of zones, of pressure. And football of quick coordinated movements with a good technical basis.'

Wenger's appointment was not greeted with unreserved enthusiasm by his new charges. 'Bloody hell,' exclaimed the club captain, Tony Adams. 'I've got to play for a Frenchman? You must be joking.' Traditional English suspicion of the French was only exacerbated when Wenger revealed his disapproval of excessive alcohol consumption. This was always going to be a little difficult at Arsenal, where the changing room was noted for its drinking culture; the players Paul Merson and Kevin Campbell had been found guilty of drink-driving in recent years, while Adams had spent fifty-six days in jail over the Christmas of 1990 for the same offence. (To the chagrin of the other inmates, he was unable to play for HM Prison Chelmsford whilst inside, because of Arsenal's insurance policy.)

Wenger's pursuit of proper nutrition also raised eyebrows. 'He's put me on grilled fish, grilled broccoli, grilled everything,' protested the club's top scorer, Ian Wright. 'Yuk!' This sort of diet might be standard fare for athletes on the Continent, but such an ethos was alien to English football. The French goalkeeper Lionel Pérez signed for Sunderland in 1996 and couldn't believe what he found: 'It's truly a different world over here. The players will eat sausages, fried eggs and beans before a game. After an away trip, the club will lay on beers for the coach trip home.'

The success of Wenger at Arsenal, as the club mounted a challenge to Manchester United's dominance, converted many in the domestic game to this new code of behaviour, and by the end of the decade English football had become a more professional, more effective and slightly less interesting sport than it had been before his arrival. The widening gap between players and supporters was generally measured in terms of income, with professional footballers at the highest level now being paid more in a week than an average fan could earn in a year. But there was another factor, too. The extraordinary levels of fitness and of physical pampering that were needed to be a successful athlete made the players seem something other than human, at least while they were on the pitch. It was increasingly difficult to imagine that one could achieve anything remotely comparable, so great were the sacrifices required to compete. As a character in the television series *A Touch of Frost* pointed out of a game: 'It was a football match, it's not real life.'

Domestic football in Britain also became much more international, and on Boxing Day 1999, in a moment charged with great symbolism, Chelsea, under the management of the Italian Gianluca Vialli, became the first English club to field a team that had no British players in it at all. These were momentous developments in the nation's favourite game and seemed to point to a new incarnation of Britain, one that was converging culturally with Europe, even if politicians were reluctant to make a similar leap. The ramifications, some felt, might be enormous and long-lasting. 'If all football players appear to come from abroad,' mused journalist Lynne Truss, 'will the young conclude that abroad is a phenomenally great place?'

Running alongside these changes in the nature of English professional football was a broadening of the support base. The new all-seater stadia at the top of the game – following the implementation of the Taylor Report, the outcome of an inquiry into the deaths of 96 Liverpool fans at Hillsborough

– had reduced capacity and increased ticket prices, and complaints began to be heard that ordinary working-class fans were being priced out of the game, supplanted by middle-class, fair-weather supporters, as the Premier League confirmed the social cleansing of a reviled and beleaguered pastime. Again Arsenal were seen to be leading the way, so that when the comedy series *The Fast Show* created the character Roger Nouveau (played by John Thomson), an archetypal middle-class fan who sips chilled white wine from his picnic hamper at half time, he was inevitably portrayed as a supporter of the Islington club.

With this influx of wealthier fans, football clubs became supremely inventive in finding new ways to extract money from their followers. 'The secret of our success is to treat the fans with respect,' announced Edward Freedman, managing director of Manchester United Merchandising Ltd, adding, with no apparent trace of humour: 'We have over eight hundred products available.' Cantona discovered that part of his deal with the club required him to put his name to a book and a video, and ultimately he found the whole experience distasteful: 'At that time they thought that merchandising was more important than the team and players. When the business is more important than the football I just give up, rather than be treated like a pair of socks, a shirt or a shit.' In 1998 the chairman of Newcastle United, Freddy Shepherd, and one of his board members, Doug Hall, were reported to have boasted to an undercover reporter about the stupidity of fans paying £50 for a shirt that cost just £5 to make. The response of the secretary of the club's supporters' association was plaintive: 'We all know we're being exploited over club merchandise but we don't need to have our noses rubbed in it by the people who are raking in the money.'

Even Tony Blair, a man not noticeably averse to business opportunities, professed himself disturbed by the commercial strategies of Manchester United, the nation's biggest club: 'Loyalty doesn't seem to be enough any more. Rather it is exploited to make us pay more.' He didn't dwell on the theme, however, and his sentiments weren't reciprocated. 'He's done a brilliant job,' enthused United's manager, Alex Ferguson, of Blair in 1996. 'The result is that the Labour Party is actually speaking for the people again.'

Paul Whitehouse's character Ron Manager in *The Fast Show* may have been a parody of the old pre-Wenger school of English management, drenched in sentimentality, but there were times when he came close to articulating a truth, despite himself. 'I wonder what Jesus makes of it all,' he ruminated, during a typically wayward studio discussion. 'He's gutted, isn't he, you know? He's thrown those money-lenders out of the temple, he looks down and sees them take up residence in the Premiership. Far cry from small boys in the park with jumpers for goalposts.'

If there was one defining moment in football's move from the public bar to the dinner party, it was the publication in September 1992 of Nick Hornby's memoir *Fever Pitch*, recounting his love of Arsenal and how it had shaped his life. It had long been possible to appreciate the aesthetics of the beautiful game, and recently even hooliganism had acquired an edgy allure in some quarters, as seen in books like Bill Buford's *Among the Thugs* (1990). But Hornby went much further and made fashionable the idea of embracing football culture in its entirety. He articulated the wit, warmth and absurdity of being a supporter in a way that *Match of the Day* had never even considered. The only place on the BBC where a comparable cultural embrace could be found was Radio 5 Live's phone-in show *606* with Danny Baker, the very embodiment of laddism, who was named Radio Personality of the Year in 1992; so alien was the world presented here that *The Times* described the show as 'quintessentially postmodern'.

In Hornby's wake, it was no longer sufficient in public life simply to enjoy football as a sport; a tribalism had also to be adopted, or feigned, if one wished to hold one's own in polite society. And those chasing votes were keen to be included, so that it became difficult to avoid knowing which club a politician had allegedly supported since early youth. Tony Blair, for example, professed his love for Newcastle United and was reported to remember watching 'Wor' Jackie Milburn play for club; as Milburn had left the Toon in June 1957, a month after Blair celebrated his fourth birthday, that would have made the future prime minister a very precocious child of the terraces, and the apparent boast attracted much ridicule. (In fact, Blair had made no such claim, although many were prepared to believe he had.) Perhaps more plausibly, John Major was a Chelsea fan, once passing a note to Chris Patten during a cabinet meeting, asking if he'd like to go to Stamford Bridge the following Saturday; Patten queried who was playing, and Major wrote back tartly: 'If you don't know, you can't come.'

Both the Archbishop of Canterbury, George Carey, and the Chief Rabbi, Jonathan Sacks, were proud to call themselves Arsenal fans, and had their first social meeting at Highbury stadium in 1991, when the home team were beaten 6–2 by Manchester United. 'It was a catastrophe,' Sacks told the press. 'We were trying to work out the theological implications. Does it mean that our prayers were not heard, that the players were relying on us or that God is a Manchester United fan?'

This permeation of football through the British class structure was unprecedented in the modern era, and it seemed to many to be symptomatic of a wider cultural colonisation. 'As if to take the piss, aspects of traditional working-class behaviour became chic,' wrote Mark Steel. 'Broadsheet critics effused over the hidden genius of *Carry On* films and 1970s ITV sitcoms. The most popular names for boys born into middle-class families were Fred, Harry and Jack. Football became a compulsory middle-class topic.' On the other hand, it appeared that football was also capable of popularising art forms previously considered remote and elitist. After a recording of Luciano Pavarotti singing Puccini's 'Nessun Dorma' was used as the theme tune for the BBC coverage of the 1990 World Cup, the single went to number two in the charts and the song became a firm favourite on the karaoke circuit. By the following year rock promoter Harvey Goldsmith was staging a Pavarotti concert in Hyde Park in front of 125,000 people, as well as a populist production of *Tosca* at Earls Court.

What was actually happening, it appeared, was that a convergence of culture was taking place. The leaking of football into the broadsheet world was merely the most visible symptom of that development, the distinction between white and blue collars concealed by the wearing of replica shirts on a Saturday afternoon (or a Sunday lunchtime, or Monday evening, or whenever Sky felt a particular match should be staged).

In the process, football grounds became safer, less violent places to visit – more family-friendly, to use an expression that was gaining currency at the time – and those who lived in their vicinity generally felt less as if they were under siege on match days. Further positive signs could be found in the grassroots campaigns that led to the creation in 1993 of the organisation Let's Kick Racism Out of Football (later renamed Kick It Out), a development that was mostly welcomed at a time when a fifth of professional players were black.

But there was, many felt, a danger that something was being lost along the way, a cultural vitality that had always thrived on impolite emotions. Football was not as other sports. It consumed supporters' lives with its passions and rivalries, and though these were mostly expressed in banter and humour, there was an undercurrent of offence and sometimes outright hatred that didn't sit well with the gentrification of the game. Up against this century-old culture, however, there now came the full weight of capitalism and commercialisation; not just Sky Television and the Premier League, but also UEFA and the Champions League and what by the end of the decade was known as the FIFA World Cup, the international administrative body having decided to lay claim to the world's most popular sporting tournament. There could be only one winner from such a conflict.

'The game's identity, its fan base, its whole image, has been cleaned up beyond all recognition,' wrote Mark Jolly in *The Times* in 1992, the year that Danny Baker moved on from *606*, replaced as host by the much less laddish David Mellor, a sitting Conservative MP. In due course Baker returned to the station with a new Wednesday evening phone-in show to demonstrate that another version of football still existed, but it wasn't an unmitigated success. In 1997 a particularly contentious penalty award, made by referee Mike Reed in an FA Cup match between Chelsea and Leicester City, sparked an entire programme of ranting by presenter and callers alike. 'There's a cancer at the heart of the golden core of football, and it is referees,' Baker declared; 'most of them need a good slap around the face.' He also suggested that listeners should target Reed personally and 'make his life hell'.

After the customary period of dithering by the BBC, Baker was sacked from the show, with Radio 5 Live announcing: 'He crossed the dividing line between being lively, humorous or controversial to being insulting. This is something we cannot tolerate.' Baker professed himself unrepentant and made clear where he felt the interests of the BBC lay: 'I don't think you can represent the true feelings of rank-and-file football fans as well as keeping your contacts with the hierarchy in the FA.' Despite the bluster, his subsequent broadcasting style was less abrasive and, as the massive commercial dominance of the Premier League grew increasingly evident in the media, he came to seem ever more nostalgic, a curator of a dying culture.

There was an element of that too in *Fantasy Football League*, which had started on Radio 5 Live with Dominik Diamond before making the leap to BBC Two with David Baddiel and Frank Skinner. The two comedians were joined by the nerdish figure of Angus Loughran, known here simply as Statto, who dressed in pyjamas and dressing-gown, drank milk and was teased relentlessly throughout the show. The affection evident in that mockery of 'boring, boring Statto', as well as the weekly appearances of former West Bromwich Albion striker Jeff Astle singing dreadful karaoke, indicated that, despite some critical interpretations, the world of the new lad was not quite as harsh or exclusive as it might be. The humour was still that of the terraces, but it was softened, gentler in tone. It revealed the sentimentality that lay in the make-up of laddism, reflecting its origins in dreams of an adolescent golden age. 'You don't even have to grow up,' was one of the reasons given by *GQ* magazine in an article titled WHY IT'S GREAT TO BE A BLOKE. Amongst the others was: 'You don't cry. Unless, that is, your team gets promoted or wins something.'

Certainly *Fantasy Football League* was a milder place than Channel 4's *The Word*, which had similarly enjoyed a post-pub broadcast slot (licensing hours were still restricted at this stage, and closing time was at 11 p.m.). *The Word* featured live music alongside more notorious segments, most famously 'The Hopefuls', in which members of the public were given the opportunity to appear on television, so long as they performed a distasteful stunt, such as immersing themselves in a bath of maggots, drinking vomit or French kissing an old woman.

Among the non-musical highlights were presenter Mark Lamarr taking reggae star Shabba Ranks to task for his views on homosexuality, and a memorable encounter between rapper Snoop Doggy Dogg and the anarchic comedy act of Rod Hull and Emu. But mostly *The Word* was distinguished by its extreme amateurishness, the last great example of a 1980s fancy that chaotic presentation and production values equated to edgy, exciting television. By the time the programme was cancelled in 1995, it had been overtaken by the newer style of *Fantasy Football League*, *Don't Forget Your Toothbrush* or *The Big Breakfast*, which were much more heavily scripted and were, in essence, a reinvention of light entertainment. Frank Skinner once claimed that he was 'the new vaudeville', and he wasn't far from the truth.

The assumption was still that many of those watching *Fantasy Football League* would have had a few drinks, but there was no aggression on display in this version of new laddism and there was room for ladettes as well. The comedy critic Ben Thompson, writing more than a decade after the incident, suggested that there had been a strong vein of misogyny about Baddiel's reaction to that discussion of *Henry: Portrait of a Serial Killer*, that 'something about the spectacle of a man humiliating a woman in public must have been especially gratifying to him'. It was a not uncommon accusation, but it felt as though it was still rooted in the 1980s world of the 'new puritans' at a time when things were changing. In a popular culture that now included girl power and ladettes, male strippers and female pornography, women who embraced football and computer gaming, some of the certainties associated with the identity politics of the previous decade had blurred.

Not all of this was to the taste of more venerable feminist thinkers. In 1999 Germaine Greer published *The Whole Woman*, a sequel of sorts to her groundbreaking 1970 book, *The Female Eunuch*, arguing that the concept of liberation had been forgotten in the drive for equality, and insisting that global politics was in danger of being abandoned. 'If you believe, as I do, that to be feminist is to understand that before you are of any race, nationality, religion, party or family, you are a woman,' she wrote, 'then the collapse of the prestige and economic power of the majority of women in the world as a direct result of western hegemony must concern you.' Inevitably the book made much less of an impact than had its predecessor, that note of seriousness again seeming to belong to another time.

Debates about gender roles would inevitably continue; on the right there were still concerns over young women's behaviour in public, on the left there were further battles for equality to be fought. But a substantial section of the country had reached some sort of compromise during the 1990s, in a spirit if not of liberation then at least of relaxation; responsibility had been abandoned in pursuit of simple pleasures and gratification. In 1997 David Baddiel took a solo stand-up show on tour, much of his set concerned with discussing his attachment to pornography, and it was noted that his audience included more women than men. From a Marxist feminist perspective, that could be seen as a simple case of false consciousness, but then for most of Britain – even for many who had been on the left in the 1980s – Marxist feminism came quite a long way down the list of priorities in the last decade of the century.

3
Events

'You're in a bad way'

COLLIN HAYE: What an ageing patient called Mr Major's government needed today was a shot in the arm. What it actually received was a bullet in the throat.
Chris Morris & Armando Iannucci, *The Day Today* (1994)

Q. What should you look for if you see a pin flying through the air?
A. John Major with a grenade in his mouth.
Denis Healey (1994)

ALAN B'STARD: John Smith is one of the few politicians left who has stuck rigidly by the Conservative 1992 manifesto.
Laurence Marks & Maurice Gran, *The New Statesman* (1992)

At the beginning of January 1993 the Conservative MP Ann Widdecombe bumped into John Major and wished him a happy new year. 'Well, it can't be any worse than last year,' he grumbled, and she felt obliged to remind him that he had actually won a general election in 1992. But he wasn't to be consoled: 'Yes, one good day in the whole year.' A few weeks earlier, Gyles Brandreth — now part of the new Tory intake in the House of Commons — had shared a dinner table with William Whitelaw, the man whose unerring instinct for the soul of the Conservative Party had helped Margaret Thatcher steer through the difficult times of her first decade as leader. Whitelaw, reported Brandreth, 'spent the whole evening sighing, shaking his head, wobbling his jowls in despair. "I don't know what's become of us."'

All governments are traditionally accorded a honeymoon period when the media tend to give them the benefit of the doubt, and when the opposition is regrouping and rebuilding. Major had been lucky that his honeymoon effectively lasted long enough to see him through a general election; he was considerably less fortunate that it came to an end so swiftly, and so spectacularly, after that victory. Seldom has a newly elected government suffered such a rapid fall from grace. Partly this was because Major had lost his novelty value for the press, and partly because John Smith had taken over the reins of the Labour Party with such apparent assurance. But mostly it was because everything that could go wrong did go wrong.

The first and most devastating blow came in September 1992, while the Commons was still enjoying its summer recess. Britain's membership of the Exchange Rate Mechanism pinned sterling to the other European currencies (which in practice meant the deutschmark), with only a narrow deviation permitted from its trading value on the international markets. But as the recession dragged wearily onwards, the idea of sticking to exchange rates that had been fixed three years earlier started to look unsustainable. Domestic problems were exacerbated by international instability; Germany had recently taken on the massive task of reunification after the fall of communism in the East, while the American economy was suffering its own problems.

Britain, bedevilled by economic stagnation, and caught as ever between Europe and the USA, the two great powerhouses of the West, was in a dangerous place, 'trapped in the dollar-deutschmark crossfire', as Major later put it. There was also the fact that the ERM found no favour with currency speculators, for the obvious reason that it had been designed precisely to reduce the amount of speculation that would be possible; markets seldom approve of being chained by politicians, and Britain was increasingly looking like a weak link.

Towards the end of the summer of 1992 the currency markets, believing that sterling was over-valued, moved to correct the position, and were thoroughly unconvinced by Britain's attempt to resist such pressures. The issue reached a crisis in a day of high drama on 16 September, nicknamed almost immediately Black Wednesday. That morning, in a two-pronged defence of sterling's membership of the ERM, the Bank of England began to throw huge sums of money at the market, buying up the currency that no one else wanted, while Norman Lamont implemented an immediate rise in the interest rate, from 10 to 12 per cent. Neither initiative made any difference whatsoever, and nor did Lamont's announcement that afternoon that interest rates would go up again the following day, this time to 15 per cent. By the early evening, it was clear that the fight had been lost. Told that for every minute they delayed the country was losing £18 million, ministers threw in the towel.

A visibly shell-shocked Lamont was sent out to face the television cameras so that he might stage a humiliating climb-down. Britain withdrew from the ERM, sterling was effectively devalued by around 10 per cent, and the proposed second interest rate rise was abandoned. The estimated £3.3 billion that had been spent by the Bank of England was written off but not easily forgotten. It was all over, and the experiment was abandoned. There was some talk of Britain rejoining the ERM 'as soon as circumstances allow', but no one really believed in such a fantasy. It had been, reflected the education secretary John Patten (no relation to Chris), 'the mother of all mistakes'.

Britain was not the last target of the speculators. In the immediate aftermath of sterling's collapse, France came under attack as well, though strong intervention by Germany protected the status of the franc, whilst Spain, Portugal and Ireland were obliged to devalue, and Sweden and Norway also withdrew from the mechanism. By that stage it was, or should have been, clear to everyone that the whole enterprise had been doomed to failure from the outset. Though the ERM survived, it was so heavily modified as to become almost meaningless; the margin by which member currencies were allowed to deviate from their central value was increased from 2.25 per cent to 15 per cent. The long-cherished dream of Europe's ruling class – the construction of a single currency, to which the ERM was but a bridge – was once again looking utopian.

Even if other countries got caught up in the near-collapse of the ERM, however, it was John Major's bad luck to be the first and most visible fall guy. The mechanism had, in one way or another, played a crucial role in ending the political careers of the three most powerful Tories of the 1980s: Nigel Lawson, Geoffrey Howe and Margaret Thatcher herself. Now it seemed as though Major might also fall victim to its curse. Having suffered such 'a catastrophic defeat', he admitted in his memoirs: 'My own instinct was clear: I should resign.' But he didn't, and nor did Norman Lamont.

The fact that Lamont remained in office was particularly surprising. When the Labour government of Harold Wilson had been forced to devalue sterling in 1967, James Callaghan had immediately tendered his resignation and, though he remained in the cabinet, he was moved from the exchequer. Expulsion from the ERM was a still greater reversal of government policy than that had been, and yet the chancellor stayed in place. The next day, the journalist Max Hastings told Lamont that he was amazed he was still in office, given that 'nobody's got any confidence in you any more', and Lamont seemed shocked that anyone would think such a thing: 'The prime minister has expressed his full confidence in me.' He was later to make clear that he had been no enthusiast for the project in the first instance, and within days, he was publicly celebrating its collapse. 'My wife said she'd never heard me singing in the bath until last week,' he chuckled. For nearly two years, he had been responsible for implementing the policy, but evidently felt little accountability for it.

The fact that no heads rolled merely compounded the political catastrophe of Black Wednesday for the Tories. It would have been unfair for Major to cast Lamont in the role of scapegoat, but it would also have made perfect sense. Instead, the perception was that incompetence had gone unpenalised, and in the absence of official censure, the public were quick to come to their own verdict; if Major had largely escaped blame for the recession, he was to find the recovery much more difficult. At the beginning of September 1992, the Conservative Party had still enjoyed a small lead in the opinion polls; by the end of the month this had disappeared entirely with a startling fall of 14 percentage points. John Major, who at his peak during the Kuwaiti War had enjoyed a personal satisfaction rating of 46 per cent – the highest recorded since Winston Churchill – now stood at minus 27 per cent, and found that his party was less popular than it had been under Thatcher at the time of the poll tax.

For a public who were feeling an economic squeeze, and who were all too aware not only of their mortgage payments but of their level of credit-card indebtedness, the idea that the government would even contemplate putting up interest rates by five percentage points in a single day made the crisis very personal indeed. The memory was to linger and Major was never again to enjoy a lead in the opinion polls.

Parliament was hurriedly recalled for an emergency debate about the events of Black Wednesday, giving John Smith, who had been in office as Labour leader for all of four weeks, an unexpectedly early opportunity to kick a man when he was down. He didn't resist the temptation. Noting that ERM membership had been Major's key policy, Smith concluded: 'With it has gone for ever a claim by the prime minister or the party he leads to economic competence. He is the devalued prime minister of a devalued government.' In the same debate Gordon Brown, now shadow chancellor, was equally severe in his verdict on the Tories: 'They may hold office for five years, but after five months they have lost all authority to govern. They have failed the country and they will never be trusted again.'

Those judgements were perfectly accurate, though one might have been forgiven for marvelling at the source of such thunderous denunciations, for Labour had been an enthusiastic advocate of the ERM even before Britain had joined, and Smith and Brown had been the principal cheerleaders. Nor had they previously raised the issue of sterling being pitched at too high an exchange rate (one of the charges now laid at Major's door). The shadow budget of 1992 had had nothing to say on the subject, while the manifesto had been explicit in its support for the government's position: 'Labour will maintain the value of the pound within the European Exchange Rate Mechanism.' 'Very little thought was given to the level of sterling's entry,' admitted Peter Mandelson, another of Labour's great Euro-enthusiasts, in his memoirs. 'It was the politics that mattered, the need for Labour to demonstrate financial discipline.'

The Labour leadership was not alone. The Bank of England, the Confederation of British Industry, the Trades Union Congress, the Liberal Democrats and most of the media – including all the broadsheet newspapers – had also urged Britain's entry into the ERM, believing it to be essential for the nation's economic well-being. Amidst such a deafening unison, it had been difficult to hear the voices of those few politicians singing from a different, darker hymn sheet, whether on the left of the Labour Party or the right of the Conservatives. Now the direst warnings of those doom-mongers had been proved right, and it was of some consequence how their respective parties would respond to the setback.

From Labour there came no sign of a rethink after the failure of its economic policy. Gordon Brown continued to operate on a mistaken assumption that the recession would persist, and made no public acknowledgement that he might have been as wrong as Major. When the future Labour cabinet minister David Blunkett wrote in his diary that Black Wednesday was actually 'White for us', it revealed only that – as Mandelson's comments implied – tribalism had become of more significance than, say, the state of the British economy; it certainly said nothing about whether the party's position and attitudes might need to be reconstructed in the light of such a disastrous outcome.

There were those on the Tory right who likewise used the term White Wednesday (or even, a short-lived phrase, Golden Wednesday). But here the ramifications were far greater, since there was still a debate to be had. 'I felt intellectually liberated,' remembered the Eurosceptic MP John Redwood of the expulsion from the ERM. It seemed inevitable that John Major would, sooner or later, come into conflict with this new-found freedom on his right-hand side.

Because the prime minister, of course, had little option but to continue defending – in principle at least – the policy he had himself implemented whilst chancellor. Others might attribute the length and depth of the British recession to membership of the ERM, but he, almost alone, maintained that the experiment had been worthwhile and had brought benefits, primarily the reduction in the inflation rate from 10 per cent in 1990 to 3.5 per cent by the end of 1992. Such arguments cut little ice with the public when set against the monthly unemployment figures, released the day after Black Wednesday, which showed a further 47,000 people had been added to the jobless total. The truth was, as Douglas Hurd later acknowledged, that 'we had for the moment neither an economic nor a European policy'. Just a couple of months earlier, Major had described the idea of leaving the ERM as 'fool's gold'; now that was his only political currency.

It was not simply the public who lost faith with Major's government on Black Wednesday. Much of the press, which had been broadly, and often narrowly, supportive of the Tories in the past, saw it as a turning point. Many right-wing commentators had been suspicious of Major all along, if for no other reason than he wasn't Margaret Thatcher, and now others too began to express reservations. The *Telegraph* titles in particular set up a rival Conservative camp, where ideology could disport itself in pride and purity, unsullied by compromise.

Max Hastings was then the editor of the *Daily Telegraph* and, although he had personally backed Michael Heseltine in the leadership election, he had been sympathetic to Major up until Black Wednesday. His deputy editor, Simon Heffer, on the other hand, had never been a fan, and the *Sunday Telegraph* was edited by another Thatcher loyalist, Charles Moore, who had interviewed Major early on in his premiership to the satisfaction of neither. 'It was clear from the outset that he and I were oil and water,' remarked Major tartly in his memoirs. 'I was never to enjoy support from his pen.' The *Sunday Telegraph* also housed Christopher Booker, whose journalistic career was seldom noted for his willingness to let go once he had sunk his teeth into an issue; he too took against Major. And its deputy editor was Frank Johnson, one of the wittiest, and therefore most wounding, writers on Fleet Street and another who had no time for the prime minister. As early as December 1990 Alan Clark had reported the dinner conversation of Johnson and Peregrine Worsthorne (former editor of the *Sunday Telegraph*): 'Both were plainly getting ready to be "disillusioned" with the unfortunate John.' When Major was told, during the 1992 election campaign, that the Tories were behind by six percentage points, he is said to have replied: 'Of those six points, three are the fault of Simon Heffer and the other three are Frank Johnson's fault.' He exaggerated, of course, but losing the loyalty of the *Telegraph* papers was to prove a running sore.

The Times also began to distance itself from Major's leadership, a situation exacerbated by the fact that the prime minister was clearly no soul-mate of the paper's proprietor, Rupert Murdoch, who was no longer the frequent visitor to Downing Street that he had been in

Margaret Thatcher's time. One of Murdoch's other daily titles, *Today*, was to declare itself for Labour, while the *Sun*, the most important publication of all, which had once been the theoretical journal of Thatcherism, commenced hostilities in its own unique way. On the evening of Black Wednesday, its editor, Kelvin MacKenzie, cheerfully told Major on the phone: 'I have a bucket load of shit on my desk and I'm going to pour it all over you.' Major's response displayed all the forbearance of a patient uncle, indulging a child with a taste for practical jokes: 'You are a one.' The following day the *Sun*'s front-page headline read: NOW WE'VE ALL BEEN SCREWED BY THE CABINET.

That headline was a typically indelicate allusion to stories then circulating about David Mellor, who had been appointed secretary of state for national heritage after the election. This was a new department rounding up responsibilities that had previously been scattered around various Whitehall offices – sport, the arts, film, broadcasting, tourism – and Mellor was immediately dubbed the 'minister of fun'. His time in office, however, was fleeting since, in Major's carefully chosen words, 'David's definition of fun ran rather wider than his departmental responsibilities.'

In July 1992 the *People* newspaper ran a story about an affair between Mellor and a young actress. It appeared that much of the report had been obtained by the covert bugging of the flat where they met. At the time this intrusion was legal – it had been conducted with the knowledge of the landlord, though not of the two lovers – and the exposé was justified by the paper's editor, Bill Hagerty, on the grounds of public interest; he argued that Mellor had 'said he was unable to write speeches because he was so tired', and that therefore his affair must be interfering with his duties as a cabinet minister. But most readers understood that it was just too good a tale for a hungry tabloid to refuse, and the fact that Mellor was not noted as the most physically attractive of MPs ('I worry about what David Mellor will do when he loses his looks,' joked the comedian Barry Cryer) only added to the merriment.

It was a story that lingered long in the memory, particularly after the woman involved – having had her personal life splashed across the papers, and facing much personal criticism because she was wrongly believed to have sold her story – decided that she might as well give her own account. The publicist Max Clifford negotiated a deal on her behalf with the *Sun*, and, at some point along the way, a few suitably salacious details were fabricated to make it all more entertaining still; Mellor was alleged to be partial to having his toes sucked and to enjoy making love while wearing a replica

Chelsea strip. (Like his friend and prime minister, he was known as a fan of the West London club.) Mellor hung on to office for several weeks, but he was now seen as fair game and, following further stories, was eventually forced to resign, making a personal statement that was notable for being wittier than most examples of the form. 'Having grown heartily sick of my private life myself, I cannot expect others to take a more charitable view,' he shrugged. It was eclipsed only by one of the *Sun*'s best ever headlines: TOE JOB TO NO JOB.

Ultimately it was all very trivial stuff, seemingly confirming Britain's reputation for absurdly puritan standards in political life. 'An affair with an actress?' puzzled the former French culture minister, Jack Lang. 'Why else does one become minister of culture?' But beyond the gossip lurked a serious issue, for Mellor had plenty of enemies in Fleet Street who saw him as a legitimate target, and had done so for some time.

Thanks to a spate of handwringing in the late 1980s about factual errors and invasions of privacy in the press, a Home Office committee had been established under Sir David Calcutt, the Master of Magdalene College, Cambridge, to investigate the newspaper industry. Reporting in 1990 it concluded that self-regulation by the Press Council had failed, and recommended that this largely ineffectual body be replaced by a semi-independent Press Complaints Commission. Calcutt also said that if this attempt to curb the excesses of tabloid reporting didn't succeed, then legislation would become necessary. Mellor was at the time a Home Office minister and issued a famous warning to the press that they were 'drinking in the Last Chance Saloon'.

On 9 July 1992, as he settled into his new department, Mellor announced that he was asking Calcutt to conduct a six-month evaluation of how the new system was working, and to look at whether 'any further measures may be needed to deal with intrusions into personal privacy'. This was reported in *The Times* under the headline: PRESS ON PROBATION AS ENQUIRY BEGINS INTO SELF-REGULATION. There was a serious risk that some sort of privacy legislation, long discussed, might this time be forthcoming. Ten days later Mellor found his private life exposed on a grand scale and, once the *People* had broken the story, spread across the pages of all the nation's newspapers.

Those parts of the press who felt most at risk from the threat of legislation were quick to link the two stories. 'This is the man charged with deciding whether Britain's press should be shackled with a privacy bill,' marvelled the *Daily Mirror*. 'How can he be left in charge of a privacy bill?' wondered the *Sun*. 'How can it be argued that a law should be passed rendering [Mellor's affair] an unfit subject for publication?' asked the *Daily Mail*. The glee occasioned in the media by his departure from office was, in short, not entirely disinterested. The national heritage select committee held an inquiry into the issues raised, starting in autumn 1992, but by the time they reported with a call for legislation to protect privacy, the government had learnt its lesson and lost any resolve to change things.

Apart from the newspapers, the other beneficiary from the affair was Max Clifford, who found himself a tabloid figure in his own right and seemed rather to enjoy the attention. He also got a taste for humiliating Tories — 'I was glad it was damaging,' he gloated — and let it be publicly known that his media skills were now available to anyone else with a scandalous tale to sell. No one quite realised at that stage how many such stories there would be in the coming years.

For John Major, there was the unwelcome departure from the cabinet of a trusted friend and ally, of whom he had all too few, as well as one of his better salesmen, of whom he had still fewer. Mellor, though mocked in many quarters for a puffed-up sense of self-importance, was a grammar-school boy with something approaching a common touch, a competent and quick-witted media performer in a government not over-blessed with such figures. In the wake of Black Wednesday, as the issue of Europe became ever more cancerous in the Conservative Party, the absence of the Euro-friendly Mellor from the top table was increasingly regretted. He found a new career in journalism and on the radio, but the ridicule that hounded him out of office was not quickly forgotten and he remained the butt of gags. 'He bestrode the political scene like a colossus,' joked Clive James, on a television review of the year, 'with one foot in his mouth and one foot in hers.' Mellor's value as a Major loyalist, commentating from the sidelines, was much reduced.

The autumn of 1992 was already proving deeply uncongenial to the government. As if to prove the old maxim about trouble coming in threes, Black Wednesday and Mellor's resignation were swiftly followed by another self-inflicted wound, this time at the hands of the cabinet's most populist figure, Michael Heseltine. In the reshuffle that followed the election, he had moved to the trade and industry department — reviving the slightly pompous old title of President of the Board of Trade — and found he had been handed a long-ticking time-bomb.

Back in the late 1980s, when the electricity industry had been privatised, the newly floated power companies had inherited contracts with British Coal to supply fuel for their generating stations. These contracts were due to come up for renewal in 1993, and it was clear that demand for coal was going to fall substantially. With memories of the miners' strike a few years earlier, the generators had no desire to preserve their dependence on an unreliable source and had already begun switching to gas as their primary fuel. And since the primary obligation of the private companies was to their shareholders, they had discovered that it was cheaper for them to buy what coal they needed from abroad. It was estimated that consumption of domestic coal would fall by at least a third, possibly by up to a half. Moreover, there were already millions of tonnes stockpiled at every power station, pit and depot in the country, and production was being heavily subsidised by taxpayers in an attempt to keep it vaguely competitive.

Only one rational conclusion could be reached, Heseltine decided, and the argument for swingeing cuts to the mining industry was strengthened by the knowledge that the miners had lost the industrial muscle they had once possessed. In Norman Lamont's words, no matter how drastic the course of action, 'The lights would not go out.'

Rational argument, however, is not the only requirement of a government, and the announcement by Heseltine and British Coal that thirty-one pits were to be closed with the loss of 30,000 jobs (more than half the workforce) caused a public outcry greater than anything since the poll tax. Certainly the protests were far more widespread than they had been during the great strike of 1984, with even the most solidly Tory parts of the country up in arms. Apart from anything else, there was fury in Conservative ranks that the closures would hit Nottinghamshire, where miners had continued working throughout that strike, standing up heroically — as it was portrayed — against the bullyboy tactics of Arthur Scargill's National Union of Mineworkers. They had even formed their own breakaway organisation, the Union of Democratic Mineworkers (UDM). Now, it appeared, they were to be abandoned, their jobs sacrificed alongside those of their militant former colleagues, with the closure of seven of the thirteen mines in the area, and the Thatcherite wing of the party was incensed. 'We have an enduring obligation to the Notts miners,' one of them exclaimed. 'I cannot believe my ears listening to ministers.'

Such outrage could not altogether be separated from the Thatcher loyalists' delight at finding a stick with which to beat Heseltine, their bête noire, but there was no doubt where public sympathies lay. A quarter of a million people marched in London against the proposals, there were demonstrations right across the country, and three tonnes of coal were dumped at the entrance to Heseltine's house in Oxfordshire. 'The trouble with this bloody government,' one demonstrator told Norman Tebbit, 'is they don't care what we think. They only care what fucking bloody foreigners think.'

Marcus Fox, chairman of the 1922 Committee of Tory backbenchers, said the cuts were 'totally unacceptable', the CBI voiced its opposition, and the press were vociferous and pretty much unanimous, with the blame attaching to Major and Heseltine in almost equal measure. The *Sun* ran a blank front page with just the headline THIS IS WHAT MICHAEL HESELTINE KNOWS ABOUT INDUSTRY (a little harsh on the man who had founded the successful Haymarket publishing company). Another asked IS MAJOR A GONER? And an editorial in *The Times* ended with a damning verdict on the prime minister: 'He looks weak. He is weak.'

Arthur Scargill suddenly found himself being courted by a media that had long ago written him off as an irrelevancy in modern Britain, and he took every opportunity to urge a strike ballot against the proposed closures. More powerful still was the image of UDM leader Neil Greatrex going a stage further and arguing that, with coal stocks at their current levels, there was a limit to what the miners could do alone; he demanded instead a general strike, a suggestion that was traditionally the preserve of the Trotskyist fringe. Indeed the front page of the *Socialist Worker* carried precisely that call and saw its weekly sales double. Meanwhile, Roy Lynk, the founder and national president of the UDM, who had been awarded an OBE in the 1990 New Year's honours list, staged an underground sit-in protest. (The *Sun* sent him a hamper from Harrods to sustain him in his struggle.)

Within days Heseltine was on his feet in the Commons announcing a climb-down. Only ten pits would close immediately, while a review examined the cases of others, and more money had been found to increase the already generous redundancy packages. It was just enough for the government to survive a parliamentary vote, despite rebellions and abstentions by Conservative MPs, though Heseltine was later to admit that, during that debate, 'I have rarely felt so alone.' It was quite an admission from a man who had considerable experience of isolation within his own party.

Ultimately the furore wasn't really about severance payments. In rejecting the notion that there was no such thing as society, the country had come to feel the loss of community and, through a combination of guilt and sentimentality, the pit villages of Yorkshire and the North-East were chosen to symbolise what was perceived to have been lost. It was a feeling reflected in two of the most cherished British films of the next few years. *Billy Elliot* (2000), the tale of a ballet-dancing son of a Durham miner, was set against the backdrop of the 1984–5 strike and – unlike the television coverage of the time – saw the dispute from the miners' side, the camera directed at the intimidating lines of riot police, rather than from behind their shields. More poignantly, *Brassed Off* (1996) was set in the aftermath of Heseltine's announcement, focusing on the works brass band of Grimley Colliery, a pit being threatened by closure.

Based on the story of the celebrated Grimethorpe Colliery Band (who, under the baton of John Anderson, provided the music for the soundtrack), *Brassed Off* depicted a close-knit community under attack and clinging desperately on to its own distinctive culture. 'If they close down the pit, knock it down, fill it up like they've done with all t'bloody rest,' argues the bandmaster Danny (Pete Postlethwaite), 'years to come there'll only be one reminder of a hundred bloody years' hard graft. This bloody band.' Other, younger members of the band are less convinced that there's anything left worth fighting for. Andy (Ewan McGregor) declares he has 'No hope, just principles', while Phil (Stephen Tompkinson) tersely sums up their obsolete status: 'Dinosaurs. Dodos. Miners.' In one of the most powerful scenes, Phil, who has lost everything – 'wife, kids, house, job, self-respect' – is seen in his alternative guise as a party entertainer. In full clown make-up, he is supposed to be amusing a group of children at a Harvest Festival, but is unable to escape the horror of his disintegrating life. He snaps, launches into an attack on the Tories, and turns to a statue of Christ, demanding to know why God hasn't yet taken Margaret Thatcher: 'What's He sodding playing at?'

Despite their despair, the miners vote for the redundancy deal and the pit closes, but in a last hurrah the band make it for the first time to the Brass Band Finals at the Royal Albert Hall, where they win first prize. Danny turns down the award in a speech that explicitly attacks the policies of the Conservatives: 'Over the last ten years, this bloody government has systematically destroyed an entire industry, our industry. And not just our industry. Our communities, our homes, our lives. All in the name of progress and for a few lousy bob.' As the band celebrate their victory on top of a London bus, they pass the Houses of Parliament, and break into a rendition of what Danny refers to as 'Land of Hope and bloody Glory'. For the best part of two centuries the brass band had been one of the most beautiful and evocative sounds in British culture, and as its elegiac interpretation of Elgar's music swells, a caption appears: 'Since 1984 there have been 140 pit closures in Great Britain at the cost of nearly a quarter of a million jobs.'

The huge and unexpected success of *Brassed Off* reflected the somewhat belated public disquiet at the virtual death of an industry that had at its peak employed over a million men. John Major was later to claim that he knew the pit-closure policy was wrong from the outset, but 'My feelings were based on instinct, which is not easy to justify against the logical economic judgements when the economy is ailing, and your chancellor and your energy secretary are sure the policy will work.' So soon after Black Wednesday, it is perhaps pardonable that he didn't fully trust his gut feeling, but for the electorate that merely compounded the problem. As an unnamed cabinet minister admitted in the *Sunday Times*: 'We all took our eye off the ball. It was a cock-up.'

As the anger of October 1992 faded away, the pit closures went ahead anyway, though more quietly and more piecemeal than originally planned. But the damage sustained by the government was not easily shaken off. In the space of four months, it had contrived to have a major sex scandal, to suffer economic humiliation in front of the whole world, and to misjudge entirely the sentiments of the nation. The misery Major expressed to Ann Widdecombe as 1992 closed was not misplaced; truly, nothing had gone right since the election. One of the few things the Conservatives had left in their locker was their reputation as the low-tax party. Then, in March 1993, the government threw that away as well.

In what proved to be his last budget as chancellor, Norman Lamont announced an extra £10 billion of taxes to be phased in over the next three years, including an increase in National Insurance contributions – NI being an income tax in all but name – and a curtailment of mortgage tax relief. There was even talk of introducing NHS prescription charges for pensioners. For a party that had campaigned just twelve months earlier on the danger of higher taxes if Labour were to win, such a policy reversal was almost indefensible, 'the biggest tax increase since the British went off to fight Napoleon'. Worse yet, Lamont had said in his pre-election budget: 'I have no need, no proposals and plans either to raise or extend the scope of VAT.' Now, in the most controversial move of all, came the introduction of VAT on domestic fuel, which had previously been exempt from tax. It was to start at 8 per cent from April 1994, rising the year after to the then-standard rate of 17.5 per cent and, when in full force, would add nearly £100 to the average annual bill.

There was a lacklustre attempt to claim this as some sort of 'green tax', designed to help combat global warming, but even loyal Tories struggled to accept that it was motivated by anything other than the wish to raise billions in revenue. For everyone else, it was immediately apparent that it would have the greatest impact upon the poorest, in a year when state pensions rose by just seventy pence a week. It was also, in effect, a new poll tax, since it applied not merely to fuel consumption, but also to standing charges about which the householder could do nothing. As might have been predicted, the new tax met with outright hostility, and in opinion polls its introduction was opposed by over 90 per cent of the population. Equally predictable was Labour's rush to capitalise on such an unpopular move. 'You can never trust the Tories on tax again,' thundered the shadow chancellor, Gordon Brown, in a neat and highly effective inversion of the long-established order.

Nonetheless, the government held firm to its policy and in December 1994 it brought the proposal to implement the second phase, the rise to 17.5 per cent, to the House of Commons. And there it was defeated by a majority of eight votes, the first substantial reverse the Conservatives had faced on a fiscal measure since their election in 1979. The defeat was largely the work of a group of Eurosceptic MPs from whom the whip had been withdrawn as punishment for not supporting the government on a previous occasion, and who therefore felt that they had no obligation to act as lobby-fodder. 'We did the party a favour,' insisted Teresa Gorman, one of the Tory rebels who voted with the opposition. 'The policy was strongly resented in the country, and widely believed to have cost us council seats.' She was right on the second count, but the damage had already been done, as Major later acknowledged: 'The VAT increase was a political millstone which cost us dearly.'

The impression given through all this was of a government of bunglers and amateurs, a political establishment for whom ridicule was an appropriate response. And the disease seemed to be spreading through other institutions. A couple of weeks after that 1993 budget, the running of the Grand National hit problems, initially with a demonstration on the course by animal rights protestors, and then with a false start which required the riders to pull up before the first fence. A second attempt to run the race was also called off after the starting tape got entangled around the neck of one of the jockeys, but this time the recall system — which still depended upon a primitive system of flags — failed, and thirty of the thirty-nine riders continued on their way, unaware that the race had been called off. Seven horses completed the course, including Esha Ness ridden by John White, who finished with the second fastest time ever recorded. The 50–1 shot never made it to the record books, however, for the race was declared void for the first time in a history stretching back over a hundred and fifty years, and there was no official winner. It was nothing to do with the government, of course, but the shambles raised parallels for some, including one reader of the *People*. 'I can't help thinking how John Major's idea of running the country is like this year's Grand National,' she wrote to the paper. 'After a number of false starts, he has simply abandoned the whole thing.'

The apparent ineptitude of the government was matched by a feeling that it had lost any sense of the electorate's wishes and aspirations. In the 1980s there had been plenty of complaints from the left that Margaret Thatcher was interested only in those who shared her vision and was prepared to neglect the rest of the country; now even traditional Tory supporters found there was little to cheer about.

At the highest level, the 1993 Leasehold Reform Act – which opened the possibility of leaseholders buying the freehold on their properties, whether their landlord wished to sell or not – prompted the resignation from the Conservative Party of the Duke of Westminster, the richest man in Britain. In a more humble world, a plan to restructure the police force was announced and provoked the biggest protest rally in the history of the British police, with more than 20,000 officers converging on Wembley Arena to make their voice heard. The home secretary, Michael Howard, declined an invitation to attend, but his opposite number, Tony Blair, made the most of his opportunity. 'The case for reform is whether it helps to cut crime,' he said, to an appreciative audience, 'not whether it allows the Treasury to cut corners or satisfies some mistaken dogma.'

Nor was the military, that most totemic issue for the dyed-in-the-tweed Tory, exempt. Proposals were brought forward to close down the Royal Navy dockyards at Rosyth and Devonport, while the Options for Change military review – prompted by the ending of the Cold War – saw the disappearance of several of the country's most venerable and cherished regiments. This hit particularly hard in Scotland where the Gordon Highlanders, with two hundred years of history behind them, were merged with the Queen's Own Highlanders (themselves the product of an earlier amalgamation of the Seaforth Highlanders and the Queen's Own Cameron Highlanders) to form the non-specific Highlanders. A protracted campaign did, however, secure a temporary reprieve for the Royal Scots, the oldest infantry regiment of the line in the army.

While it was thus busy alienating its own supporters, the government, of course, continued also to cause outrage on the liberal left. At times this seemed to be the result of little more than a desperate publicity stunt, designed to outflank and embarrass Labour, as when Michael Howard announced that identity cards would be introduced, before backing down from the proposal. At others, it seemed to reflect a genuine intolerance of civil liberties, so that the 1994 Criminal Justice and Public Order Act shifted the balance of power away from the citizen and decisively towards the police, allowing for greater use of stop and search, for the taking and retention of fingerprints and body samples, and for a suspect's silence under questioning to be raised in court. It also attacked several areas of what were seen as dissenting lifestyles, including the repeal of the duty of local authorities to provide sites for travellers, and the introduction of provisions aimed at hunt saboteurs, anti-road protestors and those who attended raves.

Indeed this Act covered so many bases that few in the legislature, let alone amongst the public, were able to keep up with it. When introduced as a Bill, it ran to 112 pages; by the time it passed into law it had nearly doubled in size to 214 pages. Additions and amendments were seemingly made up on the hoof, as the Conservatives tried unsuccessfully to find a measure so extreme that the Labour Party wouldn't back it, thus enabling the opposition to be portrayed as soft on law and order.

Then there was the government's simple insensitivity to issues that required at least the lip-service of concern. Chief amongst the culprits here was Ann Widdecombe, who had made her name in the Commons as a doughty campaigner against abortion, having been elected in 1987 as the MP for Maidstone, where the local Tories had once turned down Margaret Thatcher as their candidate. In John Major's government there were so few women – none at all in his first cabinet – that she was bound to be noticed when she became a minister, but in all likelihood she would have stood out in almost any era. She displayed such a fierce refusal to care about her look ('I am short and fat and ugly,' was her own assessment) that it became the most readily identifiable image in the House; with her dumpy stature and jet-black pudding-bowl hairdo, she resembled, thought Gyles Brandreth, 'a death-watch beetle'. Coupled with that was a willingness to express forthright opinions in plain-speaking language that was lapped up by a media ruing Edwina Currie's absence from the government. 'She is as hard as nails and as cold a politician as you would fear to meet,' one anonymous colleague told the press, feeding the myth of the most heartless Tory of them all.

She first made public waves as a social security minister in 1991 when a study published by National Children's Homes concluded that the welfare state was failing the poorest; in the families of those receiving benefits, it was claimed, 10 per cent of children under five were missing meals because of poverty, and one parent in five regularly went hungry. Widdecombe retorted that this meant the vast majority of those on benefits were eating sufficiently, and that the research should therefore have concentrated instead on the differences between those who did eat properly and those who did not, in order that the latter might be pointed in the right direction.

Her comments displayed logic but little compassion, and much of the media turned against her, particularly the *Daily Mirror*, for whom she became a hate figure to rival the position of Labour's Clare Short at the *Sun*; the paper missed few opportunities to point out that she was unmarried – a virgin, even – and apparently was thus, by definition, a woman out of touch with the mass of the people.

The biggest storm came in January 1996 with the broadcast of a Channel 4 documentary that showed a pregnant prisoner being shackled to warders as she was taken from Holloway Prison to the Whittington Hospital in North London to give birth. This was standard policy, following a disproportionate number of escapes by women prisoners on their way to hospital in recent years, and a practice with which Widdecombe, now the prisons minister, professed herself content: 'I was perfectly happy for women to be secured between prison and hospital. I was perfectly happy with the procedure that you removed the restraints as soon as medical treatment started, that was, when labour started.'

Again it was a logical position, but not one likely to attract much public support, and the *Mirror*'s abuse became ever more personal. The 'mums-in-chains minister', she was called in what should have been a muck-raking article (except that there was no muck to rake) headlined LOVELESS LIFE OF THE WOMAN THEY CALL DORIS KARLOFF. The policy was swiftly changed so that restraints would be removed from pregnant prisoners on their arrival at hospital, but the whole story followed a pattern that had become characteristic of John Major's government: an unpopular policy was allowed to fester and to attract opprobrium before being abandoned in a humiliating retreat.

Even in those areas where government initiatives were clearly progressive, poor public relations squandered opportunities to generate favourable headlines. A campaign against age prejudice at work in 1993 attracted as little attention as did the rough sleeper initiative.

The latter was a response to the homelessness that had been growing steadily since the mid-1980s, most visibly in London where thousands of people, generally young, were sleeping on the streets. These were the inhabitants of cardboard boxes to whom Labour had rightly drawn attention in the 1992 election campaign. Their plight had been highlighted in one of the better recent storylines of the television soap *EastEnders*, in which Sophie Lawrence played Diane Butcher, the sixteen-year-old daughter of Frank (Mike Reid), with whom she has a difficult relationship. Running away from home in 1990, Diane ends up living on the streets of London, encountering prostitution, violence and hopelessness – though even the grittiest soap was unable to convey the hunger, cold and sheer, numbing tedium of sleeping rough.

Homelessness in this form was an extreme symptom of a wider and deeper housing problem, a long-term shortage of accommodation exacerbated, in the words of LSE lecturer Anne Power, by a range of factors including 'the growth in family break-up, lone parenthood and the accelerated closures of mental hospitals, children's homes and other large institutions'. In the early years of the decade, when the wave of house repossessions caused by the recession meant that home ownership no longer looked an entirely secure option, a substantial layer of the population watched the story of Diane Butcher with a feeling of 'there, but for the grace of God'.

As environment secretary, Michael Heseltine launched a programme to address the issue, putting money into building new single-person flats for social housing, as well as making more basic contributions, such as the provision of mobile phones for charity workers, so that availability of accommodation at hostels could be checked in advance. Coming at the same time as other programmes, particularly the launch in 1991 by John Bird of *The Big Issue*, a street newspaper sold by the homeless to earn money, the initiative proved a modest success, reducing the numbers on the streets substantially, though it received far less coverage than had the original scandal. Solutions are, of course, far less newsworthy than problems, but in a media age it was part of a competent government's job to draw attention to its successes. Competent was not an adjective often applied to Major's administration.

Nor, regrettably, was the word 'decent', particularly after the government's behaviour over the Civil Rights (Disabled Persons) Bill. This backbench measure, sponsored by MPs from all parties, sought to ensure that access for the disabled was provided in places of employment, on public transport and in public buildings. But when the Bill came to the Commons in 1994, five Tory backbenchers submitted some eighty amendments between them, the clear intention of which was to wreck the proposed legislation by ensuring that the debate ran out of time. There were suspicions that the backbenchers were acting on government orders, a charge flatly denied by Nicholas Scott, the minister for disabled people, until it was demonstrated to be true; Scott's department was indeed behind the drafting of the amendments, anxious to scupper the Bill but lacking the courage to admit the fact in public. Calls for Scott to resign came both from the Labour Party and from journalists, including the *Independent*'s Andrew Marr: 'He blatantly misled the House of Commons but, more important than that, he was party to one of the shabbiest acts of parliamentary sabotage we have seen for years.' Even Scott's own daughter, Victoria, who worked with a campaigning group on the issue, joined in the calls: 'Resignation would be the honourable thing to do.'

Scott was said to be 'close to tears' and to have offered to step down, but was persuaded not to do so; instead he was obliged to talk out the Bill himself, speaking for more than eighty minutes in the Commons as he outlined the government's honest position that 'it would cost too much money'. As he spoke, a demonstration by disabled people outside Parliament saw thirty or so campaigners abandon their wheelchairs and drag themselves painfully up the steps of the public entrance to the House, where their progress was blocked by police officers. It wasn't the Conservative Party's finest hour. Professor Stephen Hawking, the country's best-known scientist, who was afflicted with a motor neurone disease, joined the condemnation: 'I don't think any disabled person should vote for the present government unless they do something to atone for the shabby way they killed the Civil Rights Bill.' There was subsequently some expiation with the passage of the Disability Discrimination Act in 1995, a weaker measure which made it unlawful to discriminate against people with disabilities, though without the requirement for access. Steered through Parliament by Ann Widdecombe and William Hague (the latter having replaced Scott), the Act didn't noticeably improve the Conservatives' image in the country.

As the party's future leader, Iain Duncan Smith, was later to reflect: 'Everything we did that was good was despite us, everything we did that was bad was our fault.'

It was somehow appropriate that the most popular television comedies during the tenure of this most ill-starred of governments featured such hapless central characters. ITV's big hit was *Mr Bean*, in which Rowan Atkinson played a childlike cartoon of a man whose inability to understand the grown-up world caused chaos and confusion. Meanwhile the BBC was finding success with *One Foot in the Grave*, a sitcom that contained virtually no jokes, just a succession of unfortunate incidents, coincidences and misunderstandings in a world without meaning or hope. The programme's creator David Renwick explained its rationale: 'The show has an attitude. Cynical, resigned, aware of the soddishness of circumstance and hostility of the world around us.' Many of the storylines were so dark that, with only minimal changes, it would have made a particularly bleak drama. One of the best-known sequences sees the central character Victor Meldrew, played by Richard Wilson, buried up to his neck in the garden, while his wife Margaret (Annette Crosbie) tells him she's just learnt of the death of her mother, the woman's body having lain at home undiscovered for five days. Indeed, death is a perpetual presence: a particularly disturbing scene from 1995 depicts a suicide by hanging, and in the final episode in 2000 Meldrew is killed in a hit-and-run accident.

Wilson actively campaigned for the Labour Party, and Victor Meldrew was no Tory either, as he made clear in his reflections on the 1992 election: 'I just couldn't believe that last election result. It's like hiring a man-eating shark as your children's swimming instructor. "Yes I know it bit my baby's head off last time, but I still think it deserves another chance."' Despite that, his vision of the world could have served as an epitaph for John Major's government: 'One thing you can be sure about in life is that just when you think things are never ever going to get better, they suddenly get worse.'

For there seemed to be nothing that the prime minister could do to stem the tide of hostility and even contempt that his government faced. In May 1993 he finally sacked Norman Lamont as chancellor (he offered him the environment department, but Lamont turned it down), and replaced him with the much more popular and laidback Kenneth Clarke, a cheerfully paunchy, cigar-smoking jazz lover, whose taste in Hush Puppy shoes made him seem more louche than he really was. And still the polls were unforgiving, with Major now 'less loved even than Neville Chamberlain in 1940'. The hero of David Lodge's novel *Therapy* reflected that it might all be deliberate: 'John Major has the lowest popularity rating of any British prime minister since polling began. I'm beginning to feel almost sorry for him. I wonder whether it isn't a cunning Tory plot to capture the low self-esteem vote.'

Meanwhile Lamont took his expulsion from government very personally indeed. He refused to issue the customary public letter protesting his loyalty to the prime minister, and Major revealed in his memoirs, published in 1999, that the two men hadn't spoken since the day of the sacking. There were some who detected a note of envy in Lamont's bitterness. He had arrived in Parliament after a 1972 by-election, seven years before Major, and yet by the middle of the 1980s he had fallen a significant step behind when it came to promotion. Even so, he had managed Major's leadership campaign in 1990 and clearly felt that he was entitled to continuing support from his senior colleague rather than being, as he saw it, cast in the role of sacrificial offering to the media.

A fortnight after his dismissal, in June 1993, Lamont stood up to make a personal statement to the Commons, a courtesy generally accorded to ministers on leaving office. His speech was trailed in the London newspaper the *Evening Standard* with an article from David Mellor, the most recent cabinet casualty, headlined WHY LAMONT WON'T TAKE HIS REVENGE. He couldn't have been more wrong. Lamont clearly had in mind the resignation statements of Nigel Lawson and Geoffrey Howe, which had between them helped put Margaret Thatcher out of office, and sought to replicate their effect: 'There is something wrong with the way we make our decisions. The government listens too much to the pollsters and the party managers. The trouble is that they're not even very good at politics and they are entering too much into policy decisions. As a result, there is too much short-termism, too much reacting to events, not enough shaping of events. We give the impression of being in office, but not in power.'

That last phrase – taken, Tony Benn noted, from the title of one of his own published volumes of diaries, *Office Without Power* – defined the position of the government precisely, and was often to be quoted, but it wasn't enough to rank with Howe's 'conflict of loyalties', since Lamont lacked the stature to inflict such a killer blow. Though never popular with the public, and inevitably diminished further by Black Wednesday, his move to the back benches posed a problem for the prime minister, not because he was a real rival, but simply because, with his departure, Major's flank was left exposed; henceforth he would take the full blame for economic bad news. And, in the immediate term, losing a chancellor in such an acrimonious manner could only be bad publicity. 'Norman's statement left our side numb, shell-shocked, silent, and the opposition benches cock-a-hoop,' wrote Gyles Brandreth in his diary, as Major sustained yet another not-quite-fatal wound. It was barely a year since the triumph of the 1992 general election.

None of these problems were of Labour's making, but the opposition could hardly fail to benefit from the government's travails. For the first time since the days of Alec Douglas-Home, the party could afford to lie back and wallow in the Tories' discomfort. To the annoyance of some of the self-proclaimed modernisers – primarily the fast-rising Tony Blair – this was precisely what it appeared to do. Under John Smith's leadership, the flash of the Sheffield rally was put to one side, replaced by a solid caution and a steadying of the ship.

The influence of the once ubiquitous Peter Mandelson, since the election a mere backbench MP, declined considerably under a leader who thought he was so 'devious he would one day disappear up his own something or other'. Smith even managed to do his job without benefit of a personal press officer. The focus groups and private polling, on which Neil Kinnock had come to rely so heavily, mostly melted away, and the ceaseless quest for new, middle-of-the-road policies came to an end. The one key exception to the latter was Smith's determination, following his calamitous shadow budget, that Labour should never again be cast in the role of the high-tax party.

Most disturbingly, from the modernisers' perspective, Smith was content to work with the trade unions. When he was asked in the early 1980s why he hadn't joined the SDP, his reply had reflected the fault line running through the left: 'I am comfortable with the unions.' For many who had split from Labour in those difficult days, and for others who might have been tempted but remained, this was perhaps an even more significant issue than Europe or nuclear disarmament. In 1992 Tony Blair was asked whether the Labour Party should have a more distant relationship with the TUC – somewhat akin to that between the Tories and the CBI – and he was succinct in his answer: 'Why not?'

There were new initiatives under Smith, but they were seldom in pursuit of a quick headline. In 1993, for example, a carefully considered speech floated the idea of a reconfiguration and expansion of the Security Council of the United Nations, suggesting the addition of Germany, Japan, India, Brazil and Nigeria as permanent members to augment the five victorious Allies from the Second World War. It was a long-overdue proposal, but one that did little for the narrow party interest of humiliating the government.

It didn't take long for complaints to surface. By November 1992 Clare Short was using the pages of *Tribune* magazine to bemoan the leadership's 'masterful inactivity', while from the right of the party the MP Nick Raynsford was denouncing the 'tranquillity' of John Smith's leadership: 'the party appears to be substituting a state of anaesthetised torpor for a previous mood of hyperactive aggression.' Writing in the *Fabian Review*, Raynsford warned: 'Simply relying on the incompetence and failure of the Tories to deliver us a victory in 1996–97 will not be sufficient.' Tony Benn wasn't the only one to read such comments as a thinly coded 'demand that Gordon Brown and Tony Blair take over the leadership and deputy leadership'.

Even with this air of calm, however, the party was continuing to reform itself. In 1993 the annual conference, responding to two decades of concern about the under-representation of women in the Commons, voted in favour of all-women shortlists for the selection of some parliamentary candidates; these were to be used in half of all marginal constituencies and in half of those seats where a Labour MP was retiring. It wasn't an entirely popular move – Tony Blair would later insist that the 50 per cent rule was 'a target', not a requirement – but it was accepted as a short-term, interim measure to address a historical deficit. In the event, it turned out to be even more temporary than anticipated; the policy was successfully challenged at an industrial tribunal by two men, arguing that they had faced discrimination on grounds of gender, and the practice had to be abandoned. During its brief life, however, it had already resulted in the selection of several candidates, and its fruits were to be seen at the next election.

If the modernisers had not yet taken over, there was certainly a mood in the party for moderation. Every year at the conference, the results were announced of the voting for the seven members of Labour's national executive committee (NEC) chosen by the constituency parties' rank-and-file members. Those elected were almost always MPs (as leader of Sheffield council, David Blunkett had been a rare exception in the 1980s), and for the last couple of decades they had tended to be on the left of the party. Now, with membership at a post-war low, it appeared as though the rank and file that remained were following the leadership in a drift towards the right. In the 1992 contest Bryan Gould and the leftist hero Dennis Skinner were voted off the NEC, replaced by Gordon Brown and Tony Blair. Then in 1993 came the final break when Tony Benn, after an unbroken period of thirty-four years, was removed in favour of Harriet Harman.

This truly was the end of an era, the cutting of a thread that ran all the way back to the 1959 election, when Benn himself had been the moderniser, dragging Labour into the era of television and the mass media. For the last decade and a half he had rivalled Denis Healey as the most recognisable Labour politician in the country, capable of arousing passions on both sides, of hatred and of devotion, in a way that could be matched perhaps only by Enoch Powell and Margaret Thatcher. His move to the left in the 1970s had come close to capturing the party for full-blooded socialism, had precipitated the splintering off of the SDP, and had transformed British politics. More than anything Kinnock, Smith or Blair had done or would do, the decision of ordinary party members that Benn should lose his seat on the NEC was the symbolic moment marking the birth of a new incarnation of Labour.

As the results were announced, Benn was given a standing ovation in recognition of his extraordinarily long service, but also surely in acknowledgement that his influence was now a thing of the past, that the membership had had enough of principled opposition. Labour had shrunk, both in aspiration and size. Some had left because they had been forced out – in 1991 the purge of entryists had finally forced the departure of Militant to form its own party, Militant Labour – while others had simply given up in despair. 'A lot of people have left the Party,' Benn noted sadly on the day of his defeat, 'and I think a lot more will leave.'

Ironically it was at the same 1993 conference that John Smith showed how much he had learned from Benn's strategic thinking. Benn's attempts to transform Labour in the latter days of James Callaghan's leadership had focused on changing the constitution in the name of democracy, giving more power to constituency parties to select and deselect their parliamentary candidates, and wresting control of the election of the leader away from the grasp of MPs alone. Now Smith adopted exactly the same tactic, picking up an idea, heavily canvassed by Bryan Gould in recent years, that the trade union block vote — whereby union leaders cast the votes of their members without any need for consultation with those members — should be abolished at conference, and that both unions and constituency parties should henceforth be balloted as individuals when it came to choosing the party leader. Importantly, though, the electoral college, which weighted the various component parts of the Labour movement, would remain.

As with Benn's reforms, the principle of one member, one vote (OMOV, as it was swiftly abbreviated) was touted as a move to a greater democracy, but it was controversial and by no means guaranteed of success, since it could only be passed if the trade union leaders cast their block votes against their own immediate interests. Many were disinclined so to do, arguing that if the union movement was bankrolling the party, it had a right to be closely involved in its decision-making. 'No say, no pay,' as Tom Sawyer, leader of NUPE, expressed it. Few leading politicians were prepared to risk union displeasure by campaigning hard on the issue, though Tony Blair conducted a number of interviews supporting reform, observing as he did so: 'Why can't you get Gordon or any of the others to do this?' It wasn't the last time that Gordon Brown's absence at a time of controversy was to be noted.

Meanwhile, Smith was adamant that this was a necessary change if Labour were ever to shed the impression that it was not merely the creation but also the creature of the trade unions. He had no ideological issue with the industrial wing of the movement, but he shared a common feeling that it was time to readjust the balance of power, and he let it be known that he would resign as leader if he failed to win the day. What really swung the debate, however, was not Smith's resignation threat or Blair's support, but the contribution of John Prescott.

Like Smith, Prescott had been born in 1938 and had entered the Commons in 1970 (defeating a young Conservative hopeful named Norman Lamont), but the paths the two men had taken on their way to Parliament had been very different. While Smith was winning the *Observer* Mace debating competition as a law student at Glasgow University, Prescott was working as a steward on cruise liners, gaining a reputation as a trade union activist and trying his hand at amateur boxing. Having failed the eleven-plus, he had painstakingly remedied the deficiencies of his education as a mature student at Ruskin College, Oxford and the University of Hull, though many commentators struggled to see much beyond his northern accent and his often garbled syntax.

His speech in support of OMOV was perhaps his finest moment, even if it suffered a little when transcribed: 'There's no doubt this man, our leader, put his head on the block when he said he believes, because he fervently believes, of a relationship and a strong one with the trade unions and the Labour Party. He's put his head there; now's the time to vote; give us a bit of trust and let's have this vote supported.' Linda Smith once observed, 'I suspect language isn't his first language', while Matthew Parris in *The Times* (in a piece cited by Prescott in his autobiography) wrote of the OMOV speech: 'John Prescott went twelve rounds with the English language and left it slumped and bleeding over the ropes.' But, added Parris, 'somehow, everybody guesses what he meant.' Giles Radice summed up the performance more succinctly, saying that Prescott was 'incoherently eloquent'. And he was indeed eloquent. Prescott was far from being the inarticulate fool of his caricatures, and he knew exactly what he was doing. His own account of that speech made clear his intentions: 'I had to turn it into something which was about emotion, that they would feel safe about going back to their constituencies. It was the theatre of politics.'

The following week, at the Conservative Party conference, a recording of the speech was played, with the words running backwards, over a selection of images from the film *Jurassic Park*. It was very funny, but it revealed the Tories' failure to understand the nature of Prescott. He was very far from being a dinosaur, left over from an era when extremists walked the Earth; he was amongst the sharpest politicians of his generation and one of the key players in the reinvention of the Labour Party. As he put it in the House of Commons many years later: 'I may get the grammar wrong, that's true, and I'll have to take the blame for that – that was my education, I'm responsible for it – but you know I'd sooner get perhaps the words wrong than getting my judgement wrong.' On OMOV his judgement was absolutely right, and his intervention swung the vote for John Smith. Had Smith had the chance to move on to the next stage of his proposed changes – a statement of core beliefs to augment Clause IV of the party constitution – there is little doubt that Prescott would have been there to support that as well.

Despite the criticisms from within his own party, Smith's reassuring, gradualist approach to Labour's repositioning played extremely well with the public. By the beginning of 1994 Labour held a commanding lead in opinion polls, with the Tories sometimes slipping into third place. Smith was recording the best figures of any Labour leader since Harold Wilson three decades earlier, while Major was judged by more than four-fifths of the population to be 'not really in charge'.

'What fools we were to believe this lot,' the *Sun* concluded of the government that January. 'Today our eyes are wide open. We can see we have been conned.' Even Major's former lover, Edwina Currie, shared the same perspective, reflecting in 1994 that the party should have chosen Michael Heseltine to succeed Thatcher: 'What a mistake we all made, me most of all.' The prime minister appeared on Jimmy Young's Radio 2 programme in March to be confronted by some home truths. 'Love her or hate her, at least voters took Lady Thatcher seriously,' said the disc jockey, 'while they laugh and make fun of you.'

In the only two by-elections held in 1993, the Tories had lost both seats, with massive swings to the Liberal Democrats – 28 per cent in Newbury, 35 per cent in Christchurch – and nervous glances were being thrown across the Atlantic to Canada, where the ruling Progressive Conservative Party had suffered a defeat in federal elections so comprehensive that it had been reduced from 151 seats to just two.

This appalling spectre hovered over John Major's Tories in the early months of 1994, as the volume was turned up in the whispering campaign against the prime minister. Kenneth Baker was heard to say that Major was 'dead in the water', the right-wing cabinet minister Michael Portillo was suggesting that Michael Heseltine might be useful as 'a transitional short-term figure whose virtues might win them an election', and Gyles Brandreth was recording the latest tearoom gossip in his diaries: 'Open speculation is rife again. Today's most popular prediction: a leadership challenge in the autumn, with Lamont as the stalking-horse, pre-empted by Major stepping down to be replaced by a so-called "dream team": Heseltine as PM, Portillo as deputy.' Others were more open. Edwina Currie told the prime minister bluntly that he ought to resign, and the absurdly right-wing MP John Carlisle appeared on Radio 4's *Today* programme, offering himself as a stalking-horse candidate. Major's position, many were arguing, had become untenable.

Then, just after eight o'clock on the morning of 12 May 1994, John Smith was struck down with a heart attack. He died barely an hour later, and suddenly everything was up for grabs again.

The shock of Smith's death, and the mourning that followed, was genuine, but the idea that he might not become prime minister had surfaced in various forms throughout his tenure of the Labour leadership. Bryan Gould remembered Neil Kinnock telling him in 1992 not to stand against Smith, but to keep his powder dry: 'He won't last the course. It's important that you're there to pick up the pieces.' Similarly in 1993 John Major had predicted that Smith wouldn't be leader come the next election: 'It's just a fingertip thing, a pricking of my thumbs. I'm not sure why, but I just don't believe John'll make it.' There was also the odd story of the night, about a month before Smith died, when Tony Blair woke up suddenly and turned to his wife, Cherie. 'If John dies, I will be leader,' he told her, according to his memoirs. 'And somehow, I think this will happen. I just think it will.' Perhaps it was this Macbeth-like premonition that gave him a head start on his rivals in the race to succeed.

'Britain's next prime minister died yesterday,' opened the report of Smith's death in the *Sun*, an indication of how far the Tories had fallen, and a stark reminder to the Labour Party that this time the stakes were as high as they could possibly be.

It had long been accepted that there was one outstanding candidate for the job. 'Until the 1992 election,' said Neil Kinnock, 'my assumption had been that if we had formed the government in 1992 my successor would be Gordon, and if we lost the election then John Smith's successor would be Gordon.' But things were different now. Gordon Brown was shadow chancellor, and his refusal to sanction any policy commitment that might come with a price tag had made him less popular with his colleagues than he had once been. Nor did his personal behaviour endear him to others; when backbencher Peter Hain co-authored a pamphlet arguing for a Keynesian economic policy, he was summoned to Brown's office, where the shadow chancellor 'rounded on me in a bullying rant'. In the annual elections to the shadow cabinet, after five years of topping the poll, Brown slipped to third place in 1993, behind Robin Cook and John Prescott. In his last days, Smith was said to have remarked that Brown's position as heir apparent had changed: 'He'd have no chance to be leader if there was an election now.'

Brown too had changed. The responsibility of his office seemed to weigh him down, as it had Kinnock, and he was starting to bore people, the witty and feared Commons debater now reduced to reciting reams of statistics and espousing policy positions that came in long, numbered lists. Even the sympathetic *Guardian* journalist Hugo Young struggled to stay awake. 'I have given a very poor account of what he said about economic policy,' he observed in his notes of a meeting with Brown. 'He kept coming back to it, and I fear I kept switching off.' Brown's personal awkwardness was also being noted by the likes of the BBC's political correspondent Jon Sopel, who wrote of 'his somewhat dour appearance, and the strange rehearsed smile that would appear in the middle of his answer for no discernible reason'. Others had their suspicions of his much-vaunted ability. 'Funnily enough, I have not only never spoken to him,' wrote Tony Benn in his diary after a 1993 Commons debate, 'but I have never heard him speak before and I was glad I hadn't.' He went on to conclude that Brown 'looks as if you could not trust him with a corner shop'.

By any normal standards Robin Cook, Labour's most effective Commons performer and a politician of integrity and intelligence, should have been a serious contender for the succession. But there was something a bit too prickly about Cook and he didn't inspire much warmth. 'Very irritating,' was Benn's assessment, which had a certain irony given that Peter Mandelson described Cook as 'the thinking man's Tony Benn'. Meanwhile John Prescott was wonderfully barbed: 'He was probably the most brilliant parliamentarian of our times – but he was well aware of it.' Anyway, as Cook observed: 'apparently I am too ugly to be the next Labour leader.' (Damien in *Drop the Dead Donkey* claimed he looked like the Mekon from *Dan Dare*.)

Instead the real threat to Brown's ambitions came from his closest ally in Westminster, Tony Blair. Appointed by Smith to be shadow home secretary, Blair had really come into his own in the last two years, particularly since the 1993 launch of a slogan donated to him by Brown: 'Tough on crime, tough on the causes of crime.' Repeated over and over again in speeches and interviews, this was less a soundbite than a catchphrase; although the policy implications were never fully explored, it was sufficient to send a signal that the issue of law and order, hitherto a Conservative preserve, was now on the Labour agenda. Blair had shown that – as with Brown's handling of tax increases – he could take on the Tories at their own game and score heavily, and he was clearly a bright, articulate young man who was good on television.

He was also very ambitious and in something of a hurry. Despite not standing for the leadership or deputy leadership in 1992, he had taken the trouble of inviting the right-wing journalist Barbara Amiel to his house and secured an interview that ran as the cover story in the *Sunday Times* magazine on the weekend after John Smith's election. 'Some feel the party should have skipped a generation and gone for Tony Blair,' wrote Amiel, and one felt that Blair himself was foremost amongst their number. In a 1992 episode of *The New Statesman*, Alan B'Stard had explained the kind of person Britain wanted as prime minister: 'She needs somebody young, somebody sexy, somebody twenty-first century, a sort of English Bill Clinton. Only with brains obviously.' Tony Blair, many in the Labour Party were concluding, fitted the bill perfectly.

Most importantly he appeared to be acceptable to the South-East of England, the issue that had preoccupied Bryan Gould, Giles Radice and others for so long. He was born in Edinburgh with a Scottish father, and had been educated in Durham and Edinburgh, but he had attended private schools and no surviving trace of a northern or Scottish accent was discernible; to all intents and purposes, Blair was a middle-class Londoner. Moreover, for the first time since 1976, the Labour Party would be able to present a leader from an English constituency. This was not merely a question of public perception. As Peter Shore had pointed out in 1993: 'It is difficult indeed for Scots, in their almost Nordic political culture where Labour and social democracy are still dominant, to realise the extent of the alienation in middle and southern England that still exists between the Labour Party and the electorate.'

There was no doubt that Blair grasped the extent of the problem and he made overcoming it his primary political goal. When, in the wake of Smith's death, a newly resurgent Peter Mandelson wrote to Gordon Brown making clear – as straightforwardly as he was able – that the race had a new favourite, he stressed that Blair's strongest card was his 'southern appeal', and said this was the answer to 'our overriding question, is Labour serious about conquering the South?'

Mandelson's defection to the cause of Blair was a recognition that the wind had already changed. Blair was anointed the winner by Fleet Street virtually before the starting-pistol had been fired, urged on by a team of cheerleaders that included the tabloid journalist Alastair Campbell, who would subsequently become Blair's press secretary. Within three days of Smith's death, opinion polls were being published that gave Blair a lead over his nearest challengers, Gordon Brown and John Prescott, of up to 15 percentage points, and the momentum had become unstoppable.

Brown was persuaded not to enter the contest, for fear of a humiliating defeat, and the only candidates to stand against Blair were Prescott and Margaret Beckett, the latter having served as interim leader after Smith's death. Due formalities were observed, but with bookies quoting Blair at odds of 8–1 on, the result was a foregone conclusion and he was duly crowned, having secured on the first count an outright majority of the vote amongst MPs, constituencies and unions (though not union leaders). This was unmistakably a new era, as Paddy Ashdown had noted at Smith's funeral, which was attended by hundreds of party members from around the country, 'there not just to mourn John Smith, but also the passing of the old Labour Party, of which John was almost the last bastion'.

In electoral terms there could be little question that the right person had been chosen. For that assessment of Brown's limited geographical appeal was entirely accurate; he was just too Scottish for southern tastes, and where Smith had looked like the kind of bank manager you'd approach for a loan, Brown looked like the kind who'd refuse you and probably take pleasure in doing so, thinking he was teaching you a lesson about financial prudence. Or, as a Labour whip told John Major: 'He's too like one of those undertakers in old western films that measure you for a coffin before the gunfight.'

Beyond the image, though, the political philosophies of Blair and Brown were, as far as anyone could ascertain, identical in almost all regards. The important thing, wrote Giles Radice in his diary, was that they had 'avoided the trap of self-defeating competition into which [Roy] Jenkins, [Tony] Crosland and [Denis] Healey all fell — especially when they ran against each other in the 1976 leadership election. Their rivalry fatally weakened their ideological position in the party.' Nearly twenty years on, Radice was to revise this opinion and suggest that if Brown had stood for the leadership in 1994 and had been beaten in a straight fight with Blair, 'it might have been better for the country'. Mandelson agreed. 'I now believe I should have done more to encourage Gordon to stand,' he wrote in his memoirs; 'an open contest with a clear result would have removed the temptation for him to agonise about what might have been, and brood that he had somehow been unfairly pushed aside.'

By then the story of the rivalry between Blair and Brown had become the most-analysed political soap opera since the war, fuelled by a grudge that made Edward Heath seem like a model of Christian forgiveness. But in 1994 the appearance, in public at any rate, was of a happy new order. Brown somehow looked a more substantial figure, secure in his post as shadow chancellor, while Blair, the youngest leader in Labour's history, was simply untouchable, a fresh-faced picture of innocent enthusiasm. He was nicknamed Bambi by the press, Tony Blur by the Tories, and *Spitting Image* portrayed him as a schoolboy, but there was also a sporting parallel for an increasingly football-obsessed era. 'Tony Blair has become the Gary Lineker of British politics,' complained a Conservative minister; 'anyone who criticises him ends up sounding nasty.'

4
Cool

'It's like a new generation calling'

Tony Blair's speech brought tears to my eyes.
Noel Gallagher (1996)

Britain is now the place to be thanks to the likes of Oasis.
Melinda Messenger (1997)

The Britpop movement was wrong for us because it was so awash
with this knowing irony.
Jonny Greenwood (1998)

Two weeks after the 1992 general election, the *Melody Maker* took the almost unprecedented step of giving over its cover to a group who had not yet released a record. The headline boldly announced the arrival of SUEDE: THE BEST NEW BAND IN BRITAIN, though that barely hinted at the effusiveness of the piece inside: 'the most audacious, androgynous, mysterious, sexy, ironic, absurd, glamorous, hilarious, honest, cocky, melodramatic, mesmerising band you're ever likely to fall in love with.' Given that the weekly music papers were then championing the causes of groups as pedestrian as Ned's Atomic Dustbin and Kingmaker, while the monthly magazines were still in thrall to Simply Red and Crowded House, this might be seen as damning with faint praise.

Because for once the purple prose was justified. After many years of false starts and dead ends, Suede looked like the real thing, a big and important British rock group, potential saviours of a dying tradition, as they played a series of sell-out gigs in ever larger venues, provoking what Luke Haines, singer with their support band the Auteurs, called 'genuine teen mayhem'. They released a self-titled record that became the fastest-selling debut album in British pop history and went on to win the Mercury Music Prize, and they established themselves as a familiar, swaggering presence on *Top of the Pops*. It had been a long time since a guitar group had broken out of the ghetto of indie rock with such intent and promise: in retrospect, that *Melody Maker* cover was to be cited as the dawning of a new era, a rebirth of British music that reached its fevered peak in August 1995 with a much-hyped chart battle between Blur and Oasis.

The arrival of Suede didn't come a moment too soon for a music industry that was threatening to expire from sheer boredom. Sales of singles had fallen to less than half the level they had reached at their peak in 1979, a fact made only too plain by the indie group the Wedding Present, who released a new single each month in 1992 with a limited pressing of just 10,000 copies a time; despite the tiny numbers, every one of those records made the top thirty, and in May 'Come Play with Me' even scraped into the top ten.

Rumours of the imminent cancellation of *Top of the Pops* were so widespread that the BBC had an off-the-peg statement ready for when enquiries were made: 'The future of the programme is secure and any reports of its demise are premature.' It all sounded very defensive and the qualification that 'clearly the programme will evolve' didn't help. The future, industry wisdom had it, lay not in singles, but in reselling the heritage of rock on CD to its original vinyl purchasers, now blessed with disposable income and new technology. 'Pop is dead,' sang Radiohead in 1993. 'It died an ugly death by back catalogue.' Suede turned that perception on its head.

In fact, they were not quite the first, for the early signs of what would become known as Britpop were already evident. Albeit a little awkwardly, a British response was emerging to the dominant American rock of R.E.M., Guns N' Roses and Nirvana, PJ Harvey was attracting critical attention and looked like a star of the future, while Pulp, a band who had made their live debut as long ago as 1980, were finally edging towards success; their record 'O.U. (Gone, Gone)' was jointly named single of the week with Suede's first release, 'The Drowners', in *Melody Maker*. Even a self-consciously alternative phenomenon like the crusties ('that neo-trampish, soap-loathing youth cult', according to the *Sunday Times*) could claim some chart success in the form of Carter the Unstoppable Sex Machine, whose pop-punk was blended with programmed beats, politicised lyrics and a weakness for puns on songs like 'Twenty-Four Minutes from Tulse Hill', 'Do Re Me, So Far So Good' and 'Sealed with a Glasgow Kiss'.

Most extravagantly, the Manic Street Preachers had released their debut album, *Generation Terrorists*, earlier in 1992, promising that they would sell twenty million copies and then disband, having completed their mission to rejuvenate music. In the event, the record achieved more modest, if respectable, sales of 350,000, with band member Richey Edwards left to explain what had gone wrong: 'The world had changed, perhaps more than we realised. People didn't care about such things anymore. It wasn't like 1977, when you could make a statement and get taken seriously.'

Despite the initial failure of the Manic Street Preachers to break through to the mass consciousness, their statement of ambition was significant, signalling a change of priorities in British rock. Suede matched that level of self-belief. 'We always knew the kind of band we'd be,' explained their bassist, Mat Osman, a whole two singles into their career, 'which was an important, celebratory, huge rock band. A really old-fashioned thing.'

The new bands' influences were also old-fashioned, with echoes from the glam rock of the early 1970s. The first live review of the Auteurs compared them to Cockney Rebel, while Suede were signed by a record label boss impressed with singer Brett Anderson's charisma. ('I thought: He's a star, he's like Bryan Ferry.') Suede's first feature in *Q* magazine was illustrated by a picture of Anderson under posters of David Bowie, with a headline taken from an old Marc Bolan song: WHATEVER HAPPENED TO THE TEENAGE DREAM? Also attracting attention was the singer Lawrence, who had enjoyed very minor cult status with Felt in the previous decade on delicate albums like *Forever Breathes the Lonely Word*, and who now reinvented himself with the stomping pop of his new group Denim; their debut album, *Back in Denim* (1992), was so authentic in its evocation of the 1970s that it employed members of the Glitter Band to contribute shouts of 'Hey!' at appropriate moments.

Song titles from the time indicate the extent to which the early Britpop bands plundered the lexicon of glam: 'Stay Beautiful' (Manic Street Preachers), 'Lipgloss' (Pulp), 'Show Girl' (Auteurs), 'I Saw the Glitter on Your Face' (Denim), 'So Young' (Suede). At a time of recession, there was something entirely appropriate about drawing on the influence of the soundtrack to the three-day week.

The presence in these groups of performers like Lawrence, Luke Haines and – from Pulp – Jarvis Cocker, all of whom were veterans of the indie days of the 1980s, suggested a deliberate turn towards the mainstream. And in this regard, rock music was far from being alone, for the move from the fringes of what had been alternative culture was everywhere evident in the early 1990s, nowhere more so than in comedy.

The emergence of a new generation of comedians had been perhaps the most marked feature of the 1980s counterculture. Starting in 1979 with the Comedy Store in Soho, a network of clubs had opened in London and then across the country, providing space for a wave of performers from Alexei Sayle to Alan Davies, some of whom were explicitly political, and virtually all of whom consciously eschewed what was perceived to be the racist and sexist nature of mainstream entertainment. Attracting a predominantly young, college-educated audience, alternative comedy – as it became known – found a media foothold on the newly launched Channel 4, with an occasional foray onto BBC Two, but seldom got much further. British television still only had four channels and was in constant search of entertainment that could appeal across classes and age ranges.

The first to attempt a crossover into a wider market was Ben Elton, the best known of the alternatives. As the star of the influential, though still niche, *Friday Night Live*, he had, to the irritation of some of his contemporaries, become for the public and the media the pin-up boy of anti-Thatcher satire. In 1989 he stepped in as the presenter of Terry Wogan's thrice-weekly chat show on BBC One while the host was on holiday – a stint which included an interview with former Conservative MP turned novelist Jeffrey Archer – and the following year he progressed to his own series, *The Man from Auntie*, on the same channel. The format was familiar, a mix of stand-up routines and sketches not dissimilar to the work of Jasper Carrott, and though it was still suffused with the right-on personal politics with which he had made his name, it wasn't entirely effective. It was also starting to look a little dated. 'Ben Elton thinks he's a supporter of feminism in his *Man from Auntie* series because he knows what a clitoris is,' one viewer wrote angrily to the *Daily Mirror*. 'The fact is, he's being downright patronising. If women want to educate men on the female orgasm, I'm sure they don't need Ben Elton's hints.'

He also branched out, more successfully, into writing novels and West End plays but, as the decade wore on, he was increasingly criticised for what was seen as the loss of his political edge, though he professed himself unconcerned. 'I'd had ten years of being told I was a bigoted, loud-mouthed, left-wing yobbo,' he noted in 1998. 'Suddenly it was: Where's his claws? Where's his teeth? You can't win, so frankly, fuck the lot of them.' He had moved on. Indeed, he even showed a certain frustration with those who clung to the bogeymen of the past; as a character in one of his novels observed: 'We can't blame Mrs Thatcher for everything like we used to when we were young.'

Nonetheless, Elton's subsequent attempt to create a traditional, family-friendly ensemble sitcom in *The Thin Blue Line* was widely panned as being unworthy of the man who had co-written *The Young Ones* and *Blackadder*, and his original audience gradually melted away. What critical standing he still enjoyed on the left finally disappeared altogether when he announced he was working on *The Beautiful Game*, a musical about football, with Andrew Lloyd Webber, a man who was not only irredeemably unfashionable but a loyal supporter of the Conservative Party – he had written their campaign anthem for the 1992 general election. 'I was never a big fan, but at least at some point he had a little, tiny sliver of principles and talent,' reflected Mark Steel. 'Whatever made him give all that up and go and work with Ben Elton?'

Elton's move into mainstream entertainment, and his consequent abandonment of overt politics, came at a time when the nature of the comedy scene was changing anyway. By 1990 Arnold Brown, a survivor of the alternative clubs, was getting laughs with his parody of a comic style that had often been characterised more by its political engagement than by its humour. 'Why did the capitalist elephant cross the road?' he asked. 'Because the working-class chicken had been made redundant by that woman Thatcher.' Meanwhile John Thomson was developing a character named Bernard Righton, a 'reformed stand-up comedian' who managed to lampoon both the now unfashionable style of the northern club entertainer and the new world of the anti-racist, anti-sexist alternative. 'My mother-in-law, I'm not saying she's tight,' ran a typical Bernard Righton anti-joke. 'She's not, she's very generous. She bought me and the wife some lovely wedding presents, and she's actually helping out with the mortgage. I love her.'

The new critical favourites were the likes of Vic Reeves and Bob Mortimer, purveying an anarchic style that owed as much to the old days of the music hall as it did to the alternative 1980s. 'We're just your bog-standard vaudeville,' explained Reeves. 'We're no different from Morecambe and Wise – it's just that they never sang songs about muesli.' There was also the deadpan Paul Merton, a traditionalist who would later remake a selection of Ray Galton and Alan Simpson's most cherished scripts, including some originally written for Tony Hancock. When asked in 1994 which comedians he admired, the veteran comic Ken Dodd paid due tribute to such figures: 'Vic Reeves and Paul Merton really tickle me.'

Most successful of all in reaching out to the mainstream audience without losing his original appeal was Jack Dee, whose 1992 series *The Jack Dee Show* was a hit on Channel 4. Grumpy, dissatisfied and witheringly sarcastic, he avoided material that might be sexist or racist, but he also had little time for overt politics. 'I'm interested in stylish comedy with an edge,' he told the press, 'not with scoring political points.' Instead there was a series of jokes about everyday subjects like pets, motoring and exercise regimes. In Dee's world, modern life was full of frustrations and petty annoyances, mainly because it was populated by other people, who were invariably infuriating.

If the implied attitude was alternative, however, the presentation was resolutely old-fashioned. Wearing a well-cut suit, Dee stood almost motionless, leaning into a vintage microphone in a mocked-up 1960s nightclub, and from time to time he introduced musical guests such as Georgie Fame, Sam Brown and Alison Moyet, all of whom would have been equally at home on an ITV variety show at eight o'clock on a Wednesday night. His live act of the time was much the same, with just the rare foray into more dangerous territory. 'How are you going to get people in this country to stop smacking their children?' he mused about a government initiative. 'It'd be nice to stop fucking them first of all, wouldn't it?'

Despite such occasional transgressions, it was clear from the outset that this was something new: an accomplished, funny comedian coming out of the alternative clubs who was undoubtedly of his own time, yet destined for much wider consumption. By the end of 1992 Dee had started making guest appearances on more mainstream programmes and had been approached as a possible compere for the Royal Variety Show. He declined that offer, but achieved a real breakthrough early the following year when he made the first in a celebrated series of adverts for John Smith's beer. In the spirit of postmodern playfulness that was then obligatory in the advertising industry, the commercial showed Dee insisting that he wasn't prepared to do anything to compromise his image as 'the hard man of comedy', before being offered a sack of money, at which stage he capitulated and took his place amongst a swarm of all-singing, all-dancing giant ladybirds. A later advert introduced tap-dancing penguins into the scene, while Dee continued to sneer about the 'widget' that enabled the beer to pour smoothly with a proper head.

He was the first alternative comedian of any standing to star in a major advertising campaign and it made his name. Having been used to an audience of two million on Channel 4, he was now being broadcast nightly on peak-time ITV and becoming a national celebrity. As 1993 drew to a close, the brewery claimed that sales had doubled, while the campaign was voted Advert of the Year by readers of the *Daily Mirror*.

This crossover was a conscious move by Dee. 'I know I'm doing a good job when I'm appealing beyond my peer group,' he told the press even before his Channel 4 series. 'I love it when people my parents' age compliment me.' In 1995 he was rewarded with his own prime-time variety show on ITV, *Jack Dee's Saturday Night*, featuring guests as diverse as Freddie Starr and Lily Savage, Pulp and the Chinese State Circus, all of whom he said he'd personally approved; this show, he insisted, was his creation. 'I think it's time light entertainment got up to date a bit,' he explained. 'In the past, stand-up has always been put under a kind of youth umbrella. But I see it as a legitimate form of entertainment for everyone to enjoy.' Meanwhile younger comics were queuing up to appear on venerable Radio

4 institutions like *Just a Minute* and, after the death in 1996 of Willie Rushton left a vacancy on the panel, *I'm Sorry I Haven't a Clue*.

Similarly Dawn French and Jennifer Saunders's sketch show happily featured guest stars – particularly women – from an older tradition of entertainment: Betty Marsden, Eleanor Bron, June Whitfield and Lulu amongst others. After four series on BBC Two, the show transferred to the more mainstream BBC One in 1994 at around the same time that the two main stars were launching themselves into hugely successful sitcoms: *Absolutely Fabulous* (1992) and *The Vicar of Dibley* (1994).

Having started as a deliberate reaction to the light entertainment establishment, alternative comedy was now becoming hard to distinguish from its erstwhile enemy. In the process, however, the battle over content had been won, as Benny Hill, the most internationally renowned British comedian of the 1980s, recognised. 'When you and I started in this game, you couldn't make jokes about politics and the church,' he told Bob Monkhouse shortly before his death in 1992. 'Now we can't make jokes about women and race. All these politically correct geezers have done is change the taboos.'

Some of the older comedians thrived in this world. By the time of his death in 1995, the resolutely apolitical Peter Cook had been elevated to the status of Britain's greatest comedian by fellow comics and critics alike. Less predictably, Bob Monkhouse responded enthusiastically to the new wave, making a career-changing appearance on the topical panel show *Have I Got News for You* in 1993 where he was so good that rumours spread of him taking a team of scriptwriters along to the filming. It wasn't true, he just happened to be one of the best ad-libbers in the history of British comedy, and his appearance won him a solo series on BBC One, *On the Spot*, in which he proved just that. He went on to host *Gagtag*, where Frank Skinner mixed with older club comics like Frank Carson, Jim Bowen and Ted Rogers ('that feels about right,' observed Skinner of the line-up). Similarly Barry Cryer, who had spent many years as one of the most respected writers in the business, returned to his early incarnation as a stand-up and became revered as an elder statesman of the form.

It was significant, however, that Cryer and Monkhouse had both in their early days met opposition to their presence on the comedy circuit, on the grounds that they were middle-class and educated. A cockney comedian named Leon Cortez once took Monkhouse to task: 'Variety's for the working class, on the stage as well as in the seats. Do yourself a favour and fuck off out of it.' Now variety itself was on its last legs, and the new comedy was coming almost exclusively from graduates, with the inherent danger that it might prove too distanced from the masses. BBC One, fearing unfashionability, had dispensed with the services of Les Dawson and Russ Abbot at the start of the decade, but in 1993 Alan Yentob, newly appointed controller of the channel, appeared to be having misgivings about the policy: 'We should broaden its appeal to the CD [social classes] who like light entertainment.' The following year, Jim Davidson was to take over as host of *The Generation Game*.

Some of this disconnection was simply a function of age. When Rob Newman and David Baddiel climaxed their 1993 British tour with a gig at Wembley Arena, it was rightly seen as a ground-breaking event that lifted live comedy to a new level of success. Their fan base, built from their origins in *The Mary Whitehouse Experience* on Radio 1, was younger even than the frequenters of the comedy clubs, and the atmosphere was little different from that of a pop concert. 'Fourteen-year-old girlies can say they're going to a Baddiel and Newman gig because they fancy Dave or Rob,' wrote Caitlin Moran in *The Times*, 'but in reality they're hoping to meet a sixteen-year-old boy who looks a bit like them. Just like going to a T. Rex gig.' Stewart Lee, one of those who remained a cult act with a strong political edge, observed the same phenomenon: Newman and Baddiel's 'sassy pop-literate acts and shoe-gazers' haircuts were about to create a whole new audience for Alternative Comedy – girls'.

In time, much of this audience, like that of the alternative comedians, would be found in the massed ranks at, say, a Michael McIntyre gig, when he played six nights at Wembley and four at the O2 Arena in 2009, or amongst the purchasers of the ten million DVDs sold by Peter Kay in the first decade of the twenty-first century. The enormous mainstream success of such comedians was rooted in the breakthroughs of the early 1990s, as Stewart Lee concluded: 'When Rob Newman flew up in the air at Wembley it changed comedy in Britain for ever, probably for the worse. Suddenly stand-up looked like a career option for ambitious young people, and a cash cow for unscrupulous promoters.'

If the extraordinary success of live comedy in the post-alternative era was unprecedented, it did at least grow out of an established path, with a comic gigging up and down the country before graduating to television as a guest on the time-honoured format of the panel show, a multitude of which had sprung into being. For one of the other great cultural success stories of the 1990s, there was no such model to follow.

It had been a long time since the visual arts in Britain had produced a figure who could truly be called a household name. In the 1950s the nation's favourite sitcom, *Hancock's Half Hour*, could make a joke about Henry Moore and expect the audience to share the laughter, but scarcely anyone since had been able to command that degree of recognition. There was little public interest in modern art, so that despite the storm of controversy caused in 1976 by the American Carl Andre's *Equivalent VIII*, the artist himself had remained largely anonymous; for every thousand who knew the phrase 'the Tate's bricks' there was one, at best, who could hazard a guess at his name. And while Francis Bacon, David Hockney and Lucian Freud were feted by broadsheet critics, their work was not sufficiently known to warrant attention in the tabloids or on prime-time television. Margaret Thatcher once dismissed Bacon as 'that artist who paints those horrible pictures', but most of the population would have struggled to get even that far.

There was little promise here of riches to be made, no expectation that stardom might beckon, but a diverse and creative art world had thrived in the 1980s, from the painters Thérèse Oulton and Stephen Conroy through the film-makers Derek Jarman and John Maybury to the performance artists in the Mutoid Waste Company and the Neo-Naturists. 'Everybody in the late 1980s accepted that you were never going to make money so you might as well do what you wanted,' commented Millree Hughes, then working in the 'organic and messy' art scene in London.

The same had been true, of course, of much of the music at the time. 'We had so little commercial ambition,' noted Luke Haines of his time in the indie band the Servants. 'We really were in it for the art. The aim was just to get the record out.' Just as that attitude changed in the music of the 1990s, so it did in art, with the emergence of a highly visible, controversial and profitable wave of practitioners, making Damien Hirst and Tracey Emin, in particular, the best-known living British artists for generations.

Two things were notable about the Young British Artists (YBAs), as they became known. First, much of their most celebrated work was created at the start of the decade, before they became famous: Hirst's *The Physical Impossibility of Death in the Mind of Someone Living* (1991), a tiger shark suspended in a tank of formaldehyde; Marc Quinn's *Self* (1991), a sculpture of his own head made of frozen blood; Rachel Whiteread's extraordinary concrete casts of living spaces, *Ghost* (1990) and *House* (1993). Second, their success came despite, not because of, the art establishment as represented by the publicly funded galleries; Hirst didn't have his first Tate exhibition until 2012. Rather it was the result of the very visible patronage of a handful of wealthy collectors, most famously the advertising executive Charles Saatchi, and the support of a select few art dealers, headed by Jay Jopling, whose White Cube gallery opened in 1993.

Both men were, as it happened, closely connected to the Conservative Party. Saatchi's agency had created much of the Tories' advertising since 1978, while Jopling's father, Michael, had been chief whip in the first Thatcher government. The associations didn't entirely escape notice: Tracey Emin initially refused to sell her work to Saatchi in protest at his political track record, though happily this principled opposition didn't last long enough to damage her career prospects.

The other key to the YBAs' success was the revival in 1991, after a year's absence, of the Turner Prize, now under a sponsorship deal with Channel 4. As part of that arrangement, the prize money was increased to £20,000 and the terms of the competition were changed, so that there was an upper age limit of fifty for nominees. The television channel provided coverage of the shortlisted work as well as the ceremony itself, and turned the award into a major media event. Or, in the words of Stephen Bayley, co-founder of the Design Museum in London, it was 'a classic pseudo-event in that it exists for the media and for no else except its own beneficiaries'.

Its rise to public prominence was, somewhat ironically, assisted by the noisy intervention in 1993 of the K Foundation, an extension of the pop duo the KLF, who announced that they would be giving their own prize to 'the worst artist of the year'. Their shortlist coincided with that of the Turner Prize, as did their winner, Rachel Whiteread, who was prevailed upon to accept the £40,000 award, for donation to charity, after the K Foundation threatened to burn the money if she refused to take it. The fact that they were serious about the threat was demonstrated by their subsequent performance artwork, the self-explanatory *The K Foundation Burn a Million Quid* (1994).

Despite this distraction, the Turner Prize and the YBAs went from strength to strength and over the course of the 1990s changed the parameters of public debate, so that the familiar cry of 'But is it art?' was heard less frequently even in the tabloid newspapers. Luke Haines argued that the more pertinent question – 'But is it good art or bad art?' – should perhaps have been asked more often, though the YBAs shied away from it themselves, 'because they were essentially afraid of calling themselves artists'. In a 2001 book review, Craig Brown quoted Damien Hirst's own definition: 'Great art is when you just walk round a corner and go, "Fucking hell! What's that!"' Brown went on to point out: 'Hirst is, in any real sense, far closer to an entrepreneur than to an artist; little separates him from, say, Sir Bernard Matthews of Turkey Roasts, a man who has also, incidentally, glimpsed the profit to be found in corpses.'

Nonetheless, with the temporary celebrity of the YBAs, the British public acquired a taste for modern art such as had never existed before, and when the Tate Modern gallery opened in London in 2000, it was an immediate and unexpected hit, attracting over five million visitors in its first year. Three-quarters of those visitors were British, rather than the foreign tourists who had been anticipated, and half were under the age of thirty-five. The changing perception of contemporary art was one of the most striking features of the decade.

A similar transformation was to be found in British attitudes to food. Again the development had roots in the preceding decade, when the word 'foodie' had first appeared and Keith Floyd had ushered in a new age of television chefs. But it was in the 1990s that there was a noticeable rise in the standards and diversity of food offered in public establishments across the board, rather than merely in a small number of fashionable restaurants.

Much media attention was given to the new phenomenon of the gastro-pub, but less elevated hostelries also began to include hitherto exotic items on their menus. In 1996 Clive Aslet, the editor of *Country Life* magazine, noted the fare on offer in an unexceptional pub in Hampshire: 'the dish of the day was Mexican pork, the ploughman's lunch came with chorizo (appropriate only if the ploughman was called Miguel, one might have thought), and the blackboard showed that Sunday lunch was served with a vegetable called kabosha squash.' Whether this was necessarily a good thing was debatable; much of the food thus presented was the product of a microwave, and there was a suspicion in some quarters that gimmickry was taking the place of proper cooking. In a 1995 episode of the television series *Pie in the Sky*, Richard Griffiths's character Henry Crabbe, a semi-retired police officer who is also the head chef and proprietor of a restaurant, rails against those who pursue novelty for its own sake: 'They're not gourmets. They're a bunch of miserable old foodies and faddies.'

Nonetheless, there was unquestionably a positive change in the perception of British cuisine, both domestically and internationally. ('How do you cook a chicken in England?' ran a Parisian joke of the 1980s. 'Boil it until the tyre marks disappear.') There was, moreover, a new culture of restaurant-going, so that by 2001 it was possible to say that 'eating out has become a hobby for the young' without the observation seeming risible. Drinking wine was now perfectly normal, even in pubs, where two decades earlier it had been viewed by many with suspicion: 'It's not an Englishman's drink, is it?' Wolfie (Robert Lindsay) had argued in the sitcom *Citizen Smith* in 1977. 'It's sort of new on the scene, innit?' And so ubiquitous had cooking become as a television spectacle that almost everyone could name a kitchenful of chefs: Delia Smith, Antony Worrall Thompson, Gordon Ramsay, Ainsley Harriott, Rick Stein amongst many others.

Most media-friendly of all, perhaps, was Jamie Oliver, who first appeared on television in 1997 in a documentary about the River Café in Hammersmith, where he was then working. A former industrial building, converted by the architect Richard Rogers and owned by his wife, Ruth, the River Café was at the cutting edge of fashionable eating, frequented by celebrities, media powerbrokers and New Labour politicians, and it gave 22-year-old Oliver the credibility to back up his youth, good looks and blokeish banter. 'When I'm working hard, I use slang,' he explained. 'I'll say, "Know what I mean?" or "Pukka, that's cool." It's my age and it's who I am.' By 1999 he was writing a column for *GQ* and making his own series, *The Naked Chef*, the realisation at last of the media dream that lads and cuisine would one day be brought together. Oliver's back-story — growing up in an Essex pub, playing drums in an indie guitar band — was irresistible and his attempts to demystify cooking for his mates and other geezers made him an instant star. He even dressed as if he was out for a few beers after going to a match; asked in a 2000 interview to describe what he was wearing, he replied: 'Adidas shell-toes, nice Levi's twists in a sort of a retro style, an old shirt from a second-hand shop and a Duffer Of St George T-shirt.'

He was not, however, to everyone's taste. The term 'mockney' had first been sighted by *New Society* magazine in 1986, used by 'upper-class Oxford undergraduates' to describe their affectation of speaking in a 'mock Cockney accent', and had gradually spread to embrace celebrities like the violinist Nigel Kennedy and the actress Emma Thompson. Now it was being applied widely to individuals alleged to be keen on concealing their roots, and Oliver was prominent amongst those singled out, as he adopted a classless persona for the new Britain. 'About as working class as the Duchess of Devonshire,' wrote Tony Parsons. 'It's true that this pukka mucker comes from Essex, but it is the rural, white, middle-class part of Essex where they still have morris dancing and Young Conservative balls, a place of small minds and smaller manhoods.'

Yet even with the easy-to-emulate preparations demonstrated by Jamie and Delia, the new-found British celebration of cuisine concealed a slightly less impressive reality. Surveys showed that the average outlay on food was falling as a proportion of overall household expenditure, from 17 per cent in 1971 to 11 per cent twenty years later. Partly this was the consequence of improved income and relatively deflated food prices, so that while it had taken five minutes' work on an average wage to buy a pint of milk in the 1970s, it now took just three minutes. But there was also the suspicion that cooking, like gardening, was becoming something of a spectator sport. Further surveys at the end of the decade revealed that spending on leisure had overtaken that on food for the first time ever, and that a quarter of what was eaten fell into a category euphemistically called convenience food. (There was perhaps a parallel here with the way that the rise in popularity of televised football coincided with reduced participation in sporting activities.)

It was partly in response to concerns over the national diet that official bodies became ever more committed to giving advice on what should and should not be eaten. In 1994 the Committee on Medical Aspects of Food Policy, who advised the government, recommended that each adult should consume six portions of vegetables or fruit each day, two portions of potatoes, pasta or rice and (somewhat intriguingly) four and a half slices of bread. The following year the Independent Television Commission decreed that no one should be seen in a television advert eating more than one chocolate bar, because it would encourage behaviour contrary to the government's 'diet strategy'.

Elsewhere, other creative fields were also enjoying revived fortunes. Having struggled for ten years to make an international impact, British Fashion Week really took off in 1994, with sponsorship by Vidal Sassoon and the backing of the government, and couture began to gain a level of respect that hadn't always been forthcoming in recent times.

In 1988 Vivienne Westwood, the most internationally revered designer of the age, had appeared on the *Wogan* chat show, hosted that week by Sue Lawley, and faced an audience that simply laughed at her latest collection, treating her with the same derision that greeted modern art. A few years later, her visionary reworking of classic English style was being celebrated even in her own land, while she herself was awarded an OBE. After receiving the award, she posed for the press, twirling the skirt of her frock high enough to reveal that she wasn't wearing any knickers, and promptly won Fleet Street over to her cause.

By the middle of the decade British designers were being headhunted by international fashion houses. John Galliano became chief designer at Givenchy in 1995, and when he moved on to Christian Dior the following year, he was replaced by Alexander McQueen, while in 1997 Stella McCartney took over from Karl Lagerfeld at Chloé. 'You could feel there was a change in the air, not just on the street but also within the industry,' remembered Robin Derrick, the art director of British *Vogue*, who was instrumental in promoting this new era of design. 'London seemed exciting again for the first time in years.'

The British film industry too was rediscovering its heritage with a reinvention of what had historically been its strongest and most appealing genre, the social comedy. A string of international hits emerged, including *Four Weddings and a Funeral* (1994), *Brassed Off* (1996) and *The Full Monty* (1997), all of which had received funding from Channel Four Films. Though *Four Weddings* was to face criticism – much of it retrospective – for being too saccharine in its whimsy, it broke records as the highest-grossing British film ever.

And there was much else to suggest that the future of the industry might be brighter than its recent past, in particular the emergence of an Anglo-Asian strand within the same genre, also heavily supported by Channel Four Films: *Wild West* (1992), *Bhaji on the Beach* (1993) and *East Is East* (1999). These tended to focus on the generational conflicts within immigrant families over the degree of integration that should be pursued, but they also presented a vision of the country which celebrated the common ground that underlay multiculturalism, evoking nostalgic echoes of an older Britain.

East Is East was set in Salford in 1971, a vanished world of Enoch Powell, space hoppers and *The Clangers*, where smoking is permitted in cinemas, tin baths and chamber pots have yet to be replaced by fitted bathrooms, and discos play everything from Deep Purple through Georgie Fame to Dave and Ansell Collins. *Wild West* took the clichéd rock and roll story of a band dreaming of stardom, and recast it with a British Asian group playing country music in Southall. The generational culture clash is embodied in the comic stoicism of Zaf (Naveen Andrews), whose obsession with Steve Earle and Dwight Yoakam guarantees an incapacity to fit in with anyone except his own gang. 'You don't see many Asians wearing cowboy hats,' a woman remarks, and Zaf shrugs: 'Yeah, our community's got no sense of style.'

Meanwhile *Bhaji on the Beach* featured aunts fierce enough for P.G. Wodehouse, made a comparison between Blackpool's Golden Mile and the excesses of Bombay, and was accompanied by a Punjabi version of Cliff Richard's 1963 hit 'Summer Holiday'. In one of the more touching scenes, an old English actor, Ambrose Waddington (Peter Cellier), is in a theatre with the middle-aged Asha (Lalita Ahmed) and reflects on what has been lost of his world: 'We used to have eleven live venues here before the war. Opera, royal premieres, classics, that was our popular culture then. Now? It breaks my heart. Look what we've become. Not like you, you've kept hold of your traditions.'

All these films were located in a more or less recognisable modern Britain far distant from the heritage movies that had dominated much of the country's cinema in the 1980s. The same was true of a spate of thrillers: *The*

Crying Game (1992), *Shallow Grave* (1994) and *Butterfly Kiss* (1995), the latter two marking the directorial debuts of Danny Boyle and Michael Winterbottom respectively.

The successes of British music, comedy, art, cuisine, fashion and movies in the early and mid-1990s were in large part attributable to the generation that had spent the 1980s in opposition to Margaret Thatcher. The repeated setbacks endured by the liberal left during that decade had alienated many from the political process altogether, producing a sense simply of weariness. 'There's been a depoliticisation of the intellectual classes,' noted David Baddiel in 1991. 'Lots of right-on people can't be bothered any more.'

For those who still clung to their faith, there was one last kick to come, as the results were announced of the 1992 election, a moment that finally spelt the end of the 1980s. 'Without any doubt it was one of the most awful experiences of my life,' wrote Mark Steel of that night, and he was not alone. 'I had always known it was impossible for one person to change the world on their own,' reflected John O'Farrell. 'But I felt so bitter about the outcome of the 1992 election that I stopped particularly trying.' Jeremy Hardy, writing in 1993, shared the same sense of defeatism: 'These days, my political activism is reduced to sitting in front of the television news saying "bastards" periodically.'

Out of this despair, however, seemed to come a determination to shift the battleground from politics to popular culture, to continue the fight for the soul of the nation in another form. If the Tories were unbeatable at the ballot box, that didn't mean that their values had to be accepted anywhere else. So although this generation was to prove strikingly absent from Westminster politics, it dominated the cultural renaissance of the Major era. After prolonged incubation in the 1980s underground, it broke spectacularly into the mainstream with an energy and a sense of style that hadn't been felt for many years. It was almost as though the nation had decided by the end of 1992, in the wake of Black Wednesday and the pit-closure programme, that it had made a terrible mistake in the election and had resolved to ignore the government altogether. A new Britain was to be forged, regardless of what was happening in Westminster.

At first, this cultural explosion went largely unremarked in the corridors of power. John Smith, who was born before the Second World War, made no attempt to align himself or his party with a self-consciously youthful phenomenon, and the prime minister was never going to cut a very convincing figure in the new order, even though his own tastes were far from elevated. 'There is a lot of talk going around in the upper echelons of society about the low level friends John Major has,' noted Woodrow Wyatt in 1991, recording in his diary that at a recent party thrown by Jeffrey Archer, the prime minister had chosen for his dining companions 'people like Tim Rice, Sarah Brightman, David Frost and his wife and other people in the entertainment industry or on the fringe of it'. In 1995 Major awarded a knighthood to Cliff Richard.

Such middle-of-the-road inclinations weren't sufficient to keep on top of new developments. In 1992 Major was heard saying that the pizzas available at the Pizzeria Castello in Elephant and Castle, run by Antonio Proietti, were 'the worst in the western world'. Evidently the changing tastes of a smarter set had passed him by. 'Proietti's restaurant has served the best pizzas in London since the early 1980s,' wrote the restaurant critic Jonathan Meades, in a state of shocked disbelief. 'They are far more Italian than the mass-produced English imitations. Perhaps this was lost on Mr Major, with his love of Little Chefs and Happy Eaters.'

Equally out of touch was Stephen Dorrell, the secretary of state for national heritage, who went to the Cannes Film Festival in 1995 in support of the British film industry. There he managed only to cover himself in embarrassment, not least when he failed to recognise the name of the great actress Jeanne Moreau, head of the festival jury, referring to her in a speech as 'a distinguished Frenchman'. Dorrell's successor was Virginia Bottomley, who came into office with a positive spirit. 'There will be no cuts in government spending on the arts,' she insisted, just three weeks before it was announced that government spending on the arts was to be cut by 3 per cent.

Bottomley went to Cannes in 1996, where she attended a screening of Danny Boyle's *Trainspotting*, one of the defining cultural artefacts of the decade. An adaptation of Irvine Welsh's acclaimed novel about drug abuse in Edinburgh and the corrosive impact heroin has on friendships, it featured a cast that included Ewan McGregor, Jonny Lee Miller and Robert Carlyle and was accompanied by a soundtrack featuring some of the leading exponents of Britpop. Bottomley professed to like the movie, though judging by the interview she gave the *Observer*, her preference was more naturally inclined towards heritage than heroin. 'Part of my job is to encourage tourism and our great traditions,' she explained. 'This is what films like *Sense and Sensibility* did, as well as the BBC's *Pride and Prejudice*. If we have got the country houses and the landscapes, they should be shown off on film, particularly as we approach the millennium.' It wasn't the most ringing endorsement of modernity, though she had at least seen *Trainspotting*, which was more than Labour's arts spokesperson, Jack Cunningham, could claim.

No political foray into popular culture, however, quite matched the 1996 *Guardian* article about Britpop written by John Redwood, arch Eurosceptic and Fellow of All Souls. He began by confessing that as a teenager in the 1960s he had much preferred the comedy-beat group the Barron Knights to the Rolling Stones ('I didn't like them much in the 1960s and like them even less now,' he said of the latter), before praising the recent achievements of Pulp and Blur. He focused particularly on the Lightning Seeds, a band led by Ian Broudie, and on their album *Jollification* (1994): 'The Lightning Seeds reassure us there is still an England under that English sky. There is a time and a place, here, for jollification.' The single 'Change' from that album prompted still more enthusiasm: 'They are right that there is too much needless change. We can't make everyone drink warm beer if they prefer cool lager, and we can't make a policy out of nostalgia. But we can defend Britain against senseless change – against political vandalism which would demolish our constitution, giving away powers to Frankfurt and Brussels.' Redwood's contribution attracted much ridicule, along with a warning from former Tory MP Alan Clark that was heeded by few during that era: 'He is breaking the first rule for politicians – never have anything to do with showbusiness.'

'It's embarrassing,' commented Ian Broudie of Redwood's attempt to swim with the tide. 'He preferred the Barron Knights over the Stones. I mean, doesn't that tell you everything you need to know about the Tories? They went through the most exciting decade of this century with their eyes closed.'

But perhaps Broudie's comment was just as revealing as anything that Redwood had written. For it indicated the shift that had taken place in music and was to change the tone of mass culture in general. The early Britpop groups had drawn primarily on the sounds of that darkest of recent decades, the 1970s, but as it became clear that the economy had managed to climb out of recession, the primary colours of the 1960s began to seem ever more appealing.

The key moment was the arrival of the Manchester band Oasis, whose series of hits began modestly enough with 'Supersonic' in April 1994, but whose ambitions seemed to match the boasts of the Manic Street Preachers. By December of that year they had released 'Whatever', a slight piece adorned with a string section and blown out of all proportion to well over six minutes in length, that was evidently aimed at the number one spot in the Christmas singles chart. It missed that mark, losing out to East 17's 'Stay Another Day', but nothing much else impeded the band's inexorable rise. Their second album *(What's the Story) Morning Glory?* (1995) sold upwards of twenty million copies worldwide, even succeeding in America – where Suede had failed to make an impact – and for a couple of years their music was the only serious rival to that of the Spice Girls on the soundtrack to modern Britain.

There was still in Oasis a residual influence from the early 1970s, but it was Gary Glitter and Slade, rather than David Bowie and Roxy Music, who were now the benchmarks, while the band's first top twenty single, 'Shakermaker', bore a striking resemblance to the New Seekers' 'I'd Like to Teach the World to Sing' (a song promptly revived by tribute band No Way Sis). The principal source of inspiration, however, was a lumpen Beatles obsession that steamrollered through Britpop, flattening out the subtleties, ambiguities and diversity. They were, some mocked, like a reincarnation of the Rutles, the fictitious parody of the Beatles created by Neil Innes and Eric Idle for the television comedy *Rutland Weekend Television* in 1978; consequently there was some amusement when Innes successfully sued Oasis for borrowing the melody of his song 'How Sweet to Be an Idiot' for 'Whatever'. That was a minor distraction, however, and did nothing to dent their – and the media's – fiercely held belief that the group were indeed the new Beatles.

The idea caught on that we were living through a moment of popular culture that echoed, and might even rival, the 1960s, and for a while there was no stopping it. Certainly the visual artists seemed to be looking back to that decade, to a time when Andy Warhol had turned money-making into one of the fine arts and Marcel Duchamp's concept of the readymade, originally developed fifty years earlier, had finally become fashionable. Several key artworks drew explicitly on the period for inspiration: Douglas Gordon's *24 Hour Psycho* (1993) slowed down Alfred Hitchcock's 1960 movie so that it lasted for a full day, while the most controversial work at *Sensation*, the Royal Academy's 1997 exhibition of the YBAs, was Marcus Harvey's *Myra*, a portrait made from children's handprints of the Moors murderer Myra Hindley, jailed for life in 1966.

Sensation itself was a hugely popular show, attracting 300,000 visitors in Britain before becoming a cause célèbre in New York, and its success was a sign of the other triumph of the age: the power of marketing. The increasing commercialisation of culture had started as a desire to escape irrelevant isolation in the underground: 'Who wants to be a sad little indie noise-freak who alienates everyone?' as Blur's singer, Damon Albarn, put it in 1995. That was the year in which even the television news bulletins reported on the hyped sales battle between Blur's 'Country House' and Oasis's 'Roll With It' as they fought for the number one chart position. 'The screaming at gigs was deafening,' remembered Blur's bassist, Alex James, of that year. 'From the end of summer to the start of Christmas, the screaming never stopped.' When the critics on the music magazines compiled their lists of the best albums of 1995, the top ten was comprised entirely of British acts.

The success of Britpop provoked a recovery in singles sales from the doldrums at the start of the decade. But this upturn was due as much as anything to the marketing drive of the major record labels. 'Part of the reason Britpop took off with such a flourish,' noted Louise Wener, 'is that it coincided with record companies slashing the cost of singles and selling them for as little as a pound.' Singles were now regularly released in four formats — on two separate CDs, on 12in vinyl and on cassette tape — with different combinations of bonus tracks, in an attempt to lure the hardcore fan into buying all four. Although this scheme worked well enough in the short term, it was hardly a sustainable model, and by 1997 concerns were being expressed in the industry that the proliferation of formats was out of control and was damaging profits. In a not unrelated development, this realisation coincided with the decline of Britpop.

For now, however, few doubts were being entertained, and the seemingly unstoppable wave of creativity required only a decent brand name for it to be fully exploited. It duly arrived. 'Once, cool Britannia ruled all the new waves of youth culture, alongside black Americans,' wrote journalist Cosmo Landesman in May 1992; 'alas no more.' He spoke too soon, and within a couple of years that very phrase — Cool Britannia — had been resuscitated from *Gorilla*, the 1967 debut album by the Bonzo Dog Doo-Dah Band whence it had first come, and attached to the newly vibrant youth culture. In the summer of 1996 the expression turned up as the name of a new flavour of ice cream by the American manufacturers Ben and Jerry (vanilla with strawberries and chocolate-covered shortbread) and by the end of the year it was inescapable. Britain is 'currently the coolest country in the world', declared the *Sunday Times* in September, with an impressive degree of certainty. Cool Britannia was to be the Swinging Sixties reincarnate.

There was, of course, an element of cherry-picking about this evocation of the 1960s, as Gus made clear in an episode of *Drop the Dead Donkey*, complaining about the contents of a compilation video of old footage: 'You've put in a huge chunk about the Vietnam War and hardly anything about Twiggy. I'm sorry, but we're trying to tap into the feelgood nostalgia market here. People aren't going to pay £12.99 to watch a bunch of burning foreigners.' He went on to sum up the media attitude with deadly accuracy: 'The past is a commodity. We can do what we like with it. Chop it up, move it around.'

Beyond such cynicism, there was a new myth being created here, a belief that everything good started in the 1960s, when Britain had led the popular culture of the western world, a wish that such happy times might be recaptured. And, for a brief moment, the comparisons were genuine enough. The Beatles had commissioned album covers from the pop artists Peter Blake and Richard Hamilton, now Blur had a video directed by Damien Hirst; the heroin chic of waif-model Kate Moss was clearly a continuation of Twiggy by other means; and the international press fell in line — *Newsweek* magazine announced in October 1996 that LONDON RULES and *Vanity Fair* gave its front cover in March 1997 to a story headlined LONDON SWINGS AGAIN! illustrated with a photo of the Oasis singer Liam Gallagher and his fiancée, the actress Patsy Kensit, in a bed adorned with Union flag linen. Many of the old names returned in commercial triumph. Blake designed his first album cover since *Sgt Pepper* for Paul Weller's *Stanley Road* (1995), the must-have toy for children was Tracy Island, after the BBC began screening old episodes of *Thunderbirds*, and the James Bond franchise was successfully relaunched with Pierce Brosnan in *GoldenEye* (1995). A growing, laddish appreciation of the 1960s work of Michael Caine ('the coolest English actor to step in front of a movie camera', according to the *Sun*) allowed him to reprise his role as Harry Palmer in *Bullet to Beijing* (1995), Barbara Windsor was back on television, this time in *EastEnders*, and Lulu made a return to *Top of the Pops*, collaborating with Take That on the number one single 'Relight My Fire'.

By the end of 1995 the Beatles themselves were at the top of the charts with 'Free as a Bird', their first new single in twenty-five years, the three surviving members having fleshed out an unreleased demo by John Lennon. Indeed the Beatles turned out to be the best-selling British act in America in the 1990s, with all three *Anthology* albums reaching number one in the States, while even the lightweight *Live at the BBC* compilation sold eight million copies.

For those with different memories of the period, it was somehow appropriate that a single taken from the latter album — a cover of the Shirelles' 'Baby It's You' — entered the charts in the same week that saw the funeral of the 1960s gangster Ronnie Kray. Jailed for murder in 1968, with his last years spent in Broadmoor after he was diagnosed as a paranoid schizophrenic, Kray — like his surviving twin, Reggie — had not been forgotten in the East End of London, and all the stops were pulled out for the send-off. The body lay in state until the day of the funeral, when thousands lined the route of the cortège to watch the passage of an old-fashioned, glass-sided hearse, drawn by six black-plumed horses, and followed by twenty-six black Daimler limousines. In another car — a less impressive blue Peugeot estate – was Reggie, handcuffed to a prison warder, and received by the huge crowds with a kind of hysteria, accompanied by chants for his release. He paid his tribute in a message printed in the order of service: 'Ron had great humour, a vicious temper, was kind and generous. He did it all his way, but above all he was a man.' Making the same point, the coffin entered the church to the vainglorious strains of Frank Sinatra's 'My Way'. There were wreaths from Barbara Windsor, Roger Daltrey and Morrissey, as well as some sent by necessarily absent friends, including those from 'All the boys on Reggie's wing at Maidstone' and 'Linda Calvey, Tina Malloy and all the girls at H Wing'.

The media coverage was no less restrained, with the *Daily Mirror* giving over its first five pages to the event. 'They promised a funeral to outshine Winston Churchill's,' reported the paper, and if that wasn't quite achieved, it was yet another backward reference to the good old days when psychopathic killers doted on their mums, and East End thugs were said to look after their own.

To cap it all, in the summer of 1996 England staged its first international football tournament since the World Cup three decades earlier. Euro 96 was the definitive symbol that the sport had been fully rehabilitated into society, and there was even an expectation that the England team, having failed to qualify for the 1994 World Cup, could do rather well this time. There was a new manager, the Essex-born, media-friendly Terry Venables, and a squad of players, headed by Alan Shearer, Teddy Sheringham and Paul Gascoigne, who looked as if they might just be the real deal. They didn't start well, but redeemed themselves with a 2–0 win over Scotland at Wembley, complete with Gascoigne's finest international goal, flicking the ball over the head of defender Colin Hendry and catching it on the volley to score.

This was followed by a 4–1 victory over Holland that saw England deliver a genuinely inspirational team performance, which – thanks to that one goal conceded – ensured that Scotland failed to progress beyond the group stages. A quarter-final against Spain saw a vanishingly rare win in a penalty shoot-out, before normal service was restored, and England were knocked out by Germany in another penalty shoot-out at the end of a match that attracted a record television audience for a sports event of 26.2 million. It had been a desperately close-run thing, but even without achieving the ultimate dream of a second trophy in the nation's history, the tournament inspired much of the country (at least south of Hadrian's Wall) and was an unqualified marketing victory, achieving record high gates for such a competition.

To accompany the tournament, an official single was released – 'We're In This Together' by Simply Red – while the BBC bizarrely chose the EU's anthem, Beethoven's 'Ode to Joy', as the theme music for their coverage. (ITV went for 'Jerusalem' instead.) Neither made much impression. The English FA, however, commissioned a song that caught the mood of the crowds better than any previous football record, the Britpop anthem 'Three Lions' by the Lightning Seeds with David Baddiel and Frank Skinner. With its look back to that solitary international triumph in 1966, it encapsulated the eternal optimism of England fans: 'Thirty years of hurt, never stopped me dreaming.' That summer the chorus of 'Football's coming home' was heard everywhere, as the record went to number one at the peak of Cool Britannia.

All this was now meeting with official approval. John Major, in his speech at the Lord Mayor's Banquet in November 1996, leapt unconvincingly onto the bandwagon and listed the triumphs of the age. 'Britain has won a third of all Oscars in the last thirty years,' he announced. 'Our television programmes are in demand worldwide. Our education system attracts half a million foreign students a year. Our theatres give the lead to Broadway. Our pop culture rules the airwaves. Our country has taken over the fashion catwalks of Paris.'

Not all these claims were entirely accurate. In particular, television was the one area where Britain was not a world-beater. In 1997 the BBC made just £90 million from exports, a figure dwarfed by the £257 million made through publishing and product licensing. Domestically it was a golden age for sitcoms, from *One Foot in the Grave* and *Absolutely Fabulous* to *Father Ted* and *The Royle Family*, and for satire, which had disappeared from television in the 1970s and made only a tentative reappearance in the '80s, but now flourished in the shape of *Have I Got News for You*, *Drop the Dead Donkey* and *The Day Today*. Little of this travelled well overseas, however. Even when British shows did make their way abroad, it was not always by the most direct route; the rights to Jimmy McGovern's crime series *Cracker* were sold to ABC in America, whose remake proved much more successful in the export market than the original had been.

Nor did those whose work was praised by Major necessarily appreciate his words of encouragement. Alexander McQueen, mentioned by name in that speech, was distinctly unimpressed. 'Fucking plank!' he retorted. 'So fucking typical of the fucking government! They do nothing to help you when you're trying to do something, then take the credit when you're a success. Fuck off.'

The name of McQueen, one might suspect, was not frequently on the prime minister's lips and had been fed to him by a speechwriter, a not uncommon practice in politics. The point of such references, however, is to make them sound natural, and that was a trick that Major simply couldn't pull off with any conviction. His opponent after the death of John Smith, on the other hand, was a master of the game. If there was to be a Swinging Sixties revival, then there was self-evidently a need for a new Harold Wilson, especially after the original obligingly died in 1995. And Tony Blair was very keen to fill his predecessor's shoes, making as much noise about being young and with-it when compared to those fuddy-duddy old Tories, as had Wilson when he had been leader of the opposition. 'I am a modern man,' Blair proclaimed. 'I am part of the rock and roll generation – the Beatles, colour TV. That's the generation I come from.'

Not even he, however, managed to strike quite the right note on every occasion. 'The great bands that I used to listen to – the Stones and the Beatles and the Kinks – their records are going to live forever,' he said at the Q magazine awards ceremony in 1994. 'And the records of today's bands, the records of U2 or the Smiths and Morrissey, will also live on because they're part of a vibrant culture.' In fact, the Smiths were hardly one of 'today's bands', having split up seven years earlier, and had anyway been chiefly remarkable for not being part of 'a vibrant culture'; they stood out precisely because their awkward pop was made in the glossy wastelands of the mid-1980s.

At the Brit Awards in 1996 (he was very keen on attending award ceremonies during this period), Blair took the opportunity to proclaim the good news one more time. 'British music is back once again on top of the world,' he enthused, though he gave no indication of understanding why this might be so. Indeed, McQueen's disparaging comment about 'taking the credit' seemed even more apposite when applied to Blair than to Major, for at least the latter was in government at the time, and could make some kind of claim to having created the economic conditions for the successes. It was a point that didn't escape the attention of the Conservative-supporting lyricist Tim Rice. 'Bearing in mind that he has never been slow to blame the present government for every economic failure or problem during the past few years,' he wrote of Blair's speech, 'it is strange that he failed to give it any credit for this phenomenal achievement.'

But Blair was on a roll and later the same year he was to be found paying tribute to Creation Records, the home of Oasis and Primal Scream, and to its founder, Alan McGee: 'Alan's just been telling me he started twelve years ago with a one thousand pound bank loan and now it's got a thirty-four million pound turnover. Now *that's* New Labour.' Even leaving aside the intriguing idea that the Labour movement was now expected to be seen in terms simply of capitalist endeavour, this was a somewhat revisionist version of history. That bank loan had been raised back in 1983 in order that Creation could participate in the Enterprise Allowance Scheme, the work of the employment secretary at the time, Norman Tebbit.

And Creation was not alone; much of the alternative culture of the 1980s and 1990s, however anti-Tory it professed to be, had benefited from the same initiative, from *Viz* comic to Jazzie B's Soul II Soul collective. Tebbit could, had he so wished, have proclaimed himself the most significant patron of the arts in modern times. But then Norman Tebbit, unlike Tony Blair, never posed for a photo opportunity with a Fender Stratocaster around his neck, and never made any pretence at being cool.

Nor would he have essayed such a terrible soundbite as 'Labour's coming home', as Blair did at his 1996 party conference. 'It's a bit cheap,' remarked Ian Broudie, composer of 'Three Lions', about that appropriation. Even the Blair enthusiast Giles Radice, while getting the reference, was annoyed: 'What on earth does "Labour's coming home" mean?' The answer, of course, was that it meant nothing at all. And Blair's next line – 'Seventeen years of hurt never stopped us dreaming' – flew in the face of the facts, since the cultural moment that had become known as Cool Britannia was largely created by a generation that had indeed stopped dreaming, that had lost its faith in political change altogether. But the soundbite made for a great tabloid headline, and the Blairite *Daily Mirror* duly obliged. The left-wing paper *Tribune*, on the other hand, added its own sardonic twist: LABOUR'S COMING HOME: PLEASE NOTE CHANGE OF ADDRESS.

Blair's much-vaunted love of football had also been expressed in the *Observer* in the build-up to Euro 96. 'In sport, as in politics, a well-fought campaign for second place means nothing,' he wrote, in an article whose subtext was not exactly well-concealed. 'Venables has, rightly, put his faith in youth.' His failure to mention the participation in the tournament of Scotland, the land of his birth, was a striking illustration of where his appeal was now being pitched.

In appropriating the imagery of the cultural renaissance, Blair tried to add a party dimension to it; he was to some extent successful in the endeavour, but only at the expense of stripping out any meaningful political content. He was, however, perfectly in tune with his times. His rebranding of the Labour Party as New Labour was of a piece with the marketing process that created Britpop, Cool Britannia and the Young British Artists, and was just as detrimental to creative thought.

The attempt to lay claim to the 1960s was also a mixed blessing. Blair did win the endorsement of Terence Conran, who had founded the Habitat chain in 1964 and had been instrumental in the look of that decade, but it was not a connection that met with everyone's approval, since the MSF trade union was fighting at the time for recognition at Conran's Design Museum in London. 'The Conran image is of a soft sofa in a shop window,' claimed Roger Lyon, general secretary of the MSF, 'but the harsh reality is of a medieval despot. There is a climate of fear and a sense of bullying at the Design Museum which is ill at ease with the culture of a museum and the arts.'

Amongst Blair's contemporaries, the claims of New Labour were greeted with even less enthusiasm. In 1997 Jonathon Green wrote a new introduction to *Days in the Life*, his classic oral history of the 1960s underground, and was dismissive of Blair's perspective: 'If the Tories represented those who disdained the great Sixties party, then New Labour are those who were never asked along.' Marcia Williams, who had been Harold Wilson's private and political secretary, was also unconvinced. 'He's anaesthetising the whole scene, isn't he?' she remarked in 1996. 'So it ends up bland. It's totally bland.' Most devastating of all, Vivienne Westwood wasn't even taken with Blair's dress sense. 'I prefer John Major's style,' she announced.

Nor was the most famous Barron Knights fan much impressed. 'The Blair image is of a 1960s modernism,' wrote John Redwood. 'He is looking back to gain the future. He sees Britain as a land of Carnaby Street and the Beatles, of rock bands and fashion icons, of out-of-doors *nouvelle cuisine* restaurants by the Tower of London and singles by Elton John.'

Blair's less than fastidious grasp of history meant that when he came to write his memoirs, he omitted any mention of his Cool Britannia phase, but it had played a more significant role than he was prepared to acknowledge. In the move to the mainstream, the overt politics had largely disappeared from popular culture, but a residual, implicit dislike of the Tories had helped shape the mood of the nation.

Part of the awfulness of Steve Coogan's chat-show character Alan Partridge, for example, was his parody of the way that the light entertainment establishment had traditionally endorsed the Conservative Party. 'Suffice to say,' he noted of the 1992 election result, 'I think we all, that is the whole country, breathed a very heavy sigh of relief.' As if to prove his point, the much-mocked magician Paul Daniels threatened to leave the country in 1997 if Labour won the election. Tony Blair was sufficiently in on the joke that he allowed himself to be interviewed on stage by Partridge at a Labour Party youth rally in the autumn of 1996.

'I want us to be a young country again,' Blair declared, at a time when the average age of a Labour MP was forty-eight, and that of a Tory MP sixty-two.

It added enormously to Blair's appeal that the Conservative Party looked old and tired, out of step with the country's culture, of interest only to light entertainment has-beens; in a word, unfashionable.

But Cool Britannia was not the sum total of British youth culture in the early and mid-1990s. Some of the dance music that coexisted with Blur and Oasis — the big beat of Fatboy Slim and the Chemical Brothers — was easily subsumed, but a less celebratory side could be heard in the claustrophobic paranoia of records by Massive Attack, Tricky and Goldie. That darker tendency was evident too in the Perrier Award-winning comedy of the League of Gentlemen, encountered in the cult that belatedly gathered around the fiction of Derek Raymond, and found in the dark fantasies of comics written by the likes of Grant Morrison, Bryan Talbot and Alan Moore.

It was also noticeable that the politicians who fawned over pop stars and designers were less keen to trumpet the achievements of computer games. Yet ever since the massive successes of *Populous* (1989) and *Lemmings* (1991), British games-writers had demonstrated a remarkable ability to sell their products in an international market. *Earthworm Jim* (1994) even reversed the trend for licensing existing film, comic-book and television creations into games, by creating a character that could spin off into his own television series and comics.

By the mid-1990s, gaming had become one of the most lucrative branches of the entertainment industry, with Britain amongst the leaders in such software, but it was an area that provoked nervousness in politicians. It was all a long way removed from their own cultural experience, and it seemed rather too keen on the depiction of violence, a tendency that became more marked as the technology improved. 'Until video discs came along, the characters in computer games were cartoon figures; the resolution was very poor,' noted James Ferman, director of the British Board of Film Classification, in 1993. 'I suspect that, even a year from now, they will be very different from what they are now.' Controversies about the corruption of youth were bound to come, and in due course they arrived.

December 1997 saw the release of the game *Grand Theft Auto* which, despite its setting (players took the role of a criminal rewarded for causing death and destruction in fictionalised versions of New York, Miami and San Francisco), was actually a British creation. Gleefully satirising the violence in American culture, it fed into concerns about joyriding in Britain, which had been a major media story since the last decade, often centred on estates such as Blackbird Leys in Oxford and Meadow Well in North Tyneside. In both locations riots associated with joyriding took place in 1991, at a time when over half a million cars were being stolen every year, two-thirds of them by teenage boys. Six months before it was even released, the game was the subject of questions in the House of Lords, where Gordon Campbell, formerly secretary of state for Scotland in Edward Heath's government, expressed his concern at the moral tone of the game and its apparent encouragement to break the law. As the launch approached, Campbell renewed his complaints, and was joined by others including the charity Family and Youth Concern ('This game is sick') and Fred Broughton, chairman of the Police Federation: 'So-called games like these which glorify crime and sneer at police officers upholding the law are beneath contempt.' All the denunciations ensured that *Grand Theft Auto* was an instant best-seller, to the great satisfaction of the company behind it, which had taken the trouble of employing a publicist for this very purpose. 'Max Clifford was the real genius here,' admitted the game's deviser, Mike Dailly. 'He designed all the outcry, which pretty much guaranteed MPs would get involved.'

This was treacherous ground for the cheerleaders of Cool Britannia, despite the impressive export sales, but even within music there were no-go areas. Beyond the state-sanctioned Swinging Sixties revival, there was an echo of the free festival movement that had grown out of that era. Originally manifest in the New Age travellers of the 1980s, this movement was bolstered at the start of the 1990s by a host of sound systems – Spiral Tribe, Bedlam and others – that were run by loose collectives of pseudonymous and sometimes anonymous figures, part of the fallout from rave culture.

Much of that dance scene was quickly institutionalised in the superclubs that sprang up in the new decade, most notably the New Labour-supporting Ministry of Sound, but there were those determined to keep alive the original spirit of free events, organising a string of increasingly high-profile parties in warehouses and rural locations. As such gatherings were technically private, the police had few immediate powers of regulation, and since they attracted tens of thousands of participants, physical intervention by the authorities was seldom a realistic option. For those who lived in the vicinity of these raves, they tended to be disruptive, noisy and unwelcome, while the failure of the law to prevent young people enjoying themselves infuriated some newspapers.

There was an unresolved conflict here between different views of society that had been summed up back in 1986 by the chief constable of Hampshire, talking about New Age travellers: 'If only they would return to a more conventional way of living, there would be no problem.' The dispute came to a head in May 1992 with a free festival on Castlemorton Common in the Malvern Hills that seemed to echo the glory days of such events in the hippy aftermath of the early 1970s. An estimated 30,000 people descended on the 600-acre common for a week-long party and, reported *The Times*, 'established a mini-city with full catering facilities, a large-scale drug distribution system, their own internal police force and a full programme of music and drama productions'. Local residents were quick to spot the different tribes that had descended upon them. 'The travellers bring their own shovels and when they go to the toilet they dig it in,' explained one. 'But the ravers were the ones causing all the trouble – they do it anywhere. They're a lot of yuppies from London.' A broad social mix was indeed apparent. One festival-goer declared: 'This is anarchy working as it should. The site is self-policing. It's an eco-system.' The press were pleased to discover that he'd been to Ampleforth College and had studied geology at university.

The massive media coverage of the event, however, apart from making great play of public order and drug issues, focused on the fact that many of those who attended were claiming benefits. A sketch in the comedy series *Armstrong and Miller* mocked the tabloid perceptions, with New Age travellers enthusing about the lifestyle: 'You can make nearly a grand a week on benefits easily, and leave litter all over the countryside, and steal babies.' Others were less amused, particularly the social security secretary Peter Lilley. 'Most people were as sickened as I was by the sight of these spongers descending like locusts, demanding benefits with menaces,' he quivered at the Conservative Party conference a few months later, and he vowed to reform the rules: 'We are not in the business of subsidising scroungers.' The following year he broadened his attack to bring in immigration, a perennial conference favourite: 'We have all too many home-grown scroungers, but it's beyond the pale when foreigners come here expecting our handouts.'

Apart from the sound and fury, the government's more substantial response was the deeply controversial Criminal Justice and Public Order Act 1994, which gave the police enhanced powers to suppress raves, and famously defined the music it was targeting as 'sounds wholly or predominantly characterised by the emission of a succession of repetitive beats'. The battle against the Act led to a series of demonstrations and to some violent conflicts with police.

This was a side of youth culture that definitely didn't come with government approval. Rather it was seen as an alien world that needed curbing. The same was true of the gangsta rap that was making its way across the Atlantic. In 1991 copies of the album *Efil4zaggin* by American rap band NWA (the album title was intended to be read backwards) were seized by police, and Island Records were prosecuted under the Obscene Publications Act for releasing the record. That prosecution was unsuccessful, but it did help create a climate of uncertainty, so that when the album *Death Certificate* by Ice Cube, a former member of NWA, was released in Britain, it came shorn of two tracks – 'Black Korea' and 'No Vaseline' – that were deemed to be potentially racist. Even so, an album that opened with the song 'The Wrong Nigga to Fuck Wit' was never going to make the records-of-the-year list of any British politician.

The fear about gangsta rap, like so many controversies over youth culture, was of the contamination of the middle class. The same was true of travellers. So a 1995 episode of *Pie in the Sky* centred on a senior police officer's daughter, Jane ('a weekend hippy, a traveller who doesn't travel too far,' says her sister), who joins a New Age convoy. Happily she sees the error of her ways, after getting drunk and injuring herself. 'I hit rock bottom with those people,' she admits ruefully to the avuncular figure of Richard Griffiths. 'I woke up in hospital and realised I can't live like that.'

The eponymous hero of *Inspector Morse* was less fortunate. In a celebrated 1992 episode, 'Cherubim and Seraphim', directed by Danny Boyle, he discovers that his niece, Marilyn, has been drawn into the rave scene. The day after going to a party in a disused brickworks, she is found dead, having committed suicide. Despite Morse's insistence that she would never have touched drugs, it transpires that she has indeed been under the influence of a new, experimental pill, which is being developed for treatment of the elderly, but which has also acquired a countercultural use; by expanding the blood vessels feeding the brain, it induces a sense of euphoria so intense that the comedown can inadvertently result in suicidal tendencies.

In truth, 'Cherubim and Seraphim' didn't add a great deal to the debates about raves or drugs, and its opening scene, with girls in perfect make-up and boys in leather jackets as they stumble out from an all-night party into the dawn, lacked the smack of authenticity. Its significance, perhaps, lay in the fact that it existed at all. *Inspector Morse* was far and away the most popular detective show on television, with a domestic audience that touched twenty million. It was also one of Britain's few really big television exports of the time; by 2007 ITV were to claim that a billion people worldwide (around a sixth of the global population) had seen at least one episode. The idea that such a mainstream show felt the need to address raves was an indication of how far up the public agenda they had moved, and how close the country was to one of its periodic moral panics.

That scare duly arrived in 1995 with the death of an eighteen-year-old named Leah Betts from a combination of taking an ecstasy tablet and drinking vast quantities of water. The story became big largely because she was clearly not part of an underclass that could be easily dismissed: her stepmother was a nurse and her father a former police officer, who became a key campaigner for stronger action against drug use.

For a while ecstasy became the subject of righteous moralising. Ignorant indignation was whipped up to the extent that, for example, rent-a-quote Conservative MPs like Terry Dicks and Harry Greenaway could be prevailed upon to call for the banning of the single 'Everything Starts with an E' by the E-Zee Posse, clearly unaware that the record had been released some six years earlier. Furthermore, the prominence of the Leah Betts story, at a time when it was estimated that a million people took ecstasy every weekend, suggested that it was hardly the most destructive drug in widespread use. More damaging was the prescription medicine Temazepam, used for treatment of anxiety and insomnia, which had become a street drug in the late 1980s and was still popular enough to inspire Black Grape's song 'Tramazi Parti' in 1995. Meanwhile, although media interest in glue-sniffing had peaked a decade earlier, there was, virtually unnoticed, a steady rise in the number of deaths by solvent abuse amongst those too young or too poor to acquire other drugs; lighter fuel was now the favoured source of kicks, until its sale to those aged under sixteen was banned in 1998. Legislation proved less effective in dealing with a new Scottish craze, when it was discovered that setting fire to wheelie-bins produced fumes that could be inhaled for a quick high. 'Wheelie-bins being set on fire is quite common,' marvelled a spokesperson for the Strathclyde Fire Brigade, on being told, 'but I had no idea this was the reason.'

In more elevated circles, cocaine use was reaching near-ubiquity in fashionable London society. Tabloid exposés claimed the occasional high-profile scalp, as when Richard Bacon was sacked from presenting *Blue Peter*, or Jefferson King (aka Shadow) from *Gladiators*, but mostly cocaine went by with a nod and a wink, perhaps because it was also so common within media circles. When the former New Labour spin doctor Charlie Whelan was employed by the *Daily Mirror* to write a column during the 1999 Labour conference, it was given the nudging title of A FEW LINES OF CHARLIE.

'Cocaine is the binding agent of what many are now calling Swinging London,' wrote Dylan Jones in 1996, by which stage the ecstasy-friendly sounds of rave had partially given way on dancefloors to jungle, and then to its offshoot drum and bass, whose faster beats suited cocaine rather well. By then too darker drugs were making their presence felt in the form of crack cocaine and heroin, the latter doing considerable damage to the Britpop scene in particular. As the comedian Harry Hill used to observe: 'The worst thing about heroin is it's very more-ish.'

*

Drugs played their part in the rapid decline of Cool Britannia, but mostly the era collapsed under the weight of its own self-regarding sense of importance. The third Oasis album, *Be Here Now*, was released in 1997 and was accompanied by such media hype and such absurdly inflated reviews that huge sales were guaranteed. In Britain alone, 350,000 copies were sold on the first day of release, a million in the first fortnight. As people actually heard the record, however, it became clear that it had nothing to add to its predecessors, save excess; there were more string overdubs, more guitar solos and more repeats of the same choruses, leaving just two of the eleven songs coming in at under five minutes. Most importantly, the grandiose treatments couldn't conceal the weariness and lack of inspiration in the writing; there were no songs capable of capturing the public imagination in the way that the singles 'Wonderwall' and 'Don't Look Back in Anger' had done eighteen months earlier. It was 'the same old pub rock bollocks', admitted guitarist and songwriter Noel Gallagher.

The immediate future of rock appeared instead to lie in the hands of Radiohead, whose album *OK Computer* had been released a month earlier. As with Oasis, there were strong Beatles influences to be heard here, but they came from the darker, less fab end of the legacy, with 'Happiness Is a Warm Gun' and 'Sexy Sadie' influencing 'Paranoid Android' and 'Karma Police' respectively. It sold phenomenally well and made the group international stars, despite being almost wilfully anti-commercial.

Pop music had launched Cool Britannia and now it prefigured the demise, with the experience of that third Oasis album replayed in other fields. Guy Ritchie, for example, had made his debut film as a director with *Lock, Stock and Two Smoking Barrels* (1998), a critical and popular success, acclaimed for its reinvention of the British gangster genre. His second feature, *Snatch* (2000), on the other hand, was described by film critic Roger Ebert as a piece that 'follows the *Lock, Stock* formula so slavishly it could be like a new arrangement of the same song'. *Tomb Raider II* was published in time for Christmas 1997 and won rave reviews and increased sales as it extended the Lara Croft franchise, but soon faced criticism that it had lost some of the strength and charm of the original creation. In the words of gaming historians Magnus Anderson and Rebecca Levene, 'Lara was becoming less pop culture, and more pin up.'

Similarly, as the novelty of the YBAs began to wear off, many lined up to denounce their new work as lazy and repetitive. Certainly there was nothing in the YBA catalogue from the latter years of the decade to rival in public attention the *Angel of the North* sculpture by Antony Gormley, an artist whose first exhibition had been staged at a time when Damien Hirst was considering his A-level options. Hirst did attempt to fuse the parallel worlds of art, cuisine and celebrity with the Pharmacy restaurant in Notting Hill, but it was not a notable success.

Once its moment had passed, Cool Britannia was increasingly portrayed as something of an embarrassment. Seen in retrospect, it appeared little more than a scam concocted by publicists and their media accomplices, probably in the confines of the Groucho Club, a private-members establishment in Soho, London that had opened in 1985. Craig Brown had pointed out early on that the club was written about in the media as though it were 'a cross between the Algonquin Round Table and the Bloomsbury Group, when it actually resembles nothing so much as the Radio 1 staff canteen', but such dissent was never going to stop the self-celebration. 'Jumped-up one-book novelists, poxy little film company liars, grown men who write for *Loaded*, comedians who've had lunch with someone from Channel 4,' exulted a former football journalist turned restaurant critic in Tony Marchant's drama series *Holding On*; 'we all gather together and enjoy our good fortune, the unique talent we possess.'

From the inside, it was all terribly exciting. 'Soho was fizzing,' wrote Alex James from Blur. 'There was a big mad family of extraordinary people.' James had been introduced to the club by Vic Reeves and Jonathan Ross, and found soul-mates there in the form of Damien Hirst and actor Keith Allen. Under the collective name of Fat Les, the trio had a hit single with the World Cup song 'Vindaloo', while Allen summed up one aspect of the spirit of the age with his description of a *Vanity Fair* photo-shoot that was staged in the Groucho Club: 'not only were we drunk, we were obnoxious.'

There was more, however, to Cool Britannia than a Soho coterie high on booze, cocaine and mutual backslapping. In its early incarnation, before the branding and the marketing took over entirely, there was a moment when popular culture enjoyed one of its periodic peaks of creativity. And before politicians rushed to join in, there was too a political dimension to underpin the post-1980s partying. In 1994, while John Smith was still alive, the journalist Allison Pearson wrote that 'the whole country was conspiring to look like a piece of anti-government propaganda'. Tony Blair was shrewd enough to position himself on the right side of a cultural fault line that separated the Conservatives from much of the rest of the country, and in the white heat of that anti-Tory alliance, there was lost – temporarily, as it turned out, though perhaps at a time when it was most needed – a scepticism about politics itself.

5
Bastards
'I'm singing my song for Europe'

GARY: I don't know about you, I'm worried about the European Community.
Simon Nye, *Men Behaving Badly* (1992)

Why do our people behave so badly? Do they understand nothing?
William Whitelaw (1995)

One thing I think everyone is agreed on is that the Europeans are rabid animals, hell-bent on destroying our way of life and introducing tough anti-pollution measures.
Armando Iannucci, *The Friday Night Armistice* (1996)

For governments going into general elections, the manifesto is an opportunity not merely to promise new policies but to brag about past achievements. So it was that in 1992 the Conservative Party proudly boasted: 'The Maastricht Treaty was a success both for Britain and for the rest of Europe.' Gerald Kaufman once famously described the 1983 Labour manifesto as 'the longest suicide note in history', but that single sentence ranks amongst the shortest. Almost everything about it was wrong. As a result of British squabbling over Maastricht, the country found itself consigned to the fringes of the European debate yet again, just when it seemed as though progress might be possible, while the rest of Europe departed down an inexorable path to creating a single currency, a journey that looked fraught with danger from the outset. Neither camp could really boast of 'a success'. And even the tense of that manifesto sentence was wrong, for Maastricht was by no means a done deal at this stage.

The Treaty of European Union was signed by the representatives of twelve nations in the Netherlands town of Maastricht in February 1992. It brought into existence the European Union, subsuming the European Community, formerly known as the European Economic Community

(EEC). The change in terminology was significant, and was intended so to be: it reflected a move away from merely economic cooperation towards greater political, financial and social cohesion, just as had been promised in the 1958 Treaty of Rome that had launched the European project. This was 'a new and decisive stage,' explained Helmut Kohl, the German chancellor, 'which within a few years will lead to the creation of what the founding fathers of modern Europe dreamed of after the last war: the United States of Europe.'

Foreign policy and the judicial process, collaboration on which had previously been dealt with at governmental level, were increasingly brought within the ambit of the EU, and the British people – hitherto subjects of the Queen – suddenly discovered that they had become citizens of the Union. The European Parliament was given additional powers, and the creation of a European central bank was agreed. This latter was at the heart of Maastricht, part of the schedule for a single European currency, a project that had long been the holy grail of Euro-enthusiasts.

Amongst the twelve signatories was Britain, though in the negotiations over the Treaty at the end of the previous year John Major had argued successfully for the country to be allowed to exempt itself from two of the crucial elements: the preparations for the single currency, and what was known as the Social Chapter, which provided for certain employment, trade union and social rights. The latter element, the nation was told, would have placed an intolerable burden on businesses and made the British economy uncompetitive in the wider world, which was arguable – the Labour Party certainly argued against it – but comprehensible. The position on the single currency was less clear. Britain was still at this stage a member of the Exchange Rate Mechanism, which only made sustainable sense as a precursor to monetary union; if the country wasn't going to take that next step, then it was not immediately obvious what the point was of belonging to the ERM. Nonetheless, the securing of the two opt-outs was trumpeted as a massive achievement. The government's press office briefed journalists that it was 'game, set and match' to Major and, although not everyone was convinced ('Why go to the brothel if you're not going to drop your knickers?' wondered Henry Davenport in *Drop the Dead Donkey*), this was the line that was sold to the public. Britain was actively engaging with Europe but there were still things up with which we would not put.

The insistence on claiming Major as a tough negotiator was largely a response to the lurking presence of Margaret Thatcher. She had been out of office for less than a year when the Conservative Party met for its annual conference in October 1991 in the build-up to Maastricht, and although she was seldom seen in the Commons any more ('I hate coming into this place now,' she admitted), she was far from being politically dead and buried. Unlike almost every other Tory politician, she genuinely enjoyed the conference, knowing that here she could talk directly to the rank-and-file membership, with whom she shared a kinship and a warmth largely absent from her dealings with the grandees of the party. She didn't actually address the 1991 gathering – she merely appeared on the platform, which was enough to provoke a wildly enthusiastic standing ovation – but she took the opportunity to tell journalists that she was in favour of a referendum on the key issues being proposed for the Maastricht summit, and in particular on the single currency.

Norman Tebbit, Thatcher's most loyal lieutenant, repeated in public the call for a referendum, and chancellor Norman Lamont hinted heavily that he was similarly inclined: 'I will not allow a single currency to be imposed on this country. Unlike the Labour Party, we don't want laws to be made and taxes to be raised in Brussels for which the British people have not voted.' The clamour for a referendum on Maastricht became so great that the foreign secretary, Douglas Hurd, felt obliged to intervene. 'It is not on,' he said. 'The Conservative Party voted against a referendum in 1975. It is simply not a subject for a referendum.'

That reference to 1975, when the Labour prime minister Harold Wilson, in an attempt to satisfy both wings of his party, had called a national vote on Britain's membership of the EEC, was carefully chosen. Thatcher, then the leader of the opposition, had been typically forthright in her condemnation of the tactic, accusing the government of trying to 'pass the buck' and seeking to 'bind and fetter' parliamentary democracy. During her eleven years in Downing Street, she had accordingly held not a single referendum; it was only since leaving office that she had been converted to the idea of appealing beyond Parliament to the people.

In response to the groundswell of concern, Major held a Commons debate before flying to Maastricht, seeking parliamentary support in advance for his negotiating position. Thatcher spoke in that debate, repeating the request for a referendum on a single currency, but along with most Conservatives she backed the prime minister; just six Tory MPs rebelled, and the government won with a comfortable majority of 101. On hearing, just a few days later, however, the terms of the deal that had been struck, Thatcher was less supportive: 'the country is being sold down the river,' she cried.

That, of course, was before the general election, but already the Eurosceptic MP Michael Spicer was warning that the parliamentary party resembled 'two warring armies looking at each other across the trenches'. After April 1992, the massive majorities to which the Tories had grown accustomed became a thing of the past, and nowhere was this more evident than on the thorny issue of Europe, 'the fault-line that runs through the bedrock of the Conservative Party', as Michael Heseltine put it.

According to the calculations of Richard Ryder, the Conservative chief whip, more than fifty of the Tory MPs who had retired at the time of the election were either pro-European or at least sufficiently loyal to the leadership that they could be relied upon not to rock the boat. The newly elected members were less dependable. Many had been inspired by Thatcher's long reign and were more doctrinaire than Tories of the past; indeed the parliamentary party was now more Thatcherite than it had been during her own time in office. Many too had come to see her latter-day scepticism over Europe as an article of faith, and the likes of Iain Duncan Smith, Bernard Jenkin, Barry Legg and Roger Knapp seemed to regard this issue as being ultimately more important than the survival of a Conservative government.

Others, too, were determined to put principle before party. And there was inspiration to be found in the past, in the career of Enoch Powell, whose hostility to Edward Heath's leadership of the Conservative Party – on grounds of economic policy and opposition to Europe – had caused him to rebel against the party whip on 115 occasions during Heath's four-year premiership, and ultimately led him to abandon the party altogether. He refused to stand in the general election of February 1974, and publicly announced that he had voted Labour in the hope of rolling back British involvement with Europe. Powell had never rebuilt a front-line political career, but his philosophy had played a major part in the Thatcherite takeover of the Conservative Party. Now in the last years of his life (he was to die in 1998), he continued to argue his case against Europe, speaking at the Newbury by-election on behalf of Alan Sked of the Anti-Federalist League, which was ultimately to evolve into the UK Independence Party. Amongst those he met on that occasion was Nigel Farage, inspiring the young stockbroker to take seriously the idea of a political career; Farage was later to emerge as the leader of UKIP, perhaps Powell's last contribution to British politics.

The influence of Powell, whether acknowledged or not, was felt widely amongst those Tory factions opposed to Major, his stature enhanced by biographies written by Robert Shepherd (1996) and Simon Heffer (1998). The fact that he had put his beliefs above his own advancement, and above his own party, allowed him to be recast as the great political martyr of the right, an example to all those who subscribed to his romantic vision of Britain. The former cabinet minister Nicholas Ridley, one of the small handful of MPs who had voted for Powell in the leadership election of 1965, was to be heard arguing nearly thirty years later that party loyalty was not the highest virtue when it came to Europe.

The conventional tactic for dealing with dissent was for the whips to threaten junior MPs that they were jeopardising their career prospects, but that didn't prove entirely effective when encountering passionately held beliefs about Europe. Nor did it carry much weight when it was tried with Peter Tapsell, who was then in his sixties and still on the back benches, having first been elected to Parliament in 1959. Tapsell was old enough to have known some of the class of 1938, and in particular Walter Elliott, who had considered resigning from the government over the Munich Agreement with Germany, Italy and France, but had been persuaded that it was in his interests not to cause trouble. 'Walter Elliott said that voting for Munich had not only eventually wrecked his own political career,' remembered Tapsell, 'but, more importantly, had damaged his self-esteem. He said he had never ceased to reproach himself for that vote.' Tapsell had no intention of selling his own conscience in similar fashion.

Whips' talk of careers being threatened also created its own problems as the House became home to a new wave of professional politicians, impatient that they had not yet been promoted, despite their loyalty. 'Four of the 1992 intake met the chief whip in 1993 to ask when they would be made ministers,' remembered Major, adding that this would have been 'unthinkable behaviour in previous generations'. But then in previous generations such preferment was not a serious possibility. At the beginning of the century, just forty-two of 402 Conservative MPs had a job in government; by the time that Major became prime minister, this had risen to 129 out of 376, and the election simply increased the proportion: the number of Tory MPs was reduced, the number of government posts was not. There was plenty of scope here for disgruntled young politicians to feel that their advancement was being thwarted if promotion was not immediately forthcoming.

All of which made Maastricht a difficult question for the new Parliament. Although Major had signed up to the Treaty, it had still to be ratified by the passing of the European Communities (Amendment) Bill. A hint at the scale of that task came in May 1992 when the Queen gave her first-ever speech to the European Parliament. 'We are all trying to preserve the rich diversity of European countries because, if that diversity is suppressed, we shall weaken Europe, not strengthen it,' she said. 'But at the same time we have to strengthen the ability of Europeans to act on a European basis where the nature of a problem requires a European response. That was the balance struck at Maastricht.' It was an unusually explicit piece of political argument, and the fact that Her Majesty's government felt it necessary to involve her in the issue was a clear signal of how nervous they were. A week later twenty-two Conservative MPs voted against the second reading of the Bill, while another four abstained, though the vote passed in the absence of Labour opposition. (It was, jibed Ken Livingstone, 'An issue of such vital historic significance that Neil Kinnock gallantly led the Labour Party into a fighting abstention.')

At the beginning of June, things took a turn for the worse, as far as the government was concerned. Given the chance to express their opinion in a referendum, the Danish people voted against Maastricht. The Treaty was left in a state of limbo, for it required ratification by all twelve signatory countries if it were to pass into European law. An early day motion was put down in the Commons calling on the government to postpone any further moves towards ratification and to make a 'fresh start'; it attracted wide support with ninety-one Conservative MPs signing, nearly a third of all Tory MPs and getting on for two-thirds of Tory backbenchers. Major rejected such calls, insisting that nothing had changed despite the Danish vote, but he failed to convince his own side. That phrase from the early day motion was adopted by a new dissident faction within the party, the Fresh Start group, which shared much of its ideology, and some of its members, with the already established No Turning Back group, which was devoted to keeping the flame of Thatcherism burning fiercely.

There had always been dining groups of Conservative MPs, but these modern incarnations were, some feared, dangerously close to becoming parties within the party, just as Militant had been in the Labour Party in the 1970s and '80s. Certainly they owed ultimate allegiance not to the current leader but to the previous incumbent, who had left the Commons at the general election but remained closely involved in party politics. Encouraged by the Danish vote, Thatcher adopted a stance of outright opposition to Major's position, much to his despair: 'It was Margaret's support for the defeat of the Maastricht legislation which helped to turn a difficult task for our whips into an almost impossible one.'

The issue of Maastricht was still unresolved when the government was dealt the blow of Black Wednesday, whereupon some concluded that the Treaty was already obsolete. 'When Britain was forced to withdraw from the ERM in September 1992,' wrote Kenneth Baker, 'it seemed to me that the *raison d'être* behind Maastricht had collapsed and that the right thing to do was to renegotiate the Maastricht Treaty.' He was not alone. Another early day motion, again calling for a 'fresh start', this time on economic policy, with a commitment never again to fix exchange rates, attracted the signatures of seventy-one Conservative MPs. If the consequence of monetary involvement with Europe was international humiliation such as the country had endured on Black Wednesday, then many wanted no further part of it. Others were drawing lessons from across the Atlantic, where negotiations were reaching a final stage in setting up the North American Free Trade Agreement; this created a trilateral trade bloc between the USA, Canada and Mexico, but there was no suggestion, noted some Tories, that a single currency might be necessary to make the arrangement work.

There was but one beacon of hope and that was flickering, perversely enough, in France, where the government had suddenly announced after the Danish vote that it too would hold a referendum. Despite the pretence that all nations in the Community were equal, everyone knew that some were more equal than others; Denmark was never going to be allowed to scupper the European project of monetary union, but a French rejection would have sunk Maastricht.

In Britain it was not merely Eurosceptics who were praying for deliverance at the hands of the traditional enemy. 'I could have borne its loss with fortitude,' noted Major, with characteristic understatement, of the French vote. It wasn't to be. The French people, in a much tighter result than any had predicted, came down in favour of Maastricht, with just under 51 per cent support, amidst widespread rumours of gerrymandering. Most of Europe's leaders gave thanks that they didn't have to reopen negotiations on the intricate obscurity of a 250-page document, but for Major it was a disastrous outcome, leaving him stuck with the problem of trying to get the wretched thing through Parliament in the anti-European atmosphere that followed Black Wednesday.

Part of the reason why it was such a hard sell, both in the Commons and in the country, was that few could grasp quite what was being sold. All the government propaganda centred on the fact that Major had achieved more in the negotiations than anyone could have dared dream. 'We spent much of our time showing that, given John Major's two opt-outs, the treaty would do Britain no harm,' was the best Douglas Hurd could find to say about the ratification campaign. 'But these negative arguments did not amount to a battle-cry.' There was, though, never any clear explanation of what the Treaty actually contained – rather than what had been left out

– that was quite so important and so desirable for Britain. Important and desirable it evidently was, however, for Major staked his political career on its passage through Parliament, threatening more than once to resign if he didn't get his way.

'There wasn't a lot in it that was positive for Britain,' admitted Tristan Garel-Jones, the minister for Europe. Rather, its strength was in curbing some of the excesses of the single market by introducing the idea of subsidiarity, an unwieldy word borrowed from the Catholic Church and intended to suggest that decisions should be taken at the lowest possible level. The Treaty's phrasing hardly made this an easy concept to convey to the public:

> In areas which do not fall within its exclusive competence, the Community shall take action, in accordance with the principle of subsidiarity, only if and in so far as the objectives of the proposed action cannot be sufficiently achieved by the Member States and can therefore, by reason of the scale or effects of the proposed action, be better achieved by the Community.

The Europhiles, moreover, were aware that Major's opt-outs were not irrevocable. He hadn't vetoed the Social Chapter or the process of monetary union, and Britain reserved the right to join in at a subsequent date if it saw fit. 'The doors were left open,' as Giles Radice put it. Foundations had been laid on which a more enlightened administration would be able to build. In particular – despite the travails of Black Wednesday and the ERM – the drive towards economic and monetary union was still going ahead, with a timetable for a single currency now established; Britain might not be part of that for the moment, but many still wished it to join.

That wasn't quite the government's position, though, for Major was essentially a pragmatist when it came to Europe. Without trying to destroy the single currency, he wished to delay its advent, arguing that his sole consideration was whether such a scheme were in Britain's interests. He was, he said, 'procrastinating on principle'. And he had at least the support of the last prime minister but one, who had himself been a master of that valuable political art and knew what it was like to live on a knife-edge majority. 'I think John Major made the right choice in getting us the option,' reflected James Callaghan in 1996.

That still didn't explain why the Treaty was so necessary. The suspicion was that, as the defence secretary Malcolm Rifkind put it: 'since there was a general will in Europe to have a treaty, it was essential for us to go along with that.' If the opt-outs were the price Major paid to keep his backbenchers on side, the Treaty itself was the price he paid for the goodwill of his European counterparts. In seeking to serve two masters, he was able to satisfy neither.

Nor was his cabinet particularly enthusiastic, according to the then trade and industry secretary Peter Lilley. He remembered the cabinet meeting at which each minister was asked whether Maastricht would be beneficial to the work of their department; not one person, he said, was able to answer positively. Even Douglas Hurd, seen by the right as an ardent Europhile, was by now objecting to the European Commission's habit of 'inserting itself into the nooks and crannies of everyday life'.

By October 1992, therefore, the scene was set for that rarest of political beasts: a memorable Conservative Party conference. Black Wednesday was too raw and too recent for the wound even to have started healing, while the battle of Maastricht was just about to break out in earnest. Europe was inevitably at the top of everyone's agenda. The former prime minister Edward Heath, the man who had taken Britain into the EEC, was booed as he made his glacial way to the platform, and so too was Tristan Garel-Jones, who was known as an arch-Europhile.

On the other hand, this was Norman Tebbit's moment. As the hard man of the 1980s government, he had divided opinion almost as emphatically as had Margaret Thatcher herself, hated by the left while being adored by the faithful for his adherence to the Thatcherite causes of social mobility, unfettered capitalism and aggressive nostalgia, as well as for his ability to express those beliefs in terms so clear and forthright that they could hardly be ignored. He also shared some of the sentiments of those Tory MPs who set what they regarded as the national interest higher than party loyalty. When asked by Woodrow Wyatt before the 1992 election whether he wanted the Conservatives to win, 'He went rather quiet for a bit and then said, "There isn't much difference".' Not for nothing was he cast in the role of — according to Chris Patten — 'the only man whom Major is worried about'. His potential for mischief-making was enormous.

He didn't disappoint. Unlike Heath and Garel-Jones, he received a standing ovation even before he started speaking. He then delivered what Gyles Brandreth described with some distaste as a 'vulgar, grandstanding, barnstorming performance on Europe', castigating the government's policy and pointedly turning to John Major to say: 'I hope, prime minister, you will stand by your chancellor. After all, it was not Norman Lamont's decision to enter the ERM.' Tebbit hadn't been a regular speaker at conference for a few years, so the impact was all the greater when he tore into the ERM policy: 'The cost in lost jobs, bankruptcies, repossessed homes, the terrible wounds inflicted on industry, has been savage.' Mustering all his considerable reserves of sarcasm, he added: 'But we established our credentials as good Europeans.' He sat down to an even bigger ovation.

Douglas Hurd was the man who drew the short straw and had to try to calm things down. He urged the party not to split on the issue of Europe: 'Let us decide to give that madness a miss.' Some hope. The Eurosceptic right was fired up by Tebbit and by the evident support that their position enjoyed in the wider party. 'It is something I never thought I'd see at a Tory party conference and something we did not see at Blackpool, during the Labour conference which was held the week before,' enthused Teresa Gorman. 'Ours was a real debate.' It was, in other words, just like Labour in the 1980s.

John Major's own speech to the conference seemed to be, in advance, one of the critical moments of his political career. He wasn't helped by the serialisation, in the *Telegraph* newspapers that week, of extracts from Nigel Lawson's memoirs, focusing particularly on Lawson's criticism of Major, who had served under him in the Treasury. Major got a standing ovation, of course – loyalty to the leader was too ingrained a Tory habit to disappear overnight – and his appearance even inspired, for the first time ever at a British party conference, a similar reception for the prime minister's spouse. But the speech itself was bizarrely low key, seeming to lack any sense of proportion, given the cataclysms of the previous month. Amongst the new measures Major proposed were more motorway service stations, explaining that he knew what it was like to be a parent with children who were desperate for the toilet. It was, many felt, perhaps too homely a concern to be raising quite so soon after Black Wednesday, and did nothing to reassure those with doubts about his leadership.

Meanwhile, that Labour conference at which Teresa Gorman sniffed had endorsed Maastricht as 'the best treaty available', reinforcing the party's new-found claim to be good Europeans. For John Smith at least, unlike many of his colleagues, this was not such a recent development. As a young MP in 1971 he had defied the party whip in the vote on joining the EEC, following Roy Jenkins into the Yes lobby. Unlike Neil Kinnock, he couldn't be accused of selling his principles for political advantage.

Nor was the party's position truly a sign of opportunism, but rather an admission of defeat: if it was considered too difficult to win over the British people by proposing a genuinely radical agenda, then at least a European form of social democracy was a realisable and acceptable compromise. Labour's enthusiasm for Europe in all its forms was a tacit admission of a loss of faith in Britain, just as the Eurosceptic position implied that the country wasn't strong enough to fight its corner against Germany and France. So the employment legislation contained in the Maastricht Treaty was warmly embraced by Labour, while support for the ERM was followed by an inclination to accept the single currency if it were politically feasible. The unspoken assumption was that national politicians were now powerless when it came to the rate of exchange or interest rates, but few seemed concerned with such details.

'The electorate has rejected the Labour Party at four successive general elections,' taunted the Conservative minister David Hunt. 'The front door to power has been slammed firmly shut on them. No wonder they are slinking round to the back door. It used to be beer and sandwiches at Number Ten, now they want claret and croissants with the Commission in Brussels.' There was truth in the accusation, but it missed the most significant political point: Labour was united behind its policy, while the Conservatives were not. Labour was also united in its opposition to the government over Maastricht.

The attempt to get Maastricht ratified in the Commons dominated politics in the first half of 1993. In a series of votes a stubborn group of Conservative backbenchers fought every line of the Bill, often siding with the Labour Party in what Major called 'a mad-hatter coalition'. The ensuing bitterness soured the party for years to come. 'In the voting lobbies it was not unknown for one Conservative MP to spit at another,' remembered Michael Spicer. 'Physical violence occurred during the course of one or two crucial votes.' He also recalled a senior MP being dragged by his hair into the government's lobby. Spicer was a key figure in the rebellion, but one who insisted on maintaining good relations with the whips and the leadership. He was also reluctant to attract attention to himself at a time when the open voicing of dissent guaranteed publicity. Indeed, Maastricht made media stars of several backbenchers who would otherwise have languished in obscurity.

Chief amongst them was Bill Cash, whose slight frame, unflattering pinstripe suits, greying hair and glasses made him look like Major's Eurosceptic doppelgänger. He was 'the biggest bore in the House of Commons', according to his colleague Julian Critchley, though another Tory MP, Teddy Taylor, disagreed: 'I am the biggest Euro-bore there ever was.' Cash managed to vote against his government forty-seven times during the Maastricht debates, with a further thirteen abstentions, and did what he was told just twice. He was rivalled in coverage only by Teresa Gorman, the MP for Billericay whose vocal enthusiasm for hormone replacement therapy, never knowingly understated dress sense and tattooed eyebrows (to conceal the fact that her real ones hadn't grown back after being shaved) were matched only by her splendid quotability. 'The Conservative establishment,' she once announced, 'has always treated women as nannies, grannies and fannies.' There was an equally oddball supporting cast, with notable contributions from the married couple Ann and Nicholas Winterton, dismissed scornfully by Michael Heseltine as having a knack for stumbling upon 'a populist cause waiting for a voice'. Their fellow MP Nicholas Soames was less restrained: 'You're cunts,' he told them after one Commons rebellion, 'and ugly ones to boot.'

This group of mavericks and misfits – a hard core of around twenty-five, with a similar number on the fringes – were undoubtedly motivated by high principle, albeit in some cases only recently discovered. This, however, was neither the first nor the lasting impression they made on a television audience. Every time they conducted yet another round of interviews on College Green, they came across as slightly strange, obsessed with an issue that simply didn't feel like a priority to most of the electorate. They were not, for many viewers, very endearing. The same was true of those cabinet members who were assumed to share their Eurosceptic views. The most popular ministers – Major, Heseltine, Kenneth Clarke, Chris Patten – were pro-Europe, whilst those who harboured suspicions about the EU were viewed with less warmth by the public: Michael Howard, Peter Lilley, John Redwood.

There was a very real danger that the expression of doubts about further European integration would come to be equated with Thatcherism at the precise time when the nation wished to move away from that creed. Nostalgia for the 1980s was less common in the country than it was in the Conservative Party, and the identification of Euroscepticism with Bill Cash and Teresa Gorman, let alone with the likes of John Carlisle, who had made his name as an indefatigable supporter of the apartheid regime in South Africa, brought back unwelcome memories of all that was ugly about the decade. There was a suspicion too that the underlying attitude was the one caricatured by satirists John Fortune and John Bird. 'I was talking about positive fundamental principles,' explains a fictional Eurosceptic MP, 'by which I mean something very deep in the British character, which we are in danger of losing, which is under threat, and which I think could be summed up as a proud, traditional and instinctive loathing of foreigners.' The rebels were too easily portrayed as dated and backward-looking and, despite Major's dogged attachment to the cause of Maastricht, they damaged the Conservative Party, as well as the cause of Euroscepticism itself.

They did, however, have friends in high places. Several newspapers were sympathetic, particularly the *Telegraph* titles and the *Sun*. 'The awkward-squad was RIGHT to fight Maastricht,' opined the latter, after the battle was lost and won. There was also Sir James Goldsmith (knighted in Harold Wilson's controversial resignation honours list in 1976), a multimillionaire businessman of dubious reputation who donated money to Bill Cash's think tank, the European Foundation; this despite the fact that Goldsmith was the founder of the Referendum Party, a Eurosceptic organisation which was planning to stand candidates against the Tories.

Another donor to Cash's think tank was Margaret Thatcher, now in the House of Lords as a life peer (despite her reported wish to be given an hereditary peerage as the Countess of Finchley), who was becoming something more than a figurehead for the rebel tendency within the Conservative Party. She made herself available for private meetings with wavering MPs who wished to defy the party whips over Europe, but who felt in need of having their sinews strengthened and their will stiffened. 'Did she play an active part?' ruminated Iain Duncan Smith in later years. 'Yes, in the background. But they all did, all of the grandees.' Major was distinctly unimpressed by such contributors to the debate: 'devils on the fringe,' he called them, 'living out past glories.'

'I shall not be pulling the levers, but I shall be a very good backseat driver,' Thatcher had said at a farewell party after her resignation as prime minister, and although she was actually talking about her relationship with US president George Bush and the forthcoming Kuwaiti War, her comments were widely associated with her attitude to her successor. Indeed in her constant demands and running commentary on Major's government, she did come to resemble the suburban busybody Hyacinth Bucket, as played by Patricia Routledge in the television sitcom *Keeping Up Appearances*, endlessly nagging at her mild-mannered and long-suffering husband, as he attempted to drive slowly and carefully down the road.

Thatcher's behaviour during Major's premiership was even worse than that of Edward Heath during her own time in office. Heath had been unstinting in his disapproval as he remained stubbornly on the back benches ('like a sulk made flesh,' in the words of journalist Edward Pearce), but he hadn't actively engaged in plotting against her. Even Thatcher's most devoted follower, Woodrow Wyatt, thought that she overstepped the mark on occasion. 'She can be petty and is unfair, I think, to Major,' he wrote in his diary. But then, as a minister told the BBC's John Cole: 'She was always criticising the government when she led it, so why expect her to change now?'

While Thatcher's interventions provided succour for the hardcore rebels, they began also to tarnish her reputation within the party. For every trembling disciple like trade minister Neil Hamilton ('Isn't she beautiful? It's almost too wonderful to bear'), plenty of others were coming to see her as something of an embarrassment. Edwina Currie noted in her diary that when Thatcher made an appearance in the lobby of the Commons, 'only acolytes' spoke to her; 'everyone else slides past, as if she's a turd on the pavement.'

Meanwhile, Maastricht rumbled and grumbled its way through Parliament, its painfully slow progress resembling the trench warfare of the First World War. A second Danish referendum in May 1993 finally produced the right result, after the country had been given a better deal, allowing it to opt out of the single currency, a joint defence policy and European citizenship, and Britain was now the only potential stumbling block on the road to the Treaty's ratification. In the end it all came down to a single night in July 1993. The Treaty had been approved but two votes were outstanding: first on a Labour Party amendment, calling for the inclusion at the last moment of the Social Chapter, and then on the government's final motion that would pass the Treaty into British law without the Social Chapter.

It was a moment of high drama such as hadn't been seen in the Commons since 1979, when James Callaghan's government had been brought down in a vote of no confidence. In a truly absurd situation, the Conservative rebels found themselves voting with the Labour Party for the Social Chapter, calling for the EU to be given greater power over British working life, something they regarded as an evil almost as great as a single currency. The argument was that all tactics were justified if they could defeat the Treaty, but it was far from an easy position to explain to anyone else. 'How can it be principled to vote with the opposition in favour of something which, on principle, you are absolutely opposed to?' wondered Edward Heath during the debate.

A tie on the Labour proposal was settled by the Speaker casting her vote, according to convention, with the government, since the amendment had not been passed. The second vote, however, was clear-cut: twenty-three Tories sided with the opposition and the government motion was rejected by a majority of eight. For such a major piece of government legislation to be decisively rejected on the floor of the House was almost unheard of, and the excitement was so great that even the normally aloof Tony Benn found himself joining in the uproar. 'I must admit I waved my order paper, a thing I've never done before in my life,' he confessed to his diary.

The defeat was not unexpected, and John Major's prepared response was immediately to put down a motion of confidence in the government and its position on the Social Chapter. If the government lost that vote, it would fall and a general election would follow at a time when the Conservatives could hardly be less popular; large numbers of Tory MPs would be out of a job. It was a shrewd move that outwitted the rebels. 'The prime minister's got the party by the goolies,' admitted Teresa Gorman on television the next morning. Even so, it was an unequivocal admission of weakness that for the time in post-war Britain, a majority government felt the need to call for a vote of confidence in itself.

The confidence debate ended with a speech by Douglas Hurd that, if only one could believe him capable of such subversion, sounded as though he were mocking Major as the reincarnation of Chauncey Gardiner, the naive sage played by Peter Sellers in the 1979 film *Being There*: 'Under the leadership of the prime minister, we have cultivated the land well despite much rough weather. We have sown good seed and we can now work together to bring in a good harvest.' It was enough. The government carried its motion with ease, with a majority of thirty-eight reluctant votes. More than three hundred hours of parliamentary time had been devoted to the subject and seventy-five votes taken in the Commons, but finally the Maastricht Treaty had passed onto the statute books.

The animosity that had become so evident, however, did not dissipate, and the genie of Euroscepticism, having been let out of the bottle, was reluctant to return. The dissident faction within the Conservative Party had operated as though it were a separate entity, complete with its own meetings, briefings and whips; all it lacked was a catchy name. This omission was to be rectified by John Major himself. Following that final vote, he gave an interview to Michael Brunson of ITN and, unaware that he was still being taped, continued the conversation after the formal interview had concluded. As Major tried to explain the problems of leading 'a party that is still harking back to the golden age that never was and is now invented', Brunson asked whether it was true that three cabinet ministers had threatened to resign over Europe. Major's response was amongst his more memorable quotes: 'Do we want three more of the bastards out there?' The three he had in mind were generally considered to be Michael Portillo, Peter Lilley and John Redwood.

In the 1980s the left wing of the Conservative Party had taken up Margaret Thatcher's disparaging reference to them as 'wets' and adopted it as a badge of identity. The 'bastards' — at least those outside the cabinet — did precisely the same; indeed, Teresa Gorman titled her 1993 book about the Maastricht rebellion *The Bastards*. Lord Kilmuir, who served in Harold Macmillan's cabinet, had once famously claimed that 'Loyalty is the Tories' secret weapon.' Now disloyalty had become a very public form of self-harm, and there was no sign that it might end.

Sniping from the right was to continue throughout Major's period in office, even if those in the cabinet protested their fidelity in public. 'There is no vacancy for the leadership,' insisted Michael Portillo. 'It does us great harm as a party for there to be speculation, to create the idea we are always looking to the next leader and trading in our leaders.' No one believed him, and the true allegiance of Eurosceptic Tories was mostly perceived to be more accurately reflected by John Bird and John Fortune's fictional MP: 'I'm as strong and loyal a supporter of John Major as anybody, but he is the most craven apology for a person that you can possibly imagine.' Nor was there any indication that Major might forgive and forget. A year later he was heard saying, again to Michael Brunson: 'I'm going to fucking crucify the right for what they've done.'

When the story of Major's comment about 'the bastards' became public knowledge, Gyles Brandreth wrote despairingly in his diary: 'I don't see how the prime minister can struggle on for four more years like this — lurching from shambles to disaster to catastrophe. If it weren't so heartbreaking, it would be very funny.' And from those who weren't Conservative MPs or supporters of the government, there was indeed a chuckle of *schadenfreude* to be heard.

The violence of Major's language was a long way from the calm, courteous image that had been his chief attraction, so far removed that it was hard to see him ever recovering his reputation. Worse still, his comments were seen as expressing not strength and determination but merely pique. Thatcher had very publicly sacked, demoted and humiliated the wets in her cabinet, the likes of Norman St John-Stevas, James Prior and Francis Pym; she hadn't whinged to a television journalist about how threatening their presence on the back benches might be. By contrast, no one really believed that Major was going to crucify his right-wing critics.

Nor did he. There was a moment of angered resistance when he rejected a Eurosceptic delegation urging him to make a decisive shift to the right — they wanted Jonathan Aitken, Michael Forsyth and Neil Hamilton to be appointed to the cabinet — but the pattern became depressingly familiar. Over the next few years, as the issue of Europe repeatedly resurfaced, Major again and again found that seeking the middle ground was seen only as falling between two stools; he was caught in an unenviable position where appeasing his party critics was both politically expedient and electorally damaging.

In March 1994 the imminent enlargement of the EU raised new questions. Austria, Sweden and Finland were due to join (Norway had also applied but did not pursue entry when its people rejected the idea in a referendum), and it became apparent that for the Union to continue functioning, a change would have to be made to the system of qualified majority voting. As it currently stood, each large country was allocated ten votes in the Council of Ministers, with the smaller countries having either three or four, making a total of ninety votes available. For a proposal to be vetoed, it required twenty-three dissenting votes – two large countries and a small one. Now it was suggested that the threshold should be increased to twenty-seven, making it much harder to block the will of the majority.

This, John Major made clear, was unacceptable to Britain. There would be 'no surrender' on the issue. Challenged in the Commons by Giles Radice, he played heavily to his Eurosceptic colleagues and tried his best to open a dividing line with Labour, accusing John Smith of giving in to European demands and mocking him as 'Monsieur Oui, the poodle of Brussels'. (He later apologised for that comment: 'It was a gratuitous and graceless accusation, and I knew it as soon as the words left my lips.') When he subsequently failed to make good on his promises in the negotiations, and Britain was forced into a climb-down, he looked all the weaker for having made it such a point of unbending principle. 'It was a most humiliating retreat, and it hurt badly,' he admitted in his memoirs.

He reported back to the Commons – on his fifty-first birthday – and was met with mocking jeers from the opposition and what Michael Spicer called 'an uproar of sullen silence' from his own benches. The one exception on the Tory side was Tony Marlow, a prominent backbench bastard, who pulled no punches: 'My right honourable friend has no authority, credibility or identifiable policy in this vital area. Why doesn't he stand aside and make way for somebody else who can provide the party and the country with direction and leadership?'

Marlow lacked the authority with which Leo Amery had delivered the killer blow to Neville Chamberlain in 1940 ('In the name of God, go!'), but he was articulating a commonly held view. 'The balance of probability is that Michael Heseltine will be prime minister by the end of the year,' wrote Andrew Marr in the *Independent*, while an editorial in *The Times* pointed out this was just the latest in a long line of failures by Major: 'There is a limit to the number of chances even the most naturally loyal of MPs is prepared to give him.' It concluded ominously: 'Those who want better leadership had better start planning for it now.'

Such calls were temporarily silenced just weeks later with the abrupt death of John Smith. The immediate reaction of most MPs in all parties was one of stunned disbelief, but mere mortality seldom impedes the path of politics, and it was only a matter of hours before calculations were being made on both sides. Amongst some Conservatives there was a sense of relief that the pressure was, at least for the moment, off their beleaguered leader: 'So, God's a Tory after all,' one was reported to have commented. For others, it seemed more like the end of a dream. 'By lunchtime my parliamentary enemies were briefing the press about the implications of John's death for my own future,' wrote Michael Heseltine, who had himself suffered a heart attack the previous year. Smith's unexpected demise suddenly made the idea of a Heseltine premiership look a much more risky proposition. A week earlier the BBC had commissioned a survey of people who had voted Conservative in 1992 but who now said they wouldn't do so again: 58 per cent had said that Major should resign, with Heseltine the clear favourite to replace him. Now that possibility receded very rapidly, and the consensus in the parliamentary party was that Major had to be allowed to limp on for a little longer.

Still seeking a compromise formula that would keep his warring party together, Major began to talk about 'a multi-speed Europe', with the implication that Britain would be travelling in the slow lane. It was a short-lived proposal, however. Quite apart from being contrary to the will of the EU, it suggested that everyone was headed in the same direction, which was precisely what the Eurosceptics disapproved of; it was the destination as well as the speed of travel to which they objected. In any event, the public were unimpressed. The elections to the European Parliament in June 1994 dealt Major another humiliation; Labour took sixty-two of the eighty-seven seats available and the Conservatives were reduced to less than one per cent of the vote in five constituencies.

And still the internal hostilities continued. In November 1994 legislation was required to increase Britain's contribution to the EU budget and Major tried again to demand loyalty from his MPs, insisting that this was yet another issue of confidence in the government. The European Finance Bill was duly passed, but eight Tories abstained on a Labour amendment and, belatedly displaying a trace of firm leadership, Major withdrew from them the Conservative Party whip. The group included several of those who had become such familiar faces on the nation's television screens during the Maastricht troubles — Teresa Gorman, Tony Marlow and Teddy Taylor amongst them — and they were joined by a ninth, Richard Body, who evidently had no appetite for comfort when martyrdom was on offer; he resigned the whip in solidarity.

These were still a minority, of course, and there were plenty of loyalists, including most notably on this occasion Lord James Douglas-Hamilton, who had succeeded to the title of 11th Earl of Selkirk a couple of days earlier, but renounced his peerage simply so he could stay in the Commons and support the government. (He was rewarded after the 1997 election with a life peerage.) But it was the whipless wonders, as they were immediately dubbed, who attracted all the headlines. They seemed to care nothing about being cast into the outer darkness, instead taking the opportunity to vote down the government's proposed rise in VAT on domestic fuel, and to raise their media profiles still further. In due course they were readmitted to the party in April 1995, an event they saw as a further sign of their prime minister's weakness. 'The whips capitulated,' crowed Teresa Gorman. The rebels celebrated by giving television interviews to announce that they felt no remorse for their actions. It was 'a victory parade', the new Labour leader, Tony Blair, said at prime minister's questions, before delivering what was to become his most famous jibe at Major: 'I lead my party, he follows his.'

While the arguments over Maastricht remained obscure for most of the public, there were elements of European integration that made a more immediate impact on everyday life, particularly the transformation of British shopping wrought by the arrival of European retailers. At the beginning of the decade five companies – Tesco, Sainsbury's, Safeway, Gateway and Asda – dominated British food retailing, between them controlling 60 per cent of the market. This highly lucrative business offered a profit margin of 8 per cent, way above the European average for food retail of just 2 per cent. It was a discrepancy that convinced foreign retailers to enter the British market, pitching themselves as the low-price alternative. Aldi and Netto, from Germany and Denmark respectively, arrived in 1990, followed by Lidl, another German company, and by the American discounters Costco. Yet another German firm, Rewe, became the biggest shareholder in Budgen and created the Penny Market chain.

The potential for profit was enhanced by a revolution in the weekly rhythm of shopping. In 1986 the Conservative government had suffered a rare Commons defeat when the churches and the trade unions had found common cause in rejecting a reform of Sunday trading legislation. A subsequent appeal to the European Court of Justice clarified that this was purely a matter for national governments, but the major retailers resolved not to wait any longer. In the weeks before Christmas 1990, hundreds of shops, led by DIY chains and supermarkets, simply ignored the law and opened on Sundays. The practice was repeated in December 1991 and then extended, past Christmas and into the New Year.

By the end of 1992 the likes of B&Q, Asda and Sainsbury's each had hundreds of stores open on Sundays, although it was illegal, and the newspapers were reporting that 'Sunday shopping is now a fact of life.' Twelve months later, Parliament conceded defeat, passing new legislation to permit retailers to do what they were already doing, though, in a token compromise, larger premises were restricted to just six hours of trading on the Sabbath.

Meanwhile, the foreign invasion that had started in the north was now marching rapidly southwards, accompanied by an expansion of the native chain Kwik-Save, and provoked a wave of price-cutting amongst the established supermarkets, led by Somerfield (as Gateway had been rebranded). Cheaper own-label ranges such as Sainsbury's Essentials and Safeway Savers were launched, and by late 1994 tinned goods and Christmas turkeys were being offered at prices that had reverted to the levels of the 1970s. The price of cornflakes fell so low in Shoprite that Kellogg's refused to continue supplying the chain. Other forms of resistance to the foreign threat included the introduction of loyalty cards (starting with Tesco in 1995) and an expansion into non-food categories; newsagents, chemists and clothes departments were now common, and videos, books and CDs followed. The tactics proved successful, containing the hard discounters to less than 10 per cent at the bottom of the market, and gradually the older retailers began to emphasise quality again rather than merely price; in 1995 Sainsbury's replaced its advertising slogan 'Where good food costs less' with the more positive 'Everyone's favourite ingredient'.

As the dust settled, it became clear that the winners were Asda — whose chief executive, Archie Norman, was shortly to be elected as the Conservative MP for Tunbridge Wells — and Tesco, who had taken over as the biggest food retailer in the country and were now looking further afield, opening stores in France and Hungary. The losers were the chains like Somerfield, Kwik-Save and Iceland (the first two merged in 1998), who found themselves squeezed and unable to compete with the relentless price-cutting that saw baked beans fall to a penny a tin.

Associated with this was a change in the geography of retail development. Starting in the 1970s, but reaching a peak in the ten years from 1985, the big chains had concentrated their expansion on building huge superstores on out-of-town sites, to the detriment of smaller outlets and high streets. The appeal of such ventures was clear from the numbers thronging to shop in them, but there were costs involved in the rise of the superstore. 'It's a cancer,' remarks a character in Peter Lovesey's novel *Upon a Dark Night*, 'scarring the countryside and bleeding the life out of the city centres.' The environmental impact was substantial, for the out-of-town stores came complete with massive car parks, and the average distance travelled to go shopping rose by 14 per cent between 1990 and 1995.

A potential answer to this latter issue was the introduction of statutory parking charges for such shopping centres, a policy that was tentatively proposed by the Labour Party before being dropped in 1998. Some saw a connection between the abandonment of the idea and the donations made to political parties by the supermarkets and by individuals associated with them. Tesco was a major sponsor of the Millennium Dome project, with a £12 million contribution, and a key partner in Labour's New Deal programme, while David Sainsbury, chairman of the family grocery business, was said to have become the biggest individual donor in Labour Party history; following the award of a peerage in 1997, he was appointed as a science minister the following year.

In any event, the arrival of the European retailers effectively brought an end to out-of-town expansion. The major British firms had already secured most of the sites they required, and in the mid-1990s they cooperated with John Selwyn Gummer, the environment secretary, on a change in planning procedures that made consent for any such developments in the future considerably more difficult to obtain. There was the unmistakable sound of a ladder being pulled up to prevent others from following. Instead, their power further entrenched, Tesco and Sainsbury's spearheaded a return to the high streets, now largely denuded of competition.

Meanwhile other businesses were also arriving from Europe. They included an enterprising broadcaster who took advantage of the Single Market regulations to set up the satellite television channel Red Hot Dutch, aiming the signal directly at Britain. The channel transmitted more explicit pornography than was legally available in the country at the time but, since such material was permissible in Europe, it broke no laws. The service didn't come cheap – the decoder cost £100, followed by a subscription of just under £50 a quarter – but was competitively priced compared with under-the-counter material in Soho, where a video of 'two hours of animals' would set you back £150.

Not that Red Hot Dutch, or its imitators, offered anything as extreme as footage of zoophilia. Rather their major themes were orgies, lesbian sex and anal intercourse, which was enough to horrify William Rees-Mogg, chairman of the Broadcasting Standards Council. 'It reminds me of films about concentration camps where you felt humans were deliberately reduced to subhuman status,' he shuddered. 'It is as unpleasant as being taken into an abattoir to view a series of butcheries.' More soberly, the shadow home secretary joined in the denunciations. 'I am appalled,' said Tony Blair about the broadcasts. 'There must be a risk of children seeing them. The law should be changed.' A special parliamentary screening of material culled from Red Hot Dutch attracted a substantial audience of MPs and peers, all hoping to be equally outraged, though some left disappointed. 'Seen much worse,' muttered one member of the upper chamber, as he wandered out of the screening.

The channel was officially banned in 1993, which meant only that would-be viewers had to buy a smart card on the Continent if they wished to receive the broadcasts, and the same pattern was repeated in the cases of TV Erotica in 1995 and Rendez-Vous in 1996, by which time the internet was making such Canute-like gestures redundant. The market for hardcore European pornography was in any event somewhat limited. Red Hot Dutch attracted only 20,000 subscribers in Britain (perhaps it would have been more had the rugby league club Salford accepted the offer of a million-pound shirt sponsorship deal), compared to the 135,000 who received the Adult Channel, a legal, softcore broadcaster which came under the remit of the Independent Television Commission. On the other hand, a survey of Adult Channel viewers found that 87 per cent of them wanted more explicit material. In a characteristically British muddle, no one was completely satisfied.

While the private sector was transforming these areas of retailing and leisure, the governmental institutions of Europe were still regarded with deep suspicion in Britain. During Margaret Thatcher's last days in power the *Sun* had produced one of its most striking front pages ever: a photograph of Jacques Delors, president of the European Commission, accompanied by a two-finger salute and the headline UP YOURS DELORS. The story concerned the attempt to create a single currency, but the detail was of little importance compared with the general attitude, which could have been taken as a statement of intent by much of the British media.

It was partly in an attempt to overcome such unhelpful images that the Commission announced in 1991 the creation of a 120-episode multilingual TV soap opera, *Channel 6 Live!*, centred on a European television station taken over by a foreign media tycoon, who drops European programmes in favour of American shows. 'According to the commission's media directorate,' reported the *Sunday Times*, 'the soap will deal with the "struggle" to "stem the tide of American media" polluting Europe's airwaves.' Since the *Sunday*

Times was a stable mate of BSkyB, the foreign-owned television network that provided an outlet for so much American programming, this wasn't a project that met with wholehearted approval, and the paper was pleased to reveal the following year that the plans had been quietly abandoned.

Clearly, though, there was something in the air, and in 1992 the BBC launched a thrice-weekly soap opera titled *Eldorado*, set in Spain and similarly multilingual in content, though the focus was on British expatriates. It seemed like a winner. The setting was familiar: quite apart from the longstanding attraction of the country as a holiday destination, somewhere around 160,000 Britons were by now living in Spain and the number was growing, many of them retirees with visiting families. At a time when Australian soaps — *Neighbours* and *Home and Away* — were at the peak of their popularity, bringing sun and fun to a recession-hit Britain, the idea of a soap set on the Costa del Sol was surely irresistible. Unfortunately, the public decided to resist, and did so in their droves. The show that was intended to replicate the runaway success of *EastEnders* rapidly fell out of the television top thirty and, though audiences eventually recovered a little, it was soon cancelled by a deeply embarrassed BBC, having lasted just a year.

By then, the Corporation was struggling too with its other great European project, a lavishly expensive version of Peter Mayle's 1989 book *A Year in Provence*, which starred John Thaw as the former advertising executive and dramatised his adventures in a small French village. This time, it must have been assumed, nothing could go wrong. The book had sold two million copies and Thaw, one of television's biggest stars on the back of *Inspector Morse*, had been lured from ITV: it was the dream combination. A massive publicity campaign ensured that the first episode pulled in 14.5 million viewers, but within two weeks the programme had lost over five million of them and a BBC executive was reflecting: 'It's supposed to last twelve weeks, so you wonder if anyone will still be watching it at the end.' By the time *A Year in Provence* dragged itself over the finishing line — a proposed second series having long since been jettisoned — barely seven million viewers were left. The critics were no more impressed than the public. 'What could possibly explain such a flabby blancmange of condescension and dullness?' wondered Craig Brown. 'The only explanation that springs to mind is that after a close reading of the book the director, screenwriter and actors grew to loathe the smug, misanthropic, patronising posturings of Peter Mayle with such a passion that they sought to expose them by parody on prime-time television.'

Worse yet, the programme was being routinely mocked on other shows, including *Spitting Image* and *Drop the Dead Donkey*. 'You know you sponsored me a pound for every minute I could sit through *A Year in Provence*?' said Dave to Henry, in the latter. 'Well, you owe me 90p.' Even David Blunkett was moved to write to *The Times*, deploring the state of the BBC: 'From what I gather, no one viewing *Eldorado* or *A Year in Provence* could claim that standards are improving.'

ITV, without the BBC's institutional enthusiasm for all things European, opted instead to bring William Donaldson's magnificent creation, Henry Root, to the screen with *Root into Europe* (1992). A retired wet-fish merchant, whose politics made Margaret Thatcher look soft on criminals and foreigners by comparison, Root was intended as a parody of the Englishman abroad, though the central appeal of the show was hearing him air his prejudices about Europeans. The Italians, he explained, 'can have relations with you on the dance floor without you knowing a thing about it till you get home at night'. Shot on a much lower budget than *A Year in Provence*, and starring George Cole, it too failed to win over a decent-sized audience, but at least it didn't become a source of ridicule.

Nor did European issues attract much of a positive spin elsewhere on television. In *Cold Feet* (1998) a middle-class woman, on being told by her husband that he's invested money in what he calls 'a sure thing', a golf course in a Marxist dictatorship in Africa, retorts: 'So what other "sure things" are we investing in? An off-licence in Saudi? A nightclub in Iran? Euro-bloody-Tunnel?' And he admits, somewhat apologetically, that he does indeed have shares in Eurotunnel.

That such shareholders would be met with the pitying contempt normally reserved for an *Eldorado* actor was drawn from life. The idea of a tunnel connecting Britain and France had been talked about for the best part of two centuries before the project started in earnest at the end of the 1980s. It was scheduled to cost £5 billion and to be open in May 1993. In April that year the company behind the scheme admitted that it didn't know when the tunnel would be open, but that it should come in at a shade under £10 billion. An official opening was held in May 1994, just a year late, though it took a further few months before services commenced, and no one was expecting a dividend on their shares for years to come.

The Channel Tunnel eventually worked, of course – the concept was perfectly sound – but its troubled construction seemed emblematic of Britain's difficulties in trying to integrate into Europe. There was widely believed to be greater enthusiasm amongst the younger generation, but it was not always clear that this amounted to anything more than clubbers making their way to Ibiza or 'following the herd down to Greece' (in the words of Blur's song 'Girls and Boys') on the promise of easy, no-strings-attached sex. As Club 18-30 put it in a 1995 advertising campaign, BEAVER ESPAÑA, an image satirised in Harry Enfield's film *Kevin and Perry Go Large* (2000), which sees the eponymous teenagers attempt to lose their virginity in Ibiza.

The real-life Kevins and Perrys replaced football hooligans as the British export the government was least likely to boast about. In 1998 Michael Birkett announced that he was resigning as Britain's vice-consul in Ibiza because he had seen enough. 'In a moment of anger recently I said I would like to gas the lot of them,' he told the press; 'clearly I don't mean that. But I became so angry at the degrading behaviour and the bad name Britain is getting in Europe that I knew it was time to leave.'

As the decade wore on, there was no discernible shift in cultural attitudes to Europe. Occasionally a cult movie emerged, such as *Il Postino* (1994) and *Amélie* (2001), but continental cinema never came close to the successes of the American and British film industries, and even in the foreign-language stakes, they were eclipsed by Ang Lee's *Crouching Tiger, Hidden Dragon* (2000). In music there was nothing to compete with the influence of America, despite the occasional hit record for a pop act like 2 Unlimited or a critically acclaimed band like Air or the Cardigans. Spain and France proved ever more popular places to retire to, but that merely reflected the recovery of house prices in Britain and the corresponding attractiveness of cheap property abroad. And although much of the increased tourist trade was facilitated by the EU's deregulation of the air industry, allowing the emergence of budget carriers like Ryanair and EasyJet, the EU enjoyed no benefit in terms of public gratitude. In short, the hostility of UP YOURS DELORS might have faded a little, but the suspicion still remained.

John Major's last great struggle with Europe was yet to come, though the first warning bell had been sounded in 1993, when the German health minister went on the record to say that he was not convinced of the safety of British beef. His comments provoked a consumer scare in his own country, and British beef exports to Germany, which had never been very substantial, collapsed completely. It was not the end of the story.

The issue dated back to the Thatcher years, when – following an intensification of farming methods – there had been an outbreak amongst British cattle of bovine spongiform encephalopathy (BSE), commonly known as mad cow disease. This might, some suggested, be causally linked to variant Creutzfeldt-Jakob disease (vCJD), a fatal brain condition in humans. The reality of that connection had never been conclusively demonstrated, and the then agriculture minister, John Selwyn Gummer, had shown his scorn for such concerns in a famous photo-opportunity where his daughter took a bite out of a British beefburger (though it later transpired that she hadn't actually eaten it). Even so, the existence of BSE itself was sufficient to have prompted a slaughter of infected animals and the banning in 1989 of the use of sheep and cattle carcasses in cattle feed, this having been determined to be the likely cause of the epidemic. The sale of cows' brains for human consumption was also banned.

In March 1996 the nightmare resurfaced when the government was advised for the first time of scientific concern that BSE might indeed be linked to vCJD, several cases of which had now appeared. The data were still inconclusive at this stage, but quite properly the information that did exist was passed on to Parliament. Predictably the Labour Party, which had no great stake in the votes of farmers, saw the issue as simply another weapon with which to assault the government; Harriet Harman, the party's health spokesperson, led the charge with her denunciation of 'the government's reckless disregard for public health'. Even more predictably the media — seldom noted for their capacity to understand the concept of scientific risk — responded with panic reporting and horror stories about an impending apocalypse. WE'VE ALREADY EATEN 1,000,000 MAD COWS: 'BORROWED TIME' FEAR ran the *Daily Mirror* headline, echoed by the *Sun*'s MAD COW ALERT OVER KIDS, while the *Daily Mail*, having clearly given the matter some considerable thought, ran the front-page headline: COULD IT BE WORSE THAN AIDS?

The result was an immediate crisis of public confidence and a further blow to the beef industry, which had anyway been in decline since 1980, well before the BSE scare. McDonald's and Burger King announced they wouldn't be using British beef, education authorities withdrew the meat from school menus, and sales fell by 90 per cent. There was a similar consumer boycott abroad, and the European Commission swiftly imposed a ban on British beef exports not just to other countries within the EU, but to the whole world.

This move by Europe took the debate into uncertain legal territory. The EU's actions plainly had nothing to do with genuine health concerns, for if the well-being of consumers had been the motivation, then presumably the sale of British beef would also have been banned in Britain itself. Indeed Franz Fischler, the EU's agriculture commissioner who was partially responsible for the ban, was quite clear that this was not a safety issue. 'I would not hesitate to eat beef in England,' he commented. 'I know no medical reason not to.' Instead the decision to stop all exports of British beef was an attempt to contain the political — rather than the actual — contamination, an operation designed to protect farmers elsewhere in Europe from being dragged into the mess.

It was hard to see it as anything more than the adoption as policy of those tabloid scare stories, by a European Commission that turned out to have supra-parliamentary power over a key British industry. And, not unexpectedly, it aroused the fury of Eurosceptics. 'Why the hell should the foreigners in Brussels forbid Britain from exporting beef to countries outside Europe?' demanded Norman Tebbit, while even the pro-European Michael Heseltine sounded shaken: 'For those who believe Britain's best interests are served at the heart of Europe, this has been a testing experience.'

Behind the political arguments, BSE presented a genuine problem. By the summer of 1996 two hundred new cases a week were being reported, and the first deaths from vCJD had been recorded, though by the end of the crisis these turned out to be numbered in the dozens, rather than the tens of thousands that had been threatened in some quarters. 'I have never been so worried about anything since I first came into the House,' John Major told Paddy Ashdown, as the saga started. 'I think we could be presiding over the collapse of a £20 billion industry, with incalculable consequences for jobs.' He added, somewhat plaintively: 'I'm scared stiff. I simply don't know what to do.'

The government's response was drastic but politically necessary. At an estimated cost of over £4 billion, some three and a half million cattle were slaughtered and their corpses burnt. It was a true holocaust in the purest sense of the word, as the journalist Boris Johnson took pleasure in pointing out, and it raised enormous logistical problems. Around the country there built up huge piles of carcasses awaiting incineration, some of which, it was revealed, were being secretly dumped at landfill sites in an attempt to clear the backlog. Discussions opened with the power industry to see if it was worth converting generating stations to run on dead animals, though this was not pursued, perhaps because the idea of cattle replacing coal as a primary fuel would be the mother of all PR disasters for a government already perceived to have lost its way. Public confidence was hardly helped by press stories like the *Daily Mirror*'s MAD COW GERMS MAY BE IN OUR AIR, which warned that not even fire might be sufficient to destroy the infection and that 'deadly germs' could escape: 'The bugs come from burning carcasses and could be breathed in or absorbed through the eye.'

But even without coverage couched in the language of a poor 1950s science fiction movie, the crisis would have had serious political implications. To the public, the government simply looked incompetent. No allowance would be made for the enormity of the undertaking, and every stumble on the way was greeted with a combination of fury and ridicule. Much of the latter was directed at the hapless agriculture secretary, Douglas Hogg, whose habit of wearing a broad-brimmed fedora made him a distinctively absurd figure on television news bulletins.

The sale of beef on the bone was banned, to the annoyance of those who relished T-bone steaks and oxtail soup, and the only option for the meat industry itself seemed to be grim fatalism and black humour. 'Buy our burgers,' read a sign in one Essex butcher's. 'You will not get better.' Meanwhile, on the EU front, the issue descended to a level of surrealistic bathos with the Battle of the Bulls' Semen.

In April 1996 Britain asked for a partial relaxation of the export ban in relation to three beef-related products: gelatine, tallow and bull semen. The EU turned down the request and Major lost his temper, telling the Commons that Britain would veto all European proposals until the issue had been resolved: 'We cannot continue business as usual within Europe when we are faced with this clear disregard by some of our partners of reason, common sense and Britain's national interests.'

This was precisely the kind of attitude that Eurosceptics wanted to see and the *Sun* leapt into the fray, helpfully running a list of 'twenty things to steer clear of' if we wanted 'to hit back at the nations that voted against us'. Amongst the suggestions were port wine, Hugo Boss suits, Mercedes cars, shares in Luxembourgish banks and – possibly a more plausible target for *Sun* readers – German pornography. 'All the sickest videos come straight out of Germany,' the paper noted, which must have given a boost to sales of such material.

Major's campaign of non-cooperation, paralysing Europe in the name of British bulls' semen, was not very long-lived. In June 1996 he announced he was calling it off, having been given assurances about a schedule for lifting the beef ban, though even the block on exporting meat from grass-fed cattle in Northern Ireland was relaxed only in September 1997, and it was August 1999 before it all finally ended. Even then, Germany said it wasn't yet ready to accept British imports, France decided unilaterally to maintain the ban, and at the Lord Mayor's Banquet later in the year, the French ambassador pointedly refused to eat beef (though his wife did).

Meanwhile the British farming industry had taken another beating from what it saw as centralising, standardising, politically motivated bureaucrats, whose knowledge of agriculture was regarded with little respect. If a Conservative government was unable to stand up for the interests of farmers, it suggested that the relationship between town and country was far from healthy. There was a growing dissatisfaction in rural areas with the behaviour of officialdom and the declining profitability of farming. The comedian Bob Monkhouse, who presented the National Lottery on television, used to tell a story about interviewing a cattle farmer who'd won £7 million. When asked what he'd do with the money, he replied: 'I reckon I'll just keep on farming till it's gone.'

For John Major, the BSE story was another indication of just how unlucky a prime minister he was. The real issue with vCJD, which had a long and unpredictable incubation period, lay not in present policies but in those of the past, in the BSE epidemic of the late 1980s. The same was true of many other difficulties he encountered, from coal mining to Europe itself. As the Eurosceptic MP Terry Dicks pointed out: 'The problems facing this country over Europe are the problems created by Mrs Thatcher when she took us into the Single European Act. The Maastricht Treaty, by comparison, is like a pimple on an elephant's bum.'

More broadly, the problem with Britain's relationship with Europe was that the country often felt and behaved as though it were the odd man out, for the very good reason, as cabinet minister Gillian Shephard pointed out, 'that, in many ways, we *were* the odd man out. Our legal and welfare systems had developed in different ways; our democracy was exercised differently; and we had been a unified nation for longer than the other major states.' The concept of European harmonisation had great resonance amongst those countries who had endured the consequences of two centuries of conflict between France and Prussia; it had less in Britain, which hadn't been invaded for over nine hundred years, and whose borders had remained intact for centuries. Where the British had become obsessed with preserving and venerating their history, the European project was largely concerned, in the words of Tristan Garel-Jones, with nations 'burying their ghosts'.

There was too a conflict of political style. Britain's electoral system generally produced majority governments for a single party, and its default position was one of antagonistic hostility and tribal loyalty, quite distinct from the coalition-building, consensual approach common in most European countries. No British politician, not even the usually emollient John Major, had any experience of cross-party coalition, and all had grown up in the abrasive world of the House of Commons. It left them ill-prepared to deal with their colleagues on the Continent. 'When British ministers spoke the language of Westminster in Brussels,' remarked Major, 'it was like spitting in church.'

And there was a longstanding reluctance amongst much of the population to the idea of giving up control of the nation's affairs. This had traditionally been a feature of the left in Britain. Back in the early 1950s, when the European Coal and Steel Community – the ultimate forerunner of the EU

— was being founded, Labour's former foreign secretary Herbert Morrison had been clear that Britain should have no part of the new venture. 'We can't do it,' he insisted. 'The Durham miners will never wear it.' A decade later and the Labour leader, Hugh Gaitskell, was arguing against joining in the developing project, warning that Britain risked becoming 'no more than Texas or California in the United States of Europe. It means the end of a thousand years of history.' On the Continent itself, by contrast, that very concept had long been a dream of the left; an 1867 congress in Geneva, organised by the revolutionary League of Peace and Liberty and attended by the likes of Victor Hugo, Giuseppe Garibaldi and Mikhail Bakunin, had looked forward to 'the establishment of a confederation of free democracies constituting the United States of Europe'.

By the 1990s, Labour had changed its position and was actively embracing this form of internationalism, while many right-wing Conservatives were influenced by Margaret Thatcher's belated belief that integration had gone too far. For most of the public, however, the truth was that Europe seldom featured very high on their list of political priorities. There was a vociferous minority who were adamantly opposed, and a slightly smaller number who grumbled that Britain was dragging its feet, but in the middle was a majority who, if asked, would express discontent with what was seen as interference from Brussels, but who had other concerns on their minds. The danger of the political class's obsession with Europe was that it seemed to be obscuring more immediate domestic issues, as though the electorate were being ignored. Paul Davies, a trade union official and chair of the Labour Party in the Wirral, summed up the perception in 1993: 'People are asked to take pay cuts in NHS Trust hospitals and they turn on the telly and it's some peculiar argument about Maastricht that the leadership's worried about.'

This sense of a broken connection between the interests of the people and those of their parliament was bolstered by a sense that politicians were sometimes less than conscientious about their responsibilities. Margaret Thatcher was later to confess, in regard to the Single European Act, that 'We didn't read the small print', but she failed to address the question of why they had not done so, that surely being part of the duties of a government negotiating such treaties. ('It was the small print wot done us,' reflected Michael Spicer.) Similarly in 1992 the home secretary Kenneth Clarke admitted cheerfully that he had not actually got through the whole of the Maastricht Treaty. 'Nobody out there has read it,' he said. 'I have never read it.' Furthermore, he suggested, he doubted whether John Major had read it either.

Admittedly the Treaty was a very long and very dull document, couched in the densest of legal jargon, but Clarke did have the advantage over most of the population that he was a Queen's Counsel, and presumably was therefore capable of penetrating its murky depths on the public's behalf. From the other side of the House, Peter Mandelson demonstrated an equally cavalier attitude to detail, accusing Labour opponents of Maastricht of being 'overly obsessed by the words'. None of which augured well for the future; in the absence of scrutiny, the possibility existed that troubles were being stored up for a later generation.

There was, furthermore, some confusion in the minds of the electorate as to the precise extent of the European Union. The distinction was unclear, for example, between the EU itself and the Council of Europe, the latter founded in 1949 by ten countries including Britain, to uphold the principles of human rights and parliamentary democracy. Or between the European Court of Human Rights, which came under the auspices of the Council, and the European Court of Justice, which was a part of the European Union. Even for those who did keep track of these niceties, there was a strong suspicion that the public's perplexity might not be accidental.

In 1985 the EEC adopted both the flag of the Council of Europe – a circle of twelve golden stars on a blue background – and its anthem, an arrangement of Beethoven's 'Ode to Joy' (the music that had once been the anthem of Ian Smith's white regime in Rhodesia). It also launched its own celebration of Europe Day, an annual event occurring just four days after the existing Europe Day, which commemorated the foundation of the Council of Europe. For two decades the Council of Europe and the European Parliament even shared the same building in Strasbourg. When the lines were this blurred, it was hard to avoid the notion that some kind of game was being played and that, whatever the governing class of Europe was up to, it was unlikely to be in the interests of greater democracy.

Certainly there was little in the story of John Major's relations with Europe to sound an encouraging note. Shortly after taking office he had used a speech in Bonn to differentiate his leadership style from that of Margaret Thatcher. 'My aims for the Community can be simply stated,' he explained to his audience at the Adenauer Foundation. 'I want us to be where we belong. At the very heart of Europe.' There was no reason to doubt his intentions, but his attempts at cooperation were not always reciprocated. On Black Wednesday he had asked for help from Germany and found his call unheeded. Yet still he persevered. 'I could have played to the gallery, and thrown the Maastricht Bill away, and donned a John Bull shirt,' he told his biographer, Penny Junor, in 1993. But had he done so, he argued, Britain would have been 'excluded from the decisions in Europe, when we were still in the Community but other people were making decisions for us'. He thus had every right to feel seriously aggrieved when the beef ban proved that, despite his best endeavours, others were indeed making those decisions. His loyalty to the European project had earned him no Brownie points whatsoever.

When he won the 1992 election with a majority of twenty-one seats, Major was considered to be in a strong position in the Commons, but over the course of that Parliament, his majority was cut again and again by by-election defeats, defections and expulsions. Even so, he had been dealt a better hand than had, say, the 1970s Labour government of Harold Wilson, which started as a minority administration and gained a majority of three seats only at a second attempt. Major's misfortunes were ultimately not of the electorate's making, but of his own. In his approach to Europe – the single most far-reaching foreign policy issue of his premiership – he was unable to provide strong leadership, while his failure to explain to the public why Maastricht was such a crucial question did nothing to endear the European Union to Britain.

He did, however, keep the Conservative Party just about together, at a time when it was revealing an unhealthy appetite for devouring itself. By 1995 the defence secretary, Michael Portillo, was briefing journalists that 'it would be better if the party formally split', and suggesting that, in such an event, he would be amongst the 20 per cent who could splinter off to form an out-and-out Eurosceptic alternative. The fact that no such split occurred was itself a tribute to Major's delicate balancing act, as he tried to deal with a party that was busily forgetting the nineteenth-century wisdom of Walter Bagehot. 'The principle of Parliament is obedience to leaders,' Bagehot wrote in *The English Constitution*. 'The penalty of not doing so is the penalty of impotence.' That seemed to be the fate of John Major.

6
Charters
'Caught by the fuzz'

DEAKIN: The Met has never been cleaner, I can tell you that for a
fact. It's also a fact that our clear-up rate for crime is at an all-time
low. What conclusion you draw, Mr Gordon, is entirely up to you.
J.C. Wilshire, *Between the Lines* (1992)

GUS: If this government can't even privatise things properly,
it makes you wonder what's the use of having them at all.
Andy Hamilton & Guy Jenkin, *Drop the Dead Donkey* (1994)

State schools, I used to joke, were so-called because they were in a
'right old state'.
Jenny Eclair, *Camberwell Beauty* (2000)

There is a scene in *A Parliamentary Affair*, the first novel by Edwina Currie, in which a Conservative MP is out canvassing and finds herself in a house being used as a brothel, where the inhabitants prove to be unusually receptive to her call for their votes. 'You can put us girls down. We're in favour of free enterprise, we are,' one of them tells her. 'Citizens' Charter and all that: looking after the customer, innit?' It was a rare sighting of someone with a good word to say about the Citizens' Charter, the big idea (or, at least, said John Patten, the 'medium-sized idea') that was intended to form the centrepiece of John Major's premiership.

Major launched the Charter project in a speech in March 1991, at a time when he was still expected to call an early election that summer, promising that it would reinvigorate the public services and restore their position within society. At its core was the simple principle that services should be run for the benefit of their users, not of their providers, and that there should be a clear statement of intent in each field of activity, against which performance could be judged. 'People who depend on public services – patients, passengers, parents, pupils, benefit claimants – all must know where they stand and what service they have a right to expect,' he explained, as he also raised the possibility that institutions like British Rail might be obliged to refund passengers in the event of particularly poor delivery. Charters were to be drawn up and published by all public services.

It wasn't an entirely new concept, nor was it confined to any one part of the political spectrum. Bryan Gould had already floated a Labour Party proposal that local councils should provide 'customer contracts', while Paddy Ashdown's 1989 book *Citizen's Britain: A Radical Agenda for the 1990s* had addressed the idea of enshrining the rights of individuals when dealing with the state. From the Conservative right, too, there was a growing demand – articulated by John Redwood amongst others – that the Thatcherite reforms of the 1980s should be extended into the public services, with a refocusing on 'customers' and an evaluation by results rather than by expenditure.

Much of the existing debate, however, had the appearance of being rather theoretical and, particularly on the left, of being tied so closely to the constitutional reforms that had become fashionable in recent years – the demand for a written constitution, a new bill of rights and so on – that it looked more like an afterthought than a guiding principle. For Major, by contrast, it was a personal issue and one on which, to the bewilderment of many of his colleagues, he displayed a genuine passion.

It was hard not to see in this commitment an expression of his own story. John Major was the first prime minister to have grown up with the welfare state; he was just five years old when the NHS was created in 1948, by which time his predecessors were already adults, and he made his personal experience clear from the outset. 'I know that for millions of people in this country the National Health Service means security,' he said in his first conference speech as leader. 'I understand that because I am – and have always been – one of those people.' Unlike many of his cabinet colleagues, he remained an NHS patient rather than opting for private medical care.

More than this, though, his early years 'as a young man without money or privilege', including a period of unemployment, had left him dissatisfied with poor standards of customer care and frustrated by the petty reality of dealing with 'anonymous voices and faces' at the local council and the labour exchange. His account would have been recognised by much of the country, if not by many politicians and commentators: 'Offices where correspondence or calls never seemed to be dealt with by the same person and you had to begin from first base, time after time after time.' His suspicion that things had got worse, not better, in recent years lay behind his determination to make the Citizens' Charter a key plank of his appeal to the nation.

He faced, however, two entrenched forces of opposition. First there was the cynicism of the media, many of whose leading figures still yearned for the fundamentalist iconoclasm of Margaret Thatcher's permanent revolution, and who saw all this as being pretty small beer. Much of the criticism was concerned with the everyday triviality of the policy. Was it really that big a deal that driving tests should be available on Saturdays, that parents should be guaranteed a yearly report on their child's educational progress (one child in four didn't get a school report at this stage), or that people shouldn't have to wait so long for a passport to be issued?

Major's argument was that for motorists, parents and holidaymakers, these things were indeed important. He insisted that having areas of the motorway coned off for repairs that were clearly not taking place was a source of unnecessary stress for commuters stuck in the resultant traffic jams. He argued that passengers on the London Underground should be informed when the next train was due; consequently electronic boards began to appear on platforms carrying the information, an innovation later extended to bus stops. And he drew attention to the fact that one of the biggest drains on the social security budget was trying to rectify mistakes in benefits claims; efficiency would save money, as well as removing a cause of misery in claimants' lives.

The mundane nature of these concerns failed to inspire commentators and some aspects were simply ridiculed out of existence. The Radio 2 disc jockey Terry Wogan made great fun of the motorway cones and of Major's response, a phone number, dubbed the Cones Hotline, to which motorists could report unnecessary coning where no work was in progress. For much of the media, that part of the initiative came to symbolise the whole, and when it was announced in 1994 that the Cones Hotline had taken 8,000 calls of complaint in its first two years, but that just three had resulted in cones being lifted, the sound of hollow laughter filled the columns of the press: 'a bad miscarriageway of justice for the long-suffering motorist,' giggled the *Daily Mirror*. The Hotline was quietly phased out.

Nonetheless, the Charter reforms continued, setting new standards, some of which inadvertently revealed the urgent necessity of reform. A target was set, for example, that no one should wait more than two years for treatment on the NHS. This was later reduced to eighteen months, but even so it could be seen only as an indictment of the impoverished level of the existing service that such an aspiration had to be articulated in the first place. Similarly the suggestion that 92 per cent of British Rail trains should arrive within five minutes of their scheduled time looked arbitrary if not overly onerous, but it was not met. In fact, even the BR Charter itself was two months late in arriving.

More significant than the targets, though, was the idea of providing information to consumers. And here Major ran into the second force resisting his initiative, with schools the main battleground. The educational establishment had fought the culture of Thatcherism in the 1980s more successfully than perhaps any other institution and was vociferously opposed to the proposals coming out of the Citizens' Charter. In particular, objections were raised to the testing of pupils in basic areas of literacy and numeracy at key stages in their education, and to the publication of league tables of schools based on this testing and on examination results. These tests, and indeed exams themselves, were said to be too crude a measure of the work done by schools – they provided, for example, no indication of 'added value' in places where there were particularly difficult intakes – and would give parents a distorted picture.

There was also opposition from teachers' unions and, initially at least, the Labour Party to the Office for Standards in Education (OFSTED), formed as an extension of Her Majesty's Inspectors of Schools to oversee the new regime; all schools would now be inspected on a regular basis and the reports of the inspectorate published. Ruffled feathers were not exactly smoothed with the appointment in 1994 of Chris Woodhead as head of OFSTED. Woodhead's ability to infuriate the teaching profession was unparalleled: during his tenure as Chief Inspector of Schools, which was renewed when Labour came to office, his abrasive character and fierce denunciations of bad teachers – some 15,000 of them, it was claimed, spread equally between primary and secondary schools – were to loom large in the public debate, leaving many educationalists with the feeling that their work was undervalued and unappreciated. 'Chris Woodhead had many qualities which he did his best to hide,' noted Labour's education secretary David Blunkett, 'but collegiality and modesty were not among them.'

This was one area in which the Conservative government felt that it was in tune with the public and it pressed on, despite the dissent, so that the testing and the league tables became a routine feature of British life. Many parents warmly embraced the reforms, and much of the media was happy to have statistical evidence that appeared to confirm its poor opinion of comprehensive schools.

Eighty per cent of state secondary-school pupils were now educated within the comprehensive system, but when the A-level league tables were published in 1992, they showed that 70 per cent of the highest performing institutions were grammar schools. A disparity between selective and nonselective schools was to be expected, but the gap revealed was greater than many had chosen to believe. And beyond that was the gulf that separated private from public: when *The Times* compiled a list that same year of the 100 establishments with the best A-level results, all but five were independent. 'My overriding aim is to improve opportunity for all children of whatever background in our state system,' explained the education secretary, John Patten, in 1993. 'So much so that by the end of the century the borders between the state and independent sectors will be blurred. Excellence will be available to all.' The same platitudes were to be echoed by Labour ministers and were no more believable from their mouths. State education had been chronically underfunded – a fact that was evident in the physical infrastructure of too many schools – and it seemed deeply implausible that the investment per pupil would ever match that in the private sector.

That assumed, of course, that finance was the primary issue. Plenty of commentators argued that there were deeper problems, that expectations and standards were too low and that there was a desperate need to raise them, in the interests both of pupils and the wider society. Amongst such critics was the newspaper columnist Melanie Phillips, whose 1996 book *All Must Have Prizes* launched a sustained assault on virtually all aspects of current educational theory, from the emphasis on creativity over knowledge to the collapse of moral authority. It was a controversial book ('crap by anybody's standards', in the elegant phrasing of educationalist Professor Ted Wragg), but some of the basic facts it reported were more difficult to dismiss: 'the first tests for 11-year-olds held in 1995 revealed that half were not up to scratch in English or maths', while the proportion of British pupils gaining three GCSE grades between A and C in maths, English and a science was less than half the equivalent in Germany or France. Elsewhere, research in 1993 by the Adult Literacy and Basic Skills Unit found that 40 per cent of those in colleges of further education needed help with literacy and numeracy. Such outcomes were hardly a resounding endorsement of the existing system.

There was little popular clamour for the widespread return of the previous tripartite division between grammar, secondary modern and technical schools, complete with the eleven-plus exam, but many felt that state education was simply failing to deliver. Moreover, the left, both in the Labour Party and the unions, was perceived as accepting the decline in standards – whether it were relative or absolute – and to have no coherent strategy for how it might be reversed. Opposition to change looked like little more than a stubborn defence of an unsatisfactory status quo, allowing the terms of the debate to be set by the reforming agenda of the right.

The campaign against testing and tables reinforced a widely held view that the teaching profession had become complacent and averse to scrutiny. There existed a belief – fuelled by tabloid tales of the loony left and trendy teachers – that education was the last refuge of the politically motivated scoundrel. John Morton's comedy series *People Like Us*, starring Chris Langham as a hopeless television journalist, parodied modern teaching methods where 'the pupils actually own the ownership of their own knowledge. What happens is, they sit in groups and interview each other, and then they go on to cut out things from magazines, draw graphs, so that they can establish for themselves that they don't know what the questions are.' So what does the teacher do in such a system? 'Well, he hands out the glue.'

The anecdotal experience of some parents seemed to back up this perception of wilful underachievement. When the future Liberal Democrat MP Vince Cable visited his local comprehensive in the 1980s, at a time when his oldest son was due to move into secondary education, he discovered that the school's pupils had failed to gain a single O-level in science or languages the previous year. 'When I asked to speak to a head of department about this deficiency,' he later wrote, 'I was confronted by a character modelled on Dave Spart from *Private Eye* who harangued me on the subject of pushy middle-class parents obsessed by "irrelevant" exam results.' Cable sent his son to a private school instead.

That denunciation of the 'pushy middle class' ran right through the debate on education. There were few groups, it sometimes seemed, to whom educationalists objected more than middle-class parents, especially if they took an interest in their children's schooling, and one of the complaints about the league tables was that they would encourage well-off parents somehow to manipulate the system. John Major had some sympathy with such a judgement, though he drew different conclusions. In his 1994 conference speech, he denounced those who opposed his reforms: 'They are the people who can afford the good things of life, who chortle away about our emphasis on basic standards and the three Rs – and then move to a catchment area with better schools for their own children.' When David Blunkett became education secretary, he also blamed the middle class, this time identifying them as having a stranglehold on the profession itself: 'I wasn't prepared to put up with the middle-class claptrap which assumes that everything will be well if we would just leave teachers to get on with what they were doing.' No matter one's political position, the target remained the same.

*

Cable's option of a private school was less palatable within the Labour Party, where the comprehensive system had become one of the defining tenets of the left, associated especially with Caroline Benn and Glenys Kinnock, the wives of Tony and Neil respectively. It was an issue that cut to the core of the modern party, in which some 60 per cent of delegates to the annual conference were said to be either teachers or school governors. Previous leaders, including Harold Wilson and James Callaghan, had sent their children to private schools, but that was no longer an acceptable option. There was, however, some room for manoeuvre, and Tony Blair discovered a compromise when he sent his son halfway across the capital to the London Oratory school, much to the horror of many Labour Party activists.

The Oratory was a Catholic comprehensive within the state sector, which had no selection procedure based on ability, but was nonetheless a grant-maintained school, a new category of establishment created by the Conservative government in the late 1980s, operating outside the control of the local education authorities and receiving funds directly from Westminster rather than from their councils. Such schools were few in number – less than 1 per cent had taken this route by 1992 – but they accounted for over a quarter of the best performing state schools at A-level, and places at the Oratory were much sought-after by parents, particularly those in the part of North London where the Blairs lived; state education in Islington had a particularly poor reputation. But official Labour Party policy was at that stage opposed to institutions opting out of local government control, and Blair's decision was deeply resented by some, especially since Islington was a Labour-controlled authority. This was, recognised Alastair Campbell, the political weak point: 'a Labour leader shipping his kids out of a Labour area because he thought the schools weren't good enough.' Blair was unrepentant. 'I am not going to make a choice for my child on the basis of what is the politically correct thing to do,' he insisted, and there were many even on the left who, despite their principles, quietly nodded in agreement with his decision.

The dispute within Labour about the future direction of state schooling surfaced at the 1995 conference, where Blair declared that his priorities for government were 'education, education, education'. Not necessarily convinced, the former deputy leader Roy Hattersley – hitherto regarded as a right-winger – revealed how far the party had travelled when he became something of a leftish hero merely by restating a long-held faith in the comprehensive system. In what a *Daily Mirror* leader column called 'the most unpleasant, blinkered attack on Labour's education policy', he called in vain for all grant-maintained schools to be returned to local control, and won huge cheers with his passionate plea: 'For God's sake, let us stop apologising about comprehensive schools.' Offstage he was less restrained: 'Tony has targeted middle-class votes for the last year,' he told Peter Mandelson. 'Well, I say *fuck* the middle class.'

His contribution was not much welcomed. In private, Blair was contemptuous – 'fat, pompous bugger' – while in public, David Blunkett sketched the outline of what was to become a familiar argument, denouncing Hattersley for daring to dissent: 'When socialists fall out, it's the Tories who rejoice.'

A few months later, in January 1996, the story broke that Harriet Harman, Labour's shadow health spokesperson, had sent her son to a school that not only enjoyed grant-maintained status, but was also a grammar school, still selecting its pupils on ability. Worse yet, it wasn't in the authority where she lived, the Labour-run London Borough of Southwark, but in neighbouring Bromley, which had the benefit of a Conservative council. This truly was beyond the pale for much of the party, and many who had bitten their lips over Blair's personal decision took the opportunity to attack Harman instead.

So too did many who had never really taken to Harman herself, a privately educated, well-connected feminist who didn't always mix well in male-dominated, old Labour circles. 'Not the most well-liked soul at Westminster,' according to Edwina Currie, she was seen as too middle class, too worthy, too serious, even if the latter complaint failed to recognise her particular sense of humour. When the Labour MP George Foulkes once compared Margaret Thatcher to a fishwife, Harman corrected his terminology, pointing out that the correct term was 'fishperson'. It was surely a good self-deprecating joke, though there were some who insisted that it wasn't meant as such.

Harman's choice to back educational selection in practice, whatever her party said about it in principle, was greeted with fury. John Prescott was distinctly unimpressed ('I'm not going to defend any fucking hypocrites'), and many of the older MPs, from Tony Benn to Roy Hattersley, were similarly incensed. A rare exception was Mo Mowlam, who was prevailed upon to defend Harman on television after Alastair Campbell threatened to 'reveal her stepchildren were at a public school'. Others in a similar position to Harman were annoyed that she wasn't making the same sacrifice as they had. 'I suppose Lisanne and I feel upset because we have been through the comprehensive schooling process with our five children,' confessed Giles Radice, while Glasgow MP Michael Martin stressed the therapeutic effects of living by one's principles: he 'had exactly the same choice to make as Harriet and, although the kids had a difficult time, it made us a better family'.

For the Tories, this was manna from heaven. Over the last few years, their traditional areas of political superiority had been cut from under them. Black Wednesday had destroyed their reputation for managing the economy, Blair as shadow home secretary had successfully colonised the issue of crime, and the fall of the Soviet Union had removed the ultimate bogeyman. Now they were back on safe territory and John Major enjoyed one of his most successful sessions at prime minister's questions, flinging Blair's favourite soundbite back at him: 'I just want to be tough on hypocrisy, tough on the causes of hypocrisy,' he protested.

The attacks on Harman culminated in a crowded meeting of the Parliamentary Labour Party, where several MPs added their voices to that of the *Daily Mirror* in calling for her to resign from the shadow cabinet. There was little chance of that, however, for Blair had decided to stand by her on tactical grounds. When challenged on his own children's education he had argued, 'let's not fight the war that the Tories want us to fight,' and he applied the same logic to Harman's position: 'I'm not going to allow the Tories the pleasure of crucifying any member of the shadow cabinet. That's the only issue.' It had become a trial of strength, a test of whether he would bow to pressure from the left and thereby validate the charge, repeatedly levelled at him by the Conservatives, that in office he would be unable to contain the extremists in his party.

With that much at stake, and still new to his job, he won the day, however grudging the support. Harman herself then went on to lead an opposition-initiated debate on the health service and performed so well that she took the wind out of the Tory sails. 'She is a doughty Commons performer under pressure,' noted the *Independent*, while *The Times* said she 'won genuine cheers from her own side'. It was not the last time that she would display such resilience in difficult circumstances.

One of the less expected contributions to the debate in the parliamentary party was made by Bernie Grant. MP for Tottenham since 1987, Grant was still best known for his controversial comments as leader of Haringey council at the time of the Broadwater Farm riot in 1985, when he had blamed the police for the troubles and said that, in the eyes of local youths, they had got 'a bloody good hiding'. Widely, though wrongly, believed to be on the hard left of the party, he came out in defence of Harman's choice and went on to spell out his position in public: 'The comprehensive schools in inner-city areas of London are very bad indeed, and are failing our children.' He added that many of his black constituents were sending their children to the West Indies to get a better education, where their impoverished schooling was starkly revealed: 'When they get to the Caribbean, they are put in classes two years younger than them.'

He had a point. Nationally 7.4 per cent of children were in private education, but in the capital that figure stood at 11 per cent. This could have been the consequence of higher earnings, except that the same discrepancy wasn't evident in the South-East outside London. There was a sense of desperation about the quality of state schools in the capital that even overrode the professed beliefs of liberal parents. The writer Blake Morrison lived in South London: 'Ten years ago I would not have imagined forking out for my children's [schooling]. But though defensive and shame-faced, I'm not in a minority. Most of my friends in the area have begun drifting from state education as well.'

For all the controversy, the incident of Harriet Harman's son helped focus minds in the Labour Party on a historic failing. 'I don't criticise the Harmans for their choice,' said Nigel de Gruchy, general secretary of the teachers' union the NAS/UWT. 'What I criticise is the Labour Party for ignoring until recently the fate of inner city comprehensives.' In his memoirs, Blair admitted the scale of the problem ('In my heart of hearts I knew I wouldn't send my own children to most inner-city secondary schools'), and hopes were high that a future Labour government would act decisively on education. The question of public services, which Major had chosen to highlight with the Citizens' Charter, was now firmly at the centre of political debate, even if not in the form that he would have wished.

The general suspicion was that, in the first instance, more investment was probably required, rather than endless initiatives. In *Drop the Dead Donkey* a character announces that there's a 'new government policy on education', and is met with a bored reply: 'Course there is. It's a Tuesday.' But the initiatives kept coming, and more kites were flown in pursuit of positive headlines. The situation approached farce in 1996 when the home secretary, Michael Howard, and the education secretary, Gillian Shephard, suggested they were in favour of reintroducing the cane in schools, ten years on from the banning of corporal punishment. Within hours, Shephard had been told by John Major to pull back from such talk; it wasn't government policy and would anyway be illegal under European law. But the issue, once raised, attracted widespread support on the Tory right, and the prime minister was obliged to offer a free vote on the subject in order to defuse the row.

The move was defeated in the Commons but over a hundred MPs, the vast majority of them Conservative, voted in favour. It was a foolish episode that did the government no good at all; those who supported harsher discipline in schools were annoyed that no progress was made, and that Shephard had been obliged to vote against her own views, while the contributions of some of the pro-caners merely reinforced the image of Tory MPs as a slightly odd collection of individuals. 'It was degrading,' remembered John Carlisle of his own childhood punishments, sounding rather more enthusiastic than was healthy, 'it was painful. Weals were actually put on one's buttocks, blood actually did come. And that was on the basis that because of the punishment, one did not do that particular offence again.'

Of all the public services, the highest levels of dissatisfaction were probably to be found amongst passengers using British Rail, the company that had been running the country's railways since the private companies were nationalised in 1948. For years the only predictable aspect of rail travel had been the misery of the experience, and the service offered by BR had long been a rich vein of jokes for stand-up comedians, much of the humour focused on catering, the inevitable delays and the excuses offered for late or non-running trains. For years 'leaves on the line' was the front runner in the latter category, though inclement weather in 1991 brought forth the new explanation that trains couldn't operate because they were faced with 'the wrong kind of snow'.

A new variation on an established theme appeared in 1994 when the Channel Tunnel was opened, providing a rail link from London to Paris. The contrast between the high-speed trains in France and the antiquated network in Britain could hardly have passed without notice. The 1992 Labour Party manifesto promised to end that disparity through the use of private finance, a policy that had been developed by John Prescott.

As the party's transport spokesperson, Prescott was aware of the need for spending on infrastructure, but also knew that it wouldn't feature very high on the list of a future Labour government's priorities. He came to the conclusion that 'there was an argument for private-public financing and leasing of assets in the public sector' and successfully argued his case within the party; the manifesto committed a future Labour government to 'mobilise private capital for large-scale public transport investment'. Other proposals of his included reducing the speed limit on motorways to 50 m.p.h. during peak hours, and a reduction in the permitted alcohol limit for drivers, though these failed to win many converts, possibly undermined a little by Prescott's own example; in 1991 he was banned from driving after his third speeding offence in four years.

The idea of encouraging investment by private firms, who would then lease back the new-built infrastructure to the state, was more successful. It proved to be immensely popular with politicians of both parties, who saw in it a way of increasing spending without incurring too great a short-term impact on the government's balance sheet, in effect paying for public services on the never-never. Rebranding it the Private Finance Initiative, Norman Lamont picked up the concept, much to its creator's annoyance. 'You buggers have pinched our public-private financing plans,' Prescott said to Lamont, and Lamont replied, 'Well, it's your own fault for having a good idea.'

The Tory manifesto in 1992, however, had other plans, promising to end British Rail's monopoly and displaying a distinct whiff of nostalgia for the pre-war days of the railways: 'We want to restore the pride and local commitment that died with nationalisation.' Major's original vision had been a recreation of the big regional companies – the Great Western Railway, the London and North Eastern Railway and so on – that dominated the 1920s and 1930s, but by the time the process of privatisation had passed through the government's policy-making machine, the result ended up very different. The network itself, the thousands of miles of tracks across the country, together with the associated signals, tunnels, bridges and stations, was separated from the services that ran on those tracks. The network was passed to a new publicly floated company, Railtrack, while the various services were split into dozens of franchises that were sold off to private companies. It was hard to see the logic of the split, or how it would inculcate 'pride and local commitment' when the company that owned the train on which you were travelling had no responsibility for the station at which you had embarked.

'I used to be a closet supporter of privatising British Rail,' observes the hero of David Lodge's 1995 novel *Therapy*, 'before the transport minister announced his plans to separate the track from the companies that run the trains. You can imagine how well that will work.' He was not alone, and the government found that they had created a system so complex that it even succeeded in provoking warm glances back to the days of British Rail. That company's role as the butt of easy jokes was inherited by Virgin Rail, as Richard Branson found that his normally infallible feel for popular ventures was unable to overcome the problems of running a modern railway.

Some of the previously privatised services – most notably British Telecom – had improved enormously once they were taken out of state control, and Labour's belated conversion to the cause recognised the fact, but the new rail companies remained heavily dependent on subsidy, which some felt was the worst of both worlds; it certainly wasn't an easy task to tell the public that their taxes were being passed on in dividends and bonuses. Reservations were expressed even within Conservative ranks. 'Privatising the railways was described as a "Thatcherite" policy,' observed Chris Patten, now happily remote from the fray. 'But I doubt whether she would have pursued it – too messy and likely to be too unpopular.'

If British Rail was a privatisation too far for many people, the idea of breaking up the Post Office and Royal Mail was complete anathema to the nation, even though, as its proponent Michael Heseltine pointed out, a large part of the network – some 19,000 sub-post offices, the friendly village service so beloved of romantics – was already owned privately. His enthusiasm for the project of privatising one of the country's oldest institutions was not matched by that of his cabinet colleagues at a time when the Maastricht debate was making every initiative difficult, and the proposal was quietly dropped, much to Heseltine's disappointment. 'I had been responsible for council house sales and for privatising the coal and nuclear industries, the Stationery Office and numerous smaller public services,' he later wrote, 'but this would have been the jewel in the crown.'

Even the fact that plans were drawn up upset many who felt that too much of the nation's fabric was being unravelled. As Nick Marshall, a character in Michael Palin's novel *Hemingway's Chair* (1995), explains: 'The Post Office is part of national life. Part of our national identity. It's our legacy and I'll be damned if I'll sit back and see it kicked around like the railways, the coalmines and shipping.' But Marshall is actually an arch-privatiser, who has infiltrated the Post Office hierarchy somewhat in the manner of Militant embedding itself in the Labour Party. Secretly he's determined to impose progress even where it isn't wanted, resolved to 'Fight everyone out there who wants to keep the Post Office small and cosy and cuddly.'

The novel is set in an East Anglian town and centres on the conflict between Marshall's restless pursuit of change and the values of our hero Martin Sproale, who sees community, continuity and tradition as the foundations of public service. Inevitably Marshall wins the argument and, although privatisation fails to materialise, a programme of ruthless, soulless modernisation finally ensures that the local post office is relocated and computerised: 'It was more like a freshly landed spacecraft. A stop-gap environment on the road to automation and eventually the final eradication of the human element from the whole process.' The changes are symbolised in the training given to staff: 'The full greeting, as laid down in the Customer Charter, is "Good morning", before twelve, and

"Good afternoon" after twelve, followed by personal identification and the Assistance Information Request.' In other words: 'Good morning, my name is Steve. How may I help you?'

The image of the pirate raider of public services became a commonplace of fiction. He was to be found too in Christopher Brookmyre's debut novel, *Quite Ugly One Morning* (1996), a crime thriller centring on Stephen Lime, the crooked and murderous chief executive of an NHS hospital trust, a splendidly evil character who keeps a vicious Alsatian named Tebbit. As one character explains: 'No matter what they get their PR people to say, or whatever slogans they put under their logos, the Trusts don't give a shit about patient care. They only care about pounds, shillings and pence, and that's why they were set up in the first place, and filled with accountants and bankers and a whole legion of grey zeroes in suits.' Lime has an Achilles heel, however; his enemies find that his computer proves remarkably easy to hack into, since his passwords are so predictable: Tebbit, Thatcher, Portillo.

Coming from a different direction but arriving at much the same place, Michael Aitkins's popular sitcom *Waiting for God*, which first aired on BBC One in 1990, derived most of its humour from the attempts by two elderly dissidents, Diana Trent (Stephanie Cole) and Tom Ballard (Graham Crowden), to frustrate the efficient running of Bayview retirement village. This is a private concern, owned by a group of doctors and run by Harvey Baines (Daniel Hill), whose remit is simply to keep costs down and whose incompetence as an administrator matches that of contemporary sitcom creations like the broadcasting bureaucrat, Gus Hedges, in *Drop the Dead Donkey* and Gordon Brittas, manager of a leisure centre in *The Brittas Empire*. 'I'll have you know I trained for over three weeks to run this place,' exclaims Baines, as he seeks to justify his stewardship of this run-down outpost of what he calls 'the age management industry'. He can't comprehend why his efforts are so unappreciated. 'I don't understand,' he wails. 'What's wrong with me? Why doesn't anyone like me?'

Meanwhile Diana is busy raging against his management and against politicians who seek to fob her off with token gestures. 'All we want is to be treated like human beings, respected, not patronised,' she insists. 'So you can stick your free bus passes and your free televisions right up where the sun don't shine.' In one of the best storylines, a new arrival, Daisy Williams (Jane Downs), the widow of an army officer, wants to organise the residents as though they were members of her late husband's regiment: 'More togetherness, more planning, more organisation, so we can all rattle along as one big happy family.' She naturally takes strong exception to Diana and regards her as a trouble-maker: 'I know the type. Fifth columnists. It was people like her — freethinkers — that lost us the Empire. No team spirit.' Eventually Diana and Tom defeat her, and as they reflect on their narrow escape, Tom mentions Daisy's appeal to community spirits. Diana corrects him: 'Appeal to jingoistic spirits. Forming teams, a desire to inflict your views on all around you. Fascism.' He suggests that maybe it's patriotism, and she concedes: 'It's a fine line.'

Running through it all was the sense that a social infrastructure was being eroded through the pursuit of profit, a perception that was unlikely to be transformed by the Citizens' Charter. Regardless of what had happened in the polling booths in 1992, the public were becoming angry that there was no apparent increase in state spending, even if the government had been returned to office promising no such thing.

The same feeling was evident in other shows of the era. *In Sickness and in Health* saw Alf Garnett (Warren Mitchell), the great comedy anti-hero of the 1960s, now a pensioner and surviving on food that has passed its sell-by date. 'Rationing, the good old days — we was better off then,' laments his sometime fiancée, Mrs Holingbury (Carmel McSharry). 'We was far better off when we were fighting the Germans.' Inevitably, *One Foot in the Grave* presented an even bleaker depiction. In a 1993 episode, an elderly man in a care home is seen being knocked to the ground by staff and viciously kicked while he lies helpless, before being locked in a cupboard under the stairs for the night, all as a punishment for having nightmares. The sequence was sufficiently horrific that it was edited when given a pre-watershed repeat.

Nowhere was sensitivity to the state of the public services more acute than in relation to the NHS, the condition of which was memorably summed up in the comedy *The Day Today*: 'What was once the healthy bouncing boy child of Ernest Bevin is now barely more than a disease-racked, breathless corpse.' (Characteristically, the show managed to hit two targets in a single sentence, denouncing underinvestment even as the misattribution of Aneurin Bevan's NHS satirised the vacuity of media experts.)

The problem for the government was that the NHS was essentially seen as Labour territory; there were few votes in health for the Conservatives, only a widespread suspicion that — despite Major's protestations — they didn't have much commitment to the institution. The more thoughtful Tories might complain of the sentimental British attachment to outdated institutions, but they struggled to find a way of dealing with a health service that was, in Michael Portillo's words, 'amazingly inefficient, yet popular'.

One option was to find efficiency savings by subcontracting to private companies what were seen as non-essential parts of the service. John Patten argued that one of the government's successes was the privatising of laundry, cleaning and food in the NHS: 'This approach also means that the state or local authority can concentrate more on their core business.' The subsequent deterioration of diet and hygiene in hospitals – aspects that many felt were integral to a decent health system – did nothing to improve the image of a decaying service. Nor did the opening of a restaurant by McDonald's in Guy's Hospital in south-east London, the first such outlet in a European hospital.

Meanwhile any attempts at wider structural reorganisation were met with outright hostility. During Virginia Bottomley's time as health secretary, she attempted to rationalise London's hospitals, which had grown up in a haphazard fashion over several centuries, resulting in a structure that no one would have chosen if starting from scratch. Her plan included the closure of St Bartholomew's Hospital in the City of London, founded in 1123 and the oldest surviving hospital in England. The ensuing outcry, and the popular campaign against closure, was successful in reversing the proposal, but the plan left a bitter legacy and Major was later to cite it as 'a factor in our dismal 1997 general election showing in London'.

That aborted scheme also helped make Bottomley one of the least popular politicians in parts of the country that were seeking a female hate figure to replace Margaret Thatcher. She wasn't an obvious choice for the role. Her background as a children's psychiatric social worker and with the Child Poverty Action Group was hardly the stuff of heartless-Tory mythology, while her public image – 'fragrant, intelligent, capable', drooled the *Sunday Times* – made her eminently suitable to represent the new, caring Conservative Party that Major wished to create.

Nonetheless, Edwina Currie regarded her as being 'insufferably patronising', and when the neo-punk band S*M*A*S*H released a single '(I Want to) Kill Somebody' in 1994, listing the targets of their hate, they saved a special place for her: 'Margaret Thatcher, Jeffrey Archer, Michael Heseltine, John Major – Virginia Bottomley, especially'. Others saw her femininity as a cunning trick. 'The only reason Virginia Bottomley gets away with her destruction of the health service,' suggested comedian Jeremy Hardy, 'is that she is the only person in the Conservative Party with whom anyone can imagine having sex.' But that, according to John Redwood's adviser Hywel Williams, didn't reflect the feelings aroused in some of her Westminster colleagues: 'She was the kind of assured, attractive and bossy woman whom a certain type of English professional male wants to harm physically.'

Redwood himself was then the secretary of state for Wales and seized on his position to explore a full range of policy areas, including an alternative, and possibly more pragmatic, approach to the NHS. In a 1993 speech he argued that the 'search for economies should often begin with the consultancy contracts, computer procurement, the paperwork and administration'. He also identified a 'restlessness amongst some of the medical staff about the number of men in grey suits'. It was, however, a difficult proposition for a party who were so closely associated with the growth of bureaucracy in the public services, and it was never pursued with any enthusiasm by Redwood's colleagues.

Instead the public perception was simply that the Tories were trying to close down hospitals and reduce services. And the fragility of the government majority in the Commons meant that campaigners could put pressure on local MPs which proved irresistible. In 1996 two Tory members – John Gorst and Hugh Dykes – successfully threatened to resign the whip if there was no climb-down on a proposal to close the casualty department at Edgware Hospital. Tony Blair took the opportunity to revive an aged, but still damaging, taunt: 'The prime minister's policies are determined by the imprint of the last person to sit on him.'

The reality was that spending on the NHS continued to rise every year, but the results were seldom obvious to the users. This was even more true in the one public service that seemed entirely immune to any constructive reform. In the twelve years after Margaret Thatcher's election in 1979, spending on the police had risen by 87 per cent in real terms, and there were 27,000 more officers in the force. Yet still the crime rate rose remorselessly, while efficiency continued to fall. In 1993 it was revealed, under the remit of the Citizens' Charter, that the Metropolitan Police had solved just 12 per cent of crimes committed on their patch, and that half the forces in the country had a clear-up rate below 20 per cent. As David Mellor observed of the police: 'They are overpaid, we've thrown money at them and we have the highest level of crime in our history.'

The crime rate, at least, was to be addressed. In the cabinet reshuffle that followed the departure of Norman Lamont in 1993, Michael Howard was promoted to home secretary and lost no time in making clear his intention to match Tony Blair's anti-crime rhetoric. 'The silent majority has become the angry majority,' Howard told a Tory conference, which really needed no telling. 'In the last thirty years, the balance in the criminal justice system has been tilted too far in favour of the criminal and against the protection of the public.' The centrepiece of his hardline new stance was a powerful soundbite to rival Blair's 'tough on crime'. 'Let us be clear,' he spelt out. 'Prison works. It ensures that we are protected from murderers, muggers and rapists, and it makes many who are tempted to commit crime think twice.'

Under previous home secretaries, the numbers in jail had been falling, with a move towards community-based sentencing and the introduction of early-release schemes, but Howard began a process of reversing that trend. By the end of the decade there were around a third more prisoners than at the start, with the greatest proportional increases coming amongst those given short sentences of up to six months and young offenders aged under eighteen. There were costs attached to this development, both in economic and social terms: prison was still an expensive option, crime rates in jail were calculated to be eight times higher than on the outside, and ex-prisoners reoffended at only marginally lower rates than did those given community sentences.

To keep the pressure on Howard, amongst Blair's first acts when he became Labour leader was the appointment of Jack Straw to succeed him as shadow home secretary. 'Jack was sensible and no softie on lawbreakers,' noted Blair in his memoirs, and the *Sun*'s columnist Richard Littlejohn – not a noted liberal – purred with pleasure when Straw got the real cabinet job: 'one of our most impressive home secretaries.' Others were less convinced: Paddy Ashdown made clear that, if the Liberal Democrats were offered a coalition with Labour, one point would be non-negotiable: 'none of us could be part of a government in which Jack Straw was home secretary.'

Straw made his name with a 1995 speech attacking graffiti artists, 'winos and addicts' and 'squeegee merchants', insisting: 'We have literally to reclaim the streets for the law-abiding public citizen; make street life everywhere an innocent pleasure again.' There was little here that dissented from a similar speech by Major the previous year, urging the public to report beggars to the police and calling on the courts to use the full sanctions of the law, including fines of up to £1,000. 'It is not acceptable to be out on the street,' said Major. 'There is no justification for it.' The concept of 'zero-tolerance policing' – based on the theory that the acceptance of low-level but visible anti-social behaviour adversely affected community confidence, and thereby permitted an escalation in more serious crime – had made its way across from America, and both parties were eager to claim it as their own.

But, following his master's soundbite, Straw was not content to sit back and wait for crime to happen, and in 1996 he launched himself into a series of speeches, articles and interviews in which he appeared to suggest that if only parents brought up their children with more discipline, then Britain would be a much more law-abiding country. It was time to break the taboo on talking about parenting, he insisted, calling for a curfew to be imposed on those under the age of ten, and then branching out into questions such as the time children should be in bed. He hastened to add a mild disclaimer to this latter theme: 'It is not exactly for politicians to tell parents what time to impose. But my experience is that parents would welcome more discussion in schools and the media.'

By now, some people were finding it rather difficult to take him seriously. Linda Smith began to refer to him as 'the Child Catcher from *Chitty Chitty Bang Bang*', while in Sue Townsend's books, Adrian Mole used Straw as a latter-day bogeyman to terrify his son, telling him that 'if he didn't behave in future, a man called Jack Straw would get him and put him in prison'. Straw's image was such that at one point he had to make clear to the shadow cabinet his position on flogging ('we're against it'), a revelation that prompted his colleagues to burst out laughing, much to his annoyance. 'Ooo, Jack, you're getting soft on crime,' one of them teased.

The impact on the Conservative government, however, was more serious; as William Waldegrave revealed, one of the great taunts thrown at cabinet members on the more moderate wing of the party was: 'So you're to the left of Jack Straw, are you?' In constant danger of being outflanked, Michael Howard pressed his 'prison works' strategy harder still. He could soon boast that the crime rate had begun to fall for the first time in living memory, though some pointed out that the decline also coincided with an economic upturn and a consequent drop in unemployment. It was all too late for Tory stalwart Peter Cadbury, the businessman whose grandfather had founded the chocolate company; he resigned from the party in protest at their lack of action on law and order, explaining that he himself was a victim of crime: one of his outbuildings had recently been broken into, and some garden tools had been stolen.

There was in any case some doubt about what the true crime figures were. In 1995 the police recorded just over five million crimes in England and Wales, while the British Crime Survey estimated the number to be just over nineteen million. Faced with such a massive discrepancy, the public chose not to place any faith at all in statistics, and it was generally assumed that the figures had somehow been fiddled. The opposition could also point out that, despite the recent fall, the number of recorded crimes had doubled under the Tories, though this merely followed the depressing post-war trend: in 1950 there had been 6,000 violent crimes reported; by the mid-1990s this had risen to nearly a quarter of a million.

Something of that longer view was captured in one of the most acclaimed television drama series of the decade. Peter Flannery's *Our Friends in the North*

(1996) explored thirty years of British history, depicting the slow crumbling of hope and faith on the left, ending in the present with a thirteen-year-old taking up joyriding, just as his gun-toting father had a decade earlier. The story centred on Newcastle, but made excursions to London, where corruption was depicted as endemic within the police force. 'Nobody will ever clean up the Met,' shrugs a character in 1966. 'Nothing will ever change.' Four years later, as an inquiry into the force is abandoned on the instruction of a Conservative home secretary, the decent Geordie officer, who was called in to investigate, resigns in disgust: 'I've been a copper for twenty-five years,' he says. 'I never dreamed. They've made a mockery of it.' Viewers were expected to draw parallels with the present.

Some things had changed, however, and a signal of sorts was sent when the Metropolitan Police Force was rebranded as the Metropolitan Police Service in 1989, following a report into the 'corporate identity' of the police. The change was accompanied by a 'statement of common purpose and values', to be displayed in stations across the city. 'We must be compassionate, courteous and patient,' it read. 'We need to be professional, calm and restrained in the face of violence and apply only the force which is necessary to accomplish our lawful duty.'

There were developments too in the fictional portrayal of the police. In the television series *Between the Lines* (1992), the main character, Detective Superintendent Tony Clark (Neil Pearson), has a taste for neat whisky, excessive smoking and philandering, the latter providing plenty of opportunities to take his clothes off, thus displaying an attractive range of cuts and bruises from the numerous times he gets beaten up in the course of his duty. This much would have been recognisable to Clark's predecessors in the 1970s series *The Sweeney*, but the basis of the show was fundamentally different. Where *The Sweeney* had argued that good coppering depended on bending the rules to get a result, and that the work of the police was hamstrung by bureaucracy, *Between the Lines* believed that it was important to play by the book, that banging up villains was no excuse for cutting procedural corners. Clark even argued that, despite the boozy culture of the force, officers should refrain from interviewing suspects who are over the drink-driving limit, since it would be taking advantage of someone in a vulnerable state.

The subjects under scrutiny by Clark and his colleagues in the Complaints Investigation Bureau are the police themselves, and specifically the kind of officers seen in *The Sweeney*. 'He was out of step,' a constable explains of a former colleague. 'We can't afford the hard men, sir, not any more. Not when we're living and working in a goldfish bowl. Dinosaurs like Steve, they get the job done, fair enough, but the cost is too high.'

Despite such protestations, and despite the premise underlying the show, the cumulative effect of the series was to give the impression that every police station was ruled by fear, secrecy and bullying, and that virtually every officer in the Metropolitan Police over the rank of sergeant — together with most of those below — was bent, violent and contemptuous of the public whose interests they were supposed to serve. If they weren't taking bribes, they were fitting up innocent men, and if they weren't actively breaking the law themselves, it was only because they were neglecting their duties. And this time it wasn't just the capital's police who were depicted as failing. 'Think of the police as a solid block of male attitudes,' explains one of the country's senior female officers, based in the East Midlands. 'Prejudiced, sexist, racist, ignorant, violent, a culture based on unchallengeable certainties.'

Much the same conclusion was reached in Lynda La Plante's acclaimed series *Prime Suspect* (1991), which starred Helen Mirren as DCI Jane Tennison, encountering incompetence, sexism and racism in the Metropolitan Police. Jackie Malton, the real-life officer on whom the character was based, and who acted as adviser to La Plante, was keen to stress that things had changed, and that the degree of resentment and resistance Tennison encounters from her male colleagues was becoming a thing of the past. 'That level of obstruction wouldn't happen today,' she said in 1991. 'But it might have done five years ago.' She had no doubts about the drama's accuracy, however: 'It's painful for me to watch because that's my experience. I suffered that prejudice, and if other women in the police say they didn't, I'd say they're liars.' Alan Eastwood, chairman of the Police Federation, was more dismissive, insisting that the sexism seen on screen was 'overplayed'.

Between the Lines and *Prime Suspect* weren't, of course, the only visions of law and order on offer. Conventional detective fiction continued to be broadcast, including a remake of *Maigret* (1992), this time with Michael Gambon in the title role, as well as variations on old themes, such as *Hetty Wainthropp Investigates* (1990), in which Patricia Routledge played a retired working-class woman who solves crimes in a quiet, harmless kind of way. There were also some new detectives comfortably in the old tradition: David Jason in *A Touch of Frost*, John Nettles in *Midsomer Murders*.

And there was always *Inspector Morse*, though his depictions on television were starting to diverge a little from those on the page. In the later novels by Colin Dexter, such as *Death Is Now My Neighbour* (1996), Morse is still 'arrogant, ungracious, vulnerable, lovable' and still revels in the old-fashioned aspects of detection: 'hypotheses, imaginings, the occasional leap into the semi-darkness'. But he has become a more respected, establishment figure, so much so that he's on friendly terms with real-life senior officers, including Peter Imbert, former Commissioner of the Metropolitan Police, and the current incumbent, Paul Condon, who apologises at one point that he can't stop for a chat. 'Press conference,' he explains. 'It's not just the ethnic minorities I've upset this time — it's the ethnic majorities, too. All because I've published a few more official crime-statistics.' And Morse nods in sympathy.

On screen, however, portrayed by John Thaw, he was confronting a changed world, full of women priests, acid house ravers and devil-worshipping rapists. As Morse himself became ever more reminiscent of Eeyore in the Winnie-the-Pooh stories, shaking his head sadly at the state of modern society, the series seemed to be acknowledging a new breed of fiction that was, in the jargon of the day, more 'edgy'.

This trend was represented for most by Ian Rankin, who had, by the end of the decade, become the country's biggest-selling detective novelist, and whose character Inspector Rebus, an ex-SAS hard man policing the mean streets of Edinburgh, finally made it to television in 2000. Earlier rumours of adaptations had suggested that the title role might be played by Leslie Grantham, Robbie Coltrane or Bill Paterson, though it turned out to be the 38-year-old John Hannah, fifteen or so years younger than the character in the novels. The age was important, giving the show a grittier, tougher feel than its rivals.

In fact it threatened to be too edgy, and the opening scene of the first episode had to be heavily edited. ITV felt that the proposed sequence was a little strong for transmission immediately after the nine o'clock watershed, since it depicted a man tied to a chair with a plastic bag on his head, just about to be tortured, who then throws himself out of a window to be impaled on railings. 'It was a shame,' lamented Rankin. 'It would have been a great opening.' But even with the cuts, the mass television audience commanded by Morse was not apparently inclined to switch on to this younger brand of crime. The series ran for just four episodes, dashing the hopes of those in the tourist industry who had predicted that 'Rebus will be for Edinburgh what Inspector Morse was for Oxford.' When the character returned to television five years later, he had aged rather rapidly and was now portrayed by the 52-year-old Ken Stott.

Rebus was essentially the traditional police detective, tricked out in the world-weary cynicism of the hardboiled tradition represented by Dashiell Hammett and Elmore Leonard and relocated to present-day Scotland. Perhaps the most unusual feature was that he was still a police officer, for the dominant fashion of the 1990s was to find alternative ways to explore the same themes of murder and mystery. Detectives were increasingly outnumbered by their civilian counterparts, including lawyers (*Kavanagh QC*), customs officers (*The Knock*) and police surgeons (*Dangerfield*), even chefs (*Pie in the Sky*) and a conjuring consultant (*Jonathan Creek*). One of the central characters in *Holding On* was Shaun, played by David Morrissey, an investigator from the Inland Revenue who is portrayed in a sympathetic light, chasing down tax fraud in major companies and amongst the wealthy elite. 'People say there's one law for the rich,' he sneers. 'That's rubbish. They abide by quite a few actually, the ones in Liechtenstein, Panama, Switzerland.'

Much of this was television chasing after novelty, but it also suggested an underlying dissatisfaction with the police force, a suspicion that audiences were less willing to trust the traditional guardians of the state. Certainly this was true of Jimmy McGovern's *Cracker* (1993). Here, to the full police-show panoply of identity parades, autopsies and dysfunctional private lives, was added Robbie Coltrane as Fitz, a criminal psychologist who is addicted to nicotine, alcohol and gambling, as well as possessing an extraordinary gift for penetrating, psychological monologues in the interrogation room that provoke confessions from the guilty. Fitz was a return to the days of the gifted amateur, and without his assistance, the police were as helpless and incompetent as Inspectors Lestrade and Gregson had been without Sherlock Holmes to guide them.

The popularity of *Cracker* massively raised the public status of the speculative science of criminal profiling at a time when traditional detective work was coming under close scrutiny. After confirmation that a series of miscarriages of justice had occurred in relation to the IRA terrorist campaigns of the early 1970s, the Guildford Four were released in 1989 and the Birmingham Six in 1991; in the latter year the convictions of the Maguire Seven were also quashed. All seventeen innocent men and women had served, or were serving, long jail sentences after being convicted of involvement in the bombing of pubs, and the revelation that they had been wrongly imprisoned reinforced a belief, long held in some quarters, that was expressed by Fitz in an early episode of *Cracker*: 'Good old-fashioned British justice, where a man is innocent until proven Irish.'

But these cases, we were assured, lay far in the dim and distant past, when different standards applied. Such episodes were extremely unlikely now under the reformed rules of police enquiries. There was a certain irony therefore that the success of *Cracker* fed so comfortably into what nearly turned out to be yet another such case.

The murder of Rachel Nickell on Wimbledon Common in July 1992 was a particularly horrific crime, both in the severity of the attack — she was sexually assaulted and was stabbed forty-nine times — and in the fact that the only witness was her two-year-old son, found clinging to his mother's dead body. A massive police investigation narrowed down to one man, a thirty-year-old named Colin Stagg who lived nearby and regularly walked his dog on the common. The evidence against Stagg barely deserved to be credited with the word 'circumstantial': he had been on the common that day, his older brother had earlier been convicted of rape, and he had once written a mildly obscene letter to a woman he had contacted through a lonely hearts advert. A search of his home revealed a half-hearted interest in paganism, a black-handled knife and some soft pornography, including a few copies of *Razzle* and *Escort* magazines. He was, in short, the classic 'loner' so beloved of thriller writers.

As far as the police were concerned, this tied in perfectly with the profile of the murderer they had been given — and which they had broadcast on the ever-accommodating BBC One programme *Crimewatch* — by the country's leading forensic psychologist, Paul Britton, 'the man dubbed Britain's real-life Cracker' by the press. The investigating officers concocted a scheme whereby a policewoman would go undercover and befriend Stagg, trying to draw out his 'extreme sexual personality' with the aim of prompting a confession.

For seven months she stuck to her task, recording every conversation and writing letters directed by her superiors as she became a proxy pen-pal, urging the suspect to develop ever more lurid fantasies that he might satisfy her pretended interest in extreme sex. The lack of reciprocation was farcical, at times resembling the 1970s sitcom *George and Mildred*, with its depiction of a sexually voracious siren and her timid husband. She 'revealed' a past relationship that involved inflicting pain, and he was baffled. 'I do not understand,' he wrote back. 'Please explain as I live a quiet life.' In a later phone call, he began to glimpse what she was going on about: 'Is it kind of, what are they called, sadomasochism kind of thing?' But even then, he needed clarification: 'Is it of a sexual nature?' Finally, she made it explicit: she would have sex with him — he was a virgin — if only he would admit to being the Wimbledon Common murderer. 'I'm sorry,' he replied, 'but I'm not.'

Despite the complete absence of a confession, or of any forensic or eyewitness evidence, the police somehow persuaded the Crown Prosecution Service that a charge of murder could be brought. Stagg, they claimed, had demonstrated a personality indistinguishable from that of the kind of person who murdered Nickell; according to Paul Britton, the chances that two such people had been on the common at the same time were 'vanishingly small'. In September 1994 the case came to court and the evidence collected by the policewoman was thrown out in short order by a judge who was clearly horrified by the undercover operation: 'a blatant attempt to incriminate a suspect by positive and deceptive conduct of the grossest kind'. Stagg was acquittted and released after thirteen months in custody, displaying some understandable bitterness: 'My life has been ruined by a mixture of half-baked psychological theories and some stories written to satisfy the strange sexual requests of an undercover police officer.'

Those responsible for his prosecution were less coherent. Barbara Mills, the Director of Public Prosecutions, and Paul Condon, the Commissioner of the Metropolitan Police, gave a joint press conference in which they defended the 'honey trap' operation and insisted that there had been sufficient evidence to bring charges, no matter what the judge might think. There was, however, a growing suspicion that the police were becoming seduced by pseudo-science at the expense of traditional methods. 'In the old days, we'd be searching for the evidence,' explains a detective, hot on the trail of burglars in the drama series *Hamish Macbeth*. 'But nowadays it's all psychological profiling. What do we know about these characters? We've got to get behind them, know their hopes, their fears, where they go, what they do.' Stagg was also quoted as saying: 'I hope that now the police – the fat, lazy bastards – will go out and find the real killer.' Unfortunately, it was already too late. Even before Stagg came to court, Robert Napper, the man who eventually confessed to the killing of Rachel Nickell, had murdered again, his victims a young woman and her four-year-old child.

A subsequent case, the murder of an eighteen-year-old A-level student, Stephen Lawrence, in South London in 1993, revealed another aspect of police failings. Five white youths – all of whom lived locally – were identified as the prime suspects in the killing, but the Crown Prosecution Service decided there was insufficient evidence on which to proceed, and the case did not come to court. A private prosecution was subsequently mounted, though it did not secure a conviction. For many, the failure of the police and the CPS to bring anyone to account compounded the original crime and merely confirmed the widespread perception that racism was endemic to the judicial system; it seemed unlikely that, had the colours of the victim and the alleged perpetrators been reversed, there would have been a similar level of inaction.

There had been similar cases in the past, but what made the difference in this instance was the dogged determination of the Lawrence family – particularly Stephen's parents Neville and Doreen – to fight an establishment that denied them justice. Their cause received a massive boost in February 1997 when, following an inquest verdict of unlawful killing, the *Daily Mail*, in an unprecedented act either of journalistic courage or trial by media (depending on one's perspective), devoted its front page to named photographs of each of the five men with the unequivocal headline: MURDERERS. It added: 'The *Mail* accuses these men of killing. If we are wrong, let them sue us.' From here on, the campaign could scarcely be ignored, and later that year the incoming home secretary, Jack Straw, set up an inquiry into the case, headed by the impeccably establishment figure of William Macpherson, a retired judge who had served with the Scots Guards and the SAS.

Macpherson's report was published in February 1999 and told a depressingly familiar tale. The police handling of the murder had been incompetent (though there was no finding of corruption), lessons had not been learned from the 1981 Scarman Report about relations between the police and members of ethnic minorities, and the Metropolitan Police were declared to be 'institutionally racist'. This last finding was something new in an official inquiry. Scarman had shied away from such a damning verdict, but Macpherson heard evidence from, amongst others, the Chief Constable of Greater Manchester, who admitted that 'internalised' prejudice affected the behaviour of officers, and concluded that there was such a thing as institutional racism at work, even if it were difficult to pin down: 'It can be seen or detected in processes, attitudes and behaviour which amounts to discrimination through unwitting prejudice, ignorance, thoughtlessness and racist stereotyping which disadvantages minority ethnic people.'

The charge went down extremely badly with much of the press. A phrase previously confined to what had been dismissed as 'the loony left' was now being given legitimacy by the state, and many were not prepared to accept the inevitable implication articulated by Ian Jack in the *Independent*: 'The loony left weren't so loony after all.' Even before the publication of the report, *Times* columnist Michael Gove had compared the behaviour of the Lawrences' lawyers to that of Joseph McCarthy in the 1950s and had denounced the idea of institutional racism as 'making sweeping assumptions about groups instead of forming reasoned judgements about individuals'. Within the force itself, there was said to be a severe fall in morale and, as the findings were digested, Paul Condon, the Metropolitan Police Commissioner, came under intense pressure to resign; he survived, having belatedly accepted the concept of institutional racism.

The impact of Macpherson was considerable and prompted a season of soul-searching in other institutions. In cabinet, the health secretary Frank Dobson claimed that it wasn't just the police, but that 'the NHS was riddled with racism' as well, while Herman Ouseley, chair of the Commission for Racial Equality, said that the same was true of the education system. A spokesperson for the Church of England joined the breast-beating: 'We have recognised for a long time there is some degree of institutional racism. We are working on it.'

But it was in the police force that the effects were felt most profoundly. Straw was determined that the report should be implemented in full and could justifiably boast in his memoirs that 'Sixty-seven of the seventy recommendations had a concrete result, in changes of practice, or law.' A long process of rebuilding trust commenced, though the size of the task was made clear by an opinion poll conducted for the *Guardian* before the report's publication; it showed that a quarter of the public thought that 'most police officers tend to be racist or very racist', while a third felt that, regardless of personal intentions, the operations of the force discriminated against ethnic minorities.

Evidence that such feelings might be based in fact had come in 1995 with an edition of *World in Action* that addressed racism in the force. It included, most controversially, secretly filmed footage of the comedian Bernard Manning entertaining four hundred off-duty officers from Manchester at a police charity dinner. Manning had made his name on the series *The Comedians* in the 1970s, but had found television work increasingly hard to come by as the tide turned, both in comedy and society, against material deemed to be sexist and racist. Undeterred, he upped the offensiveness of his live performance, revelling in his status as the least politically correct entertainer in the country to the extent that, despite being a very gifted comedian, for much of the time he simply gave up on the pretence of being humorous. Amongst the jokes about 'shooting niggers' that got the police laughing, were also some simple statements about identity: 'They actually think they're English because they're born here. That means if a dog's born in a stable it's a horse.' Manning's routine was roundly denounced, not only by the usual suspects but also by the likes of the *News of the World*, though it did rather feel as if the wrong target had been chosen: Manning told gags, those laughing at them were responsible for policing the country.

For now, major reform of the police remained a step too far for the Conservative government. Instead Michael Howard was promising to abolish the centuries-old right to silence for defendants, even though –

given the spate of miscarriages of justice – some might have concluded that it was the behaviour of the police, not that of the accused, that required attention.

As John Patten surveyed the state of modern Britain in his book *Things to Come* (1995), and considered where we went from here, he also noted that 'the undermining of institutions in the United Kingdom seems in the mid-1990s to be endemic', and pointed to the urgent need to 'rekindle respect for our institutions'. After sixteen years of Tory government, much of which had been devoted to attacking the establishment of the country both on left and right – from the trade unions and the BBC to the Church of England and the professions – it was perhaps unsurprising that little respect still remained.

Even in those areas of public service that had the wholehearted support of the government, things were far from rosy; the use of the police for political ends in the miners' strike and the attacks on New Age travellers and those attending raves had not done much to enhance the force's standing in society. And although the NHS continued to enjoy widespread public approval, its image too was damaged by two of the most sensational murder cases of the decade. In 1993 a nurse named Beverley Allitt, working in a Lincolnshire hospital, was given multiple life sentences for the killing of four children in her care and the attempted murder of several others. Five years later Dr Harold Shipman, a GP in Manchester, was arrested and was found guilty on fifteen counts of murder, though it transpired that this was little more than the tip of the iceberg: an inquiry reported that he had probably killed around 250 of his patients over a career that lasted more than a quarter of a century. These were, of course, exceptional examples of a betrayal of trust and could be seen as isolated cases. The same was not true of the discovery late in the decade that human tissue, including the organs of hundreds of children, had been retained by Alder Hey Children's Hospital in Liverpool without the consent of the patients or their families. A subsequent investigation revealed that the unethical practice was not confined to that institution alone.

Nor could individual members of the public be exonerated in the breakdown of social relationships that had once been taken for granted. A generation earlier, the family doctor had enjoyed unquestioning esteem, but in 1991 a study published in the *British Medical Journal* showed that over 60 per cent of GPs had been abused or assaulted by patients or by patients' relatives in the previous twelve months. Similarly, a 1997 survey of clergymen in London found that 70 per cent had been assaulted or threatened with violence, while schools were found to be 'at a higher risk of arson than any other buildings used by people'.

Moreover, there was a nagging feeling on the part of many that long-term underinvestment in the physical infrastructure of public services was eroding the quality of life in Britain. The story was not, of course, quite so simple. Much work was done in regenerating some parts of the country: in Manchester, for example, not only was the notorious Hulme estate redeveloped but a velodrome, a swimming pool and a new concert hall were also constructed. (The sports facilities, part of a failed bid to stage the Olympics, were later important in the successful attempt to secure the 2002 Commonwealth Games.)

There were also new initiatives to revitalise areas that had festered for decades. In 1988 the government had brought forward the idea of allowing council residents to vote on whether they wished to remove their estates from local authority control and pass them to a newly constituted Housing Action Trust. The legislation to create these bodies struggled initially – the Labour opposition scored one of its few victories of the Thatcher years when the House of Lords voted against the proposal – but it was subsequently passed and the first of the new organisations was approved in 1991. By the end of the decade the Labour minister Chris Mullin was visiting one such trust, which had taken over some of the worst council housing in Liverpool and, having demolished the existing high-rise horrors, had replaced them with good quality low-rises. Mullin noted in his diary: 'I can't remember what Old Labour's line on Housing Action Trusts was, but I bet we were opposed. Something else the Tories were right about.'

But such was the Conservatives' reputation by the mid-1990s that these successes passed by mostly without mention and certainly without credit. The impression had taken root that public services were being neglected because the Tories believed there was 'no such thing as society'. And it was because John Major recognised the problem more clearly than any of his colleagues that he had proposed the Citizens' Charter; by giving people the right to information, they would gain a stake in society, would cease to be merely units in the erratic functioning of the state and would become involved.

Had it been communicated with sufficient enthusiasm, the Citizens' Charter could genuinely have been a big idea. But there seemed little appetite for it amongst Major's senior colleagues, some of whom seemed more inclined to join in, albeit discreetly, with the sneering of commentators. Initially Labour attacked the entire project as, in the words of Gordon Brown, 'a cosmetic public relations exercise', but it was hardly that. After a flurry of excitement in 1991, the media simply lost interest in the entire enterprise, and although over half a million pounds was spent on press advertising in 1993, it did little to compensate for the Charter's absence from the news columns. Perhaps the problem was with Major himself. His appeal had largely rested on the fact that he seemed like a normal human being, and the Charter had been built in his image, but as his position crumbled in the aftermath of Black Wednesday, so too did the everyday concerns of the Charter come to seem merely trivial.

'We don't want a leader who is ordinary,' fretted Gyles Brandreth, after meeting the prime minister towards the end of September 1992. 'We want a leader who is *extraordinary* – and decent, determined, disciplined, convincing as he is, JM isn't that.' A few months later Brandreth watched Major being interviewed on television by David Frost and could only express the exasperation felt by many in the Conservative Party: 'Maastricht, Mellor, the ERM, unemployment, the pits; we judder from shambles to catastrophe to disaster and *still* our leader speaks of the Citizen's Charter.'

7
Basics
'I'm a weirdo'

The spectacle of a cabinet minister making a fool of himself convulsed the nation as they read their newspapers, eyes rounded and popping in every corner of the land. In a dismal world it was wonderful to have something ridiculous to laugh at.
Edwina Currie, *A Parliamentary Affair* (1994)

NICKY: The great moral issue facing modern British politics is corruption.
Peter Flannery, *Our Friends in the North* (1996)

Too many Conservative MPs have been exposed as perverts, liars and conmen.
The Sun (1997)

If it was John Major's intention that the Citizens' Charter should be the enduring soundbite of his premiership, he was to be disappointed. Far more resonant, it transpired, was a phrase he came up with in his speech to the 1993 Conservative Party conference, even if it was wrenched out of context and used against him. It was intended to be a positive message, reclaiming the ground he had occupied at the start of his premiership, before everything had gone wrong. Casting an eye back to the 1950s and '60s, he denounced fashionable theories that had led to wrong turns being taken on education, family life and housing ('we pulled down the terraces, destroyed whole communities'), but argued that the innate character of Britain had survived these onslaughts.

'Underneath we're still the same people,' he urged. 'The old values – neighbourliness, decency, courtesy – they're still alive, they're still the best of Britain.' Then came the killer phrase: 'It is time to return to those old core values, time to get back to basics, to self-discipline and respect for the law, to consideration for others, to accepting a responsibility for yourself and your family.' His audience understood entirely what he was talking about, and responded with genuine warmth and affection for a decent man who dreamed of simpler, happier times.

Party conferences, however, are not primarily about the activists in the hall, but about the country beyond, for whom the events are filtered through the words of the assembled journalists. The former Tory MP Matthew Parris, now working for *The Times*, was at the pre-speech press conference and saw how the phrase 'back to basics' would be received: 'Within seconds, journalists were asking sceptical, cheeky or downright lewd questions about divorce, adultery and waywardness among Major's own colleagues.' And that did indeed become the interpretation, aided by briefings from the Conservatives' director of communications, Tim Collins, that the prime minister 'was intent on rolling back the permissive society'.

Major had wished to signal that policy development should reflect traditional values in education and in law and order, which in itself was a slightly dangerous gambit. The economic news was all positive — in May inflation had fallen to 1.3 per cent, its lowest level in nearly three decades, growth in GDP was averaging over 3 per cent and the unemployment rate was starting to fall — and it might have been politically more astute to return to his earlier theme: yes, it had hurt, but yes, it had worked. To focus attention instead on areas in the public and private spheres where society had taken a wrong turn was merely to invite people to consider, after four Conservative election victories, which group of politicians they would like to blame for these failings. If Major's message had been understood as he wished, it would have reinforced the growing impression that Thatcherism had left society in a poorer ethical state; when he said that the country needed 'more Conservatism of the traditional kind', the unspoken implication was that this had been absent in the Thatcher years.

'Back to basics' avoided that frying-pan only to be consumed by the fire of personal morality. And the reason was not hard to discern. For it was not just the media who had stoked up the flames; the right wing of the cabinet had been making an issue of private morals for some time. At the previous conference Peter Lilley had embarrassed himself and viewers by breaking into a parody of the song 'As Some Day It May Happen' from Gilbert and Sullivan's *The Mikado*:

There's those who make up bogus claims in half a dozen names,
And councillors who draw the dole to run left-wing campaigns —
They never would be missed, they never would be missed.
There's young ladies who get pregnant just to jump the housing queue,

And dads who won't support the kids of the ladies they have kissed.
And I haven't even mentioned all those sponging socialists –
I've got them on my list.

The focus on single mothers, in particular, was becoming a common theme. John Redwood delivered a speech condemning the 'trend in some places for young women to have babies with no apparent intention of even trying a marriage or stable relationship', and John Patten made his position clear at the 1993 conference: 'To me there is no greater betrayal than having a child and then walking away.' Meanwhile Michael Portillo was explaining at a fringe meeting: 'Conservatives do make value judgements. For us there is a difference between right and wrong.' As the right-wing backbencher Edward Leigh saw it, Back to Basics was the opportunity to make these value judgements part of public policy: 'This is our chance to tackle the permissive society. Let's speak up for family values.'

It was partly in response to this tide of feeling within the party – and perhaps in the country beyond – that the Child Support Agency was established in 1993, charged with tracing absent parents and ensuring that they made a proper contribution to the financial maintenance of their children. This would, it was argued, reduce the burden on the state, whilst also helping to inculcate a sense of responsibility in feckless parents.

Again, though, the charge could easily be laid that this problem had largely developed on the Conservatives' watch. The proportion of children living in single-parent households had doubled since Margaret Thatcher had taken power and now stood at around one in five. To argue that the Tories were now the solution to a problem they had helped to create was always going to be hard; there might be rejoicing in heaven over the repentant sinner, but the electorate tended to be less forgiving. In any event, the entire Back to Basics agenda was hijacked from the off, as the press seized the opportunity to go after any transgressing Tories they could track down.

The first story to break was entirely atypical. Within a fortnight of Major's speech, the papers were salivating over stories about Steven Norris, the transport minister, a married man who was said to have (or to have had, it was never entirely clear) five mistresses. His wife, it transpired, knew about the mistresses, though they didn't know about each other, and she had no desire to play the media game, which made his life a great deal easier. And since Norris was also a popular figure at Westminster, the whole incident passed almost as rapidly as it had arrived, leaving him still in his ministerial office, albeit with the popular nickname 'Shagger'.

Much the same had been true when, in 1992, it was revealed that Paddy Ashdown had, some years earlier, had an affair with his then-secretary. Aware that the story was about to break, Ashdown seized the initiative by announcing it himself at a press conference, while the woman in the case refused to speak to the press. Again he acquired a nickname – Paddy Pantsdown, donated by the *Sun* ('dreadful, but brilliant', he acknowledged) – but little harm was done. In fact, there was a short-term gain; in response to the question of whether he would make a good prime minister, his opinion poll rating leapt from 34 to 47 per cent.

If this suggested that there was a new tolerance abroad for politicians displaying human foibles, another story from 1992 provided a more depressing perspective. The weekend before John Major announced the start of the general election campaign, a hitherto unknown junior minister, Alan Amos, was arrested on Hampstead Heath in North London. The Heath had long enjoyed a reputation as a cruising area for homosexual men – the previous year the gay campaigner Peter Tatchell had led a team clearing up the area, filling twenty-five bin liners with 'discarded condoms and other fascinating debris' – and, although Amos was not charged with any offence, the newspapers drew their own conclusions. GAY SEX SHAME OF TORY MP, ran the *Sun* headline, while the *Daily Star* adopted a suitably sanctimonious tone when lecturing him about 'wandering at dusk at a place which has been turned into a no-go area for decent families by perverts'.

Amos himself denied that he was homosexual and would admit only to having engaged in a 'childish and stupid' act, but still felt obliged to stand down as a candidate in the forthcoming election, 'in the best interests of my constituents, the Conservative Party and the re-election of John Major', as he put it. 'Yet another victory for squalid reporting,' he said, 'a dangerous abuse of freedom in an open society.' And there was some justification for his resentment. Had the press not been informed of his arrest and caution, his majority of 8,000 in Hexham would have ensured that he was safely returned to the House of Commons. Once the story was in the public domain, however, he stood no chance, as was demonstrated by the performance of the Liberal Democrat candidate in the constituency, Jonathan Wallace; he took the opportunity to announce that he was 'gay and proud of it' and was rewarded with a 10 per cent drop in support.

The respective stories of Ashdown and Norris on the one side and Amos on the other sketched out the ground rules for political sex scandals at the start of the decade, a set of standards summed up by the Conservative MP Rupert Allason in his political whodunit *Murder in the Commons* (published in

1992 under the pen name Nigel West): 'Mere infidelity could probably be survived, but a wholly legal act of homosexuality spelt catastrophe for the upwardly mobile.'

There were other cases too that would once have meant ruin but which no longer rated serious or prolonged attention. In the summer of 1992 the *Independent* ran a story that Virginia Bottomley had had her first child in 1967 before marrying the child's father, another future Tory MP, Peter Bottomley. Andreas Whittam-Smith, the paper's editor, defended the disclosure: 'As Mrs Bottomley speaks to the nation about teenage mothers, I think it is a significant fact worth recording that she was once herself an unwed teenage mother.' But since neither of the Bottomleys had ever made an issue of the evils of unmarried parenthood, the story disappeared very quickly.

Similarly, when Clare Short was reunited with the son she had given up for adoption back in 1963 when she was just seventeen, she was fearful of the publicity that would result — 'My expectation was that I would be criticised and drummed out of politics as a wicked woman' — but the revelation actually brought her widespread support and sympathy in a way she hadn't previously known. It was simply seen as a feelgood story, all the more so when her son was seen on television accompanying her to the count on election night in 1997.

One other incident from 1992 illustrated the slightly strange state of what constituted a scandal in modern Britain. Norman Lamont, eighteen months on from his Miss Whiplash episode, was reported to have exceeded the limit on his Access credit card, and it was alleged that the last purchase made was for twenty Raffles cigarettes and a bottle of Bricout champagne from a Threshers off-licence in Praed Street in the Paddington area of London. The details were important. Praed Street was repeatedly described as being in a 'seedy' part of Paddington, from which we were meant to infer that it was a red light district, while Raffles cigarettes — apart from bearing the name of the most famous amateur thief in English literature — were mostly smoked by women; had the brand been Marlboro or Benson & Hedges, it would have been less fun. The fact that Lamont didn't smoke cigarettes was also reported, leaving the public to draw their own conclusions.

Unfortunately all these details, while fascinating, were also wrong. Lamont had used his card in the Connaught Street branch of Threshers, half a mile from Praed Street, and hadn't bought cigarettes, but rather two bottles of claret and one of Château Margaux. It transpired that journalists had approached the Praed Street branch, and that the staff there — manager David Newton and sales assistant John Onanuga — had simply concocted the story that the media wanted to hear. Threshers issued an apology, saying that the two men had 'admitted totally fabricating the story' and 'had no intention of damaging Mr Lamont's reputation'. They deeply regretted their actions, but it did neither much good; Newton was sacked by Threshers, and in March 1994 Onanuga was deported for having overstayed his visitor's visa.

Lamont survived this piece of fluff, of course, but it was indicative of how feverish the atmosphere at Westminster and in Fleet Street had become that such a non-story made it into the newspapers at all, let alone onto the front pages for several days. A few months later, in February 1993, the magazine *New Statesman & Society* reported on this absurd level of gossip, illustrating their piece with reference to an article in the little-known scandal magazine *Scallywag*, which had printed an entirely baseless rumour about John Major himself having an affair with a woman who provided catering services in London. Major promptly issued writs against both magazines, which were settled out of court.

The 'back to basics' speech, however, gave free rein to rumours, and from here on in, it was open season on Tory MPs. A few days after the 1992 conference, the junior health minister Tim Yeo had called for new rules that would permit adoption by single-parent households to be used only as 'a last resort'. When it transpired more than a year later that during the conference he had been engaged in an extra-marital liaison that resulted in the birth of a child, thus creating another single-parent household, he was obliged to resign from his new job as an environment minister, even though several of the more liberal figures in his party – Douglas Hurd, Norman Fowler, Virginia Bottomley, Emma Nicholson – weighed in on his behalf. Similarly, the obscure MP Gary Waller briefly visited the front pages with another story of an illegitimate child, as did the civil service minister Robert Hughes and junior Welsh minister Rod Richards, who were both reported to have had affairs.

And so it went on, an endless litany of affairs, mistresses and Commons researchers. 'They run off with these silly girls,' bemoaned a character in the sitcom *Dinnerladies*. 'We never had any of that with dear old Ted Heath.' The list of miscreants was extended on what felt at times like a weekly basis, so that the details of each case blurred with those of the last, and it became difficult to remember which of the obscure figures propelled into the headlines had done what. Nor did it seem particularly important; if one case were missed, then another was bound to come along shortly, so that *The Day Today*'s invention of a Conservative Party post, the Vice Chairman for Resignation Issues, seemed all too appropriate. Each weekend would inevitably produce, in the words of a *Sunday Mirror* headline, ANOTHER BACK TO BASICS BOMBSHELL.

That particular headline related to the man who had inherited Margaret Thatcher's old seat in Finchley. Hartley Booth, a 47-year-old married man who was also a Methodist lay preacher, was said to have become infatuated with a 22-year-old art student. Booth denied any sexual impropriety, but the fun here lay in the details of the allegations: that the affair had quite possibly not been consummated, that he had written love poems to her, and that she was discovered to have previously worked for Peter Mandelson. Elsewhere Richard Spring, the MP for Bury St Edmunds, was said to have enjoyed 'a three-in-a-bed romp with a woman and a man', though since all three of the alleged participants were unmarried, it was hard to know what business this was of the newspapers.

And although John Major himself had seen off the rumours about his own conduct (the story of his relationship the previous decade with Edwina Currie had yet to enter the public domain), his son, James, was caught up in the media storm, when news broke that he had been having an affair with a woman who was not only married but thirteen years older than himself. Few newspapers could resist the detail that 'her husband found them cuddling in the kitchen at their home in Cambridgeshire, with James in drag', though it was hard not to feel slightly disappointed when this turned out to refer to an incident at a fancy-dress party for which he had turned up in 'a frilly garter, bra and silky knickers'.

Currie herself was in no doubt where the fault for all these stories lay: 'the bloody "Back to Basics" campaign is to blame, for it outlawed the one protective factor the Tory Party has always relied on – hypocrisy.' As Sarah Keays, who had been Cecil Parkinson's lover in the 1980s, put it: 'They apply one standard to themselves and another to the rest of the country.'

Through it all ran the saga of former MP Alan Clark, who published the first volume of his diaries in 1993, complete with accounts of his philandering, in both his real and fantasy lives. 'I will be a figure of fun, like Mellor,' he worried as publication approached, though in his case the public were simply entranced. He was seen as an old-fashioned bounder, a rogue who operated on a scale so much more impressive than that of his erstwhile colleagues. Even better was the response of his wife Jane, who stood by her husband: 'I still think he's super,' she told the press. 'I know he's an S-H-one-T, but that's it.' She also exhibited heroic levels of aristocratic disdain: 'Quite frankly, if you bed people that I call "below-stairs class", they go to the papers, don't they?'

This latter comment was occasioned by the story that Clark had seduced a married woman as well as both of her daughters, which gave him enormous lad credentials. It got even better when the whole family arrived in Britain from South Africa ('a sad old cuckold with a couple of hard-faced slappers', in Ian Hislop's words), and the woman's husband, Judge James Harkess, threatened to seek out Clark and horsewhip him. Sadly, Harkess backed out of this nineteenth-century course of action, and instead resorted to employing the publicist Max Clifford to make his case. Nonetheless, Clark had managed to find the political equivalent of the Philosopher's Stone, transmuting bad behaviour into an improved public image. The same could not be said for the Conservative Party, for whom the Clark stories kept the pot of scandal bubbling.

Even Clark's airing of his dirty linen, however, was as nothing compared to David Ashby, a Leicestershire MP, who was alleged by the *Sunday Times* (for by now it was not only the tabloids who were indulging in such tales) to have left his wife of twenty-eight years because of his 'friendship with another man'. It was claimed in subsequent reports that he had shared a bed with a man whilst on holiday in France, which he agreed was true but only for reasons of economy, adding pointedly: 'I have got to keep my wife in the style to which she is accustomed.'

Rather than keeping his head down and waiting for the storm to blow over, Ashby sued the *Sunday Times* for libel over a related story — that he had also shared a bed with a man on holiday in Goa — and thus launched a court case that provided more information than anyone could truly be said to need. His wife called him 'queenie' and 'poofter', he alleged in court, she physically assaulted him, he said, and taunted him about his impotence (he called a doctor to testify that he was indeed impotent). Giving evidence against him, she denied much of this, but claimed that he had told her of his homosexuality when he moved out of the marital home. At one point in the trial Ashby also burst into tears in the witness box, and proceedings were further enlivened when he gave a demonstration of the bizarre contraption he wore in bed to prevent his snoring.

After twenty days of this, the jury found against Ashby, leaving him with huge legal costs to meet and a wrecked political career that never recovered. In 1996 he was deselected by his constituency party as their candidate in the forthcoming general election. 'It is the usual blind prejudice,' he explained: 'love the Queen Mum, hate queers, hate foreigners, get out of the Common Market, keep the Queen's head on the coins.' He later expanded on this in a live radio interview, saying of the local Tories: 'They're a bunch of shits, aren't they, and we know they are.'

The fact that Ashby, however misguidedly, felt obliged to parade the most private details of his life in court was an indication of the bitter human cost of the newspapers' gleeful assault on the government. The other side of the story, the experience of families caught up in the storm, was the subject of one of the better television dramas of the time.

In Paula Milne's three-part series, *The Politician's Wife* (1995), Trevor Eve played Duncan Matlock, a highly ambitious politician who is minister for families and has designs on the leadership. When he is revealed to have had an affair with a Commons researcher, who turns out to be a former prostitute, an all-male establishment closes ranks, trying to spin his infidelity as a brief fling, even though the party hierarchy know that it was a long-term relationship. Duncan's wife Flora (Juliet Stevenson) is initially persuaded to do the right thing, both for her husband's career and for the party. 'Bloody bad time, Flora,' the chief whip (Ian Bannen) tells her. 'We're being ravaged by publicity-hungry dissidents who think nothing of defying the leader, the whips, every loyalist ethic the party ever stood for.' When she subsequently discovers the truth, however, she goes about exacting a quiet, convoluted and devastating revenge in which she engineers a political and financial scandal, manipulating the party machine to destroy him. 'I came to see,' she tells her local association, with heavy irony, 'that, important though the family is, the real issue here is duty to the party.'

For many of those whose private lives were opened up to the vulgar gaze, the real issue was the media. Writing in the aftermath of his trial, Ashby bitterly denounced 'the press who wildly throw phrases like "public right to know" and "exposing hypocrisy" around as if that is a valid reason for destroying a person's family and career'. It was also true, though, that newspaper readers happily colluded with the media, revelling in the discomfort of men who – with the occasional exception of David Mellor or Norman Lamont – could scarcely be called household names.

And much of the pleasure derived from the fact that it was the Tories who were the victims of the muck-raking. There were Labour stories of misbehaviour, such as the revelation in 1994 that Dennis Skinner had a mistress in London to complement his wife in his Derbyshire constituency, but they made little impact since the public appeared uninterested. Two years later *Our Friends in the North* ran a fictionalised account of local government corruption that echoed the days of T. Dan Smith and John Poulson. It seemed deeply unhelpful to the Labour cause ('Bloody Labour Party!' exclaims one character. 'Crooks, the bloody lot of 'em') and came hot on the heels of allegations about corruption and accusations of religious sectarianism and nepotism in the Labour authority of Monklands, where John Smith had had his constituency.

Yet none of this was allowed to interfere with the dominant media narrative of Tory sleaze, a word that was gaining political currency even before Major's 'back to basics' speech. 'Sleaze-baiting is particularly evident now,' wrote Andrew Marr in June 1993, 'because it seems to reflect a deeper truth: disgraceful news seems somehow more credible, more authentic, than good news.' The headline to that piece was HOW MUCH WORSE CAN IT GET?, suggesting that things had reached rock bottom for the government. They hadn't, and the opposition could scarcely contain its glee. 'It was perceived that Labour were above reproach, and the Conservatives beyond redemption,' fretted John Major, while Alan Clark reported a former Tory minister asking in frustration: 'Is the Labour Party made up of two hundred virgins?'

By now there were too many groups with a vested interest in keeping the stories flowing. Much of the public felt almost personally betrayed by a government that, having been returned with such huge support, had then proved to be incompetent; with retaliation at the ballot boxes still a long way off, the best revenge was to turn them into a laughing-stock. There were those on the right of the Conservative Party who happily, if covertly, joined in, seeing in the Back to Basics fiasco a chance to discredit for ever the non-Thatcherite wing of the party. And there was a press equally keen to ensure that no privacy law, of the kind once threatened by David Mellor, should be allowed to surface; the more scandals that were published, the stronger the argument became that politicians only wanted such regulations because they had things they wanted to hide from the electorate.

Mixed up in this farrago of moralising indignation were a couple of genuine tragedies. In January 1994 the wife of Lord Caithness, a transport minister, killed herself with a shotgun, reportedly after learning that her husband was leaving her for another woman. He resigned his post immediately and the story made very few waves, suggesting that perhaps personal loss still had the power to instil a sense of proportion. Such a theory, however, was exploded the following month when the death was announced of Stephen Milligan, the MP for Eastleigh.

The circumstances of Milligan's demise could hardly fail to escape notice. His body was found at his home, dressed in women's underwear, with a satsuma in his mouth and a bin liner over his head. He had died from strangulation with a length of flex, the apparent victim of a session of autoerotic asphyxiation that had gone wrong. Again his was hardly a name instantly recognisable to the public, though at Westminster he was popular and highly regarded. A former journalist with the BBC and the *Sunday Times*, he had been elected in 1992 and was the first of the new intake to get a government job, making his presence felt with his loyal contributions to the Maastricht debate. At the age of forty-five, he was a rising star in the party and he had high aspirations. 'I would like to be foreign secretary,' he told his friends the day before he died. His death represented a real blow to the Tories, beyond even the loss of his seat to the Liberal Democrats in the ensuing by-election. 'Bad not just for the Tories, but for the whole political class,' was Giles Radice's conclusion, though there was no doubt who took the brunt of the scorn. WOULD THE LAST DECENT PERSON IN THE TORY PARTY SHUT THE CLOSET DOOR, trumpeted a less than sympathetic *Daily Mirror* headline.

The details were too much for John Major to comprehend; he was out of his depth when it came to such arcane sexual practices as breath-play. It was, said the prime minister, 'a desperate personal tragedy', concluding that 'he must have been pretty unhappy and pretty miserable'. That verdict drew instant criticism. Judge Tim Milligan, a cousin of the dead man, insisted: 'Stephen was neither miserable nor unhappy. On the contrary, he was thoroughly fulfilled in his work at Westminster and his Eastleigh constituency.' Gyles Brandreth, one of his closest friends in the Commons, was equally unimpressed. 'Stephen was gloriously happy,' he wrote in his diary. 'He'd had another good week in parliament. He was looking forward to promotion. I imagine he went for his round of golf and came home and thought he'd play his little sex game as a weekend celebration – as a treat.'

It was left to Ian Jack, a former journalist colleague of Milligan, to point out a truth largely ignored – that, despite the regrets of unfulfilled potential and the embarrassment caused to the bereaved family and friends, none of this was of much consequence to the dead man himself: 'Personally, I hope Stephen Milligan died a happy man. There seems every possibility that he did.'

If Major struggled to deal with the fallout from Milligan's death, the police certainly failed to cover themselves in glory. As with Alan Amos, details of the incident reached the media with remarkable speed, so much so that Milligan's father found out his son was dead via a news bulletin, and the first his mother heard was when a newspaper reporter phoned with the question: 'How do you feel about your son being strangled?' A Scotland Yard inquiry was launched to discover how this apparent breach of protocol, not to say decency, could have happened; it reported that no police officer was to blame, and hinted that the story was probably leaked by political figures. Commissioner Paul Condon also took the opportunity to deny 'suggestions that officers regularly took bribes from reporters'.

Even if that were true, there were other elements in the police handling of the case that left something to be desired. In the initial reports a detective was quoted as saying: 'The first indications are that he died during a homosexual bondage-type encounter. We believe he was a homosexual.' There was no reason whatsoever for such a conclusion to be drawn, save, it seemed, that, like John Major, the police were unable to believe that 'normal' people might indulge in such minority practices.

There were, of course, scandals involving gay MPs during this period, as well as persistent rumours about senior members of both main parties, including Michael Portillo, Peter Lilley and Gordon Brown. But the tone was changing in response to a new mood in society. In separate incidents Michael Brown and Jerry Hayes, MPs for Brigg and Cleethorpes and for Harlow respectively, were pilloried in the press not for homosexuality as such, but for allegedly having sex with 'underage' lovers. In both cases the other people involved in the stories were not yet twenty-one, which was until the autumn of 1994 the age of consent for male homosexual acts, though it was a near-run thing. The coverage of Hayes's alleged lover – Hayes always denied that they had had sex – was splashed in the *Sun* in 1997 but related to events at the beginning of the decade, while Brown was outed in the period between the vote to lower the age of consent and the implementation of that change in the law.

That vote had come about largely because of the contribution made by a handful of MPs on the liberal wing of the Conservative Party, at a time when John Major was signalling the need for greater tolerance. In the late 1980s Margaret Thatcher's government had identified homosexuality as the most vulnerable element in the supposed permissive legacy of the 1960s and, with Section 28 of the Local Government Act, had sought to prevent the 'promotion' of 'homosexuality as a pretended family relationship'. In the struggle against that measure, the actor Ian McKellen had come out and, with the launch of the group Stonewall, had become a leading figure in the campaign for gay rights; now he was not only invited to Downing Street to discuss the issue with the prime minister, but was also given a knighthood in the first honours list of Major's premiership.

Neither of those developments was uncontroversial. Major's invite was attacked by the right ('another chance to show that he is "nicer" than his predecessor', sneered Frank Johnson in the *Sunday Telegraph*), and the acceptance of a knighthood was denounced as a sell-out by some in the gay movement. Even so, the gestures were partially successful in their aim of trying to signal an end to overt Tory prejudice. Major also changed the regulations that discriminated against homosexuals in the civil service, and let it be known that he was in favour of decriminalising homosexuality in the armed forces.

But the real target for reformers was the unequal age of consent, the key provision written into law that institutionalised discrimination. This was not merely a symbolic piece of legislation. Although the level of police harassment of male homosexuals had fallen from its peak in the late 1980s, the most recent year for which figures were available showed that in 1992 there had been 244 prosecutions for consensual gay sex involving men aged between sixteen and twenty-one.

In 1994 Edwina Currie proposed an amendment to the Criminal Justice Bill that would reduce the homosexual age of consent from twenty-one to sixteen, the same as that for heterosexuals. Sponsors of the amendment included MPs from all parties and amongst those voting for it were forty-two Conservatives, including cabinet ministers Tony Newton and William Waldegrave, as well as such prominent figures as William Hague, Michael Brown, Jerry Hayes and Steven Norris. The more traditional Tory attitudes, however, were also much in evidence. 'What Mrs Currie is seeking to do,' complained Tony Marlow, 'is to get this House to vote to legalise the buggery of adolescent men.' The veteran backbencher Elaine Kellett-Bowman was already on record with her thoughts: 'Sodomy is unhygienic, unhealthy and still the major cause of the spread of AIDS.'

Nor was this a divisive issue for one party alone. John Smith said it was 'a matter of equality and freedom', and Labour's home affairs spokesperson, Tony Blair, made what Currie called 'a humdinger of a speech'. (She also observed: 'He will make a fine and popular PM some day, if his party have the sense to choose him.') But the amendment was defeated with the assistance of thirty-five Labour MPs, including David Blunkett, Ann Taylor and Michael Martin, the future home secretary, government chief whip and Speaker of the House respectively.

The House then proceeded to the next vote, as a result of which approval was given to a compromise proposal – a reduction to eighteen years of age. Although it failed to satisfy the thousands of demonstrators gathered in Parliament Square, this was at least a step towards equality. The reform had the backing of John Major and of the home secretary Michael Howard, who explained that he couldn't go any further because 'We need to protect young men from activities which their lack of maturity might cause them to regret.' As an aspiration for legislators, that seemed a trifle ambitious.

Some European countries were starting to introduce legal recognition for same-sex partnerships, but for now the reduction in the age of consent was as far as the British Parliament was prepared to go. In 1996 Glenda Jackson, the former actress turned Labour MP, tabled an amendment to the government's Housing Bill that would have given homosexuals living in council or housing association properties the same rights as heterosexuals enjoyed, so that if the person in whose name the tenancy was held died, his or her partner could take over the tenancy and remain in the property. The provision was opposed by the environment secretary, John Selwyn Gummer, and defeated at committee stage.

That same year the ban on homosexuality in the military came to the fore. Until 1994 there had existed a curious state of affairs whereby all homosexual acts were illegal in the armed forces, and an offender could both be given a dishonourable discharge and sentenced to a jail term; since the forces had no provision for such imprisonment, the sentence was served in a civilian prison, even if the offender had committed no crime recognised by civilian society. That situation changed with the decriminalisation of homosexuality in the armed forces and merchant navy, but it remained a sacking offence, and the defence secretary, Michael Portillo, was unwilling to cede any further ground. He had most of Fleet Street on his side, expressing an attitude that was summed up in the *Sun*'s typically forthright leader column: 'The British soldier needs to worry about the enemy ahead. Not some queer behind him.'

An amendment to the Armed Forces Bill was tabled in the names of a cross-party trio of Edwina Currie, Gerald Kaufman and Menzies Campbell, but was easily defeated, largely because the Labour leadership decided that this was too controversial an issue to be addressing so close to an election. As shadow home secretary, Tony Blair had been quite clear where he stood. 'People are entitled to think that homosexuality is wrong,' he had said. 'What they are not entitled to do is use the criminal law to force that view on others.' As leader of the party, however, he displayed little inclination to pursue gay rights too vocally, and abstained on the armed forces vote, although it was official Labour policy.

There was, in this debate at least, a clash of values. On the one side was the claim to individual human rights and equality before the law, on the other an insistence that the overriding priority of the armed forces was efficiency. An army that retained an officer class was never going to be a model of democratic values, civil rights or egalitarianism, and there was a case to be made that one of the few public services capable of doing its job shouldn't be interfered with in the name of equality. The presence of homosexuals, explained the retired Air Chief Marshal Sir Michael Armitage, would have 'quite a serious impact on unit cohesion, on unit discipline and therefore on fighting effectiveness'. It was hard, however, to separate such arguments from what mostly came across as simple prejudice, as satirised on Chris Morris's television show *Brass Eye* by a character worried about the possibility of homosexuality in the Royal Navy: 'Homosexuals can't swim, they attract enemy radar, they attract sharks, they insist on being placed on the captain's table, they get up late, they nudge people while they're shooting, they muck about. Imagine the fear of knowing you have a gay man aboard a boat.'

But the tide was turning, and the pressure from outside Parliament was building relentlessly. During the 1994 debate, twenty agony aunts – including such household names as Claire Rayner, Marjorie Proops and Anna Raeburn – had written to *The Times* in support of Currie's amendment: 'How can a law be said to protect teenagers when it turns them into criminals and threatens to prosecute them for expressing love for another person?' The fact that such a message was promoted on a weekly basis by the advice columns of almost every popular newspaper did more than any politician ever could in changing public opinion. The *Daily Telegraph* acknowledged as much when it marked Proops's, death in 1996 with a leader column imagining a *mea culpa* letter written by the dead woman from Heaven. 'I said they should change the laws to allow homosexuality, abortion and easier divorce,' it read. 'From where I sit today, some of those old teachings don't look so stupid.'

Also influential was the inclusion of gay male characters in films like *The Full Monty* and *Four Weddings and a Funeral*, and of lesbians in the television series *Between the Lines* and *Drop the Dead Donkey*, as well as in the soaps *Emmerdale*, *The Bill* and *Brookside*. The last of these famously featured in 1994 the first pre-watershed lesbian kiss on British television, between Beth Jordache (Anna Friel) and Margaret Clemence (Nicola Stephenson), the same year that two boys were seen kissing in the teen drama *Byker Grove*.

Britpop was making its own contribution. In 1992 the Manic Street Preachers had produced a T-shirt bearing the slogan 'All rock 'n' roll is homosexual', a typically provocative overstatement, and the new music also found room for openly gay stars like the bisexual David McAlmont and Skin, the lesbian singer with Skunk Anansie, each of whom received extensive coverage in the mainstream press in a way that would have been difficult to imagine just a few years earlier. Brett Anderson of Suede had proclaimed early on that he saw himself as 'a bisexual man who's never had a homosexual experience' (prompting Blur's Damon Albarn to retort: 'I'm more homosexual than Brett Anderson'), and amongst those lobbying MPs for a change to the age of consent was Simon Gilbert, the group's drummer. 'I first had gay sex when I was thirteen,' he told the papers. 'By the time I was sixteen it was the law which was my biggest fear.'

There was also Huffty, the lesbian co-presenter of *The Word* who looked, in her words, like 'the stereotypical dyke, with the shaven head and the big boots'. She only lasted for one series of the show and her career then stalled, leaving her unable to realise her dream of making a Geordie soap opera titled *It's Queer Up North*: 'I'd play a lesbian ram-raider in a shell-suit and big trainers, kd lang would play my mother and Kevin Keegan would play my father.'

With the glaring exception of football, the world of Cool Britannia, even in its more laddist corners, seemed happy to accept homosexuality. When Tony first arrives in *Men Behaving Badly*, Gary suspects that he might be gay and is deeply troubled: 'I won't be happy till he's out of my flat.' His middle-aged, frumpy secretary Anthea, however, is the voice of reason. 'I don't think that matters, does it?' she says. 'My nephew's gay. He told us last year during the *Top of the Pops* Christmas special.'

It had been argued in the 1960s that the great liberalising reforms of Harold Wilson's government were largely driven by a political elite against the wishes of most of the country, so that even Lord Arran — whose campaigning had largely been responsible for the limited legalisation of male homosexuality — was anxious that public opinion should not be challenged too openly. 'Any form of ostentatious behaviour, and form of public flaunting, would be utterly distasteful,' he told the Lords, as the Sexual Offences Act was passed in 1967. Thirty years on, however, it appeared as though Britain was changing despite the government, not because of it.

The fact that politicians were now running behind the wider culture was entertainingly illustrated in 1994 when the married-couples game show *Mr and Mrs*, perhaps the blandest programme on British television, announced that it would henceforth consider applications from gay and lesbian couples who wished to compete. The following year London Transport announced that it was modifying its rules to allow those undergoing a sex change to hold two travelcards, with photographs of themselves in both genders, so that they could travel more easily. Also in 1995 Guinness commissioned Britain's first unequivocally gay advert, showing a male homosexual couple in a domestic setting, complete with a decorous but definite kiss, all accompanied by the strains of Tammy Wynette's 'Stand by Your Man'. When word got out about the commercial, however, it attracted some negative criticism and Guinness appeared to lose their nerve. The advert was never shown, to the regret of its director Tony Kaye: 'I think it was charming and it was very funny and would sell a hell of a lot of beer.'

Indeed one of the most striking features of the 1990s was the public's growing acceptance of what were becoming known as minority lifestyles, and it was the perception of gay sex that symbolised the transformation. When the British Social Attitudes survey reported in 1990, the number of those believing homosexual relationships to be wrong was recorded at 69 per cent – down a little from its high point during the right-wing backlash a few years earlier, the time of Section 28 and AIDS – and the gap between that figure and those who believed that such relationships were not wrong stood at 55 per cent. When the same questions were asked a decade later, the gap had narrowed to just 10 per cent, and those believing homosexuality to be wrong were now in a minority.

Some of this change was indirectly the result of AIDS, the response to which had focused the energy of gay campaigning groups. Similarly when the police began a series of raids on London fetish clubs, a cause was found around which different minority groups could coalesce. These clubs were primarily concerned with fetish clothing, particularly rubber and leather, and were allied to the sadomasochistic scene (though most operated a 'no fur' policy in deference to animal rights, a development that would have horrified Leopold von Sacher-Masoch). Typical was Club Whiplash, raided by police in 1994 following an undercover operation by 'vice squad officers who hired leather outfits to infiltrate the S&M subculture'. The intention was clearly to intimidate – stalls selling leatherwear and belts had their goods confiscated, as though possession of a leather cap were itself illegal – and charges were brought under the Disorderly Houses Act, 'a 250-year-old law prohibiting public dancing'. When the case came to trial in 1996, the jury returned verdicts of not guilty. That was the same year in which the tenth staging of the Sex Maniacs' Ball was also stopped by the police, prompting the creation of the Sexual Freedom Coalition to fight further such actions.

The information and guidance produced by government and charities in response to the AIDS epidemic had also, it was argued by some, demystified gay sexual practices. Related to this was the resolution of a longstanding legal anomaly. Ever since the Sexual Offences Act of 1967, it had been legal for male homosexuals over the age of twenty-one to engage in anal intercourse, but it remained strictly illegal for heterosexual couples, even if they were married. In popular mythology, anal sex remained the preserve of gay men, though the National Survey of Sexual Attitudes and Lifestyles, published in 1994, revealed that the lines were less clear-cut than generally depicted; between 12 and 14 per cent of heterosexuals had some experience of the practice, while nearly half of gay men aged between 25 and 34 did not. One consequence of the change in the age of homosexual consent was that for the first time, anal intercourse became legal for anyone over the age of eighteen, and there was a rapid rise in the open discussion of the activity, breaking its status as a taboo and its exclusive association with homosexuality. ('I am the Billy Graham of anal sex,' claimed Frank Skinner, whose live act included a great deal of material on the subject.)

The growing acceptance of homosexuality was in inverse proportion to the public fury directed towards paedophilia, and in 1997 a story broke to delight the hearts of all tabloid editors. Back in the early 1970s Gary Glitter had made some of the best singles of the era, irresistibly monolithic stomps with call-and-response choruses that were guaranteed to fill the floor at every youth club disco. He was also one of the sharpest manipulators in the pop business and, having waited eleven years between his first record and his first hit, he was determined never again to slip away into obscurity.

After the hits had dried up, he had rebuilt his career through sheer perseverance and established himself as a major live draw, turning his Christmas shows into a sell-out event, an annual rock and roll pantomime, while he was also to be found appearing on prestigious bills like the 1996 Prince's Trust gig in Hyde Park, alongside Bob Dylan, Eric Clapton and the Who. 'Amongst great British institutions,' wrote *Q* magazine, 'Gary Glitter now stands somewhere between Paul McCartney and the Queen Mum.' His position as one of the ironic icons of Cool Britannia was confirmed when Oasis included the chorus of 'Hello, Hello, I'm Back Again' on the opening track of *(What's the Story) Morning Glory?* and when he was invited to perform in the Spice Girls 1997 film *Spiceworld*.

That movie appearance never happened. In November 1997 Glitter took his computer in for repairs to a branch of PC World, where a technician discovered images of child pornography on the hard drive and reported the fact to the police. At the same time a woman sold her story to the *News of the World* (via Max Clifford) alleging that Glitter had had a longstanding relationship with her, starting when she was fourteen years old. As the police investigations proceeded, he still played his traditional Christmas shows, though they weren't sell-outs as normal, and the following year he was charged. The trial itself didn't come to court until November 1999, when he faced charges that he repeatedly abused a girl from 1980, when she was fourteen, through to 1982.

The reporting of the case was not without its salacious side (GLITTER LIKED ME TO WEAR WHITE UNDIES AND CALL HIM DADDY, leered the *Sun*) and ultimately it was tabloid excess that scuppered the prosecution. The court was told that the alleged victim's deal with the *News of the World* meant that she stood to earn a further £25,000 – in addition to the £10,000 already paid – if Glitter was convicted. This, it was felt by many, brought her evidence into doubt, and though the arrangement was legal the presiding judge deemed it 'a highly reprehensible state of affairs'. Glitter was acquitted, but immediately after that verdict he pleaded guilty to fifty-four charges of making indecent photographs of children, these being sample charges relating to a computer collection of around 4,000 images, some of them featuring the torture of the very young. The judge sentenced him to four months in jail, and Glitter completed the transition from loved pantomime dame to loathed hate-figure.

Other sexual minorities, whose social status lay somewhere between homosexuals and paedophiles, took longer to find acceptance, but ground was gradually gained (or lost, depending on one's perspective). At the end of the 1980s a police investigation, under the codename Operation Spanner, was launched after a video made for private consumption was discovered, depicting scenes of sexual torture so extreme that officers suspected that serious assaults and possibly even murder had been committed. What they discovered instead was an extensive network of homosexual sadomasochists, most of them middle-aged, spread across the country.

Over four hundred men were arrested at one time or another, before sixteen were prosecuted and fifteen found guilty in December 1990 of criminal behaviour under the 1861 Offences Against the Person Act. The splendidly named Judge James Rant presided and was at pains to make clear that there was no prejudice in his courtroom: 'This is not a witch-hunt against homosexuals. The unlawful conduct before the court would result equally in the prosecution of heterosexuals or bisexuals. Nor is it a campaign to curtail the private sexual activities of citizens of this country.' But, he added: 'The courts must draw the line between what is acceptable in a civilized society and what is not. In this case, the practices clearly lie on the wrong side of that line.'

The case turned largely on the question of consent, on whether inflicting sexual violence on another person should legally be construed as assault if the other person agreed to the act, and therefore on whether it was permissible to allow oneself to be assaulted. At one end of the spectrum, of course, was sexual intercourse itself: which in the absence of consent was very definitely a crime but which was perfectly legal between consenting adults. The acts involved in the Spanner case were somewhat to the other end of the continuum, ranging from urtication, through branding, the insertion of wires into penises and the sandpapering of testicles, up to the nailing of a foreskin to a board.

Much of this, though unorthodox, was far from being confined to gay men. The practice of driving nails through the foreskin, for example, had featured in an early Gérard Depardieu film, *Maîtresse* (1976), while Nick Broomfield's documentary *Fetishes* (1996) was to record similar heterosexual acts in a professional establishment in New York. In any event, as one of the defendants put it, 'it's really no worse than having your nose or ears pierced'. He added: 'It's the same as going potholing really. Unless you have done it, you can't understand what the thrill of it is.'

The case went to appeal in 1992. The judgement was upheld by Lord Lane (best known for keeping the Birmingham Six in jail), who cited as precedent a 1934 trial in which a man who caned a woman in the context of sex was found guilty of assault. From there, it proceeded to the House of Lords, by which stage the story was becoming a cause célèbre, with even *The Times* concerned at the implications. 'Consensual sadomasochism should not be made a crime,' argued a leader. 'If the activities in the Operation Spanner case are to be made illegal, why not spanking or whipping for sexual gratification, both of which take place by consent, sometimes even in houses owned by famous men?' Indeed, not only men. According to reports in 1997, a group of British expats in Hollywood, including most prominently the actress Elizabeth Hurley, enjoyed an after-dinner game in which they took turns to be spanked and had to guess the identity of the spanker. It was, Hurley was quoted as saying, 'silly and naughty'.

The appeal was nonetheless rejected, with one law lord arguing that 'there must be some limitation upon the harm which an individual can consent to and receive at the hands of another'. In 1999, a decade after the initial arrests, the case reached the European Court of Human Rights, which again upheld the original verdict, on the grounds that it was a matter for individual states to determine where the line should be drawn on inflicting harm, even between consenting adults.

During the course of that decade, however, society had adjusted its opinions and the judiciary too began to reflect the changing times. In 1996 a man was prosecuted for using a hot knife to sear his wife's buttocks with his initials. He had been reported to the police by her doctor and was convicted of assault causing actual bodily harm, even though she had been a willing party to the act, indeed had initiated it. The conviction was overturned on appeal on the grounds that 'sexual activity between husband and wife in the privacy of the matrimonial home is not, in our judgement, a matter for criminal investigation, let alone criminal prosecution'.

There had also been a tentative start to building bridges between the police and the gay community, at least in London. The career of the serial killer Colin Ireland, sentenced in 1993 to five life terms for murdering five gay men in sadomasochistic bondage sessions, necessitated a degree of cooperation that had long been absent from the Metropolitan Police's dealings with gay men.

In broader cultural terms, there was a notable move of sexual minorities into the mainstream. Some developments were not entirely obvious, as when the British designer Craig Morrison, who had previously exhibited his work at events such as the Rubber Balls organised by *Skin Two* magazine, launched spiky rubber rucksacks onto a market that was only too happy to make them fashionable items for everyday use. At the same time, tattoos and body piercings – once seen as the preserve of sailors and outlaws – became increasingly commonplace.

Other manifestations were surprising, to say the least. 'How Deep Is Your Love?', the last single by the decade's biggest boy band, Take That, was accompanied by a video of the four remaining members tied up by a dominatrix wearing a scarlet dress and Dr Martens boots. At the end of the decade even Steps, the most innocuous of pop groups, were seen in a video wearing outfits designed by the fetish label House of Harlot.

And running right through the period was Channel 4's cult series *Eurotrash*, 'an extraordinary programme' in the judgement of Tony Benn. 'You wouldn't have believed this could appear on television. There has been such a change in public standards. There is a whiff of decadence about it.' More positively, as Elizabeth Coldwell, then editor of *Forum* magazine, pointed out, the show 'poked fun at bizarre sexual practices while subtly condoning them'. It was increasingly difficult to be shocked by minority tastes after a couple of years of exposure to jokey features on cyber sex, foot fetishists and masturbation machines made from cows' tongues (this latter was before the BSE crisis, of course).

There was also the emergence of star comedians including the transvestite Eddie Izzard, who described himself as a 'male tomboy', Steve Coogan's incarnation as Pauline Calf, and Lily Savage, the drag character created by Paul O'Grady. Savage had spent much of the 1980s as the sensation of London's gay cabaret venue the Vauxhall Tavern before breaking into a wider comedy circuit (billed as a 'Radical Marxist Sex Kitten') and then into television.

With Savage's rise to fame, the longstanding camp element in light entertainment finally came out. 'I'm not really a queer or a homosexual,' gay comedian Larry Grayson had insisted back in the 1970s. 'I'm just behaving like one. That's the big difference.' The public didn't necessarily believe such protestations, but it was deemed necessary to keep making them for the sake of a mainstream audience. Grayson continued his denials of homosexuality when he took over as host of *The Generation Game*, but O'Grady made no such concessions when Lily Savage hosted a revival of the BBC game show *Blankety Blank* in 1997. Nor did other television presenters like Graham Norton, Dale Winton or the newly out Michael Barrymore.

The trailblazer for this was Julian Clary, who had become a familiar television presence at the start of the decade, appearing in a series of startlingly theatrical costumes and delivering some of the wittiest put-downs of the age that took camp homosexuality onto prime time. 'I always wanted to be mainstream and successful,' Clary reflected in 1995, 'but I got bored with it.' At the time his career was still suffering from the effects of a single joke, delivered while presenting a prize at the 1993 British Comedy Awards and broadcast live on ITV. Appearing in pristine black tie, Clary noted that the stage set reminded him of Hampstead Heath, and then took the opportunity to have a little fun at an ex-chancellor of the exchequer who was in the audience. 'I've just been fisting Norman Lamont,' he said, though the punchline — 'Talk about a red box!' — was sadly lost in the audience laughter.

Lamont had earlier been booed while presenting an award to the makers of *Drop the Dead Donkey*, but was keen to show he could take a joke. 'I've enjoyed the evening immensely,' he told the press afterwards. His equanimity wasn't enough to shield Clary from criticism, however, and the tabloids had a field day expressing their shock and horror at the gag. An on-air apology for Clary's comments was subsequently broadcast and the comedian found television work hard to come by over the next few years. John Junor, the great Fleet Street veteran of outraged morality, was one of many keen to express his indignation, but also noted in his *Mail on Sunday* column the presence of Stephen Fry on television and Channel 4's alternative Queen's speech on Christmas Day, due to be delivered by the venerable Quentin Crisp. 'Aren't the gays taking over our culture?' he wondered. Though as Clary observed, fisting wasn't restricted to homosexuals: 'It's an activity open to anyone lucky enough to be born with a hand and an arsehole.'

By the end of the decade, Clary's comments might not have made such an impact. In 1999 the drama series *Queer as Folk* debuted on Channel 4 and opened with a sequence in which a 29-year-old man picks up a

15-year-old boy outside a club in Manchester's Canal Street and takes him home for a sex session, where he asks whether the boy likes rimming. The ensuing scene was bound to upset some tabloid critics: 'witty, well-acted and totally repulsive', concluded the *People*, with 'stomach-churning sex scenes'. It also caused some commercial problems; Beck's Beer publicly withdrew its sponsorship of the show, 'which proves we can make a difference by making a fuss', gloated the *Sun*'s Garry Bushell. But as the show's creator Russell T. Davies pointed out, there were still curious double standards in operation: 'If Stuart had taken Nathan home and murdered him rather than had sex with him, it would be on at 9 pm on ITV rather than Channel 4 at 10.30 pm.'

The real significance, however, was that for the first time there was a British drama in which all the central characters were gay, and which took great delight in teasing the heterosexual world. 'It's all true. Everything we've ever been told,' reported one character in mock horror, having ventured into a straight pub. 'There are people talking in sentences that have no punchline and they don't even care.'

Meanwhile the word 'transgender', a political umbrella term covering those previously known as transvestites and transsexuals, began to be heard, and such people became visible for the first time. A 1995 advert for Levi's showed a drag queen having a shave in the back of a New York taxi, to the surprise of the cabbie who had assumed his passenger was female; it was passed for British television by the Independent Television Commission, albeit with screenings restricted to post-watershed broadcasts. In the same year Loughborough College of Art began offering a short dressmaking and fashion course for transvestites, while a 1999 documentary in the BBC Two strand *Trouble at the Top* told the story of Divine, a firm in Northamptonshire who rescued a failing shoemaking business by concentrating on shoes for transvestites and fetish footwear, an episode that inspired the 2005 film *Kinky Boots*. Even Bruce, Hyacinth Bucket's posh brother-in-law in *Keeping Up Appearances*, is a cross-dresser in private.

Perhaps the most significant development in this field, however, came in 1998 with the arrival in *Coronation Street* of Hayley Patterson (played by Julie Hesmondhalgh), the first transsexual in a British drama series, let alone in a soap. The following year she changed her name by deed poll to Hayley Cropper, following a ceremony that united her with Roy Cropper (David Neilson). At this stage, transgendered people were still considered legally to be their original gender, so they couldn't marry; the law was changed in 2004, and Roy and Hayley were able to wed.

*

That legal development reflected the way that politicians were now running to catch up with public taste. As ever, the question of gay rights was the touchstone and in 2000 the Sexual Offences (Amendment) Act finally brought the age of consent for male homosexuals down to sixteen, in line with that for heterosexuals, though a new limit of eighteen was also introduced for those whose partner was 'in a position of trust in relation to that person', following an amendment by Labour MP Joe Ashton. The Bill passed the House of Commons with a big majority, but was twice rejected by the House of Lords, following strong opposition from the churches; the government invoked the Parliament Act to force it through their Lordships' chamber.

Those changes were made, of course, by a new government. During John Major's premiership, despite his undoubted inclination to liberalise the law, he was hampered by the right wing of his party, with whom he was already at war over Europe.

There was no obvious reason why a Eurosceptic position should be allied to an illiberal attitude towards sexual morality, but the fact remained that there was a strong correlation, at least on the government benches. In the 1994 vote on the compromise amendment, reducing the gay age of consent to eighteen, a majority of Conservative MPs voted in favour of the change: 169 for, 134 against. But amongst those Tories who had voted at least once against their leaders on Maastricht, there was an overwhelming majority against the amendment: thirty-two out of forty-five rebels voted to keep the age limit as it stood, with a further three abstaining. In terms of how the future of the party would be shaped, the voting patterns of the three cabinet ministers referred to by Major as 'bastards' were intriguing. None of the three voted for a reduction to sixteen, but both Michael Portillo and Peter Lilley supported the compromise at eighteen; John Redwood was the only one to vote against. A similar phenomenon was evident in Fleet Street, where the *Daily Telegraph*, the *Daily Mail* and the *Sun* – the most Eurosceptic national newspapers – were adamantly opposed to any change in the law.

Perhaps the convergence of two issues that seemed so disparate stemmed from the knowledge that such decisions would soon be taken out of the hands of the British legislature altogether, that the European Court of Human Rights was shortly to rule – as it did – that the ban on homosexuality in the armed forces was illegal and that having different ages of consent was discriminatory. The perception of a meddling Europe intervening in what the British liked to think of as moral concerns was reinforced in 1999 when the European Commission issued a handbook for those seeking to improve standards in prostitution. 'Even a "madam" who has never had sexual contact with her clients may want advice on how to sterilise her whips,' it suggested.

There was a limit on how far the parliament elected in 1992 was prepared to go on issues of liberalising the law, and on how much of his rapidly dwindling political capital John Major was prepared to expend, particularly at a time when sexual scandal was engulfing his government on such a frequent basis. Meanwhile, the Labour Party, fearful of saying anything that might appear controversial, made no promises on sexual rights in its manifesto for the 1997 general election.

Despite this silence, however, it was symbolically important to Tony Blair's government that things should be seen to have changed, and the law was subsequently amended in fits and starts. The new, more relaxed attitude had the additional benefit that fewer politicians were likely to see their careers end in tabloid scandal. There were still examples — most notably the tragic case of Paisley South MP Gordon McMaster, who committed suicide in 1997, alleging that others in the Labour Party were spreading rumours that he was homosexual — but they were now exceptions rather than the rule.

The change was apparent in 1998, when the *News of the World* proposed running a story about Nick Brown, then Labour's agriculture minister, and his alleged relationship with a rent boy. Brown denied the allegations but, rather than wait for publication, he was encouraged to offer the paper an alternative story in which he would come out as a gay man. 'The result was,' reflected Tony Blair, that 'the story turned from a sordid scandal into an honest confession and Nick was saved.' It was a slightly odd use of the word 'confession', but by no means unique; even the *Guardian* report of the time used the same terminology: 'Brown confessed to being gay.'

Elsewhere the *Sun* greeted the story with a comment column headlined ARE WE BEING RUN BY A GAY MAFIA?, which called on all homosexuals in public office to come out, but insisted that it didn't wish to invade anyone's privacy, while the paper's columnist, Richard Littlejohn, linked the outing of Brown to 'the government's determination to lower the age at which schoolboys can be sodomised'. Perhaps the best response to such hysterical coverage came from Michael Gove, then writing for *The Times*, who suggested mischievously that John Prescott might also be gay: after all, he had joined the merchant navy, had waited on tables and was married to a woman who was 'a camp icon to rank with Bet Gilroy or Barbra Streisand'.

In fact, such mockery was no longer necessary, for this was effectively the last great flourish of the *Sun*'s longstanding campaign against homosexuality in all its forms. A fortnight before the Nick Brown story broke, Matthew Parris, a columnist on *The Times* and the *Sun*, had appeared on BBC Two's *Newsnight* programme and mentioned in passing that there were two out homosexuals in Blair's cabinet: 'Chris Smith is openly gay and Peter Mandelson is certainly gay.'

It was hardly a shock revelation, for Mandelson had been outed by the *News of the World* in 1987 and again by the *Sun* in 1995, and he made no secret of his homosexuality in his everyday life. 'I know he's that way,' worried Neil Kinnock in the 1980s, 'but why does he have to flaunt it?' But Mandelson had never made any public comment or declaration on the subject and seemed to have no inclination so to do, presumably on the grounds that it was no one else's concern; consequently it was seldom mentioned explicitly. Parris's casual comment, therefore, caused a certain panic, particularly at the BBC where the director general John Birt, a former colleague of Mandelson on LWT's *Weekend World* programme, issued instructions that no further mention was to be made on air of the minister's sexual orientation.

Mandelson's network of media contacts extended beyond even Birt, however, and a couple of weeks after the *Newsnight* interview, David Yelland, the editor of the *Sun*, informed Parris that his column in the paper was to be terminated. 'From the conversation I had with Mr Yelland,' remarked Parris, 'I drew the impression the two things are linked.' At the same time Yelland announced a change of policy: 'From now on the *Sun* will not out homosexuals unless there is a major public interest reason to do so.' There was a degree of irony that this should be coming from the flagship of the News International empire, whose proprietor, Rupert Murdoch, had only recently been heard remarking that 'The trouble with Blair is that he spends too much time listening to that poof Mandelson.' Nonetheless, the shift in tone was welcomed as evidence that Fleet Street, like the political class, was finally catching up with public opinion.

As a final indication that a new social order had been established, Peter Tatchell found himself in 1999 acclaimed as a hero by the right-wing press. Tatchell had been the victim of extraordinary tabloid vilification since the mid-1980s, first when he stood unsuccessfully as Labour's candidate in the Bermondsey by-election, and then when he came out and became the most famous gay campaigner in the country. A leading figure in the direct action group OutRage!, he had courted further controversy with stunts that included a demonstration during a sermon by the Archbishop of Canterbury, intended to highlight the Church of England's position on homosexuality. On that occasion he had been prosecuted for 'indecent behaviour in a church' under the obscure Ecclesiastical Courts Jurisdiction

Act, and given a witty fine of £18.60, a reference to the date of the legislation. The press reaction to his campaigning was less than supportive. 'Odious is too polite a word to describe Peter Tatchell,' opined the *Sun* in 1997. 'But the more accurate words cannot be printed in a family newspaper.'

The portrayal of Tatchell as a 'loony left' extremist changed, however, in November 1999 when he attempted to effect a citizen's arrest of Robert Mugabe, the president of Zimbabwe who had taken over from the likes of Idi Amin and Jean-Bédel Bokassa as the British media's favourite African hate figure. Tatchell's actions, undertaken at considerable personal risk, drew attention to Mugabe's virulent hatred of homosexuality – 'British homosexuals are worse than dogs and pigs because they do not differentiate between males and females,' he argued – and thereby struck another blow for gay equality, for few in Britain wished to associate themselves with Mugabe. (Mugabe was later to claim that Africa minister Peter Hain was Tatchell's lover, which provoked mixed reactions: 'Hain is taking it calmly,' reported Robin Cook. 'Tatchell is furious.') It wasn't long before Richard Holloway, the former Bishop of Edinburgh, was praising Tatchell as 'a classic Christ-type figure' who 'refuses to be deflected from his mission, in spite of having been beaten up more times than St Paul'.

By 1997 *Midsomer Murders* was happy to use the expression 'arse bandit', so that DI Barnaby could correct such terminology, and it was clear that things had changed. In 2001 a gay man named Brian Dowling won the second series of the reality television show *Big Brother*, having come out to his family shortly before going on the show. His mother's response summed up the transformation of attitudes in Britain: 'Are you trying to be fashionable?'

It was all a long way from the days of Alan Amos and Michael Brown. That dictum of Rupert Allason (another who voted against the lowering of the age of consent) that 'a wholly legal act of homosexuality spelt catastrophe' for an ambitious MP no longer applied. Being gay, even being openly proud of being gay, was no longer an impediment to holding office. In 2012 Ken Livingstone, the former Mayor of London who had in the 1980s been amongst the first major politicians to fight for gay equality, looked back to the early days of Blair's premiership. 'As soon as Blair got in, if you came out as lesbian or gay you immediately got a job,' he remarked. 'It was wonderful.' It was also a piece of sound practical politics, learned from the catastrophe of Back to Basics.

8

Resignation

'I get knocked down but I get up again'

There are at least two oppositions in the House of Commons and one of them is Conservative.
Gillian Shephard (1994)

After the defeat there will be the mother of all battles over the future of the Tory party.
John Biffen (1994)

UNLUCKY ALF: Oh, bugger!
Paul Whitehouse & Charlie Higson, *The Fast Show* (1994)

On Thursday, 22 June 1995 John Major took the second of his twice-weekly sessions of prime minister's questions, where observers noted that he seemed more confident and relaxed than he had been for some time. Asked about stories that divisions within his party were undermining negotiations on the future of Northern Ireland, he casually brushed such talk aside, while also finding time to point out – in a characteristic piece of understatement – that 'terrorism is unpleasant and should be resisted'. An hour or so later, having caught up with the third-place play-off in the rugby world cup (England were being comprehensively trounced by the French), he stepped out into the rose garden of 10 Downing Street, a blue-spotted tie providing the only colour in his otherwise monochrome appearance. A crowd of journalists were gathered, summoned there for a press conference and left waiting in the hot sun. The atmosphere was less of eager anticipation than of slightly irritated boredom, since none had any inkling what the content of the prime minister's message was likely to be, and few expected that they would be recording anything of any note.

They were wrong, for the prime minister of Great Britain and Northern Ireland had called them together to announce that he was resigning as the leader of the Conservative Party. This meant, he explained, that there would now be an election in which Tory MPs would be balloted to choose who they wished to be leader of their party, and therefore who would be the prime minister. The short, three-minute statement caught politicians, journalists and public entirely by surprise, but the real shock came in the second half of the announcement, when Major declared that he himself would be a candidate in that election. It was, he explained, an attempt to flush out all those who had been whispering behind his back, destabilising his premiership. 'I am no longer prepared to tolerate the present situation,' he said. 'In short, it is time to put up or shut up.'

The move was entirely without precedent in British politics — premiers had left office before, but never as a temporary tactic to wrong-foot their political opponents — and it was of slightly dubious constitutional propriety, for Major intended to continue serving as prime minister during the election period, although he would not be the leader of his party. It was though, according to Matthew Parris in a *Times* article that bore all the hallmarks of an off-the-record Major briefing, a genuine question: did the party really wish him to remain as leader? 'He just wants an answer, one way or the other,' wrote Parris. 'I believe Major would regard losing this contest as second best, but a good deal better than carrying on as before.'

The motivation was plain to see, for the news continued to be resolutely dreadful for the government and for Major in particular. In the local authority elections of May 1994 — the last fought by Labour under John Smith's leadership — the Tories had shed 429 seats, losing control of half the councils they had held. The performance was repeated in May 1995, leaving them now firmly in third place in terms of numbers of councillors, having been overtaken by the Liberal Democrats. A poll in the *Daily Telegraph* the following month suggested that at least seventy Conservative MPs supported the idea of a leadership election. A challenge was surely going to come.

Major himself was looking ever weaker, the arrival of Tony Blair having reduced still further what little was left of his dwindling appeal. A survey in September 1994, for example, had asked who in public life would make the ideal next-door neighbour; this would once have been Major's long suit, but now he was eclipsed by Blair, who came in at number twelve, with Major ranking fifteenth, just one place ahead of television prankster Jeremy Beadle. (The top slot went, somewhat surprisingly, to Jack Charlton, who had recently coached the Republic of Ireland football team in the World Cup.) Perhaps in response to Blair's encroachment on his territory, the prime minister stepped up the homely rhetoric in which he had always specialised, though by now the folksiness was becoming almost self-parodic. Spotting a squirrel in a park, hoarding nuts for winter, he slipped into characteristic Chauncey Gardiner mode: 'Sometimes I feel like that about the British economy. We need to conserve the wealth we have and use it wisely.' His speech at that year's party conference, which the press was told he had written himself, opened with the defiantly low-key greeting, 'Glad you could make it,' and went on to offer such bathetic insights as: 'Running a country isn't like walking down a road.'

Meanwhile the murmurs of backbench discontent were growing ever louder. Word got out that a meeting in mid-June 1995 between Major and sixty or so MPs from the Fresh Start Group, which was supposed to resolve differences within the party, had been a bad-tempered disaster, with backbenchers barracking their leader. 'It was a terrible meeting,' confirmed Iain Duncan Smith. 'He was the prime minister and you've got to treat him with a bit of respect. I think a lot of people forgot that and it got quite disrespectful. It got too personal.' According to other accounts, Duncan Smith was amongst those heckling and interrupting Major's speech. Certainly the encounter was one of the factors that prompted Major's decision to resign, calculating that he could never compromise with such people, and that he should strike before they did. 'They were very rude,' said Douglas Hurd. 'It meant that any lingering tendency he might have to move a bit towards them had vanished.' But if Major was starting to look like a liability, who could possibly replace him and restore Tory fortunes?

Given a free choice of who to lead the party into the next election, Conservative voters in the country would probably at this stage have opted for Michael Heseltine, who retained high levels of public support despite his attempts to close down the mines and privatise the Post Office. But he was never really an option, certainly at the outset. He had proved personally loyal to Major, to whom he owed his current position, and he was firmly identified with the Europhile wing of the party. Above all, he had too much form, having been the man responsible for Margaret Thatcher's demise; to remove one prime minister might be regarded as doing the party a service, to remove two would start to look like appallingly naked ambition. Loyal Thatcherites were inclined to agree with Norman Tebbit's recent comment that anyone considering Heseltine as a leader should 'lie down in a dark room until the feeling goes away'. Nonetheless, the aspiration was evident enough to be mocked on television by the satirist Armando Iannucci: 'I fully support the prime minister, though if he were to fail to secure sufficient votes to avoid a second ballot, and if I were in turn asked to stand in the interests of the party – I'd love to.'

Iannucci's mention of a second ballot referred to the option that still existed within the Conservative voting system for a stalking-horse candidate: a no-hoper whose function in a first ballot was to attract protest votes and thus destroy the incumbent, so that more substantial candidates might enter in the second round, without having dirtied their hands in the process. Various names were put forward for this role, from the unknown Barry Field through the embittered Norman Lamont to the publicity-hungry Teresa Gorman. ('I'm ready to stand if no one else will,' she told her colleagues. 'It's about time we had another woman at the helm.')

The idea of a stalking-horse, however, was a side issue; the real question was whether one of the three 'bastards' that Major had identified within his cabinet might be prepared to stand against him in the open at the first time of asking, thus removing the need for a stalking-horse altogether. To do so would require considerable political courage, for it couldn't be done from within the cabinet, and resignation as a minister would guarantee becoming a political pariah should the challenge fail; it was hardly the best career move, unless there was a real chance of success. It was on the horns of that dilemma that Major wished to skewer his opponents.

There was no doubt about the identity of the principal target of the ploy. Michael Portillo had been promoted into the cabinet following the 1992 election, had now risen to become the secretary of state for employment and was very clearly the emerging star of the government. The son of an exiled Spanish Republican, he was, by the normal standards of politics, a very handsome man. 'He preened, he spat, he flicked his hair, he pouted his luscious Latino lips,' wrote Emma Forrest in the *Sunday Times* of a 1994 appearance on *Question Time*. 'He is the Mick Jagger of the 1990s.' If that was a little too effusive and extravagant when talking of a cabinet minister, it did capture some of the narcissism evident in those politicians who mistake good looks for charisma, and some of the delusion of their followers; 'he attracts the same kind of fervour and devotion as a pop star,' noted the BBC journalist Jon Sopel. *Private Eye* evoked François Mitterrand's famous description of Margaret Thatcher (the eyes of Caligula and the mouth of Marilyn Monroe), saying Portillo had 'the eyes of an assassin and the lips of a tyrant'.

Politically, Portillo had been very careful to position himself on the right of the party, enjoying his status as Margaret Thatcher's anointed one. He was the latest in a long list of such sons and heirs that had once included Major himself; as far back as 1991 she had suggested that if John Major lost the next election, the answer was to 'Skip a generation: go for Portillo.' His heavily trailed speeches ranged far beyond his cabinet brief, but seldom ventured much deeper than a tabloid leader-column about scroungers and single mothers. 'We must listen to the still small voice of Britain's quiet majority,' ran a typical passage, delivered in his disconcertingly deep, booming tones. 'The quiet majority is dismayed by much that goes on around it: standing in the Post Office queue watching handouts going to people who seem capable of work; reading of yobbos sent on sailing cruises; being told that competition in schools is divisive or demoralising.'

Amongst the party membership, he was irresistible, seen as a younger, more right-wing Heseltine, with a similarly impressive coiffure. The foreign origins were forgiven by the faithful since he was so unequivocally opposed to the European project, while others saw a connection between these two facts; Tristan Garel-Jones likened him to 'a Jew overcompensating for foreignness'. Beyond the party, however, he aroused deep distrust bordering on hatred, seeming to represent all that was most unpleasant about the younger Thatcherite Tories. When the comedy writers Laurence Marks and Maurice Gran were developing the idea for their sitcom *The New Statesman*, they approached Portillo (Marks lived in his Southgate constituency) for advice, and he happily showed them around the Commons, answering their questions. Some interpreted the broadcast result, in which Rik Mayall depicted a pushy, amoral, quasi-fascist Tory MP, swaggering and murdering his way through the ranks, as a caricature of Portillo. As his star continued to rise, the Family Cat, a North London indie group, enjoyed some success with their song 'Bring Me the Head of Michael Portillo'.

A 1994 leader column in the *Independent* tried to discover what made this 'privately courteous, publicly arrogant' man tick, and concluded that he was 'a peacock, but not a pea-brain, who squawks some of the crudest messages that are currently to be heard in mainstream British politics'. Hugo Young of the *Guardian* was no more enthused. 'Portillo struck me as totally ambitious, utterly calculating and perhaps not as chastened as he should be by his lack of experience,' he wrote, after meeting him. 'It's a long time since I've met a more coldly dedicated politician.'

He was also capable of foolish misjudgements. In 1994 the *Sunday Telegraph* revealed that to celebrate the tenth anniversary of Portillo's arrival in Parliament, a party was being planned for a thousand people at Alexandra Palace in North London, complete with a firework display, a guest list headed by Margaret Thatcher and Norman Tebbit, and the screening of a specially commissioned film about the great man's life, from his appearance in a Ribena advert at the age of eight onwards. Once news of the party got out, however, it was drowned in a sea of ridicule. Ten years as an MP might deserve some kind of commemoration – Virginia Bottomley had recently held a barbecue at a friend's house to celebrate her first decade in the House – but this all seemed a touch too extravagant, smacking of hubris when humility might be more appropriate. As the *Sun* observed: 'There's nothing worse than blowing your own trumpet.'

In a state of embarrassed panic, the planning was scaled back, the fireworks cancelled, the film pulled at the last minute. Thatcher and Tebbit failed to turn up, and the five hundred or so guests who did arrive for the £30-a-head black-tie dinner had to be escorted in through the back entrance by police in riot gear, there to provide protection from a crowd of protestors armed with eggs and flour and chanting: 'Choke on your champagne, you bastards.' In fact, although Dom Pérignon was available, most settled for less elevated refreshments – Penfolds Bluestone Ridge from Australia (£8.50 a bottle at the cash bar) proved the most popular choice – as they tucked into an unadventurous menu of smoked salmon, fillet of beef and baked Alaska. Meanwhile a string quartet fought to be heard in the vast hall, decorated for the occasion with pink bows and purple and white balloons, before giving up the attempt and handing over to the amplified, but still tasteful, sounds of the cabaret band Tuxedo Class.

The highlight came with a slightly low-key speech from a clearly uncomfortable Portillo. 'I could tell from the way his voice was wobbling and his leg was shaking,' noted Gyles Brandreth, the MC for the evening, 'that Michael was hating every second of it.' Indeed he was. 'It was horrible, horrible,' he moaned in an interview some years later. 'The whole thing was a living nightmare.' For some of the guests, however, his mere presence was enough; one young woman was reported to have travelled down from Scotland for the occasion and was in raptures: 'He's an orgasmatron. I just hope I don't faint if he talks to me.'

Despite the perceived arrogance, and the charges of insincere playing to the gallery, the last few years had been successful ones for Portillo. The entire political world knew by the end of 1994 that he was Major's greatest potential rival, and when the prime minister announced his resignation, the call went out immediately for him to enter the lists. The Conservative Party needed 'a man who speaks the language of the people', announced the *Sun*. 'That man is Michael Portillo. He must not be kept waiting in the wings.' But not all Portillo's flaws had yet been revealed, and it now transpired that his ambition was not quite as ruthless as had been assumed. He dithered and dallied, unwilling to take on the responsibility for striking the fatal blow, and eventually declared his support for Major, thereby ruling himself out of the first ballot.

Yet the right remained convinced of the need for change, and a candidate had to be found. Otherwise the Eurosceptic wing would look impotent, capable of sniping from the sidelines but unable to fight openly and honestly. So if Portillo wasn't prepared to risk a challenge to Major, and if his colleague Peter Lilley, who did consider the possibility, was also unwilling to put his head above the parapet, who else was there?

The answer was John Redwood, who had come into the cabinet as secretary of state for Wales in the reshuffle following the departure of Norman Lamont, and who was being described in the press as 'the cabinet's most junior member and its resident rightwing rottweiler'. In his memoirs, Major hinted that Redwood acted because 'he had heard gossip that there was a sporting chance that he might not survive the reshuffle planned for July', but that was ungenerous. Redwood was a politician of deep conviction and principle, and his decision to resign from the cabinet to put himself up for the leadership took real political guts. Though little known to the public, he was still only forty-four, he had an ultra-safe constituency and he could confidently look forward to more senior posts in government.

He was, however, lacking the aura of leadership, to an even greater extent than Major. Having catapulted himself into the headlines, he now came under serious media scrutiny for the first time, and he never really recovered from the footage that was discovered of him on a platform in his early days as Welsh secretary trying to mime to 'Hen Wlad Fy Nhadau', the Welsh national anthem, with hilarious ineptitude. His head wobbled, his face seemed petrified into vacancy and he managed to look both feeble-minded and patronising, like an Oxford don reading a storybook to a primary-school class. But that was just a single incident, albeit one re-broadcast frequently over the period of the leadership election. The real problems came when he actually spoke. Because, although no one ever really defined it, something wasn't quite right about Redwood's public persona.

He was self-evidently the most constructive and gifted thinker in Major's cabinet, the one Tory working to develop new policies that could extend the Thatcherite revolution without being enslaved to her memory. His track record was impressive; he had been one of the first to advocate privatisation of state assets, long before Thatcher herself espoused the concept, but he had later argued with her against the introduction of the poll tax. He also had a keen understanding of the aspirations of first-generation suburban families. This was the same constituency to whom Major made his pitch, but the difference between the two men was instructive: in place of Major's apparent empathy, there was a remoteness to Redwood, a lack of warmth, an inability to communicate a sense that politics was anything more than a cerebral conundrum.

This perception was unfortunate and unfair, for Redwood was certainly a practical politician, not an abstract intellectual, but it proved impossible to shake. And it was most commonly associated with Matthew Parris's description of him as resembling Mr Spock from *Star Trek*. In fact Parris did not restrict his characterisation to Redwood alone; the conceit, spread over several political sketches in *The Times* from 1989 onwards, was that the Conservative Party was being taken over by members of the Vulcan tendency, 'infiltrators from a strange and distant planet' who were 'courteous, clever and ruthlessly logical'. Included in their ranks were Francis Maude, Peter Lilley, David Curry, Alan Howarth and Michael Portillo as well as Redwood, while in 1994 Parris revealed that the military strategists on Vulcan had now refined their design and that Tony Blair was 'an improved version, with added charm'. It was only with Redwood, however, that the tag stuck, seeming to capture something of the awkwardness of the man.

In terms of other politicians, he was most often compared to Keith Joseph, the self-flagellating prophet of Thatcherism in the 1970s, and to Enoch Powell in his romantic reverence for the nation. But there was also an element of Tony Benn: polite, calm, uncontaminated by scandal ('John has never been exposed to germs,' according to a colleague) and absolutely convinced that what he was saying was blindingly obvious common sense. 'The key to Redwood was that he had very simple views expressed in a subtle and original manner,' wrote his adviser, Hywel Williams. 'Hence a view of the history of England that was not so far removed from the stories of the Boys' Own Bumper Book of History.' When interviewed on television, Redwood exhibited a strange half-smile, suggestive of a private joke at the audience's expense and, although those who knew him insisted he was a witty man, his attempts at humour in public mostly displayed a clumsy jocularity. He once said that he'd like to be Mr Blobby – 'He's nice and everyone likes him' – but if comparison with a children's television character was sought, then rather more accurate was Gyles Brandreth's suggestion of Daddy Woodentop.

Major claimed in retrospect that Redwood was the ideal opponent – 'beatable, Eurosceptic and a cabinet colleague' – but it seems unlikely that at the time, with Portillo refusing to break cover, he was expecting such a heavyweight challenge. For despite his obvious limitations as a communicator, Redwood was a serious candidate, with a plausible alternative vision of where the Conservative Party should be heading. This was not simply a stalking-horse campaign, preparing the way for others, but the action of a man who had ideas above his station as Welsh secretary, even if these had hitherto been confined to dreams of the chancellorship. To the surprise of many, he turned out to be a fighter, and the fact that he was prepared to resign from the cabinet to battle for his beliefs won him some grudging respect.

There was, of course, little chance that Redwood would actually win – certainly he didn't expect to do so – and none at all that he would win at the first ballot, but there was a very real danger that he could do Major sufficient damage to force the prime minister's departure. In that event, it was assumed, Michael Heseltine and Michael Portillo would enter the race and decide the leadership between them, though the memory of 1975 – when Margaret Thatcher stood in the first round and built up sufficient head of steam to knock out supposedly more weighty candidates – was never far from the minds of protagonists, electorate or commentators.

Nor was there any possibility that a Conservative Party led by Redwood would win the next election. Indeed his own analysis was that, following the 'decisive disaster' of Black Wednesday, the Tories were destined to lose regardless of what they now did (a feeling shared by Major). But he was, he pointed out, one of the few who had argued against membership of the ERM from the outset; he could at least present himself as a clean pair of hands.

Redwood's cause did go on to attract a handful of serious players, including Norman Tebbit and Iain Duncan Smith, one of the more highly regarded of the new intake of MPs, but it was the campaign launch that shaped much of the coverage that was to come. Recognisable faces alongside the candidate were in short supply – the only major figure was Lamont – and the rest looked a distinctly unimpressive crowd, dominated by Teresa Gorman in characteristically overstated outfit (a shoulder-padded, puff-sleeved jacket in vivid green, worn over a turquoise blouse) and by Tony Marlow, the man who had the previous year demanded Major's resignation in the House of Commons and had recently called him 'a nice guy, but a loser'. Remarkably, Marlow's outfit overshadowed even that of Gorman, a striped blazer that, thought Major, 'would have looked good on a cricket field in the 1890s'. In fact it was the official blazer of the Old Wellingtonian Society, reflecting the fact that, unlike Major, he was a public schoolboy. In an early indication of sympathy for Redwood's challenge, the *Daily Telegraph* delicately cropped the photo of the launch to exclude Marlow.

Indeed Redwood enjoyed far more support from the press than he might have expected, though virtually everything else was against him.

The stock market plunged seventy points after his announcement, with £15 billion lost in the value of shares, the cabinet remained publicly loyal to Major (though Virginia Bottomley did say she would be prepared to serve in a Redwood cabinet if asked), and a poll in *The Economist* showed that the Conservatives would fare even worse under Redwood than under the current prime minister. The same was true, it appeared, of Michael Portillo and Kenneth Clarke, while the best option was Michael Heseltine; with him as leader, the Labour lead would be cut, though it would still stand at nineteen percentage points.

But the dislike of Major in the Tory press meant that Redwood attracted some powerful backers. Rumours circulated that Rupert Murdoch, Viscount Rothermere and Conrad Black – proprietors of News International, Associated Newspapers and the Telegraph Group respectively – had met and decided to throw their weight against Major. Certainly Redwood met Black, in an encounter arranged by Simon Heffer, and won his qualified support. It was, though, only a temporary position. During the feverish leadership speculation the previous year, just before John Smith's death, Portillo had met with Conrad Black in the company of Michael Spicer, who recorded in his diary that Black 'will back Portillo and will get Murdoch alongside'.

The headlines as the ballot approached were horrendous for the prime minister. TIME TO DITCH THE CAPTAIN said the *Daily Mail*, REDWOOD VS DEADWOOD mocked the *Sun*, while the *Times* spelt it out on polling day: 'Today good Conservatives should vote against Mr Major.' Most enduring, though it played no real part in the contest at hand, was an article by Simon Jenkins in *The Times* that was headlined THE NASTY PARTY – the phrase captured so perfectly the public perception of the modern Conservative Party that it was to stick for a decade and more.

These papers' overriding concern was the European Union, Britain's membership of which was opposed by both the Canadian Conrad Black and the Australian-born American Rupert Murdoch. With Major now held to be guilty of 'appeasement' in relation to Europe, and with Margaret Thatcher and Norman Tebbit too far into retirement for recall, there was a need to find a new face of Euroscepticism that would be acceptable to the public; the logic was thus to build up Redwood as Major's assassin, enabling Portillo to emerge from the ensuing fray and lead Britain away from the EU.

There was therefore considerable excitement when it was discovered that Portillo's supporters were preparing a campaign headquarters for him. In anticipation of the contest going to a second ballot, a bank of phone lines were installed in – and furniture removed from – a house in Lord

North Street in Westminster that had been earmarked for Portillo's use. It was a development that brought one of Major's better jokes. Asked at prime minister's questions about the indecent haste with which twenty telephones were being installed, he replied merely that the speed of the operation was 'a tribute to privatisation'.

Those phone lines proved unnecessary. When the MPs were balloted on 4 July 1995, John Major secured just about enough support to survive as leader. He registered 218 votes, with 89 voting for John Redwood and 22 abstaining. Though far from impressive – a third of the parliamentary party had failed to support their leader – it was nevertheless a technical victory. Major had privately set himself a minimum of 215 votes and just about scraped over his own hurdle. 'It was not really enough,' he reflected later, 'but it was three votes too many to allow me to walk away.'

This being a secret ballot, the dissidents had no obligation to out themselves, and only twenty-eight did so. As Redwood identified, however, many of those who supported him were from marginal constituencies, where the need to find a new leader was at its most acute. Even amongst those who voted for Major, enthusiasm was not always apparent; he was merely 'the least worst option', according to transport minister Steven Norris.

Major's own comments revealed how beleaguered he felt, with the press in open opposition to him. 'The election has been decided by MPs in Westminster, not by commentators outside,' he said, and the *Daily Telegraph*, one of his chief tormentors, conceded the point: 'It is healthy for democracy when MPs, or the electorate at large, force a spell of humility upon the scribblers.' Rupert Murdoch's papers weren't such good losers. 'Yesterday Conservative MPs threw away their last best opportunity to win the next general election,' seethed *The Times*, while the *Sun* gave up all hope of the party: CHICKENS HAND IT TO BLAIR ran their headline.

Indeed the outcome of the vote was received with glee by the Labour leader – 'That's perfect, exactly the result we want' – though it was the narrowness of the victory rather than the identity of the winner that counted. Far from strengthening Major's position, the episode left him looking even more wounded. 'None of us could help cheering,' noted Peter Mandelson, of the response of those gathered in Blair's office to hear the result. 'It was a rather brilliant tactic,' Tony Blair was later to write of the resignation and re-election, but 'Major made the same error as Labour had in the 1980s: he appealed for unity rather than a mandate. So the bold tactic was not accompanied by a bold strategy.' There was some truth in the analogy, though at least Labour had waited until it was in opposition before really settling down to internecine warfare. The Tories had this period of self-indulgence yet to come.

'My re-election ended the frenzy in the party, but not the conflict,' was Major's mature verdict on the episode, though he also admitted that, had he not jumped the gun, he would have faced a leadership challenge that autumn and would probably not have won. Whether a change of leader would have served the party any better, however, is doubtful. Major did at least have a proven track record, having succeeded against the odds in 1992, and no other potential candidate could claim a remotely comparable achievement. Heseltine seemed like a more popular option, and would have been more combative in taking the fight to Blair, but he too would have struggled to unite a party determined to be divided. 'I don't think it settled anything,' reflected Iain Duncan Smith of Major's gamble. 'He said it was to clear the air, but you never clear the air of something like that, it is unclearable. It didn't win with the public, because the public believed that that was it: the government was no longer in control of its destiny.'

Meanwhile John Redwood returned to the back benches not quite in triumph but certainly with his reputation on the right enhanced. He set up a think tank, Conservative 2000, under the leadership of his former adviser, Hywel Williams, to generate new policy initiatives, and he continued to argue for his view of where the Tories should be heading. In any future leadership contest, he was now certain to be a candidate, even if he hadn't quite eclipsed the claim of Michael Portillo to the succession, and even if he was still regarded with suspicion by many Thatcher loyalists ('slightly loopy', was Alan Clark's assessment).

In the mini-reshuffle that followed the election, Heseltine was promoted to deputy prime minister and first secretary of state, and given wide-ranging authority over other departments. He set up a presentation committee that was intended to coordinate initiatives and announcements, though the fact that no such body already existed was something of a comment on the government's management thus far. Both he and Major denied that his career advancement was the result of any pre-contest deal between the two men, though inevitably that was how it was seen; it was 'some kind of Faustian bargain,' reflected Major's press secretary, Christopher Meyer, 'but I could never work out who was Faust and who the Devil.'

The other major development, though its significance was not yet obvious, was the promotion of William Hague to take over from Redwood as Welsh secretary. At the age of thirty-four, Hague became the youngest cabinet minister for nearly fifty years.

*

If the main impression of the Conservative Party was now one of disunity, it was compounded by a growing reputation for corruption, potentially threatening the perception of politics in Britain more widely. This was regularly lumped in with all the sexual improprieties under the banner headline of sleaze, though as with the Back to Basics circus, some of the stories were less important than others.

They included a 1994 *Sunday Times* campaign in which undercover reporters, posing as businessmen, approached twenty MPs with the offer of £1,000 in exchange for putting down a question in Parliament. All refused save for two Conservatives, Graham Riddick and David Tredinnick, who accepted the proposal, only to find themselves featured prominently in the paper the following week. There was some justifiable resentment amongst Tories of the tactics used; it was little more than entrapment, in the same way that plain-clothes police officers had once loitered in public lavatories, hoping to provoke homosexual men into making an approach – though, in this instance, there was little condemnation from the liberal left. It was even possible to see the results of the investigation as being relatively reassuring, since they revealed that 90 per cent of the sampled MPs (and one had to assume that it was a targeted selection) were honest; of the two MPs who did accept the offer, Riddick thought better of it later, and had already returned the cheque before the story was printed.

Among the more serious cases were those centring on the controversial figure of Mohammed Al-Fayed. In 1985 Al-Fayed and his brothers had bought the Harrods department store in a deal that prompted an investigation by the Department of Trade and Industry. When that investigation finally reported in 1990, it was critical of the brothers and, while it did not recommend that any action be taken, it did somewhat tarnish their image, concluding that they had 'misrepresented their origins, wealth and business interests'. The story really took off, though, in October 1994 when Al-Fayed claimed that, during the 1980s, Ian Greer, the lobbyist he had retained to represent his interests, had asked for money in order to acquire the services of a couple of Conservative MPs, Neil Hamilton and Tim Smith, so that they might ask questions in the House on his behalf. The cash was said to have been passed on in what were always referred to as 'brown envelopes', a phrase that had overtones of the 'plain brown wrappers' in which pornography was traditionally posted.

In another phrase that stuck in the public consciousness, Al-Fayed alleged that Greer had said: 'You need to rent an MP just like you rent a London taxi.' Al-Fayed added: 'Every month we got a bill for parliamentary services and it would vary from £8,000 to £10,000, depending on the number of questions.' Both Hamilton and Smith were now ministers, and were obliged to resign, with Smith admitting that he had indeed taken Al-Fayed's money (though not via Greer). Hamilton, on the other hand, denied the allegations; he and Greer issued writs against the *Guardian*, which had broken the story, although they withdrew their case in 1996. It was not, however, the end of the matter.

Also caught up in Al-Fayed's orbit was Jonathan Aitken, the chief secretary to the Treasury, who was accused – again by the *Guardian*, this time in conjunction with the ITV programme *World in Action* – of some dubious business dealings, including a stay at the Fayed-owned Paris Ritz hotel, paid for by a Saudi businessman. There were further allegations that the arms company, BMARC, of which Aitken was a non-executive director, had broken an arms embargo on Iran in the 1980s. 'He was a man with whom one could do business,' Michael Heseltine noted drily of Aitken. 'Unfortunately, others felt the same and there arose a series of allegations about his business relationships, especially in the Middle East.' Aitken too launched a libel action against both the *Guardian* and *World in Action*, issuing a clarion cry that was to come back to haunt him: 'If it falls to me to start a fight to cut out the cancer of bent and twisted journalism in our country with the simple sword of truth and the trusty shield of British fair play, so be it. I am ready for the fight.'

As these stories broke, an opinion poll in October 1994 found 61 per cent of the public agreeing with the statement that 'the Tories these days give the impression of being very sleazy and disreputable'. If it had been only individual MPs, such tales might have made little impact on the public; it was less fun to read about a politician seemingly found with his hand in the till than one caught with his trousers down. They acquired greater significance, however, for coming in the wake of the much more serious arms-to-Iraq affair.

The story started in October 1989, shortly after the Iraqi invasion of Kuwait, when three directors of Matrix Churchill, a machine tools company based in Coventry, were charged with having supplied parts to Iraq which, it was suggested, could have been used for making munitions. Such sales were potentially in breach of a United Nations embargo and of British government regulations, introduced earlier in the decade, banning the export of lethal equipment to either side in the Iran–Iraq War.

The resulting controversy hinged on the use of public interest immunity certificates (PIIs), a procedure that required a minister to sign a paper requesting that certain documents should not be made available in a courtroom for reasons of national security. These became known – largely thanks to the persistence of Labour's Robin Cook – as 'gagging orders', though that was slightly misleading; it was up to the judge in a case to decide whether or not to act upon a PII, and although in practice the presumption was likely to be in the government's favour, no politician had the right to demand silence.

In the Matrix Churchill case, which came to court in 1992, several PII certificates were issued, and their effect was to prevent the defendants from arguing that the government both knew and approved of what they were doing, the regulations having been secretly relaxed. Their case rested upon the claim that the Ministry of Defence had knowingly helped them to evade restrictions on arms exports to Iraq, but in the absence of the relevant documentation, this would be hard to prove. On the government's side, the argument was that intelligence secrets had to be protected at all costs; indeed one of the defendants was himself working unpaid for British intelligence. But there was a general suspicion that this had nothing to do with national security and everything to do with avoiding embarrassment for the government and the civil service. Michael Heseltine at the Department of Trade and Industry was prevailed upon to sign a PII relating to a time before his incumbency, though he insisted: 'The more I looked through the files, the more appalled I was.' He later said that it seemed 'everyone knew' what was going on.

It was, however, a previous minister in the department who brought the sorry episode to an end. Alan Clark, a man who, in Geoffrey Howe's memorable phrase, 'couldn't see an apple-cart without wanting to overturn it', gave an interview admitting the truth: that he saw it as his job to encourage exports 'despite guidelines which I regarded as tiresome and intrusive', and that as far as he was concerned, 'the interests of the West were well served by Iran and Iraq fighting each other'. He subsequently acknowledged in court that he had knowingly helped the Matrix Churchill directors obtain an export licence, in defiance of the arms embargo, by being 'economical with the *actualité*'. The trial collapsed, amidst much talk of cover-up and conspiracy.

There was a suggestion that Clark might be prosecuted for giving false evidence in his original written statement in the case, but – with his usual flair for escapology – he ended up as the hero of the hour. Had it not been for the belated honesty of his testimony, the public believed, the government would happily have seen the men go to jail (they faced a possible sentence of up to seven years) rather than own up to its collusion in the sales of arms to Iraq, a country that had waged a genocidal war against its Kurdish minority population. 'How can they believe this of people like Michael [Heseltine] and me?' protested John Major, but sadly the truth was that even he was looking tainted by the relentless media focus on sleaze.

Major set up an inquiry under a high court judge, Richard Scott, to which he himself gave evidence that failed to enhance his image. 'I can't be expected to read everything,' he complained, to little public sympathy. 'He came out,' concluded Giles Radice, 'with little respect left. "Don't blame me, I'm just the PM" might be the best summing up of his approach.' The former foreign secretary, Geoffrey Howe, also gave evidence, explaining – in words that deserved to become as notorious as Clark's phrase – that the government hadn't announced its change in policy after the Iran–Iraq War ended in 1988 because of 'the extremely emotional way in which such debates are debated in public'.

Worse still for the government, the inquiry dragged on for years and did not report until 1996, ensuring that the story remained alive well beyond what would normally have been its expiry date. To keep the pot boiling, a judicial review in 1994 concluded that the Thatcher government's provision of funds for a project to build the Pergau Dam in Malaysia had been unlawful, a misallocation of overseas development money in reciprocation for an arms deal. Although this happened before Major's time, it implicated his former foreign secretary, Douglas Hurd, and further added to the perception of dishonesty.

When Scott's report did finally emerge, it was a vast document comprising a million words and 2,400 pages, without a summary and couched in the most convoluted language. 'I accept the genuineness of his belief that he was personally, as opposed to constitutionally, blameless,' wrote Scott of Nicholas Lyell, the attorney general. 'But I do not accept that he was not personally at fault.' Parliament had been 'designedly' misled, but ministers had not 'acted with any duplicitous intent'. Other parts revealed that the careful circumlocutions of *Yes, Minister*, which had so entertained the nation in the previous decade, were rooted in reality; the danger of the truth being found out was translated into civil service jargon as: 'we could find ourselves in a presentational difficulty.'

In such a morass of meaning, it was hard to pin down any specific criticisms, and the government – in the form of Ian Lang, who had succeeded Heseltine as president of the Board of Trade – managed to find enough material to feel able to claim: 'There was no conspiracy. There was no cover up.' William Waldegrave was amongst those ministers criticised, though he professed himself unconcerned: 'It will be hairy for ten days. But that will be all.' The political response was to quote selectively from

Scott's words and thus claim that a clean bill of health had been given. Civil servants colluded with this spin operation, issuing a Cabinet Office paper that blandly, and misleadingly, stated: 'Answers given to Parliamentary questions gave an accurate description of the government's policy on exports to Iran and Iraq.'

A subsequent Commons debate was dominated by a bravura performance by the shadow foreign secretary, Robin Cook, who – having had very little time to absorb the report – broadened the attack to take in the whole of 'an arrogant government that has been around too long to remember it is accountable to the people'. It was 'one of the most startling speeches I have ever heard in the House,' wrote Paddy Ashdown. 'Quite the best piece of debating I have ever seen, and a Parliamentary occasion to match Geoffrey Howe's resignation speech.' So rattled was the government that yet another threat of a confidence motion was required in order to secure a majority, albeit by just one vote.

But the government did survive and no ministers resigned over the issue. Nor was anyone prosecuted, though the perception remained that ministers and civil servants had facilitated a breach of regulations, perhaps believing that in pursuit of foreign earnings the country could not afford what Alan Clark called 'the luxuries of moral posturing'.

Such episodes further damaged John Major and the Conservatives. It was probably true that the party's standing with the public was already at an all-time low, but the appearance of being, in Paddy Ashdown's words, 'grubby and wheedling' certainly helped keep it there. Even the phraseology was unfortunate. Clark's expression 'economical with the *actualité*' derived from the cabinet secretary, Robert Armstrong, in 1986. Giving evidence in the government's attempt to ban Peter Wright's book *Spycatcher*, Armstrong had spoken of the need sometimes to be 'economical with the truth' and, although the phrase was not new, it attached itself to the Tories, all the more so now that Clark had revived it. By the mid-1990s, it had been transmuted, in the hands of comic novelist Tristan Hawkins, into 'being conservative with the truth'.

As the scandals mounted, Major responded in 1994 by appointing Lord Nolan to head a committee on standards in public life, charged with leading an inquiry into the outside financial interests of politicians, civil servants and members of quangos. The committee reported in May 1995 with a broadly positive message – 'much of the public anxiety about standards of conduct in public life is based upon perceptions and beliefs which are not supported by the facts' – and an uncontroversial list of attributes that should be exercised by those in office: selflessness, integrity, objectivity, accountability, openness, honesty and leadership. It also, however, brought forward fifty-five recommendations that included a ban on MPs working for lobbying companies, the full disclosure of all extra-parliamentary income and the ending of MPs' self-regulation, to be replaced by a newly created Parliamentary Commissioner for Standards.

The proposals raised the hackles of many members. 'We in this House know far more of what is going on with our fellow members than any bureaucrat brought in from outside,' protested Edward Heath, to loud cheers from the Tory back benches. 'I deeply resent the inference in Nolan that all of us are crooks,' added the respected MP Anthony Steen. That hadn't actually been Nolan's message, but such protestations helped fix the idea in the minds of the public that it might well have been so. Insisting, correctly, that implementation of Nolan was a matter for Parliament, not the government, Major allowed a free vote in the subsequent debate, and twenty Tory members joined the whipped opposition MPs in accepting the proposals. It was undoubtedly another political victory for Labour, and did nothing to remove the impression of corruption which had so indelibly tainted the Conservatives.

Nolan also voiced concern about the way in which ministers who had been responsible for privatising various industries seemed destined, once they had left office, to end up on the boards of the resulting companies, so that Norman Fowler, Peter Walker and Norman Tebbit, for example, found paid employment with National Freight, British Gas and British Telecom respectively. Similarly John Wakeham, the former energy secretary who had been responsible for privatising the electricity industry, was appointed to the board of NM Rothschild, a bank that had advised regional power companies during that process. 'What is really sleazy,' wrote Richard Littlejohn in the *Sun*, 'is the number of Tories sticking their noses into a trough they have created themselves.'

Some of these appointments dated back to the days of Margaret Thatcher's premiership, but the controversy over them remained, particularly as a storm grew over the remuneration being offered to the heads of privatised companies. Huge profits were being made and much of the money appeared to be finding its way into the pockets of directors. In 1991 it was reported that, amongst other cases, the chief executive of PowerGen had enjoyed a pay rise of over 250 per cent in two years, prompting Frank Dobson, the shadow energy secretary, to promise that a future Labour government would impose pay controls on those he referred to as 'fat cats'. Since many of those in such positions were the people who had been running the companies when they were in public ownership, the argument that high pay was needed to attract the best candidates seemed not to apply. 'You're doing the same job you used to do before privatisation,' spits Pascoe at an executive of Mid-Yorks Water, in Reginald Hill's novel *On Beulah Height*. 'And if what they paid you then was peanuts, what's that make you now but a monkey with a bloated bank balance?'

The popular perception that the government looked after its own was widespread. In 'An Innocent Man', a 1994 episode of *Pie in the Sky*, 'an old hippy' who has become 'a very rich bastard' bids unsuccessfully for one of the new rail franchises. A colleague advises him: 'Join the Tory Party. Give them a hundred grand, and you might squeak in, "Sir" Duncan.' It was also noted that politicians' wives seemed to get more than their fair share of plum jobs. 'We should ask why the Tories put so many of their wives on quangos,' suggests Helen in *Drop the Dead Donkey*, and Henry provides an answer: 'It's so their wives are out while they're shagging their mistresses.'

These arguments – about Tory ministers on boards, about profits and about salaries – were brought together by Gordon Brown in 1993, as he called for a one-off tax on the privatised companies to be used to subsidise job creation schemes. 'We are unearthing a scandal,' he said, linking the issue to a broader Labour theme of standards in public life. It was a highly effective line of attack, especially when attached to Dobson's 'fat cats' phrase, and by 1995 the *Daily Mirror*, which had been making much of the running, was able to declare that this was 'the number one issue in the country'.

Labour was no longer proposing to curb remuneration in the private sector, but the stories of massive pay rises continued, with Cedric Brown of British Gas coming in for particular condemnation as he took a 75 per cent increase in late 1994, soon after 25,000 workers were laid off by the company. The political damage to the Conservatives was considerable. 'Government was powerless,' admitted Michael Heseltine, 'but the criticism was nonetheless intense and damaging.' Meanwhile the idea of a so-called 'windfall tax' – borrowed without attribution from Thatcher's first term, when it had been applied to bank profits – had taken root.

A suspicion was growing that during the hard times of the recession, those at the top of business had been protected, and that now recovery was under way, they were taking every opportunity to line their pockets. Even when wrongdoing occurred, it felt to many as though appropriate punishment was not forthcoming. The trial of four men for fraudulent dealings in shares of the brewer Guinness produced guilty verdicts in 1990, but the chief executive of the company, Ernest Saunders, served just ten months of his five-year sentence, after an appeal judge accepted that he was suffering from premature Alzheimer's disease. Happily, the symptoms of this appalling condition eased with his release.

In 1993 Asil Nadir, a businessman whose Polly Peck company had collapsed a couple of years earlier and who had been a major donor to Tory funds, fled to Northern Cyprus rather than face sixty-six charges of theft and fraud. Not only did he thus evade justice, but he also caused the resignation of a Northern Ireland minister, Michael Mates, who had written to the attorney general complaining about Nadir's treatment. Mates had also, in 'a light-hearted gesture', given the failed businessman a watch inscribed with the message: 'Don't let the buggers get you down.'

Labour had its own embarrassing associations, most notably with its former MP Robert Maxwell. As the proprietor of the *Daily* and *Sunday Mirror*, Maxwell had become a major figure in British public life during the 1980s and, despite widespread concern that he was not entirely scrupulous in his business practices, he was feted by politicians. In November 1991 his body was found floating off the Canary Islands, after he fell – or possibly jumped – from his yacht. 'This is truly tragic news,' lamented Labour leader Neil Kinnock. 'Bob Maxwell was a unique figure who attracted controversy, envy and loyalty in great measure throughout his rumbustious life.'

After Maxwell's death, it emerged that the scale of his misbehaviour had been massively underestimated; hundreds of millions of pounds had been appropriated from the Mirror Group's pension funds to bail out a company that was in deep financial problems. He was indeed a crook and a fraud, despite the denials issued by his writ-happy lawyers and printed in his papers. His connections with Labour would surface from time to time, but seldom in a way that actually damaged the party, mostly because Maxwell was such a larger-than-life character that he was easily recast in the public mind as an absurd pantomime villain. A year after his death, he was featuring as the punchline to 'A Bigger Splash', an episode of *The New Statesman*. Here he is shown to have faked his own death, only to find himself in a crate being thrown off his yacht, which by now is owned by Alan B'Stard.

Such jovial treatment was not extended to the Conservatives. With his ministers continuing to be washed away by the waves of sexual and financial sleaze, Major was in a hopeless position. And still the sniping from the right continued.

Shortly before his re-election as Tory leader, Margaret Thatcher had published the second volume of her memoirs, *The Path to Power*. The story ended on page 461 with her 1979 election victory, but there followed a further 150 or so pages about her time after leaving office, many of which were devoted to attacking her successor's performance. 'The problem with John Major's alternative approach,' she explained, running through the Maastricht Treaty saga one more time, was that 'it left the fundamental problems unresolved'. Hers was not a noticeably helpful intervention, though the response of Major loyalists only stoked the fire still further: off-the-record briefings by senior Tories described the former prime minister as 'an irrelevance', 'out of touch' and 'suffering the effects of sour grapes', which served to infuriate those who still venerated her.

Under continuing pressure, and with the leadership election results showing how large the problem was within the parliamentary party, Major began to modify his tone and then his position on Europe. 'We are all Eurosceptics now,' gloated Norman Lamont in a speech on the fringe of the 1995 Conservative conference. The following year came the crucial decision, a public commitment that there would be a referendum before Britain joined the proposed single currency. 'His own intellectual analysis of Britain's interests remained the same,' reflected Douglas Hurd, 'but he would no longer show any personal enthusiasm for the EU.' Kenneth Clarke, the leading Europhile in the cabinet, was saddened by the new stance. 'The truth is,' he noted, 'that, privately, John Major has changed his mind. He's changed sides.'

Clarke himself came under pressure, as media stories circulated that he was threatening to resign over the issue of Europe and that Brian Mawhinney, chairman of the Conservative Party, was flirting with the idea of 'new chancellor, new chance'. Clarke reportedly told Mawhinney to stop briefing the press, coining the memorable phrase: 'Tell your kids to get their scooters off my lawn.' (It was an allusion to Harold Wilson's 1969 words to the engineering union leader Hugh Scanlon, during pay negotiations: 'Hughie, get your tanks off my lawn.') Clarke was subsequently obliged to issue a statement to the effect that he had no intention of resigning as chancellor; the announcement itself revealed how much damage the government had sustained.

Others who shared Clarke's dismay at the way things were going proved to be less loyal, and several defections by MPs reduced still further the government's majority. In 1995 Alan Howarth, who had been a minister for education and science until the 1992 election, became the first Tory MP to defect straight to Labour, while later that year Emma Nicholson also crossed the floor to become a Liberal Democrat, explaining that the Conservative Party now seemed 'class-ridden, prejudiced, fratricidal and distanced in ignorance from the mass of the people'. Always on the liberal wing, Nicholson had nevertheless given the appearance of being a solid, traditional pearls-and-twinset Tory – if there was no room for her in the modern Conservatives, it didn't augur well for the party. A couple of months later Peter Thurnham, MP for a marginal Bolton constituency, announced that he had resigned the whip and was now an independent Conservative; he too subsequently joined the Liberal Democrats.

The sense of hopelessness touched even those not yet in Parliament. Alan Clark had chosen not to stand for re-election in 1992, but had been regretting that decision ever since and was actively seeking a constituency that would be prepared to take him on, despite his controversial reputation. His moment came in the autumn of 1996 when Nicholas Scott, the MP for Kensington and Chelsea, was found lying drunk and unconscious in a gutter in Bournemouth during the Conservative conference. Scott was subsequently deselected as the candidate by his local party and replaced by Clark. How committed Clark was to the cause, however, was doubtful. 'What I hope, quite firmly now,' he wrote in his diary, 'is that the Tory Party is smashed to pieces and a huge number of people lose their seats. Then, at last perhaps, my particular brand of radicalism can grow.'

Others who stayed outwardly loyal were also committing treason in their hearts. 'There are bad moments when I pray that Blair wins with a big majority to get this shower out,' confided Edwina Currie to her diary in 1996. Michael Portillo, it seemed, was not prepared to wait for such an eventuality. Having been promoted to defence secretary in the reshuffle following Major's re-election, he electrified the 1995 conference with a speech that encapsulated his public persona. It was a transparent bid for his future leadership, using the defence brief as a loose metaphor for his other concerns, particularly the European Union, which, he mocked, would soon want to 'harmonise uniforms and cap badges, or even to metricate them', and would seek to impose a forty-hour working week on British forces. But he also took in education – calling for the teaching of British history, 'the real history of heroes and bravery, of good versus evil, of freedom against tyranny, of Nelson, Wellington and Churchill' – and hinted heavily at his opposition to the single currency, as well as insisting that Britain would not join a 'single European army'. British troops were prepared to die 'for Britain, not for Brussels', he declared, momentarily forgetting the role of the Welsh Guards in liberating that city in 1944 and the contribution made to the defeat of Nazism by the Free Belgian Forces based in Britain.

He ended with a notorious peroration: 'Around the world three letters send a chill down the spine of the enemy: SAS. And those letters spell out one clear message: don't mess with Britain.' This was not quite so gratuitous a reference as it was portrayed; the European Court had recently ruled that the SAS's shooting of three IRA activists in Gibraltar in 1988 had been in contravention of the terrorists' human rights. Even so, it appeared a little presumptuous – and inappropriate, given his own timidity in the leadership election – when he appropriated the motto of the regiment, 'Who Dares Wins', for his resounding conclusion: 'We dare. We will win.'

It all went down a storm in the conference hall, and won a huge standing ovation, but few others were impressed. 'Cheap and nasty,' decided the *Daily Mirror*, while Andrew Marr wrote of how 'grown newspapermen were slack-jawed and white-faced at the sheer gung-ho relish with which he took on the factual world and defeated it with overwhelming verbal force'. Jacques Santer, the president of the European Commission, was said to have found the speech 'deplorable' and 'grotesque', John Redwood dismissed it as 'rabble-rousing', and Leon Brittan – former Tory home secretary and now an EU commissioner – was outraged: 'He has damaged the Conservative image and he has actually damaged himself.' Most worryingly, many senior army officers and SAS sources shared those views. Even Portillo was a little embarrassed by himself, according to Gyles Brandreth who bumped into him on the evening of the speech: 'He knows he went too far. He's had a good summer, been taken seriously, impressed and surprised the brass hats. This devalues the currency.'

The speech did, however, allow Portillo to regain from Redwood the mantle of the right's favoured candidate for the succession. It was his name that was again mentioned most often, although the prospect of a leadership challenge was fast receding. Officially there was an election for the leader's job every autumn, even if this was seldom enacted and the incumbent was assumed to have been returned unopposed. In a pre-emptive strike, the executive of the backbench 1922 Committee announced in February 1996 that, with a general election impending, that provision would be suspended for one year. This was presumably intended to silence the whispers, though in fact it merely allowed for the emergence of a new rumour: that John Major would voluntarily step down in favour of Heseltine before the election.

But most of the stories were now about the battle that would follow the widely expected defeat at the ballot boxes, with new names emerging at Westminster and in the press on a regular basis. Malcolm Rifkind, Michael Howard, Michael Forsyth, Stephen Dorrell, Kenneth Clarke – all joined the proposed list of candidates, alongside the familiar nominations of Heseltine and Portillo. *The Times* even allowed room for William Rees-Mogg, its former editor, to float the outlandish suggestion that Alan Clark might be the man for the job: 'he is rash, amusing, grand, Eurosceptic, outspoken, scandalous, clever, arrogant, the extraordinary rather than the ordinary.' (Rees-Mogg's inability to foresee the future had long been a standing joke at *Private Eye*, though the best gag came from Boris Johnson, who once wrote of him that he 'has predicted twelve of the last two recessions'.)

The rumours grew into open speculation during that final year before the general election, which was now widely expected to be held in May 1997. This was the last possible date that Major could call it, and the assumption was that he was holding on in the hope that the public might change minds that had been made up years ago. The Tories had been behind in the opinion polls since Black Wednesday and the gap between them and Labour was now hitting levels in excess of thirty-five percentage points, with over half the country saying they were going to vote for Tony Blair's party.

Yet for almost exactly the same period, the economy had been growing. The recession that had opened the decade had long since come to an end, and the opinion polls showed that the public understood that to be the case. But they gave no credit to the Tories, believing that, in John Redwood's words, 'the recovery took place in spite of rather than because of the government's policies'.

Part of the problem was that the price of that recession had been so painful, as Major admitted: 'Unemployment rose from 1.75 million on the day I became prime minister to a peak of just under three million.' This was the price that had apparently been worth paying for getting inflation under control, and, in this respect at least, it had been a success; although there was no prospect of a return to full employment, the high rates of inflation, once so familiar, had been vanquished and did not reappear. Keeping inflation at bay during the subsequent recovery was seen by some as a tribute to the work of Kenneth Clarke as chancellor of the exchequer – the combination of growth and low inflation had last been achieved under Roy Jenkins back in the 1960s – but it brought its own problems. Annual wage increases were smaller and, though this merely reflected low price rises, the illusion of a fast-growing pay packet wasn't in evidence to help build what was known in the jargon of the time as 'the feelgood factor'.

Economic growth did, however, feed into the mood of the country in other areas, and it helped shape the celebratory nature of the national culture in the mid-1990s. Unfortunately for the government, the political benefits from the good times were enjoyed almost entirely by the Labour Party, with Tony Blair being widely regarded as the prime minister in waiting; there was a simple impatience with the Tories that they didn't know when to leave the stage for the rightful incumbent. Perhaps the last hope for the Tories was that England might win Euro 96 and send the country into a fever of patriotic rejoicing, with the government deriving some vicarious credit. Alastair Campbell was among those attending the semi-final, where 'for political reasons I found myself rooting privately for Germany', and noted that Major looked 'a bit ashen' as England fell at the penultimate hurdle. The corresponding relief in the Labour camp was summed up by Blair: 'Jetzt sind die Tories gefuckt.'

The real reason why the Conservatives got no thanks for the recovery, however, was that by now they were getting no credit at all for anything from anyone, with the possible exception of Inspector Morse, who experienced 'a wholly unprecedented sense of gratitude to the Tory government for its reform of the Sunday licensing laws'. Everyone knew that the end was coming for John Major, no matter how long he waited for the polls to turn. This time he knew it too and, unlike 1992, he had no faith in victory. He was 'mildly depressed', observed Tristan Garel-Jones. 'At times, I can't conceal it, he gets into black despair, very black moments.'

Signs of the government's unpopularity were everywhere evident. Just before kick-off in an England rugby international at Twickenham, an announcement was made on the public address system that Virginia Bottomley was present and a chorus of boos and jeers was heard from every corner of the ground. The Labour MP Dennis Turner, who had once been a bingo caller, revealed that the call for the number 10, which had been 'Major's Den' (following on from the better known 'Maggie's Den'), had now changed to 'Blair's Lair'. A 1995 film of a book by Sister Helen Prejean had popularised the phrase *Dead Man Walking* and it was hard to resist applying those words to the prime minister. Even Edwina Currie, on the day before the election was called, was talking openly about the need for a clean and quick leadership race after the coming defeat: 'If there's going to be a contest, please John, please don't make us hang around.'

As the general election approached, there was finally a feelgood factor abroad, though it was hardly of the kind Major had hoped for. 'As I look around me, I see more and more faint traces of a smile on people's faces,' wrote Armando Iannucci. It came, he concluded, from the knowledge that 'very soon the whole damn load of clammy, innumerate, Europhobic, rate-capping, utility whoring, supergun smuggling, wayward penised carcasses who've been incompetently slabbering around the corridors of power for the last eighteen years will be really, actually and measurably out on their arses for ever'.

9
Election
'Things can only get better'

A tidal wave has burst over the Conservative Party tonight, and it's not a matter of putting your finger in the dike. The sea wall is collapsing all around us.
David Mellor (1997)

It is a great rising up of we, the nation, against all the greed, lack of principles and of respect for real people and their problems.
Helen Fielding, *Bridget Jones: The Edge of Reason* (1999)

Because I haven't always been a Conservative, I know how a lot of people see us. People loathe the Tories. That's why we lost.
Daniel Finkelstein (1997)

In August 1992, during John Major's glorious summer between the landslide election vote and the disaster of Black Wednesday, nineteen Tories, both MPs and officials from Conservative Central Office, flew out to America to attend the National Convention of the Republican Party in Houston, Texas. There was something of a valedictory tone to the gathering, with a final appearance by Richard Nixon, the most controversial president of recent times, and the last-ever speech by Ronald Reagan, the man who had – with Margaret Thatcher – dominated western politics in the previous decade. Many feared that it might also prove a farewell for the incumbent president. With an election just ten weeks away, George Bush was trailing in the opinion polls, some considerable distance behind his younger, more charismatic Democrat rival, Bill Clinton.

In this company, the visiting Tories were greeted as loyal allies in the cause, especially in light of the story (denied by the British government) that the Home Office had been prevailed upon to check its files, seeking any dirt there might be on Clinton from his days as a Rhodes scholar at Oxford. They were also received as conquering heroes for having triumphed against the odds earlier in the year. The Conservative Party organisation was 'half a generation ahead of anything in the United States', enthused the senior Republican congressman, Newt Gingrich, and there was much that the Americans could learn from their British friends. How much was actually learnt, however, was unclear, for George Bush was subsequently unseated by Clinton. And by the time of the presidential election, Major's moment in the sun had passed; it seemed entirely in keeping with his new image as the unluckiest man in British politics that his party had been seen so ostentatiously to have backed a loser.

That election, though, was not exactly a resounding success for the Democrats. Clinton won with just 43 per cent, the lowest share gained by a winning candidate in modern times, making him the first president since Nixon in 1968 to be elected on less than half the vote. His victory was less an endorsement of his campaign than a reflection of the way that Bush haemorrhaged support to the wild-card candidate, businessman Ross Perot, who secured the largest third-party turnout in eighty years. Clinton in fact attracted a lower share than had his predecessor as Democrat candidate, Michael Dukakis, when losing in 1988.

Nonetheless, it was a welcome win for the centre-left, the first time the Democrats had taken the White House since 1976, at a time when the Republicans were irredeemably tainted by the Watergate scandal, ending a run of defeats almost as long as that endured by the Labour Party. If the British right had turned out to have nothing to teach their American counterparts, maybe there were things to be learned in the other direction on the left. And so, in January 1993, as Clinton took office, Tony Blair and Gordon Brown, the rising stars of Labour, made their way across the Atlantic to pay tribute and to see if their party could benefit from the new president's experience. They were followed shortly afterwards by Peter Mandelson.

The key lessons, it appeared, were to distance the party from its past image and to avoid anything so definite as a policy, so that one might instead confound one's opponents with a moving target. In the days after his election, one of Clinton's close aides said that his first task was to demonstrate 'that things are going to be different, that these are new Democrats and that he has a positive agenda for change'. That phrase 'new Democrats' stuck in the minds of the British visitors. So too did the concept of triangulation, whereby the left-wing and right-wing positions on an issue were worked out and a place found distinct from the two, the alternatives being vehemently denounced as extremist. This process didn't necessarily mean that a midway position should be adopted; if Labour had traditionally been seen as insufficiently tough on low-level crime, for example, then the answer was to outflank the Tories on the right.

This was the tactical expression of what was becoming known as the Third Way, an increasingly popular political concept in the English-speaking world that promised to blend free-market economics with a leftist social policy of 'fairness', though its exact definition remained obscure at best. In an attempt to explore what it meant, several conferences were to be held over the next few years, including a major gathering staged in New York in 1998, which was addressed by Blair, Clinton, the Bulgarian president, Peter Stoyanov, and the Italian prime minister, Romano Prodi; amongst those attending was Christopher Meyer, now the British ambassador to America, who concluded that 'the Third Way was less a coherent philosophy of government, more a tactic for election-winning'.

On their return to Britain in 1993, Blair and Brown found that their enthusiasm for Clinton's brand of politics was not matched by others in the Labour Party. John Smith was still the leader and was content to continue ploughing a more traditional furrow. There was a sense that Clinton was doing little more than Neil Kinnock had tried, chasing after focus groups and attempting to tailor policy to the supposed middle ground. 'All the ideas from Clinton are an elite few running a party on the basis of the information they get from the polls,' observed John Prescott in 1993. 'That is not the way the Labour Party has been run, and while we've tried it in the last couple of elections, it does seem to be that we've lost, doesn't it?' Smith was more forthright: 'We don't need any of that fucking Clinton stuff over here.'

The feeling that there was no need for a change in direction was supported, as it happened, by the very polls that Prescott professed to despise. In the last opinion poll published before Smith's death in May 1994, Labour stood at 45.5 per cent, with the Liberal Democrats and Conservatives neck-and-neck, more than twenty points behind. The assumption on the part of the electorate was that Labour could, almost certainly would, win the next election and that Smith was a serious leader. Westminster too was increasingly impressed by his performance. On the night before his death, a clip of Smith was shown on the television news and Paddy Ashdown recorded in his diary that he turned to his wife and 'said that for the first time he looked like a potential prime minister'.

Almost uniquely in modern British politics, Smith avoided ridicule. As Tony Benn pointed out, *Spitting Image* 'doesn't mention the Labour Party now. There is nothing to say about the Labour Party — the whole of British politics is completely stagnant.' What Benn found objectionable, however, cheered others; Smith's Labour wasn't mocked because it was too unthreatening to warrant attack. 'John was making the party feel more and more comfortable with itself,' reflected Clare Short in 1996. 'My own view is that he would have done that with the country.'

He did not, of course, get the chance to do so, and his replacement by Tony Blair ushered in a frantic new phase of jettisoning the luggage of Labour's history. Much of the groundwork for this had already been laid by Smith, under whom one member, one vote had been introduced, and during whose time Gordon Brown, as shadow chancellor, had proclaimed: 'Labour is not against wealth, nor will we seek to penalise it. The next Labour government will not tax for its own sake.' In an interview shortly before his death, Smith had stressed this point to the BBC's John Cole, saying that tax was the big issue: 'he was not going to add to the burdens of what he unselfconsciously called "our own people".' His core values also foreshadowed those associated with Blair: 'An abiding theme, in this and other conversations, was restoration of the role of the family in British society.'

But Blair undoubtedly accelerated the so-called modernisation of the party, stressing the 'southern appeal' of which Peter Mandelson had spoken. Blair himself was quite clear where he stood. 'I was middle class and my politics were in many ways middle class,' he wrote in his memoirs. He understood the need to appeal to the suburban South, the non-unionised private-sector workers and self-employed who had come to see Labour as the enemy of enterprise, the party of high taxation that wished to penalise middle England, though even here the groundwork had already been laid. In the elections to the European Parliament that were held between the death of Smith and the accession of Blair, Labour enjoyed an average swing of 12 per cent nationally, with the figure rising to 15 per cent in London and the South-East.

In 1993 Andy McSmith, Kinnock's former press officer, had predicted the emergence of a Labour Party that would be 'more European than the Tories, very strong on law and order, with a promise of electoral reform, and social welfare without excessive tax increases'. This would be 'a party where the upwardly mobile could feel at home, not unlike the one which David Owen tried to create a decade ago'. In essence this was the party that Smith was creating and very much the party that Blair wished to lead, though preferably without any public nod to Owen, whose recently ended career as an MP was littered with broken parties and with personal and political animosities.

*

Unusually for Labour, Blair became leader as the head of a clearly defined faction. Previously, figures such as Harold Wilson, Michael Foot and Neil Kinnock had been associated with the left, Hugh Gaitskell, James Callaghan and John Smith with the right, but all were broadly acceptable to most sections of the party and all were cautious about campaigning on a ticket of transforming the party in their own image. Blair, on the other hand, came in saying from the outset that he was going to change everything. And he began as he meant to carry on, by deliberately picking a fight with the left of the party.

In fact, it was an old battle, albeit one that seemed to have been settled more than thirty-five years earlier. The Labour constitution contained in Clause IV a statement of the aims and values of the party, including a broad definition of the socialist society to which it aspired, committing Labour 'to secure for the workers by hand or by brain the full fruits of their industry' and stating that the way to achieve this was through 'the common ownership of the means of production, distribution and exchange'. Written in 1917, the year of the Soviet revolution in Russia, the intention was clear: the anarchy of the market should be replaced by state planning and state ownership of industry. It was, wrote Jack Straw, 'one of the most explicit statements of Marxist-Leninist values of any left-wing party in western Europe'.

Though never pushed to its logical conclusion, this philosophy had inspired both the great reforming government of Clement Attlee in 1945 and, subsequently, some of the more radical thinkers on the left. It had come under threat, however, during the leadership of Hugh Gaitskell in the late 1950s, with an attempt to rewrite the clause. 'The changing character of labour, full employment, new housing and the new way of living based on the telly, the fridge, the car and the glossy magazines – all these have had their effects on our political strength,' argued Gaitskell. 'We have to show we are a modern, mid-twentieth century party, looking to the future not to the past.' But his attempt to rewrite the party's aims was defeated at the 1959 conference, and thereafter the relevant passage from Clause IV was printed on every membership card as a token of a covenant.

For some in the party, however, this was still a stumbling block. Amongst them were Jack Straw, who published a pamphlet 'Policy and Ideology' in 1993 proposing a new statement of the party's aims, Will Hutton, who wrote that year of the need to change Clause IV, and Giles Radice, who met Blair a week after the results of the leadership election were announced in 1994, urging him to revise the clause. The debate having been started, Blair decided that this was indeed to be his great statement of intent to the British people.

Towards the end of his first conference speech as leader, he included the line: 'It is time we had a clear up-to-date statement of the objects and objectives of our party.' That was as far as he went in the hall, with no mention of Clause IV at all, but backstage his spin doctors were briefing the media that this was precisely what he was talking about. There was a certain irony that a man who was insisting in public, 'Let us say what we mean and mean what we say,' was doing nothing of the kind, and leaving his publicists to join the dots for journalists. But it was also an entirely successful strategy, ensuring that there was no shocked outrage to disrupt his standing ovation, while making his point to the wider public. 'Tony Blair yesterday delivered the ultimate proof of his determination to change the Labour Party by sounding the death knell for Clause IV,' was the opening to *The Times*' coverage of the speech, which continued: 'A source close to Mr Blair confirmed that Clause IV would be replaced, and that Mr Blair regarded it as a "narrow and inadequate" description of socialism.'

The fact that some concern would have been voiced if Blair had come out into the open was demonstrated later that week when the conference voted for a resolution in support of the existing Clause IV, but by then it was too late to halt the momentum, much of it generated by the media. Alastair Campbell recorded in his diary that David English, chairman of Associated Newspapers who published the *Daily Mail*, 'was in raptures', and Campbell also found himself fielding interview requests from such unlikely sources as the editor of the society gossip magazine *Tatler*: 'She said *Tatler* readers were flocking over to Labour.' By the end of the year even Sir Royston Merchant, the fictional mogul behind GlobeLink News on *Drop the Dead Donkey*, had swung into line, and Gus Hedges, Sir Royston's jargon-spouting henchman, had installed a huge photograph of Blair in his office. 'We're underachieving in the team togetherness department,' Gus would urge an office full of cynics, and he sounded as though he might fit rather well into the new model Labour Party.

The key to getting a revised Clause IV through was said to be John Prescott, the hero of the leadership's OMOV battle the previous year, and he was assiduously courted by Blair and Campbell. It was not so much that Prescott represented the left, as that he was in the mould of the old-fashioned trade union fixers who had always dominated party conferences and who had, except for the occasional lapse, ensured that the left was kept firmly under control. Now, boosted by his victory in the election to choose the party's deputy leader – on his third attempt to get the job – he had no intention of rocking the boat. Nor did anyone else much, so averse had the party become to appearing divided. Blair staged a series of meetings around the country, arguing persuasively for a redefinition, and creating a mood in which a postal ballot of the membership endorsed the change overwhelmingly.

In April 1995 a special conference was held in the Methodist Central Hall in London, where the original Clause IV had been adopted in 1918, to approve the new wording issued by the leadership. One of the few to speak against was Arthur Scargill, the miners' leader, whose speech was accompanied by slow handclapping. 'That began making me feel as if I was at a Nuremberg Rally,' wrote Tony Benn in his diary, which seemed slightly to be overstating the case; certainly the reception was discourteous and intolerant, but it was no more than Benn's own supporters had meted out to his opponents in the 1980s. In any event, Scargill's was an isolated voice ('Yesterday the loony left became the lonely left,' gloated the *Sunday Times*) and early the following year he turned his back on Labour to found the Socialist Labour Party, though it was not a notable success – at a 1996 by-election in Barnsley, Scargill's home town, the SLP won fewer than a thousand votes. Also to leave Labour, though without quite as much fanfare, was Bruce Kent, who in the 1980s had been the public face of the Campaign for Nuclear Disarmament.

The new statement formally adopted in 1996 was hardly the most inspiring call to arms, combining the crashingly obvious ('by the strength of our common endeavour, we achieve more than we achieve alone') with vague thoughts about empowerment (we should all have 'the means to realise our true potential'). It also reasserted one of Blair's common themes about the position of the individual in society: 'the rights we enjoy reflect the duties we owe.' The blandness of the aspiration was the point of the exercise. Blair wished to let the electorate know that his party, which he was already referring to privately as New Labour even during his leadership campaign, was moderate, mainstream and safe.

The episode encapsulated much of Blair's leadership style. There was the less-than-honest conference speech, illustrating the way that statements would now be made not in public view, but behind the scenes, announced first to the media, rather than to elected representatives and party members. There was the emphasis on the process of change rather than the end result: 'I was surprised how little thought had gone into what might take its place,' mused Robin Cook. There was the fascination with words and technicalities that made absolutely no difference in real terms – it had been a long time since the party thought of Clause IV as a guide to economic policy – but which sent signals to the media that progress was being made.

And there was the studied non-involvement of Gordon Brown, remaining aloof from the fray.

How successful, or necessary, any of it might have been, was hard to tell. At the start of 1994, when John Smith was still alive, a Gallup poll had found 79 per cent agreeing with the statement 'Labour is a much more moderate and sensible party than it used to be'; in the month that the new Clause IV was adopted this proportion had risen by a negligible fraction to 80 per cent. A great deal of energy had been expended to no measurable end.

Meanwhile, the reforming radicalism of which Blair spoke so often bore little fruit in terms of actual proposals. In his memoirs, he insisted that 'there was no room for compromise on essentials', going on to list those areas where New Labour was prepared to accept the changes wrought during the eighteen years of Conservative government: trade union legislation, privatisation of utilities (including the railways), income tax levels, nuclear defence and grammar schools. He added: 'On the NHS and schools we also compromised.' With the best will in the world, it was hard to discern what remained of the 'essentials' on which compromise was ruled out.

In any event, policy was never going to be the strong suit of a Blair-led Labour Party, though there was at the time an unusual public appetite for new thoughts on how society and the economy could be reconstructed. The mood was evident in the runaway success of *The State We're In* (1995), a book written by Will Hutton, economics editor of the *Guardian*, which was said to have achieved sales of 150,000 in hardback alone. It was a powerful assault on the short-termism of British capitalism and the Conservatives' economic liberalism, coupled with a call for 'the recognition that the market economy has to be managed and regulated', and it was devoured with great enthusiasm on the left. For a while Hutton's language – 'social citizenship', 'the stakeholder society' – was seldom far from the lips of New Labour, though the phrases didn't last.

In the highest echelons of the party there seemed to be little time for innovative thought, despite the appointment of a clever young man named David Miliband, who was clearly on the right wavelength, as head of policy. ('The old answers are inadequate, and our generation has the chance to play with new ideas,' enthused Miliband in 1993.) Those who were closest to the leader and whose opinion really counted, however, were more focused on short-term goals, especially Alastair Campbell – much more involved in decision-making than his title of press secretary would indicate – and Philip Gould, a pollster first employed by Peter Mandelson for the 1987 election and subsequently involved in Bill Clinton's 1992 campaign. The experience of the latter was spelt out in an article co-written with Patricia Hewitt: 'The lessons which the British left can learn are not so much about *content* as about *process*.'

Gould specialised in running focus groups, small gatherings of a dozen or so people who were encouraged to discuss their views and perceptions with the others, thereby — it was claimed — giving a deeper sense of the public mood than crude opinion polling could provide. The technique was sufficiently new to Britain that the year before Blair's elevation to leader it was still being referred to in inverted commas in the press. Gould's role lay in interpreting the results of his research, which more often than not reinforced his leader's gut instinct. 'He trusts his own judgement more than anything else,' Gould said of Blair. 'He just somehow thinks he is in touch with the British people.' Equally influential, though, was the philosophy of politics that Gould brought with him, and which chimed with the approach of Campbell and Mandelson. The job of a leader in the modern world, argued Gould, was the winning of 'a daily mandate in which strength comes from popularity'. The pursuit of the news agenda and the attempt to dominate it each and every day was to become more important to New Labour than the development of policy. In the campaign to win power, detailed proposals were less important than broad-stroke buzzwords. The crucial issue was the building of an image of resolution and determination.

For if there was one thing that Blair admired in the political arena, it was strength, an attribute that always prompted the same epithet: Rupert Murdoch 'had balls', Alastair Campbell and Michael Heseltine were both said to have 'clanking great balls', while Peter Mandelson had 'balls of steel'. Blair was not so immodest as to claim the same for himself — though he made sure to place on record Murdoch's praise for his 'brass nerve' — but he did like to talk about himself as a conviction politician in the hard-hitting mould of Margaret Thatcher.

This overlooked, however, a critical difference. Certainly Blair was prepared to take his party in unfamiliar and unloved directions, but it was always in pursuit of a wider popularity, whereas Thatcher had imposed unwelcome and difficult changes both on her party and on the country itself. In his acceptance speech on becoming leader, he had talked of 'tough choices', and that was to remain a familiar catchphrase over the next decade, but there was little evidence in domestic policy of decisions being made that a moderate Tory, say John Major, would have found particularly tough.

And perhaps it was because his first priority was to find out where the people were and then follow them, that Blair tended to sound less like Thatcher and more like Major, even in his phrase-making. The new Clause

IV, for example, included the promise to create a society where 'power, wealth and opportunity are in the hands of the many, not the few'; the formulation echoed Major's speeches, in which he rejected 'the notion that excellence for the few excuses mediocrity for the many', and said that the elimination of inheritance tax would bring 'wealth for the many, not the few'. Blair's rhetoric about the welfare state — that it should provide 'a hand up, not a hand out' — was often attributed to the influence of Bill Clinton, but had been foreshadowed by Major too, in a 1991 speech to the Conservative Party's women's conference: 'Our Conservatism is about developing personal independence. It is designed to give people a hand up, not a hand out.' Similarly, Blair may have borrowed 'with opportunity must come responsibility' from Clinton ('we offer opportunity; we demand responsibility') for his 1994 conference speech, but it wasn't a radical break from Major's speech earlier the same year: 'our policies are based on individual choice, individual opportunity, individual responsibility.' It was a theme that both men stressed. Absolutely central to the concept of the Third Way, argued Blair, was the creation of 'a modern relationship between the responsibilities of the citizen and those of society', a refusal to be fooled by the false dichotomy between self-interest and the collective good. Or, as Major put it in 1991: 'Some people tend to see individualism and social responsibility as mutually exclusive. We make no such mistake.' Major himself noticed the debt: 'The language of New Labour may have been first-rate, but it was second-hand.'

What was new, both to the Labour Party and to British politics, was an obsession with the press and the broadcasters. 'We paid inordinate attention in the early days of New Labour to courting, assuaging and persuading the media,' Blair acknowledged in later years. 'In our own defence, after eighteen years of opposition and the, at times, ferocious hostility of parts of the media, it was hard to see any alternative.' Lessons had been learnt from the way in which Michael Foot and Neil Kinnock had been destroyed by the press, and there was a determination that nothing of the sort should happen again.

Part of the answer was the assiduous courtship of proprietors, so that famously Blair and his entourage flew to Australia in the summer of 1995 to speak to Rupert Murdoch and his senior executives. At the same time John Major was on holiday in the south of France with Nicholas Lloyd, the outgoing editor of the *Daily Express*, a much less powerful figure.

Just as important, though, was the engagement in what Blair called 'hand to hand fighting' to shape the news agenda. It was in pursuit of this goal that Labour invested millions of pounds in its Excalibur computer system in late 1995, and began the process of feeding in thousands upon thousands of articles, speeches and statistics that could be searched instantly to reveal any contradictions or discrepancies in the words of Conservative politicians. Excalibur lay at the heart of Labour's anti-government campaigning, based on a simple insight articulated by Dave Hill, the party's media spokesperson: 'Journalists are inherently lazy and our rebuttal unit has made it easier for them.' From now on, any speech by a Tory cabinet minister was followed almost instantly by a Labour Party press release commenting adversely upon it. Sometimes the rebuttal even preceded the announcement, the so-called 'prebuttal', while the use of electronic pagers meant that even during a statement in the House of Commons, information could be fed to key MPs so that they might intervene more effectively.

The success of the approach partially depended upon the recent proliferation of media outlets, and the consequent dilution of resources available to any one organisation. Since the late 1980s, newspaper revenue had come under pressure from the growth in magazine publication and from a long-term decline in circulation, much of it among the young, while the broadcasters were confronted by the rise of satellite and then internet outlets. As a result, there was a coming together of the media, a growing mutual dependence.

It was seen first in the now ubiquitous radio phone-in shows, which were based almost exclusively on listeners' reactions to stories that had appeared in the newspapers. That pattern then became standard on television, where commentators were struggling to fill 24-hour news channels. But since the papers were themselves cutting back on their reporting staff, they in turn found television and radio a useful source of material for comment. The rising number of outlets was sold as a broadening of choice, but actually brought into being a much more monolithic news establishment that spent more and more of its time examining itself, chasing its own tail in ever decreasing circles. New Labour bought into this system entirely, adding a postmodern politics to a postmodern media, in which story became more important than reality.

And since Labour's own policy was being deliberately kept to a minimum, to avoid making any promises beyond the most mundane, its own positive message – as opposed to its attacks on the government – mostly consisted of press conferences that proclaimed for a second or third time, in excited tones, longstanding and already announced commitments. The fact that this simple tactic worked, that it was accepted by a media world increasingly devoid of a sense of history, set the tone for much that was to follow.

At the same time, any comments by frontbenchers that smacked of old Labour were curbed. When such statements did slip through, retaliation was swift. A few months after Blair had made such a stout defence of Harriet Harman's choice of school for her son, Clare Short casually mentioned in a television interview that 'in a fair tax system people like me would pay a little more'. At the time, MPs received a salary of £34,000 and the idea that 'middle income families' might be more heavily taxed under a Labour government was precisely the image that Blair did not wish to project; official policy was that no one under £40,000 would face an income tax rise. There was fury at the way Short had 'fucked up', in Alastair Campbell's words. 'She cannot be trusted to behave in a professional or competent way,' was his verdict, while John Prescott was more succinct: 'That woman is fucking mad.'

Short's offence was minor compared to the dissent being heard from within Conservative ranks − 'We won't win under Major,' ran a fairly unexceptional comment, this time from the MP Graham Riddick; 'he and his cabinet are a load of deadbeats and has-beens' − but caused a huge over-reaction in leadership circles. Battered into submission by a barrage of briefing, Short fell silent for a while, but later in 1996 was to be found in the *New Statesman* criticising the 'people who live in the dark' behind Blair. She was, in a phrase that first surfaced that year and that became the ultimate denunciation of those who said anything hinting of Labour's past, 'off message'.

'How can I be off-message when I am the message?' John Major was once quoted as saying, and Tony Blair would have understood the point entirely, for he too was the message made flesh; nothing else in New Labour came remotely close to the importance of getting Blair elected as the prime minister. This was the sole item on the agenda of what was touted as the 'New Labour project'. (That terminology, incidentally, was not itself new; there were Labour MPs in the 1980s who had talked disparagingly about the 'Mandelson project', while the party's press officer Andy McSmith used to refer to 'the Kinnockite project'.)

Not even Gordon Brown was of much significance in terms of public presentation, and his best-known speech in opposition had been the one containing the explanation in 1994 that 'Our new economic approach is rooted in ideas which stress the importance of macro-economic, neo-classical endogenous growth theory.' The subsequent discovery that this had been written by Brown's youthful adviser, Ed Balls, prompted one of Michael Heseltine's crowd-pleasing gags at the Tory conference, when he announced of the policy that 'It's not Brown's, it's Balls'.

The response to Blair in the Labour Party was mixed. Membership rose sharply in the first years after the leadership election – it had 'the fastest-growing membership of any party in the western world', boasted Blair in 1996 – but many comrades of longer standing weren't enthused to the same degree. The openly expressed admiration of Thatcher alienated traditionalists, who shared Neil Kinnock's feelings: 'That woman fucking killed people.' And the distrust wasn't confined to the left. 'They all loathe Blair,' wrote Tony Benn of the old right-wing councillors in his Chesterfield constituency. 'Blair doesn't inspire anyone. Nobody loves him, because he doesn't want them to do anything except admire him, obey him and give money.'

There was, indeed, something unlovable about Blair's persona, even in those early days. Unlike Bill Clinton, he was not a charismatic figure, but he had learnt the trick of behaving as though he were, of projecting an ostentatious self-belief that stood in stark contrast to John Major's diffidence. His performances were reminiscent somehow of Kevin Keegan, at that time the manager of Newcastle United, a man who during his playing career was generally considered to have turned himself into a great footballer by sheer application, compensating for a lack of natural brilliance by working harder than anyone else; it seemed entirely appropriate that in 1995 Blair staged a photo-opportunity with Keegan, playing keepie-uppie for the cameras. The long-honed professionalism acquired a new polish now that he was leader, but increasingly it came at the price of warmth and spontaneity. 'At times his competence is almost chilling,' observed Matthew Parris in 1996.

Similarly, Blair was not blessed as an orator, but he had studied hard ('If only I could speak like that,' he yearned, after seeing Tony Benn, then at the peak of his powers, in the early 1980s) and he developed, at his best, a conversational style, with flashes of humour and lashings of self-confidence, that projected a relaxed tone. It was a studied informality, as analysed by Alan Partridge: 'He'd take his jacket off and throw it over his shoulder, as if to say: I'm a regular guy, not a stick-in-the-mud, I like a pint, why not vote for me?' The same nonchalant note was evident in public when talking about opposition from within the party; asked about comments from the left-wing MP Dennis Canavan that he was too authoritarian, Blair's typically jokey response was: 'I thought I told him not to say that.'

That relaxed image, of course, had also been the hallmark of John Major, before the Eurosceptic rebellion wore him down and, for all their differences, there were points of comparison between the two men. 'One of his skills is that everybody thinks he agrees with them. It's not because he says one thing to one person and another to another. It's the way he expresses his views.' That was Kenneth Clarke on Major in 1993, but it became too a common assessment of Blair. 'Tony has a habit of saying things people want to hear,' wrote John Prescott. 'They believe him, because they are charmed by his smiles and nods.'

Blair's mode as a platform speaker was less convincing, a jerky series of staccato sentences, often untroubled by verbs, that was intended to convey passion and vision, but sounded rather as if he were in a brainstorming session at an advertising agency. 'Standing together, stronger together, weaker apart. Better off together, worse off split apart,' he urged, when discussing Scottish devolution. Or again, in a characteristic flourish at the 1996 Labour conference: 'The buck stops here. For the future, not the past. For the many, not the few. For trust, not betrayal. For the age of achievement, not the age of decline.' It was a style ruthlessly parodied by satirist Craig Brown. 'Yesterday has gone and past,' declaimed one of his characters, Barbara Vacant, in the television comedy *Norman Ormal*. 'Today is the day before tomorrow. Tomorrow is another day. Yesterday is two days away from tomorrow. Tomorrow will be today tomorrow. And the day after tomorrow will be the day before yesterday.'

Even when Blair was at his most eloquent, there was a certain hollowness where the fire should have been. Some of his earlier speeches as opposition leader read better on the page than they sounded in the flesh: 'I have spent sixteen years being angry, passionate and indignant about young people huddled in doorways, families made wretched by unemployment, the poor unable to make ends meet. I am fed up with anger. They don't need our anger, they need action. And they will not get it through the rage of opposition.'

That speech encapsulated his greatest appeal for the Labour Party. He was driven above all else by the wish to win elections. 'My ambition is clear and simple: to get Labour into government,' he said, while still shadow home secretary, and there was much more of the same after he became leader. 'Power without principle is barren,' he declared in 1994, 'but principle without power is futile. This is a party of government and I will lead it as a party of government.' Many in the party suspected that the power element of that equation meant more to Blair than did the principle, but twenty years on from the last general election victory, most were prepared to sacrifice a few sacred cows if it meant winning. After all, so much of the movement's identity and history had been given up already.

'What's got into Labour?' wondered Henry Davenport in *Drop the Dead Donkey* during John Smith's leadership. 'It's full of Perrier-drinking PR prannies who want to replace "The Red Flag" with "The Sun Has Got His

Hat On", and think the Tolpuddle Martyrs are an American football team.' For the 1994 Labour conference, Blair did indeed try to ditch the traditional singing of 'The Red Flag', but was persuaded that it was a symbolic step too far; instead a jazz version of the anthem was played, and delegates were issued with little Union flags to wave during its performance, lest television viewers might think the lyrics hinted at a solidarity with the international working class. It was not to be the last such assault on tradition. As Blair told Paddy Ashdown: 'From my experience, you have to take your party members and shove their faces in it before they really understand.'

The Conservative response to Blair, on the other hand, was simply confused. Even the normally acute Matthew Parris managed, in the space of a single article in 1994, to depict him as 'a vampire', as 'general secretary of a small, service-sector union' and as the 'manager of a small plastics factory in Enfield, where he is also sidesman in the local church and takes his daughters to pony classes in a newish Volvo'. The question of how best to tackle this threat was never satisfactorily resolved, and the early attempts to characterise Blair were simply confused.

Some senior figures, like Michael Heseltine, believed that he was an opportunistic thief of Tory clothing. 'The greatest con job of modern times,' seethed Heseltine. 'Blair is a total cynic.' The implication of that position was that in office the new Labour leader would resort to more left-wing policies, to high taxes and high levels of spending, because he wasn't really convinced of the need to change; he was, in effect, Neil Kinnock in middle-England clothing. But others, including the more astute Chris Patten, recognised that Blair represented a genuinely new political force and argued from the outset that it would be 'a mistake to try and pretend he is a lefty'.

The Conservative campaign that eventually emerged, at the beginning of 1996, attempted to straddle both approaches and fell squarely in the middle. NEW LABOUR, NEW DANGER ran the strapline to the posters, managing both to emphasise the newness of Blair's approach — the single most desirable attribute for any product, according to conventional wisdom in the advertising world — and to offer the left a crumb of comfort, suggesting that their compromises were being made in a good cause.

The most enduring image from this campaign was the one that showed Blair displaying his over-toothed grin with a strip ripped across the centre of his face to reveal a pair of badly drawn red eyes. It immediately became known as the 'demon eyes' poster and was controversial from the outset. The Advertising Standards Authority ruled that it was dishonest and ordered it not to be used again, while Peter Mandelson professed himself outraged. 'Tony Blair is a practising Christian,' he protested; 'to portray him as the devil is a crass, clumsy move.' On the other hand, *Campaign* magazine, the industry's weekly journal, named it campaign of the year, saying that it 'drew on the public's underlying concerns about Tony Blair: that he smiles too much to be sincere and will do or say anything to be elected'. Neither response was particularly appropriate, serving only to inflate further the self-importance of advertisers, since, despite all the media attention, the poster made no impact whatsoever on public opinion.

Nor did the government make up ground with a follow-up poster, NEW LABOUR, NEW TAXES, which merely provided an opportunity for Labour to talk about the promises on tax made by the Tories during the 1992 election and since broken. In January 1997 Gordon Brown revealed that there would be no increases in income tax or VAT under a Labour government and that, as chancellor, he would adhere to the spending levels already announced by Kenneth Clarke. The most important pledge to be made in the run-up to the general election, it worked because it confirmed everything that Labour had been saying since that controversial shadow budget nearly five years earlier.

Against this, the Tories – the party that had increased VAT and had then applied it to domestic fuel – had no answer whatsoever. Polling in 1992 had shown that 75 per cent of the electorate thought a Labour government would increase taxes; in 1997 that belief was still held by 64 per cent, but it was significant that more now thought that the same would be true of a re-elected Tory government. The one possible angle of attack on Labour's tax announcement, that it was a flagrant breach of party democracy, a decision taken by Blair and Brown without consulting even the shadow cabinet, would simply have reinforced the perception of Blair as a strong leader.

And anyway, none of it really mattered. The first opinion poll conducted after Blair became leader showed Labour pulling still further ahead of the Conservatives, and by the end of 1994 the gap had widened to a record level of thirty-nine points. Meanwhile Blair himself was recording an approval rating of 68 per cent, the highest ever for a leader of the opposition and considerably in excess of John Smith's best figure of 53 per cent. Victory had been certain under Smith, but now a landslide seemed the most likely outcome of the next election. In fact, it appeared Labour had won a landslide the last time around, so great were the numbers now telling the pollsters they had supported the party in 1992. Public disillusion was such that the electorate was rewriting its past, denying that it had ever voted in a Conservative government.

The only slight concern for Labour was that support was running higher amongst men than amongst women, and in November 1996 the *Financial Times* ran a story — immediately decried and denied — that Blair had 'flattened his bouffant hairstyle as part of a campaign to build bridges with women voters'. It was an echo of a story in *The Times* four years earlier, claiming that John Major was 'worried enough about his wan appearance to go to the trouble of having his hair tinted at Trumpers, the Curzon Street hairdressing salon'. That too was denied, though rather more convincingly. 'If I really were dyeing my hair,' reasoned Major, 'would I have chosen this colour?' The fact that serious newspapers were prepared to publish such inconsequential stories was seen by many as an indication of how trivial the British media had become. 'It was a black day in the history of *FT* journalism,' was the official response of Alastair Campbell, the man credited with having created the myth that John Major tucked his shirt into his underpants. He was later to complain: 'Political coverage in this country is a joke. Most of the national media treat politics as a soap opera.'

There was also an argument, however, that this frivolity was all that was left now that policy differences had largely disappeared. The accusation that the two major parties were almost indistinguishable had often been made in the past — in a different context it had been at the heart of Jonathan Swift's Lilliputian satire nearly three centuries earlier — but this time it really was difficult to find differences of opinion between Major and Blair on what had once been the defining issues of British politics: the operation of the free market, nuclear weapons, Europe, trade unions, taxation, crime, welfare, the virtues of competition, the legacy of Thatcherism. This was what Daniel Finkelstein, director of the Social Market Foundation think tank, dubbed 'Blajorism', in tribute to the Butskellism of the 1950s. Not to be left out, Paddy Ashdown complained that 'Labour has stolen our ground comprehensively' and worried that, following the election: 'Our policies are too close to Labour's for us to be a genuine opposition.'

The key difference between Blair and the others, though, was that he was leading a party so exhausted by pessimism, so scarred by defeat that it was prepared to unite behind him, pretty much regardless of what he said. Debate was discouraged, but for now there were few indications that it was much missed.

It was in response to Blair's occupation of Tory territory that some in the Conservative Party called for a move further right. There was talk of putting 'clear blue water' between them and New Labour, if not before the election, then certainly after the coming defeat.

That phrase, 'clear blue water', which first appeared in the month that Blair was elected leader, rapidly became something of a cliché; it was used, for example, as the title of a pamphlet compiling extracts from speeches by Michael Portillo, put together by the Eurosceptic MP George Gardiner. Other voices, though, urged caution. Phillip Oppenheim, conscious that his Amber Valley constituency in Derbyshire was a very tight marginal, was one of the more moderate MPs warning against abandoning the traditional centre-right ground: 'there's real danger in diving off your own patch of land just because someone else is muscling on to it. Initially bracing though the clear blue water might be, you may not find any other firm land.'

Amongst those articulating the case for an extension of Margaret Thatcher's reforming radicalism, the boldest were John Redwood, David Willetts and John Patten, the latter calling for further privatisation of state-held assets: 'We should now dispose of everything that remains by 1999, so that the new century can begin with a clean slate.' But there was little appetite in the media or the electorate for a continuation of the Thatcherite permanent revolution. Attention instead focused on personalities, with Portillo still the clear favourite to succeed Major, even if it was hard to pin down precisely where he differed from the government of which he was a member in terms of actual, concrete policy; it was another indication that style was becoming more important than substance.

And the style was now out of step with public taste. Every time the right spoke, it seemed only to reinforce the now widespread perception of the Tories as 'the nasty party'. In March 1997 David Evans, MP for Welwyn and Hatfield and one of Redwood's declared supporters two years earlier, gave what he termed 'a light-hearted interview' to sixth-formers at a school in his constituency, in which he said that Major was 'unforgiving and vindictive', that Virginia Bottomley was 'dead from the neck up' and that Melanie Johnson, the Labour challenger for his seat, was 'a single girl' with 'three bastard children'. He also outlined his theory, in the context of the recent rape of a schoolgirl by 'some black bastard', that rapists should be castrated. The *Sun*, which – in the absence of a Portillo-led Conservative Party – was becoming an avowedly Labour paper, declared his comments to be 'appalling', though the *Daily Telegraph* backed him (it was 'the prissy ideologues who express deep shock at his words who are out of touch'), perhaps revealing more about the triumph of doctrine over manners at the *Telegraph* than it did about Evans. Certainly his comments didn't seem likely to inspire a Tory revival in the polls.

Nor was it simply the opinion polls that were prophesying disaster; every time the people had the opportunity to cast a vote, the message was the same. In May 1996, in the last local elections before the general election was due, the Conservatives fared even worse than in previous years, seeing the Thatcherite totem of Basildon taken by Labour, as well as losing heartland councils like Hastings and Wokingham (where John Redwood had a 25,000-strong majority as MP). Meanwhile Tunbridge Wells fell to the Liberal Democrats.

In February 1997 the last by-election of the parliament was held in Wirral South, where Barry Porter had been the Conservative MP ever since the seat was created in 1983, never receiving less than 50 per cent of the vote. Now that was overturned and Labour took the seat, itself winning more than half the vote. It was the twenty-sixth by-election to be fought since John Major had become prime minister, and the Tories had failed to win a single one. In fact it was the thirty-fifth straight Conservative defeat on the mainland, dating back to 1989 (there were also two contests in Northern Ireland in that period). The party's only shred of hope was that such losses in the past had not precluded victory at the polls in 1992.

But no one really believed that another surprise success was on the cards, and in the last days of the Major government a number of senior figures began casting around for seats that might provide some shelter when the inevitable storm came. In a process that became known as the chicken run, the party chairman Brian Mawhinney left Peterborough to become the candidate for North West Cambridgeshire, social security secretary Peter Lilley similarly abandoned St Albans for Hitchin and Harpenden, and health secretary Stephen Dorrell moved from Loughborough to Charnwood. In a less high profile but more symbolic example of the phenomenon, David Amess, whose triumph in Basildon had set the tone for election night in 1992, quietly made his excuses and left for Southend. Each individual decision was vindicated; the original constituency was lost while the newly adopted seat was retained. The sight of so many Tories running for their political lives, however, did nothing to suggest faith in the government's future.

Tony Blair, with 1992 still in mind and wary of over-confidence, did his best to dampen down expectations on the Labour side in that last year, but in private his frontbenchers could scarcely contain their excitement. 'I've been here for seventeen years,' exclaimed Jack Straw in 1996. 'We've been in opposition for all the time I've been here. And soon we're going to be in government.'

Finally, on 17 March 1997, John Major called an election for May Day, ten years on from Margaret Thatcher's last victory and more than twenty-two years since Labour had last won a general election. With just over six weeks to polling day, it was to be one of the longest election campaigns of modern times, reflecting a Micawberish hope that something would turn up, that some good news might emerge to persuade the voters to return to the Tory fold, that the Labour Party might implode into factional in-fighting or be struck down by a terrible scandal, that the country might get cold feet about entrusting its future to an untried, inexperienced group of politicians. Nothing of the sort happened. Instead there was a demoralising continuation of the sleaze and splits that had so damaged the Conservative Party's image in the long, miserable slide from the peak of April 1992.

Because even during the campaign, the negative stories continued to emerge. Allan Stewart, the Conservative MP for Eastwood, the safest Tory seat in Scotland, announced that he was withdrawing his candidature after stories of an extra-marital affair emerged. It wasn't the first time he had made headlines. Two years earlier he had resigned from his government job after an encounter with anti-motorway protestors campaigning against the M77 development in his constituency, in which he was alleged to have waved a pick-axe 'in a very threatening manner'. His own account of that incident hadn't sounded very different: 'I picked up the pick-axe first of all to avoid anybody else picking it up and secondly in possible self-defence. There was then a robust discussion.' Now he was leaving Parliament altogether and, almost immediately, the man expected to replace him as the candidate in Eastwood, Mickey Hirst, resigned as chairman of the Conservative Party in Scotland just before the *Sunday Mail* revealed 'a series of homosexual encounters'.

Meanwhile the MP for Beckenham, Piers Merchant, was alleged to be having some sort of relationship with a seventeen-year-old who worked as a hostess in a Soho nightclub. He denied any sexual involvement and was backed by his constituency party, despite an unequivocal public warning from Michael Heseltine that he should be deselected.

This failure of the Conservative leadership to impose its will on local parties was in stark contrast to the iron discipline of the Labour Party, where the NEC had the right to overrule a candidature even after a constituency had made its selection. In 1995 Liz Davies was removed as the candidate for Leeds North-East after the leadership decided that she was too left-wing and that her association with the newspaper *London Left Briefing* was too controversial. Tony Blair insisted that people like her were 'piggybacking' on the Labour Party: 'If they stood on a *Labour Briefing* platform, they'd get 500 votes,' he pointed out. He was quite correct, of course, though the same charge could have been laid against him, as a candidate who had won his parliamentary seat in 1983 on a manifesto calling for British withdrawal from Europe, unilateral nuclear disarmament and the involvement of trade unions in government.

Worse for the Tories than the cases of Allan Stewart and Piers Merchant, however, were the continuing repercussions from the Mohammed Al-Fayed affair. One of the MPs involved, Tim Smith, announced that he wouldn't be standing for re-election, but the other, Neil Hamilton, remained defiant and secured the support of his constituency association in Tatton, Cheshire, where he had a majority of nearly 16,000. In a brilliant tactical move, dreamt up by Alastair Campbell, the local Labour and Liberal Democrat parties were persuaded not to field their own candidates, but rather to unite behind an independent 'anti-sleaze' figure, the BBC television reporter Martin Bell.

This became one of the more memorable stories of a rather monotonous campaign, since it provided more amusement than any other contest. The star was not Hamilton himself — an intelligent, witty man who was strangely incapable of portraying himself as anything other than smug and bumbling — but his wife, Christine, who turned out to be terrifically entertaining. A former secretary to the lurid 1960s MP Gerald Nabarro, she clearly knew a thing or two about self-promotion, and made her mark early on, hijacking Bell's first appointment with the press in the constituency and demanding to know whether Bell accepted that her husband was innocent until proved guilty.

It was a rare moment of cheer for the Hamiltons, though not for the Conservatives more generally, since it reminded the country that there were still outstanding accounts in the sleaze files. Perceptions weren't improved when John Major, on an election walkabout in Braunton, Devon, found himself in a hardware shop run by a man named Frank Slee: a photo-opportunity under a shop sign reading Slees was hardly what the spin doctor ordered.

And still the divisions over Europe would not heal, particularly in relation to the single currency promised at Maastricht. The manifesto had carefully laid out the compromise position: 'If, during the course of the next parliament, a Conservative government were to conclude that it was in our national interest to join a single currency, we have given a guarantee that no such decision would be implemented unless the British people gave their express approval in a referendum.'

It wasn't enough for some, and Stephen Dorrell was soon to be heard on the radio saying that Britain would definitely not be in the first wave of countries joining the single currency. His subsequent apology was one of the more impressive examples of the form: 'My thought process was blurred at that particular moment. I had the government line. The truth is I couldn't remember precisely at the right moment precisely what the formula was.'

More damagingly, over a hundred Conservative candidates explicitly stated in their election addresses that they would certainly not support joining the single currency during the course of the next parliament. Their actions 'made a mockery of any attempt to find a common approach', raged Michael Heseltine, and Major jettisoned both the script of a press conference and a proposed party political broadcast so he could address the issue directly, urging his party not to 'bind my hands'. It was one of his more impressive performances. 'He sounds tough and courageous,' noted Giles Radice. 'Perhaps if he had been like this earlier, the Tories would not now be in the mess they are in.' Major's intervention was portrayed in Eurosceptic quarters, however, as being binding in precisely the way he didn't wish, picking up on his reference to a referendum: 'I will not take Britain into a single currency. Only the British nation can do that. Upon that, you may be certain.' This, said the *Daily Mail*, was 'his most dramatic personal pledge yet in defence of the pound'.

A couple of days later, a poll in the *Guardian* reported that Labour were just five points ahead of the Tories, causing a moment of panic in the opposition camp, though other polls continued to show leads of up to twenty points. Rapidly dismissed as a 'rogue poll', this was actually, insisted Iain Duncan Smith, an endorsement of the Eurosceptics, as the faithful began coming back to the Tories: 'What they thought was a blip, I don't think was a blip; it was a reality.' An alternative explanation also offered itself. If it were a real, though short-lived, phenomenon, it could equally have been in response to Major's rare moment of determined self-confidence.

The issue of Europe was also being exploited by the Referendum Party. Announced in January 1995, and backed by £20 million of businessman James Goldsmith's money, the organisation had a single aim: to secure a referendum on whether Britain should reject any moves towards a more federal European Union. 'This is a single-issue, bio-degradable party,' proclaimed Goldsmith, 'which will be dissolved once we have achieved our aim.'

Initially dismissed as the folly of an old man who had drifted out of touch with Britain since his retirement to Mexico in 1987, the new party soon began to worry the Conservatives, both with the scale of its ambition – it fielded over five hundred candidates in the general election – and its ability to generate headlines. It attracted the support of Margaret Thatcher's old financial adviser, Alan Walters, and the former Tory chairman, Alistair McAlpine, as well as media-friendly names like the actor Edward Fox, the broadcaster David Bellamy, the novelist Frederick Forsyth and, to the amusement of many, Robin Page, presenter of the television programme *One Man and His Dog*, a title that seemed to sum up the enterprise rather well. Even Norman Tebbit, when asked whether he would support the Referendum Party, was prepared at least to entertain the idea: 'I would not go that far – not yet – but I can understand why many people who do not have such a strong attachment to the Conservative Party are doing so.'

The Referendum Party had little chance of winning a seat, let alone the election, but its very existence was a threat to the Tories, providing a right-wing alternative for disaffected Eurosceptics. A poll in 1996 showed the party on 14 per cent, enough to suggest that Goldsmith might yet play the role of a British Ross Perot, taking support away from a right-wing incumbent. 'He is in part an anarchist,' wrote Hugo Young, after meeting Goldsmith; 'counter-typical as a business tycoon, he is the loosest of all cannons at large in a system he despises.'

The Referendum Party did in fact go into the election with an MP to its name. Serial rebel George Gardiner had finally been deselected by his Reigate constituency party and announced that he was leaving the Conservatives to join Goldsmith's organisation. Amongst his offences had been a description of John Major as 'Ken Clarke's ventriloquist's dummy', suggesting that the prime minister was under the control of Europhiles. By ironic coincidence, the most striking poster of the election campaign showed Tony Blair sitting on the knee of the German chancellor, Helmut Kohl, with the slogan DON'T SEND A BOY TO DO A MAN'S JOB, suggesting that a Labour government wouldn't be able to fight its corner in Europe.

It was a powerful image, if somewhat in contradiction to the message of the 'demon eyes' advert, but it aroused a storm of fury amongst Europhile Tories including Edward Heath. A 'pitiful piece of publicity,' he thundered, 'absolutely contemptible.' The poster, inspired by an old Vicky cartoon of Harold Macmillan sitting on the lap of John F. Kennedy, had been dreamt up by Michael Heseltine, long regarded as a Europhile himself, but now thought to be subtly shifting his ground in anticipation of a leadership bid. Few were convinced by his later protest: 'This was not a Eurosceptic concept – it was a Blair-sceptic concept.' There was no such equivocation about the Referendum Party's subsequent advert, showing Kohl with both Major and Blair, one on each of his knees.

*

Through all this, the Labour campaign sailed serenely onwards, adhering to a long-planned programme. Its ruthless, relentless professionalism ensured that there were no mistakes, no slip-ups, no excitement, just a repetitive routine of photo-opportunities and stage-managed set-piece speeches that contained not a single memorable sentence. The entire message was to be found in the modest aspirations of the title of the campaign song, D:Ream's 'Things Can Only Get Better'. As Alastair Campbell acknowledged to the journalists travelling with Blair: 'I know you're bored shitless with it.'

Faced with the New Labour machine, John Major dug out his soapbox in an attempt to revive the spirit of '92, but it didn't really work second time around. He looked, wrote the retiring Tory MP Julian Critchley, as though he were 'clinging to his magic soapbox like a small child with his comfort blanket'. The routine lacked the appearance of spontaneity that had been its main attraction five years earlier. Alan Clark saw one such appearance on College Green and noted that it was a 'papered house', with an audience supplied by Central Office. When Major did meet the public, he was again faced by hecklers, but this time round, in Luton at least, they were supporters not of the SWP but of the Referendum Party. Europe simply wouldn't go away. And when the Tories tried to get beyond that issue, they seemed still to be fighting the election before last, attacking Labour for its links with the trade unions and its position on privatisation. As with some on the left, there was here a willing suspension of disbelief, a deluded insistence that Blair didn't mean what he said.

But for most of the left, Blair's position didn't really matter any more. So hated were the Conservatives that the sole objective was to ensure they were thrown out of office; what came next was very much of secondary importance when compared to the eagerly awaited joy of seeing the Tories humiliated. Amongst the wider public, the anger had turned into simple irritation at the long-delayed departure of the government. 'There's none of the bitterness of 1992 when memories of the poll tax were still fresh, we were in deep recession and the pit closures were round the corner,' wrote Phillip Oppenheim, about the experience of canvassing in his constituency. 'Instead, just an uneasy boredom which is almost harder to handle.'

By now even Major himself had privately conceded defeat. Iain Duncan Smith came across him one evening at Conservative Central Office. 'He was sitting, slumped, looking very down, nobody with him at all. So I poked my head around the corner and said: We've had some quite good stuff from my area. And he looked up and smiled and said: That's good. Then he said: It's not going to change anything.'

The banishment of any doubt that the government would fall was, at least in part, a tribute to Tony Blair's leadership. The pain of 1992 had convinced many at the time that the Tories would never be beaten, but there was now no trace of that sentiment anywhere in the country. Most of the destructive work had been done by the Conservatives themselves, as they staged a slow-motion political suicide, but the absolute certainty of Labour's victory in the campaign, the inevitability of the coming landslide – that was largely Blair's work. For nearly three years he had been the most convincing and authoritative leader of the opposition in living memory, looking more prime ministerial than the current office-holder, and the public had long since taken it as read that he would be moving into Downing Street.

Gordon Brown talked about ending 'the long night of Tory rule', but the ending itself was a protracted process, resembling the tactically delayed appearance of a superstar on stage, whipping the crowd into a frenzy of anticipation. Blair's progress around the country acquired something of the feel of a messianic crusade for the faithful, particularly for those not old enough to remember anything save a Conservative government. The veteran BBC political correspondent Nicholas Jones talked to young Labour activists and detected a new note: 'I discovered not just admiration but adoration for Blair, and I had to force myself to remember that they were talking not about a pop star but a politician.' He also reported that his daughter had phoned him during the campaign to say excitedly that she had met Blair: 'I touched him.'

The press too was becoming increasingly animated and there was a scramble to get aboard the bandwagon. The *Sun* came out in favour of Blair at the start of the campaign and even swallowed its Euroscepticism in order to stay on message, the courting of the paper's owner, Rupert Murdoch, having proved worthwhile. Ever since its declaration for Margaret Thatcher in 1979, the *Sun* had been implacably opposed to Labour and its return to the party fold was greeted with the fatted calf of better access to stories than was given to the *Daily Mirror*. But then, as media commentator Roy Greenslade pointed out: 'the *Mirror* is merely preaching to the converted. The *Sun* is attempting a much more difficult (and unprecedented) task: to educate its readers into loving the old enemy.' In fact, of course, most of those readers had already made their minds up.

Meanwhile the *Daily Telegraph*, *Sunday Telegraph*, *Daily Express*, *Daily Mail* and *Mail on Sunday* all endorsed the Tories but without any conviction at all, and the impression was of noses being held with the fingers of one hand while a cross was pencilled in with the other. The *Daily Express* said that it would stick with 'the devil we know', but didn't offer any direct advice to its readers, while the *Daily Mail* suggested voting Conservative 'however reluctantly'. Regardless of any recommendations, though, the damage had already been done with the long campaign of sniping from the *Daily Mail* and the *Telegraph* titles in particular.

The Times had a less clear party allegiance. While still evidently on the right, it was quite prepared to flirt with the idea of supporting Tony Blair, and ended up suggesting that voters should opt for individual candidates, regardless of party, who would explicitly reject the single currency. London's *Evening Standard* was particularly damning in its editorial before the election, listing all the calamities of the previous five years and concluding: 'None of these farces and fiascos on its own could explain the public contempt for John Major's government, but putting them all together shows a pattern of unrelieved incompetence the like of which has rarely been seen before.'

The lack of enthusiasm for the government in Fleet Street infuriated traditional Tories. 'There is widespread umbrage that an unelected media should presume to dictate to the voter the way in which he or she should vote,' wrote Julian Critchley, conveniently forgetting the decades of unwavering support his own party had enjoyed. In 1992 some 70 per cent of newspaper circulation supported the Tories; in 1997 around the same proportion was supporting Labour.

The lack of self-knowledge was replicated on the other side of the Fleet Street–Westminster divide. On election night, as the shocking news flashed across television screens that Margaret Thatcher's old seat in Finchley had fallen to Labour, Paul Dacre, editor of the *Daily Mail*, was reportedly outraged: 'What the fuck's going on? These are fucking *Mail* readers!' Having spent the last few years undermining the prime minister, it seemed a little late in the day to be expressing surprise.

If the campaign itself was marked, for most of the public, by a tone of bored impatience, election night itself was an extraordinary occasion, a unique moment in the history of political broadcasting in Britain. 'It was one of the most brilliant evenings of television I've ever seen in my whole life,' said Ian Hislop on *Have I Got News for You*, and he was not alone. Books about election campaigns had long been a feature of political journalism, but so big a shared event was the 1997 coverage, that for the first time a book – Brian Cathcart's *Were You Still Up for Portillo?* – was published that documented the television results programmes themselves.

And even that wasn't quite enough. While BBC One and ITV provided their traditional Dimbleby-led shows, BBC Two broadcast *The Election Night Armistice*, in which Armando Iannucci and his usual accomplices tried to maintain some degree of impartiality, despite a clearly partisan audience and a panel of guests largely comprised of alternative comedians (Phill Jupitus, Jo Brand, Kevin Day) who made no attempt to conceal their gloating over the long-delayed defeat of the Conservatives. The show also gave Alan Partridge the opportunity to reveal that even he had had a change of heart: 'The Referendum Party – insults aside – have probably got more integrity than the whole of the other political parties put together.' (Sally, the snobbish newsreader in *Drop the Dead Donkey*, was another supporter of James Goldsmith's party, on the grounds that 'So many rich people can't be wrong.')

To start with, 1 May 1997 had been a beautifully sunny day. Outside the ranks of the Conservative Party itself, there was a sense of hope and optimism abroad, a feeling that the spell cast long ago by the White Witch to make it always winter but never Christmas was about to be broken. That expectation was confirmed when, shortly after the polls closed, the BBC predicted that the landslide would be so great that the seats of cabinet ministers Malcolm Rifkind, Michael Forsyth and John Selwyn Gummer were at risk of being lost. In the event, Gummer held on to his seat, albeit with a 12 per cent swing against him, but the others were less fortunate. It is a rare thing for a cabinet minister to lose an election; Chris Patten had been defeated in 1992, but before that one had to go back to 1979, when Shirley Williams lost in Hertford and Stevenage. This time, no fewer than seven members of the cabinet found themselves being made unemployed on live television, as the votes were counted. Had so many Tories not swapped seats in the chicken-run days, the number would have hit double figures.

Notable casualties outside the cabinet included Neil Hamilton, who shed over 13,000 votes to be thoroughly beaten by the independent Martin Bell, Jonathan Aitken in South Thanet, and Norman Lamont, whose constituency of Kingston had been abolished and who failed to take what should have been a safe seat in Harrogate and Knaresborough.

The wrath of the voters fell on Eurosceptics and Europhiles alike. On the right, Tony Marlow, Toby Jessel, Ivan Lawrence and Rupert Allason all lost their seats, as did Nicholas Budgen in Wolverhampton South West, a constituency he had taken over from Enoch Powell and which had been Conservative since 1950. George Gardiner, the solitary Referendum Party MP, was beaten into fourth place in Reigate, which did therefore give the Conservatives a gain, even if only on a technicality and even if the party's majority was reduced by 10,000 votes compared to 1992. On the left, Edwina Currie lost in Derbyshire South, as did Sebastian Coe, the former Olympic athlete who, ever since his election in 1992, had been rather wasted as an asset, buried from public sight in the whips' office.

Most famously from this wing of the party, David Mellor was beaten in Putney, where James Goldsmith himself was a candidate. Goldsmith's own vote was an insignificant 1,500, not enough to have swayed the result in a constituency taken by Labour with a 3,000 majority, but the personal animosity between the two men was one of the highlights of election night. Mellor's speech conceding defeat was punctuated by chants of 'Out! Out! Out!' led by Goldsmith, but he still made his point: 'I would like to say that fifteen hundred votes is a derisory total, and we have shown tonight that the Referendum Party is dead in the water. Sir James, you can get off back to Mexico, knowing your attempt to buy the British political system has failed.' In a subsequent interview with Michael Buerk, Mellor added a lovely soundbite: 'Up your hacienda, Jimmy.'

If one way to measure the government's rout was by the massed ranks of departing MPs, another was by geography. The Tories lost all ten Scottish and all six Welsh seats that they had held. The northern English cities inevitably proved even more hostile territory than they had been in the 1980s, but the battle was also lost in the South-West, where there was now no Conservative representation in cities like Bristol and Plymouth. It could no longer be suggested that this was a national party; the surviving Tory rump was confined almost exclusively to rural areas and, particularly, to the South-East. Not that there was much comfort even here. The Conservatives had gone into the election with forty-one London seats and emerged with just eleven. The national swing to Labour was 10.5 per cent, but this concealed some truly remarkable results, particularly in the London suburbs. Constituencies in places like Harrow, Wimbledon, Croydon and Hendon all saw swings against the Tories of over 15 per cent, while in Brent East a swing of nearly 19 per cent unseated Rhodes Boyson, one of those who could claim to have been a Thatcherite before Thatcher.

There was a warning here for the Labour Party, had it been in a suitably reflective frame of mind. The fact that the southern suburbs registered above-average swings meant that the reverse was true in Labour's heartlands, where the vote was noticeably less enthusiastic. Peter Mandelson described the 1997 election as a 'revolution' and he may well have been right; no one was quite sure what would come next, but there was an overwhelming wish to see the toppling of the *ancien régime*. It was, though, 'a bourgeois revolution', in the words of Hywel Williams, and for MPs who had spent the last few weeks campaigning in traditional Labour areas, the scale of the national victory came as a shock. 'Nothing prepared me for what happened.

During the campaign I saw no particular enthusiasm among my own electorate,' remarked Chris Mullin of his Sunderland South constituency. 'I've been involved in every election since 1970 and I've never seen such apathy and indifference.' Mullin's majority in a solid Labour seat went up by more than 5,000, but his actual vote declined by more than two thousand. Just down the coast, in Mandelson's constituency of Hartlepool, turnout fell by over ten percentage points.

Labour did increase its national vote by some two million, but still polled lower than John Major had five years earlier, while its share, at 43.2 per cent, was only marginally higher than the 43.1 per cent registered by Harold Wilson when losing the 1970 election. And this was on the worst turnout since 1935. Indeed the turnout was perhaps the real story of the election, though it wasn't widely recognised as such at the time.

The Conservatives had shed four and a half million votes. Even allowing for natural wastage, for Labour's improved showing and for the interventions of the Referendum Party and the UK Independence Party (who accounted for around 900,000 votes between them), that meant a great many people had absented themselves from the polling booths. They included traditional Labour voters, as in Sunderland, but most attention was fixed on Tory truants. 'Up and down the country they stayed at home, our people,' reflected Ann Widdecombe. 'They stayed at home on a grand scale.' Amongst those who didn't bother with the ballot box was Julian Critchley, who couldn't bring himself to vote for his Eurosceptic successor in Aldershot. Whether someone like Critchley could be regarded as typical of the stay-at-home Tories was a matter of some dispute, though the anti-Europe parties' comparatively poor showing suggested that he might well have been; it seemed unlikely that the absentees were distressed by the lack of right-wing policies. The debate over who those missing supporters were, and how to win them back, was to preoccupy the Conservative Party for the next decade.

For now, Labour had the luxury of simply ignoring the details. Thanks to the vagaries of the first-past-the-post system, the party had a majority of 179 seats in the Commons, more than 63 per cent of the MPs, and – taking into account boundary changes – had gained 145 seats. In parliamentary terms, it dwarfed even the 1945 landslide of Clement Attlee (though he had won a shade under half the popular vote), a moment that had largely passed into the realm of fable. Meanwhile the Liberal Democrats actually polled fewer votes than in 1992, but more than doubled their number of MPs, a fact which simply revealed the extent of the anti-Tory tactical voting at work. And the Conservatives lost more than half their seats.

Amongst the bedraggled company of 165 Tory MPs who slunk back to the Commons was the former education and employment secretary, Gillian Shephard, though her judgement seemed a little affected by the trauma. 'The scale of the defeat in terms of parliamentary seats was enormous,' she subsequently wrote; 'in terms of actual votes cast, less shattering.' But whichever way one cut it, the Tory performance was a catastrophe. The disappearance of four and a half million votes gave the party just a 30.7 per cent share – the lowest it had recorded since 1832 – while barely one in five of the registered electorate had been persuaded to come out in support of the government.

More than the raw statistics, however, it was in the atmosphere of election night, and of the next couple of days, that the defeat of the Conservatives truly became tangible. When Tony Blair arrived in London from his Sedgefield constituency and made his way to the South Bank, where a victory party was being staged at the Royal Festival Hall, there was an air of excitement quite unlike that of normal elections. For those on the left, even for many in the centre, this was something more than a success at the ballot box. If there was a recent parallel, perhaps it was with the spirit of the victory parade staged in 1982 to celebrate British success in the Falklands War. 'This was what it was about,' Enoch Powell had said of that occasion. 'England had known itself, it had recognised itself.' There was a similar sense on the morning of 2 May 1997; it felt as if a country that, some considerable time ago, had decided to divorce itself from the excesses of Thatcherism had finally got round to signing the papers.

It was, wrote Sue Townsend's character Adrian Mole in his diary, 'a glorious new dawn of optimism and a celebration of the transcendence of all that is best in humankind'. However absurd that came to seem in retrospect, it wasn't too much of an exaggeration. Even amongst the large majority who hadn't cast a vote for the new government, there was a desire to share in the mood of rejoicing. An opinion poll taken shortly after the election showed more than half the population claiming to have turned out for Labour, regardless of the facts. Amongst them was Bridget Jones's mother, a lifelong Tory, who happily joined in the new order, proudly announcing: 'We're having a Tony and Gordon Ladies' Night at the Rotary! Everyone's going to call each other by their first name and wear casual wear instead of ties.' Few, though, can have been happier at the turn of events than George Elliot, a taxi driver in the North-East, who had been so impressed in 1983 by the newly elected MP in the back of his cab that he placed a £10 bet at odds of 500–1 that Blair would be prime minister by the end of the century.

As the results became clear on election night, John Prescott expressed the mood of the moment, riding with his team in his battle-bus around Smith Square in Westminster, where the Conservative Party headquarters were located, and singing as loudly as possible: 'Out, out, out, at last you're out, out, out!'

But nothing that night came close to the moment late on in the proceedings when the results were announced from Enfield Southgate in North London. It was one of the safest Conservative seats, with a 15,000 majority, and no one gave the thirty-year-old Labour challenger, Stephen Twigg, a ghost of a chance. Simply the fact that an openly gay man had been selected was a sufficiently welcome sign in itself for many. 'It's marvellous that there's going to be at least one gay candidate fighting the Enfield Southgate constituency and pledged to fight for homosexual equality,' noted Peter Tatchell. The implied dig was at the incumbent MP, Michael Portillo, the man widely tipped to be John Major's successor as leader of the party. Indeed the *Daily Mail* ran an article on election day under the headline PORTILLO POISED TO SEIZE VICTORY FROM DEFEAT, predicting precisely that event. The news that instead his vote had collapsed and that Twigg had taken the seat with a swing of 17 per cent was greeted with disbelieving glee around the country.

'It was the defining moment of a generation, like VE Day or the moon landing,' remembered Mark Steel. 'Portillo had lost.' It was all the more potent for coming just when celebration fatigue seemed to have set in. 'It was so relentlessly bad for us, the other parties' supporters had stopped cheering. They just looked on amazed,' wrote Gyles Brandreth of the count in Chester, where he was losing his own seat. Even so, 'poor Portillo's defeat prompted a standing ovation'. A man having a cigarette outside an election party in North London was reported to have come rushing in, demanding to know what had prompted the 'cheering and shouting coming out of all the houses'.

Even without the national indulgence in schadenfreude, it was the most significant personal defeat of the night, and a vindication of Tony Blair's tactics since assuming the leadership. For a Conservative parliamentary party without Portillo suddenly looked a very different beast altogether, one that was unlikely to pose any serious threat. Had John Smith still been Labour leader, there is little doubt that the party would have won the 1997 election, but almost certainly without the same landslide. In particular the London suburbs, where Blair scored most heavily, would have been a much more difficult proposition, and the strong likelihood is that Portillo would have survived to lead a more substantial opposition. That possibility no longer existed and, for the man who had dithered in 1995 over whether to challenge John Major, there appeared to be a sense of relief that the decision had been taken out of his hands. 'One thing alone I will not miss,' Portillo said in his concession speech, 'and that's all the questions about the leadership.'

For John Major, the defeat was the event for which he had been preparing himself for the last five years. On the day after the 1992 victory he had discussed the result with Chris Patten and concluded that winning next time was unlikely: 'I believed we had stretched the democratic elastic as far as it would go.' That had become conventional wisdom over the ensuing period. 'You can ask the people to elect you once or twice or even three times, and to do so with fair conviction,' the journalist Robert Harris had written in 1996. 'But once you start going back and demanding fourth or even fifth helpings of power, you cannot help but look greedy.'

That everything had gone so badly wrong merely confirmed this accepted wisdom, so that there were few options left save for gallows humour. 'If I had stood unopposed,' joked Major in 2000, 'I would still have come second.' Even so, the enormity of the humiliation was beyond nightmare, and there was a great deal of truth in Robin Cook's jibe on election night. 'This is a time to be magnanimous,' he smirked. 'It would be churlish to deny the Conservative Party their part in our victory tonight.'

In a better world, Major would have stayed on as leader of his party, just as James Callaghan had after the 1979 election, to give the Tories a chance to adjust to their new circumstances and to conduct a proper inquiry into what had gone so appallingly wrong. But, unsurprisingly, he'd had enough by now. For over four years he had been under constant attack from members of his own party, and he announced his resignation immediately, much to the disgust of at least one erstwhile colleague: 'it was disgraceful to resign when he did,' complained Portillo, fifteen months later. 'Totally selfish.' There was, of course, a certain self-interest in this position; had Major stayed on, it would have given Portillo a chance to get back into the Commons in a by-election and fight for the succession.

Major's exit was as dignified as had been his entrance and – for the most part – as had been his conduct during his time in office. 'When the curtain falls, it's time to get off the stage,' he told the assembled media, while quietly he left behind a bottle of champagne for the newly elected prime minister, with a note saying: 'It's a great job – enjoy it.'

Any sober judgement on Major's conduct of economic policy in office would have to take account of the terrible slump of 1990–2, exacerbated by membership of the ERM – the mass unemployment, bankruptcies and home repossessions – and of his role, first as chancellor and then as prime minister, in those events. When he came to write his memoirs, however, he glossed over 'the recession I inherited', and relied instead on a simple audit of the position to which he had succeeded, as compared with the one he passed on: interest rates had fallen from 14 to 6 per cent, unemployment from 1.75 million to 1.6 million and, most importantly of all, the inflation that had bedevilled Britain for decades was finally under control, reduced from 9.7 to 2.6 per cent. The tax burden had increased as a share of GDP, but only marginally, from 36.3 to 36.6 per cent, and the economy had been growing for sixteen consecutive quarters. Inequality in wealth, having grown dramatically under Margaret Thatcher, had reached a plateau under her successor. On two measures of Thatcherite policy, the number of owner-occupied houses continued to grow, but the number of shareholders fell from its peak of eleven million in the late 1980s to just seven million by the time Major left office.

There had been hard times in the early 1990s, when 'all the economic indicators worsened', but overall, he was happy to conclude: 'It was a fine legacy.' As Treasury officials told Gordon Brown, when outlining the economic position immediately after the election: 'These are fantastically good figures.'

Major could have gone further and claimed, with some justification, that spending on health and education was increasing in real terms – though the electorate failed to discern the impact – and that the official crime rate, once considered impervious to political initiatives, was falling, even if no one believed the figures. He had also articulated a post-Thatcherite, Conservative vision of where the country could go, had anyone cared to listen. And, in political terms, there was one towering achievement which none could deny: he had won in 1992, finally persuading the Labour Party to adopt the Tory agenda. 'Margaret Thatcher buried old Labour,' reflected Tristan Garel-Jones, 'but John Major laid a lump of granite on the grave.'

Yet this was the man who had led the Conservative Party to its worst election result for a century and a half. But perhaps 'led' is too strong a word, for there was little inclination in the parliamentary party to accept the discipline of leadership. And there was only one real, underlying cause for the disasters of the last few years. All the sleaze and the scandals, whether sexual or financial, all the errors of judgement about closing down mines, adding VAT to domestic fuel or the shackling of pregnant prisoners, all the awkwardness about a new cultural movement and about the tolerant society it ushered in – ultimately these should have been the flotsam and jetsam of politics, bobbing impotently on a rising tide of prosperity. Even the recession might have been forgiven, if not forgotten. But they were given significance, and the state of the economy was deemed irrelevant, because there was Europe, and because Thatcher and all those loyal to her memory had finally decided that Enoch Powell had been right after all; this was the question that transcended all others.

Ultimately, everything came back to this one subject, whether it manifested itself in Black Wednesday or the Maastricht Treaty, the beef ban or Red Hot Dutch. The position of Britain in relation to the rest of Europe had become the defining issue of post-Empire politics, and a group of obstinate Conservative MPs insisted on regarding the question as one of principle rather than pragmatism. 'I felt it was beyond the normal ability of someone who felt strongly about constitutional issues that he simply obey the party line,' said Iain Duncan Smith, and there were enough others who agreed with him, supported by a substantial section of the Tory press, to make Major's period of leadership almost impossible.

In the process they almost destroyed the Conservative Party. Way back in 1961, Harold Macmillan had warned that membership of the European Community 'could break the Tory Party', though he added privately that he wasn't overly concerned about the possibility: 'It never hurt the Party to split over something that was really in the national interest.' The reality had been worse though: the party had not split, so that the acrimony and the disloyalty and the factionalism had bubbled away inside, until every part of the body was diseased. When it came to the critical moment, and Major put down one of his confidence motions, the Eurosceptics could just about be relied upon to fall into line, but the damage caused by the rebellions and squabbles in the periods between those votes was enormous. The prospect of perpetual Tory government, that had loomed so large in 1992, now looked merely risible, replaced by the likelihood of opposition for the foreseeable future.

From a purely party perspective, the actions of the Eurosceptic MPs and their journalist cheerleaders were entirely negative; the bitter divisions that were opened then would take more than a generation to heal. The Tories split between ideologues and managers, with the supposed leader desperately trying to ride both horses. 'Majorism', as defined by John Cole, was 'doing the best a prime minister could in difficult circumstances'. But neither Major, nor probably anyone else, could unite a sullen, dissatisfied tribe. 'There's no banter, no joshing, no camaraderie,' observed John Patten of the parliamentary party in 1997. 'Can't you feel the terrible hatred that there is in this place?'

In terms of their overriding concern, on the other hand, the Eurosceptics could claim a qualified victory. The drive towards European integration continued, but on the biggest question of all they had prevailed: Britain was unlikely to join the single currency when it was launched. Moreover, the case had been made with sufficient force that it became a toxic issue for the incoming government as well. Opinion polls at the time had shown a majority against Maastricht and that tendency grew; the proportion of people favouring a complete, unequivocal withdrawal from the EU rose from 29 per cent just before John Redwood's leadership challenge to 38 per cent at the start of 1997. Whatever else the Tories left behind for Labour, there was precious little enthusiasm for the European project.

Happily for John Major, that was no longer his concern. In 1995, having announced his resignation as Conservative leader in his 'put up or shut up' ultimatum, he had gone to Lord's cricket ground to watch the third day of England's Test match against the West Indies, and had taken heart from the applause that ensued when a shot of him was projected onto the big video screens: 'I was warmed and encouraged by this response.' Now, having resigned for a second and final time, he went to the Oval, where he watched Surrey play the British Universities in a fifty-overs match. For a man who had fought so hard all his life to overcome the limitations of his education, there was something entirely appropriate that the county club he had supported since childhood (and of which, in 2000, he was to become president) should triumph over the combined universities by six wickets, with nearly twenty-five overs to spare. It was even more pleasing that they should do so at the ground so close to his heart that he had chosen it as his luxury item when appearing on Radio 4's *Desert Island Discs*.

Again Major encountered the warmth that he so often brought out in people he met in person. 'You had a rough decision, mate,' one of the spectators called out to him, and the simple dignity of his response encapsulated some of the character that had helped him win that extraordinary victory, five long years ago: 'Perhaps. But the umpire's decision is final.'

Intermission
Patriotism
'The England he knew is now no more'

You cannot suppress the individualism of an island race.
John Major (1994)

England is obsessed with the war. It is the only nation in the world
that has decided to make the Second World War a sort of spiritual
core of its national self, understanding and pride.
Michael Naumann, German culture minister (1999)

We are forging a new patriotism based on the potential we can fulfil
in the future. There is an energy about Britain at the moment.
Tony Blair (1998)

In 1994 the news broke that during the prime minister's weekly audience
with his monarch, John Major had come to blows with the Queen, and
that a fist-fight had ensued. In a state of panic, all the television channels
switched to a patriotic piece of film that had long been kept in reserve for
just such a constitutional emergency. 'Britain is a nation built on the very
scowling face of adversity, its dauntless spirit unbowed by any crisis,' intoned
a reassuring voice, over the strains of 'I Vow to Thee, My Country', while
a series of pictures were shown of characteristic British images: a fluttering
Union flag, a bulldog, the white cliffs of Dover, city workers playing with
skipping ropes, a white policeman smoking a joint while dancing with a
black woman, leafy country lanes in villages with names like Manford
Thirty-Sixborough and Wabznasm, where a man in expensively casual
clothes doesn't have a match for his cigarette and is instantly surrounded by
children with lighters, eager to help. 'This is Britain,' concluded the voice-
over. 'And everything's all right. Everything's all right. It's OK. It's fine.'

It was one of the best sketches in the comedy series *The Day Today*, delivered
in a warm, paternalist tone that parodied the BBC's role of nanny, wrapping
the nation in a comfort blanket during its darkest hours. And the humour

came in part from the appallingly anachronistic nature of such attitudes at a time when opinion polls were showing that half the population, given a chance, would like to emigrate and that 40 per cent of adults under the age of thirty-five believed that Britain would become a worse place to live over the next ten years. In 1996 the *Daily Telegraph* commissioned Gallup to repeat a survey investigating the mood of the nation, using questions originally put in 1968. The picture it painted was not encouraging. In a reversal of the previous results, people believed that the country was becoming less healthy, less educated and less honest; behaviour was deteriorating and peace of mind was in decline. The contrast between *The Day Today*'s mocking evocation of an unchanging country and the public perception of national decline was self-evident.

Elsewhere in the schedules, of course, the BBC was continuing to produce programmes that provided exactly the consoling warmth held up to ridicule by *The Day Today*, and in the process was securing much larger audiences than a BBC Two satire could ever aspire to. The one sitcom that lasted throughout the decade, for example, was *Last of the Summer Wine*, in which three elderly Yorkshiremen enjoyed a second childhood. It had just completed its twelfth series when John Major became prime minister and, in the week that Tony Blair went to the polls in 2001, it came to the end of its twenty-second, showing no signs of going away. Equally it showed no signs of changing, save for the occasional adjustment in cast, necessitated by age and infirmity rather than discontent and restlessness.

Roy Clarke, the writer of *Last of the Summer Wine*, also created *Keeping Up Appearances*. This, the most old-fashioned sitcom to debut in the 1990s, depicted a world long since thought to have vanished from light entertainment, in which a visit from the vicar is fraught with danger, the working class are always feckless and any suggestion of sex is inherently laughable. The cast of characters was equally dated, from the sexually frustrated sister to the browbeaten middle-management husband, but was saved from cliché by Patricia Routledge's portrayal of Hyacinth Bucket, a monstrous embodiment of suburban snobbery who pronounces her surname Bouquet and is obsessed with maintaining standards in a world of moral decline. Every episode sees her efforts end in humiliation, undermined both by her family and by her own foibles, but nothing can shake her faith in the eternal virtues of cleanliness and rank, property and propriety. She was, for many viewers, the ultimate caricature of a certain kind of Tory woman, in the tradition of other sitcom battle-axes like Sybil Fawlty and Margo Leadbetter, and if she lacked their redeeming features, she did at her best exhibit the same pithy turn of phrase, as when worrying (needlessly) that her neighbour has taken a lover: 'I warned her against watching Channel 4. She'll come to no good identifying with the continental classes.'

It was an image of Britain that exported rather better than many might have wished. When television viewers in New England were asked in 1995 to vote for their favourite programme, *Keeping Up Appearances*, somewhat surprisingly, emerged as the winner, having built a cult following on the Public Broadcasting Service.

If that popularity remained intriguingly unexplained, the attraction for a domestic audience was clear. 'I think an essential part of the appeal of these comedies,' reflected Clarke, who had also given us *Open All Hours*, 'is that they portray small worlds, which people find reassuring. People's lives, until not so long ago, used to be circumscribed by small boundaries. They didn't travel much and if they went a few miles they would experience a culture change. Today things are becoming more and more evened out from one end of the country to another. I wonder if these little individual comedy worlds provide something in people's lives that has been lost.'

When A.J. Cronin's characters were revived for a new series of *Doctor Finlay* in 1993, twenty-two years after its hugely successful first run had ended, and now set in the 1940s, its executive producer, Robert Love, shared Clarke's perspective: 'If there is a desire for a bit of nostalgia, a return to simpler and older values, I wouldn't blame the audience for that frankly. After all, we live in pretty shitty times.'

In a similar vein, the biggest television hit of the recession years was *The Darling Buds of May*, adapted from the novels by H.E. Bates (and produced by his son, Richard Bates) about the happy-go-lucky Pop and Ma Larkin and their seven children, living an idyllic life on twenty-two acres of Kent countryside in the 1950s. Seventeen million viewers tuned in for the first episode, mostly attracted by the idea of seeing David Jason in his first role since Del Boy in *Only Fools and Horses*, which had recently come to the end of its regular run.

In truth Pop Larkin wasn't far removed from being Del Boy's country cousin. Relentlessly cheerful, and displaying much the same repertoire of shrugs, stretches and tics, he has no truck with officialdom and is one of nature's anarchists. 'Since when has the state had a conscience, eh?' he asks, in a tone of fair-minded reason. Even his optimistic new catchphrase ('Perfick!') echoes that of his previous incarnation ('Lovely jubbly!'), and in case there's any doubt, he's also trying to find someone on whom to offload three hundred army-surplus catering tins of pickled gherkins.

Exhibiting a casual, even negligent, attitude toward both public and private morality, the Larkins are far from paragons of Conservative virtue. Pop has never paid tax ('I think you should get it off them before they get it off you'), while his unmarried daughter is pregnant and doesn't know who the father is. Nor was the series much interested in defending the rule of law; in the first Christmas special the family harbour an escaped convict, so that he might see his children in the festive season, and the story was treated in an unashamedly sentimental manner. Elsewhere, an unsympathetic official voices the authorities' dislike of Pop: 'Here we are, a nation even now still recovering from the economic wounds of the Second World War, and parasites like this Larkin seem to think they have a God-given right to exist outside the system.' But there was never a sliver of doubt as to whose side we were on in this evocation of Arcadia.

The series opened with a visit from a tax inspector (Philip Franks), looking not unlike a young John Major with his glasses, earnest manner and slight stoop. He's come to investigate tax arrears, but chooses to stay on, unable to resist either the bucolic paradise of Pop's farm or the charms of Mariette (Catherine Zeta-Jones), whom he first encounters when she's clad in jodhpurs and riding boots. Much of the country could see the considered wisdom of his decision, and the viewing figures increased still further, reaching a peak of twenty million, to outscore even *EastEnders*. The appeal of the series was self-evident. It had all 'the joie de vivre, the sunshine and the easy sexuality traditionally associated with France', wrote Craig Brown, while another reviewer, Patrick Stoddart, concluded that 'John Major would call it "extremely agreeable", and you can't argue with that.' He may well have been right that the show would prove popular in Downing Street, for David Jason was awarded an OBE shortly after the third and final series aired.

Some remained unconvinced, however, amongst them the leader writers at the *Sunday Times*. Under the headline DARLING BUDS OF MAJOR, an editorial in February 1993 called for more radical thinking by the government: 'The prime minister seems to hanker after a *Darling Buds of May* Britain, circa 1955, when every summer was warm, every village had its bakery, life revolved round the Rotary Club and the Women's Institute and every child sat attentively in front of a teacher in a cardigan reciting Shakespeare's sonnets.' It added sternly: 'Nostalgia has its attractions. But its relevance to the increasingly nasty and brutish world that too many of today's Britons endure, even after fourteen years of Tory rule, is something of a mystery.'

Undeterred by such criticism, John Major delivered perhaps his best-known speech a couple of months later, on the eve of St George's Day, appearing to articulate precisely the position that had attracted the disapproval of the *Sunday Times*. Addressing the Conservative Group for Europe, with the storm of Maastricht still breaking around him, he spoke about the continuity of national identity: 'Fifty years from now, Britain will still be the country of long shadows on county grounds, warm beer, invincible green suburbs, dog lovers and – as George Orwell said – old maids bicycling to Holy Communion through the morning mist. And, if we get our way, Shakespeare will still be read, even in school.'

The intention of the speech, Major insisted, was not to celebrate nostalgia, rather it was to suggest that international cooperation did not mean the death of distinct cultures, and he was later to lament the way his words were used as 'a caricature of my political philosophy'. The problem, however, was that his speech was, in John Redwood's words, 'too easily caricatured', resonating with a public perception of Major as a decent man who would have been perfectly comfortable in a 1950s suburb. This image was not improved by a choice of slogan for the 1997 election – 'Britain is booming. Don't let Labour blow it' – that consciously echoed Harold Macmillan's in 1959: 'Life's better under the Conservatives. Don't let Labour ruin it.'

And so, despite Major's protestations, the public did see his speech as a reflection of his philosophy. They detected a wistfulness about his words that might be endearing – for there was something attractive about a patriotism that had no need to resort to xenophobia, much less to racism – but was a little lightweight, conveying a spirit of Sunday-night television that seemed faintly inappropriate in the country's supposed leader. There was a touch of the sad, lovelorn aristocrat Ralph, as played by Charlie Higson on *The Fast Show*, a man inclined to wax lyrical on catching sight of a slightly overcast sky. 'So typically English. That's a Constable sky, isn't it?' he muses. 'It's Turner, Gainsborough, it's the music of Elgar and Vaughan-Williams. It's picnics with Scotch eggs and pork pies and the rain just spattering onto a white linen tablecloth. It's summer holidays on the beach, huddled beneath the blanket, sheltering from the wind. Some memories are so vivid.'

It was easy to mock, but there was undoubtedly a part of the British psyche that yearned for the old certainties. Major's creation of a cabinet post for national heritage (which didn't outlast him, being reconstituted as the department for culture, media and sport) reflected not only the public taste for those period dramas of which Virginia Bottomley approved, but also the standing of the National Trust. Founded in 1895, the organisation had celebrated its fiftieth birthday at the end of the Second World War with 8,000 members; by the end of the century it numbered two million, far in excess of all the political parties put together. Major's desire to wallow in the past was not unique to him.

It was his reference to Orwell, however, that provided a field day for the prime minister's critics. The allusion was to a passage in a 1941 essay 'The Lion and the Unicorn', where Orwell sought to capture something of the diversity of England, though Major wisely avoided other examples from the same sentence about 'the queues outside the Labour Exchanges' and 'the rattle of pin-tables in the Soho pubs'. In no spirit of helpfulness, an editorial in the *Independent on Sunday*, headlined WHAT A LOT OF TOSH, quoted further from the essay, contrasting Orwell's 'solid breakfasts and gloomy Sundays, smoky towns and winding roads, green fields and red pillar-boxes' with the reality of modern Britain: 'that solid breakfast known as muesli, that winding road called the M25, that gloomy Sunday spent in Tesco, that bright-yellow field of rapeseed, that old mill town where the only smoke is on bonfire night, that pillar-box which may be privatised.'

That slightly pessimistic vision of where Britain now stood was itself becoming dated, however, as the waves of Cool Britannia began to wash across the country. Martin Jacques, the former editor of *Marxism Today*, was closer to the new spirit of the age in his response to Major's speech. 'We desperately need to make a new start, to draw a line under the past, to reinvent ourselves,' he argued, calling instead for a celebration of a cosmopolitan, meritocratic, ethnically diverse country that could be part of Europe, and citing as symbols of this new Britain the likes of Vivienne Westwood, Stephen Hawking, Richard Branson and the Olympic gold medal-winning athlete Linford Christie. This was to be the dominant strand of thinking on the centre-left over the next few years, an attempt to shed much of Britain's past and to discover a new identity in a post-Thatcher world.

It reached its most articulate expression in Mark Leonard's pamphlet *Britain*™, published by the think tank Demos in 1997. Leonard emphasised the role now played in the economy by the creative industries (pointing out that design, fashion and music were 'our strongest export sector with a £1.1 billion turnover in 1996'), saluted retail entrepreneurialism ('Britain has more shop workers than either France or Germany'), and celebrated diversity ('Indian restaurants now have a higher turnover than coal, steel and shipbuilding combined'). Britain was already 'the global hub' for business and culture, but there was a gap internationally between the reality and the perception – hence perhaps that American fascination for *Keeping Up Appearances*. The solution was the rebranding of Britain, the development of a national character that reflected the country's true nature, both for export purposes and to assist the building of a better society domestically.

Although it became associated with the Cool Britannia phase of New Labour, *Britain*™ didn't share the same fascination with the 1960s, nor was it quite as obsessed with newness for its own sake as Tony Blair sometimes appeared. Alongside his acceptance of what had changed in Britain, Leonard also stressed older values that would have been recognisable to those on the right: a British tradition of non-conformism and eccentricity, an ethos of fair play and support for the underdog, a tradition of silent, peaceful revolution.

Nonetheless, it was all a long way from old maids and Holy Communion. And there was still the issue of Britain's history to deal with. This turned out to be one of the recurrent themes of the decade: appeals to historical episodes made regular appearances, however trivial they might seem. In 1992 Gillian Shephard told the Conservative Party conference that the May Day bank holiday was to be abolished, because it was 'socialist', and suggested that it might be replaced by a holiday on 21 October, Trafalgar Day. The proposal was said to have worried the Foreign Office, fearful of sending the wrong diplomatic signals, but it attracted the support of novelist Kingsley Amis at least: 'If it's going to get up the noses of the French, then I'm all for it.' Like so many government initiatives in the 1990s, it came to nothing; May Day survived, and the Trafalgar Day idea was still being floated by Tory politicians twenty years later.

The latter years of the decade also saw a boom in Tudor history that was to prove remarkably durable. In 1997 Fiona Buckley launched her Ursula Blanchard series of mystery novels with *To Shield the Queen*, set in Elizabethan London, while the following year, two actresses were separately nominated for Oscars for their portrayal of Elizabeth I: Judi Dench in *Shakespeare in Love* and Cate Blanchett in *Elizabeth*. (Sadly, Quentin Crisp's incarnation as the Virgin Queen in Sally Potter's 1992 film *Orlando* had gone unrecognised by the Academy.) Meanwhile Vivienne Westwood took to dressing in the manner of Elizabeth I, and a Hula Hoops advert on television starred Harry Enfield and Paul Whitehouse in their characters as the Self-Righteous Brothers at the Elizabethan court (the *mise-en-scène* was clearly derived from *Blackadder II*).

At a slightly more serious level David Starkey, who had already strayed beyond academia into a more public role on Radio 4's *The Moral Maze* and as a shock-jock on the short-lived independent station Talk Radio, became a television star with his documentary series on *Henry VIII* (1998) and *Elizabeth* (2000). His camp foppishness was in the grand media tradition of eccentric experts, but he broke with convention by cultivating a persona that was smug, rude and unattractive; consequently, he enjoyed a smooth passage into television, where a willingness to be loathed is a rare and precious commodity. Starkey seemed to revel in his status as a hate figure, and the commentators duly built up his reputation, David Aaronovitch suggesting in the *Independent on Sunday* that even modern saints would be hard pressed to tolerate him: 'From time to time, Mother Theresa and Princess Diana may well have interrupted their ministrations to the dying, and cursed him for a fuckpig.'

Starkey's key selling points to a wider audience were his treatment of historical events as soap operas – albeit 'soap operas which had the quality of Greek myth' – and the drawing of parallels between the Tudors and the current royal family. He was also keen to address contemporary politics. 'The target of Tony Blair's Cool Britannia is, fundamentally, Henry VIII's England,' he argued. 'Henry cut us off from the pan-European, Catholic church; Blair will take us back to the heart of Europe. Henry turned England on itself and back to its past; Blair will have us look forward and outward.' Meanwhile Mark Leonard was keen to claim the Tudors for Blairism: 'In those days foreigners regarded this country as one of expressive, emotional people, not of stiff upper lipped types.' It was only in the last couple of years, he suggested, that Britain had started to reclaim this honourable tradition.

This rise of media interest in the sixteenth century was not paralleled in schools, where the Midlands Examining Group, the most popular supplier of history GCSE exams, announced in 1997 that it was dropping its papers specialising in particular periods of British history. The previous year just 97 pupils had sat its Tudors and Stuarts paper, while 52,000 had opted instead for world history. A rival board, the Southern Examining Group, likewise dropped its 1509–1689 paper, replacing it with modern world history.

One area on which pretty much everyone was agreed, however, was that the Second World War was of central significance to understanding Britain, whatever one's perception of the country, whatever lessons one wished to learn.

There were, to start with, those for whom the war years still burned brightly on a personal level. They included some of the Maastricht rebels – both Bill Cash and Nicholas Budgen had lost their fathers on active service – as well as Laurence Passmore, the hero of David Lodge's novel *Therapy*, who is reluctant to buy a Japanese car because 'I'm old enough to remember World War Two, and I had an uncle who died as a POW working on the Siamese railway.' That meant that he was now in a minority in Britain, but if anything the veneration of those who had served had grown still stronger in some quarters. They were, wrote journalist Tony Parsons, 'the best generation that this country ever produced – the generation that fought World War Two and then built the welfare state, the men and women who fought for Churchill and voted for Attlee'.

Parsons returned to the theme of the sacrifices made by his father's generation in his best-selling novel *Man and Boy* (1999). 'His youth might have been marred by the efforts of the German army to murder him,' the flawed protagonist, Harry Silver, reflected of his father, 'but at least in his day a father's role was set in stone. He always knew exactly what was expected of him.' That sense of a simpler time when a man knew his position in the family and in society ran through much of the literature of the era. 'I'm happy to be a bloke, I think,' worries Rob Fleming in Nick Hornby's *High Fidelity* (1995), 'but sometimes I'm not happy being a bloke in the late twentieth century. Sometimes I'd rather be my dad.' It surfaced too in John O'Farrell's *The Best a Man Can Get* (2000), whose hero argues that his inability to be a responsible parent is the result of his own father having walked out of the family home in his childhood; but even that goes back to the war, because his father, as a child, had similarly been deprived of his parents: 'I mused that if Dad hadn't been evacuated, then he would have had a father as a role model, which might have made him stay around to be a role model for me, which would have made me a better father.'

Part of the yearning for a more straightforward era, when being a man didn't require the construction of an ironic laddishness, was a kind of war envy, a feeling that no man was truly complete until he had stared death in the face. It was a romantic notion that war was life painted in the starkest black-or-white tones, when men were 'tested in battle', and was an indulgence made possible by half a century without British involvement in major conflict. Eddie Izzard once talked of the time when, as a child, he had been taken by his father to the beaches of Normandy, recalling the impact that had made on him. 'I don't know what it is; I just feel I should have been there to *do a bit*,' reflected Izzard. 'It was just something I wanted to be involved in.' The tendency found some odd expressions, none more so than in Nigel Planer's *The Right Man* where the narrator encounters a tree surgeon hanging out of a tree and is filled with admiration and envy for 'a man's legs, tough, sinewy, bloody British legs. Not pumped up with steroids, vitamins or gym machinery.' And the thought strikes him: 'Men's legs must have been like this at Agincourt.'

Nor was the theme restricted to male writers. 'My father has carried grown men with bullet wounds through the jungle, he has cut the heads off his enemies and carried them back to base in a rucksack,' reflects the heroine of Jenny Eclair's *Camberwell Beauty* (2000). 'We are all so wet these days. Maybe it's time we had another war to put things into perspective, and as I say that I almost laugh; it is impossible to imagine either Henry or Jed in combat.' Given subsequent events, the most ironic such comment came from Adrian Mole in 1997: 'Due to Mr Blair's obvious hatred for war I am never going to be tested in battle. A shame.'

'Our fathers, they did national service,' moans Gary Sparrow (Nicholas Lyndhurst) in the sitcom *Goodnight Sweetheart* (1993). 'Their fathers fought in the war. Experiences that marked their shift into manhood.' Now, there was no equivalent rite of passage, no way of symbolising the end of adolescence. Except that Gary stumbles upon the solution. A television repairman living in a starter home in Cricklewood, dissatisfied with his life and feeling threatened by his wife — a personnel manager who's studying for a psychology degree — he discovers a time portal that takes him back to an East End pub during the Blitz in 1940. Over the course of fifty-eight episodes, he lives a double life, balancing the normality of the present with the excitement of the past, where he poses as a glamorous secret agent. And as his fantasy becomes all too real, he finds himself caught up in action and discovers that he too can be a war hero.

Throughout the series the contrasts between then and now are repeatedly pointed out, whether it's Gary's best friend Ron (Victor McGuire) lamenting the growing complexity of masculinity — 'Men were allowed to be gross in those days, before Women's Lib' — or his present-day wife, Yvonne (Michelle Holmes), who can see why he's become so obsessed with the past: 'I can understand why the forties appeal so much. It's a time of certainties, a time when people knew what they were doing and why they were doing it.'

Related to this feeling was the phenomenon of the SAS memoir, one of the big success stories of 1990s publishing. It began with Andy McNab's *Bravo Two Zero* (1993), which sold 350,000 copies in hardback to become Britain's best-selling war memoir ever, as well as being a book 'which actually improves with every read', according to Alan Partridge. An account of a failed SAS raid behind enemy lines in the Kuwaiti War, it was followed by Chris Ryan's *The One that Got Away* (1995), which gave another version of the same incident, complete with heavy digs at McNab. (Both names were pseudonyms, of course.) McNab went on to write the autobiographical *Immediate Action* (1995) — 'the book they tried to ban' — before launching a fiction series starring an SAS character named Nick Stone, that opened with *Remote Control* (1997), while Ryan also created a fictional SAS hero, Geordie Sharp, in *Stand By, Stand By* (1996).

Effectively these books replaced the *Commando* comics and the Sven Hassel novels that had proliferated in the 1960s and '70s, supplying tales of violence and endurance to keep the *Loaded* generation entertained between gangster movies. They did, however, represent something new, for there hadn't previously been much of a tradition in Britain of popular memoirs and fiction from the other ranks; demand was satisfied instead by translations of Hassel and, on a somewhat higher literary plane, Erich Maria Remarque. For an older generation, there was ITV's *Soldier, Soldier* (1991–7), a popular drama series that launched a brief but hugely successful singing career for its stars Robson Green and Jerome Flynn. As with cooking and gardening, it appeared that the less soldiering that was actually being done, the greater the public appetite for its depiction on screen and in print.

Memories of the Second World War were also kept alive in the coverage of sport, particularly when England qualified for a football tournament, since Germany always seemed to be lurking in the same half of the draw. 'We beat them in 1945,' said the *Sun* in the build-up to the 1990 World Cup semi-final. 'Now the battle of 1990. Herr we go again.'

Most notorious of all was the *Daily Mirror*'s front page on the day of the Euro 96 semi-final. 'ACHTUNG! SURRENDER — For you Fritz, ze Euro 96 Championship is over', ran the main headline, illustrated with pictures of Stuart Pearce and Paul Gascoigne wearing Second World War helmets and accompanied by a front-page editorial: MIRROR DECLARES FOOTBALL WAR ON GERMANY. The leaden attempt at humour continued over the next two pages: 'There is a strange smell in Berlin and it's not just their funny sausages, it's the smell of fear.' The *Daily Mirror* also approached the owner of a Spitfire to ask whether, in the event of an English victory, he would perform a victory roll over the hotel where the Germans were staying, though England's defeat meant that this proved unnecessary. (To be fair to the *Daily Mirror* and its editor, Piers Morgan, the xenophobic abuse was not restricted to combatant nations; England's quarter-final against Spain prompted a list of TEN NASTIES SPAIN'S GIVEN EUROPE, which opened with syphilis, Spanish flu, carpet bombing and the Inquisition.)

With such willing cheerleaders, it was unsurprising when a friendly match in Berlin between Germany and England, scheduled for 20 April 1994, was cancelled on the grounds that Adolf Hitler's birthday was probably not the ideal date for such an encounter.

The war-obsessed coverage of football was hardly new. On the day of the 1966 World Cup final, the *Daily Mail*, showing little confidence in the prospects for Alf Ramsey's team, got its excuses in early: 'If Germany beat us at Wembley this afternoon at our national sport, we can always point out to them that we have recently beaten them at theirs.' But that was a very different time, and the distance that had been travelled was brought home by the death in February 1993 of Bobby Moore, captain of that World Cup-winning England team. 'He looked like a Greek god, with his clean-cut limbs and short golden curls,' mourns Laurence Passmore in *Therapy*. 'They don't make them like that any more. They make overpaid lager louts plastered with advertising logos, who spit all over the pitch.' Like so many in Britain, Passmore has a weakness for the 1960s: 'It was a time of hope, a time when it was possible to feel patriotic without being typecast as a Tory blimp. The shame of Suez was behind us, and now we were beating the world in the things that really mattered to ordinary people, sport and pop music and fashion and television.'

The mostly hostile reaction that greeted the *Daily Mirror*'s Euro 96 front page illustrated how fine the line was between jocularity and offence, and how difficult it was to judge the tone when invoking the war. It was a lesson that the government learnt the hard way in 1994 as the fiftieth anniversary of D-Day on 6 June approached.

Clearly such an occasion would not be allowed to pass without recognition, and a state ceremony was scheduled in Normandy. There was some debate over the involvement of Germany, but it was soon decided that perhaps it would be best to hold over any official participation by the vanquished until the anniversary of the liberation of Europe the following year. The problems for John Major came with the events that were planned at home. 'We'll have spam and spotted dick for dinner,' enthused an official from the British Tourist Authority, 'and then a singalong with all the old wartime favourites.' There were to be fun days and street parties all over the country with fireworks, fancy-dress parties and sandcastle-making competitions, while pubs were to be encouraged to sell beer at 1944 prices.

No sooner had the plans been announced than they began to run into political trouble. Major promised 'celebrations and commemorations', which many felt struck entirely the wrong note. An operation that cost thousands of British lives should not be the cause of celebrations, regardless of how worthy the cause or how successful the ultimate outcome might have been.

Peter Mandelson put down a motion in Parliament describing the proposals for 'festivities and public relations stunts' as 'inappropriate and in bad taste', and calling instead for a 'single, respectful national service of thanksgiving in grateful memory of those who gave their lives so that others could live in freedom'. The broadcaster Ludovic Kennedy, himself a veteran of D-Day, also suggested that the government was cynically exploiting the anniversary for political ends, noting that it fell just three days before the elections to the European Parliament, in which the Conservatives were expected to perform poorly.

This much could have been expected and dealt with. But Mandelson's complaints were heard elsewhere as well. The Conservative MP Winston Churchill, grandson of the wartime prime minister, weighed in: 'They have their history wrong,' he said. 'They don't seem to know the difference between D-Day and VE Day.' The Royal British Legion revealed that they hadn't even been consulted and suggested that the arrangements smacked of 'trivial light entertainment'. And then the light entertainment veterans themselves added their voices. Vera Lynn, who had been booked to sing in Hyde Park, said that she didn't wish to perform in a 'carnival atmosphere', and Ann Shelton was equally condemnatory: 'It's a bit like saying we should have jugglers at the Cenotaph.'

When asked by pollsters, the public made clear that they shared these opinions. Just about the only person who seemed untouched by the criticism was Tim Bell, the public relations executive famous for his work for Margaret Thatcher, who had been paid handsomely for dreaming up the festivities. 'If someone wants to mess up the party by moaning and groaning, that's their problem, not mine,' he sniffed.

John Major could not afford such disdain, and the plans were radically scaled back in what was inevitably seen as a humiliating climb-down. 'The debacle and retreat over the D-Day celebrations has confirmed the impression of John Major's government being accident-prone and incompetent,' concluded the *Independent*, and a leader in *The Times* agreed: 'The D-Day anniversary could have been an opportunity for the government to prove some competence and for Mr Major to justify his claim to be in touch with ordinary people. Instead it has revealed flaws that have become all too familiar.'

Having got D-Day so entirely wrong, Major was unlikely to gain much credit for the fiftieth anniversary of VE Day on 7 May 1995, even though it proved to be one of the most impressive occasions of the decade. This time the tone was judged perfectly. A service of thanksgiving in St Paul's Cathedral gathered together more world leaders than any event since the Coronation; a memorial service in the oldest synagogue in the country was attended by the Chief Rabbi, the Archbishop of Canterbury and the Archbishop of Westminster, the first time all three figures had ever gathered at a synagogue service; and Radio 4's *Today* gave its 'Thought for the Day' slot over to Prince Charles to reflect on the need for remembrance. A two-minute silence was also held across the country.

The sombre side having been catered for, many of the abandoned plans from D-Day were then revived, centring on Hyde Park, where there were indeed spam fritters, the world's largest hokey-cokey, and a concert of community singing led by Vera Lynn, Harry Secombe and Cliff Richard. It was all a huge success, with around a quarter of a million people gathering in The Mall to see the Queen Mother and her two daughters appear on the Buckingham Palace balcony, just as they had fifty years earlier. In what was not a notably successful decade for royalty, this was the high point, the moment when all the clichés about embodying history, continuity and the British spirit resonated with the nation.

For the government, reeling from yet another appalling performance at the polls, this time in local elections, there was little positive to be taken from the occasion. 'The most potent political image was of Blair walking down the Mall acclaimed by the cheering crowds,' remarked Hywel Williams, and a leader column in the *Observer* spelt out the potential parallels: 'a seductive, subterranean folk memory is being activated. Might Blair be about to repeat Attlee's post-war landslide?' *Private Eye* made the same point with a front cover headlined THEN AS NOW that pictured revellers in 1945 complete with a speech bubble: 'Hoorah! We're all voting Labour.'

Some commentators, including the *Independent*'s Polly Toynbee, regretted that the VE Day celebrations were all so 'deliberately backward-looking, in praise of a better past, and fearful of the future'. The very next day, she lectured her readers, had been Europe Day and yet, so obsessed had we become with history, it had passed by without any commemoration at all. Such an absurdly sour note — surely the anniversary of the defeat of Nazism was worth throwing a party for — was rare, however, and even many of those who professed themselves cynical were caught up in the emotion of the moment. The comedy critic Ben Thompson went to a VE Day festival on Hackney Downs in East London, where he was surprised to find himself so moved. 'Looking around at the genial multifariousness of the crowd,' he wrote, 'there was no other option than to be temporarily overwhelmed by a profound sense of patriotic pride.'

Nor was Toynbee entirely right about it all being nostalgia. Some features of that long weekend most certainly pointed the way forward, albeit to a corporate future in which even patriotism was available for sponsorship. The only cola for sale at official events in London was the newly launched Virgin Cola, which had secured exclusive rights to slake the revellers' thirst, while it was impossible to escape brand advertising by everyone from Eurostar to Sainsbury's. 'Serving the nation, then and now' was the latter's slogan, which wasn't everyone's concept of war service. Vera Lynn was among those to notice that such major companies were much less interested in the more muted celebrations for VJ Day on 15 August; the Forgotten Army had been overlooked once again.

And yet there were still doubts on the liberal left about how to celebrate. 'Is it possible to have kitsch ironic VE Day party – like for the Royal Wedding?' worried Bridget Jones. 'No, you see, you can't be ironic about dead people. And then there's the problem of flags. Half of Tom's friends used to be in the Anti-Nazi League and would think the presence of Union Jacks meant we were expecting skinheads.' She had touched on one of the central issues of a decade that worried deeply about national identity: how acceptable in modern Britain were the emblems of nationhood and patriotism?

The question had caused some controversy in 1992 in relation to the singer Morrissey, whose album that year, *Your Arsenal*, was acclaimed as his best ever, with David Bowie's ex-guitarist Mick Ronson giving the music a glam polish. But songs like 'We'll Let You Know' and 'The National Front Disco' struck some critics as overly sympathetic, even dewy-eyed, in their treatment of football hooligans and skinheads. 'We are the last truly British people you will ever know,' he sang on the latter, and there were concerns in some quarters that his fascination with the more violent, disreputable end of English youth culture was getting a little dangerous.

Undeterred, he appeared as the special guest at Madstock, a reunion concert by the group Madness in Finsbury Park, North London that August, and stole all the headlines. Singing in front of a backdrop picture of skinheads, he produced a Union flag and waved it around, to the evident excitement of some of the skins in the crowd. The following week's edition of the *New Musical Express* devoted its front cover to a photograph of the singer with the flag and allotted more than 6,000 words to addressing the question: 'Has Morrissey gone too far this time?' The answer was, not unexpectedly, in the affirmative; stopping just short of calling him a racist, the paper denounced the way that the former Smiths frontman had 'continued to pick away at the scab of race relations in this country'.

Morrissey was unapologetic. 'I like the flag,' he insisted. 'I think it is very attractive. When does a Union Jack become racist?' He also pointed out that he was far from the first pop musician to employ such imagery, and indeed precedents could be found for much of the *NME*'s charge sheet, which included a selection of remarks from previous interviews with the singer. 'When I see reports on the television about football hooliganism,' Morrissey was quoted as saying, 'I'm actually amused.' This supposedly damning observation in fact sat fairly happily with, say, the comments of former

Clash singer Joe Strummer on the behaviour of England fans during the 1990 World Cup: 'I get a strange swell of pride when I hear of our football hooligans causing trouble abroad.'

But Morrissey's protestations about the national flag ran counter to the accepted values of the industry that provided him with a living. Ever since the formation of Rock Against Racism in response to comments by Eric Clapton and David Bowie in 1976, the music world had been justly proud of its part in making discrimination on grounds of colour unfashionable and unacceptable; it was largely through the endeavours of popular culture that racist language and behaviour had become the great taboo in Britain.

In the process, racism had somehow been conflated with patriotism, so that any expression of Britishness was itself suspect. When, in 1993, Blur issued a publicity photo which showed them wearing clothes from the mod and skinhead cults, posed in front of a wall bearing the slogan: 'British Image 1', the *NME* said they were 'flirting with fascist imagery'. One of the babies apparently discarded with the bathwater was the country's flag, which had for some become a deeply controversial symbol, associated with days of Empire and with a British nationalism that was felt to be at the heart of continuing colonialist attitudes. This feeling was not unrelated to the fact that the flag was employed so ostentatiously by the National Front and their successor groups on the far right.

Such sensibilities, however, were rapidly passing out of fashion. The sleeve of the first Oasis demo tape in 1993 bore an image of the red, white and blue colours swirling inwards as though disappearing down a plughole. Liam Gallagher explained the significance of the symbolism: 'It's the greatest flag in the world and it's going down the shitter. We're here to do something about it.' When the group played two gigs at the Maine Road stadium in 1996, their biggest concerts thus far, Noel Gallagher's guitar was emblazoned with the flag, and at the Brit Awards the following year Geri Halliwell of the Spice Girls captured the front pages by wearing a Gucci mini dress with a Union flag tea-towel sewn onto it. In 1997 too, David Bowie was pictured on his new album, *Earthling*, wearing a distressed Union Jack frock-coat, and – somewhat tardily – Annie Lennox wore a similar jacket when she performed at the Brits two years later. By this stage, the furore over Morrissey's appearance at Madstock felt like a very long time ago. It was one of Cool Britannia's legacies that the Union flag was reclaimed from the right wing to become a truly national symbol.

In a parallel development, the flag of St George – an emblem with little resonance in recent times – also became a fixture, particularly at Euro 96, asserting an English identity that had hitherto felt no need to project itself, but which now seemed a little threatened by the inexorable rise of nationalism in other parts of the United Kingdom. 'No wonder the English have become so desperate to wave the flag of St George,' reflected the hero of Tony Parsons's novel *Man and Boy*, 'to remind ourselves that our roots are just as deep and defined as those of the Irish or the Scots.' Clinton's Cards even began making greetings cards for St George's Day and several authors published books in which they made attempts to define Englishness. The television journalist Jeremy Paxman concluded his exploration of the theme with a checklist of traits: 'individualism, pragmatism, love of words and, above all, that glorious, fundamental cussedness'.

The ease and speed of this cultural embrace of the flags suggested that earlier fears on the left of extreme nationalism had been misplaced. There was little political charge to this appropriation, merely another echo of the Swinging London years. For politicians, on the other hand, it was territory that should have been entered with great caution, for the exploitation of the flag had always been regarded as slightly suspect, even unBritish.

In *Stalky & Co*, the 1899 school novel written by the great poet of Empire, Rudyard Kipling, an MP visits a fictionalised version of the United Services College to address the boys on the subject of patriotism. The majority of his audience are the sons of servicemen, themselves intending to join the forces, but his speech, which culminates in the unfurling of a Union Jack, leaves them in appalled silence. In the lives of these future members of the imperial officer class, the flag is not intended for such use, nor for everyday display: 'It was a matter shut up, sacred and apart. What in the name of everything caddish, was he driving at, who waved that horror before their eyes?' The MP leaves the flag behind, donated to the school's cadet corps, with the result that the corps quietly disbands itself rather than be associated with such a loathsome gesture.

That example hadn't put off subsequent generations of politicians. In particular, Margaret Thatcher, fresh from victory in the Falklands War, had been enthusiastic about being pictured in front of the Union flag. Such opportunities included a 1987 election broadcast that featured footage from the two world wars, suggesting a belief within the Conservative Party that it had 'a monopoly of patriotism', in the words of David Owen. 'When you see Mrs Thatcher's kind of Tories wrapping themselves in the flag,' remarked Neil Kinnock, 'it does make you very suspicious when they have done so much damage to people who live under it.' Exactly the same charge was made eight years later by Tony Blair about John Major's Conservatives: 'It is no good waving the fabric of the flag when you have spent sixteen years tearing apart the fabric of our nation.'

The Labour response, however, was very different this time. At the party's last conference before the 1992 election, a tentative toe had been dipped in the water and delegates had been treated to a backdrop that featured the Union flag 'discreetly woven into the slogan "Opportunity Britain"'. Now, with the endorsement of Cool Britannia, New Labour simply took the flag for themselves, flaunting it boldly along with other symbols of nationalism. 'Let us say it with pride,' declaimed Blair at the 1995 conference: 'we are patriots. This is the patriotic party, because it is the people's party.' A speech he made during the election campaign was originally intended to contain, until it was deleted at the demand of Robin Cook, a more radical declaration still: 'I am proud of the British Empire.' (Blair was later to record that, as control of Hong Kong was passed to China, he felt at the handover ceremony 'a tug, not of regret but of nostalgia for the old British Empire'.)

The first Labour Party broadcast under Blair's leadership ended with a suitably patriotic peroration — 'We can change the course of our history and build a new confident land of opportunity in a new and changing world' — as the sound of Elgar's 'Nimrod' swelled on the soundtrack. An election broadcast in 1997 went one step further, using 'Land of Hope and Glory' as it showed patients lying on trolleys in hospital corridors, street muggings, car theft and drug dealing, as well as a Union flag being lowered, all juxtaposed with pictures of leading Conservatives laughing and looking smug. The final shot was of a sandcastle surmounted by a little Union Jack being washed away by waves. It was a slick, cynical, manipulative piece of scaremongering, and it was very effective indeed.

Less successful was another broadcast during the campaign that attempted to put the positive case for voting Labour. It featured that other great symbol, a British bulldog, even though, as Clive Aslet pointed out, the breed had, in modern times, 'become a wheezing caricature of its former self: overbred, prone to buckling of the legs and devoid of the old athleticism, tenacity and aggression of the sporting dog'. The effect was further undermined when it became known that the animal in question had been rather too well-endowed for media exposure, and had therefore had his testicles airbrushed out; the revelation prompted a slew of jokes about Blair not really being the dog's bollocks after all.

Some on the left of the Labour Party struggled to accept the rebranding project. When Tony Blair's speech to the conference in 1996 ended with a back-projection of the Union flag, it was all too much for Tony Benn to bear: 'It was the National Front, it was everything I feared, and it made me absolutely sick.' But he was in a dwindling minority, and many of the party were carried along by the way in which New Labour's unashamed wrapping

The Conservative Party celebrates social mobility on a 1992 poster. *Getty Images*

John Major visits British troops in the Gulf after the Kuwaiti War, 1991. A year later, his Labour rival, Neil Kinnock, addresses the pre-election Sheffield Rally. *Mirrorpix*

The advent of the new lad is proclaimed in *Loaded* magazine and the sitcom *Men Behaving Badly*. Amongst the heroes of the movement is Eric Cantona, particularly after he deals forcefully with an abusive fan.

Right: Rex Features;
below: Brendan O'Sullivan/Rex Features

The political dimension of 1990s comedy is evident in Harry Enfield's incarnation as Tory Boy and Chris Morris's parody of the news media in *The Day Today*, as well as in the support actor Richard Wilson (of *One Foot in the Grave*) gives to the Labour Party.

Above: BBC Photo Library; right: © Trinity Mirror/Mirrorpix/Alamy

The future belongs, however, to the non-political comedians epitomised by Jack Dee.

Above: BBC Photo Library; right: Rex Features

Following their victory in the 1992 election, the Tories implode: Norman Lamont announces Britain's withdrawal from the ERM, and David Mellor and his family present a united front in the wake of stories about his personal life. Both men were out of office by 1993.

Right: Mirrorpix; below: Murray Sanders/ Daily Mail/Rex Features

At the height of Britpop Geri Halliwell of the Spice Girls and Noel Gallagher of Oasis are amongst those reclaiming the imagery of the Union flag. In 1992 Morrissey had attracted controversy by dancing with it at a concert. *Top and below: Redferns/Getty Images; left: Getty Images*

The bucolic nostalgia of the hugely popular TV series *The Darling Buds of May* finds an equally warm counterpart in a new wave of cinema that celebrates community in modern Britain, including *Bhaji on the Beach*, *The Full Monty* and *Brassed Off*.

Top: ITV/Rex Features; below: Moviestore Collection/Rex Features

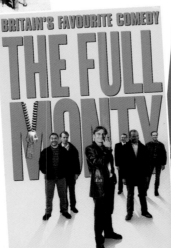

The outcome of the 1997 election is a foregone conclusion, as recognised by the *Sun*'s endorsement of Tony Blair, allowing Alastair Campbell to coordinate a campaign chiefly notable for its dullness.

Above: Getty Images; left: © Homer Sykes Archive/Alamy

The new government is dominated by the rivalry between the self-conscious modernity of Tony Blair and the self-proclaimed prudence of Gordon Brown.

As the alternative culture of the 1980s moves into the mainstream, it makes household names of indie rock star Jarvis Cocker, Paul O'Grady's drag queen Lily Savage (presenter of BBC One's *Blankety Blank*) and the computer game character Lara Croft. Meanwhile the rise of the docusoap turns ordinary people into minor celebrities, including Maureen Rees from the series *Driving School*.

Top: Redferns/Getty Images; middle: FremantleMedia Ltd/ Rex Features; above: © Joe Bird/Alamy; right: Mike Forster/Daily Mail/Rex Features

John Redwood's challenge
for the leadership of the
Conservative Party in 1995
proves unsuccessful but
damaging to the party.

Times Newspapers/Rex Features

William Hague becomes
leader in 1997 but fails
to convince the country,
even with the support of
Margaret Thatcher and
Ann Widdecombe.

*Above: Stefan Rousseau/Press
Association Images; left: AFP/Getty Images*

The nation's response to a fire at Windsor Castle in 1992 concludes the monarchy's *annus horribilis*, though popular support returns for the anniversary of VE Day in 1995: the Queen, Queen Mother and Princess Margaret had appeared on the same balcony fifty years earlier.

Tim Graham/Getty Images

A turbulent decade for the royal family is dominated by the death of Princess Diana in 1997 and the wave of public grief leading up to her funeral.

AFP/Getty Images

Above: A Sinn Fein delegation, led by Gerry Adams and Martin McGuinness, in Downing Street for talks during the Northern Ireland peace process. *Mirrorpix*

Below, left to right: The Labour candidate, Frank Dobson, concedes defeat to the independent Ken Livingstone in the first mayoral election for London in 2000. In 2001 Peter Mandelson resigns from the cabinet for the second time in a single parliament, and the foot-and-mouth epidemic revives the imagery of the BSE crisis of John Major's premiership. *Left: AFP/Getty Images; below: Getty Images*

The start of the new millennium is greeted by protests over fuel tax and the adornment of Winston Churchill's statue with a grass Mohican.

Left: AFP/Getty Images; below: Adam Butler/Press Association Images

of itself in the flag succeeded in defusing the allegations of anti-patriotism which had served the Tories so well throughout the previous decade. 'We have reclaimed the flag,' declared Peter Mandelson. 'It is restored as an emblem of national pride and diversity. Restored from years as a symbol of division and intolerance.'

The Conservatives struggled wearily to fight back against the barrage. Where once there had been talk, given Labour's plans for devolution and its enthusiasm for Europe, of a 'Union Jack election', it was becoming increasingly difficult for the Tories to construct a patriotic argument: so many of the symbols had already been taken. An election poster was produced that smacked of desperation, depicting, over the slogan NEW LABOUR, EURO DANGER, a lion with a blood-red tear dripping from its eye. It proved to be the least popular piece of propaganda in the entire campaign. 'People haven't got a clue what it's about,' complained Sebastian Coe. 'They wonder what we did to the poor lion to make it cry blood.'

Running through Labour's campaign, underlying all the patriotic imagery, was the theme with which Blair ended his 1995 conference speech: 'This coming election is not a struggle for political power. It is a battle for the soul of the nation.' His words echoed sentiments associated with Margaret Thatcher: 'Economics are the method,' she had said. 'The object is to change the soul.' Nonetheless it was still a powerful theme, and one that he had begun to explore in his days as shadow home secretary.

In February 1993 James Bulger, a two-year-old from Kirby, was abducted from a Bootle shopping centre by two ten-year-old boys and brutally tortured to death. It was a particularly horrific murder, even without the added factor of the killers' age, and the public reaction was one of shock and distress, amplified by the release of grainy CCTV images showing the toddler being led away by his murderers. There were further parallels here with the 1960s, though of a less desirable kind: the crime echoed those of Mary Bell in 1968, while the only point of comparison in terms of public revulsion was with the Moors murders case of 1965. 'Wherever you go, whoever you talk to,' wrote Andrew Marr, a week after the killing, 'there is only one subject that interests people at the moment. The murder of James Bulger hangs over the whole country like a dark cloud.' The crime sparked a national outpouring of emotion and comment as the country tried to find some meaning in a meaningless act of violence. There was an insatiable need to discover what had gone wrong with Britain that such a thing could happen.

Into this debate stepped Tony Blair. 'Very effectively I made it into a symbol of a Tory Britain in which, for all the efficiency that Thatcherism had achieved, the bonds of social and community well-being had been loosed, dangerously so,' wrote Blair in his memoirs, admitting that he personally benefited from the intervention: 'at the time, politically, there was a big impact on my standing, which rose still further.' Blair acknowledged, as the Labour Party had too rarely done in recent years, that it was not enough simply to talk of social deprivation, that there was a question of morality here: 'If we do not learn and then teach the value of what is right and wrong, then the result is simply moral chaos which engulfs us all.'

He spoke too of the need for community, and if none of this came with much idea of how it was to be achieved, other than by locking up more offenders, it undoubtedly did its job of stoking public unease. An opinion poll published a fortnight after the Bulger murder showed that law and order was now second only to unemployment as the issue causing greatest concern to the public, the numbers mentioning it having doubled in the last month. Levels of youth criminality, many felt, had reached crisis point.

The belief that there was a terrifying rise in juvenile crime was hardly borne out by the statistics; the number of young people under eighteen cautioned or convicted of an offence had fallen by nearly a third in the last six years. But the perception was allowed to remain and, without offering any way forward, Blair found that his rhetoric captured the public mood more effectively than did that of the government. There was a look of campaigning zeal about him, which outflanked John Major's more reassuring tone, even when the prime minister promised a 'crusade against crime' and adopted a strange position that ignorance was the best policy: 'We should condemn a little more, understand a little less.' Major's 'back to basics' speech the following autumn was perhaps a more considered response, though any chance that it might steal Blair's thunder faded away with the first whiff of Tory sexual impropriety.

Meanwhile the home secretary, Kenneth Clarke, was shocked out of the political complacency he had displayed just a few months earlier at the Conservative conference. 'We are the party of law and order,' he had bragged; 'the Labour Party know it, and the general public know it.' That was in the wake of Black Wednesday and the David Mellor affair, and offered some reassurance that there was one issue where the Tories remained untouchable. Now, though, with Blair outflanking him in talk of hard-hitting measures, Clarke responded in kind, promising that more detention centres for juveniles would be built, though many experts in the field felt that the contest to be tough failed to shed much light on the problem of teenage criminality. 'The two of them arguing about whose penal institution is bigger gets us nowhere,' shrugged Frances Crook, director of the Howard League for Penal Reform.

When Michael Howard became home secretary shortly afterwards, he ramped up the rhetoric still further. He also took pot shots at tried and tested targets, announcing 'the toughest-ever crackdown on violent videos'. (The judge in the Bulger case, followed by much of the media, had wrongly suggested that videos, including the 1991 film *Child's Play 3*, had played a part in the murder.)

It didn't take much foresight to predict that the proposed measures would do little to prevent another case arising to capture the public mood of anguish. In December 1995 Philip Lawrence, the head teacher of St George's Catholic School in Maida Vale, London, was stabbed to death outside the school gates after he intervened to stop a gang of children who were attacking a thirteen-year-old pupil with an iron bar. His widow, Frances, wrote an open letter to the pupils of the school, which was read at assembly: 'Violence is not a knife in the hand. It grows, like a poison tree, inside people who, unlike yourselves, have not learnt to value other human beings. Now I trust you to work as hard as you can, in school and at home, to create a world in which goodness is never again destroyed by evil.' She later expanded on this, calling on 'the government and those who shape society' to lead a moral crusade 'to re-evaluate what on earth is going on in society now, to try to provide a framework, a guidance for people'.

Philip Lawrence was subsequently voted Personality of the Year in the annual poll of listeners to Radio 4's *Today* programme and an award scheme, funded by the Home Office, was launched in his name 'to show everyone just how many groups of young people are doing extraordinary things for their communities'. A month-long knife amnesty was also called by police forces across the country; as a result, 40,000 weapons were handed in, not just knives, but also machetes, swords, bayonets and knuckle dusters.

Worse was to follow just a few months after Lawrence's murder, when a 43-year-old man named Thomas Hamilton walked into Dunblane Primary School in March 1996 and shot dead sixteen children and one teacher before killing himself. The scale of the massacre was deeply shocking and again demanded a political response. The government set up the Cullen Inquiry, which called for tighter gun control, and subsequently passed legislation that banned the ownership of almost all handguns.

But the Tories were again outflanked by Labour. Even before Cullen produced his report, the party had invited Ann Pearston of the Snowdrop Petition, a campaign to outlaw all gun ownership, to speak at the 1996 Labour conference. The Liberal Democrat conference that year also voted in favour of a ban, even if one delegate expressed a distaste for such opportunistic resolutions: 'I don't believe, emotional as it is, that we should be, in effect, grave-robbing those children for votes.' When the Labour government was elected, it passed new legislation that finally ended the owning of handguns (except, incongruously, in Northern Ireland); nonetheless, the incidence of crimes involving firearms more than doubled over the next five years.

Equally ineffective was the response to Dunblane by the culture secretary, Virginia Bottomley, who followed Michael Howard's lead and decided that violence in fictional films was somehow to blame. She announced that the government would introduce legislation to ensure all new television sets came fitted with what was known as a V-chip, a device that supposedly allowed parents to stop their children seeing violent and sexually explicit material. This requirement had recently been passed into law in the United States, but it met with little enthusiasm in Britain, partly because, by venturing beyond 'video nasties' into television, it trod on the toes of those newspaper proprietors who had a stake in broadcasting. The proposal had 'flaws' thought *The Times*, was 'unworkable' according to the *Financial Times*, and took us into 'a thorny area' in the eyes of the *Independent*. The *Sun* was more forthright still: 'she's wasting her time.' Within a week, the government had dropped the idea.

Horrific crimes like the killings of James Bulger, Philip Lawrence and the children at Dunblane quite rightly dominated the headlines for days and even weeks, as all such events will, but there was a new element in the desire of politicians to make quite so much capital out of them. It was hard not to see their contributions as cynical, opportunistic and — worse still — politically foolish.

Tony Blair's wish to weave the murder of James Bulger into the narrative of a crumbling Britain under the Tories could presumably be extended, so that one might point, say, to the Moors Murderers in the 1960s and the killing career of Peter Sutcliffe in the late 1970s as an illustration of the kind of thing that happened under a Labour government. That would be an absurd claim, of course, but so too was Blair's implication that a government led by him would prevent such things happening. Yet this was the path he was heading down. Because although it was a short-term success, Blair's rhetoric stoked up unrealistic expectations for the future, which could surely never be met.

'This generation, my generation,' he said at the 1995 conference, 'enjoys a thousand material advantages over any previous generation, and yet we suffer a depth of insecurity and spiritual doubt they never knew.' The suggestion that we were about to witness a spiritual rebirth of the nation, a sea change in morality, the very idea that these things were in the gift of the government – all were allowed to run unchecked, until even some of the senior figures in New Labour began to be concerned. 'I think that if we win the election,' commented Jack Straw in 1996, 'the greatest burden on Tony Blair and the rest of us will not be delivering on the economy so much as the huge expectation that we will somehow be the agents of a different ethical order.'

A year later, after the election had duly been won, Giles Radice was surprised to be visited at his constituency surgery by a woman who 'complains that we haven't yet managed to "change people's behaviour towards each other" and asks what I am going to do about it'.

And while the Labour Party in opposition was bemoaning the state of the nation, its continual attacks on the current government's 'sleaze' similarly fuelled the hope that politics itself would be transformed. It was another hostage to fortune, and one that would come to be the source of some regret. 'We made a very big mistake in allowing the impression to be gained that we were going to be better than the Tories,' wrote Blair in his memoirs; 'not just better at governing, but more moral, more upright.' The implication was that it was the electorate's fault, that the nation had somehow got a misunderstood message into its muddled head, but perhaps that wrong 'impression' owed more than a little to the attitude summed up by a headline in the party's election manifesto: WE WILL CLEAN UP POLITICS.

These suggestions that morality was at stake were all the more improbable since they came at a time when concrete policy commitments were being kept to an absolute minimum, for fear of promising real things that couldn't be delivered. In this, as in so much else, the role model seemed to be Harold Wilson in the months before the 1964 election, another young politician thrust prematurely into the leadership by the early death of the incumbent, another who sought to end a long period of Tory government.

The comparison was made explicit in the first episode of *Our Friends in the North*, broadcast in 1996 but set just before that 1964 election. 'What actual guarantee have we got that a Labour government will do any better?' queries Nicky (Christopher Ecclestone). 'Wilson's making no promises at all, as far as I can make out. We've got the white heat of the new technology, but that could mean more of the same old con trick.' And in case the contemporary reference isn't entirely clear, Nicky is seen delivering copies of the Labour manifesto, which that year carried the slogan THE NEW BRITAIN. It was a phrase that Wilson had used extensively, inspiring many in his party, including the young Tony Benn, who talked of 'changes just as exciting as at any time in the past' as he looked forward to 'the implementation of Labour's New Britain programme'.

Blair adopted much of the same language, particularly in his 1995 conference speech which returned to the theme over and over again, as he promised 'to build a new and young country'. He referred to the people who had called out to him on The Mall on the anniversary of VE Day, and said they were 'decent people, good people, patriotic people. When I hear people urging us to fight for "our people", I tell you: these are our people. They are the majority. And we must serve them, and build that new Britain, that young country, for their children and their families.' At the same conference, John Prescott went a daring step further and appropriated a Tory slogan that pre-dated the existence of the Labour Party itself, saying that the future now belonged to 'One-nation Labour. The party that speaks for the whole country.'

The conceit caught on, at least in New Labour circles, and the 1997 manifesto made the extraordinary assertion that the party was now 'the political arm of none other than the British people as a whole'. That rhetoric was to survive Blair's first term in office: on the night of the next election, in 2001, the Labour MP Shaun Woodward was to claim that his newly adopted party was 'a party for everyone, not of any particular class or any particular view'.

On the day after the 1997 election the Labour MP Tony Wright had said of Tony Blair that he was 'good at being a man of his time. That is to say, he well expresses the fact that there is no Big Idea. Maybe the Big Idea is that there is no Big Idea.' But perhaps that was to miss the scale of Blair's ambition. His wish was to elevate his party to such a level that it rose above mere politics and could embody Britain itself. Or perhaps, as so often, Blair was merely perfecting a more voter-friendly version of John Major, of whom Giles Radice had written in 1992: 'He is clearly going to be the Baldwin of the 1990s, taking the politics out of politics.'

Blair's moral crusade, intended to reshape the conduct of politics and the nature of the country, came ultimately from his faith, as he made clear in his memoirs: 'I had always been fortunate in having a passion bigger than politics, which is religion.' Along with Gordon Brown, Jack Straw, David Blunkett and other leading members of New Labour, he was a member of the Christian Socialist Movement, and in the 1990s there was a notable trend away from the more secular character of the party. When the *New Statesman* magazine conducted a survey in 1994 of what Labour MPs considered the most important books in their lives, the results showed a marked change since the last such survey two decades earlier; then Karl Marx had been cited as the most popular author, now he had fallen behind the Bible in popularity, and the leading place had been taken by John Ruskin.

In the wider society, however, religion was looking like a quaint, eccentric leftover, unable to retain its moral authority. In his finest novel, *The Vicar of Sorrows* (1993), A.N. Wilson satirised a Church of England that had lost its way, from the high Anglican priest who still owes his true allegiance to Rome and spends his spare time either cottaging or railing against the ordination of women, via the progressively minded Archdeacon ('Sin isn't a word we use much nowadays'), all the way down to the evangelical parishioners who yearn for 'jollier forms of service in church'. At the centre is the tormented figure of Francis Kreer: 'A married man, for nearly twenty years, he did not love his wife. A priest of the Church of England, he did not believe in God.'

Kreer's life falls apart, he suffers a breakdown and in his madness stumbles upon an extraordinary discovery: the fact that there is a direct correlation between the Bible and *Who's Who*. It's played for tragicomic effect, but by the end of the decade 'the Great *Who's Who* Biblical Conspiracy' would have looked perfectly sane in a world where the best-seller lists included works such as Michael Drosnin's *The Bible Code* (1997). That book argued that the Hebrew Bible was written by extraterrestrials who placed hidden messages in the text, including a prediction that the world would end in 2006. Within days of the al-Qaeda attacks on America in 2001, three of the top five best-selling books on the internet retailer Amazon were by or about the sixteenth-century mystic Nostradamus. It was only a short step to the conspiracies of Dan Brown's *The Da Vinci Code* (2003).

The decline of the Anglican church as a social force had been a long, gradual process, but its virtual disappearance into irrelevancy was painfully apparent in the 1990s. On Easter Monday in 1992 a concert was staged at Wembley Stadium in memory of Freddie Mercury, the singer with Queen, who had died the previous year. At the end of his set, David Bowie spoke of Mercury and of others who had died from AIDS and, grasping for a way to express his feelings, dropped to one knee to recite the Lord's Prayer. There was a time when such a gesture would have been recognised as a communal statement, embracing not only active Christians but pretty much everyone in the country, a ritual of social solidarity; now it was merely embarrassing, for those in the stadium, those watching on television and, it looked, for Bowie himself. Such things were no longer part of the nation's shared language.

The same phenomenon was apparent elsewhere. There had always been a convention, for example, that both the major television channels would screen a religious programme at the same time early on a Sunday evening, the so-called 'Godslot', so that neither would gain an unfair advantage while the other went through the motions of public service broadcasting. But the nature of those programmes had changed, so that the BBC's holy warhorse, *Songs of Praise*, which had been on air since 1961, began introducing more 'human interest' interviews, with a consequent reduction in the number of hymns sung.

In 1993 ITV went further and cancelled its own religious series *Highway*, presented by Harry Secombe, after ten years on air. The decision provoked more letters of complaint to the Independent Television Commission than had any other single issue, but ITV's commercial logic couldn't be doubted. They began to screen instead a feature film early on Sunday evening, increasing the channel's audience share and eclipsing *Songs of Praise* on BBC One. (With less fanfare, Radio 4 also ended *Morning Has Broken*, which used to broadcast hymns early on a Sunday morning.) By the end of the decade the only spiritual dimension to be found on the major channels in prime time was the appearance of Mystic Meg, the *News of the World*'s astrologer, on the draw for the National Lottery.

Elsewhere the mockery of religion, once a taboo subject, had become sufficiently commonplace that it barely merited mention. In 1994 the gay performance troupe the Sisters of Perpetual Indulgence were reported to the Broadcasting Standards Council for a television routine in which they dressed as nuns. The BSC concluded that the performance was 'unlikely to cause widespread offence', and the Sisters issued a press release to apologise for not having done so.

There were still occasional attempts to protect religious sensibilities, as the jeans-manufacturer Diesel discovered in 1998 when it ran a promotional campaign, in places like *Minx* magazine, as well as on the London Underground, that showed nuns and the Virgin Mary wearing jeans, under the slogan: SUPERIOR DENIM. A spokesperson for the company laughed off the complaints that were received — 'Diesel's advertising tends to be on the ironic side and our target customer would understand the advert and not take it literally' — but the Advertising Standards Authority banned the campaign, saying that depicting 'nuns as sexual beings was unacceptable'. By then, of course, the images had done their job.

Less conventional forms of spirituality, however, continued to grow in popularity, a trend reflected not only in the proliferation of New Age non-fiction, but in the massive rise of the fantasy genre. At one end of the market were the satirical fantasies of Terry Pratchett, whose first book, *The Carpet People*, had been published in 1971, and who achieved success with his Discworld series from 1983 onwards. By the 1990s he was regularly hitting the best-seller lists, sometimes twice a year, as well as attracting the backhanded compliment of being the country's most shoplifted author, but Discworld remained essentially a cult. Those who hadn't read any of the books might recognise his name, and perhaps the name of his imagined world, but nothing else; he didn't impact on a general culture in the way that fantasy writers like C.S. Lewis or J.R.R. Tolkien had.

Or indeed as J.K. Rowling was to do. Her first novel, *Harry Potter and the Philosopher's Stone*, was published in June 1997, and by the end of that year had sold 30,000 copies. Thereafter, as word spread, sales really took off and by the time of the fourth volume in the series (*Harry Potter and the Goblet of Fire* in 2000), bookshops were opening at midnight on the day of publication to feed the fan frenzy. The first American printing of 3.8 million was said to be the biggest ever, while the British print run of 1.5 million similarly set a British record. Rowling's success ensured that the novels encountered some hostility, and reports soon emerged of them being banned in Church schools. 'The Bible is clear about issues such as witchcraft, demons, devils and the occult,' explained one head teacher. 'Throughout it insists that God's people should have nothing to do with them.'

For those of a like mind, there were dangers everywhere. In 1993 the Reverend Ian Cook of Manchester had objected to a promotion by Kellogg's in which plastic figures were given away in boxes of Frosties and Weetos cereals. 'Three of them – Astaroth, Lamia and Alu – are actual demon gods,' he complained, saying the campaign was 'grotesque and occult'.

Concern was expressed, too, at the rise of overt paganism. There were said to be a quarter of a million pagans in the country – and Leeds University became, in 1994, the first university in Britain to acquire the services of a pagan priestess to provide spiritual guidance for students – though even devout Christians must have struggled at times to see their activities as being overly sinister. In 1994 a group in Milton Keynes applied to the local council for permission to use a patch of wasteland for their ceremonies, where a small group wished to congregate with lighted candles and an open fire, the latter intended to provide light and 'to warm up food, such as jacket potatoes'. The group's leader portrayed its activities in terms of a very British domesticity: 'If we are denied the right to worship publicly, we are forced to retreat into our homes. This is what happens at the moment, and quite frankly I'm sick of clearing the candle wax off the carpet.'

*

The decline of the mainstream churches was not a new story; having risen during the 1950s, attendance at Anglican services had been in decline ever since. Nonetheless a noticeable marginalisation of religion, a hastening of that decline did occur in the 1990s. In a parallel manner, another long-running narrative was given a new twist as the debate about immigration shaded into a fear of asylum seekers.

This was an issue that occupied a great deal of media attention during the decade, for there had been a rapid rise in the numbers of people who arrived in Britain claiming that, in the words of the 1951 United Nations Convention on Refugees, they had 'a well-founded fear of being persecuted for reasons of race, religion, nationality, membership of a particular social group or political opinion'. In the mid-1980s around 4,000 such people came to Britain each year; by the start of the 1990s this had risen to 20,000 and it continued to increase until it reached a peak of 50,000. Similar increases were being seen all over Europe, particularly in Italy, where a third of Genoa's population was soon reported to comprise recent immigrants, and in Germany where there were 400,000 applications for asylum in 1992 alone, though even these numbers were dwarfed by those seeking refuge in countries like Iran and Pakistan.

Much concern was expressed about this level of immigration and how it might impact upon the nation's coherence. There was also anger at the inability of the system to deal with the number of applications, hampered by a computer system that didn't work as well as had been promised. By the end of the decade nearly 100,000 people were waiting to see whether they would be granted permission to remain in the country. The response by some politicians of both major parties was to present refugees as authors of their own misfortunes, and to talk about a 'flood' of 'bogus' asylum seekers, who were merely seeking refuge from poverty. Measures must and would be taken, the public was assured, to prevent Britain being overwhelmed.

This was considered particularly treacherous terrain for Labour, the assumption on both sides having long been that immigration was an area where the Tories were always stronger. 'Immigration, an issue which we raised successfully in 1992 and in the 1994 Euro-elections campaign, played particularly well in the tabloids and still has the potential to hurt,' wrote Andrew Lansley, the party's director of communications, in a memo leaked to the press in 1995. In fact it hardly played in the subsequent election campaign at all, and warranted barely a mention in the Conservative manifesto, which was more concerned with trumpeting British virtues: 'Tolerance, civility and respect have always been the hallmark of our nation. It is thanks to them that we have an excellent record on race relations.'

If that sounded very much like John Major himself speaking, the same message could also be heard elsewhere. 'I understand Britishness as being outward-looking, open and internationalist,' said Gordon Brown, in a speech in 1998; 'a commitment to democracy and tolerance, to creativity and enterprise and to public service, and to justice or, as we often put it, to fair play.' And, despite the carping about asylum seekers, this was Britain's self-image as it emerged during the 1990s: a country that prided itself on a tolerant diversity, and that saw itself as a modern nation while still cherishing its past.

It was striking, however, that culturally so much of that diversity was rooted in the country's former colonies, with increasing visibility for minorities who had hitherto been seen as peripheral. The decade saw, for example, not only the wave of British Asian films, but also the emergence of musicians including Cornershop, Asian Dub Foundation and Apache Indian, and television comedies like *The Real McCoy* (1991) and *Goodness Gracious Me* (1998, following its radio debut two years earlier), while the nation's favourite boxer was the world featherweight champion Prince Naseem Hamed, born in Sheffield to Yemeni parents. But there was no comparable embrace by the mainstream of the European heritage, a fact that continued to irritate forward-thinking politicians.

Frustration with this lack of interest in Europe was evident in a speech made in 2001 by Robin Cook about Britain's membership of the EU. 'I do not accept that to acknowledge our European identity diminishes our Britishness,' he argued. 'None of our European partners, with their own proud national traditions, seem afflicted by this self-doubt and insecurity.' That, at least, was the message that Cook wished to put across, though actually the part of his speech that received the widest coverage related yet again to the theme of national identity, and the tension between past, present and future. 'Chicken tikka masala is now Britain's true national dish,' he explained, 'not only because it is the most popular, but because it is a perfect illustration of the way Britain absorbs and adapts external influences.'

It was as good an image as any had come up with to symbolise the new Britain, though he didn't draw the obvious conclusion, that the influence of the former Empire remained more powerful than that of Europe. In any event, he had already gone too far for some. Tony Blair was said to have regarded the speech as 'a "catastrophic intervention" because it seemed to want to dump our history'.

PART TWO

NEW ANGELS OF PROMISE
1997–2001

If there's such a thing as reincarnation, I hope Tony Blair comes back as a politician.
Bernard Manning (1996)

What we want to know is what kind of society this government is trying to create.
Barbara Castle (1998)

The strangest Tory ever sold.
The Economist (1998)

10
Enter Tony Blair
'I bet this is as good as it gets'

A media-friendly, highly electable platoon of smiling, capitalist thugs.
Peter Baynham (1997)

The Blair government is mostly government by bilateral meeting.
Donald Dewar (1998)

I think the [Conservative] Party will slowly destroy itself.
Alan Clark (1997)

Like so many of the country's dealings with the Continent, Britain's involvement in the Eurovision Song Contest has been a patchy, semi-detached affair. The event was created by the European Broadcasting Union and first staged in 1956, but the UK was not represented that year. It had meant to participate, but failed to get its timings right; the contest was held in May, while the Festival of British Popular Song, which was intended to choose the British entry, didn't happen until October. The UK entered in 1957, but then was absent again; only from 1959 did the country become fully committed to the event, televising it every year and sending in songs which might not have been at the cutting edge of pop music, but were at least competent. And for some while, Britain was a major Eurovision power, averaging a third-place finish and winning the competition four times in fifteen years from 1967.

That run ended with the success of Bucks Fizz's 'Making Your Mind Up' in 1981, a year when Margaret Thatcher was busily handbagging the European Community, securing a rebate on British contributions to the EC and showing no sign of wishing to be seen as a good European. Offence was taken, the Eurovision gods were displeased, and over the subsequent fifteen-year period the UK slid to an average sixth place, with no winners at all. Even when established chart acts like Michael Ball or Sonia were entered, they failed to carry off the prize.

The contest had never been very highly regarded; as far back as 1960 Maurice Richardson, the *Observer*'s television critic, had described the broadcast as 'torture', and later in the decade Michael Billington was to wonder in *The Times* whether, given the homogenised Europop sound of the entries, he was 'listening to twenty-two singers with one song or twenty-two songs rendered by one singer'. Now, however, the public perception of the contest fell into disrepute, reduced in Britain to the level of a laughing-stock. During those fifteen lean years the highlight for many viewers became the commentary of Terry Wogan, relentlessly mocking the songs, the clothes, the voting and the event itself.

By 1997, then, there was little expectation of entertainment, let alone victory. 'Each year you say this is dreadful, but there is always next year,' remarked Wogan in the build-up. 'Well, now it is next year and it is worse.' Britain's entry was the bookies' third favourite, 'Love Shine a Light' by Katrina and the Waves, a group whose sole top twenty hit ('Walking on Sunshine') had been in 1985, and whose continued existence came as something of a surprise even to those who thought they knew about pop music. It was an unusually strong song, written by the band's guitarist, Kimberley Rew, formerly of cult favourites the Soft Boys, but that meant little in this context.

Much more important was the fact that the contest was staged on 3 May, the day after it became clear that the Conservative government had fallen; its replacement, Tony Blair's Labour Party, were widely believed to be bent on reversing the country's Eurosceptic history. Clearly things had changed, and that night in Dublin the goodwill towards Britain was unstoppable. Katrina and the Waves scored a record number of maximum points, a record points tally and a record margin of victory.

The result was accepted in the manner it had been delivered: as an endorsement of the new government. 'Britain proudly took centre stage in Europe last night,' opened the *Daily Mirror*'s report, while Michael Leggo, the head of BBC entertainment, who was now to be responsible for hosting the next event, seemed to be confused about which competition he was staging: 'We are delighted to be bringing the contest back after an absence of eighteen years,' he declared, evidently forgetting that it had only been sixteen years, and that his eighteen took us back instead to the last Labour government. And in a manner that was to become all too familiar, Tony Blair was amongst the first to leap in with his congratulations. 'It's been a long time since Britain was walking on sunshine,' he enthused. 'Britain is now well and truly back in the spotlight.'

The Eurovision triumph was no isolated incident. On the day before polling, the French daily paper *Libération* had dedicated thirty-four of its forty pages to an account of Britain, including fashion, the arts and sport, but focusing on the election. 'If Blair succeeds in power,' commented the editor, 'we will have hope.' Helmut Kohl talked of his impression that 'the Labour Party is the one that is more Euro-friendly', and Jacques Santer, president of the European Commission, urged greater involvement: 'Never more than now has the EU needed strong British commitment, with its unique combination of pragmatism and efficiency.' In a speech in 1995 Blair had made his intentions clear – 'I have no doubt at all that the future of my country lies in being at the heart of Europe' – and although John Major had used exactly the same phrase at the start of his premiership, Britain's European partners believed that this time it was sincere.

The Foreign Office, embarrassed for many years by the Conservatives' detached attitude to Europe, was said to be ecstatic at the election result, with one diplomat quoted as saying of the new foreign secretary: 'If Robin Cook went into negotiations in Brussels dressed as a clown, refusing to speak any language other than Swahili and ended the day by urinating in the German chancellor's coffee, his negotiating stance would still be seen as an improvement over his predecessors.' Some of this enthusiasm survived the early days, so that when a poll was conducted in France in March 1998, shortly after Blair had addressed the National Assembly (speaking much better French than any of his predecessors since Anthony Eden), it found that he would win a majority in that country as well.

Acclaim abroad was more than matched by a sense of euphoria at home. 'This was our Velvet Revolution, and yesterday the population went wild,' reported Matthew Engel in the *Guardian*, seeking to draw comparisons with the overthrow of communism in Czechoslovakia. 'There was an almost tangible sense of enjoyment,' wrote David Blunkett in his diary, 'the sheer exhilaration of people revelling in the feeling that the Tories had disappeared – as if the whole nation was letting out a huge sigh of relief.' As Peter Hain summed it up: 'It was a joy to be Labour that spring.' Even the opposition observed the same phenomenon. 'A great sigh of relief seems to have gone up across Britain at the removal of the Tories,' noted Paddy Ashdown. 'Tony starts his prime ministership with a tidal wave of hope and goodwill behind him.'

Seldom in modern times had a new government been elected with such optimism and enthusiasm; one had to go back – the inevitable comparison – to the days of Harold Wilson in 1964. It was all too much for some, almost unbelievable. 'I am sure we will all wake up in the morning and find that the Tories have won again,' said David Miliband, at the victory celebration.

The media too were well satisfied. Like their readers, viewers and listeners, they were bored with stories about the travails of the Major government. At the very least, they were happy to find a new narrative, and in more liberal quarters, the joy was unconfined. Jane Garvey, then a presenter on BBC Radio 5 Live, recalled arriving for work on the morning after the election and encountering the detritus of what had clearly been some serious celebrations: 'The corridors of Broadcasting House were strewn with empty champagne bottles.'

There was undoubtedly an abundance of positive energy, but given Blair's stated objective – 'the journey's end had always been changing the country' – the real question was the one posed by Giles Radice: 'What will Tony's success consist of: election victories or something more permanent? The jury is out.'

'When Tony Blair came to power,' reflected the writing team on the Channel 4 programme *Rory Bremner, Who Else?*, 'we thought, "That's it. What on earth are we going to do now?"' They weren't alone. John Major's government had, after a hesitant start, proved such a rich source of material for comedians and satirists that there was some confusion about where to go from here. *Drop the Dead Donkey* disappeared entirely in the election year of 1997, and although it returned for a final short series of six episodes the following year, this was only a brief revival in which it concentrated most of its fire on the media, with a story arc concerning the imminent closure of Globelink News. Similarly Armando Iannucci's *Armistice* series was absent in 1997, save for its election night special.

Private Eye was to come up with the 'St Albion Parish News', mocking Blair as a trendy vicar – a figure which proved durable enough to survive into his more self-righteous incarnation – but initially it too struggled to find an appropriate tone. An early attempt showed the new prime minister posing with an electric guitar as the lead singer of a pop band called Blairzone: 'Hey listen – me and the band are going to put together a totally new sound,' he enthused. 'Not so new that you don't like it but more a sort of classical progressive rock fusion sound – like Barclay James Harvest's "Galadriel" – remember that?' New Labour might be laughably light on policy, might have sold its heritage in pursuit of power, might be, in the words of Iannucci, 'the party of the left that bashed the unions, was tough on spending, is in the pockets of media barons and is run by flash southern bastards who'll privatise anything that moves', but even so it was seen to represent a break from the morality-free zone of Conservative sleaze. And, despite the repeated playing down of expectations, there remained the belief that the party represented a fundamental change after eighteen years of Tory government.

The man in whom so many hopes were now vested seemed a very different proposition from his predecessor as prime minister. Tony Blair's privileged background, complete with private education and Oxford degree, was a long way removed from John Major's childhood in South London, but there were points of connection, in particular their family history in entertainment. Blair's paternal grandparents had, like Major's father, been stalwarts of the music halls: Celia Ridgway as a dancer and Charles Parsons, her third husband (though they were unmarried at the time of the birth of Blair's father), as a comedian who called himself Jimmy Lynton. It was in his grandfather's honour that Blair was gifted his middle names, Charles Lynton. Major was similarly bequeathed a stage name; his father's real name was Tom Ball, only adding the Major when he formed a double-act called Drum and Major. The music hall roots were even of similar vintage, Jimmy Lynton being born just eight years after Tom Major-Ball.

Those roots expressed themselves in both men, but while it took the 1992 election to get Major onto his soapbox playing to the crowd, Blair followed the more conventional, self-indulgent path of a middle-class man of his generation. 'I have always been crazy about rock music,' he later commented, and while at Oxford in the early 1970s he sang with a student group, named Ugly Rumours, also featuring the future music journalist Mark Ellen on bass. 'We were rather tragic, and had precisely zero presence on stage,' remembered Ellen. 'We were yards of unconditioned hair in cowboy boots.' Blair sported a cut-off T-shirt to reveal his midriff as he posed like Mick Jagger, though the setlist was dominated by covers of West Coast American bands like the Eagles and the Doobie Brothers, and his voice was described by his future wife (one of the few people to have a tape of the band) as 'reedy'. There appears to have been little serious intent in the venture, nor in Blair's vague attempts to promote rock gigs in London, but he showed more commitment to the project than he ever did to student politics.

There was a show-business element too in his marriage in 1980 to Cherie, daughter of Tony Booth, the actor who appeared in the *Confessions* movies and whose best-known role was as Mike, the socialist son-in-law of working-class Tory Alf Garnett in the sitcom *Till Death Us Do Part*. By this stage, the long hair and the bared midriff had been consigned to history; Blair was an active member of the Labour Party, was working as a lawyer, having reverted to more immediate family precedent – his father had practised and lectured in law – and was beginning to think about Parliament.

His first opportunity came at the 1982 Beaconsfield by-election, held during the course of the Falklands War. Largely as a result of that conflict, it turned out to be the only by-election in the eighteen years of Conservative rule that saw a swing to the government, but perhaps more significant was the homogenisation of the main candidates. All three main parties were represented by men with 'a civilised, middle class pedigree', reported the *Guardian*. 'Three Oxford-educated chaps, considerably dressed and properly spoken, all from decent public schools.' Anthony Blair, as he was then known, didn't exactly stand out from the crowd, and he lost his deposit.

The following year he was parachuted into a safe seat in Sedgefield, County Durham for the 1983 general election and was ready to start working his way to the top. He shared an office at Westminster with another newly elected MP, Gordon Brown, and the pair were identified early on as future stars of the parliamentary party, not least by Peter Mandelson, who took every opportunity to place them on view in the media. Both men voted for the fashionable candidate, Neil Kinnock, in the leadership election held shortly after their arrival in the Commons, and both threw themselves into the campaign to ditch the left-wing image that Labour had acquired during the ascendancy of Tony Benn. Often seen in these years as being almost joined at the hip, there were key differences; unlike Brown, Blair had not been born into the movement — his father, once a communist, had long since been a staunch Conservative — and his background was of a kind to cause suspicion in a party that still genuflected to proletarian purism. He had to work harder than his friend and colleague to shed some of his past; it was noticeable, for example, that he was no longer Anthony, just plain Tony.

Of the two, Brown was acknowledged by everyone — including Blair himself — as the senior; a potential leader who was capable of ferocious performances in the Commons, he had age, experience and expectation on his side, and was elected to the shadow cabinet by his fellow MPs a year earlier than was Blair. He was also regarded as the intellectual heavyweight, although much was to be made in later years by Blair's supporters of their man's unflinching re-examination of where the party should stand. 'I developed a theory about the basis of socialism being about "community",' Blair explained in his memoirs; 'i.e. people owed obligations to each other and were social beings, not only individuals out for themselves.' The word 'theory' seemed a little grandiose.

As the defeats for the party continued to mount up, however, it was Blair's distance from a traditional Labour image that increasingly attracted the approval of colleagues and opponents alike. 'He could be one of us,' wrote Gyles Brandreth in his diary in May 1993: 'public school, Oxford, decent, amiable, well groomed, no known convictions.' That use of Margaret Thatcher's favourite phrase of approval — 'one of us' — was carefully judged. Labour in the 1980s, for all its left-wing image in the media, had seldom looked like a genuinely radical party; rather it spent most of its time desperately defending the status quo against the assaults of the Conservative government. Blair, however, leant towards the Thatcherite model of activity at all times, perpetually looking for roots that might be torn up, even if he had little insight into what might be put in their place.

The showbiz element had never quite left him, but as leader it was channelled into his major speeches to the annual conference and elsewhere, occasions that appeared to be treated with a degree of serious preparation not always in evidence when it came to detailed policy-making. He no longer looked like a rock star manqué, though he was clearly conscious that, by the standards of politics, he was a good-looking man. 'Tony Blair is the first prime minister I can completely imagine having voluntary sex with,' drooled Bridget Jones, and she wasn't the only one. A poll in *Forum* found that Blair was the sexiest man in British politics (not a particularly competitive field) and when, in the summer of 1997, the women's pages of the *Sun* ran their annual poll for the 'top 100 hunks', he came in as a new entry at number sixty-five, one place ahead of Brett Anderson of Suede, though he was a couple of places behind David Essex and a long way off the pace set by David Beckham, who had supplanted George Clooney in the top spot.

Beyond Blair himself, the new Parliamentary Labour Party looked very different from any that had gone before and, at first sight, much more like the country it represented. The impact of all-women shortlists, about which Blair had been sceptical at best, had paid dividends: the number of women in the Commons more than doubled, from 57 to 120, the overwhelming majority of them on the government benches (the Conservatives had fewer women MPs than in 1992). Amongst the beneficiaries of the shortlist policy were Maria Eagle, whose twin sister Angela was already an MP; Anne Begg, a 32-year-old teacher who suffered from Gaucher disease, a degenerative cell disorder, and who became the first wheelchair user elected to Parliament; and Gisela Stuart, a 41-year-old lecturer of Czech-German parentage who was born in Bavaria and had come to Britain at the age of seventeen.

Stuart's cosmopolitan background was matched by that of Rudi Vis, a 46-year-old Dutch-born lecturer who took Finchley and Golders Green, incorporating Margaret Thatcher's old seat of Finchley. Pleasure was found too in the election in Exeter of Ben Bradshaw, a gay 36-year-old BBC reporter, who recorded the biggest swing in the South-West. This was at the expense of Dr Adrian Rogers, the director of the Conservative Family Institute, who had used the campaign to denounce homosexuality as a 'sterile, disease-ridden, God-forsaken occupation' and had referred to his rival as 'Bent Ben'; one Conservative election leaflet had warned that if Bradshaw won 'schoolchildren would be in danger'. And if his sexuality weren't bad enough, Bradshaw unashamedly outed himself as 'a European who can speak German and Italian'.

Labour in 1997 looked and sounded like a different party from any that had previously governed in Britain. It was more diverse in terms of ethnicity, gender and declared sexuality, and – under the youngest prime minister since Lord Liverpool in 1812 – it was more youthful too. Indeed the average age of MPs after the election was just forty-seven. (The Tories meanwhile could also claim to have changed; for the first time in three hundred years, there was no Old Harrovian MP to be seen.)

Whatever encouragement might have been taken from these outward signs of diversity, however, was not to last. Despite the increased number of women elected, they still amounted to fewer than one in five of MPs and, particularly on the Labour side, there was a media tendency to see them as a single amorphous block, collectively nicknamed by the press 'Blair's babes', a term that started out patronising and swiftly became derogatory. Within a few months, the Labour MP Brian Sedgemore was dismissing them as 'the Stepford Wives, those female New Labour MPs who've had the chip inserted into their brain to keep them on-message'. In the same speech, Sedgemore made similarly dismissive comments about 'all New Labour MPs', and though those remarks were less well reported, he had a point, for it rapidly became clear that it didn't really matter much what the parliamentary party looked like, let alone thought.

A very different approach to government was soon in evidence, one in which – given the massive size of the majority – MPs barely counted as lobby-fodder, and even the cabinet itself was of little significance. All the crucial decisions were instead to be taken by the intimate groups that surrounded Tony Blair and Gordon Brown, very few members of which had any claim to electoral legitimacy. Blair's confidants included his childhood friend and diary secretary Anji Hunter, his former flatmate Charlie Falconer and his political secretary Sally Morgan. There was also, as chief of staff, Jonathan Powell, a former diplomat (and brother of Margaret Thatcher's foreign policy adviser, Charles) who Blair had met during that 1993 trip to Washington. 'Tony was wise enough to take advice from lots of different people,' remarked Powell, with no apparent trace of irony: 'from Alastair Campbell and Peter Mandelson, but also from John Burton, his constituency agent, Gail, his mother-in-law, and Jackie, his children's nanny.'

The future had been spelt out in Blair's first public remarks as prime minister elect outside the Royal Festival Hall victory party in the early morning of 2 May 1997. 'A new dawn has broken, has it not?' he began, in a phrase that he later claimed to regret, not because it was so terribly trite, but because it might have raised unrealistic expectations of what he was capable of delivering. The crucial proclamation came a few moments later: 'We have been elected as New Labour and we will govern as New Labour.' An inadvertent echo of Neil Kinnock at the Sheffield rally in 1992 ('We will govern as we have campaigned'), as a statement of intent this related to style more than it did to substance, promising a continuation of the centralised control structure that had brought the party to power.

In pursuit of the New Labour project, the key relationships were between the inner circles and the media. The shadow cabinet, on the other hand, was effectively sidelined. Neither Blair nor Brown had shown much enthusiasm for the body even as shadow ministers under Kinnock ('They didn't always turn up,' a colleague remembered), just as Blair had been reprimanded for his non-attendance at meetings of the parliamentary party.

During his own leadership, the shadow cabinet had met, but Blair had been continually irritated by the way that its proceedings found their way into the press, presumably as a result of unauthorised briefings. 'I'll have to tell them that if they cannot be trusted to have serious discussions in the shadow cabinet, we won't have them,' Blair huffed in 1995. Given how much damage Labour was doing to the Major government by the judicious use of leaks from within Conservative ranks, such caution was perhaps understandable, if undesirable. Less tolerated should have been the continuation of the practice into government, when cabinet meetings were downgraded still further. 'They're a farce,' remarked Ivor Richard, leader of the House of Lords, in 1998; 'nobody says anything.' Lance Price, one of Blair's spin doctors, attended a meeting of the cabinet in 1999 and concluded that all he had learnt from the experience was 'how little real influence it has as an institution'. When someone tentatively suggested that a decision might be made, Blair replied: 'Oh, I don't think we should go that far.'

The inherent problem with a cabinet, of course, whether shadow or real, was that it shared power between its members, leaving its leader with the basic principle that his position was that of 'first among equals'. Since Blair didn't wish this to be true in his own case, it was self-evidently a system desperately in need of reform. Peter Mandelson addressed the issue in his 1996 book *The Blair Revolution* (co-written with Roger Liddle), arguing that 'The cabinet is a rather inflexible body', and that decisions should rather be taken in 'bilateral and ad-hoc meetings'. As Will Hutton pointed out in a review of the book: 'No prizes for guessing who plans to attend as many ad hoc meetings as possible.'

Mandelson, officially at that stage no more than a backbench opposition MP, was indeed at the heart of New Labour policy- and decision-making and, initially at least, was the figure who attracted the greatest public and press attention. He had been instrumental in the creation of New Labour, assisting Neil Kinnock's repositioning of the party as well as playing a central role in Blair's election as leader. Never entirely satisfied with a position of power backstage, however, Mandelson craved the spotlight and in 1990 had resigned as the party's director of communications to seek a parliamentary seat of his own.

To tide him over and to help fund that ambition, he got a part-time job on the *People* newspaper writing a column under the heading 'People in Power'. It was not a notable success and few went to it in search of political wisdom. Just three days before Black Wednesday in 1992, Mandelson was to be found staunchly defending John Smith's muddle-headed opposition to the possibility of devaluing sterling, though he also made room to comment on a reported romance between singer Barbra Streisand and tennis player Andre Agassi: 'If he's game, and she's set, it should make quite a match.' Some years later, Alastair Campbell was to confess that not only had he helped Mandelson get the job, he had also churned out some of this guff himself. 'Writing was never his strong point,' nudged Campbell; 'he had to look to his friends to help him out. Know what I mean?'

After the election victory of 1997, many continued to see Mandelson as the power behind the throne, though in reality his great days were already past, the kingmaker now become merely another courtier, vying for his master's ear alongside new favourites. Nonetheless, his public image as the pantomime baddie was important in those early days, helping to deflect criticism from Blair himself. In 1995 the ever-outspoken Brian Sedgemore claimed that Mandelson was disliked right across the parliamentary party: 'The level of hatred is consistent throughout every geographical area and cuts across gender, class, social background and occupation.' As Mandelson himself put it: 'They dare not attack Tony Blair directly, so they go for the next best thing, which they think is me.'

While not disagreeing with that perception, the journalist Frank Johnson believed that it stemmed ultimately from a sense of self-disgust amongst Labour MPs. Mandelson was the man identified with the changes Labour had made in order to become electable, but 'they do not like to be reminded of that. Mr Mandelson's presence reminds them of it all the time.' Rather more direct was the attitude of Harry Enfield, as relayed on *Have I Got News For You*. 'You're ghastly,' Enfield was reported to have drunkenly said to Mandelson at a Downing Street party in 1997. 'No one likes you. You should go. You're horrible.' As Max Clifford, who knew a thing or two about being disliked, observed of Mandelson: 'The public views him as slimy and he only has himself to blame.'

Fast eclipsing Mandelson as Blair's right-hand man was Campbell himself, whose job title of press secretary merely hinted at his position. 'He was indispensable, irreplaceable, almost an alter ego,' gushed Blair in his memoirs, valuing the instinctive tabloid touch of a man who had graduated from writing for *Forum* magazine to being a political journalist on the *Daily Mirror* and *Today*. There were others, even in opposition, however, who felt that the relationship between the two men was not entirely healthy. Joy Johnson, formerly the political news editor of the BBC, spent just under a year as Labour's director of communications, and compared Campbell's role unfavourably with that of Margaret Thatcher's press secretary in the 1980s. 'When you heard Bernard Ingham speaking, you heard Margaret Thatcher,' she noted, 'and when you heard Margaret Thatcher speaking you heard Margaret Thatcher. When you heard Tony Blair, very often you heard Alastair Campbell.'

Ingham himself regarded Campbell and his henchmen as a new development in British politics. 'They're bullies,' he cried. 'They break every rule. I'd have been thrown out on my ear in a minute if I'd tried any of it. They're an appalling bunch.' Max Clifford wasn't much impressed either: 'It seems that either his position went to his head, or he didn't understand the fundamentals of PR, because instead he upset a lot of people and only fed stories to his friends, which anyone can do and requires absolutely no skill.' Nor were they alone in voicing early doubts. In 1996 the notoriously litigious Conservative MP Rupert Allason brought a libel case against Campbell and the *Daily Mirror*. The case was lost, but not before the judge had expressed serious reservations about Campbell's conduct, saying he was 'less than completely open and frank', and adding: 'He did not impress me as a witness in whom I could feel one hundred per cent confidence.'

Those opinions did nothing to impede Campbell's rise to eminence within Blair's camp at the expense of Mandelson, a fact that Mandelson clearly resented. In his diaries, Campbell recorded an inconsequential argument between the two of them about what their leader should wear for a photo-opportunity, a dispute that rapidly developed into a row and coming to blows before Blair was obliged to step in to separate them. 'He went off,' reported Campbell, 'still shouting at me from the corridor, saying I was undermining him and Tony.'

Both men were effectively competing for the same post, that of chief spin doctor to the prime minister. And since spin was at the heart of New Labour, the job was of some significance. 'If "spin" means presenting your policies and your programme as coherently as possible when others have every intention of distorting it, then I'm all for it,' remarked David Blunkett, but of course that wasn't what it meant. It also involved manipulation, dissembling and obfuscation. As Mandelson once explained, the objective of the spin doctor was 'to create the truth'.

Rivalries like that between Campbell and Mandelson were far from uncommon in the higher echelons of the Labour government. Campbell had problems with Clare Short ('he couldn't stand her,' observed Blair); John Prescott hated Harriet Harman and fell out with David Blunkett ('a rift gradually opened between us,' noted the latter); and neither Prescott, Blunkett nor Jack Straw got on with Gordon Brown ('they don't trust him,' according to Campbell). Meanwhile the enmity between Brown and Robin Cook, dating back to their days as the bright young things of the Scottish Labour Party in the 1970s, was described by the *Guardian* as 'one of the most bitter feuds in British politics'.

And Brown, of course, hardly spoke to Mandelson, who he believed had stabbed him in the back in the 1994 leadership election; like their 1960s namesakes Peter and Gordon, they lived in a world without love. The grudge was perpetuated by Brown's own spin doctor, Charlie Whelan who, like Mandelson, had in his early years been involved in the Communist Party, where factionalism and splits were *de rigueur*. Meanwhile Cherie Blair hated Brown and all his circle. None of it was exactly comradely, as Clare Short pointed out. 'We can't go on carving each other up,' she lamented in 1996. 'You have to behave in a way that you preach.' Her words were wasted. As one civil servant drily remarked of the new government: 'We found that some of them really weren't very nice to each other at all.'

Above everything else there was the split between Blair and Brown, the two men who had once been so close that they were nicknamed 'Pushmi-pullyu' by other MPs, in reference to the two-headed llama in the 1967 film *Doctor Dolittle*. Millions of words were to be written analysing their fractious relationship, though at heart the issue was very simple, as Blair recognised: 'The truth is I got the leadership and he wanted it.' Other issues crept into the dispute, from the personal (Blair's choice of Jack Straw to manage his leadership campaign) to the political (Blair overruling Brown's wish to introduce a top rate of income tax at 50 per cent) to the downright trivial (a dispute over who was going to use the soundbite 'Labour's coming home'), but the essence remained the same. Brown resented the fact that he had been overtaken by his younger colleague.

And so, for more than a decade after that leadership contest, Brown staged a slow-motion mutiny against the elected leader of his party, while Blair appeared to do nothing to resolve the issue. On the one side, there was bitterness and hostility, on the other, fear and indecision. The result was an uneasy, unsatisfactory compromise, by which Brown was installed as chancellor of the exchequer and was to remain there for the duration of Blair's premiership.

Little of the dispute was rooted in policy or philosophy. 'There is but a cigarette paper between the politics of Brown and Blair,' wrote Polly Toynbee in 1996, but ultimately that didn't matter, for 'most of politics is far more about personal rivalry, jealousy and suspicion than usually gets reported'. If there was a difference between the two men, it was temperamental, not political, and lay more in their attitude towards the past than the future. Brown saw himself as part of the continuing romance of the Labour movement – a character in a new chapter perhaps, but not the author of a new volume – while Blair was eager to make a complete break. That was sufficient for many in the party, who saw in Brown a hope for the left, once Blair had worked his electoral magic; concrete evidence of difference was hard to find, but there was a tribal loyalty to be discerned in Brown's speeches. In 1995 the comedian Caroline Aherne, in her character as chat show host Mrs Merton, asked Ken Livingstone a beautifully barbed question: 'Which would you prefer to be – leader of the Labour Party or prime minister?' Brown, one assumed, would have chosen the former, Blair the latter.

Consequently the language they used, the names cited as inspirations, the poses that were struck – these things sometimes varied, even if they led to no real divergence on what should be done now. Brown specialised in broad policy, Blair in warm generalities, but neither was at home with detail. Blair liked to talk about the radical centre, Brown of being a progressive, but both refrained from referring to socialism; similarly both avoided mention of the working class, favouring the much woollier 'hard-working families', a phrase imported from America. For a decade they had made for a complementary team; now, once victory was assured, that was being thrown away, and it was hard not to lay most of the blame at Brown's door. 'You can't go on just sulking,' Blair told him in mid-1995, but it appeared that he could and would.

Like Blair, Brown surrounded himself with courtiers who lacked any power base of their own and were dependent solely on their master's patronage. Similar circles accompanied key figures elsewhere in New Labour, with diminishing returns as they got further away from Blair himself. 'John is hopelessly insecure, ever afraid of being shown up by one of his underlings,' Chris Mullin was warned when he became a minister in John Prescott's vast empire at the newly created Department of the Environment, Transport and the Regions. Once in office, he discovered the reality of departmental meetings helmed by Prescott: 'Our main role is to laugh sycophantically at his jokes. This is how it must be at the court of Boris Yeltsin.'

The turf war at the heart of New Labour firmly entered the public domain in January 1998 when Paul Routledge published a biography of Brown, with the cooperation of its subject and his intimate circle. For the first time, the extent of the feud between Blair and Brown became known not merely to the public, but also to many within the party, who hadn't realised how bad things had become. 'I certainly think it was unwise of Gordon to talk to Routledge,' wrote Giles Radice in his diary. 'It suggests that he is still nursing a grudge.'

Indeed he was, and the book spelt out the chancellor's account of the pair's shared history, hinging on that dinner in Granita. Blair had always promised Brown a clear run in any leadership election; Brown only yielded on the point in order to preserve party unity; and the price for his non-candidature was that 'He would have full charge of economic policy and a powerful influence across the range of social policy.' All three points were fiercely disputed by Blair's followers: there was no such agreement, Brown didn't stand because he knew he would lose, and no deal was made. The book, said one Blair supporter, was 'deliberately reopening old wounds to refight a battle that was never actually fought, because Gordon never stood'.

Those anonymous briefings against Brown began appearing even before the book was published. On the day the first extracts were serialised in *The Times*, Brown himself was to be found in Eastbourne, attending the wedding of the next generation's most powerful Labour couple, Ed Balls and Yvette Cooper, an event covered by Routledge in his day job as political correspondent of the *Independent on Sunday* (he noted that the bride and groom wore Vivienne Westwood and Hugo Boss respectively). But back in London, members of the Blair camp, when not 'screaming abuse' at their counterparts in the Brown team, were working overtime behind the scenes to seize back the initiative. Their efforts paid off the following weekend, when Andrew Rawnsley in the *Observer* quoted 'someone who has an extremely good claim to know the mind of the prime minister' as saying that Brown had 'psychological flaws'.

That comment was immediately attributed to Alastair Campbell, though he denied authorship, and the phrase was considered sufficiently apposite that it remained attached to Brown for the rest of his political career. Cherie Blair was later quoted as saying of the remark: 'That was an understatement.' Her preferred formulation was that Brown was 'fucked up'. Meanwhile Donald Dewar, the secretary of state for Scotland, was privately voicing his opinion that although Brown had 'the finest mind in British politics', he was an 'incomplete character'. A decade later Robert Harris, the novelist and former friend of Blair, suggested a more specific diagnosis, writing that Brown 'suffers from a kind of political Asperger's syndrome. Intellectually brilliant, he sometimes seems socially barely functional: a little bit odd.' Even if all this were true, however, Charlie Whelan had a point when he complained that Blair's camp were not exactly helping government stability: 'We can't have someone in Number Ten briefing that the chancellor is bonkers. It's fucking madness.'

The perception that there was something slightly strange about Brown had been around for some time, though a lot of the speculation had previously been fixated on his bachelor status, with several in Westminster asserting 'as a fact' that he was gay. In 1996, while still shadow chancellor, Brown had appeared on the Radio 4 programme *Desert Island Discs*, where he was questioned by presenter Sue Lawley about his private life and why he was neither married nor known to have a steady partner: 'People want to know whether you're gay or whether there's some flaw in your personality.' Brown was understandably tetchy in his reply: 'Look, I don't have to answer these questions.' But he did go on to say: 'I'm not married. It just hasn't happened. I hope it does. It may yet. It probably will do.'

The incident caused a minor controversy. Diana Wong, whose late husband Roy Plomley had created *Desert Island Discs*, and who owned the rights to the show's format, expressed her displeasure at the intrusive line of questioning, while the actor Michael Cashman, a gay rights activist and future Labour MEP, also objected, on the grounds that there was no issue of 'hypocrisy' here: 'If Gordon Brown had sought to discriminate against homosexuals in his economic policies, then issues pertaining to his sexuality would be pertinent.'

The interview cast an interesting sidelight on life in modern Britain, where an apparent lack of interest in sex had become suspect, and where it was now permissible to demand details of someone's sexual proclivities. It also fuelled stories that Blair's camp was responsible for spreading the rumours about Brown's supposed homosexuality. ('I told Gordon ages ago,' Blair was reported to have said at the time of the leadership election in 1994, 'that he could not be leader of the party without a wife and kids.') The truth, that Brown was an intensely shy and private person who had no wish to expose himself to media scrutiny, didn't seem an immediately obvious option. Yet in an era when most politicians leapt at the opportunity to flaunt their families at photo-opportunities, his insistence on maintaining a strict division between his personal and public lives was amongst his most endearing attributes.

'I don't try to be secretive,' Brown insisted, but it was hard to avoid the impression that he did. When the *Express on Sunday* reported in January 1997 that he had become engaged to his girlfriend, Sarah Macaulay, he was quick to produce a flat denial: 'It's nonsense,' he said, and the story disappeared for a little. When the couple did marry, in August 2000, it was in a private ceremony held in his own front room in Scotland. Tony Blair was not present, having been informed only the day before of the imminent wedding, and nor were any other stars of the political firmament. Nonetheless, the relationship did link Brown to the left-leaning elite of North London: Macaulay had been a pupil at Camden School for Girls, whose other alumni included Fiona Miller, now married to Alastair Campbell, and Nina Temple, the last general secretary of the Communist Party of Great Britain. More recently, she had, after the collapse of one public relations firm, founded another in partnership with the daughter of the Marxist historian Eric Hobsbawm.

By contrast with Brown's lack of disclosure, Blair was ostentatiously a family man. Cherie was the most visible prime ministerial spouse there had been; the closest that Britain had ever come to having a First Lady on the American model, she existed in a different world from that inhabited by Norma Major, who had shunned the spotlight whenever possible. The Blairs were the first couple to bring up children in Downing Street, and in 2000 added to their number a fourth child, Leo, conceived – as Cherie explained in her autobiography – at Balmoral, on a trip for which she 'had not packed my contraceptive equipment, out of sheer embarrassment'. That self-proclaimed modesty was not apparent in her book, nor in her husband's memoirs, which contained an account of their sex on the night after John Smith's death. 'I needed that love Cherie gave me,' he remembered. 'I was an animal following my instinct.'

The public flaunting of Blair's personal life was not entirely to Brown's taste. 'The whole issue of my being a family man is very sensitive to him,' Blair admitted to his wife, and it became yet another source of tension. The attempt to keep the split between the two men from public view was unsuccessful. Repeated denials of any division — claims that it was the 'froth of politics', whipped up by the media — were met with frank disbelief, and as leading figures in the New Labour world began publishing their memoirs and diaries some years later, the full horror, the sullen insolence with which Brown treated the man he referred to in person simply as 'Blair', was gradually revealed. 'In retrospect, we probably should have made it public,' wrote Blair's chief of staff, Jonathan Powell, in 2010, 'but the moment never seemed quite right. We were fighting a form of asymmetric warfare. Gordon seemed to be prepared, if necessary, to burn down the citadel in order to capture it.'

The continual denials that any problem existed did nothing to resolve the issue, and Blair's approach in private was equally irresolute, as Powell acknowledged: 'His way of managing Gordon was to string him along indefinitely without ever addressing frontally the difficult issue of who was in charge.' Blair prided himself on being a strong leader, willing to make tough choices; his failure to deal with Brown's insubordination was an early indication of a weakness that was to mar his premiership.

In the immediate aftermath of the election victory, however, such questions seemed insignificant. And initially it was Brown who had the biggest announcement to make, even if it hadn't been solely his idea.

The concept that the Bank of England should determine the level of interest rates, free from the dictates of the chancellor of the exchequer, had been around for some time. Tony Blair said that he had first been persuaded of the case in the mid-1980s, listening to Roy Jenkins arguing for it in the House of Commons, and within a few months of becoming Labour leader had resolved that it was the way forward. Gordon Brown had also been talking about the idea for a couple of years in private, encouraged by meetings with Alan Greenspan, the long-serving chairman of the US Federal Reserve.

It had, in fact, already been proposed by Norman Lamont, but rejected by John Major for what seemed like impeccable reasons: 'I disliked this proposal on democratic grounds, believing that the person responsible for monetary policy should be answerable for it in the House of Commons.'

Even before that, John Smith had come to much the same conclusion, when he was shadow chancellor: 'Don't think that having been elected to Parliament and given responsibility for running the economy by the prime minister, I would hand over a large chunk of my responsibilities to the Bank of England.' New Labour had no such reservations. Four days after the election, the government announced that it was giving the Bank control of base rates.

The principal argument for such a change was that the chancellor would always be tempted by short-term political considerations to act in ways that might be against the longer-term economic interests of the country. Some, such as the campaigner for constitutional reform Anthony Barnett, saw it as a positive step, suggesting that the Bank would become 'more accountable as sovereignty over a crucial area of decision-making, the base rate, is openly shared'. But in addition to such high-minded wishes, Blair admitted, there were also 'very good political reasons', since the move would be 'the perfect riposte to those worried about the economic credentials of an incoming Labour government'. For those with longer memories, there was the added element of one more deliberate rejection of Labour's history. Back in 1946, one of the first acts of Clement Attlee's chancellor, Hugh Dalton, had been to nationalise the Bank of England; now that was effectively to be reversed.

Even accepting the case for handing over monetary policy to the Bank, there were a number of details to be considered. First, the question of disclosure. If one of the key economic levers was to be taken out of the democratic arena, it seemed reasonable to consult the electorate, particularly since the move had clearly been planned before the election. Blair, it was said, wished to make the proposal public as part of the campaign, but was talked out of it by Brown. Instead knowledge of the move was kept within a tight group at the top of New Labour, though Brown did phone previous chancellors after the election to inform them of what he was going to do. 'You'll be pleased to hear that I'm introducing your policy,' he told Norman Lamont, thus ensuring that a former Conservative politician, who had failed to be re-elected to the Commons, heard the news before the Labour Party or the electorate. When Labour MPs were told, some voiced their disapproval. 'Who elected Eddie George?' asked Dennis Skinner and Ken Livingstone, in reference to the Bank's governor.

Second was the matter of who at the Bank of England should actually make the monthly decision on interest rates. John Patten, one of those who argued for the Bank's independence, had suggested that to retain some form of democratic accountability, the governor and deputy governors should, when appointed, be subject to confirmation hearings in front of a Commons committee. That proposal resurfaced after Brown's announcement, but was spurned. Instead, Brown established a monetary policy committee, comprising nine members, four of whom – all economists – were to be appointed by him, the other five coming from the Bank itself. He rejected the idea of confirmation hearings.

And third was the question of what the new committee's frame of reference should be, the factors that they should bear in mind when setting interest rates. It was not, as it turned out, a particularly wide remit. Brown set the Bank the sole task of achieving an inflation rate of 2.5 per cent; no other considerations – unemployment, for example, or economic growth – were to be taken into account. Again, there was little new here. In the wake of Black Wednesday, Lamont had set an inflation target of between 1 and 4 per cent, to be reduced to 2.5 per cent by the end of the parliamentary term, an ambition that had very nearly been met; inflation was running at 2.6 per cent when the Tories left office. Brown was merely continuing the established Conservative policy; New Labour had bought into monetarist doctrine and inflation took precedence over all other aspects of the economy.

But if the chancellor believed his primary responsibility to be the control of inflation, and yet had handed over that duty to an unelected body, then what, one was entitled to ask, was the point of the chancellor? Or, more pertinently still, asked Bryan Gould: 'what is the point of democracy?' Gould, one of the few serious commentators not to celebrate the development, argued that 'politicians should be made to bear responsibility for the performance of the economy – something they are constantly trying to escape'.

Others were occasionally to be heard expressing their doubts in private. David Blunkett confided to his diary in September 1997, as interest rates were put up, his uncertainty that 'the decision to give interest rates to the Bank of England and to fail to take into account the manufacturing base of the country in the Monetary Policy Committee of the Bank of England has been the right one'. The Liberal Democrats backed the move, but writing in 2009, their economic spokesperson, Vince Cable, described the Bank's independence as 'a policy that, until the recent economic crisis, was the most successful and enduring of New Labour's years in office'. It was a hint that perhaps in retrospect the idea hadn't been quite such a long-term triumph as envisaged.

By then, too, as the country plunged into a bank-driven recession, there were those querying Brown's decision later in 1997 to put the supervision of British banking in the hands of the Securities and Investment Board. The previous system, with the Bank of England as the regulatory body, had failed to prevent the collapse of the banks Johnson Matthey, BCCI and Barings, and its credibility had been damaged thereby. The new arrangement, however, went on to fail in a similar manner, suggesting that the problem was not structural but political, a capitulation in the face of big money.

The intention of the Bank moves was, as both Blair and Brown never tired of pointing out, to bring an end to the economic policies that had given the country decades of 'Tory boom and bust'. As so often with New Labour, the slogan had been purloined, this time from the last Conservative chancellor, Kenneth Clarke. 'This chancellor does not want a boom because boom gets followed by bust,' Clarke had said in 1994, making the point yet clearer in his budget speech the following year: 'no return to boom and bust.' There was a strong streak of continuity from the one incumbent at the Treasury to the next. Brown himself was later to admit that his Bank of England policy was largely to do with symbolism, not ideology or even practicality, and that it stemmed from fear, rather than courage: 'We gave the Bank powers in order to be trusted and not for any fundamental economic reasons.'

Whatever reservations some might have expressed about handing over control of interest rates to the Bank of England, it was on the surface a bold move. And that was something of a surprise. Labour had come to office in a state of extreme nervousness, less about the current election, which was as good as in the bag, than about the next; in order to spike the Tory guns next time round, there was a determination not to promise anything that couldn't be delivered. Before the election a pledge card was printed and distributed to every household. It bore five key undertakings: to cut class sizes in years 1 to 3 to a maximum of thirty, to fast-track the punishment of persistent young offenders, to cut NHS waiting lists by 100,000, to get a quarter of a million young people off benefit and into work, and to set rules for government borrowing with the aim of ensuring low inflation and strengthening the economy.

This was such a modest programme that it ran the risk of making Labour look like a government that would have much to be modest about. When asked in opposition whether his policy was the provision of universal nursery education, Blair had hedged his bets in a formulation of which Harold Wilson, at his most shifty, would have been proud: 'We will make it a priority to make such a commitment.' In that context, the Bank decision came as something of a shock. Perhaps, after all, it would be a reforming administration, just as Blair had promised in the last days of the election campaign. 'I'm going to be a lot more radical in government than many people think,' he'd claimed.

Other early decisions, however, suggested that this would not be the case. There were a series of announcements that sounded good and caught the eye of headline writers, but which amounted to little more than gestures — the grabbing of 'low-hanging policy fruit', in the words of Peter Mandelson. The rate of VAT on domestic fuel was cut from 8 to 5 per cent; the previous government's ban on union membership at GCHQ in Cheltenham was reversed; entrance charges to public museums and galleries were abolished (a recognition, perhaps, of a less elitist cultural mood); a Food Standards Agency was set up; and — as a way of increasing spending without raising taxes — the rules of the National Lottery were changed to allow a billion pounds over the next four years to go to health and education, as promised by Blair in an election soundbite: 'the people's lottery, the people's priorities'. (Inevitably the phrase 'the people's lottery' came from John Major in the first place.)

More substantially, a promised windfall tax on the privatised utilities was introduced and the money directed towards the so-called New Deal, providing training schemes for the young unemployed. The country also finally signed up to the social provisions rejected by John Major during the Maastricht negotiations, though this was not much trumpeted for fear that Labour would be portrayed as left-wing extremists.

And there was the minimum wage, one of the few trade union demands that had survived the party's transition into New Labour. During the 1992 election campaign, when Tony Blair had been the employment spokesperson and had made a 'passionate defence of the minimum wage', the proposal had been that it should be set at £3.40. In 1997 there was no such pledge, nor was the proposed level revealed during the passage of the legislation through Parliament. When it did emerge, in time for its implementation in April 1999, it turned out to be set at £3.60 an hour, with a lower rate of £3 an hour for those aged between eighteen and twenty-one (for anyone under eighteen, it didn't apply at all). Had the 1992 figure been maintained, it would, allowing for inflation, have been £4.06. On this measure, therefore, there had been a 12 per cent devaluation in Labour aspirations since the days of Neil Kinnock.

The Low Pay Commission suggested that the figure should be set at £3.75, a proposal that, according to Alastair Campbell, infuriated Blair: 'He was off on one, ranting that they were all going native and not understanding the big picture and have they thought of the effect on business?' For even at the less than onerous level that was introduced, many major companies were affected by the legislation and were obliged to raise their levels of pay. Employees of McDonald's and Burger King were amongst those to gain, as were many agricultural workers, and, as the conscience of the cabinet, Clare Short, pointed out, 'the major beneficiaries would be low-paid women'.

It was clear, however, that the minimum wage would not do much to solve the issue of poverty, which was one of Gordon Brown's stated objectives, as he promised to reform the welfare state as radically as had the governments of 1906 and 1945. In pursuit of this goal, he introduced the child tax credit and the working family tax credit, direct payments made by the state to the lowest-paid workers. The bill for this came in at £5 billion, which was raised by hitting pension funds through the abolition of advance corporation tax, penalising savers in order to redistribute wealth. 'This is the tax bombshell which was waiting to be exposed during the election campaign,' wrote Alex Brummer in the *Guardian*, adding that 'it will affect almost everyone in Britain in an occupational pension scheme'. The policy, in the words of Charlie Whelan, was 'to milk the middle class', though again this was not proclaimed in public.

The new system was an extension of the family credit that already existed, but hugely expanded and based on lessons learned by Brown's economic adviser Ed Balls while studying at Harvard. It had, some felt, a structural flaw. 'In the longer term, there is a worry that the state is subsidising low-paid employment,' reflected Short, though she concluded that it 'created a new sense of hope in constituencies like mine'.

And, arguably, that feeling of optimism was New Labour's major economic achievement in its early days. Objectively, nothing much changed. The economy had been growing for almost five years by the time the party came to power, the unemployment rate had been falling since its peak of nearly 11 per cent in early 1993, and Brown did little to change course. But the election added the feelgood factor that had proved so elusive for John Major's government.

Most of the changes introduced by Labour were opposed by the Conservatives, though the size of the government majority made such opposition fairly academic. And anyway, neither the media nor the public was much interested in what the party did or said, and each found its lack of concern reinforced by the other. Gillian Shephard recalled an occasion when one of the frontbench Tory spokespeople was invited to do a television interview, addressing precisely that point of why the party was failing to make itself heard: 'When he arrived, he was told the interview had been cancelled.' In December 1997 a meeting of the 1922 Committee was held to discuss significant and far-reaching reforms to the party structure, but, wrote Alan Clark, 'when we came out into the corridor there was not a single journalist waiting'. His conclusion was sad but accurate: 'We have become irrelevant.'

Those proposed party reforms were the responsibility of the new leader, and for a couple of weeks at least, the contest to see who would succeed John Major did manage to generate a little press interest. The assumption had long been that it would be a fight to the finish between the two Michaels – Portillo and Heseltine – but neither actually made it to the starting line. Portillo was disqualified by reason of losing his seat and Heseltine missed out when he was rushed into hospital a couple of days after the election with a recurrence of his heart problem; with the example of John Smith going before him as a warning, he stood no chance. There were other big names around, however, and Michael Howard emerged as many people's favourite before his progress encountered an unexpected setback.

The issue was somewhat obscure and dated back several years. When Howard became home secretary in 1993, he had inherited a director general of prisons named Derek Lewis, with whom he had a strained relationship from the outset. Early on there was a series of bad news stories about jails, most notably the escape of six convicted IRA terrorists from Whitemoor Prison in September 1994. Lewis could point to the fact that jail escapes had fallen substantially on his watch, but the mutual distrust between him and his political master worsened. The dispute came to a head when the report was published of an inquiry into another breakout, this one from Parkhurst Prison in January 1995, in response to which Howard decided to suspend the governor of Parkhurst, John Marriott. When Lewis rejected that decision, Howard took legal advice and found that he had no authority to overrule Lewis. He did, however, have the power to dismiss Lewis, and promptly did so.

In a subsequent Commons debate, Howard defended his actions vigorously and emerged triumphant, having emphasised that he couldn't be held accountable for everything that went wrong in the prison service. He drew a distinction between those things for which he was responsible (which he defined as policy matters) and those for which he was not (operational matters), a separation that was not only established practice but also fairly obvious. So low had the Tories fallen in public opinion, however, that outside the House the argument seemed to many to be pettifogging legalese, designed simply to distance Howard from his officials and to save his skin. It lent itself to satire, exemplified by Armando Iannucci's mock news item on *The Friday Night Armistice*: 'On Friday a high court ruling declared that all of Britain's remaining convicted armed robbers were to be released on the grounds that using guns to thieve was an operational matter rather than a policy decision, and therefore one for which they shouldn't ultimately be responsible.'

What went unnoticed at the time was that Ann Widdecombe, as the prisons minister serving under Howard at the Home Office, sided entirely with Lewis and bitterly resented his treatment at the hands of her boss. She kept her resentment private until Howard emerged as the front runner for the Conservative leadership, at which point she broke cover, giving interviews in which she suggested that there was 'something of the night' about the man.

A killer phrase, echoing Clare Short's description of Peter Mandelson and Alastair Campbell as 'people who live in the dark', it nailed Howard's image perfectly. The BBC's political correspondent Nicholas Jones had earlier referred to Howard's 'Machiavellian talent for media management', arguing that he was the Tory 'answer to Peter Mandelson', and pointing out that he was known to some journalists as 'the cabinet's Geoffrey Boycott' for his ability to stonewall endlessly. That talent was now to be put to the ultimate test, as he was invited onto the BBC's *Newsnight* for an interview with Jeremy Paxman. Howard was asked whether he had threatened to overrule Lewis over the future of John Marriott, and gave an evasive answer, so Paxman asked the same question again. And again, and then again. Twelve times in a row, he put the question to Howard without getting a straight answer. It was not Howard's finest moment, and the interview became a cult classic, encapsulating for many what was seen as the shiftiness of modern politicians.

Howard's hopes of becoming Conservative leader were probably ended with that performance, but to be on the safe side, Widdecombe followed it up with a speech in the House of Commons that comprehensively destroyed his reputation. She began by focusing on Howard's treatment of Lewis, insisting that 'We demean our high office if we mistreat our public servants', before broadening this out into a more general analysis of the state of modern politics: 'Many of our great institutions are falling into disrepute. I was wretchedly unaware of how many people to whom I talked during the election uttered the sentiment that politicians of all parties are sleazy and corrupt and principally concerned with their own interest and survival.' It was time, she declared, for Parliament to clean up its act and discard its soiled image.

If this was bad news for Howard, it was the making of Widdecombe. She had on her wall a framed poster of the cartoon cat Garfield, with the caption 'If you want to look thinner, hang around with people who are fatter than you', and she seemed now to be applying this to her own political career. Long denounced as the epitome of the heartless right-winger, she had attacked a senior right-wing colleague with such ferocity that it changed her image almost entirely. No longer Doris Karloff, the shackler of pregnant prisoners, she was now the fearless assassin of Michael Howard, and henceforth, it seemed, she would always be associated with coining that soundbite: 'something of the night'.

In the first round of voting for the Tory leadership, largely as a result of Widdecombe's intervention, Howard finished last in a field of five, beaten by two other candidates from the right, Peter Lilley and John Redwood. Some distance ahead, however, came the two who were clearly going to fight it out for the top spot. Slightly in the lead was Kenneth Clarke, though his vote was less strong than anticipated, with the former Welsh secretary, William Hague, in second place.

Every poll – of the public, of party members, of peers and of MEPs – was quite clear: Clarke was the preferred candidate of everyone who was not entitled to vote. Those who did have a vote, however, the remains of the parliamentary party, were less convinced. Clarke was regarded as being deeply suspect on the issue of Europe, and he struggled to convince the relevant electorate to look at the larger picture. 'The British people did not vote for Blair because they thought the Conservatives were insufficiently right-wing or Eurosceptic,' he pointed out in a letter to MPs, but already the tide was turning. Both Howard and Lilley dropped out of the contest, pledging their support to Hague, and it became clear that he was now likely to win.

It was an unexpected development for the public, but not necessarily for bookmakers. Hague had been joint favourite at William Hill even during the general election campaign and, in the absence of Portillo, had been pushed up as odds-on favourite before the leadership voting began. John Major's own private comment on hearing that Portillo had lost his seat was said to have been: 'I suppose it will be William.'

Hague still trailed Clarke in the second ballot, which saw Redwood knocked out of the race, but then faced a development that genuinely took the political world by surprise. Redwood struck a deal with Clarke, pledging his support in return for being effectively his running mate. It was a deeply improbable alliance, bringing together two men who represented entirely opposing positions on what was supposed to be the single most important issue – Europe – but it did unite a pair of big players with weight and experience to recommend them, suggesting a degree of political maturity.

The move came with the backing of Michael Heseltine: 'This is, I think, a historic moment in the history of the Conservative Party,' he was reported to have said. 'It is the end of years of conflict.' Others shared his belief that the implausible coalition might signal a move away from the ideological infighting that had shaped the party for the last few years, a return to the Tory tradition of power at any price. It was, wrote Hugo Young in the *Guardian*, 'the Conservative Party we used to know and fear. Ideas, it turns out, matter less than hatred, calculation and power.' The now retired veteran Julian Critchley was less convinced: 'Is this another Hitler-Stalin pact? Is the move too clever by half? Will it swing opinion Hague's way by its very outrageousness?'

Critchley's doubts were well founded. The deal was seen as naked opportunism at a time when intellectual purity was sought, and in the third and final ballot Clarke found he had gained only six votes out of the thirty-eight who had supported Redwood. Hague – who was now being backed from outside Parliament by Margaret Thatcher and Michael Portillo – won with a comfortable, if not huge, majority. Clarke announced that he would return to the back benches, and it was widely assumed that his career as a front-rank politician was over.

There was much in this election that echoed the condition of the Labour Party in the 1980s. In electing Hague, where Labour in 1980 had opted for Michael Foot, the Tories had chosen youth rather than age, but the underlying intention – of pleasing the party rather than the public – was strikingly similar. Just as Labour had then rejected the obvious option, Denis Healey, because it feared he was out of step with the membership, so too did the Tories reject Kenneth Clarke, and in both instances the failed candidate was attacked for being pro-Europe. Most of what Clarke had done as chancellor had the support of the party's right wing, but he was seen as wrong on the EU, so 'he was doomed to fall at what they believed to be the only fence on the course', as Heseltine put it.

There was too, as with Labour in the 1980s, a desire to appease the fringes, in this instance the UK Independence Party and the Referendum Party. Back in the 1960s, Harold Wilson had famously said: 'You don't need to worry about the outside left. They've got nowhere else to go.' In the 1990s, the Conservatives did have to worry; there was in UKIP an alternative, a potential home for disaffected purists. And, just as in 1981, the real hero of the radicals was absent. Then, Tony Benn had refused to stand, believing that the election lacked legitimacy, while now Portillo was out of Parliament (as Benn had been when Labour chose its next leader in 1983). The great achievement of the left in the previous decade had been to entrench Thatcher as prime minister by provoking a split in the Labour Party; the Eurosceptics didn't quite manage to split the Tories, but they did succeed in keeping out Kenneth Clarke, thereby ensuring that New Labour had a pretty free run.

Hague's victory was built on two key factors. First, he was seen as a moderate Eurosceptic, sufficiently opposed to the EU to attract right-wing support, but not so opposed that he would panic Europhiles into leaving the party. In fact he had, on this and on other issues, kept his head down during his eight years in Parliament, remaining sturdily loyal to the leadership. 'It's not the job of a junior minister to go rampaging round taking up positions on the wings of the party,' he explained in 1994. And second, he was considered by some to be the Tory answer to Tony Blair. A 36-year-old, state-educated Yorkshireman, with a voice somewhere between those of Harold Wilson and of Peter Sallis in the *Wallace and Gromit* films, he was seen as the young, classless embodiment of the Conservative Party's future. Rather neatly, he promised a 'fresh start', borrowing the slogan of the Maastricht rebels while hinting at a Blairite clean slate.

Hague's age was, initially, one of the few things that attracted attention. The youngest leader of the Tories since William Pitt the Younger, more than two centuries earlier, he seemed to the public even more youthful than that, for his image was still dominated by his appearance as a sixteen-year-old at the 1977 Conservative conference. Then, as a pudgy-faced schoolboy, his hair (long by Tory standards) clashing somewhat with his tweed jacket and sensible tie, he had caused a sensation, urging a future Thatcher government to 'roll back the frontiers of the state' and to 'create a capital-owning, home-owning democracy for the young people'.

Twenty years on, he still stood for the same principles, but the memory of that speech now merged all too easily with the character of Tory Boy, the smug, intolerant adolescent, created and played by Harry Enfield, who sneered his contempt for the unemployed and those on benefits. (Tory Boy's rebirth in Enfield's 1997 Christmas special as Tony Boy, an equally smug, intolerant adolescent, this time in New Labour colours, made less impact.) Julian Critchley referred to Hague as 'a juvenile lead', while Labour's Tony Banks joked that the Conservatives had 'elected a foetus as party leader', adding maliciously: 'I bet there's a lot of Tory MPs that wish they hadn't voted against abortion now.'

Hague also faced some criticism from the *Daily Telegraph* for saying that he wasn't opposed to the idea of gay marriages, and during the leadership election rumours circulated about his sexuality. His team was full of 'bachelor boys', ran a jibe said to have originated with Iain Duncan Smith, who was running John Redwood's campaign, though Hague was by now engaged to Ffion Jenkins, a civil servant he had worked with in the Welsh Office. 'I like women so much I have even decided to marry one,' he joked.

Despite some impressive performances at prime minister's questions in the Commons – for he was a witty, quick-thinking debater and won the *Spectator*'s Parliamentarian of the Year award in 1998 – Hague's cause wasn't helped by some early misjudged attempts at photo-opportunities. Most notoriously these included a ride on a water-chute at Flambards theme park in Cornwall, for which he sported a personalised baseball cap, and an appearance at the Notting Hill Carnival, posing with Ffion, as they sucked through straws at a rum punch served in coconut shells. He looked game but awkward and no one believed he would be doing such things had cameras not been present.

The ridicule he faced for these ventures was matched only by the media's studied refusal to recognise him at other times. He was 'the only person to have one of those "Where are they now?" features written about him whilst leader of the Conservative Party', mocked Peter Baynham on *The Friday Night Armistice*, and the right was no more convinced. 'The Tories are a waste of space,' wrote Richard Littlejohn in the *Sun*, 'and by choosing William Hague have replaced Captain Mainwaring with Private Pike. Stupid boy.' As often, Frank Johnson had the best line, comparing Hague to an asylum seeker: 'a man with a well-founded fear of persecution in his own country'. Of all the many negative comments, however, perhaps the most perceptive was that of Alan Clark, who described Hague as a 'shifty little bureaucrat'. For, in keeping with his role model, Tony Blair, the new leader saw his primary objective to be not policy development but structural reform of his party.

Hague faced an appallingly steep uphill climb as leader of the opposition. Not only were the ranks of Conservative MPs severely depleted, but the possibility existed that an end to the slaughter might not have been reached. Dozens of once-safe Tory seats were now held by such slim majorities that they had to be considered marginal, and could fall next time around. In two of the first three by-elections fought under Hague – at Winchester and at Beckenham, six months after the general election – the Tory share of the vote fell still further.

Outside Parliament, an even more sorry story was to be found. The average age of members was sixty-four (twenty years older than the Labour average) and estimates suggested that membership numbers had fallen by as much as two-thirds since 1992. 'It's getting older, weaker and smaller,' Edwina Currie had noted of the party, while it was still in government, bemoaning the absence of young people: 'without them we have no future – only nostalgia and unpopularity.' A couple of years earlier a vice-chairman of the party had admitted privately that the grassroots were withering to the extent that 'We couldn't get candidates for the local elections.' And when Michael Spicer tried to form a new local branch in his constituency in 1994, the meeting attracted just five people, three of them – including a woman celebrating her ninety-second birthday – having turned up by mistake. An eighty-year-old wondered why she was being thanked and had to be told that she'd just been appointed to sit on the branch committee. 'Thus was the new branch formed,' wrote Spicer in his diary, with bleak humour, 'vigorously to bang the drums for the Conservative message and to take it into the future.'

Nationally the party was overdrawn by £3.5 million, having spent more than twice as much when losing the election as it had when winning in 1983, even if inflation was taken into account. And there were far fewer major donors around to make up the shortfall, now that, as the BBC's political editor Robin Oakley pointed out on election night, 'it looks as though Labour will be there for a couple of terms'. The only real big spender left in the Tory camp was the businessman Michael Ashcroft, appointed by Hague as the party treasurer despite concerns about his tax arrangements and overseas business interests. Meanwhile, many of those groups who had once been considered soul-mates of the Conservatives – the churches, the universities, the professions – had been driven away during the Thatcher revolution, when big business was courted at the expense of the traditional establishment.

Just to rub it in, for those who hoped the election of Hague might truly mean a fresh start for the Conservatives, the old image of sleaze made an unwelcome reappearance. The day after the leadership question was settled, Jonathan Aitken withdrew his libel action against the *Guardian*, when evidence emerged to prove that he'd lied in court; it was now inevitable that he would himself be prosecuted, and in due course he received a seven-month sentence after being found guilty of perjury. A fortnight later, a parliamentary investigation concluded that Neil Hamilton had indeed taken money and freebies from Mohammed Al-Fayed. Though that report was only partially endorsed on appeal, the *Sun* had already covered its publication under the uncompromising headline LYING SLEAZEBAG.

'Our current organisation is not up to the job,' admitted Hague, as he gazed around at the ruins of what had, until very recently, been the most successful party machine in the history of modern democracy. 'No change is not an option. We need to renew our organisation, rebuild our membership and rejuvenate our party.'

He was right. Unlike the Labour Party, for whom the rewriting of Clause IV had been a largely cosmetic exercise in what was widely called 'sending out signals', the Conservative Party really was in desperate need of reform. Even its name was slightly misleading, for there was no such legally constituted entity as a Conservative Party. Rather there were three separate bodies: the parliamentary party, together with peers and MEPs; the full-time staff at Central Office, reporting to the leader of the parliamentary party; and the National Union, which brought together the voluntary organisations and constituency associations. Formally and technically these three groups had no influence over each other.

This had once been seen as a virtue (before the election, Labour's general secretary, Tom Sawyer, had expressed his admiration of the ease with which a Tory leader could manoeuvre since 'internal democracy is virtually non-existent'), but it had also caused enormous strain in recent years. However much, for example, John Major might have wished that Neil Hamilton had not been a candidate in the general election, ensuring that sleaze remained in the headlines, there was nothing he could do about it. 'The selection of a candidate is the responsibility of the association,' he pointed out, with a barely concealed note of frustration. At Hague's instigation, a single structure was now to be created, with representation from all sections of the party on a ruling board, akin to Labour's national executive committee. Inevitably the net effect was to concentrate more power in the centre.

And there was to be a change to the MPs-only voting system that had given the Tories a succession of leaders, from Edward Heath to Hague himself. After some arguments between those who wished the MPs to retain the lion's share of the votes when choosing their leader, and those prepared to hand over power to party members, a compromise was found whereby the MPs would vote on candidates until there were just two remaining; these would then go to a ballot of the whole membership (which meant that for the first time a national list of members had to be created). A further change made it much more difficult to challenge an incumbent leader, in the way that had led to Margaret Thatcher's removal; previously a candidate needed just a proposer and seconder, now 15 per cent of MPs were required to agree before a contest could be called.

There was something quite impressive about the way Hague pushed the reforms through, for he was hardly in the most secure position as leader. He had secured only a quarter of MPs' first-preference votes when elected, and the last-minute support of Michael Portillo – while undeniably welcome –

had been something of a barbed compliment; the suspicion was that Portillo was plotting a return to the Commons, and didn't want to find anyone as substantial as Kenneth Clarke in situ when the next leadership contest came along. That certainly seemed to be the perception of Thatcher, who was reported to be momentarily nonplussed when asked about the new leader: 'William? Oh, William. He'll only be around for eighteen months. Until we get Michael back.'

However significant the changes, the public was understandably less than fascinated by the preoccupation with procedure, and by the summer of 1998, things were looking even worse for the Tories than they had in the latter days of John Major. Opinion polls were showing Labour support at over 50 per cent, with the Conservatives scraping along at under 25 per cent. Rumours were circulating that Hague might not complete a whole term as leader, and Blair was expressing his concern that Clarke might be called upon to take over, 'something he really fears'.

Part of the Conservatives' problem was that they were still seen as 'the nasty party', unforgiven by the electorate. During the leadership contest, Hague had seemed to recognise that this had to change: 'The free and prosperous society that we had championed became tainted with the image of sleaze, greed, self-indulgence and division.' But he seemed unsure how to combat it, and anyway there were still many in his own ranks who had yet to be convinced. An initiative was launched under the banner of 'Listening to Britain', in which the shadow cabinet and other MPs would hold public meetings to see where they had been going wrong. Widely dismissed as a gimmick, the kind of project that politicians always pursue when lost for a sense of direction, it was in this instance a real educational exercise for some of its participants. 'I truly believed that I was not out of touch with people's preoccupations and concerns,' wrote Gillian Shephard, 'but experience of the meetings proved me wrong.'

There was still room in the parliamentary party, however, for the likes of Eric Forth, a communist in his Glasgow youth, who now espoused a hard right-wing position with diminishing returns. 'There are millions of people in this country who are white, Anglo-Saxon and bigoted,' he argued, 'and they need to be represented.' He'd backed Hague for the leadership, possibly in sympathy with Hague's earlier support for the reintroduction of hanging, birching and the stocks, but that was the kind of thing from which the new leader was seeking to distance himself; figures like Forth made it all the more difficult. Nor did the appointment as party chairman of Cecil Parkinson, a figure identified entirely with the 1980s, play particularly well except amongst the ageing faithful.

Beyond the public perceptions, though, was perhaps a deeper problem still. One of Tony Blair's key insights into the fortunes of the Labour Party was that it had been too successful for its own good, that by fighting to improve the lot of the working class, it had enabled many to escape their backgrounds. At that point the conventional wisdom, embodied in his own father, kicked in: 'You made it; you were a Tory: two sides of the same coin.' As Blair saw it, there was an attitude on the intellectual left that failed to connect with people's aspirations: 'In a sense they wanted to celebrate the working class, not make them middle class – but middle class was precisely what your average worker wanted himself or his kids to be.' In an increasingly middle-class country – largely thanks, claimed Blair, to Labour's achievements in the past – the only way forward for the party was to embrace and reflect those aspirations, to appeal beyond its natural constituency.

From the perspective of the Conservative Party, there was a very real danger that it was suffering a parallel process of having made itself surplus to requirements, that it too might be the victim of its own success. It had been elected in 1979 at a time when the trade unions were believed by many to be too powerful, when inflation was rampant and the economy in decline. After eighteen years of often very hard times indeed, including two huge recessions, it had broken the unions and delivered low inflation and steady growth. It had done the difficult things that it was meant to have done, and had convinced the other parties that this was the only sound approach to handling the economy. At which point, it could reasonably be asked what its continuing function was. The electorate had no obligation to feel gratefully loyal, and every right to decide that the time for unpleasant medicine had passed.

Over the course of the twentieth century, the Conservative Party had spent more years in power in Britain than had the Communists in China. But that was history, and Blair was urging the country to 'Forget the past'. In 1993 Margaret Thatcher had speculated that perhaps James Callaghan had led the last-ever Labour government. Five years later, Hywel Williams was one of the first prepared to ask in public the reciprocal question: 'Was John Major the Conservative Party's last prime minister?'

11
Royalty
'Storm the Palace'

I've never discussed private matters and I don't think the Queen
has either. Very few members of the family have.
Prince Philip (1994)

I sometimes sense that the world is changing almost too fast for its
inhabitants, at least for us older ones.
Queen Elizabeth II (1997)

Diana's power is born out of emotion and there's nothing wrong
with that.
Tony Blair (1998)

Queen Elizabeth II and Prince Philip celebrated their forty-fifth wedding
anniversary on Friday, 20 November 1992. They weren't, however,
together to mark what should have been a happy occasion, for he was away
on a trip to Argentina, in his capacity as president of the World Wide Fund
for Nature. She was therefore alone when she heard the news that a fire had
broken out at Windsor Castle.

She arrived from Buckingham Palace some hours after the start of the
conflagration, at which point firefighters were still struggling to bring the
blaze under control. Hundreds of staff were joined by Army personnel as a
priceless collection of paintings, books, carpets and porcelain was removed
from the burning building; in their midst, television cameras filmed the
Queen, in off-duty headscarf and wellingtons, cutting a distraught and
forlorn figure. 'Her Majesty is utterly devastated,' Prince Andrew told news
reporters, the formality of his words somehow distancing viewers from
what was clearly a deep personal disaster.

It was also a potential disaster for the country, whether one accepted the
idea that this thousand-year-old building and its contents were held in trust
and that the loss was to us all, or whether one merely counted the financial

cost of the damage. For Windsor Castle, like the other royal palaces, was not insured – the premiums would have been prohibitive – and the repairs were, announced the national heritage secretary Peter Brooke, to be paid for from the national purse. 'The heart of the nation went out to the Queen last night,' he said. 'I am sure the Queen will want to see her home restored in the way which we all see fit.'

It wasn't supposed to be a startling revelation, merely a statement of the obvious, but the idea that taxpayers were expected to pick up the estimated tab of £60 million unexpectedly aroused considerable hostility, even while the embers were still glowing. 'With the greatest respect, Ma'am, you should foot the bill,' said the *Sunday Mirror*, and its sister paper ran a telephone poll for readers in which 95 per cent of the 40,000 callers agreed with the proposition that the Queen should contribute to the restoration costs. The *Sun* also asked its listeners to phone and received 60,000 calls saying she should pay, against just 4,000 disagreeing. It was a response that caused genuine shock. 'We must have got it wrong,' lamented one courtier. 'At the moment of her desolation, this woman, who had done nothing but give service to her country, didn't even have the solace of her people's sympathy.' A public appeal was launched and raised just £25,000.

Attitudes were changing, but those in royal circles seemed not to have noticed. 'The suggestion that the taxpayer might foot the bill raises the question of why the Queen, in her private capacity, should not be a taxpayer also,' pointed out Labour MP Alan Williams. This awkward issue had been in the air all year, ever since the publication of Philip Hall's book *Royal Fortune*, which examined in great detail the finances of the royal family since 1688, fuelling the argument that the Queen should pay income tax, as had her great-great-grandmother Victoria. The practice had in fact been discontinued only in 1910, when David Lloyd George, as chancellor, had done a deal with Edward VII whereby the monarch was exempt in exchange for bearing the costs of state visits. 'Pay your taxes, you scum!' the Queen was heckled in June 1992, at the official opening of a refurbished Leicester Square.

In fact, according to John Major, she had already agreed to do so, but had been waiting for an opportune moment to announce her decision. In the wake of the Windsor Castle fire, the announcement was rushed forward, but even then it was hardly received with unalloyed approval in all quarters. H.M. THE TAX DODGER, mocked the front page of the *Daily Mirror*, with a sneering article by Alastair Campbell accompanied by a caricature of the Queen doing her sums on a pocket calculator. The following week an opinion poll commissioned by the *Daily Telegraph* showed that only a quarter of the population agreed with the statement that 'the monarchy is something to be proud of'.

Something had clearly gone wrong in the relationship between the monarch and her subjects. She noted as much in a speech to commemorate the fortieth anniversary of her accession to the throne: 1992 was, she said, 'not a year on which I shall look back with undiluted pleasure. In the words of one of my more sympathetic correspondents, it has turned out to be an annus horribilis.'

Much of the unpleasantness was purely personal, for this was the year that Princess Anne divorced her husband, Mark Phillips, and Prince Andrew and Prince Charles announced their separations from their wives. With her only other child, Prince Edward, yet to marry ('nature has blessed him with a disinclination towards matrimony', nudged the novelist A.N. Wilson), this meant that three of her children, as well as her sister, now had failed marriages.

The royal-family brand, so carefully cultivated by George VI as a way of rebuilding the monarchy's image after the abdication crisis, was looking distinctly fragile. The only stable relationship in the entire family appeared to be the Queen's own, and even that was called into question in 1992, when Prince Philip was asked directly by the writer Fiammetta Rocco about his much-rumoured marital infidelities. It was a presumptuous question, but he laughed off such suggestions: 'Have you ever stopped to think that for the last forty years, I have never moved anywhere without a policeman accompanying me? So how the hell could I get away with anything like that?' He was perhaps one of the last people in the country to believe that the presence of a police officer guaranteed moral rectitude. But his patience could also be tested; when he presented an honorary degree that year to the French philosopher Jacques Derrida, the father of deconstruction theory, he was heard to mutter that his own family seemed to be deconstructing.

The official announcements that accompanied each marital breakdown were only a minor part of the problem. Much worse were the media stories documenting every twist and turn of the royal relationships, and the suspicion that some of the participants were fuelling such stories themselves.

In June 1992 a new low seemed to have been reached with the publication of *Diana: Her True Story*, a book written by journalist Andrew Morton with – it was claimed at the time – the collaboration of 'some of the Princess of Wales's closest friends and family'. All the rumours about the misery of her marriage to Charles were here confirmed, with eye-catching details of her repeated, if ineffectual, suicide attempts. There were stories of her throwing herself down a flight of stairs when pregnant, of hurling herself against a glass cabinet, of self-harming in front of Charles, using his penknife. This was sensational stuff, more akin to a show-business exposé than a traditional royal book, and the media and public lapped it up. There was little doubt in anyone's mind that the stories came directly from Diana herself, a perception Charles apparently shared. 'I can *hear* my wife saying those words,' he was said to have remarked, on reading newspaper extracts.

Diana's ability to command media attention, at the expense of her husband, had become one of the marvels of the modern age, but Morton's book took her in a new direction. Previously she had specialised in making her point through pictures rather than words, culminating in her overseas trips the previous year. Back in 1980, Charles had been the first Prince of Wales in six decades to visit India and commented that he would one day like to return, bringing his future wife to see the magnificence of the Taj Mahal. In 1991 the couple did travel to India, but while he was otherwise occupied on official business, Diana visited the Taj Mahal without him, making sure that photographers caught her looking forlorn and beautiful, the shrine to marital devotion forming a perfect backdrop to her abandoned loveliness. A couple of months later she set up a similar shot in front of the Pyramids, raising the possibility that she might yet tour every great monument in the world and press them into service for photo-opportunities.

Diana: Her True Story fleshed out the background to the imagery, telling 'the story of her transformation from victim to victor'. Although retailers like Tesco and Harrods refused to stock the book, it was an immediate popular hit, selling a million copies worldwide in its first week, the only bar to its success being the publisher's difficulty in reprinting the book quickly enough. Some politicians and reviewers condemned its very existence, and many attacked the Diana depicted in its pages, but much of the country was unambiguously on her side.

The public relations triumph of Morton's book was not allowed to stand unchallenged. Two months after its appearance came reports of a taped mobile-phone conversation between Diana and a friend, James Gilbey, a car dealer who was part of the gin-distilling family and one of Morton's named sources. The origins of the tape were murky, to say the least. The conversation apparently dated from December 1989, but the recording seemed to have been made by an eavesdropper a few days after the event, suggesting that someone had taped the call and then replayed it, possibly with the deliberate intention that it should be overheard.

In any event, the recording finally made its way to the papers in August 1992 and was immediately dubbed the Squidgygate tape, since Gilbey referred to Diana by the pet name of Squidgy. Transcripts were printed, and for those who wished to hear the original (some forty thousand of them on the first day alone), the *Sun* made it available on a premium-rate phone line at 39p a minute, meaning that for just £11.70 anyone could listen to the Princess of Wales sharing her thoughts on how shabbily she had been treated. 'Bloody hell!' she exclaimed. 'What I've done for this fucking family!' She didn't emerge with a great deal of credit, seemingly as self-indulgent and in need of continual reassurance as Charles himself appeared to be, and obsessed with what her husband called her 'Mother Teresa act'. 'I understand people's suffering,' she explained. 'It's not only AIDS, it's anyone who suffers. I can smell them a mile away.'

Amongst the revelations in *Diana: Her True Story* had been confirmation that, a few years after his wedding, Charles had revived his relationship with Camilla Parker Bowles, who as Camilla Shand had been an early girlfriend before either of them got married. And in January 1993, a rival to the Squidgygate tapes appeared in the form of another recorded phone conversation dating back to the 1980s, this time between Charles and Camilla. ('Talking on a mobile phone is a bit like discussing your private life with a gossip columnist,' warned a character in the television series *Bugs*.) Again the provenance of the item was unclear, but by now leaking and counter-leaking of material from the rival camps of the warring royal couple – and from other unidentified parties – seemed unstoppable. The most famous section of what was unavoidably dubbed the Camillagate tape was a good-natured exchange about reincarnation, heavily punctuated by mutual laughter:

CAMILLA: I need you all the week, all the time.
CHARLES: Oh God, I'll just live inside your trousers or something. It would be much easier.
CAMILLA: What are you going to turn into? A pair of knickers? Oh, you're going to come back as a pair of knickers.
CHARLES: Or, God forbid, a Tampax, just my luck!
CAMILLA: You're a complete idiot!

This embarrassing episode brought down much mockery on Charles's head, but it was actually rather endearing. There was a genuine warmth and humour to the exchange, and it revealed Camilla to be – in contrast to the public perception of Diana – sexy, funny and supportive. ('Papa doesn't embarrass me. Mama does,' said Prince William, according to one of Charles's more sympathetic chroniclers.)

The transcript was first published in Australia and there was some nervousness about reprinting it in Britain, though the *Daily Mirror* soon broke ranks, allowing others to follow. But at a time when press intrusion into privacy was being debated, the *Sun* pronounced itself reluctant to publish: 'We're worried that we are being set up. Being given enough rope to hang ourselves. Wouldn't the Establishment just love that?' A few days later, the paper's editor, Kelvin MacKenzie, appeared in front of the House of Commons' heritage committee and said that the *Sun* had taken its decision 'because we are in a curious sort of way cowed in relation to the future of the press'. But he added that he would be perfectly justified in publishing the transcript, since the public had a right to know 'whether the next Defender of the Faith was going to be someone who cuckolded someone else's husband'.

The sight of the *Sun* seeking to occupy the moral high ground was not entirely convincing. More serious was the idea that the media was being used as a battleground in a high-profile marital dispute. 'I do not want to help either side in all this,' said Ian Hislop, the editor of *Private Eye*, explaining why he wasn't publishing the tape. 'Would you want to join in the biggest washing of public laundry of the decade?'

Despite Hislop's reservations, plenty did want to join in, and the two protagonists' rival camps were eager to encourage them. Just as the Conservative Party had lost any sense of loyalty and privacy, conducting its internal feuds in public, so too did the royals actively seek to let daylight in on the magic. Lord Rothermere, chairman of Associated Newspapers (publishers of the *Daily Mail*), acknowledged in 1991 that 'the Prince and Princess of Wales had each recruited national newspapers to carry their own accounts of their marital rifts', and there was no let-up in the stories, most of them unsourced.

Rumours circulated that Diana, at her lowest point in the 1980s, had taken to phoning Camilla in the middle of the night with threatening messages: 'I've sent someone to kill you. They're outside in the garden. Look out of the window; can you see them?' Charles was quoted in the *Daily Mail* as asking rhetorically: 'Do you seriously expect me to be the first Prince of Wales in history not to have a mistress?' And it was reported that *Paris Match* had acquired nude photos of the Prince. An anonymous employee was impressed: 'He looks *magnifique*. You English can be proud of him.'

Eventually the whispers and briefings moved from the dark corners into the full gaze of the television cameras. Charles was first to break cover, cooperating with Jonathan Dimbleby on a 1994 documentary titled *Charles: The Private Man, the Public Role*, in which he confessed openly for the first time his adultery with Camilla. 'Did you try to be faithful and honourable to your wife when you took on the vow of marriage?' asked Dimbleby, and Charles replied: 'Yes. Until it became irretrievably broken down, us both having tried.' Retaliation was inevitable, though it took more than a year to arrive.

Martin Bashir, a reporter on the BBC current affairs show *Panorama*, began in 1995 to investigate rumours that the security services were involved in the Squidgygate and Camillagate episodes. He approached Diana herself for an interview and, having secured her consent, found the programme turning into a different animal altogether. Broadcast in November that year, the show turned out to be a simple encounter between Bashir and Diana, in which she gave one of the greatest television appearances in the history of the medium, capturing the essence of that Taj Mahal photo-shoot and combining it with a first-person version of the Andrew Morton revelations. With head lowered to emphasise her upturned, kohl-laden eyes, she admitted her own adultery, talked about her self-harming, post-natal depression and eating disorder, and delivered a series of soundbites that were to dominate the media for days and years to come.

'There were three of us in this marriage, so it was a bit crowded,' she said, referring to Camilla, and repeated the formulation later in case it had been missed. She identified herself as a fighter for feminism: 'I think every strong woman in history has had to walk down a similar path, and I think it's the strength that causes the confusion and the fear. Why is she strong? Where does she get it from? Where is she taking it?' She talked of how she saw herself in the future: 'I think the British people need someone in public life to give affection, to make them feel important, to support them, to give them light in their dark tunnels.' And she wrote the headline for the coverage: 'I'd like to be a queen of people's hearts.'

The programme attracted the largest audience in *Panorama*'s history — nearly twenty-three million — and, somewhat surprisingly, more viewers in Britain than had watched Charles and Diana's wedding in 1981. It was seen as an open acknowledgement that a state of war existed between the most famous couple in the country, and the majority of viewers knew whose side they were on. Any doubt was dispelled by the appearance on television later that evening of Nicholas Soames, Tory MP for Crawley and a friend of Charles, whose corpulent appearance had earned him the nickname 'the Butter Mountain from Crawley'. The sight of him dismissing Diana's claims as symptomatic of an 'advanced stage of paranoia' helped ensure that sympathy swung her way.

'I've never been so overwhelmed in my life,' said Tony Hall, the BBC's director of news and current affairs, recalling his first sight of the edited interview. 'Here was a royal talking like a real human being with all the traumas of a real person's life.' That was certainly a large part of the appeal, though there was more. By claiming universality, that she suffered as others suffered, hinting even that she took on their suffering, Diana sought to channel everyone's pain. In the 1950s, the journalist Malcolm Muggeridge had coined the phrase 'the royal soap opera', but hitherto the drama had largely been conducted without dialogue from any of the principal characters. Now they were heard to speak and the effect was startling, a combination of the mundane and the extraordinary that captivated the public. There was little at a personal level that was particularly novel about the breakdown of the relationship; the misery and bitterness on display merely reflected the experience of many mismatched couples in the country. But the scale continued to fascinate; few couples announcing their separation had to worry about the division of the family butlers, as did Charles and Diana.

None could question that genuine distress was being paraded. Yet even in this tale there were moments of comic relief, many of them provided by James Hewitt. A cavalry officer who first met Diana before her marriage, Hewitt subsequently had an intermittent, though long-running affair with her that finally ended in 1992. He then gave his first full interview, to *Daily Express* journalist Anna Pasternak, in which he denied any relationship and suggested that the two hadn't even met until after the birth of Diana's second son, Harry. Though that wasn't true, a rapport had clearly been struck between interviewer and subject, for in 1994 there emerged *Princess in Love*, Pasternak's account of the affair, written with Hewitt's cooperation. Couched in the language of a romance novel, while giving a full account of the Princess of Wales's adultery, it was a very strange book, full of tremulous prose. 'He lay flat on his back in his bed,' ran a typical passage, 'not noticing the chill of the sheet, his body still warm with the feel of her, the muscles in his arms still carrying the imprint of her, where he had held her so long and so tight.'

It was not well received. 'A terribly, terribly bad book', wrote William Rees-Mogg; 'horse manure', concluded Melvyn Bragg; while Buckingham Palace affected a lofty disdain. 'Grubby and worthless', was the official response; 'we are not going to waste any more time on this tawdry little book.' Worse still, the tabloids decided that it was open season on Major

Hewitt, who, as an officer and a gentleman, should never have spilt the beans. 'A revolting creep', opined the *Daily Mirror*, while the *Sun* wondered whether he might be hung, drawn and quartered for treason, and the *Star* sniffed that he was 'bad in bed'.

His reputation in shreds, Hewitt found that even his ghost-writer was prepared to turn on him. Asked about whether she too had enjoyed a dalliance with her source, Pasternak professed herself offended. 'I wouldn't have an affair with him,' she retorted. 'He's far too thick for me.' Hewitt became a minor celebrity, though there was little he could do to exploit his fame. The same was not true of others. Roger Moore, a 26-year-old strippogram performer from Bath, adopted the persona of Hewitt, performing a routine at hen parties for £50 a time; during his act he would reportedly 'strip down to his Union flag boxer shorts to the tune of the national anthem'.

The nation's amusement at finding such a splendid bounder was not, of course, shared by Diana. 'Yes, I adored him. Yes, I was in love with him,' she said of Hewitt on *Panorama*. 'But I was very let down.' She accepted that much of *Princess in Love* was true, but added: 'there was a lot of fantasy in that book and it was very distressing for me that a friend of mine, who I had trusted, made money out of me.' And behind it all, there was the persistent – but consistently denied – rumour that Hewitt, not Charles, was actually the father of Prince Harry.

The response to Hewitt suggested that public sympathy for Diana did not extend to the rest of her entourage, and the same story could be found in the treatment accorded to the Duchess of York. In the 1980s when, as Sarah Ferguson, she first became famous, the Duchess had been a popular figure, credited with bringing a sense of unstuffy fun into the royal soap. But in more recent times she had been recast and vilified by the tabloids as a sponger and a bad mother; in 1991, by which time her marriage to Prince Andrew was clearly falling apart, *Drop the Dead Donkey* could run a joke about a cat that was named Fergie because 'It costs a fortune to feed and keeps abandoning its kittens.' Reporting on gossip from the inner circles of the royals, Woodrow Wyatt noted: 'The Duchess of York is utterly childish and low level, like a barmaid who has got into some money. She is bereft of education and taste.'

Her contribution to the Queen's annus horribilis came in August 1992, when in long-lens photographs spread across seven pages of the *Daily Mirror*, she was shown sitting by a swimming pool on holiday in France, topless and having her toes sucked by an American financial adviser named John

Bryan. (The toe-sucking detail was, of course, later reworked into the David Mellor story.) The justification for this breach of privacy was provided by a pretence at moral outrage that she had behaved in such a manner while her daughter, Princess Eugenie, was present.

'How much shrapnel can this family take?' wailed Harold Brooks-Baker, the publisher of *Burke's Peerage*. 'This is not just a nail in the coffin, it's a whole handful of nails.' But the *Mirror* had judged its readership perfectly. The pictures were trailed by an advertisement screened during an episode of *Coronation Street*, and the paper later claimed that it had been obliged to reprint after selling out its entire print run. Nor was much offence caused; the Press Complaints Commission reported that, instead of the deluge of phone calls it had been expecting, it received just one objection. And for those who missed the *Mirror*, the pictures appeared the next day in *Today* and the *Sun*, the latter coming up with the memorable headline: JUST HOW MUCH FINANCIAL ADVICE CAN A GIRL TAKE?

Both Sarah and Bryan sued for damages in a French court, seeking £1.2 million each. They won their case, but not the damages; she received just £60,000 and he £25,000, though her payout did equal the French record for such an award. (The man who took the photos, on the other hand, was said to have made upwards of £1 million.) The money can have been little compensation for the final destruction of her public image. The incident passed into popular folklore, recreated the following year in *One Foot in the Algarve* (the Christmas edition of *One Foot in the Grave*), with Peter Cook giving his best impression of a paparazzo photographer. It also prompted a comparison in *Drop the Dead Donkey* with the state of the country: 'Both being screwed by their financial advisers.' The implied adultery confirmed the negative perception that already existed, while the setting fed into the perception that she was not the most active of royals. 'If she cannot be photographed when she is on holiday,' wrote Lynne Truss, 'it leaves precious few days in the year when she is visible. Or are we paying her £249,000 a year to remain out of sight?'

Two years later, Sarah was again in the news, explaining in an interview that she practised safe sex. 'What has to be, has to be,' she said, of her use of condoms. 'But I agree there may be a cut in spontaneity.' She also said that she had had two HIV tests, which served only to fuel groundless gossip that her estranged husband had AIDS. That rumour became one of the first internet urban myths ('The story went global after Internet boffins circulated it by computer,' reported the *News of the World*), acquiring such wide currency that in 1996 Buckingham Palace felt obliged to issue an official denial that Andrew had contracted AIDS.

Stories of sexual misdemeanours among the royals became commonplace, fuelled by a spate of gossipy books published in 1993 by the likes of Nigel Dempster ('the girls' talk was that he wasn't a great lover, not even a very good one', he reported of Charles), James Whitaker (Charles and Diana 'never slept together again' after a 1986 holiday) and Lady Colin Campbell (the Queen's own marriage was a loveless façade). The gossip was unrelenting, with even the romantic novelist Barbara Cartland, who was also Diana's step-grandmother, keen to explain to anyone who would listen what the problem was in that relationship: 'She wouldn't do oral sex, she just wouldn't. It's as simple as that.'

Equally unrelenting were the jokes, with comedians taking aim at all parties in the various disputes. Armando Iannucci reworked the Conservatives' election slogan ('Charles is booming — don't let Camilla blow him'), while Kevin Day reflected cynically on the revelations in Andrew Morton's book: 'Princess Diana threw herself at a glass cabinet. Presumably in an effort to display herself to death.' Even the children's television series *Maid Marian and Her Merry Men* slipped in a few gags; having taken all the peasants' food to give to King John, the Sheriff of Nottingham explains why they should be pleased to contribute: 'The royal family is a wonderful institution, right? They give us hours of pleasure, reading about Princess Marjorie's weight problems and little Prince Herbert's hilarious adventures at nursery school.' In response to which, Robin Hood can only tut: 'Honestly! The royals can be so middle class!' Tony Clark in *Between the Lines* was more vituperative: 'A family of below average intelligence and unbelievable wealth whose powers belong in the middle ages.'

None of this might have mattered quite so much had it not come at a time when the people's affection for royalty was already at a low ebb. For many years the publisher Letts had produced a royal diary on an annual basis; in 1991 it announced that it would not be doing so any more, since demand had fallen so heavily. 'It has turned into a disaster,' commented a company spokesperson. 'People would now rather have diaries with beauty tips than information on the royal family.' The Queen's Christmas broadcast that year attracted just ten million viewers, a healthy audience, but substantially down from the seventeen million it was getting just a few years earlier. Even those who traded on royal associations were becoming reluctant to promote the fact: the Royal Automobile Club redesigned its logo in 1997, dropping the image of the crown after ninety years. 'The most serious threat to the Monarchy's future,' according to a *Daily Telegraph* editorial in 1991, 'stems not from the few who are directly hostile to it, but from the growing number who are indifferent.'

Respect for the royals was in decline, and the endless stream of personal revelations and rumours simply strengthened that trend. 'Before they came along,' a senior courtier observed of Diana and Sarah, 'the monarchy was in a healthy condition and looked to have a long and stable future. Now look how things have changed.'

In the years since the Second World War, the monarchy had effectively been off-limits for writers and artists, to the extent that the Sex Pistols not only had their 1977 single 'God Save the Queen' banned by the mass media, but also faced physical assault in the streets for having released such an abomination. Now the institution was seen as a prism through which the reality of modern Britain might be revealed.

Sue Townsend's novel *The Queen and I* (1992) was premised on the election of a republican government, leading the royal family to be rehoused on a rundown council estate where some fare better than others. The Queen and Princess Anne adapt reasonably well to their changed circumstances, but Prince Philip goes into terminal decline, morally, mentally and physically: 'How squalid he looks, thought the Queen, and she had a glimmer of understanding of how easy it was to slide into such a state and how difficult it must be to get out of it.'

Despite the familiar characters, the book is essentially a depiction of the grinding material and spiritual poverty of much of Britain. Here public services are so chronically underfunded that hospital wards are being closed down and the local school has a rain alarm to signal to the bucket-monitors that it's time to put containers under the myriad leaks in the roof. And, as Prince Charles discovers, the benefits system that is supposed to alleviate the hardships is almost impossible to navigate: 'What he did work out is that they could not claim Housing Benefit until their Income Support was known; and they could not claim Income Support until their Housing Benefit was assessed. And then there was Family Credit, which they were yet to benefit from, but which seemed to be included in the total sum.'

It was hard, too, not to see *The Madness of King George*, the successful 1994 film of an Alan Bennett stage play, as at least in part a commentary on current affairs. 'To be Prince of Wales is not a position,' despairs Rupert Everett, playing the role of the 1788 occupant of the office. 'It is a predicament.' He's shown having an affair with Mrs Fitzherbert, while he plots to take over as king. Elsewhere the politicians are arguing about the role of monarchy. 'The king will do as he's told,' insists William Pitt the Younger, to which Charles Fox retorts: 'Then why not be rid of him? If a few ramshackle colonists in America can send him packing, why can't we?'

Such a sentiment was heard increasingly often. In the 1970s the Labour MP Willie Hamilton had found that expressing anti-monarchical opinions was enough to guarantee him a public profile, but now he would have struggled to be heard amidst the clamour. 'There is no republican movement in this country,' declared Julian Critchley in 1992, and he was correct in that no major party campaigned for the abolition of the monarchy. The cause of republicanism was, however, gaining a great deal of ground. Alongside the books of gossip, there emerged also from 1993 onwards some serious volumes that called into question the entire institution. In a sign of the times, a book by the academic Stephen Haseler was given the provocative title *The End of the House of Windsor* and adorned with a photograph of Diana on the front and an endorsement from Andrew Morton on the back; a thoughtful study of British social structures was being sold as a piece of populism. The same year came A.N. Wilson's *The Fall of the House of Windsor* (a title previously used for a book by Nigel Blundell and Susan Blackhall).

There was also, for the first time since the war, a political expression of the tendency. A poll published in the *Sunday Telegraph* in January 1993 suggested that a quarter of Labour MPs now favoured republicanism, not all of them on the left. In a speech that month, Jack Straw talked about the need to reform 'eighteenth-century institutions like the House of Lords, the judiciary and the honours system'. He went on to say: 'What I think is increasingly clear is that the current royal system, with its large number of participants and its emphasis on show business, has little serious future.' He didn't quite call for the removal of the royal family — most of the talk in political circles was of following the scaled-down Dutch or Scandinavian model, the so-called 'cycling royals' — but the fact that a senior member of the shadow cabinet was going even so far was a shock to the system. And that linking of the theme with other areas of reform was characteristic of the period. Campaigners for constitutional reform, the idea of which had been gathering momentum since the mid-1980s, were keen to associate Britain's decline as an economic power in the world with its 'outdated' institutions. Even Margaret Thatcher was reported to have said that 'Britain could never make progress until it abolished the monarchy.'

Tony Blair had long regarded Jack Straw as one of the modernisers in the Labour Party, someone on whom he could call for support, and Straw's comments were an early indication that for some on the Blairite wing of the party, the monarchy was potentially an anachronism in the much-touted 'New Britain'. Certainly that was the view of Mo Mowlam, who made news in 1994 when she suggested that the royal family ought to move out of Buckingham Palace. Asked later about these comments, in a 1997 interview in the Irish rock magazine *Hot Press*, she made the connection explicit, saying that she hoped when Charles became king, 'he does begin to adapt to what Blair represents as part of our culture'.

Charles was believed by many to be something of a problem, and not simply because of the personal unpopularity he experienced as a result of Diana's high-profile feud. He was now in his mid-forties and there seemed little immediate prospect of him ascending the throne; his grandmother was still alive, and looked likely to remain so for some time, let alone his mother. At the start of the decade there had been speculation that the Queen might consider abdicating in his favour, but she used her Christmas broadcast in 1991 to make clear that she had no intention of stepping down, now or ever. 'I feel the same obligation to you that I felt in 1952,' she said, pointedly. 'With your prayers and your help, and with the love and support of my family, I shall try to serve you in the years to come.'

By 1993 whispers of abdication had given way to much more preposterous ideas, including the suggestion by Simon Courtauld, deputy editor of the *Spectator*, that after the Queen's death, the crown should pass to the Duke of Buccleuch, descended from the Duke of Monmouth, son of Charles II. A.N. Wilson, meanwhile, nominated Richard, Duke of Gloucester, a grandson of George V whose mother was another Buccleuch. Only slightly more plausible was the proposition that the crown might skip a generation, missing out Charles and passing directly to William.

It was never going to happen, but if an announcement had been made to this effect, it would have pleased a great many people on both sides of the political divide. The left objected to the institution of monarchy itself; the right to Charles as an individual. That latter distrust was expressed in the second of Michael Dobbs's Francis Urquhart trilogy, *To Play the King*, published in 1992 and adapted for television the following year. This depicted a Conservative prime minister coming into constitutional conflict with a new king, clearly based on Charles, who insists on meddling in politics. 'I happen to believe that if there was a bust-up between the government and monarchy, it would be much more likely with a Conservative government,' Dobbs explained at the time of publication. He had formerly been an adviser to Margaret Thatcher, who had never been entirely enamoured of Charles's patrician liberalism.

There were, too, those on the left who disapproved specifically of Charles. Ron Davies, the shadow Welsh secretary, took the opportunity of St David's Day in 1996 to share his thoughts on the Prince of Wales with a television audience. 'He spends his time talking to trees and flowers, yet encourages his sons to go out to kill wild animals,' he ruminated. 'You must ask the question, is this person fit to continue the tradition of the monarchy, and come to the conclusion: No, he isn't.' Davies was immediately sat upon by his New Labour masters and obliged to retract his remarks — 'My comments on the effect on the monarchy of the troubles faced by the Prince and the Princess of Wales were wrong and I will be writing to Prince Charles to apologise' — though he was presumably satisfied, as an avowed republican, to have at least raised the issue.

Davies's original conclusion was, for different reasons, shared by others. 'I have to wonder if Charles is fit to be king,' said Richard Parker Bowles, younger brother of the man cuckolded by the Prince. 'He made a fool of my family. We had no right of reply.' Elsewhere, the highlight of the 1994 British Comedy Awards was the presentation of a lifetime achievement award to Spike Milligan, during which Jonathan Ross read a letter from Charles enthusing about the former Goon's work but was continually interrupted by Milligan himself, calling the Prince a 'grovelling little bastard', much to the amusement of the crowd and the television audience.

Republicanism was still a minority cause, but it received a boost in 1994 when the *Independent on Sunday* became the first mainstream paper to declare itself in favour. If there were to be an elected president, it asked its readers, who should it be; the leading candidates were, in descending order, Tony Benn, Betty Boothroyd, Jarvis Cocker and Helena Kennedy, the lawyer who was also chair of the constitutional reform group Charter 88. The highest ranked royal was Princess Anne in eighth place, just behind Richard Branson. (Boothroyd had, coincidentally, been the nomination of Alastair Campbell, back when he was writing for the *Daily Mirror* and denouncing the royal family as 'the apex of a class system that exposes John Major's "classless society" for the slogan that it is'. As Campbell put it: 'Queen Betty has a rather truer ring than Queen Diana.')

There was another potential candidate, however. In his 1996 book *Faces of Labour*, Andy McSmith suggested that, in the event that the monarchy collapsed, Tony Blair might have a claim as a potential 'President of the Republic of Great Britain who will stand above the sordid routine of party politics and speak for the nation'.

It was a dangerously intoxicating idea at a time when Blair harboured the delusion that his party was 'the political arm of none other than the British people', and there were signs early on in his premiership that he might be tempted to think along the same lines. At the state opening of Parliament in 1997, the Blairs breached protocol by walking from Downing Street to the Houses of Parliament, waving at the crowds and upstaging the procession of the Queen from Buckingham Palace, a move that captured the attention of Fleet Street and, in the words of one report, 'effortlessly relegated the sovereign to a minor role on what used to be one of her biggest days'. Although the prime minister's office insisted that it was nothing more than a spontaneous display of informality, it outraged constitutionalists and, reportedly, earned a rebuke from the Queen herself.

In the places where it counted, however, it was welcomed enthusiastically. Blair was, said the *Sun*, 'the leader of the party of the people, in touch with his people'. The paper also quoted an anonymous minister as saying: 'Tony wants to show he is the people's premier.' That choice of phrasing would come to look rather prescient. Soon afterwards, Bill Clinton visited Britain to stage a joint press conference with Blair, but didn't see the head of state. Buckingham Palace was allegedly furious: 'They think Tony Blair is getting too grand,' a courtier told the *Mail on Sunday*, 'and that prime ministers should play second fiddle to monarchs.'

The relationship between the newly elected Labour government and the royal family was always going to be a slightly awkward one. Blair had no intention of reforming the monarchy, but the words of Jack Straw, Mo Mowlam and Alastair Campbell indicated that such thinking was not unknown in New Labour circles, where the only royal who met with complete approval was Diana.

'In temperament and time, in the mood she engendered and which we represented, there was a perfect fit,' Blair was later to write, and even Campbell was swept up in what Peter Mandelson called a 'near-teenage infatuation' when he actually met her. 'She had perfect skin and her whole face lit up when she spoke and there were moments when I had to fight to hear the words because I'm just lost in the beauty,' Campbell gushed. 'And I'm thinking how could I have written all those vile things about her.' In return, Diana appeared also to have found common ground, according to Hugo Young. 'She thinks Tony Blair is a nice chap,' he noted, after her visit in 1996 to the *Guardian* offices; 'you could almost tell she sort of fancies him, unlike Major.'

By now Diana had scaled back heavily her involvement in charitable and other public works. That didn't mean, however, that she was any less visible, and she continued to campaign in a handful of specific areas, most notably against the use of landmines. And she was still capable of generating huge media attention when she chose. Holidaying in the Mediterranean with her new partner, Dodi Al-Fayed – son of Harrods owner Mohammed – in the summer of 1997, she celebrated the fiftieth birthday of Camilla Parker

Bowles by diving off Al-Fayed's yacht in a suitably revealing swimsuit, thus ensuring that it was she rather than her ex-husband's mistress who dominated the newspapers.

She also gave an interview to the French newspaper *Le Monde*, in which she demonstrated that it was not only Charles who could meddle in politics. Describing the former Conservative government as 'hopeless' on the issue of landmines, she expressed her belief that Labour would do 'great work'. (The Blair government had already announced a moratorium on the 'operational use' of landmines, though the right was reserved to use them in circumstances where they were considered necessary for the security of British forces.)

Her relationship with Al-Fayed had already occasioned some concern. 'Many will question the wisdom of our future king mixing so closely with a man who sees nothing wrong in buying power and who played a large part in the downfall of the last government,' pronounced Rupert Murdoch's *Sun*. Now, Diana's comments on John Major's government were seen as a step too far.

'It's a pity Gucci don't make designer face zips,' suggested Carol Malone in the *News of the World*; 'then when Princess Diana was on the verge of opening her ill-informed mouth and causing an international incident (an increasingly frequent occurrence these days) she could just zip her trap shut.' Barbara Gunnell in the *Independent on Sunday* mocked 'the inane Sloane-ish inarticulacy of a woman with fundamentally nothing to say about anything', while the *Observer*, in a column titled 'Mrs Blair's Diary', described Diana as 'a woman who, if her IQ were five points lower, would have to be watered daily'. Petronella Wyatt in the *Sunday Express* was not much more supportive: 'She seems to relish her role as a martyr. God help her if she ever finds happiness – it would make her miserable.' In the same paper, Bernard Ingham dismissed her and her new partner – 'I'm told she and Dodi are made for each other, both having more brass than brains' – and in the *Sunday Mirror* Chris Hutchins drooled at the possible emergence of another taped conversation with James Gilbey: 'this one is hot, hot, hot!'

It was, of course, unfortunate for all these writers that their words had already gone to press by the time the news came out from Paris in the early hours of Sunday, 31 August 1997 that Diana and Dodi had been killed in a car crash.

The news of Diana's death at the age of thirty-six was deeply shocking and yet somehow not entirely surprising. The image of her as a middle-aged, let alone elderly, woman had never been easy to conjure up, and the manner of her passing, pursued through the Parisian night by a pack of paparazzi photographers, seemed almost immediately to make sense, an appropriate end to a life that had long since lost any semblance of reality. It felt fated.

Still it caught the country and the country's media unawares. None had anticipated that hers would be the next royal death. Instead there had for many years been plans in place at both Buckingham Palace and the BBC to cover the death of the Queen Mother: eight days of mourning including three days of lying in state in Westminster before the actual funeral. In fact that event had been planned for nearly half a century; as far back as 1952, mere months after the death of George VI, the BBC had nominated Macdonald Hobley – the actor best known as the host of *Come Dancing* – to deliver the official announcement of the Queen Mother's death. No such forward thinking had taken place for Diana.

The confusion of the early reports added to the immediate difficulties of coverage. BBC Two broke the news of the car crash at 1 a.m., followed within the hour by ITV, but it was still understood at this point that Diana had suffered only minor injuries. ITV closed down its rolling news programme around 4.20 a.m., believing that the story was finished, only to have to return to the screens twenty minutes later to announce her death. Thereafter black ties were compulsory, even for weather forecasters. All scheduled programmes on BBC One were dropped in favour of a rolling news show, Radio 4 and Radio 5 Live trod the same ground with a joint broadcast, while Radio 3 played only slow movements from popular works of classical music and Radio 1 only slow pop songs – for the first time in the latter station's existence, it did not broadcast the chart show. ITV made the commercially painful decision to abandon all advertising, at least until the evening. Tributes were relayed from other revered figures – Nelson Mandela, Mother Teresa, Margaret Thatcher – and interviews were given by the likes of David Mellor, demanding action against an intrusive press, while Jeffrey Archer and David Starkey drew comparisons respectively with the murder of John Kennedy in 1963 and the death of James Dean in 1955. The state of the nation was captured best on GMTV: 'You might not believe this,' said newsreader Anne Davies, sounding as though she couldn't quite accept it herself, 'but I'm afraid it is true.'

The continuous media coverage was more than matched by the public's response. Radio stations reported the greatest number of phone calls ever received, their switchboards jammed with people who felt the need to talk about the event, even if there was nothing in particular to say. The same phenomenon could be observed across the country. There was just one topic of conversation and one overriding emotion: stunned disbelief. For want of words to express something largely inexpressible, crowds began to gather outside Buckingham Palace and, particularly, outside Diana's own home of Kensington Palace, where they laid flowers. By the end of the week, it was estimated that £50 million had been spent on these floral tributes.

Some details emerged over the next few days, establishing that Diana hadn't been wearing a seatbelt, that her driver was well over the legal alcohol limit and had been speeding, but beyond that, there was nothing new to say, and hours and hours to be filled saying it. The newspapers followed the lead of the broadcast media, though some had first to scramble to claw back lost ground, none more so than the American magazine the *National Enquirer*: 'We apologise for the Princess Diana page one headline DI GOES SEX MAD, which is still on the stands at some locations. It is currently being replaced with a special 72-page tribute issue: A FAREWELL TO THE PRINCESS WE ALL LOVED.'

It was later calculated that Diana's death generated more newspaper and magazine coverage than any other single event in the history of humanity, appropriately enough for the most photographed woman in the world. In life, she had been a banker for any publication wishing to increase sales, and in death she continued to work her magic: the *Sun* sold an extra million copies that Monday.

As the week wore on, the response of some was to question how genuine any of this public passion was, so perfect a media story did it seem. Adrian Mole's fifteen-year-old sister chose not to go to Kensington Palace to lay flowers: 'Rosie preferred to watch the Diana-mourning on television. She said it was "more real".' Tony Benn shared the same sense of unreality from another perspective: 'I hope by this time next week we will be able to re-enter the real world again, because there is something slightly sick about this,' he observed. 'It was also,' noted Giles Radice, 'a generational thing – it was the twenty- and thirty-year-olds, especially women, who felt Diana's death most. It was my daughters and stepdaughters who were most touched.'

The response of those at a more elevated social level was to look to their own position. 'They're all going to blame me, aren't they?' fretted Charles, while Blair saw opportunities as well as challenges: 'I also knew that this was going to be a major national, in fact global event like no other. How Britain emerged was important for the country internally and externally.' Blair it was who seized control of the moment. Having decided that he ought to speak to the media on his way back from church that Sunday morning ('Anything before that would look tacky,' he agreed with Alastair Campbell), he delivered perhaps his most enduring soundbite: 'She was the people's princess. And that is how she will stay, how she will remain in our hearts and memories – for ever.'

It wasn't an entirely new phrase. The title 'the people's princess' had already been used of the Duchess of York, of Princess Anne (most recently in 1996) and of Diana herself, the title being bestowed upon her by Julie Burchill in 1991 and by James Whitaker in 1992. In November 1993 the *Daily Mirror* had published photographs of Diana taken by a hidden camera above a machine in an LA Fitness gym in West London; although Diana sued for this invasion of her privacy (the paper settled out of court for £200,000 damages and around £1 million in legal fees), the article was largely sympathetic and was headlined THE PEOPLE'S PRINCESS. Never, though, had the epithet struck such a chord. It was clearly a terrible cliché, yet at the same time it sounded like an entirely original thought, and in that contradiction it encapsulated the public mood. It also, of course, implied that the other royals didn't belong to, and weren't part of, the people.

In a trembling voice, Blair described himself as being 'utterly devastated', and summed up the mood of the country: 'We are today a nation in a state of shock, in mourning, in grief that is so deeply painful for us.' That came dangerously close to using the royal 'we', but it was no accident, as Jonathan Powell wrote in his diary: 'he obviously feels real grief but also feels he needs to express it for the nation.' Later that day, as he waited at RAF Northolt for the plane carrying Diana's corpse to arrive from Paris, Blair reflected 'that this was a moment for the country to unite. There had to be love for Diana; respect for the Queen; a celebration of what a great country this was.'

He had been prime minister for just four months. Still riding his own wave of acclaim and popularity, he was confronting a situation for which no one was even vaguely prepared. Had Diana still been married, there would have been some precedent, some protocol upon which to draw, but there was no known procedure for the sudden death of a divorced Princess of Wales who had, just a year before, been stripped of her right to be called Her Royal Highness. In the absence of any comment from the royal family themselves, Blair stepped in to speak for the country and did so convincingly. He was quite correct in assuming that there were points of comparison to be made between Diana's emotional appeal and the nebulous values of New Labour, but he resisted the temptation to make this a time for scoring political points and he was cautious about stepping too far into the limelight. 'We have to be careful,' noted Alastair Campbell the next day, 'that it doesn't look like we are writing our script, rather than hers.'

There were plenty of others who did wish to write her script. 'You cannot be a sentient human being and not feel grief and horror,' judged the historian Ben Pimlott, but he found himself topped in his garment-rending by other highbrow journalists. The novelist Piers Paul Read said that a 'comparison could be made with the Virgin Mary', a sentiment with which Paul Johnson could only concur: 'I am reminded of the Blessed Virgin.' Norman St John Stevas believed she had 'a real and charismatic gift for healing', and David Aaronovitch wrote: 'We therefore crucified her, with our strange appetite for celebrity. And however much we attempt to read paparazzi for Pharisee we know that it is really our fault that she died.' This angle, hovering between the beatified and the messianic, had already been covered in her lifetime by Adrian Mole: 'Princess Diana's cleaning bill must be enormous. She is always wearing white clothes lately, giving her the appearance of a virgin or a saint.'

As the initial disbelief turned to shock, a new narrative began to emerge. Apart from the grief, there was also anger at the actions of the paparazzi, chasing after the photographs that the British people had so often enjoyed seeing in their newspapers. This was not, for obvious reasons, an angle that the press wished to pursue in any great detail, and instead a new target was sought onto which the public rage could safely be deflected. It was found in the form of the royal family.

A few months earlier, Armando Iannucci had written: 'In time of national crisis or tragedy, the royal family doesn't share grief through the expression of recognisable emotion. They express it through staring at flags and inspecting rubble.' The Queen, Charles and Diana's sons were at the time in Balmoral, far from the rising tide of flowers in West London, and the absence of 'recognisable emotion', of any direct response at all, was seized upon by the newspapers, anxious to deflect attention from themselves.

Media scorn focused initially on Charles, plumbing new depths on the Tuesday, when the *Daily Mail* ran a months-old photograph of him under the headline CHARLES WEEPS BITTER TEARS OF GUILT. And then it was turned on the Queen herself. 'There has been no expression of sorrow from the Queen on behalf of the nation,' regretted the *Sun* on Wednesday; 'not one tear has been shed in public from a royal eye. It is as if no one in the Royal Family has a soul.' On the same day, Blair spoke to the media in Downing Street, asking that people respect the royal family's right to grieve in private, but even he was unable to halt the growing atmosphere of recrimination. 'The mood was really turning against the royals and everyone seemed helpless in the face of it,' wrote Campbell on Thursday. 'The press were now fuelling a general feeling that the royals were not responding or even caring. The ugliness of the mood was growing.'

Bizarrely, though in keeping with the Cool Britannia era, the dispute over the royal response to the tragedy homed in on the symbol of a flag. Convention had it that the Royal Standard flew over Buckingham Palace when the Queen was in residence, and no flag at all when she was not; since she was in Scotland, there was therefore no flag available to be flown at half-mast. For reasons that defied explanation, this became a major point of issue. WHERE IS OUR QUEEN? WHERE IS HER FLAG? demanded the *Sun* on Thursday. Meanwhile, it was reported in outrage, the Royal Standard continued to fly at full-mast over Balmoral; the explanation, that this was the symbol of the monarchy itself and was never lowered to half-mast even when the monarch died, fell on deaf ears.

By now the contrast was being made between the stuffy old uncaring royals and the emotionally literate public. 'What upset people,' wrote Tony Parsons the following week, 'was that the royal family seemed blind to the country's sadness.' He was right that there was a chasm between, on the one side, the public outpouring of anguish for someone known only through the media, and on the other, the private response of those who might reasonably be considered to have the best interests of Diana's children at heart, but how this alleged neglect of the nation could be resolved by the display of a flag was far from obvious. Nonetheless the tabloids' twin demands – that the royal family should parade their grief in public, and that a break with protocol should be made – were echoed elsewhere. As a leader in *The Times* put it, 'The mere presence of the Sovereign at Buckingham Palace would mean much to many mourners. So would a little flexibility in the purely symbolic matter of flags flown at royal palaces.'

The campaign worked. Behind the scenes, Blair and Campbell had been advising the royals and persuaded them that action was needed. On Thursday, the young princes – William was fifteen, Harry twelve – were sent in front of the cameras at Balmoral, a Union flag was installed at half-mast on Buckingham Palace, and it was announced that the Queen would broadcast a message on television. THE QUEEN BOWS TO HER SUBJECTS was the headline in the *Independent*, though the best response by far came from the unlikely source of the *Sport*, a publication so downmarket and reliant on advertising by premium-rate sex lines that it barely qualified as a newspaper. Under a witheringly sarcastic headline – ARE WE HAPPY NOW? – the paper declared this to be 'The day Britain should have died of SHAME', and followed it with a denunciation of Fleet Street and of the crowds at the Palace gates. 'The unstoppable, irrational and hysterical wave of mourning which has swept through Britain has been allowed to swamp the very two people we are supposed to be protecting,' wrote the editor, Tony Livesey.

'What the f*** do you want William and Harry to do next? Bottle their tears and sell them on Saturday on The Mall?' Livesey himself had lost his mother when he was thirteen and knew where his sympathies lay: 'I didn't want to speak to strangers. I didn't feel the need to prove my love for my mum.'

And all the time, the crowds continued to gather, the cellophane sea of flowers continued to rise, and intolerance for dissent became ever more vocal. The issue of *Private Eye* published that week bore a cover mocking the double standards of the press and the public, while an apology inside regretted that the magazine, 'in common with all other newspapers, may have inadvertently conveyed the impression that the late Princess of Wales was in some way a neurotic, irresponsible and manipulative troublemaker who had repeatedly meddled in political matters that did not concern her'. It added: 'We would like to express our sincere and deepest hypocrisy to all our readers on this tragic day and hope and pray that they will carry on buying our paper notwithstanding.' The humour was lost on many and the magazine promptly found itself banned by several leading retailers; a third of sales were lost, though postal subscriptions increased as a response.

Out on the streets, two elderly Czech ladies were caught removing teddy-bears from the piles of tributes and were sentenced to a month in jail, though this was reduced on appeal after two nights behind bars. A Sardinian tourist was also spotted taking a teddy-bear and was arrested after members of the public gave chase; he was given a seven-day sentence, later reduced to a £100 fine, and on his way out of court was punched in the face by a 43-year-old man who later explained: 'I did it for Britain.'

It wasn't just teddy-bears that were to be found nestling amongst the flowers, cards and poems. A friend of the comedian Stewart Lee told him about seeing a model of E.T. lying in the piles, from which Lee developed a celebrated routine in which he tried to picture what could possibly have been in the minds of those who thought this was an appropriate gesture for mourning. The reality was even stranger. Upon the death of Mother Teresa of Calcutta, which also occurred that week, some enterprising street traders saw an opportunity to offload unsold stocks of E.T. dolls; newly wrapped in miniature blue-and-white saris, they were offered as alleged effigies of the famous Catholic nun. Truly, it was an extraordinary, surreal week.

When the Queen did broadcast her message, it was not quite the unifying event that was hoped for. In what the *Daily Telegraph* called 'the most remarkable and personal message of her reign', she spoke of herself in the first person singular (rather than using her customary 'one'), described Diana as an 'exceptional and gifted human being' and, at Campbell's suggestion, said she was speaking 'as a grandmother'. Blair's evaluation was that her tone had been 'near perfect. She managed to be a queen and a grandmother at one and the same time.' But others, primarily those who placed themselves in Diana's camp, were less receptive. The Queen was 'clipped, formal, utterly without warmth and affection', wrote Alan Clark. Those who steadfastly remained aloof from the entire event could only marvel at the state to which the monarch had been reduced. 'She looked like a battered hostage paraded in front of the cameras to explain how well she was being treated,' observed Linda Smith.

Then, on the Saturday, came the funeral itself, which – despite the rival claim of Ronnie Kray – really was the biggest such event since the death of Winston Churchill in 1965. And Britain's long-asserted status as the world leader in ceremonial was triumphantly vindicated. In the space of six days, an entirely new format had been created, a blend of ritual and informality that was a breathtaking piece of theatre. To the sound of a single tolling bell, and of weeping crowds, the coffin was drawn through the streets from Kensington Palace to Westminster Abbey on a gun carriage, followed by five men in dark suits and black ties: Philip, Charles, William, Harry and Diana's brother, Charles Spencer. The coffin was draped in the Royal Standard and flanked by members of the King's Troop, but the civilian simplicity of that small group, the absence of the usual military trappings of a state occasion, was enormously affecting.

Inside the Abbey, the service included the hymn 'Make Me a Channel of Your Peace', the patriotic song 'I Vow to Thee, My Country' and Elton John's reworking of his old tribute to Marilyn Monroe, 'Candle in the Wind', while Tony Blair read the lesson, the first prime minister to do so at a royal funeral (convention suggested that it should have been the Speaker of the House of Commons).

The headlines were stolen, however, by Earl Spencer, whose eulogy paid due tribute to his sister's life and work, but also found room to attack the paparazzi and the press for making her 'the most hunted person of the modern age'. He took a sideswipe at the way Diana's royal title had been stripped from her on her divorce and, in a thinly veiled passage of criticism, addressed his dead sister on the subject of her two sons: 'I pledge that we, your blood family, will do all we can to continue the imaginative way in which you were steering these two exceptional young men so that their souls are not simply immersed by duty and tradition but can sing openly as you planned.' As he finished speaking, applause broke out amongst the massive crowds outside, to whom the service was being relayed, and spread, hesitantly at first and then in an unprecedented wave, into the Abbey itself.

This really was informality, breaching every known convention of British funerals. 'Protocol changed forever during that ovation,' wrote Tony Parsons, who was a member of the congregation. 'It was the final reminder that Diana's death has shown us that we need to invent protocol and traditions that reflect the needs of our own age.' Even Tony Benn, who had no more time for the English aristocracy than he had for the monarchy, couldn't help but be impressed: 'that speech is worth really thinking about.' After the service, there was a further break with tradition. Hundreds of thousands lined the roads along which the hearse drove, carrying the coffin to the Spencers' ancestral home at Althorp in Northamptonshire, and as the procession passed, flowers were thrown in the path of the car.

Not everyone approved of the unconventional nature of the occasion. Amongst those in the crowds were members of the Edwardian Drape Society, a purist organisation of Teddy boys. When interviewed by the media, the Society's founder Ritchie Gee explained their position: 'Everyone here had come to pay their respect at a funeral wearing trainers and zip-up anoraks. Nobody's got any respect anymore. Why aren't they wearing a suit?' Nor was Gordon Brown best pleased to discover that he wasn't being invited to the funeral, though space was found for deputy prime minister John Prescott, and Robin Cook, the foreign secretary with whom Diana had worked on the landmines issue.

William Hague was also invited, despite having signally failed to impress over the last few days. Formal and restrained in his response, he had – on the recommendation of his young adviser, George Osborne – suggested that Heathrow Airport be renamed in Diana's honour, a proposal so irrelevant that it was scarcely noticed. The Conservatives had convinced themselves that they were starting to make up some ground on Labour, but the death of Diana halted any such advance: 'That single event stopped our recovery in its tracks,' commented one shadow minister. Instead they looked entirely lost in this new Britain, where public displays of emotion ('Latin American peasant hagiolatry', in the words of Boris Johnson) were not only acceptable but almost compulsory. A former cabinet minister expressed the confusion that had descended on the Tories: 'I walked through the crowds in St James's and realised this was no longer a country I truly understand.'

Tony Blair, on the other hand, was universally judged to have played a blinder, and an opinion poll a month later showed him achieving record levels of approval. In terms of popular acclaim, this was the high point of his premiership.

It was also the start of the restoration of the monarchy's fortunes. A Gallup poll published in the *Daily Telegraph* the following week showed that half the country felt that Diana's death and funeral had damaged the public standing of the Queen and the royal family, and 71 per cent thought that the monarchy should move towards the much-vaunted Dutch model. But these were instant responses that faded rapidly, and were in any case balanced by the 51 per cent who believed that William, not Charles, should be the next king. For the image of the two young princes accompanying their mother's coffin was more potent even than the naked flagpole on Buckingham Palace. 'Their dignity and bravery in the face of such overwhelming grief wrenched the heart of a nation,' wrote Tony Parsons. 'How could anyone talk about getting rid of the royal family when these two boys are its future?'

The crowds on the streets, and the tens of millions watching on television, were expressing not republican sympathies but, at most, an annoyance with the royal establishment for failing to recognise that Diana was the kind of royal the country now wanted; aristocratic and privileged still, but glamorous, impulsive and emotional as well – heritage, celebrity and the common touch all rolled into one. Traditional values in a modern setting, as John Prescott liked to say of the Labour Party.

In Sue Townsend's *The Queen and I*, even the Queen was to be found admiring the Republican prime minister, Jack Barker, and 'his obvious flair for public relations. If only *she* had been able to call on the skills of somebody like Jack in the Buckingham Palace Press Office!' Now, in real life, she had been able to see the workings of Alastair Campbell and his team close up, as they coordinated the funeral arrangements and choreographed the royals' public response. From here on, the publicity was to be handled a little more deftly than it had been in the past. Prince Charles was photographed with the Spice Girls, and found that his official overseas trips attracted considerably more media attention than they had in the past. The Queen was photographed in a pub, and in her husband's privately owned black cab, which had been converted to run on natural gas, though it was still driven by a liveried chauffeur – an environmentally friendly mix of deference and democracy.

Underneath, however, nothing fundamental had changed. Tony Blair had captured the public mood perfectly in that week, demonstrating, in Andrew Rawnsley's words, 'that his own instincts were often his most reliable focus group. He defined public sentiment and by doing so surfed and channelled the emotion that was washing across much of Britain.' But then Blair seemed to get cold feet, unsure what to do with this popular mandate. The logic of his politics demanded the reform of the monarchy, but no attempt was made to implement any transformation. Perhaps he recognised that any serious changes to the constitution would impact less upon the monarchy than upon the enormous powers enjoyed by the prime minister by virtue of exercising the royal prerogative.

Or perhaps it was simple confusion about what that week really meant. 'I couldn't work out if it was all about her, or all about them, or all about a desire for a new way of doing things,' puzzled Alastair Campbell of the floral tributes, and he was not alone in his bewilderment. In retrospect, it seemed clearer that it was all of those things. There was genuine shock at the loss of Diana, the closest that Britain had ever come to the death of John F. Kennedy, but there was also a collective wallowing, followed by a slightly guilty sensation that the indulgence might have been a little more pleasurable than decorum demanded. 'Those weeping crowds and daytime telly presenters may feel something but it's not grief,' observed Linda Smith. 'It's New Grief, Virtual Grief, grief with most of the pain taken out. It's the feeling you get from a sad film.'

That was true up to a point, but it missed the communality of the experience. Chris Smith, the culture secretary, talked of 'a real feeling that we are coming together as a nation, in shared grief but in shared purpose too', and if that perception soon came to seem trite at best, it nonetheless reflected the deluded mood of the moment. The fact that almost everyone, certainly everyone whose voice was heard in public, was expressing the same thing was a source of great reassurance. It seemed as though there was such a thing as society, after all. There was even a suspicion that it might be classless, since the masses felt such a personal connection with their chosen representative, the daughter of the 8th Earl Spencer.

Diana had set new standards for royalty, embracing the media age in a way that none had attempted before, and her actions and her persona over the last few years had constituted an implied rebuke to tradition. She represented a leap into the unknown for a monarchy that was still largely transfixed by the memory of how it had behaved during the war, pursuing her own happiness at the same time as doing her duty. And that 'new way of doing things', identified by Campbell, had a wider resonance. 'Taking on the establishment was applauded, but few people thought it could succeed,' reflected Mark Steel, 'so it felt as if many people wanted someone else to rebel on their behalf. Part of the Diana phenomenon was a curious manifestation of this mood.'

Steel also, however, discovered that the mood of the moment was less than friendly towards those who weren't swept up in the fervour. Appearing on a television show, he tried out a joke about how we would be able to remember the marriages of the current royal family more easily than those of Henry VIII: 'Divorced, divorced, divorced. Divorced, divorced, crashed.' He reported: 'There was a collective yelp, and I wasn't asked back.' In due course, jokes about Diana did gradually emerge, so that in 1998 Angus Deayton could talk on *Have I Got News for You* about growing calls for a bank holiday to be instituted in memory of Diana: 'It's felt that the best way to commemorate her death would be for everyone to get in their cars and drive out of the cities as fast as they can.'

But the veneration in the press continued. When, at the end of 1998, the *News of the World* drew up a list of the hundred greatest Britons of the last millennium, it put Diana at number one, beating Winston Churchill, Charles Darwin and William Shakespeare.

Diana's death had some curious consequences. There were marketing opportunities: Pizza Express added leeks to their vegetarian pizza and rebranded it the Pizza Diana (with 25p of the £5.80 price going to the Princess Diana Memorial Fund), while Elton John's 'Candle in the Wind 1997' sold 33 million copies worldwide, reaching the top of the charts in twenty countries and spending forty-six weeks at number one in Canada. Hardly more elevated was the Spencer family's announcement that tickets would be made available for those who wanted to visit the grave, at just £9.50 a head; the ticketing switchboard was reported to have received eight million phone calls on the first day.

Predictably the Press Complaints Commission issued a new code of conduct in response to the death, stating explicitly: 'Everyone is entitled to respect for his or her private and family life, home, health and correspondence.' It also said that 'the use of long-lens photography to take pictures of people in private places without their consent is unacceptable'. No one really expected this code to make any difference, and indeed it didn't. Nonetheless, Rupert Murdoch was said to have expressed some satisfaction that his papers would no longer have to pay inflated sums for paparazzi photos of Diana.

There were also odd casualties. In December 1997 Channel 4 aired a documentary, *Looking Like Diana*, in which three Diana lookalikes explained that the bottom had dropped out of the market since her death; after a decade of living off their looks, they'd all moved on to other jobs. The Swedish indie pop band the Wannadies found airplay hard to come by, given their name, and Kylie Minogue's record company felt obliged to delay the release of her new album and to retitle it from its original *Impossible Princess*. Most regrettable of all, in terms of music, was the case of Britpop founders

Denim, who, after five years of failing to sell records, finally seemed on the verge of a breakthrough. They had signed to a major record label, EMI, and their new release was Radio 1's single of the week. Unfortunately it was due for release on the day after Diana died, and it was pulled from the schedules, its title — 'Summer Smash' — being deemed inappropriate in the circumstances.

In fact, the non-appearance of that Denim single was symbolic of the times. For Britpop and Cool Britannia did not long survive Diana. Her death seemed to mark the end of the brief period in which control of popular culture had lain in the hands of the anti-Thatcher generation, for that strange week allowed no space for the ironic detachment that had been characteristic of so much of the early 1990s.

It was a theme explored in David Baddiel's second novel, *Whatever Love Means* (2000), which opened with the death of Diana and depicted its far-ranging effects on a small group of friends. Joe knows that, for those who appear consumed by grief, 'it wasn't her they connected with, but hysteria — the clamour of it, chiming with their own needs, saying to them what they most wanted to hear, come, here is identity'. Unfortunately his partner, Emma, is one of those people, devastated by Diana's death, who find their world shattered. Dissatisfied by Joe's unfeeling response, she goes to see their friend Vic, who's actually even more unfeeling, though in his case the lack of concern is concealed by an attack of hay fever that makes it look as though he too has been crying. In pursuit of mutual comfort and reassurance — she genuinely, he cynically — they rapidly find themselves having sex on the sofa, while in the background *Richard and Judy* continues to broadcast the same archive footage of Diana that has been a constant television presence all week.

The day after the funeral, Vic's partner, Tess, is on a Eurostar train back from France, where she has been shielded from the reaction at home. Finding a copy of the *Star*, she makes a joke about its front page (a picture of a cloud in the shape of Diana's face, headlined DI IN THE SKY). In reply, the woman sitting opposite her bursts into tears, and the rest of the carriage is so appalled that 'H.M. Bateman would've turned in his grave to think he'd missed the chance of caricaturing it'. She'd assumed that 'she would find, away from the predictable outpouring of plebeian grief, that most people thought like her, and that she could easily chime with her own kind by being funny about it all'. But she is wrong, and her mistaken perception of the national mood reflects the confusion of a generation that found its sense of irony had become out of date overnight.

12
Government
'It all breaks down at the first rehearsal'

ERIC: Take it from me, mate. White lies have a habit of turning into seething, bubbling red-hot lies that pour down mountains.
Tim Firth, *All Quiet on the Preston Front* (1994)

We'll sell you down the river
Just remember that we said we'd deliver you.
Mansun, 'Taxloss' (1997)

I think you'd prefer to have us than the others.
Tony Blair at the TUC conference (1999)

The Labour government that came to power in 1997 was the least experienced in living memory. A handful of members – Jack Cunningham, Margaret Beckett, Ann Taylor, Michael Meacher, Gavin Strang – had served as junior ministers in the 1970s, and attorney general John Morris was a solitary former cabinet minister (he had been Welsh secretary under James Callaghan). Beyond those few, the leader of the House of Lords, Ivor Richard, had been British ambassador to the United Nations and then a European commissioner, and Derek Scott, an economics adviser under Denis Healey when Labour was last in government, returned to Downing Street in the same capacity.

But that was about the sum total. More typical was Tony Blair, who hadn't even been a member of the party the last time that Labour won an election. One had to go back to Ramsay MacDonald in 1924 to find a prime minister who similarly had no experience of government, and MacDonald had been at the head of a minority administration in a hung parliament, very obviously a brief trial period that wasn't destined to last a year. It was in no way comparable to the situation in which Labour now found itself. As Merlyn Rees, a former home secretary, observed: 'None of them know how to do it. None of them have been there before.'

It was perhaps this lack of experience that prompted such suspicion of the existing structures of government. There seemed to be a belief in New Labour circles that the civil service was inherently untrustworthy, corrupted by long exposure to a Conservative administration, with which it was assumed to be in agreement. Much anecdotal evidence suggested that the reverse was true — that familiarity had bred a level of contempt for what some saw as Tory arrogance — but nonetheless it appeared that a clean sweep was required, particularly when it came to presentation. Of the nineteen directors of communication in Whitehall departments at the time of the election, all but two had been replaced within a couple of years, and the new incumbents were aware that they relied on the patronage of the Downing Street press office.

Meanwhile, the numbers swelled of those employed to deliver their masters' message, until by the end of the decade there were 1,100 press officers in Whitehall. This was the new powerhouse of government, where Alastair Campbell held sway. He was the first prime ministerial press officer to be a political appointee, rather than coming from within the civil service, and amongst the first acts of the new government was a change in the regulations to give Campbell and chief of staff Jonathan Powell the status and authority, though not the responsibilities, of civil servants.

The blurring of the boundaries between political advisers and the civil service was new — John Major's press secretary had played no part in the 1992 election — and it caused considerable distress in the latter camp. Richard Wilson, who served as cabinet secretary through most of Blair's first term, ended his time in office with a speech as thunderous as a civil servant could be: 'It is fundamental to the working of our constitution that governments should use the resources entrusted to them, including the civil service, for the benefit of the country as a whole and not for the benefit of their political party.'

Such concerns initially fell on deaf ears, particularly within the Labour Party. For it was a longstanding demand of the left that the civil service be brought to heel under democratic control. The television comedy *Yes, Minister* had been based on the experience of the Callaghan government, and the party retained strong folk memories of policy conflicts between elected ministers and unelected officials. The changes under Blair, however, were not a noticeable gain for democracy: Campbell was even less accountable for his actions than was a permanent secretary.

As Campbell spread his wings, he became the first press secretary to sit in on cabinet meetings, and he effectively took over much of the disciplinary power of the whips' office as well. The newly elected MP Oona King, planning to vote against her government's support for the bombing of Iraq in 1998, recorded in her diary a summons to see the whips, where she found that she could stall and laugh her way out of a serious confrontation. A subsequent encounter with Campbell, on the other hand, when she refused to do his bidding, ended on much less jovial terms. 'I know it's the end of my political career,' she said, and he replied: 'Just the next five years.' As she left the room, she reflected: 'Alastair was sort of joking, and sort of not.' There was certainly no question which episode inspired more fear. Just to make the point explicit, in 2001 the chief whip's office was moved out of 12 Downing Street, to be replaced by the prime minister's press team.

By then the impressionist Rory Bremner was regularly airing a routine in which Blair himself was seen to be bullied mercilessly by Campbell. 'The press *are* the country. There isn't anything else,' the Campbell character says. 'I tell you; you tell the great unwashed. That's why we're never wrong. And you're just Little Miss Echo Tony, just a spokesperson.' Blair was said to detest the sketches, while Jack Straw thought they were 'genuinely damaging', and Bremner was banned from travelling on the prime minister's tour bus in the 2001 election. But a documentary made by Michael Cockerell in 2000, *News from Number 10*, seemed only to confirm how very closely the routines reflected the actual nature of the relationship. In particular, a scene in which Blair wanders into Campbell's room, without realising that the camera crew are there, was much cited as evidence of the press officer's power. It was 'like the schoolboy coming into the headmaster's study', said Cockerell, while Hugo Young detected 'no respect, no authority. Just two lads together. Serious lads. But, as it seemed, equal lads.'

Campbell did, however, have the advantage of competence. His accumulation of power might be a source of concern, as was his centrality to policy-making, but when it came to understanding and controlling the media, he was undeniably effective. For, unlike the rest of the cabinet, he had the benefit of many years' experience in his field. Others simply floundered. When Chris Mullin was appointed as a minister to John Prescott's Department of Environment, Transport and the Regions, he found that the deputy prime minister had failed to make a positive impact: 'there is a barely concealed contempt among both civil servants and ministers for his absolute lack of management skills, his inability to see wood for trees and his flat refusal to listen to anything anyone is telling him.' He added, with a note of sorrow: 'Deep down I am sure he, too, realises that he is out of his depth.'

'Of course we want to use the media,' Peter Mandelson had said in the post-Michael Foot days of the 1980s, 'but the media will be our tools, our servants;

we are no longer content to let them be our persecutors.' This attitude now became central to the conduct of government. Statements were made not to Parliament, but to the press, a practice hinted at back in 1989 when Blair was to be found advising a Conservative minister that 'if he is going to say something, he should make sure it is said in the form of a press release'. Even announcements concerning Parliament itself received this treatment, as when Blair – immediately after the 1997 election – revealed that the existing format of two fifteen-minute sessions of prime minister's questions each week would now be replaced by a single thirty-minute session, so as not to disrupt his schedule quite so much.

The apparent marginalisation of Parliament was one of the most notable features of the early Blair government, and it drew the attention of commentators from the start. Blair himself had the worst voting record of any modern prime minister, and was seldom seen in the House. His vote was scarcely necessary, of course, but for a politician obsessed with 'sending out signals', it suggested a lack of faith or interest in the parliamentary process. In his absence, analysis of new legislation was actively discouraged, just as it was in cabinet. During the eleven years of Margaret Thatcher's premiership, the government had used a parliamentary guillotine to curtail debates in the Commons on forty occasions; Blair's government used the tactic sixty times in its first three years.

Meanwhile the parliamentary term was substantially reduced, so that the summer recess of 1997 was the longest for decades. Even when the House was sitting, there were plenty of absentees, since the majority was so huge that Labour backbenchers were urged to spend more time with their electorates; some were away from Westminster for as much as one week a month. A new perception grew that the chief function of a Labour MP was to represent the government in his or her constituency. Harold Macmillan had once instructed Julian Critchley that his 'task was to be the Member for Aldershot in Westminster and not the Member for Westminster in Aldershot'; that was now turned on its head, with the result that government policy was subjected to less scrutiny than it might otherwise have faced. There was also a knock-on effect on local democracy: why bother contacting a local councillor with a problem when there was so often an MP on hand? As Francis Pym had observed in 1987: 'Landslides, on the whole, do not produce successful governments.'

Anthony Barnett argued in 1997 that the downgrading of Parliament was a consequence of eighteen years of futile opposition: 'Current contempt reproduces Labour's real experience. They *know* that the House of Commons is not a modern, democratic institution.' This might have been a more convincing argument had New Labour's approach not been consistent throughout, replicating in government what it had practised in opposition. In 1996 Clare Short, chairing that year's party conference, was shocked to discover how much manipulation was employed to remove dissent, as she was given a list of delegates who were to be invited to speak from the floor. 'Those who are called to speak at conference are pre-chosen and "helped" with their speeches,' she wrote later. 'Similarly "clappers" are placed around the hall, to lead a storm of applause for platform speakers whom there is a wish to favour.'

The same year, Blair attempted to suspend the annual elections to the shadow cabinet, fearing that Harriet Harman would be punished by MPs for the choices she had made regarding her son's education. He was persuaded by John Prescott that suspension was unacceptable, but the result was still manipulated; frontbench spokespeople who hadn't previously been elected to the shadow cabinet were warned not to put themselves forward as candidates if they valued their jobs. Consequently the existing members were returned effectively unopposed. It was, said Ken Livingstone, 'like the old Soviet Union, where everybody got re-elected by near-unanimous votes'.

With Parliament now of little consequence, both the media and the public lost what scant interest they had in the proceedings. Radio broadcasts of the Commons had started in 1978 and for the first two decades of their existence were most frequently consumed as 'Yesterday in Parliament', a strand within Radio 4's *Today* programme. In 1998 it was announced that the broadcast would lose its FM slot and – although increased from fourteen to twenty-three minutes a day – would henceforth be confined to the ghetto of long wave. There were protests from MPs, but significantly none from Blair's inner circle, who weren't themselves much interested in the subject. Anyway, there was by now little appetite for the show; 350,000 listeners were said to switch off or switch over the moment that the broadcast began. Already *The Times* had given up the page it had previously devoted to parliamentary coverage on the grounds, as editor Simon Jenkins put it, that he 'couldn't find anyone who read it except MPs'. The only regular press coverage that survived was in the form of parliamentary sketches; more weighty consideration was reserved for big set-pieces, preferably those involving the prime minister or the leader of the opposition. This only increased the perception that the cabinet, let alone the Commons, was of limited concern.

The power of patronage exercised by the new government shaded over into what became termed cronyism. The expression pre-dated the 1997 election, when the Conservatives accused Blair of bribing veteran Labour MPs with the offer of peerages if they would step down from their constituencies to make way for more modernising members. Amongst those being pushed forward, it was said, was Yvette Cooper, who took over the Pontefract and Castleford seat formerly held by Geoffrey Lofthouse (Baron Lofthouse of Pontefract, as he became immediately after the election). 'Tony's cronies are being parachuted into the House of Commons,' declared Michael Heseltine, and the phrase was picked up by Conservative Central Office: 'These are jobs in the Lords for Tony's cronies. And jobs in the Commons for Tony's boys and girls. It is Labour sleaze.' Not until 1998, however, did the matter really gain traction in the media.

Similarly the phrase 'control freak', first applied to Blair in 1995 by Matthew Parris ('the little shit Parris', as Alastair Campbell referred to him), became commonplace only in 1998. Steadily, however, the impression grew of, in the words of *Drop the Dead Donkey*, 'The paranoid control-freak tendency that lies at the heart of this government.' Even Harold Wilson's former political secretary Marcia Williams thought Blair went too far, saying that he was 'a control freak, he is so determined to have total control that he's really taking out everything altogether'.

Like New Labour's obsession with the media, the wish to exert centralised control was understandable, its roots lying in the 1980s when the deep splits in the party had damaged its public standing. It was hard to forget, however, that more recently Blair had been amongst those vainly urging John Smith to lead a mutiny against Neil Kinnock, and that Blair and Peter Mandelson were then chiefly blamed for trying to undermine Smith once he became leader. Loyalty to the party, never Blair's most obvious characteristic, was equally lacking in most of New Labour's officer class, who showed little inclination to abide by the iron discipline imposed upon the foot soldiers.

The insistence that MPs had to hold whatever line had been determined by the prime minister's office didn't augur well for the future of the party or of the country more widely. As the 1992 Convention on Biological Diversity, adopted by a United Nations conference in Rio, made clear, variety is the central feature of life, its greatest asset when faced with a hostile, changing environment. It was a concept in which New Labour professed to believe when it came to public services — 'Diversity must become the norm, not the exception,' Blair said of education — yet was unwilling to tolerate within its own ranks. Dissent was stifled wherever possible, even though the creation of New Labour itself had relied on the availability of space within the party to examine new ideas. As Clare Short argued, 'for parties to be able to renew themselves and be open to new thinking and policy' there needed to be room for unpopular minority opinions to develop. 'I fear that New Labour's party-management style allows for little such diversity.'

The pattern had been set at a very early stage. 'Opposition is meant to be a time for thinking,' observed Hugo Young, after a meeting in 1993 with Gordon Brown, but concluded that he had found no evidence of it. Instead, 'the longer these people stay in opposition the more they are driven to mimic the hyperactivity of the ministers they may never be'. The danger was that there would be little time for such reflection when confronted with the pressures of office, that the opportunity was being missed to create a coherent set of policies to see a government through the unforeseen events that would inevitably occur. It could be argued that this had been a problem for the Conservative administration of John Major, a man who had spent no time at all in opposition, and had barely a chance to stop and reflect on how to bring his dream of a classless society to reality, before being buffeted by the storms of Europe and sleaze.

But New Labour behaved in opposition as though they were in government, brushing aside any attempt to discuss new thought, and restricting themselves to ideas that had originated in the offices of Blair or Brown, or those recycled from the Tories. The party took over the reins of power almost bereft of serious policy in such major areas as the NHS and social security, to the extent that the 1997 manifesto's summary of health policy was reduced to banalities: 'The key is to root out unnecessary administrative cost, and to spend money on the right things – frontline care.' Even with its courting of think tanks and sympathetic intellectuals, it had trodden so carefully that few radical thoughts were aired. 'We are asked to think the unthinkable without rocking the boat,' shrugged one senior think-tank figure in the run-up to the election.

Instead New Labour insisted that it would prove itself through competence. Asked in 1996 to outline where he disagreed with Michael Howard's strong law and order agenda, Jack Straw simply replied: 'We have an approach that is more likely to work, whereas his has failed.' In the same year Roy Hattersley was invited to share with a group of Labour MPs and candidates what he had learnt as a minister. He tried to explain that they needed to be guided by principles and philosophy, and was met with heckles demanding 'What's wrong with managerialism?' With so little experience of government between them, it seemed a tall order for incoming ministers that they should prove quite as capable as they believed themselves to be.

It wasn't long before the problems began to appear. A fortnight after the election victory, the Queen's Speech outlined the government's priorities for its first Parliament, including a Bill to ban completely the advertising of cigarettes and tobacco. Briefing the press after the announcement, Tessa Jowell, the public health minister, explained that a white paper would be published in the summer, which would also address the question of how to end sponsorship of sporting events by tobacco companies. This was a little more tricky, since some sports were heavily dependent on cigarette money, had contracts in place for the next few years and might struggle to find new deals. But still the intention was clear, as the health secretary, Frank Dobson, spelt out: the Bill would cover 'all forms of tobacco advertising, including sponsorship'.

As the date for the proposed white paper began to drift, first to the autumn and then to the following year, there were reports in the press of heavy lobbying by tobacco firms and sports bodies, and of disagreements within the government, with the sports minister, Tony Banks, said to be deeply opposed to a sponsorship ban. Then in November 1997 *The Times* revealed that 'after long negotiations with the Fédération Internationale de l'Automobile (FIA)', Tessa Jowell 'has concluded that it would be counter-productive to bring in the ban for Formula One'.

The news was greeted with some dismay by health campaigners, and by defenders of other sports that were going to struggle to find replacement sponsors. The likes of snooker, darts and cricket were in for a considerably tougher time than the cash-rich glamour world of Formula One, and within Labour ranks there was concern that working-class pastimes were to be penalised while motor racing was to escape.

There was some speculation that Jowell had been unduly influenced by the fact that her husband, David Mills, had until a few months ago been a non-executive director of Benetton Formula, one of the Formula One teams. This, it soon transpired, was a red herring – though who had thrown it to the press remained obscure – for Jowell's anti-smoking credentials were impeccable, as Bernie Ecclestone, the head of Formula One, had already discovered. He had lobbied her and, getting no joy, had gone over her head to the prime minister; in October he and Max Mosley, president of the FIA, went to a meeting in Downing Street to plead their case with Tony Blair himself. They explained that if Formula One packed its bags and decamped from Britain, it would cost tens of thousands of jobs, as well as millions of pounds in exports, an assertion that seemed to convince the prime minister. In his memoirs, Blair recounted the situation as he saw it: 'Europe was looking to ban tobacco advertising in sport, and because Formula One was so heavily dependent on it, Bernie wanted time to have it phased in.'

Apart from the characteristically slack grammar, this description of the government's predicament was, at best, only a partial recollection; at worst, it was a little disingenuous. For it wasn't merely a looming European directive that was at issue, but the implications of Labour Party policy, outlined by Dobson and Jowell earlier in the year as they tried to make a reality of the manifesto's tough stance: 'Smoking is the greatest single cause of preventable illness and premature death in the UK. We will therefore ban tobacco advertising.' There was a European dimension, for the EU had become increasingly keen on anti-smoking measures, having already banned television advertising in 1991 (albeit at a time when the Common Agricultural Policy was pumping £900 million into subsidising tobacco production), but the real question was why Blair had been so easily persuaded at that meeting.

One possible answer was not long in emerging. It turned out that Ecclestone, once a major donor to the Conservative Party, had switched his financial allegiance to Labour, and earlier in the year, before the election, had given the party £1 million. It required something of a leap of faith not to question whether there might be some connection between the donation, the meeting and the decision.

Dobson and Jowell were in the clear, for they only now learned of the donation ('Cor, fuck me!' was the former's response to the news). Rather, this was a Downing Street issue, and Blair's inner circle rushed to counter the impression of scandal. Patrick Neill – Lord Nolan's successor as chairman of the Committee on Standards in Public Life – received a letter informing him of Ecclestone's donation, telling him there was the possibility of a second gift, and asking his advice on how to deal with any further money 'to avoid any possible appearance of a conflict of interest'. The letter was sent in the name of Labour's general secretary, Tom Sawyer (who didn't actually write it), and failed to make clear either the sum involved or the fact that it was Labour who were soliciting the second donation, rather than it being volunteered by Ecclestone. To the horror of Downing Street, Neill's response dealt also with the first donation and recommended that the money should be sent back whence it had come. 'Who the hell was he to decide?' raged Alastair Campbell, to which the response was presumably that he was the man recently appointed by the Labour government, and the man to whom it had turned for advice. Nonetheless, the £1 million was duly returned.

Meanwhile Gordon Brown was appearing on Radio 4's *Today* programme, denying any personal knowledge that Ecclestone was a donor to the party. According to allegations published in the book *Servants of the People*, by the *Observer* journalist Andrew Rawnsley, in 2000, this was untrue. The same accusation was also levelled against Blair's subsequent claims in a television interview that he had refused any further gifts from Ecclestone when in office, and that Labour had approached Neill for his advice on what to do with the original donation. More significantly, Blair's statement to the House of Commons on 12 November 1997 contained another falsehood: that the decision to exempt Formula One was only taken 'at the beginning of last week', thus seeking to put a distance of more than two weeks between the meeting with Ecclestone and the decision to exempt Formula One from any sponsorship ban. The truth was that Jonathan Powell had been instructed to phone Jowell on the day of the meeting, and that the following day a memo had been sent to her, making the situation explicit: 'The prime minister would like your ministers to look for ways of finding a permanent derogation for sport in particular, F1.'

Documentary evidence was thin on the ground, as no minute had been taken of the meeting, but for some the conclusion was inescapable: the decision on Formula One was taken by Blair and his closest advisers in direct response to representations by Ecclestone, and when the story of the original donation threatened to break, they engaged in a clumsy and incompetent cover-up, misleading the public and Parliament. On the more substantive issue of whether government policy had been influenced by the donation, no conclusive proof was ever going to be produced. For his part, Blair consistently denied that the money had been a factor, but in the eyes of many onlookers it strained credibility to suggest that the very substantial gift had played no part in subsequent deliberations.

The story was instructive in several respects. First, it demonstrated that the new government was no better than the last. Indeed it was considerably worse. Nothing in the sorry saga of Tory sleaze had come close to a suspicion that the prime minister had changed policy as a favour to a very rich man; this was in a new league entirely. 'Have we slain one dragon only to have another take its place with a red rose in its mouth?' asked the independent MP Martin Bell, warning that 'the perception of wrongdoing was as damaging to public confidence as the wrongdoing itself'. As John Major was quick to point out, this was 'hypocrisy on a grand scale'.

It further revealed that the public was not yet ready to abandon its hope that things had changed. Blair went on the BBC television show *On the Record* to be interviewed by John Humphrys and insisted that he was still to be trusted: 'I think most people who have dealt with me think I'm a pretty straight guy and I am.' It was an extraordinary display of chutzpah, but it worked. Barely seven months on from the election, he was given the benefit of the doubt.

And finally it showed that, for all its pre-election talk about fat cats, New Labour had a dangerous attraction to affluence. Most famously this was expressed in Peter Mandelson's much-quoted comment: 'We are intensely relaxed about people getting filthy rich.' (His attitude wasn't entirely altruistic, as he later made clear: 'I saw what others enjoyed and I wanted to share it.') Some felt that Blair too displayed a personal fascination with wealth. The film producer and Labour donor David Puttnam, recently ennobled as Baron Puttnam, noted of the prime minister that 'he is very interested in money', while the union leader John Edmonds heard him muse that 'Most of the people I went to school with are now millionaires.' Mandelson's former assistant, Derek Draper, was once quoted as saying that 'Peter goes gaga in the presence of rich people', and Chris Mullin commented: 'Not only Peter's problem. New Labour's, too.'

But since Ecclestone ended up keeping his money and gaining the exemption he sought for Formula One, there was also a suggestion that this was not a government likely to come out on top in its encounters with the wealthy. Adair Turner, director general of the CBI, marvelled that the new government was 'so craven' in its dealings with big business. Meanwhile, those within New Labour circles who did have some money were keen to hold on to it; another story that broke in November 1997 concerned Geoffrey Robinson, the paymaster general, and the millions of pounds he kept in a trust in an offshore tax haven.

Most notable in retrospect, though, was the way that the Ecclestone affair suggested New Labour's tendency to regard falsehood as a weapon of first resort. A cavalier approach to fact was evident elsewhere, often in the most trivial of stories. There was, for example, the tabloid-friendly tale of Blair saving a Danish tourist from drowning while on holiday in the Seychelles in January 1998, which proved to be no more than the product of a publicist's imagination. Or the appearance on Des O'Connor's television show, when he related an anecdote about how, at the age of fourteen, he had stowed away on an aeroplane that he thought was going to take him from Newcastle Airport to the Bahamas. 'I snuck onto the plane and we were about to take off when the stewardess came up to me and said: "I don't think I actually saw your boarding pass."' Blair claimed this to be 'one of the craziest things I have ever done'. It was subsequently discovered that the furthest scheduled flight from Newcastle at the time went only as far as Jersey, while his father admitted that the stewardess was fantasy: 'He made it only to the airport.'

None of this was of great significance, it was just a little odd. Meanwhile the constant, and deceitful, denials of any rift between Blair and Brown were understandable as a political tactic. But the mendacity displayed in the Ecclestone case suggested a dangerous ease with dishonesty.

The same trait seemed to be evident in yet another story from November 1997, that of Lord Irvine's wallpaper. A barrister in whose chambers both Tony Blair and his future wife Cherie Booth had been pupils, Derry Irvine was consequently a familiar figure in Blair's intimate circle, though his influence pre-dated New Labour; he had been at university with John Smith and had expected to be appointed lord chancellor in the event that Labour won the 1992 election. In good New Labour fashion, he also had a long-running feud with a senior colleague; three decades earlier, Donald Dewar's wife had left him for Irvine, and the two men had been enemies ever since, their relationship described by Jack Straw as 'excruciating' to witness.

In 1997 Irvine did finally become lord chancellor, and he made it his first priority to get his official apartments in Parliament refurbished. When it became known that this would end up costing the nation some £650,000, with nearly a tenth of that going on wallpaper alone, some concern was expressed at the expense of the project. (A subsidiary complaint came from the design critic Stephen Bayley, who objected to the 'garish demonstration of camp sensibility' in slavishly recreating nineteenth-century style.)

Irvine's response was to insist that this was all part of an already planned programme of restoration by parliamentary officials and had nothing to do with him. The previous incumbent, Lord Mackay, however, was unconvinced that any work needed doing: 'The residence is quite beautiful, sumptuous and palatial and, in my view, in very good order.' And he had no doubt that it was 'all being done at the whim of the lord chancellor, who is a whimsical sort of man'. The controversy rumbled on for weeks, losing the lord chancellor a great deal of sympathy, particularly on the part of Ivor Richard, the leader of the Lords. 'I'm ashamed of Derry,' he said in private. 'He has behaved dishonourably. He has tried to shift the blame on to the officers of the House. He shouldn't get away with it. He's supposed to be head of the judiciary.'

Again, had this story emerged in the John Major years, it would have been unforgivable. There was a perfectly reasonable claim to be made that, if paper was to be hung in the Gothic Revival splendour of an apartment designed by Augustus Pugin, then clearly it had to be a step up from the stuff one might buy in Homebase, but much of the electorate were unconvinced by wallpaper at £350 a roll, and concluded that Irvine was engaging in self-aggrandisement at their expense. When Irvine later appeared in front of a Commons select committee, his disdainful manner provoked even Blair to fury as he contemplated the popular response: 'They think we got rid of the Tories because they were out of touch, pompous, up themselves and couldn't care less about ordinary people, and then we have this and they think what's different?' It looked even worse than Geoffrey Robinson's trust funds. 'They say a man is judged by his friends,' remarked the *Sun*, giving Blair the benefit of its thoughts. 'With friends like Robinson and Irvine, who needs the Tories?'

Such indulgences sat very uneasily with the most controversial government initiative of that first winter. Gordon Brown's pledge to stay within the spending limits previously announced by Kenneth Clarke had to be observed, even though Clarke himself was later to say that he wouldn't have done so. To meet those targets, Brown decided to implement a proposal made by Peter Lilley to remove a benefit paid to single parents, mostly to single mothers. It was a comparatively small sum in terms of government expenditure, but at £6 a week made a considerable difference to the lives of some of the poorest in the country.

More than a hundred Labour MPs signed a letter urging him to reconsider, and polls showed the public to be against the cut, but Blair and Brown and their advisers assessed that it would look like 'weakness' if they gave in, deciding that their image was more important than any other consideration. It became a test of New Labour's toughness, a rerun of Harriet Harman's choice of school for her child, though this time – as the social security secretary and minister for women – she was cast in the role of fall guy, and sent to the Commons to push the measure through.

Forty-seven Labour MPs rebelled against their government, and many of those who voted in favour did so with deep uneasiness. 'For the first time, I voted for something I strongly disapproved of,' wrote Clare Short, several years later. There was though no question of defeat, since it had been a Conservative idea in the first place and opposition support was therefore available. Peter Lilley stood in the voting lobby, cheerfully welcoming in Labour MPs with a call of 'This way for the cuts.' When Brown appeared in front of the Commons treasury committee to talk about welfare reform, noted Michael Spicer, it was not a particularly lively session. Tory members were 'reticent to ask questions because we like what he is doing', while Labour members were 'silent because they don't like what they think he is doing'.

Not present for the Commons vote was Tony Blair. He was busy hosting a showbiz party in Downing Street, where the guest list included the radio disc jockey Zoë Ball, actors John Thaw and Kevin Whateley, and actress Liz

Dawn, who played Vera Duckworth in *Coronation Street*. Another to attend was the broadcaster Chris Evans, who had that morning signed a contract with Channel 4, worth £3 million a year, that made him Britain's highest paid television star. The reception was no one-off event; the government had recently been revealed to be spending £1.5 million a month on hospitality.

Buried deep under the benefits cut had been an awareness that there was a particular issue in Britain with lone parents. 'A quarter of all mothers under twenty-four in the United Kingdom are single, and have never been married,' John Patten had noted the previous year. 'This is compared with only about ten per cent on average over the rest of the European Union.' A connection had been made between this fact and the supposedly high level of available benefits, and over the last few years the expression 'single-parent family' — originally coined as a euphemistic alternative to 'broken home' — came to be seen in political circles as a term of abuse. The reform was intended by the Tories to be a first step towards rectifying the situation. In Labour hands, however, it came across as simple penny-pinching, and on that criterion it was singularly unsuccessful. The outrage that greeted the measure forced a rethink and a rejigging of other benefits that ended up costing more than the original system. But at least it was all sufficiently complicated that it generated no headlines.

Meanwhile, Brown was calling on Harriet Harman to make £1 billion worth of cuts to disability benefits. This time there was a definite policy objective. The numbers claiming disability benefit had increased sharply over the last decade, partly — it was suspected — as a way of reducing the headline rate of unemployment, and there was a belief that people were being encouraged to rely on state support even when it wasn't necessary. David Blunkett reported an occasion when he was a guest on a radio phone-in in 1998 and spoke to a 42-year-old caller who had had a heart bypass operation; having now recovered, the man objected strongly to having his disability benefits threatened. 'The fact that we had enabled him to become independent,' marvelled Blunkett, 'to take responsibility for his life and to contribute to his own well-being for the rest of his life — when hopefully he had as much of his life before him as behind — seemed to have passed him by.'

Even so, Blunkett, who was both blind and the child of a single-parent family, objected to Brown's proposed cuts, saying that they would 'make a mockery of our professions on social exclusion and the construction of a more just society'. Others too made their voices heard. 'It is no use being tough with the poor,' insisted Michael Cashman. 'Be tough with the people who are breaking the rules, close up the tax loopholes, and then you will be able to balance the books.' Most damaging of all, a group of disabled protestors overturned their wheelchairs outside Downing Street and threw red paint on the railings, in an uncomfortable echo of the demonstrations in 1994 against Nicholas Scott.

Tony Blair continued to insist, in a characteristic attempt to play to popular culture, that he was prepared to 'go the full monty' on welfare reform, but he wasn't proof against that kind of negative publicity. Having come into office with the determination to transform for ever the British attitude to the welfare state, he now discovered that it was a much tougher challenge than he had been expecting.

The immediate casualty was Harman, who had taken most of the flak over single parents and, never loved in the Labour movement, was plumbing new depths of unpopularity. Janet Jones, wife of Ivor Richard, recorded a joke then circulating in which Sleeping Beauty, Tom Thumb and Saddam Hussein boast about their claims to be respectively the most beautiful, the smallest and the most hated people in the world. Consulting the *Guinness Book of Records* to check their claims, Sleeping Beauty finds herself listed as the most beautiful, and Tom Thumb as the smallest, but Saddam is disappointed: 'Who's Harriet Harman?'

No one was much surprised when Harman lost her job in a cabinet reshuffle in July 1998, her cabinet career assumed to be finished. Also leaving office, though, was Frank Field, the minister for welfare reform and supposedly Harman's junior.

One of the most awkward of Labour MPs, Field had twice served on the opposition front bench since his election to Parliament in 1979, lasting for no more than a year in either instance; he now repeated the feat in government. He could also boast of having been 'booted out of the young Tories' for organising an anti-apartheid boycott, of having lost his seat on the General Synod of the Church of England for supporting the ordination of women, and of having only narrowly defeated an attempt by Militant members to deselect him in his Birkenhead constituency. Unmarried, teetotal, owning neither a car nor a television set, he was constitutionally incapable of fitting in, with a persona somewhere between a nineteenth-century social reformer and a saint. The fact that the resolutely nonconformist Margaret Thatcher was a friend of his (she referred to him as 'a good man') vouched for his outsider credentials. He was also a curiously old-fashioned politician, harking back to a time when voluntary societies, trade unions, cooperatives, churches and workers' education groups created a sense of community and shared values.

Yet he was precisely the kind of figure that Blair needed around him if New Labour's claim to be a radical government was ever to hold water. Field had spent the 1970s working for the Child Poverty Action Group and the Low Pay Unit, and had argued longer than anyone else in politics about issues of poverty and of the underclass that, in his eyes, had emerged during the 1980s: the millions left exposed and stranded, cut off from society in the wake of the two great recessions. Much of this came from the experience of living in and representing a constituency that had once been dominated by the Cammell Laird shipyard and was now scarred by unemployment, drugs and crime.

Initially a keen supporter of Blair, he celebrated the way that the new leader was breaking fresh ground. 'For fifteen years we've done nothing but follow the Tory agenda,' he said in 1994. 'Now we can leapfrog the Tories and make them follow our agenda.' A couple of months later, he was to be found making an even more controversial claim for a Labour politician: 'We are leapfrogging over the old social democracy.' And some of the message he had been espousing for years undoubtedly chimed with Blair's vision, particularly his emphasis on individual morality, responsibility and self-improvement. There was also, however, a fervent belief that the stability of society could only be secured by a return to full employment, exactly the kind of ambitious objective that New Labour was keen to avoid.

Blair brought him into government, charged with 'thinking the unthinkable', with reframing Labour's traditional position on the welfare system. Field proceeded to do just that, outlining a massive programme that centred on a reinvention of National Insurance, an end to means-testing, an attack on benefit fraud, tighter controls on who should receive incapacity benefit, and the encouragement of private pensions – in short, a rolling back of dependence upon the state combined with a focus on collective insurance. The estimated cost of his proposals, around £8 billion, would, he argued, be recouped once the programme was fully implemented, but it scared the life out of both Blair and Brown and ensured that his ideas stood no chance of making progress, particularly since he had few supporters in government. For Field hadn't shaken off his reputation as a maverick to whom the newly fashionable expression 'team player' meant nothing, and his abrasive relationship with Harman, his immediate boss, was marvelled at even in a government riven with such conflicts ('she wanted Frank hung, drawn and quartered', according to Peter Mandelson).

His departure from office in 1998, when he refused to serve in any other capacity than as secretary of state, relieved Blair of the need to find a round hole capable of taking this square peg. 'Some are made for office, some aren't,' wrote Blair. 'He wasn't.' But Field's return to the back benches also suggested that the entire project of welfare reform had been quietly abandoned, leaving behind only cost-cutting attacks on benefits that hit the poorest without providing a broader philosophy in justification. The new government was looking very much like its Conservative predecessor.

Other events in that first year of New Labour merely confirmed the impression that little had changed save news management. In August 1997 the *News of the World* discovered that Robin Cook had been having an affair with a member of his staff, precisely the kind of story that had periodically rocked the Major government. This time, it was dealt with at a speed which ensured that the account actually came out quite positively. 'It barely read like a *News of the World* exposé at all,' remarked Alastair Campbell approvingly. Conservative scandals, on the other hand, were treated far less favourably. 'The upper-crust daughter of a top Tory MP is today exposed as a £500-a-time hooker,' splashed the *News of the World* six months later, though the 'top Tory' in question turned out to be Tim Boswell, a former whip and now the party's trade and industry spokesperson; hardly a household name.

On a more serious level, New Labour's eagerness to change policy in order to protect jobs in Formula One was not matched by its commitment to more traditional industries. Even as the Ecclestone story broke, the government was explaining that it couldn't intervene in UK Coal's decision to make somewhere between 5,000 and 8,000 miners redundant, with a massive knock-on effect on other jobs. A leader in *The Times* warned that, without political action, 'we will see the once unthinkable situation of a Labour government presiding over the ultimate death of the mining industry'. A temporary deal was hurriedly put together, and Peter Mandelson staged a photo-opportunity at Kellingley colliery in order to show that this wasn't like the days of Michael Heseltine. Nonetheless, pits continued to close under Labour.

If a certain shame was apparent here in pursuing what had been Conservative policies, such an emotion didn't linger. At the last conference before the election, Labour's transport spokesperson, Andrew Smith, had railed against the Tory proposal to privatise the national air traffic control system, promising: 'Labour will do everything it can to block this sell-off. Our air is not for sale.' In June 1998 Gordon Brown announced that a majority stake in air traffic control would indeed be sold, along with the Tote bookmaker and the Royal Mint. 'There is no great principle at stake,' shrugged Chris Mullin, 'unless you believe that state ownership is by definition safer than the private sector. In which case presumably you would prefer to travel Aeroflot than British Airways.'

It was a fair point, but one that presumably could have been made with equal force in opposition. Similar reversals were seen elsewhere, from the involvement of the private sector in prisons through the introduction of tuition fees for higher education to an attempt to privatise the Post Office. Policies thunderously denounced in opposition were adopted with enthusiasm in government.

The same was true of the two big areas of public service that had so long preoccupied the Labour Party: health and education. 'I am, all said and done, a public service guy at heart,' wrote Blair in his memoirs, and Jonathan Powell was later to explain the new government's objectives: 'Our strategic aim was to shift from producer-driven public services to health and education services driven by the patient, the parent and the pupil.' There was little to distinguish this vision from that of John Major, save that, thanks to the growing economy, the new government had greater funds at its disposal (though as a share of GDP, government spending fell during Labour's first term).

But Blair's 'essentially middle class view of public services' came into conflict with Labour's traditional role of representing service-providers rather than users, and initially it was the latter that took precedence. Consequently, the first actions of the New Labour government were to wipe out many of the programmes they had inherited. Some were to disappear for ever, including the assisted places scheme, which had sent some 85,000 academically gifted children on state scholarships to independent schools. Others were simply to resurface, so that although more than a thousand grant-maintained schools had their status abolished in 1998, Blair was to be found later that year worrying that perhaps they had been a good thing after all: 'we need to be more radical to improve standards more quickly. Maybe even abolish all LEAs.' And in due course the same concept came back in 2000, this time rebranded as city academies. Somewhat belatedly, Blair had come to the conclusion that initiatives like the grant-maintained school or GP commissioning in the health service were not quite so misguided as first imagined: 'their essential direction was one that was in fact nothing to do with being "Tory", but to do with the modern world.'

In the process of learning that lesson, and accepting the idea that public services should have a customer-first ethos, a great deal of impetus had been lost and goodwill squandered. In the meantime there arose instead a series of government-driven projects intended to address such issues as the reported 40 per cent of children leaving primary school still functionally illiterate.

More often than not these schemes were accompanied by celebrities and populist gimmicks, so that when a 'year of reading' was launched in September 1998, Blair went on Radio 4's *Woman's Hour* to promote a 'dads and lads' initiative, intended to encourage fathers to read with their sons. He nominated his suggested texts for the enterprise, giving every indication of having been carefully briefed beforehand: *Lord of the Rings*, the Narnia and Sherlock Holmes books, Roald Dahl, Brian Jacques, Paul Jennings and Robin Jarvis.

Similarly, when in March 1999 Blair and his education secretary, David Blunkett, staged a conference to launch Maths 2000, 'a campaign to make next year the year of maths in schools', they were accompanied by Carol Vorderman from Channel 4's game show *Countdown*. When the year eventually got under way (the pre-announcement was a familiar routine), it featured as a support act Johnny Ball, a children's television presenter who had hosted maths and science shows like *Think of a Number* in the 1970s and '80s, though it was hard not to conclude that his appeal for New Labour had something to do with the celebrity status of his daughter, Zoë Ball.

Some of the actual proposals behind 'all the usual razzmatazz' (as Blunkett put it) also seemed more geared towards headlines than education. There was to be an hour of maths every day in primary schools, with mental arithmetic and recitations of the multiplication tables, there were to be summer schools and family numeracy classes and – in case this all seemed a bit serious – lessons in fantasy football to encourage numeracy in boys. The reality was, as ever, a little more modest than the surrounding hype; for example, just 3,000 places were available in those family numeracy classes.

Positive news stories were duly garnered, though the sense that there was a publicity stunt at the heart of such initiatives also meant that the media seized gleefully upon any minor mistake. In a radio interview Stephen Byers, the minister for school standards, was asked to multiply eight by seven and came up with the answer 'fifty-four', while posters promoting literacy were sent to all 24,000 primary schools in the country and then had to be recalled when it was discovered that they contained the word 'vocabluary'. Whether any of this noisy activity worked or not would, of course, take some time to evaluate, as future generations left school. On the pledge card issued during the election, Labour had been careful not to specify any outcomes on education policy, just that limit on class sizes for the youngest pupils. The NHS promise, on the other hand, was more specific – a reduction of 100,000 patients on the waiting list – and could therefore be evaluated; a year on from the election, and the numbers had actually grown by 150,000.

And therein lay a problem for the government. New Labour picked up the concept of the Citizens' Charter, with its emphasis on setting targets, and took it to extraordinary levels, making a bundle of rods for its own back. 'To bridge the gap between reform and aspiration,' explained Blair, the government set 'a swathe of performance targets to eliminate the longest hospital waiting times, raise school literacy and numeracy and GCSE scores, etc'.

That simple 'etc' barely hinted at the resulting culture in Whitehall, as good intentions came gushing out of every department. 'Tony was seduced by the idea of targets,' wrote Peter Mandelson. 'We all were.' So there were central targets for the quantity of cars, cycles and pedestrians on the road, as well as for traffic casualties and dog mess; for the numbers of smokers, heroin addicts and pregnant teenagers; for the incidence of robberies and building-fires; for how many children visited museums and galleries, and for the proportion of school-leavers going on to higher education. (The latter was set at 50 per cent, an increase on the Major government's ambition, which had been for a third.) In June 2001 John Hutton, a minister in the Department of Health, enquired of a civil servant how many targets had been set by the department since the 1997 election and was shocked to discover that the answer was somewhere around eight hundred.

In the 1960s Harold Wilson's administration had prided itself on issuing a National Plan for the economy; New Labour seemed determined to repeat the experiment, this time for everything but the economy. There was even a target for the number of otters to be found in the wild, a project which broke new ground by bringing in funds from the water companies and from Biffa Waste Services, enabling newspapers to report that 'the otter has secured the largest corporate sponsorship for an endangered British species'. The micromanagement of everyday life, as wish-lists became a substitute for action, created a danger that was spelt out by Chris Mullin: 'We are getting a reputation as a party of busybodies.'

Much of this derived from the days of Conservative rule, and the desire to measure productivity in services that didn't necessarily lend themselves to such analysis. Funding to universities, for example, became dependent on the quantity of published material, sparking a boom in academic journals, the value of which was not always apparent; in the early years of the new century, research showed that the average readership of an article in such a journal amounted to just five people. The result was the creation of a new layer of bureaucracy to monitor performance, which was answerable to a centralised authority, further damaging local accountability and the independence and authority of professionals working in the field, whether they were lecturers, police officers or hospital consultants. The same thinking was also applied to government itself, so that the setting of targets and the passing of ever greater numbers of laws came to be a substitute for governance. Output meant more than results.

As environment secretary, Michael Heseltine had decided to issue a white paper every year, the equivalent of an annual report, 'to set targets and to report systematically against them'. He was able to boast proudly: 'Our first-year report detailed over 400 measures already taken towards the White Paper's goals and listed over 400 commitments to further action.' The attitude underlying this approach was that government was somehow analogous to a group of companies, that business practice could be imported wholesale. It was replicated in New Labour's announcement that there would be an annual government report, though few showed any enthusiasm for the initiative ('God knows who invented this idea,' grumbled David Blunkett) and it was soon dropped, without anyone really noticing.

Key to this way of thinking was an awareness of the language to be employed. Again the seeds were there in John Major's charters – which had turned rail passengers into 'customers' and introduced such verbiage as 'the next station stop' – but came to fruition under a Labour government full of people who had cut their political teeth in the 1980s, when language had been the ground on which was fought the battle to shape thought and behaviour.

Few were as excited as Tony Blair. 'It's the signals that matter. Not the policy,' he remarked at the time, and even on mature reflection, he remained convinced that changing the language was a prerequisite for changing attitudes: 'the whole terminology – booked appointments, minimum guarantees of service, freedoms to innovate – spoke of a coming culture of change, oriented to treating the NHS like a business with customers.' If improving the delivery of services was a hard nut to crack, then the vocabulary was the soft option, and New Labour came to specialise in management jargon, forever talking about accessing, passporting and rolling out. It was a development noticed and mocked by many, including the always semi-detached Chris Mullin: 'Keith Hill and I amused ourselves over lunch compiling a New Labour lexicon. We came up with the following: pathfinders, beacons, win-win, stakeholders, opportunities as well as challenges, partnership, best value.'

The one major development in public services was the extension of the private finance initiative (PFI), which had grown out of John Prescott's thoughts on transport while in opposition, and had been adopted by the

Conservative government of John Major and Norman Lamont. Under John Smith, Labour had accepted that this was the way forward, but the scale of New Labour's embrace was still something of a surprise.

It was argued that the private sector was more competent in its management and delivery, but no one doubted that the real reason for the popularity of PFI in Westminster and Whitehall was the way that it enabled large capital projects – particularly schools and hospitals – to be undertaken at no immediate cost to the public purse. The bill was spread over a number of years, a privilege that enabled the companies involved to charge more. It was, in effect, a government version of credit card debt and would, wrote Nick Cohen in the *Observer*, 'result in the public paying a fortune for the services of corporations for decades to come'.

Notwithstanding the good intentions to reform welfare, health and education, however, there was one overriding political issue as the new government took over. John Major's opt-out at Maastricht had meant that Britain was unlikely to be in the first wave of countries – some eleven of them – launching the single European currency, which was now scheduled for 1 January 1999, barely eighteen months away. Nonetheless the project then known as EMU (economic and monetary union) could hardly be ignored by a government that prided itself on its European credentials. It would be, said David Blunkett in February 1997, 'the biggest decision of the next parliament'.

Tony Blair's position on the currency, which was to be called the euro after much argument, was ambivalent. In 1986, before the Labour Party became enthusiasts for the ERM, he had urged caution, saying that it was 'important that our choice is informed and not a careless embrace of anything with the word "European" in it', and that it was 'not an ideological argument but a practical one'. More than a decade later, he stood by that latter position, saying that when it came to the euro, 'it is economics not politics that will decide'. In this respect, he was at one with John Major, who had fallen out with those in his party who insisted on seeing the issue as one of principle.

Both men were likewise unconvinced that the programme set down was achievable. The 'single currency will not come about before the end of the century', Major said, as early as 1994, since 'the economic circumstances will not be right'. 'I still retain a very strong doubt that it will happen at all,' Blair told Paddy Ashdown two years later. 'I have no doubt about the commitment of other European leaders to it, but I am not at all sure they can withstand the pressures from their populations brought about by the austerity which will be necessary to meet the Maastricht conditions.' It was a perceptive analysis, though it underestimated the EU's willingness to fudge the entry requirements, thereby postponing the problem of austerity to the next generation of leaders.

Blair was broadly sympathetic to Britain's adoption of the euro but, despite his protestations, it was unavoidably a political decision. Those driving the project were clear about this, as Wim Duisenberg, president of the European Central Bank, explained: 'EMU is and was always meant to be a stepping stone on the way to a united Europe.' It was also true of the domestic argument. When Major in 1996 had committed the Conservatives to a referendum before entry into the single currency, it had forced Labour's hand, and the election manifesto had been explicit that there would be a triple-lock: 'first, the cabinet would have to agree; then Parliament; and finally the people would have to say "Yes" in a referendum.'

Even the first of those stages seemed unlikely, given the vanishing rarity of cabinet debate on such serious questions. The real problem was the third stage, referred to by Blair as 'the wretched referendum'. Giles Radice had been one of seven Labour MPs to sign a letter to the *Independent* in 1996 calling for Britain to be part of the first wave of entrants, but even he could see the problem. 'The real obstacle is not economic but political,' he wrote. 'Tony and Gordon, especially Tony, are "shit-scared" of the Murdoch press. This is the real weakness of this government.' The reality of that concern was manifest in June 1998, when the *Sun* gave its front page over to an editorial illustrated with a picture of Blair and the headline: IS THIS THE MOST DANGEROUS MAN IN BRITAIN?

That the *Sun* could still be driven to such hyperbole was an indication of how confused the government's message had become. Robin Cook was openly expressing doubts about British involvement in the euro in the short to medium term, while Gordon Brown was said also to be sceptical. In October 1997 an attempt to clarify the position was concocted by Brown and his advisers, in conjunction with Alastair Campbell, and resulted in an article in *The Times* under the headline BROWN RULES OUT SINGLE CURRENCY FOR LIFETIME OF THIS PARLIAMENT. The Euro-friendly Peter Mandelson had not been informed of the briefings and phoned Blair in a fury, demanding to know what was going on, only to discover that Blair had also not been consulted and was equally unhappy.

A panicked weekend of retractions, re-briefings and repositioning ensued, and the confusion and conflicts became the story. The headlines were unequivocally bad: LABOUR SPINS INTO A CRISIS (*Guardian*), EMU POLICY IN A SPIN (*Financial Times*), BROWN IN A SPIN OVER EURO POLICY (*Daily Telegraph*).

Some £20 billion was lost on the stock market that morning, just as Brown arrived in the City for a prearranged photo-opportunity. Only the *Daily Mirror*, doggedly loyal despite New Labour's open flirtations with the *Sun*, stayed onside: EU CAN TRUST LABOUR TO GET IT RIGHT, reassured the headline, explaining that the government's position 'is quite simple. It knows Britain has to be part of monetary union. The question is not IF but WHEN. Naturally enough, that will depend on when the time is right for this country.'

To answer the question of when it would be right, Brown and Ed Balls came up with five tests to determine whether Britain was ready to enter the euro. It was a largely cosmetic exercise, designed to save face in the midst of a self-induced squall of bad publicity, but for the next few years, the five tests were constantly referred to as though they had some objective meaning, even if few government ministers or spokespeople could ever remember when asked quite what they were. The tests were framed so loosely that they could mean almost anything, and could be interpreted in almost any way one wished. The only one that revealed anything much was the question of whether joining the euro would be good for the City of London, which at least demonstrated how large the City loomed in Brown's thinking. Derek Scott, then Blair's economic adviser, was later to observe that 'making a decision on one industry is like making a view on the Gold Standard based on what was good for the textiles business'. He concluded: 'The five tests on the euro are economically illiterate.'

Nonetheless, the invention of the five tests was politically shrewd on the part of Brown. The decision on whether and when to adopt the euro had now been taken out of the prime minister's hands and left entirely at the discretion of the chancellor. Blair's refusal to admit that the issue was one of politics had allowed him to be written out of the equation.

Meanwhile William Hague had pledged that there would be no application to join the currency over the course of the next parliament, in the unlikely event that a Tory government were elected. 'For the first time Conservatives sounding clearer than Labour on this matter,' rejoiced Eurosceptic Michael Spicer, though there was little domestic benefit to be found. Rather, Hague's position served to shore up Britain's credit within the EU for not having a Conservative government. When the European Central Bank was officially launched in June 1998, Blair was invited to the ceremony. The Maastricht male voice choir dignified the occasion by singing songs from the various European nations, including 'Land of Hope and Glory', which, thought Blair, struck 'an appropriate note'. The choir's final choice, however, a rendition of 'Money Makes the World Go Round' from the musical *Cabaret*, was perhaps less encouraging – evoking the spirit of Weimar Germany was not entirely auspicious.

Back home the mixed messages continued. In February 1999, with the euro now a fact, Tony Blair made a statement to the House of Commons, explaining the logistics of how Britain would move to abolish sterling and adopt the new currency. But there was no indication of when the process outlined would actually begin; it was just another holding exercise, making gestures in the absence of a real policy. 'Our intention is clear,' protested Blair. 'Britain should join a successful single currency, provided the economic conditions are met. It is conditional. It is not inevitable. Both intention and conditions are genuine.' By this stage, though, Britain had long since been excluded from the decision-making process that brought the euro into being, and once again stood isolated in European Union circles.

Derek Scott later identified the real underlying flaw, beyond even the fear of the media: 'One of the problems for the Blair government has been that in opposition Labour never worked out what being pro-European meant; it was simply part of rebranding and repositioning the party.' And, he noted sadly, 'In government the focus on positioning has continued.' That was written in 2007, a full decade on from New Labour's accession to power, and still no decision had been taken, no definite policy adopted. With every passing month, it had become more difficult to commit to the course that Blair would have liked to follow. In that first flush of enthusiasm, when he had sufficient support that he could be forgiven for the Bernie Ecclestone scandal, it might have been possible to win a referendum on the single currency, but the moment passed. 'Blair is mad not to have already made a clear sign that he wants to go into the euro,' observed former chancellor Geoffrey Howe in 1999. 'He is wasting his big majority. After the election, it may be even more difficult.'

Blunkett was right that the question of whether to join the euro was the biggest decision of the parliament. When the eurozone plunged into a sovereign debt crisis in 2009, and Blair's forebodings about the austerity measures implicit in EMU proved all too real, many expressed their relief that Britain had not signed up to the single currency. The reality, though, was that a prime minister who boasted of his ability to make tough choices had flunked this one, and that he had ultimately adopted little more than the policy referred to by John Major as 'procrastinating on principle'.

Blair's hesitancy was in large part due to his awareness that this was the one issue on which clear blue water separated the two main parties. William

Hague's Conservatives had made opposition to the euro the central and most effective plank of their political positioning. The big Europhile beasts of the party were no longer significant players; Michael Heseltine and Kenneth Clarke had retreated to the back benches while Chris Patten, returned from Hong Kong, was busy chairing a commission on policing in Northern Ireland and was soon to become a European commissioner, courtesy of Tony Blair. In their absence, the Eurosceptics now had the party pretty much to themselves and the defence of sterling was the one issue on which they could garner some public support.

Beyond that, however, things continued to look bleak for the Tories. In January 1998 the *Friday Night Armistice* team ran a stunt in which they offered cash prizes to members of the studio audience if they could identify pictures of various members of the shadow cabinet and what portfolio they held. The sums started at £10 for Michael Ancram (devolution) and rose through £150 for Francis Maude (culture), £1,000 for Andrew Mackay (Northern Ireland), all the way up to £30,000 for John Maples (health). Only the prize for Ancram was successfully claimed. It was an eye-catching gimmick, even if a little unfair, for there were some better-known faces surrounding Hague, principally that of Ann Widdecombe who was rapidly emerging as the star of the party.

Following her character assassination of Michael Howard, Widdecombe became shadow health spokesperson and took the 1998 party conference by storm. Speaking without notes, and roaming the stage in a manner that would one day become associated with David Cameron, she earned a huge standing ovation with a speech that combined passion and humour in a way not seen since the great days of Heseltine. Mocking the Labour health minister Tessa Jowell, whose picture appeared thirty-two times in an eighteen-page booklet designed to promote public health policies, Widdecombe shrugged: 'Now I could understand it if she had my good looks . . .' She became the Conservative equivalent of John Prescott – the butt of media jokes, but seen by the rank-and-file membership as their plain-speaking representative at high table.

What the media really wanted, however, was the return of Michael Portillo, so that stories of leadership challenges could be dusted off. But Portillo had changed during his time out of office as he took stock of his first professional setback. Denied the comfort of a berth in the Commons, he seemed to think more clearly and rapidly than did others about the state the Tories had got themselves into, and he resolved to make a genuinely fresh start. Still Eurosceptic, he softened his positions on social issues, recognising that times had moved on, as Hugo Young discovered in an interview: 'He notes the fact that even old people are liberal, through being forced by circumstance to have to come to terms with the children and grandchildren who are single parents, drug-takers or whatever. They have come to terms with a social reality.' He also engaged in some media work that did wonders for his image, making various television documentaries and going to work as a porter at St Thomas's Hospital in London for a series of articles published in the *Mail on Sunday*.

Through it all, he came across as a slightly tortured man, as though he were engaged in a process not only of political reinvention but of personal discovery. It would have taken the hide of a rhinoceros to emerge unscathed from the humiliation of election night, but even so Portillo gave the impression of having seen himself for the first time as others saw him, and of not caring much for the sight. His speech at the post-defeat party conference in 1997 struck a very different note from his SAS days. He decried 'a grabbing and inhumane society made up of greedy and selfish people', claimed that 'tolerance is part of the Tory tradition', and even spoke out for single-parent families: 'We admire those many people who are doing an excellent job raising children on their own.'

Having paid some sort of penance and demonstrated his repentance, Portillo was soon offered a chance to re-enter the political arena. In September 1999 Alan Clark died of a brain tumour, leaving behind a safe Tory seat in Kensington and Chelsea that proved irresistible to high-profile candidates. (Even Geri Halliwell had once suggested that she'd be prepared to stand for the constituency: 'If the people want me, I could not refuse,' she said, with all the mock humility of a real politician. 'I'd be like Glenda Jackson, but better.') Portillo was the front runner from the outset, but more than a hundred other hopefuls put themselves forward to be the Conservative candidate, amongst them a clutch of ex-MPs including Angela Rumbold, Rupert Allason and Phillip Oppenheim.

There was also the self-promoting challenge of Peter Hitchens, an *Express* columnist who had been in the International Socialists as a young man and who still displayed the self-righteous fervour of a teenage Trotskyist, even though he had now become a self-proclaimed reactionary. He had taken against Portillo for not being nearly right wing enough. 'Is he really a Tory at all?' demanded Hitchens crossly, in what was to become almost a catchphrase. 'As defence secretary he did nothing to halt the crazed policy of bringing women into almost all branches of the forces.' Hitchens himself was described by his rival Oppenheim as 'a sort of Ann Widdecombe in trousers'. Meanwhile the actor Alan Rickman, still riding high on his triumph as the Sheriff of Nottingham in *Robin Hood: Prince of Thieves*, was being touted as a possible Labour candidate, though regrettably that didn't come to pass.

Portillo's candidature had one major obstacle to overcome. For years there had been rumours in Westminster and beyond that he was homosexual, even – absurdly – that he was having an affair with Peter Lilley. In a 1999 interview with *The Times*, the publication of which fortunately turned out to coincide with the death of Alan Clark, he took the opportunity to set the record straight. He had never had a relationship with Lilley and the two had only ever talked about the rumours 'to discuss whether to conduct libel proceedings', but there was some truth in the stories about his student days at Cambridge: 'I had some homosexual experiences as a young man.'

It was a revelation that excited the media, and gave them licence to track down fellow students. 'There was this louche community which you had to be part of if you wanted to make it to the top in politics,' a former colleague, who was on the executive of the Oxford University Conservative Association, told the *News of the World* of the Cambridge Tories. 'It was like a rogues' gallery of high camp. And Portillo, with his long hair and big lips, was right in the middle of it.' But in the wake of Stephen Twigg and Ben Bradshaw, the interview made little political impact. Even Norman Tebbit, whose interest in such matters had long been noted, professed himself unconcerned. 'We live in a world where we are going to have to write off the indiscretions of youth,' he shrugged, until he discovered the full extent of Portillo's past activities and exclaimed in horror: 'We now know his deviance continued for almost a decade.' In a sign of the times, however, Tebbit also admitted: 'My views have not changed but society has.'

Portillo was duly adopted as Conservative candidate for the constituency and in November 1999 went on to achieve a swing towards the Tories in a by-election packed with fringe candidates, ranging from the Earl of Burford all the way up to Lisa Lovebucket. Within three months of returning to the Commons, he was back on the front bench as the shadow chancellor in a reshuffle and, on his first day, he stamped his authority on the party by reversing Tory policy to accept not only the independence of the Bank of England – which had been opposed pretty much for the sake of opposition – but also the minimum wage, which was complete anathema to the Thatcherite tradition.

Even with those concessions to Labour, coupled with the limited profile and resources of the parliamentary party, the Conservatives did at least try to provide some form of opposition. It was hard to say the same of the Liberal Democrats, whose role in the early days of New Labour government seemed largely surplus to requirements.

In the 1980s its forebear, the SDP/Liberal Alliance, had proclaimed its intention of supplanting Labour as the chief opposition to the Tories. That hadn't happened and, under the leadership of Paddy Ashdown, the merged party had, in the early 1990s, steered a course of 'equidistance', favouring neither of the main parties. It had, for example, largely backed John Major in the Maastricht debates, acting on pro-European principle rather than pursuing the opportunistic option of defeating the government with whatever weapon came to hand. But Ashdown felt that they had received little in return for this support, and by the middle of 1993 he was writing in his diary that 'there is real animosity between me and Major now'. From here on, the likelihood was that the party would move ever closer to Labour. The discussions about coalitions, hung parliaments and cross-party cooperation that had surfaced during the last week of the 1992 election campaign came back to mind and the idea of an anti-Tory alliance was floated in various quarters.

There was, however, a stumbling-block in the shape of John Smith, who had no interest in such speculation. He talked instead of 'the importance of party, of tribal loyalties, of the need to be fighting for a cause and a group', and concluded: 'All this makes the idea of deals quite impossible.' Ashdown found a more ready welcome at the door of the shadow home secretary, with whom he had dinner at the end of 1993, recording that Tony Blair 'believes there is a desperate need to reformulate the politics of the left and that he and I could prepare the ground for this'.

That early contact was followed by increasingly serious discussions after Blair became Labour leader, the two men plotting how they might drive the Conservatives out of office and keep them in opposition for a decade to come. Ashdown was keen on the idea of a joint project whereby issues of electoral reform and policies on health and education could be explored, without the requirement of a formal pact. Moreover, he recognised that 'I have more in common with Blair than he has with his left wing', and was prepared to make the next leap, believing that the existing party structure was outdated. Far more logical than the present arrangement – so long as one ignored history – would be a reconfiguration that saw both Labour and the Conservatives split, so that a new, pro-European centre party could emerge, positioned between a Eurosceptic right and an old Labour left.

Blair understood the concept perfectly. 'Except on law and order, I am by instinct a liberal,' he was later to write, and although he used a small 'l', it could just as easily have been a capital. There was no tribalism in his membership of the Labour Party, no family ties to the movement, and from his perspective, there was no reason why the New Labour project shouldn't be extended in the way that Ashdown sought. Indeed, many of those around him had previously been members of the SDP, including his advisers on Europe and economics – Roger Liddle and Derek Scott – and he had struck up a particularly close relationship with Roy Jenkins, the founder of that party, who became something akin to a mentor.

But in terms of the Labour leadership, Blair was effectively on his own. Gordon Brown had a deep dislike of the Liberal Democrats, who he tended to refer to as 'the Liberals', implying that he couldn't be bothered to keep up with their name changes. So too did John Prescott, another with no enthusiasm for close ties with the third party. 'No way, I'm not going down that road,' he declared, to which Blair nervously replied, 'So can I take that as a tentative yes, then?'

The other obstacle was that, despite Ashdown's talk of turning 'a Conservative defeat into a Conservative rout' through cooperation between the two parties, Labour went ahead and won a massive landslide on its own. After the election, there was no possibility of, or need for, any kind of coalition. A joint committee of senior Liberal Democrats and Labour ministers was formed, discussing the perennial subject of electoral reform amongst other items, but it amounted to no more than a half-hearted talking shop; the fact that it met in the cabinet room – where no serious decisions were now made – indicated its lowly standing. Long gone were the days of opposition when Blair could vaguely intimate that he was willing to appoint a couple of Lib Dems to the cabinet. Not even his authority over the Labour Party extended that far, though he was to be heard a year after the election reflecting: 'I still wish I had put Ashdown in the cabinet.'

In 1999, after eleven years in office, Paddy Ashdown announced that he was stepping down as leader of the Liberal Democrats. From the messy wreckage left behind by the 1988 merger of the Liberals and the SDP, he had managed to salvage a workable third party, and build its representation substantially in the Commons. His association with Blair had yielded some fruit – legislation on human rights and freedom of information were partly due to Lib Dem campaigning – but the ultimate goal remained as elusive as ever. The party, in its various guises, had been waiting to achieve a share of power longer than Britain had been waiting for a men's singles champion at Wimbledon, and still it hadn't materialised.

Perhaps his successor, the much younger Charles Kennedy, might be the one to make the breakthrough, though Ashdown didn't seem very convinced. Kennedy was 'a very attractive personality but he could be lazy and foolhardy', was the verdict he delivered to Blair, who was later to come to the same conclusion: 'All that talent. Why is he so idle?' On the day he was elected leader, Kennedy received a phone call from Blair with an invitation to a private dinner that evening. His casually unimpressed response set the tone of his new style: 'Terribly sorry; I'm already fixed up.' When he did finally meet Blair in Downing Street, his first question was, 'Do you mind if I smoke?', deliberately breaking the ban on cigarettes imposed by Cherie. He subsequently began to pull away from Labour, opening the possibility that the Lib Dems might return to being a party of opposition.

There was a need for such opposition. A MORI poll in April 1999 showed Labour on 56 per cent, the Conservatives on 25 per cent and the Lib Dems on 13 per cent, almost exactly the same results as a Gallup poll had found in August 1994. If that suggested that no mid-term slump was in prospect for the government, Labour's performance at the ballot box was less impressive. In local elections that month the Conservatives gained control of forty-eight councils, adding over 1,300 councillors to their ranks at the expense of both other parties, and a couple of months later they took 36 per cent to Labour's 28 per cent as a share of the vote in elections to the European Parliament. Meanwhile the UK Independence Party won its first seats, its three new MEPs including future leader Nigel Farage.

But the real story of those Euro-elections was the appalling turnout of only 23 per cent. This meant that just 6.5 per cent of the registered electorate had shown their support for a government that had won a landslide two years earlier. Turnout was particularly low in the Labour heartlands: 14 per cent in Sheffield Brightside, 12 per cent in Barnsley and barely 10 per cent in Liverpool Riverside. In all these constituencies, Labour historically achieved a share of over 70 per cent in parliamentary elections. One polling station in Sunderland reported turnout of 1.5 per cent. 'Mind you, does it really matter?' reflected Lance Price. 'So what if we do badly today? Victory at the next general election is all but certain.'

He was undoubtedly correct. These were, after all, merely European elections, which never attracted a great deal of support and were frequently used to register a protest vote. The same day, however, there was a by-election in the safe Labour seat of Leeds Central, and although it ensured the arrival in Parliament of a fourth generation of Benn, in the form of Tony's son Hilary, turnout had again slumped, down from 55 per cent at the general election to only 20 per cent.

Despite John Prescott's claim that the low voting figures reflected 'a culture of contentment', something more unnerving was happening here, and it reflected badly not only on the Labour Party but also on the democratic process. The leader of Sunderland council, Colin Anderson, was elected on a turnout of 17 per cent. 'The fact that 83 per cent did not vote says something about the legitimacy of the overall political system,' he commented, 'but I do not blame the people who have not voted. This is one of the country's poorest wards. If your daily life is struggling to survive, voting is not a top priority.'

Tony Blair was later to claim that he knew all along how disenchanted the *Guardian*-reading liberal element of his cross-class coalition would become, and professed himself unconcerned: 'I was sure that although in north London and elsewhere a certain type of Labour voter was going to defect, the more aspiring lower-middle-class voter – the core of New Labour – were sticking with us.' The reality, though, was that it was not merely in his adopted homeland of Islington that a decline of hope was evident, but also in places like the North-East of England, the region that included his own constituency. And even if those Labour seats were secure enough to withstand mass absenteeism, there was less certainty about their equivalents in Scotland, where a viable left alternative existed in the Scottish National Party. It was noticeable that the next Labour-held seat to enjoy a by-election – Hamilton South in September 1999 – saw a much more respectable turnout and a huge 23 per cent swing to the SNP, reducing a Labour majority from nearly 16,000 to barely five hundred.

The disillusion of traditional Labour supporters had been noted even as Blair was taking over the party. 'We have had three elections of warm words,' observed John Prescott during the 1994 leadership election. 'I'm not convinced it did us a great deal of good. It does not convince enough of those who want to switch over and it knocks the heart out of our own people.' New Labour had calculated that 'our own people' could be taken for granted, allowing the emphasis to be placed entirely on winning over the southern suburbs, and in the electoral short term, the strategy had undoubtedly been a success. In the longer term, however, there was a very real danger that the base of the Labour movement was being so heavily eroded that the party itself might cease to exist in any recognisable form. By the end of the decade, the pursuit of the affluent voter had left the committed activist feeling neglected and alienated. 'There are five people in my household and we all voted Plaid. Including me,' admitted a Labour councillor in Wales in 1999. 'I can't see the past anywhere', lamented the Manic Street Preachers in their song 'Socialist Serenade', released the same year; it ended with a contemptuous: 'Change your name to New; forget the fucking Labour'.

Again, the warnings had been issued. Peter Hain, formerly a leading light in the Young Liberals but now one of the more left-wing figures towards the top of Labour, argued in 1994 that the process of modernisation was creating 'an empty shell of a party', saying: 'It is hardly surprising that activity rates have fallen sharply, that branch meetings are badly attended and general committees barely quorate.' There was nothing for members to do, now that campaigning was dominated by the mass media and policy-making lay entirely in the hands of Blair, Brown and their inner circles; increasingly, the route into power started and ended at Westminster.

The effects of this development were concealed for a while as membership of the Labour Party rose in the early days of Blair's leadership, reversing what had been a long-term decline. But the nature of those members was changing, and a study in 1996 showed that 57 per cent earned more than £20,000 a year, and 30 per cent more than £30,000; the equivalent figures for the Conservative Party were 45 and 25 per cent. (At the time, someone working on, say, a supermarket checkout might expect to earn around £8,000 a year, while a backbench MP was on £43,000, following a 26 per cent rise.)

The new member was likely to be middle-aged, middle class and not particularly committed to the party, its history or its practice, a development that worried Robin Cook at least. 'A number of us on the moderate left of the party are becoming increasingly concerned that we are abandoning the underclass and our historic mission to work for the poor, in favour of the middle class,' he observed, adding that the new members weren't very useful: 'when we started mentioning delivering leaflets and knocking on doors, their eyes glazed and they all said they had Rotary meetings to go to. I am not sure there is enough substance here on which to build a sustainable political movement.' In 1992, Tony Benn had identified another danger when he noted 'the disappearance of the working class from the Labour Party; that's a real tragedy because many of them may be attracted to the fascists, where there's a high class consciousness and a low ideological consciousness, and racism'.

As the membership figures began to fall with the fading of election fever, the reality of Hain's 'empty shell' became ever more exposed. The election agent in Chris Mullin's Sunderland South constituency noted that there was an ageing process amongst the membership: 'I joined the party when I was nineteen or twenty, and now I am forty-one and I am still one of the youngest people in the party in Sunderland.'

A parallel process in the post-Thatcher Conservative Party was one of the main factors driving the party inwards in ever decreasing circles. 'More anti-European and right-wing views mean fewer party activists, and fewer party activists mean more anti-European and right-wing views,' wrote Chris Patten. 'By the mid-to-late 1990s, it was tough being a moderate pro-European Tory MP in any constituency, and well-nigh impossible for anyone with such declared views to get selected as a parliamentary candidate.' The same phenomenon had already been noted by Edwina Currie. 'The nice people will drift away to run their businesses,' she speculated, in 1995, 'and the nasties will remain, with Portillo at their head.' Within Labour, however, the effect was rather to shore up the power of the leadership.

By now, the traditional forces of old Labour were all but silenced. Having no time for the historic links between the party and the union movement, Blair was infuriated in 1995 when the TGWU issued a statement emphasising those links. 'These people are stupid and they are malevolent,' he raged. 'They complain that we want to distance ourselves and then give us all the evidence why we should distance ourselves.' He subsequently met with the leaders of the TUC in an Indian restaurant, accompanied by John Prescott. 'What amazed me was their timidity. It was obvious to me that he was challenging them, expecting them to complain or argue, but the response was muted,' remembered Prescott of the union men. 'I felt that evening that Tony had got the measure of the trade union movement, which I regretted.'

But by this stage, the unions had been battered more than most by the long period of Tory rule, and – despite a membership of nearly seven million – were little more than a shadow of their former selves. There had been a time in the 1960s and 1970s when the general secretary of the TUC was more famous than most cabinet ministers, when men such as George Woodcock, Vic Feather and Len Murray were household names. Even Norman Willis, who served in the job for nine years from 1984, during which time the movement suffered a series of setbacks, was a recognisable face on television. His successor, John Monks, spent a decade in office and went largely unremarked by the public.

The unions' acquiescence to the New Labour project was matched by much of the parliamentary left. The desire to win was so great that it overcame ideological considerations. And there was too the tribal factor. For all his obvious lack of sympathy with Labour history, Blair was a member of the party and had been elected in its dark days. 'I still had the feeling he was an SDP type,' remarked Prescott. 'But at least he had never left the Party, so I'd always rated him.' The visceral hatred of the Tories was sufficient even to persuade Dennis Skinner, who had long been a thorn in the side of the leadership, to swallow his much-vaunted principles and come to the party's aid. During the 1997 election campaign, he was called upon to telephone wavering trade unionists: 'I'd be frank with them and say we could argue all evening about Blair. But I'd warn them that if the Conservatives got back in, then another Tory government would have a licence to do what they liked with the health service and the old age pension.'

After the election, Skinner remained loyal to the leadership and established a friendly relationship with Blair, who listened to his advice. ('Blair's a piece of cake,' he had reportedly said in 1996; 'he stands for nothing so you can push him over with ease.') As Tony Benn noted sadly in his diaries: 'It isn't that Dennis is moving to the right, but as you get older you want to be respected and he hasn't been keen on the recent revolts.' So toothless had the parliamentary left become that in 2000 Benn was offered his own column in the *Sun* by that paper's political editor, Trevor Kavanagh.

In those first couple of years of New Labour government, the project to reassure the party's longstanding enemies seemed to have been a complete success. 'I am very strongly in favour of the current government. I don't regard it as left wing,' remarked Madsen Pirie, founder of the right-wing think tank the Adam Smith Institute. 'Gordon Brown is definitely to the right of Kenneth Clarke on markets.' The core of old Labour – not so much the remnants of the left as the working-class centre – was less impressed. 'It seems that what we fought for is now just running the status quo, and running it on whichever flavour of the month the voters will buy,' wrote MP Joe Ashton, the very incarnation of mainstream Labour traditionalism.

The tension apparent here was not sustainable. Perhaps Paddy Ashdown had been right to think about a complete realignment of the political parties, but the moment had passed, and Britain was left with two main parties that appealed to diminishing constituencies. Tony Blair boasted that the New Labour machine was 'close to unbeatable, like Manchester United at their best', but if a football analogy was sought, a more accurate comparison might be with Newcastle United. Blair's own professed club promised so much under the management of Kevin Keegan, only to fall at the final hurdle, unable to translate potential into real achievement. Or possibly the party was closer to Blackburn Rovers, the sleeping giants who, having enjoyed a massive infusion of cash (courtesy of businessman Jack Walker's astute management of tax regulations), came back in 1995 to win their first League championship for eighty-one years, but were unfortunately relegated just four seasons later.

The problems of that first flush of government – the Bernie Ecclestone affair, Derry Irvine's wallpaper, the failures to reform social security and public services, the U-turns on privatisation, the bottling of a decision on the euro – came to a head in December 1998 with the downfall of New Labour's original talisman, Peter Mandelson.

The issue was relatively straightforward, and related to the purchase of a house in the fashionable Notting Hill area of London. 'Peter Mandelson had been given a loan by Geoffrey Robinson, the paymaster general, to buy a house,' explained Blair in his memoirs. 'The sum was large, certainly in those days: £373,000.' (It was an indication of how far Blair had drifted from those who Prescott called 'our own people' that he failed to realise that, even after the tripling of average house prices during his premiership, this was still a large sum of money to most of the population in 2010.)

The loan was, insisted Mandelson, 'private rather than secret', and there was nothing illegal, or even necessarily improper, about the arrangement, though he had failed to mention it either to his mortgage company or, on being appointed trade and industry secretary, to the permanent secretary in his department. The former omission was sloppy, the latter had the potential to be deeply awkward, for Robinson was at the time under investigation by the Department of Trade and Industry in relation to his links with the late Robert Maxwell. The DTI's subsequent report found no wrongdoing by Robinson, but the affair raised again the Labour ghost of Maxwell and risked creating the impression that Robinson had bought his way into office. More importantly it reinforced the appearance of a Labour government hypnotised by wealth. As David Blunkett put it, 'it all feels wrong'.

The main issue for Blair – who also hadn't been told of the loan – seemed to be how the story had ever reached the media. He was convinced that it had been passed to them by members of Gordon Brown's camp as an act of spite: 'it was a political assassination, done to destroy Peter; but it was done also to damage me and damage me badly,' he wrote. 'What is the mentality of such a person? Determined, vengeful, verging on wicked.' Cherie Blair was similarly incandescent. 'You have been the victim of a vicious and selfish campaign,' she wrote to Mandelson, making it clear that she blamed Brown personally. 'My only consolation is that I believe that a person who causes evil to another will in the end suffer his returns.'

For everyone else, however, it seemed like a catastrophe that had long been waiting to happen. Even before the general election Andy McSmith had observed the discrepancy between the media skills of the spin doctor and his own apparent recklessness: 'Mandelson's acute judgement of political realities sometimes deserts him when he tries to judge his own situation.' John Prescott put it all down to what he saw as Mandelson's 'vanity and arrogance' and Alastair Campbell largely agreed: 'How many times had I warned him that what I called his "lifestyle ambitions" would do for him?' Mandelson was, concluded Rupert Murdoch, 'a star-fucker'. In private, Campbell was more direct still, telling the trade secretary that he was a 'stupid cunt'.

In contrast to the lingering political deaths of John Major's ministers, the execution was swift. Mandelson was prevailed upon to resign, as were both Geoffrey Robinson and Charlie Whelan, Brown's spin doctor who, despite his repeated denials to the contrary, Blair suspected had spread the story ('Tony had never liked or trusted him,' according to Mandelson). But there was no pretence that this was the end of Mandelson's career. 'We've briefed that Peter can expect to return to high office after a reasonable interval,' recorded Lance Price, and the headline-writers duly obliged: GOODBYE . . . FOR NOW, said the *Guardian*.

Notwithstanding the awareness that Whitehall was probably yet to see the last of Peter Mandelson, his departure nonetheless suggested the end of an era, as the first really high-profile cabinet resignation took down the architect of the Blairite revolution. Blair himself admitted to feeling 'a sense of doom' at his departure, but there were others who simply rejoiced. 'I think it is the end of New Labour,' wrote the ever-hopeful Tony Benn, 'because Blair without Mandelson is lost.'

13
Generations
'I've become so cynical these days'

> You do get this feeling that the socialist/anti-socialist divide is partly the old versus the young.
> Tony Benn (1992)

> 'We're the lost generation!' Martin Finkelstein, the clever boy from South Wimbledon, used to say. 'We're the children of the eighties! We have no hope!'
> Nigel Williams, *East of Wimbledon* (1993)

> Politics isn't showbiz, okay? What counts is what you say.
> Steve Hilton (1994)

In February 1993 the Marxist academic Ralph Miliband dropped in for tea at the Westminster office of the former Labour cabinet minister Tony Benn. The two men were senior figures on the left – Miliband was then sixty-nine years old, Benn a year his junior – but they had not always seen eye to eye politically. Back in the early 1960s, as Benn was fighting his long campaign to renounce his hereditary peerage so that he might remain an MP in the House of Commons, Miliband had published his best-known book, *Parliamentary Socialism*, attacking the Labour Party's reformist allegiance to Parliament. Benn's continuing membership of Harold Wilson's government in the 1970s had also met with Miliband's criticism: 'With such rebels,' he wrote scathingly, 'Mr Wilson has no great need of allies.' Even so, they had much in common, sharing an optimistic and longstanding commitment to the building of the socialist future, and a passionate pride in their respective families. Now, in their mature years, they found that it was the latter that brought them together.

Miliband was worried that his two sons, David and Edward, had little commitment to the revolutionary socialism that he had made his life's work. Indeed both were now active members of the very Labour Party that he had abandoned nearly three decades earlier. Why, he wondered aloud to Benn, did his boys seem to have so little faith in socialism, constantly challenging his pronouncements. 'Oh, Dad, how would you do that? Would it work?' they would demand of him. 'Well,' replied Benn, on hearing this sad tale of youthful conformity, 'it's the same with my sons.' His second child, Hilary, had by then already failed twice to be elected as an MP, but would in due course find his way into the House of Commons and end up sitting around the same New Labour cabinet table as David and Ed Miliband.

It sounded a somewhat melancholy meeting, but Ralph was, concluded Tony, comforted by the knowledge that he was not the only ageing socialist to find that the younger generation were going off the rails: 'I think he thought that he was very out of date.'

Perhaps he was right in so thinking. When Miliband died the following year, the former Trotskyist Tariq Ali mourned his passing: 'His death has now left a gaping void in times which are bad for socialists everywhere.' Britain was not exempt from those bad times, and even the mainstream, parliamentary left was looking in danger of extinction. The withering away of the tradition had already been manifest in Ken Livingstone's failure to collect enough nominations to stand for the Labour leadership against John Smith, and in the 1991 closure of *Marxism Today*, a journal with influence far beyond its small circulation. Above all it was evident in the fact that the recession of the early 1990s had passed by with virtually no organised resistance by the working class; the unions had lost their strength in terms of numbers, legal rights and solidarity, while many of those most affected had still not recovered from a decade of decline, and were looking cowed. As a police officer commented in an episode of *Between the Lines*, looking at an anti-cuts demonstration outside a town hall: 'It's hardly '84, is it?'

A number of factors contributed to this decline, most spectacularly the unqualified victory of the West in the Cold War, and the subsequent collapse of communism in the Eastern bloc. In 1989, while the Berlin Wall was still standing, the American commentator Francis Fukuyama had published his essay 'The End of History', arguing that the world's ideological conflicts had been resolved in favour of capitalist democracy. Whether or not this were true, the proposition found a receptive audience and confirmed what had become unavoidably apparent over the last decade: that the intellectual tide had turned in favour of free-market economics. Ideas about state ownership of manufacturing and services, or about how to plan and regulate the economy, were unlikely to get much of a hearing in the foreseeable future. As Tony Blair explained in opposition: 'People will look back on the present century and say that, in a curious way, it was an aberration – that you had this war to the death about ideology.'

In Britain the reinvigoration of the right had taken a very specific turn, under the influence of that doughtiest of cold warriors, Margaret Thatcher. The European Community had once been embraced by Conservatives as a bulwark against both international communism and domestic socialism, but now that the external threat was imploding and the power of the trade unions had been curbed at home, there seemed little further need of anything save the free market, operating on as wide a basis as possible. Everything else about the EU – its aspirations to exert influence in social matters and foreign affairs, for example – was inherently suspect.

The fall of the Berlin Wall allowed an instinctive patriotism to reassert itself, while the Manichean rhetoric of the Cold War era survived, to be directed now at the EU; any hint that it might seek to impede the free workings of capitalism was portrayed as socialism in disguise, a return to the bureaucratic statism of Eastern Europe. 'Maastricht, and most of the Euro-legislation which had gone before it,' insisted Teresa Gorman, 'is essentially socialist in nature, designed to create a centralised structure for Europe.' The Eurosceptic press barons tended towards the same view; Conrad Black was happy to explain that he was 'against the EU because it is a "socialist organisation"'. The more philosophically minded argued further that the collapse of the Soviet bloc signalled the end of the era of the superstate, thereby necessitating a rethink of the European drive towards ever closer union.

Such claims helped bolster the new-found enthusiasm for Europe evident in the Labour Party, where Euroscepticism was a fading memory, associated with old folk like Tony Benn, Bryan Gould and Peter Shore, and where debate on the issue had virtually ceased. In his 1989 book *Livingstone's Labour: A Programme for the Nineties*, Ken Livingstone argued for a wider internationalism, suggesting that a future Labour government should work with 'progressive forces in both Eastern and Western Europe as well as in the USSR', but he actually had far less to say on the subject of the European Community than on the Soviet Union. And what he really wanted to talk about was the neo-colonialism and economic imperialism of the USA.

Hatred of America had long been a defining characteristic of the British left, and had led to a slightly ambivalent attitude towards the Eastern bloc. On the one hand, very few – even within the Communist Party of Great Britain – wished to adopt that system, after the crushing of Hungary and Czechoslovakia; but on the other, the existence of the Soviet Union and China was seen as a counterbalance to America. In some quarters, open criticism was considered inappropriate, so that when Benn spoke at a rally in support of the demonstrators killed in Tiananmen Square in 1989, he could observe, slightly surprised at himself: 'It was the first time I had ever spoken in public against a communist government.'

It was a bit late by then, of course, and the established sections of the British left made little contribution to the hurried recalculations that followed the dismantling of communism in Eastern Europe. Outside the Labour Party, a group like the Socialist Workers Party could claim that events had proved their theory that the Soviet Union had long since descended into state capitalism, but no one much was listening. The whole political spectrum in Britain shifted as a result of the fallout blowing from the East, the right attracted again to nationalism, the left abandoning its attempt to accommodate both capitalist and socialist impulses. In the words of Jack Straw: 'the Labour movement would no longer uneasily have to straddle the theoretical divide which had so hobbled it since its foundation.'

Blair was to confirm this shift, but it was evident within Labour long before his Clause IV adventures. 'By driving out communism from their own countries, the peoples of central and eastern Europe have driven the threat of socialism from ours,' wrote Madsen Pirie of the Adam Smith Institute in August 1992, a couple of weeks into John Smith's leadership. 'The reformed Labour Party in Britain no longer threatens to undo what privatization has achieved.' As a consequence the Tories were deprived of one of their defining characteristics in recent years, now that the Labour Party shared their faith in markets as the only economic model in town. The need to find a new dividing line between the parties was instrumental in the elevation of Europe to the top of the political agenda.

Amongst a younger generation, however, those who might have been expected to carry the socialist banner forwards, the appeal of the Soviet Union had never been particularly marked. For someone inclined to the left and born between, say, the Suez Crisis and Rhodesia's Unilateral Declaration of Independence, the campaigns against the hydrogen bomb and the Vietnam War, let alone the memory of the Soviet part in the crushing of Nazism, played no formative role. Nor did Europe rank very high among this generation's concerns.

Instead the focus, despite the campaigns against apartheid and nuclear weapons, was much more domestic. The greatest galvanising event was the advent of Thatcherism, and the moment of crisis came in 1992 when Labour failed to remove the Tories from office. If, after all those years, the best that could be hoped for was a tame accommodation with Majorism, then it was hard to escape the conclusion that political parties in general — and the

Labour Party in particular – were no longer suitable vehicles for social or political change. The death of the left was due as much to this generation's rejection of politics as it was to the fall of the Soviet Union.

It was a development articulated most clearly in a series of roles played by the actor Robert Carlyle, born in 1961 and described in the press as 'a Labour voter who never quite recovered from the party's election defeat in 1992'. 'People need to believe. People need to congregate. But there's nothing left to believe in, nothing left to congregate for,' explains his character, Albie, in 'To Be a Somebody' (1994), the best-known story from *Cracker*. Albie is a *Guardian*-reading manual worker who didn't go to university but is sufficiently self-educated that he can identify a Mozart piano concerto or a Rossini opera from a few bars, and is sharp enough to trade verbal blows with Robbie Coltrane's Fitz. He's also feeling lost and unwanted in society. 'We get treated like scum,' he complains. 'We're socialists, we're trade unionists, so we look to the Labour Party for help. But we're not queers, we're not black, we're not Paki. There's no brownie points in speaking up for us, so the Labour Party turns its back. We're not getting treated like scum any more, we're getting treated like wild animals.'

In a desperate search for meaning in his life, he shaves his hair to a skinhead cut and kills a 'robbing Paki bastard' of a shopkeeper, revelling in the sense of power that using a forbidden racist epithet gives him. He goes on to commit a number of other murders, including those of a criminology lecturer and a senior police detective, though he fails in his attempt to kill a freelance journalist who works for the *Sun*.

Carlyle returned to the theme of the dispossessed white working class as Gaz in *The Full Monty*, struggling to find a role as a father now that he's unemployed. With no money in his pocket, he doesn't know what to do with his son, Nathan, when he spends time with the boy. 'You're always making me do stupid stuff like last night,' says Nathan, referring to a failed attempt to steal a girder from a disused steel mill. 'Other dads don't do that.' Gaz is inspired to try his hand at stripping in an attempt to get enough money to pay maintenance, so that he doesn't lose access to Nathan, but it doesn't address the underlying problem of what a man is supposed to do in a rapidly changing world: 'A few years and men won't exist. Except in a zoo or summat. I mean, we're not needed no more, are we? Obsolete. Dinosaurs. Yesterday's news.'

Less celebrated was Carlyle's depiction of Ray in Antonia Bird's *Face* (1997). Like Quentin Tarantino's influential *Reservoir Dogs*, the film was the tale of a heist that goes wrong in a sea of blood and broken friendships, here given a

Britpop makeover with a soundtrack that included music by the Longpigs, Gene and Paul Weller, and with a debut acting role for Blur's Damon Albarn. Ray used to be a communist – nicknamed Red Ray – who was active on the picket line at Wapping during the News International dispute in 1986, but he has abandoned political struggle for a life of crime because he feels that the radicalism of the 1980s has been so comprehensively defeated: 'I thought: fuck it, that's it, it's war, them against us.'

Even in his criminal life, though, he's still being beaten by the system. Without knowing it, he's working for a bent copper, who explains why Ray and his kind will never win: 'You really don't get it, do you? You and your sort are always on your own, which is why the odds are always against you. I, on the other hand, belong to an institution.' The one sign of hope comes from Ray's mother Alice (Sue Johnston), who's still campaigning, albeit on a smaller, less dramatic scale. 'It's over,' despairs Ray. 'Didn't you read the news? They won.' And Alice replies: 'They haven't won, Ray. We're still here and we're still fighting. Now, you may have given up, but that doesn't mean everybody else has.'

There were common threads between those three characters. Albie, Gaz and Ray were quick-witted, articulate men, with enough intelligence to resist the role of victim, but frustrated by their failure to find a place in society and driven to an amoral nihilism. It was a type that occurred repeatedly in the culture of the era. In Mike Leigh's film *Naked* (1993), David Thewlis played Johnny, another man for whom society has no discernible use. 'Why do you feel the need to take the piss?' he's asked, and the unspoken answer is that there's no other way for him to express the futility of his life. He's cobbled together some kind of philosophy from scraps of Nostradamus, the Book of Revelation and chaos theory, but it's hardly enough to sustain any sense of hope. 'I don't have a future,' he rages. 'Nobody has a future, the party's over. Take a look around you, man, it's all breaking up.'

The voice of a generation that spent its teenage years in the punk era, with the Sex Pistols' sneer that 'We're the future, your future', it was echoed again in the words of Albie: 'You're looking at the future. This country's going to blow. And people like me are going to light the fuse. The despised, the betrayed, we're going to light the fuse, and this country's going to blow.'

The implausibility of that apocalyptic threat was yet another cause for despair. The truth was that those exiled to the fringes of society might be growing in number but they possessed no power to bring the nation to its knees, however alluring the fantasy might appear. But nor were they likely to form part of the new Britain that John Patten (in another Tory precursor of Tony Blair's Third Way) had called for in 1993, a country in which people were 'concerned as much about their responsibilities as their rights, opportunities as much as entitlements'.

Some of Albie and Johnny's real-life counterparts found their way into what survived of the New Age travelling communities. Battered by years of struggle with police and local authorities, the travellers had sustained a near-fatal blow with the 1994 Criminal Justice and Public Order Act, and by the second half of the decade their numbers were thinning considerably. 'Ten years ago, we felt like an army, but how many's still left today? Five thousand?' a convoy member despaired to the journalist Nik Cohn. 'And what's our crime, once you get past the scapegoating? We don't know our place, that's all.' The battles had taken their toll on the broad coalition seen at Castlemorton earlier in the decade, and now only the desperate were left: 'Some people may show up with a lot of fancy ideas, full of utopian dreams, but they never last long. Hardcore travellers, the ones who endure, have no choice.' As he put it: 'The nine-to-five world has no further use for them; they're seen as garbage.'

That opposition between travellers' values and those of the 'nine-to-five world' was explored, in the mid-1990s, by several novelists for whom the image of the convoy offered an escape from modernity. In 1960 E.M. Forster had reflected that his then-unpublished Edwardian novel *Maurice* was set in 'an England where it was still possible to get lost'. Things had changed: 'There is no forest or fell to escape to today, no cave in which to curl up, no deserted valley for those who wish neither to reform nor corrupt society but to be left alone.' The New Age travellers appeared to suggest that some of this heritage might yet be reclaimed, both in a negative and a positive way: a convoy is seen as a potential refuge for a criminal in Reginald Hill's *On Beulah Height* (1993) and for Francis Kreer experiencing his spiritual crisis in A.N. Wilson's *The Vicar of Sorrows*.

The theme was developed most fully in *The Anarchist* (1996), the brilliant second novel by Tristan Hawkins, who died shortly after its publication, aged just thirty-three. *The Anarchist* tells the stories of Sheridan Entwhistle, a magazine publisher in his forties, and Yantra, a traveller who, like Johnny in *Naked*, has pieced together for himself a patchwork of philosophies and religions, ranging from Greek mythology to a belief — vouchsafed to him in an acid dream by Jimi Hendrix — that 'Stonehenge was an alien chess set'. Tempted by the image of freedom, wisdom and honesty that he perceives in Yantra, Sheridan abandons his life of suburban comfort, only to discover the shocking truth that humanity is much the same wherever it finds itself: 'Suburbia celebrates its newborn, mourns its dead and worships its gods with no less intensity than anyone else on this cruel, chaotic planet – the only difference being that it wears a tie to do it.' The encounter also provides the opportunity for Yantra's travelling companion, Jayne, to return to her own middle-class family in Hemel Hempstead, another of those who came to travelling 'full of utopian dreams' but didn't last the course.

During their time together, Yantra, Sheridan and Jayne also find themselves participating in an anti-roads protest, although there is some confusion about quite what the issue involves. 'The justification, the logic behind it, doesn't matter,' explains Jayne. 'If it helps undermine the bloody establishment then it's always right. You don't have to know what a demo's about to join in. It's a demo. And yeah, I s'pose it is a bit of a grin.' Much of that motivation could indeed be discerned in the anti-roads movement that flourished briefly, and vividly, in the mid-1990s, though there was too a genuine concern for the environment, an expression of the new creed that had supplanted socialism amongst idealist youth.

The campaign to stop ancient woodlands and natural habitats being bulldozed so new roads could be built first became a major news story in July 1995, when work began on the Newbury bypass. Over the next eighteen months, thousands of protestors occupied the land in an ultimately doomed attempt to halt construction work, using tactics – including the building of tree-houses and tunnels – that ensured maximum disruption and intense media attention. They were emulated in subsequent protests, including the demonstration against the A30 extension in Fairmile, Devon, which made a star of a 23-year-old Newbury-born activist named Daniel Hooper, better known under his *nom de paix* Swampy.

By the time he was pulled out of a tunnel in February 1997, having spent nine days underground, Swampy had become 'the nation's favourite activist', famous enough to appear on *Have I Got News for You*. A quiet, well-spoken young man, his commitment couldn't be faulted. 'We are living in a car culture,' he explained. 'Without this protest, I don't think people would be aware that they are building a super-highway all the way through the country.' None of the individual battles were won, but the raising of environmental concerns – as well as the enormous cost of dealing with such protestors – did have an impact on future planning procedures.

The numbers involved in such campaigns were relatively small, and the participants' activism marked them out as unusual at a time when political commitment was in retreat. Much more common was the atmosphere of sullen defeat found in those parts of the country devastated by the decline of heavy industry. Such places had been hit hard by the recession of the early 1980s, had remained untouched by the later boom years of Thatcherism, had barely noticed the second great Tory recession, since there was no further to fall, and had again been forgotten in the recovery of the mid-1990s.

In the North-East, in the 1970s, the shipyards had employed 30,000 and the coalfields 65,000; these figures were now down to 2,000 and 200 respectively. The flight of employment had left behind little evidence of the property-owning democracy that had been promised. A man in Newcastle explained that he had bought his house in 1960 for £2,000 and seen its value rise and fall: 'In 1980 it was worth around £25,000, now it's worth around £2,000.' Others reported trying to give their houses to the council and being refused, since the cost of maintenance was greater than the value of the property.

The same stories could be heard in Liverpool, one of the few major cities in the western world that ended the century with a smaller population than it had started, where police officers were routinely issued with bulletproof vests and school vandalism was said to cost millions of pounds every year. A clergyman returning to Liverpool after ten years' absence was shocked at what he found: 'The great quality of Liverpudlians was that we had hope, however bad things got. But the hope has gone now and everyone seems dragged down by a general depression.' Edwina Currie, born and educated in the city, was also unimpressed on her trips back. 'Liverpool is still awful,' she wrote in 1995: 'greedy envious eyes on the car, so you're scared to leave it out of your sight.'

Private enterprise, for all of Michael Heseltine's activity in the 1980s, was still conspicuous by its absence. 'We're living in a grantocracy here. That means we spend half our lives sitting on our arses and waiting,' commented an unemployed community activist in Toxteth. Despite all the money spent in the attempt to regenerate the area, decline had continued: 'There's been about six billion so far, spread over the last four decades, and here we are today, still living in shit.'

Large parts of the country were similarly lost to any sense of national prosperity, and concern was expressed particularly for the young. In the weeks before the 1997 election, Tony Parsons toured some of the more deprived parts of the country, reporting, for example, the perspective of a woman in Bristol: 'I work with children and teenagers. After eighteen years of Tory rule, many of them are apathetic. They have low self-esteem, low expectations.' The celebrated photo-journalist Nick Danziger, who specialised in covering the darkest and most dangerous places on the planet, undertook a similar journey around Britain, finding a primary-school head teacher who had little time for formal education: 'her primary objective was not to teach reading and writing, but to provide the children with a safe environment.' The desperation of the early 1980s was being replicated, fifteen years on, and there seemed little likelihood of arresting the descent into hopelessness. Another lost generation was in the making.

Danziger's perception was that 'as the British government rolls back the safety nets for the poor, the excluded and marginalised people of British cities are in many ways less able to deal with relationships and circumstances than the shanty town dwellers in Third World countries'. The pseudonymous doctor, Theodore Dalrymple, who wrote a column in *The Spectator* reporting from the front line of general practice in an inner-city area, came to much the same conclusion: 'having worked in several countries of the so-called Third World, and having travelled extensively through all the continents, I am convinced that the poverty of spirit to be found in an English slum is the worst to be found anywhere.'

In a previous era this was the natural constituency of the Labour movement, with the workers' education programmes and self-help groups that formed the backdrop to Frank Field's vision of society. In 1996 the Manic Street Preachers scored their biggest hit thus far with 'A Design for Life', its opening line – 'Libraries gave us power' – sounding epically nostalgic for a vanished world. Both Labour and the Tories had once been a part of the warp and weft of everyday society, but no longer. John Prescott talked wistfully about 'my old days when being a member of your local Labour Party meant sports days, parties, tons of amusements and games. Much of that sort of fun went out of politics when the flowcharts flooded in.'

Instead New Labour was, as Tony Blair repeatedly pointed out, concerned first and foremost with success in general elections; there was no acknowledgement of the idea that the movement had a role to play in improving lives even when in opposition. As a consequence the pursuit of the suburban vote left many believing themselves to be unrepresented, and the courting of 'middle England' made those in the North, let alone those in Scotland and Wales, feel marginalised. A man living on a South Wales estate where unemployment stood at over 90 per cent, told Danziger of the loss of identity: 'We no longer work, so I suppose I'm no longer a member of the working class.'

Instead he categorised himself as belonging to the underclass. A term that had travelled from America in the 1980s, this was now widely used to describe a sector of society occupied by, in the words of academic Mary Kaldor, 'the unskilled, unpowerful and often unwaged or low-waged' – the 'socially excluded', as New Labour preferred to express it – amongst whom material and spiritual poverty was said to be passed down from generation to generation. Gordon Brown pointed out in 1996 that '20 per cent of all households have no employed person in them, even though unemployment is running at about 7 per cent'.

The concept of an underclass was hardly new — it had precedents in nineteenth-century concepts of the 'undeserving poor' and the *lumpenproletariat* — but its supposed growth in recent years was a matter of political dispute. From a Conservative perspective, it was a left-wing problem. 'The cause is twofold,' argued John Major. 'It's a combination of poor schools, run on fashionable 1960s theories, which have let pupils down, and misguided council policies in the inner cities, which have driven out the sort of employers who would have given school-leavers work.' From the left, there was no hesitation in ascribing it to the effects of Conservative policy in the 1980s, the 'ugly face of Thatcherism', as Michael Meacher wrote in 1984, claiming that thirteen million people in Britain were 'living in chronic insecurity'. But few doubted any more the problem's existence.

Mostly the underclass was depicted in terms of youth, employing the twin stereotypes of the drunken lout and the teenage single mother; the former inspired fear of anti-social, violent behaviour, the latter attracted moral indignation and mockery. As with so many cultural trends, it was captured in the pages of *Viz* comic, which had pre-empted the ladette phenomenon with its creation of the Fat Slags, a pair of sexually promiscuous, drunken women who shared the favours of a married and unemployed petty criminal. Now it produced Kappa Slappa (soon renamed Tasha Slappa after complaints from the sportswear manufacturer), a teenage version of the same type, seen with a succession of unwanted and abandoned children, dreaming of spending her entire life on benefits. She was to be followed on television early in the next century by Matt Lucas's character Vicky Pollard in *Little Britain* and Catherine Tate's Lauren Cooper, by which time the term 'chav' had made its way into the nation's vocabulary.

Such figures were not always presented in a particularly harsh light. Steve Coogan first made his name playing both the mullet-haired, student-hating Mancunian slob Paul Calf and his tarty, promiscuous sister Pauline, and both were treated with some tolerance, at least when compared to others in Coogan's stable. So too was 'teenage temptress' Bianca Jackson, played by Patsy Palmer, who made her debut in *EastEnders* in 1993; her appalling dress sense, her sulky demeanour, punctuated by temper tantrums, and her colourful private life weren't allowed to conceal a warm heart of pure soap. There were also Hyacinth Bucket's working-class sisters Rose and Daisy, together with Rose's layabout husband Onslow, in *Keeping Up Appearances*. Warmer still were the portrayals in *The Royle Family*, a sitcom created by and starring Caroline Aherne and Craig Cash, which recreated the claustrophobic working-class family-home environment of *Till Death Us Do Part*, but without the political shouting matches in which Alf Garnett and his son-in-law engaged. And perhaps this was the most marked difference between the working-class comedies of the 1990s and those of a generation earlier. In the 1970s, series like *Love Thy Neighbour*, *Rising Damp* and *George and Mildred* had featured political – and often explicitly party political – arguments as an integral part of the comedy; that element had now disappeared.

The warmth of those depictions of socially excluded families was countered in the bleakest British film of the decade, *Nil by Mouth*, written and directed by Gary Oldman. A tale of drink, drugs and random violence set amongst the desperate, lawless white underclass on a high-rise council estate in south-east London, *Nil by Mouth* had none of the gloss of *Trainspotting*, none of the human spirit of *Brassed Off*, none of the occasional flashes of wit seen in *Naked*. There was, however, a level of impotent, profanity-laden fury that few others had ever matched. 'Get that cunt out of my fucking house,' rages Ray (Ray Winstone) at his wife Valerie (Kathy Burke). 'Get him out or I'll kill him. Then I'll fucking kill you and I'll kill your fucking slag shit cunt family.' She subsequently has a miscarriage after he gives her a severe kicking in a misguided fit of jealousy. As her mother (Laila Morse) says: 'We're unlucky, ain't we?'

This did not, of course, reflect the totality of life in Britain, even as experienced by youth. 'There are more adolescents in the Girl Guides and the Sea Scouts than there are teenage junkies, but nobody ever makes a film about them,' observes a character in Ben Elton's novel *Inconceivable*, and he had a point. The established organisations for children had become deeply unfashionable, as Chris Mullin discovered when a group of Girl Guides refused to have their photograph taken with him for the local paper in Sunderland: 'The other kids at school would make fun of us,' they explained. 'It's not cool.' (Meanwhile *Viz* brought us Boy Scouse, a strip in which teenage boys win badges for such good deeds as Multiple Identity Signin' On and Gerrin' a 14-Year-Old Baird Preggas.) But the underclass and its association with criminality became a favourite theme of film-makers in the 1990s, in what looked at times like slum tourism of the kind targeted in one of Britpop's finest moments, Pulp's hit single 'Common People':

You'll never get it right,
'Cause when you're laid in bed at night,
Watching roaches climb the wall —
If you called your dad he could end it all.

The political dimension to 'Common People' marked it out, alongside the work of the Manic Street Preachers, as an anomaly in the Britpop canon. More generally, there was little reflection of working-class life — let alone of rebellion — in the lyrics to the songs of, say, Oasis. Instead that band's success made fashionable a proletarian style and presentation that fed into the mockney tendency of the new lads; from Blur to Jamie Oliver there was displayed an attitude of chirpy matiness that owed more to the music hall than it did to Marxism. And behind that apolitical image was hopelessness, a lack of faith in future progress. After a decade and a half of defeat for the working class in much of the country, few were left with any commitment to the idea of fighting back, and New Labour was unlikely to fill the void where once there had been a sense of social optimism.

Similarly, much of television and cinema also displayed a decreasing interest in politics. Channel 4's soap *Brookside* faced criticism for abandoning the agenda that had portrayed Bobby Grant (Ricky Tomlinson) as a trade union activist in the mid-1980s. Now it became ever more sensationalist, so that even when addressing the issue of domestic violence, it resorted to the melodrama of murder and the burial of a body under a patio, a plotline that achieved high audience figures and a two-year cliffhanging story at the expense of realism. The programme's creator, Phil Redmond, was unrepentant. 'With a lack of any great vision from the Conservative government and the arrival of the cult of the individual, our stories became more introspective,' he shrugged. His new series, *Hollyoaks*, was — like *Eldorado*, but more sustainably — a response to the shiny vacuity of the Australian youth-soaps.

Meanwhile the elder statesman of social drama, Ken Loach, was entering a purple patch in his career, films like *Riff-Raff* (1991), *Raining Stones* (1993) and *Ladybird, Ladybird* (1994) making him the most acclaimed British director of the era, at least on the Continent where he was more venerated than he was at home. Here too, however, there was a turn towards the introspective. Loach's best film of the decade, *My Name Is Joe* (1998), was the story of a recovering alcoholic in Glasgow (played by Peter Mullan), who's been dry for nearly a year and is building a new life, largely centred on the amateur football team that he runs. He's optimistic, funny and charming, and he falls for Sarah (Louise Goodall), a health visitor who's in a different league:

'She's got a wee car, a job, a cheque at the end of every month, a pension, her own house,' whereas he's thirty-seven years old 'and I've got fuck all'.

Much of the film is close to romantic comedy, though the class conflict is more prominent than it would be in, say, a Richard Curtis script. With the best of motives, Joe helps out a young ex-junkie who's in trouble with gangsters, but in the process he finds himself sucked back into a shady world he's left behind, much to Sarah's horror. He tries to explain his reality to her: 'I'm really sorry but we all don't live in this nice, tidy world of yours. Some of us can't go to the police. Some of us can't go to the bank for a loan. Some of us can't just move house and fuck off out of here. Some of us don't have a choice.'

The misery of neglected parts of working-class Britain was also a reliable standby for newspapers wanting to make their readers' flesh creep. In 1993 there was tremendous excitement over a thirteen-year-old from the Byker Wall estate in Newcastle, who was too young to be named but was given the moniker Rat Boy by a local journalist. The nickname (shared by Tasha Slappa's half-brother in *Viz*) referred to the boy's supposed practice of living in ventilation shafts on the estate, though he vehemently denied any such suggestion and insisted that he was merely hiding there from the police when he was caught.

The story that emerged was uninspiring. Coming from 'a respectable working-class family', the child had first been cautioned for burglary at the age of ten and had gone on to commit a string of such crimes, typically picking on the homes of pensioners, though it appeared that, for all his instant notoriety, he wasn't exactly a master criminal; he stole very little, was easily scared off and was regularly arrested. He would then be put in council care and would promptly abscond. By the time he was fourteen, he had escaped from care more than thirty times, had admitted over a hundred crimes, and was still going strong when he reached seventeen and was sentenced to four years in jail, at which stage his identity could be revealed in the papers.

In his wake came other examples of what were becoming known as 'feral children', including Spider Boy and Blip Boy ('because he single-handedly alters crime figures'), though none made quite the same impression. The media handwringing was mocked by Ron Manager in *The Fast Show*: 'Small boys. On remand. Car stereos for goalposts? That's the way it is these days, isn't it?' Caroline Aherne played a schoolgirl in the same series: 'He's great, my dad, but he's so old-fashioned, you know? He still thinks that you shouldn't have a baby till you've left school.'

The wider context of the Rat Boy story was the lack of appropriate accommodation in which such youngsters could be held, and Kenneth Clarke, as home secretary, responded by launching a policy of building Secure Training Centres. At the time, Tony Blair was in his 'tough on crime' phase, but even he sided with penal reform groups, seeing the centres – effectively prisons for children from the age of twelve upwards – as a step too far, saying that they risked creating 'colleges of crime'. Nonetheless Clarke's successor, Michael Howard, pressed on with the plans. After the 1997 election, Labour's Jack Straw intimated that the programme was to be scrapped, to the relief of many, including the National Association of Probation Officers, whose spokesperson explained: 'We would welcome the abandonment of Secure Training Centres. They went ahead against all professional opinion. They will be extremely expensive to run and will do nothing to reduce crime.'

Then Straw announced that he'd changed his mind, and was implementing the policy after all. When the first such unit, the Medway Secure Training Centre, opened in Kent in 1998, the cost of keeping an offender imprisoned there was said to be £5,000 a week, six times as much as an adult in maximum security and eighteen times as much as sending a child to Eton. (This was later claimed to be an exaggeration, the actual cost being just half that figure, no more than a decent room at the Ritz.) Within the first seven months, there had been nearly a hundred assaults on staff, with twenty-six adults hospitalised, and morale was so low that thirty-five employees had resigned, including two senior managers. Since the centre held a maximum of forty children, overseen by a hundred staff, this appeared to represent fairly serious disruption. Meanwhile, the company running the institution, Rebound, had been fined by the government for breaches of its contract. Rebound was a part of Group 4, a private security firm that, five years earlier, had won the contract to escort prisoners between jails and courts in Humberside and the East Midlands, as part of a privatisation initiative. The company's involvement received a fanfare of early publicity, for reasons made clear in a *Daily Mirror* editorial: 'To lose one prisoner may be bad luck. To lose four in as many days reeks of incompetence.'

The reversal of policies espoused in opposition was not untypical, for the Labour government proved adept at picking up Conservative ideas on crime. It was equally fond of media-friendly initiatives that never fully, or even partially, materialised, ideas such as mandatory three-year sentences for those convicted of a third burglary charge and courts sitting at night. Most famously, Tony Blair suggested on-the-spot fines for yobbish behaviour: 'A thug might think twice about kicking in your gate, throwing traffic cones around your street or hurling abuse into the night sky if he thought he might get picked up by the police, taken to a cash-point and asked to pay an on-the-spot fine of, for example, £100.' The proposal was roundly ridiculed and denounced by pretty much everyone, from chief constables to the Liberal Democrat Simon Hughes: 'Punishing people who are not charged and not found guilty is fundamentally against civil liberties.' Even Ann Widdecombe, the Conservative home affairs spokesperson, dismissed it as 'just another headline-grabbing gimmick' (though that didn't stop her a couple of months later proposing £100 on-the-spot fines for drug takers). Again the proposal came to nothing, and Blair was to dismiss it in his memoirs as being all Alastair Campbell's fault: 'It was a great piece of Alastair tabloidery.'

The one initiative that did survive to become part of the social landscape was the anti-social behaviour order, or ASBO, introduced as a way of dealing with disruptive individuals by allowing a local authority or a police force to apply to a magistrates' court for a banning order, circumscribing that individual's permitted behaviour. As they evolved, it turned out that these could be applied to anyone over the age of ten and required a lower burden of proof than that demanded in criminal cases, even though the breaching of an ASBO was itself a criminal offence. At times, they were far-reaching in their imposition of curfews and restrictions on movements; in 2001 a fifteen-year-old was banned from entering the Fallowfield district of Manchester, and part of Rusholme, for the next ten years.

There were soon reports, however, that having an ASBO was regarded as a matter of pride in certain quarters, evidence of a rebellious individualism. 'People knock ASBOs,' joked Linda Smith, 'but you have to bear in mind, they are the only qualifications some of these kids are going to get.' How effective the policy was remained the subject of debate. Fewer than five hundred such orders were issued in the first three years, and by 2002 the new home secretary, David Blunkett, was promising to reform the system.

Undeniably, however, the talk of feral children and teenage thugs reinforced an impression that society was slipping out of control and needed the firm hand of authoritarian government to restore order. But such an image was far from new; it had been a commonplace for centuries, from the gin-sodden 1740s, 'when multitudes of men and women were rolling about the streets drunk', to the 1820s, when Surrey magistrates expressed concerns about 'the almost unchecked parading of the streets by the notoriously dissolute and abandoned of both sexes'. One could even go back to the twelfth-century historian William of Malmesbury, writing about the people encountered by the Norman invaders in 1066: 'They were accustomed to eat until they became surfeited and drink till they were sick.' As Harry Pearson noted, when considering the pitch invasions and hooliganism that marred professional football in the late Victorian era, it was only the alleged causes that changed, not the behaviour: 'In the days before violent videos and the abolition of corporal punishment in schools you just had to face up to the sad truth: some people like fighting.'

In recent years the cause of social disorder was said, by those on the right of politics, to be the breakdown of discipline that resulted from the liberalisation of the 1960s. New Labour's rhetoric suggested that it shared that perspective, implying a moral failure on the part of working-class youth and their families.

Its response was an endless introduction of new initiatives. In its first term, the government brought forward thirty-one Bills on law and order and introduced new criminal offences at a rate of around two per week. Yet still the stories of badly behaved youth continued to make headlines, embarrassingly so when they came close to home. Jack Straw's own seventeen-year-old son was arrested in 1998 for alleged drug dealing, and Tony Blair's son, Euan, two years later when he was found drunk in Leicester Square, lying on the pavement vomiting, after celebrating his GCSE results ('they weren't a huge cause for celebration,' remarked Blair in his memoirs). More significantly, the prison population continued to rise, far beyond the levels inherited from Michael Howard.

Beyond the issues of anti-social behaviour and 'neighbours from hell' on council estates lay another trend that caused concern to politicians, but against which it was impossible to legislate. There was, it was felt, a disconnection from society evident amongst middle-class members of the generation that reached adulthood in the Thatcher years. 'I must say,' points out the hero of Nigel Williams's novel *East of Wimbledon*, 'that I don't really feel part of British society.' He's not motivated by politics, or by anything else much, just disillusioned by everything, denouncing Britain as 'a squalid little place, full of people who don't believe in anything. Am I making that clear? I don't believe in *anything*. I think it's all a load of toss really.'

That sense of a generation that didn't quite feel as though it fitted into normal society was evident in Robert Carlyle's most mainstream and successful role of the decade. *Hamish Macbeth* (1995) was a prime-time Sunday evening series on BBC One that looked at first sight as though it were a Scottish version of the popular ITV police drama *Heartbeat*, a piece of television nostalgia starring Nick Berry as a Yorkshire policeman and set in the early 1960s. Certainly that was Carlyle's initial impression when offered the title role: 'A Sunday night show about a policeman in a rural setting. It didn't take a genius to work that out. No disrespect to that programme or Nick Berry. It's just not the kind of thing that I'd be interested in personally.' It turned out to be something rather different.

Macbeth is a police officer who's escaped from the big city to take up a post in the idyllic Highland village of Lochdubh, and the series came complete with a title sequence so drenched in Scottish clichés that it could have doubled as a shortbread advert. Beyond that, however, it turned out to be akin to an Ealing comedy, depicting a community warmth and a love of eccentric normality that slyly subverted expectations. The first episode was a light-hearted tale of drug-taking, domestic abuse, filicide and cannibalism, celebrating a lax attitude to law-breaking, even on the part of the police. It rapidly evolved into one of the few shows where you might expect to see discussions of existentialism, the effects of cannabis on cows or modern-day resurrection men. And Macbeth himself, as Carlyle was quick to make clear, was a more subtle character than he might have been: 'He'd joined the police during the Thatcher years, and to come out of that and have no ambition whatsoever seemed to be quite interesting.'

A similar lack of ambition could be seen in another of the BBC's quirky takes on the police drama. *Jonathan Creek* (1997) starred the comedian Alan Davies as a long-haired, duffel-coated figure obsessed with the golden age of illusion, the days of Robert Houdin, John Nevil Maskelyne and David Devant. 'I was born a hundred years too late, basically,' claims Creek, and the sense of being stranded out of time is emphasised by the theme tune (Saint-Saëns's 'Danse Macabre') and by the influences of G.K. Chesterton and John Dickson Carr on writer David Renwick. But Creek is also a product of his own time, someone who's chosen to turn his back on a conventional career path in search of freedom. 'They can never get behind me opting out from college,' he complains about his parents; 'like it's a cop-out to try and escape.'

It was a theme explored extensively in the literature of the period, in a spate of novels that effectively reworked George Orwell's 1936 classic *Keep the Aspidistra Flying* for the post-punk generation. The pattern was set by Nick Hornby's *High Fidelity* (1995), in which the narrator, Rob Fleming, has, like Jonathan Creek, given up on his college career and opted out of the suburban future that lay before him, seduced by a cultural rather than a political opposition to the mainstream. He's made progress since, setting up his own record shop to cater to the needs of the more discerning rock and roll obsessive, but now, thirty-six years old and approaching middle age, he's aware that something has gone wrong. 'We got to adolescence and just stopped dead,' he reflects; 'we drew up the map then and left the boundaries exactly as they were.'

At the heart of this arrested adolescence is a value system that defines character by subcultural credentials, the belief that 'what really matters is what you like, not what you *are* like'. Consequently Rob is baffled when one of his friends starts going out with someone who has the wrong taste in music: 'It is as hard for me to understand how he has ended up with a Simple Minds fan as it would be to fathom how he had paired off with one of the royal family, or a member of the shadow cabinet.'

In one of the novel's key scenes, Rob goes to a dinner party with people of his own age who have, unlike him, followed the middle-class path mapped out for them, and he feels adrift in a world where 'they have smart jobs and I have a scruffy job, they are rich and I am poor, they are self-confident and I am incontinent, they do not smoke and I do'. Silenced and dissatisfied, he identifies the point where it all went wrong, the year when he dropped out of college and Margaret Thatcher came to power, and concludes: 'I want to go back to 1979 and start all over again.' Instead, in a slightly unsatisfactory resolution, Rob achieves maturity through the redeeming power of golden oldie singles.

High Fidelity was one of the biggest-selling novels of the decade, and in its wake came a host of other accounts of men in their thirties tentatively re-engaging with society. In John O'Farrell's first novel, *The Best a Man Can Get*, the narrator, Michael Adams, seems to have achieved the perfect life—play balance, living with his wife and children in North London while pursuing a secret parallel existence, sharing a flat in South London with three other men and behaving as though he were still a twenty-something bachelor. But he too feels the call of adulthood and finds a metaphor for the onset of maturity as he looks back through a twenty-year collection of the *New Musical Express*. 'I flicked through a few of the interviews with my boyhood heroes – snarling punks spouting nihilistic notions of no future and anarchy, postures I'd once adopted myself,' he records, before deciding: 'I'd better drop all these newspapers off at the recycling depot.' In fact, by the end of the century, the idea of arrested adolescence, which had featured so prominently in *Men Behaving Badly* and had been embodied in the new lads, was looking decidedly dated, so that when Linda Smith appeared on the television show *Room 101* she denounced 'this culture of middle youth, this idea that we don't grow old'.

The publication of *High Fidelity* saw Hornby acclaimed in the press as the 'chief British iconographer of the 1990s' and, if that overstated the case a little, he did remain a significant chronicler of a key section of the Thatcher generation. His second novel, *About a Boy* (1998), returned to the theme with a central character, Will, who is a childish grown-up finding some meaning in his disengaged life through the medium of a grown-up child, Marcus. Through Marcus, Will meets the boy's mother, Fiona, a vegetarian music therapist, with whom he has nothing in common save for their mutual dislike of John Major, but he goes to dinner at her house anyway, only to be horrified when she tries to entertain him by playing the piano and singing from the 1970s singer-songwriter repertoire. She's not very good, but what really embarrasses him is that instead of the knowing irony he's expecting, there's a sincerity to her performance. 'Fiona meant it. She meant "Knocking on Heaven's Door", and then she meant "Fire and Rain", and then she meant "Both Sides Now". There was nothing between her and the songs, she was inside them. She even closed her eyes when she was singing.' It's a painfully excruciating evening for him – as it would have been for the smart young cynics in *Queer as Folk* – and as soon as he gets home 'he put a Pet Shop Boys CD on, and watched *Prisoner: Cell Block H* with the sound down. He wanted to hear people who didn't mean it, and he wanted to watch people he could laugh at.'

Fiona represents another side of the same generation, those still committed to the legacy of a left-wing lifestyle, but equally marginal to mainstream society. 'A peculiarly contemporary creation with her seventies albums, her eighties politics and her nineties foot lotion', she comes from a world Will 'knew nothing about and had no use for, like music therapists and housing officers and health-food shops with noticeboards and aromatherapy oils and brightly coloured sweaters and difficult European novels and feelings'. There is no doubt, however, where the reader's sympathies are expected to lie; Marcus asserts his independent identity with the declaration: 'I bloody hate Joni Mitchell.' Even with Will's return from the cultural fringes, the tone of cynicism remained intact here and elsewhere. Personal redemption might be found in relationships, but wider society was still the subject of mockery, ridicule and distrust. And it was that note of hostility against which politicians railed, desperate to prevent it contaminating the emerging sense of a new national identity.

Both Will and Fiona, one felt, would have voted for Tony Blair and New Labour, though she with greater expectation than he, putting her faith in Blair's message of bright-eyed optimism. 'We must awaken in our people the hope that change can bring,' Blair proclaimed, in a speech used for a 1997 election broadcast. 'Because the last weapon the Tories have is despair and cynicism.'

Yet again, the same angle had been tried out first by the Tories, and particularly in this instance by Michael Portillo, who had adopted the message as his theme tune. In a speech delivered in January 1994, he attacked 'the self-destructive sickness of national cynicism', claiming that 'Too many politicians, academics, churchmen, authors, commentators and journalists exhibit the full-blown symptoms of this new British disease.' A few months earlier, Portillo had visited the offices of the *Guardian*, where, noted Hugo Young, he had spoken about how 'British self-irony had grown from minor to major in the pageant of decline.'

As so often in the 1990s, however, it was New Labour that profited from a changing mood. Whatever the merits of Portillo's arguments, they seemed less than convincing when voiced by a leading member of a government that looked tired and jaded; the British could hardly fail to apply their longstanding traditions of scepticism and mockery to such an administration. Similarly, when Prince Charles weighed in with an attack on the 'all-pervading cynicism' sweeping the country, it was hard not to see special pleading on the part of the royal family, a formerly revered institution.

Blair's enthusiasm in opposition, on the other hand, promised a new era, and temporarily he carried much of popular culture with him. 'Bugger my career,' said Martin Rossiter, singer with Britpop band Gene and a member of the Labour Party; 'this is my one chance not to be cynical, and I'm grabbing it with both hands.' Following the 1997 election, the editor of BBC Two's *Newsnight* programme, Peter Horrocks, wrote a memo that announced the formal end of the age of cynicism: 'Ennui is over — for now. Much of our tricksiness and world-weariness was an appropriate way of capturing the repetitiveness of the dying days of Conservatism.'

The death of Diana seemed to suggest that the day of the cynic had indeed passed, but old habits weren't to be shaken off quite so easily. The alliance between New Labour and Cool Britannia scarcely lasted to the end of election year. As the government began to stumble, so its fashionable new friends made their excuses and left, returning to the time-honoured practice of sniping from the sidelines. By January 1998 Harry Enfield was already on the attack ('They are turning out to be worse than the Tories, even more mean-spirited'), followed in short order by Red or Dead designer Wayne Hemingway ('There is a very grave danger that by simply inviting a few, mostly naff pop stars and comedians to drinkies at No 10, the very people Blair is trying to impress will be turned off'), and by Ben Elton. 'The most gruesome aspect of the Cool Britannia thing is the way that politicians are trying to latch on to it,' he remarked. 'Leaders should never, ever try to look cool — that's for dictators.'

Within a couple of months, the *NME* was publishing disparaging comments from the likes of Jarvis Cocker, Alan McGee and Damon Albarn, and putting a picture of Blair on the front cover with the single-word headline: BETRAYED. 'I'm not ashamed to be an old rocker,' shrugged the prime minister, responding in the *Daily Mirror*. 'Pop stars are perfectly entitled to have a go at the government.' Elsewhere, the Manic Street Preachers were making a donation to Arthur Scargill's Socialist Labour Party.

If there was a moment that captured the disenchantment of popular culture with New Labour, a symbol of the fury that this was just another government pursuing pretty much the same set of policies, it came at the Brit Awards in February 1998. While Bill Clinton's favourite soft-rock band, Fleetwood Mac, were on stage, running through 'Go Your Own Way' one more time, Danbert Nobacon of the group Chumbawamba leapt onto the table occupied by John Prescott and emptied a bucket of iced water over the deputy prime minister, while shouting in support of a group of Liverpool dockers who had been in dispute with their former employers for over two years. 'I lashed out with my fist, into his ribs,' remembered John Prescott. 'I hit him so hard he fell off the table.' Only the presence of photographers crowding round prevented him from planting his foot firmly on Nobacon's neck.

Perhaps Julian Clary's jokes at the expense of Norman Lamont should have warned Prescott, but for the last few years awards ceremonies had become a happy hunting ground for politicians and public figures seeking a cheap photo-opportunity. Now they suddenly seemed less hospitable places, as the Duchess of York was to find at the MTV Music Awards later in 1998. Presenting an award to Massive Attack, she was upset when the group's singer 3D refused to shake her hand. 'Someone's having a fucking laugh. Fuck you very much,' he said, in disbelief at her presence, and later explained why he was uncooperative: 'What the fuck has she got to do with music for a start?' (His mother was reportedly unimpressed: 'There was no excuse for this kind of behaviour. He was very well-mannered as a child.')

Prescott's contretemps with Chumbawamba was a world away from the heady days of Cool Britannia, when Paul Conroy, managing director of Virgin Records, could enthuse of Blair: 'Here is a person of our generation who understands us and the music industry. It's like when Kennedy dawned on the politics of America.' Even then, however, some had harboured doubts. When Blair revealed his favourite singles of 1996, there was a definite sense that – like his 'dads and lads' reading list – it was a selection designed by committee to catch all constituencies: Oasis, Simply Red, the Fugees, Bruce Springsteen. Even worse were the inclusions of

Annie Lennox's anaemic version of 'A Whiter Shade of Pale' (a hit from the previous year, as it happened) and David Bowie's 'Hallo Spaceboy' in its tame Pet Shop Boys remix.

'We enjoy music not just because it's an export,' protested Labour's culture secretary, Chris Smith, eager to distance himself from the Tory approach to the arts, but attempts to prove the point were often unconvincing. The comedian Bob Mills interviewed Blair in opposition for MTV and came away distinctly unimpressed: 'I was very suspicious of him. He talks about music like he's just read a bluffer's guide.' The Spice Girls too were prepared to break with consensus. 'We met Tony Blair and he seemed nice enough,' said Victoria Adams in 1996. 'His hair's all right, but we don't agree with his tax policies.' Geri Halliwell went further: 'The real problem with Blair is that he's never had a real job. In the olden days a politician could be a coalminer who came to power with ideals. Not Blair. He's just a good marketing man.'

That marketing ability was more than evident in Blair's identification with popular culture. In his memoirs, he recalled talking with Billy Bragg about the limitations of Red Wedge, the movement set up in the 1980s to encourage political participation by the young. 'I felt, in art and culture, we should represent all strands, avant-garde through to basic popular art, that our voters might go to watch or listen to.' The comment raised more questions than it answered. Why should politicians feel the need to 'represent' culture? Was he really concerned with the avant-garde? And why did he see popular art as 'basic'? As so often with Blair, the words didn't repay close examination.

When a generation had, in the wake of the 1992 election, turned away from Westminster politics and set about building the foundations of Cool Britannia and new laddism, there had remained a deep antipathy to the Conservative Party, which had passed into mainstream culture. In her second set of diaries, Bridget Jones discovers that her ideal man, Mark Darcy, is actually a Conservative, and she is deeply shocked: 'never, ever in a million years suspected I might have been sleeping with a man who voted Tory.'

There was no corresponding love for Labour, old or new, however, simply an embrace of Blair as the man who would drive the Tories out of office. Once he was installed in Downing Street and showed no sign of making any concessions whatsoever to the left – the benefit reforms being, at the outset, the policy most often cited as evidence that the new regime was indistinguishable from the old – the tide turned rapidly. Hatred of the Tories was all too easily extended to Labour.

By this stage, the absence of that generation in active politics was already becoming apparent. Most of the key figures in New Labour — Tony Blair, Gordon Brown, Jack Straw, Robin Cook, David Blunkett, Peter Mandelson — had been born in the decade following the end of the Second World War. The next wave of cabinet ministers, those who made their impact early in the twenty-first century, were of the same vintage: John Reid, Alan Johnson, Charles Clarke, Hilary Benn. What was missing was any serious challenge from those ten years younger, in their mid-thirties; precious few of those knocking at the gates of the cabinet had any adult memory of a time before Margaret Thatcher. 'Where are the people?' demanded Blair. 'Why don't I have more of them? I need some better people at the top. I know it. Where are they?' The answer was that far too many had already turned their backs on the electorate and on party politics.

Some felt, too, that the atmosphere surrounding Blair's sofa-government was doing little to encourage participation. For all the celebration of the new wave of women MPs, many believed that little had really changed. At the end of the New Labour era, when Gordon Brown had finally become prime minister, Caroline Flint, the outgoing Europe minister, was to accuse the government of treating women in the cabinet as 'little more than female window dressing', but that tendency had been noted almost from the outset.

'The men remain in charge,' wrote Helen Wilkinson, from the think tank Demos, in 1998, 'with old Labour's macho labourist culture replaced by a subtler, covert and insidious laddishness — all the more alienating for being steeped in predominantly middle-class values.' Harriet Harman, temporarily out of government, marked International Women's Day in 1999 with a Commons speech criticising the 'militaristic, macho, hierarchical language and behaviour' of the Labour Party: 'I don't believe that women feel that this is their government as strongly as men feel that this is their government.' And Tess Kingham, one of the newly elected MPs of whom great things were expected, instead announced in 2001 that she would be stepping down from Parliament after just four years, disillusioned with the entire process: 'I believed I was elected to get results, not recreate a boys' public school debating club, so I gradually withdrew from activities in the Chamber.'

In the absence of the anti-Thatcher generation, promotion came rather more rapidly than might have been expected to those born in the second half of the 1960s. Among these people could be discerned a new, much more sober and dedicated attitude. The political commentator Peter Riddell wrote in his 1993 book *Honest Opportunism: The Rise of the Career Politician* that politics was rapidly becoming 'confined to those who have made a youthful commitment to seeking a parliamentary career. It is like a religious order which requires an early vocation.'

Signs of this phenomenon could be observed in Conservative Central Office during the 1992 general election campaign, when the team working with Chris Patten offered an intriguing snapshot of what was to come. It was headed by Shaun Woodward, the party's director of communications, who failed to impress the former chairman, Kenneth Baker ('not notable for either directing or communicating'), but went on to become a cabinet minister, albeit in a Labour government, having defected from the Tories after his election in 1997. The youthful group under Woodward included 27-year-old Tim Collins, formerly an adviser to Michael Howard, 25-year-old David Cameron, 22-year-old Steve Hilton and 27-year-old Edward Llewellyn; eighteen years on, the latter three would enter Downing Street as prime minister, director of strategy and chief of staff respectively. In 1992 they were derisively known within the party as 'Patten's puppies' or the 'brat pack', and not unnaturally they felt vindicated by their surprise victory, provoking one of Cameron's earliest public comments: 'The brat pack hits back!' he exulted. 'Whatever people say about us, we got the campaign right.'

After the election, all made rapid progress both inside and outside the party. Hilton had worked with the Saatchi advertising agency during the campaign (he was credited with the tax bombshell poster) and now moved there full time, under the patronage of Maurice Saatchi himself. 'No one reminds me as much of me when young as Steve,' gushed the advertiser. Hilton remained involved in political campaigning, gaining international experience as he helped Fianna Fáil to their narrow victory in the 1992 Irish election and Boris Yeltsin to success in a 1993 referendum, securing greater constitutional power for the Russian president. The slogans he devised gave an indication of how he viewed politics – 'Ireland needs strong government now' and 'A strong leader for a strong Russia' – which perhaps explained why he was less than convinced by John Major's premiership. 'He is undoubtedly our weakness,' Hilton said in 1994. 'I expect that the Labour Party will go for Major in a big way, portraying him as a wimp.' He also dismissed the Back to Basics campaign, saying it 'meant nothing', though 'the core aspects are very popular – more people locked up, kids forced back to school. I don't care what liberals with a small "l" think.' Nonetheless, he returned to the fold for the 1997 general election, devising the controversial – if unsuccessful – 'demon eyes' poster.

Meanwhile, Cameron ('a suave Old Etonian' according to the *Guardian*, and 'one of the brightest young men in the party' according to *The Times*) went on to become adviser to Norman Lamont, for whom he was said to have coined the phrase 'green shoots of recovery'. After Lamont's fall, he made an easy transition to a similar position under Michael Howard. A subsequent spell of employment with Michael Green at Carlton Communications ('the most powerful man in the ITV network') was seen by no one as an end to his political ambitions. Having been touted as a possible candidate for the doomed Newbury by-election in 1993, he emerged in 1997 as the candidate for Bill Cash's old seat in Stafford, after Cash had moved to safer pastures in Stone. He failed there, but he was to return.

If Cameron's experience of standing alongside Lamont on Black Wednesday was traumatic, so too was the early career of another future star of the party. George Osborne, two years younger even than Hilton, was an adviser to Douglas Hogg at the Ministry of Agriculture during the BSE crisis. Having survived that harrowing introduction to politics, he hitched himself to William Hague's rising star in the leadership election and went on to write many of his speeches.

Acting in a similar capacity, by the end of the decade, was Osborne's contemporary, Daniel Hannan. He too had campaigned in the 1992 election, though he had then sided with Alan Sked, who stood for the Anti-Federalist League against Chris Patten in Bath and was later to found the UK Independence Party. Like the others, Hannan slipped comfortably into the role of political adviser as the first step to becoming an elected politician. Working for Michael Spicer, with whom he set up the European Research Group, a Eurosceptic think tank, and then for Michael Howard, he also wrote leader columns for the *Daily Telegraph* and was elected to the European Parliament in 1999.

There was in all this an emerging pattern, summed up by Michael White of the *Guardian* as 'the all-party trend towards the professionalization of politics: school, university, party functionary, MP'. For it wasn't only in the Conservative Party that candidates were increasingly selected from a procession of what Edwina Currie called 'identikit young men'. The term 'Blair's babes', later applied to the women MPs elected in 1997, had originally surfaced three years earlier as a Labour equivalent of 'Patten's puppies', referring to the youthful advisers surrounding the key figures in New Labour. Some of them remained backstage figures, but others went on to be elected to Parliament, including James Purnell, Pat McFadden, Ed Balls and the Miliband brothers, David and Ed. Then there was Yvette Cooper, who had been part of John Smith's team even before the 1992 election, and Derek Draper, a researcher for Peter Mandelson. All were still in their twenties when Blair became leader of the party.

Also known as 'the crèche', this group – the youth wing of the modernisers – was not to everyone's taste. 'Some of us have been around this place longer than you,' snapped Labour MP Ann Clwyd at David Miliband, while Mike Marqusee of *Labour Briefing* was deeply unimpressed: 'They may be young, but they are socially conservative, they exist in a self-enclosed world and they are utterly unrepresentative of young people. What have they got to say, for example, about the huge grass-roots campaign against the Criminal Justice Bill?' It was a purely rhetorical question. The reality was that policies, philosophies and positions were less important now than the appearance of competent management, in emulation of Brown and Blair. 'This generation exudes an air of responsibility,' remarked Dominic Loenhis, the 25-year-old adviser to the Conservative minister Peter Brooke, in 1993, 'but I don't think there is any visionary feel or coherent philosophy.'

The career path identified by Michael White was not entirely new. Jack Straw, for example, had come into politics by such a route, first through the National Union of Students and then as an adviser to Labour cabinet minister Barbara Castle, whose Blackburn seat he subsequently inherited. But this had been comparatively rare in the past, a more normal background being an apprenticeship in local government: Robin Cook, David Blunkett, Frank Dobson, Alistair Darling, even Peter Mandelson, had all been elected councillors. Now the role of political adviser was starting to look like the most straightforward route to the summit, particularly since there were so many of them; the numbers of advisers in government nearly doubled in the eighteen months following the 1997 election, with Blair accounting for seventeen full-time advisers in his own right. While in office, Michael Heseltine had been asked why he didn't have any political advisers, and he replied: 'I do. They are called ministers.' Those days were fast being forgotten.

Straw also prefigured another key element in the new generation, for he had spent two years working on the television series *World in Action*. And the media was to become an important training ground for the new breed of politician, their one chance to claim that they weren't merely postgraduate policy wonks, that they had work experience in the outside world. David Cameron and James Purnell had stints in television, Ed Balls and Yvette Cooper were journalists on the *Financial Times* and *Independent* respectively, while Boris Johnson of the *Daily Telegraph* and Michael Gove of *The Times* were biding their time, waiting for a chance to enter Parliament, and Steve Hilton had a fortnightly column in the *Guardian*. Tim Allan and Peter Hyman – two other twenty-somethings in Blair's inner circle – had also come from television.

There had always been common ground between media and politics, but in a political landscape shaped by the likes of Peter Mandelson and Gordon Brown (again both had a background in television), the two classes were rapidly converging. The new world was encapsulated in the figure of Alastair Campbell who, as a writer for the *Daily Mirror* and *Today*, had always seen political journalism as a partisan commitment, and had been rewarded with the ear of the prime minister. It might even be identifiable in a single moment, as in 1998 when Mandelson's protégé Derek Draper was sacked as a columnist by the *Daily Express* after admitting that he ran his copy past his old boss before submitting it. Or, on the other side of the political divide, in 1999 when Daniel Hannan, as a committed anti-federalist, announced that he wasn't prepared to sit in the European Parliament as part of the European People's Party group; it was a controversial move, but he did at least enjoy the support of the *Daily Telegraph*, unsurprisingly perhaps since it was he who wrote the leader column backing his own decision.

This coming together of politics and the media might have caused more concern had the majority of commentators not decided essentially to ignore its implications. New Labour's PR machine, at least in its first decade, was so effective that it swept much of Fleet Street before it. Access to the court of Blair was strictly controlled, and restricted to those with a supportive attitude, as though the prime minister were a rock star or Hollywood actor, and most complied with the new regime, whether through conviction or – more normally – a recognition that this was the only show in town. 'For nearly two decades,' wrote Steve Richards, the *Independent*'s chief political commentator, in 2010, 'political journalism became largely defined by whether a writer was sympathetic to Tony Blair or Gordon Brown.'

There had always been a distance between the political class on the one hand and much of the country on the other – even the sainted Clement Attlee was a public schoolboy – but the growing disparity of wealth through the Tory years and into the New Labour era, even as politics was mouthing a populist rhetoric of inclusion, made the discrepancy hard to ignore. The reduction in the variety of voices heard in the corridors of power inevitably meant that large parts of the country went unrepresented. What politicians denounced as cynicism was often nothing more than the recognition of this fact. It was difficult to believe that Rat Boy was part of the same world as Tony Blair and Peter Mandelson, even less plausible that he lived just a few miles from their constituencies in the North-East. The likes of Ed Miliband and George Osborne were, as Mike Marqusee implied, much the same age as, say, Swampy, though they were not easy to mistake for him. In short, the characters played by Robert Carlyle had been disenfranchised by the political rush for the centre ground of Blajorism.

This was, it was said, a new political consensus, a post-Thatcherite settlement. The difference between Butskellism and Blajorism, however, was the latter did not carry the country in the same way as had the former. In the three elections from 1951 onwards, the two main parties attracted between them the votes of three-quarters of the registered voters; in the three elections from 1992, they secured only a half. Whatever causes one wished to ascribe to this trend – the drop in turnout, the rise of the third party, the decline of ideology – it came to the same point: the only two parties capable of forming governments were fast losing the consent of the people. And as the gap between politicians and the nation widened, it was the younger generations who felt it most acutely. According to a survey published in the Demos pamphlet *Britain*™, 68 per cent of those aged fifty-five or over were proud of British democracy; just 7.5 per cent of those aged under fifty-five felt the same.

Nonetheless, the new establishment was proving capable of replicating itself, of finding members of the younger generation who might be trained up for future office. If, as Tony Blair claimed, 'the only purpose of being in politics is to make things happen', and if the power to do this was now believed to reside solely in the office of the prime minister, then there was little point wasting one's time in local councils or the House of Commons, let alone in jobs outside politics. The special advisers, born in the second half of the 1960s, already had much greater influence over events than most MPs or even ministers. 'Britain under Tony Blair,' wrote Nick Cohen in 1998, 'is a country governed by a clique of children.'

Douglas Alexander, a former researcher for Gordon Brown, was the first of this new generation to make it into Parliament, inheriting Gordon McMaster's constituency in a 1997 by-election, and – in time for the 2001 general election – both David Miliband and Ed Balls were given safe seats, to the fury of many in the party. No one expected them to remain long on the back benches; they were, after all, the future of New Labour. It was, perhaps, little wonder that Ralph Miliband and Tony Benn shook their ageing heads as they contemplated the next generation.

14
Power

'I don't want control of you'

Too much power is held at the centre.
John Smith (1993)

SIR MICHAEL JAFFA: Democracy is all very well in its place – ancient
Greece, for example – but nowadays, oppositions are in favour
of democracy until they get elected. Because once you're in
government, you realise how frightfully negative democracy can be.
Chris Langham, *Look at the State We're In!* (1995)

Honk if you hate the English.
bumper sticker seen in Scotland (1994)

A year after Margaret Thatcher's third successive election victory, Britain
celebrated in 1988 the three hundredth anniversary of the Glorious
Revolution, the moment when a constitutional monarchy had been
established and the independence of Parliament asserted, as set out in the
Bill of Rights. Three centuries on, there were those who felt that it was
time for Britain's piecemeal accumulation of constitutional documents –
of which the Bill of Rights occupied pride of place, alongside Magna Carta
and the Petition of Right – to be replaced by a written constitution in the
way of all properly modern democracies. And so was born Charter 88, a
campaigning group that launched itself via an advert in the *Guardian*, signed
by 250 prominent figures, amongst them actors and academics, comedians,
writers and lawyers, from Rik Mayall to Ralph Miliband.

'Three hundred years of unwritten rule from above are enough,' the
Charter declared, as it set out its demands for proportional representation,
a reformed House of Lords, freedom of information and a new Bill of
Rights that would enshrine 'the right to peaceful assembly, to freedom of
association, to freedom from discrimination, to freedom from detention
without trial, to trial by jury, to privacy and to freedom of expression'. In

the wake of Thatcher's re-election, these basic rights, it was felt, were in danger of being eroded, whether through neglect or deliberate action. 'It is now the turn of the body politic to be brought up to date, by bringing the extraordinary powers of the British state under democratic regulation,' wrote Anthony Barnett, the organisation's first director.

Charter 88 lit a slow-burning fuse. Ignored by the government of the time, it nonetheless did much to set an agenda on the left, its warnings about slipping into an elected dictatorship only heightened by the talk of a one-party state that followed the 1992 election. Some in the upper echelons of New Labour regarded the organisation with a certain suspicion, seeing it as little more than a middle-class North London talking shop, but it had by then diffused its ideas widely enough that they would be hard to resist. And in any event the concept of constitutional reform chimed rather well with Tony Blair's own approach to politics.

For the one organisation that Blair had ever run was the Labour Party; this was his sole qualification for being prime minister, and the experience he gained there was in structural change. The rewriting of Clause IV, the centralisation of policy-making, the neutering of the national executive committee, the conference and the shadow cabinet — all had been concerned with form rather than content. Now, embracing much of the thinking of Charter 88, that experience was to be applied to the political structure of the country as a whole, with somewhat mixed results.

Amongst the resulting changes was the incorporation of the European Convention on Human Rights into British law. First ratified by the UK in 1951, the Convention had previously existed as a final recourse, available only to those who had exhausted the British courts and had won leave to appeal to the European Court of Human Rights in Strasbourg. As Labour leader, John Smith had committed the party to bringing the process into domestic law, so that British courts would also be able to interpret the provisions of the Convention and make judgements accordingly. Enacting this proposal was one of the Labour government's early moves, and went a long way to addressing Charter 88's call for a Bill of Rights.

It wasn't entirely coincidental that the advent of the Human Rights Act should be accompanied by television drama series that depicted lawyers as campaigners for justice. There was a precursor to this trend with *Kavanagh QC*, in which the main character met his wife in the 1960s when he defended her after she was arrested on a pro-abortion demonstration, but it reached new heights with *Judge John Deed* (2001). Created by G.F. Newman, best known for his novels and dramas about corrupt police officers, the series starred Martin Shaw as the most liberal judge imaginable. 'You still think like a defence barrister,' he's told, as he gives his full support to his daughter, arrested while destroying a field of genetically modified crops. 'Sometimes direct action is the only way,' he concludes. Similarly the legal drama *North Square* (2000) opened with a group of trendy young middle-class barristers singing along to the Clash's song 'Bankrobber'. Tastes would soon change, as right-wing newspapers began a sustained assault on human rights legislation, but for now it was possible to present fictional lawyers in a heroic light.

The other great constitutional change that came out of the Home Office was – for politicians at least – more controversial. 'We are pledged to a Freedom of Information Act, leading to more open government,' promised Labour's 1997 manifesto, though as Jack Straw later admitted, 'those few words were about all the serious intellectual consideration that the PLP or the shadow cabinet had given to this inherently complex issue'. Only when a white paper was published did the newly elected government recognise the dangerous waters into which they were drifting and begin to row back as fast as possible. The resulting Act was passed in 2000, its provisions becoming fully operative in 2005. Campaigners were furious at the watering down of the proposals – even the normally loyal John O'Farrell, now a *Guardian* columnist, complained that the measure had 'suffered a death by a thousand caveats.' – but their disapproval was as nothing compared with that of the prime minister, when he realised that he had given away the privilege of privacy.

'You idiot,' Blair wrote in his memoirs, addressing his younger, less experienced self. 'You naive, foolish, irresponsible nincompoop. There is really no description of stupidity, no matter how vivid, that is adequate.' He didn't dwell too long on his own culpability, however, swiftly moving on to criticise the civil servants who he felt should have stopped him from making good on his election pledge. The consequence was to reinforce Blair's existing tendency for what became known as 'sofa government', the taking of decisions in informal, off-the-record meetings; if no minutes were kept, there could be no paper trail available to inquisitive journalists. A move intended to illuminate the corridors of power had, in the short term, the effect of making government less accountable.

The drive for constitutional change was most evident in the pursuit of devolution, the passing of powers from Westminster to some of the United Kingdom's constituent nations. This hadn't been one of the original demands of Charter 88 (though the preamble to the launch advert had recognised the issue, declaring 'Scotland is governed like a province from

Whitehall'), but for the government, it was painful, outstanding business left over from the last time Labour was in office.

Back in 1979 referendums had been held in both Scotland and Wales on whether to establish devolved assemblies, and had met with contrasting fates; the 'yes' campaign secured 52 per cent of the vote in Scotland, but just 20 per cent in Wales. Even with that Scottish majority, however, the proposal was defeated, since an amendment to the legislation governing the referendums had introduced an additional hurdle, which required that a change to the constitution must achieve the support of 40 per cent of the electorate; in the event, the turnout proved too low, under a third of registered voters approving the proposal. Believing that they had been cheated of victory, the Scottish National Party responded by withdrawing its support for what was then a minority government, and in a subsequent vote of no confidence, James Callaghan was defeated by a single vote, precipitating the general election that brought Margaret Thatcher to power and shut Labour out for eighteen years.

For more than a decade, the idea of devolution had been off the Westminster agenda, and it wasn't until 1992, with the possibility of a Labour victory, that it returned as a live issue. During that campaign, John Major took up the cause of the Union with some enthusiasm, denouncing Labour's plans for Scottish and Welsh assemblies as a threat to the wider nation. 'The United Kingdom is in danger,' he warned at an election rally. 'Wake up, my fellow countrymen. Wake up now before it is too late.' And his words may have had an impact, for the Conservatives bucked the national trend in Scotland, marginally increasing their vote, their share of the vote and their number of MPs.

It was, however, only a temporary setback, and in 1997 Labour went into the election with much the same proposals. Once more Major talked of how devolution would 'undermine the unity of the United Kingdom', but fewer seemed prepared to listen this time; the Tory vote fell by eight points in Scotland, relegating the party to third place behind the SNP. With the Nationalists calling for full independence, and Labour and the Liberal Democrats both supporting devolution, there was a clear majority for constitutional change (far surpassing that 40 per cent threshold), and a new Westminster government prepared to enact it.

The approach this time round differed from the 1970s. There were again to be referendums in Scotland and Wales, which in itself annoyed some ardent devolutionists – in 1992 the manifesto had promised the creation of assemblies without need for further consultation – but this time there would be no threshold; a simple majority of the votes cast would be sufficient to determine the outcome. More significantly, the referendums would be held before detailed proposals were laid before Parliament. In the 1979 votes, the question had been whether to ratify legislation that had already been passed in Westminster; now the order of events was reversed. 'The tactic was obvious,' said Blair: 'get the people to say yes, then the Lords could not say no.' Others saw it as yet another example of encroachment on parliamentary sovereignty, a break with constitutional tradition.

Blair's commitment to the project was, in any event, lukewarm at best. 'It's Gordon's passion,' he shrugged. 'So we're doing it.' And indeed the issue was largely driven by Gordon Brown, who had supported devolution in the 1970s, when the idea hadn't been universally popular in the Labour Party – his great Scottish rival, Robin Cook, for example, had been opposed. It had too a personal resonance for Brown, as one of the few totems from his more left-wing youth to which he could still cling. So many compromises had been made that, in the words of the Welsh historian Martin Johnes: 'Devolution seemed to be the only radical thing New Labour was offering.'

When first appointed shadow trade and industry spokesperson in 1989, Brown had made clear the strength of his national allegiance: 'I am particularly pleased to be one of four Scots in the new shadow cabinet.' Now he was part of a cabinet in which nearly a third were Scottish, and he wasn't going to miss a chance to make good on the long-delayed promise of a fully fledged new Parliament (the proposal of an 'assembly' had by now been upgraded) in Edinburgh.

Brown was backed heavily by Donald Dewar, the party's Scottish spokesperson through the 1980s and now secretary of state for Scotland. Like others in the Scottish Labour Party, Dewar was aware of the potential threat from the SNP if devolution wasn't carried through. 'People should not underestimate how fragile the Union now is in Scotland,' he explained in 1996; the next election was secure, 'but the 2001 election could be a different matter if Labour messes it up'. The ambition was, as the 1997 manifesto made clear, to see 'the threat of separatism removed'. As even Blair recognised: 'in Scotland disillusioned Labour voters have somewhere to go.'

The passage of the campaign was not entirely smooth. A key question was the power that would be exercised by a Scottish Parliament and, in particular, whether it would have the ability to set different tax rates from those laid down in Westminster. It had long been accepted that this would be within the authority of a devolved government, but it became an increasingly pressing concern as the election approached. In 1995 John

Major appointed Michael Forsyth as secretary of state for Scotland, and Forsyth began a powerful rearguard action against devolution. Amongst his initiatives were the granting of new powers to the Scottish Grand Committee – a parliamentary body that included all those MPs who sat for Scottish seats – and the propaganda coup of returning the Stone of Scone from Westminster Abbey to Scotland in 1996, the 700th anniversary of its removal by Edward I.

These gestures hadn't been entirely successful in changing attitudes. 'It speaks volumes for the attitude of Westminster,' fumed the *Scotsman*, 'that they should expect Scotland to be grateful for being awarded this useless lump of sandstone in lieu of self-government.' But Forsyth had more luck when he coined the phrase 'the tartan tax' to warn that devolution would hit voters in the pocket. Blair, desperate to shed Labour's reputation as the high-tax party, was rattled and decided, to the fury of many, that the referendum should have two separate questions: first, whether there should be a parliament at all, and second, if such a parliament were established, whether it should have tax-raising powers.

Having thus raised the possibility that a toothless parliament would be created, Blair went on during the general election campaign to compound his perceived fault. Asked in an interview with the *Scotsman* about the tax issue, he answered: 'Once the powers are given, it's like any parish council, it's got the right to exercise them.' He was trying to explain that in the event of Labour forming a government in Scotland, it would not – if he had his way – exploit that right to raise taxes, but the ham-fisted use of the phrase 'parish council' provoked outrage, drowning out the launch that day of the Labour manifesto for Scotland.

The manifesto itself was ostentatiously adorned with the Blair tartan in a desperate attempt to flaunt the leader's Scottish credentials. (It was perhaps the same desire that prompted him, when asked what he loved most about England, to reply: 'Walking in the Scottish highlands.') It didn't work, and Blair faced a far greater degree of hostility in the Scottish media than he did in London. Alastair Campbell, who encountered the same antagonism, put it down to resentment that he and Blair were both perceived to have abandoned their roots: 'they view us as ultra English,' he complained, adding rather plaintively in his diary that 'I play the bagpipes' as proof of his true identity. In a reversal of roles, Blair was considerably blunter about Scottish journalists, dismissing them as 'unreconstructed wankers'.

Despite his clumsiness, Blair led Labour to a handsome victory in Scotland in the general election and swiftly made good on the promised referendum. It was scheduled to be held on 11 September 1997, though there was some concern that it might be postponed following Princess Diana's death. It is far from clear what impact such a postponement would have made, since Scotland's response to the death was noticeably less dramatic than that of England; a World Cup qualifying match against Belarus, scheduled for the day of the funeral, was put back by a day, but only after a great deal of pressure had been exerted on the Scottish FA by Downing Street and, more importantly, after three senior players announced that they wouldn't play on the original date. The saga of whether the match would be rescheduled ran through the week after Diana's death and suggested a semi-detached attitude north of the border to the woman who was said to be uniting the nation in grief. The opening line of Elton John's tribute song ('Goodbye, England's rose') didn't feel overly inclusive either.

In any event, the referendum went ahead as planned and produced a resounding double yes vote: 74 per cent supported the creation of a parliament, 63 per cent agreed that it should have 'tax-varying powers'. Even under the terms of the 1979 referendum, devolution would have gone ahead. The following year saw the passing of the Scotland Act, and in 1999 the first elections were held for the new 129-seat Parliament. Donald Dewar became the first minister, heading a coalition government of Labour and Liberal Democrat MSPs, as the new members were known.

Amidst this progress towards devolution was a worrying sign of New Labour's refusal to countenance dissent. An official list of approved candidates for the Scottish Parliament pointedly excluded several perceived trouble-makers, most notably Dennis Canavan, who had been the Falkirk West MP for a quarter of a century. Canavan was undoubtedly seen by the party leadership as difficult, a left-winger who objected to benefit cuts and tuition fees, but to judge that he was unsuitable for Edinburgh after his long service in Westminster seemed perverse. The selection procedure was a stitch-up, he complained with some justification, the work of a faction that was 'similar to the Militant Tendency – there's a party within a party'. He subsequently stood as an independent and was returned with a majority of over 12,000, the largest margin of victory recorded by any candidate in the election. Meanwhile Labour, while emerging as the largest party in the Parliament, saw its share of the vote reduced to 39 per cent, considerably down from the 46 per cent achieved in the general election.

Nonetheless, the rapidity with which devolution was delivered did at least address Dewar's fears about a possible nationalist backlash, reducing the risk that an anti-English sentiment would become the defining characteristic of Scottish culture. That such a feeling existed was evident from the fact that by the end of the 1990s three-quarters of all cases reported in Scotland to the Commission for Racial Equality were from English people feeling discriminated against by Scots. It was also to be heard in the rhetoric of the SNP, which spoke of the country as a colony and pointed out, in its 1997 election manifesto, 'Over fifty countries have become independent from Britain since 1945 and none of them have applied to become colonies or dependencies again.'

The same terminology had been employed, rather more forcefully, in the hugely successful *Trainspotting*. 'It's shite being Scottish,' rants Renton (Ewan McGregor). 'We're the lowest of the low. The scum of the fucking Earth. The most wretched, servile, pathetic trash that was ever shat into civilisation. Some hate the English. I don't. They're just wankers. We, on the other hand, are colonised by wankers.'

There was also *Braveheart* (1995), the Oscar-winning tale of William Wallace's fight for Scottish independence against the forces of the English king Edward I in the thirteenth century. It was a gloriously old-fashioned Hollywood yarn of heroism which, in the tradition of swashbuckling epics, quite properly played fast and loose with the minor details of historical fact, romanticising the past to the point of sentimentality. And, just like the classic works of Douglas Fairbanks and Errol Flynn, it succeeded largely thanks to the presence of its star, in this instance Mel Gibson, who also directed the piece. Perhaps unsurprisingly for an American movie made by an Australian about Scottish history and filmed in Ireland, the English don't come out too well. But although Wallace's prime objective is to avenge 'a hundred years of theft, rape and murder', he also finds himself constantly at odds with the Scottish aristocracy, which is portrayed as a class of squabbling collaborators ('a nest of scheming bastards who couldn't agree on the colour of shite') who will happily betray Scotland in pursuit of their own interests. Robert Bruce's message to Wallace is not substantially different from that of Renton: 'From top to bottom, this country has got no sense of itself.' The film was, said comedian Billy Connolly, 'pure Australian shite', though Gordon Brown adjudged it 'terrific'.

There was a new cultural mood in Scotland; the shortbread-and-tartan, heather-and-haggis image gently subverted by *Hamish Macbeth* was being cast off. The nomination of Glasgow to be the European City of Culture in 1990 was greeted with some incredulity at the time – previous recipients of the honour had been more conventional choices: Athens, Florence, Paris – but proved successful, while from the 1980s onwards, a succession of novelists had emerged, ranging from cult writers like Alasdair Gray and A.L. Kennedy through the controversial Booker Prize-winner James Kelman to best-sellers including Ian Rankin, Iain Banks and Irvine Welsh.

Between them, they articulated a grittier, more contemporary vision of Scotland, a cause helped by Danny Boyle's films *Shallow Grave* and *Trainspotting* and Gillies MacKinnon's *Small Faces*.

The Glaswegian satirist Armando Iannucci was amongst those keen to ridicule received images of the country, particularly in a nightmare recounted in *The Armando Iannucci Shows* in 2001: 'Scottish heaven consists of a bald man who tells me what a great country Scotland is because it invented golf, it discovered penicillin and it has the songs of Runrig,' he fantasised. 'And Scottish hell consists of a portrait of Ally McLeod, a frightening tartan drummer girl and a giant computer scoreboard flashing up what Scotland's goal difference is and why it means we'll go out after the first round.'

'I don't want Scotland to be presented as simply a nation living in the past,' observed Gordon Brown on *Desert Island Discs*. 'We want to be a modern country with a vibrant, dynamic economy and culture.' He went on to introduce Runrig's version of 'Loch Lomond'.

The demand for political separation was much less striking in Wales than in Scotland, as witnessed by the results of the 1979 referendum, though it was on occasion more aggressive. At the start of the 1990s, holiday homes owned by English people were still being firebombed, acts for which the nationalist group Meibion Glyndŵr claimed responsibility, though these began to tail off after the conviction in 1993 of Sion Aubrey Roberts. He was jailed for twelve years for sending letter-bombs to several targets, including Wyn Roberts, a minister at the Welsh Office, the first successful prosecution of a member of the group after more than a decade of action.

There was a certain amount of sympathy for the cause even outside Wales. In one of Rupert Allason's novels, a member of Meibion Glyndŵr is given the chance to articulate his position: 'We don't kill people or maim them,' he explains, 'we destroy property. It's Welsh property, but it's owned by outsiders who exploit the region, push up property prices, and force our youngsters to move elsewhere.' The result, as he sees it, is entirely positive: 'It scares off the money from the Midlands. The weekenders aren't prepared to take the risk. That reduces the pressure on the property market, and for the first time in years there are houses available that local people can afford.'

The group Cymdeithas Yr Iaith Gymraeg had also carried out a campaign of vandalising post boxes, telephone kiosks and similar targets that displayed signs written solely in English. Hundreds were prosecuted in the 1980s, but the actions did help provoke the passing of the Welsh Language Act in 1993, which – though criticised for enforcing bilingualism in the public sector alone – was a landmark in the history of the language. So too was the introduction of Welsh to the country's national curriculum; by the 2001 census, over 40 per cent of children were reported to be Welsh speakers, compared to just 25 per cent a decade earlier.

There had been a marked shift in popular opinion since 1979. Even so, the devolution referendum – held a week after the Scottish vote in the hope of building momentum – produced a perilously close result; if just 3,361 people, out of an electorate numbering more than two million, had switched their votes, the result would have been overturned. The proposal was passed by a margin of less than a single percentage point, would have failed the 1979 criterion (just a quarter of the electorate came out in support), and achieved a majority in only half the local authority areas, but still it was won, and plans to introduce a sixty-seat Welsh Assembly duly went ahead.

Key to the success, it was widely felt, was the recent history of Conservative government and the appointment over the last decade of English MPs as the secretary of state for Wales; most notable was John Redwood, who had won few friends in Welsh politics during his term in office. His ideological objections to big government collided with the realities of a country where 35 per cent of jobs in the capital city were in the state sector, and when he announced that he'd found sufficient savings in his budget that he could return £112 million to the Treasury, there were many who felt that the money might have been usefully spent.

'The people of Wales are sick of being treated like a colonial outpost,' declared Alex Carlile, leader of the Welsh Liberal Democrats. 'The new viceroy, Mr Redwood, is the last straw.' Peter Hain wrote that Redwood 'was almost single-handedly responsible for all Welsh Tory MPs losing their seats', and he put the case for an Assembly in purely anti-Tory language. 'This is a loyalty vote in your new Labour government,' pleaded Hain. 'Do not side with the Tories in undermining such a crucial part of our programme by voting No or by not bothering to vote at all.' Others in Labour shared the feeling that this was indeed the critical factor: Rhodri Morgan, who went on to become first minister of Wales, argued that the drive for devolution was a desire to build 'a bulwark against the return of a Margaret Thatcher, the return of a John Redwood'.

As in Scotland, there was a feeling that the country had been ignored and neglected by a Westminster government. 'We voted Labour, we got Thatcher,' read a graffito in Caerphilly shortly after the 1987 election. Sensibilities were further affronted by the reported remarks of Welsh Office minister Rod Richards in 1994, in which he described Labour councillors in Wales as 'short, fat, slimy and fundamentally corrupt', adding that the Welsh had 'no sense of self-worth' and that Labour-dominated education authorities had 'created the inferiority complex that is part of us as a nation'.

The campaign to establish the Assembly was led initially by Ron Davies, the first secretary of state for Wales to represent a Welsh constituency since Nicholas Edwards in 1987. He had developed the policy in opposition and was expected to become the leader of the new Assembly, until in October 1998 he found himself at the centre of a curious incident that recalled some of the sex scandals from John Major's days.

The details of the story never fully emerged, but it appeared that Davies had been mugged at knifepoint by a man whom he met on Clapham Common in South London. Given the Common's reputation as a cruising area for male homosexuals, in conjunction with rumours that were already circulating in the party, it was assumed that Davies had simply picked up the wrong man, though when he reported the robbery to the police, they were sympathetic, wondering whether he was part of a local pattern of attacks on cabbies. 'Are you a minicab driver?' they asked, and he replied with as much dignity as he could muster: 'No, I'm the secretary of state for Wales.' Davies became the first cabinet minister to resign (or, rather, to be resigned, for it was against his wishes) from the Blair government. The resignation letter that was written for him included a phrase contributed by Blair himself, saying that he had suffered from 'a moment of madness'.

His replacement as the party's choice for the post of first secretary for Wales, by any normal criteria, would have been Rhodri Morgan ('the talismanic Rhodri', in Peter Hain's words), who had only narrowly been defeated by Davies in a vote at a Welsh Labour conference to select a candidate. But Blair and his circle had taken against Morgan, seeing him as a maverick who didn't really belong in New Labour. Morgan's tough questioning of Alastair Campbell in front of the Public Accounts Committee probably didn't help his case. Instead Alun Michael – who was briefly appointed to the cabinet as Welsh secretary – was told that he was being sent to Cardiff. It didn't prove to be a happy experience.

Following Blair's wishes, Michael did become the candidate for the post of first secretary, having been selected in an electoral college vote that revealed how unpopular a choice he was; he was backed by union leaders and MPs, but secured amongst party members barely half the number of votes that Morgan achieved. The feeling that he had been imposed by Westminster helped Plaid Cymru to their best-ever performance in the subsequent election, mostly at the expense of Labour, though Morgan (like Dennis Canavan) bucked the trend. As in Scotland, Labour was the largest party in the Assembly, but with an even steeper fall in vote share, down from 55 per cent in the general election to just 38 per cent, so that although Michael became first secretary, it was at the head of a minority government. 'What sort of election is it,' wondered a senior Labour figure, 'where we lose the Rhondda?' Blair was said to be furious, railing against the 'Fucking Welsh'.

Worse was to come for the leadership. Within a year Michael was obliged to stand down, rather than face a vote of no confidence, and was replaced, at last, by Morgan, under whose stewardship, which spanned almost the whole first decade of the new century, the Assembly established a clearer identity and acquired greater legitimacy. Support for further devolution of powers was not marked, but a growing sense of national identity could be seen in the 2001 census, when 'Welsh' was not offered as an option for ethnicity; over 400,000 respondents added it in for themselves.

Perhaps more significant than politics in forging that new identity was a cultural renaissance, largely centred on music. The rock and pop heritage of the country was rich but disparate, ranging from mainstream acts like Shirley Bassey, Tom Jones and Bonnie Tyler to blues-rock bands Love Sculpture, Budgie and Man, as well as providing a home for the rock and roll revival movement with Shakin' Stevens and the Sunsets and Crazy Cavan and the Rhythm Rockers. A tighter focus developed in the 1990s with the success of the Manic Street Preachers, who came from Blackwood in Neil Kinnock's constituency. Their Welsh identity, proclaimed on stage with the display of the national flag, became more marked as their career progressed: their album *This Is My Truth Tell Me Yours* (1998) took its title from a speech by Aneurin Bevan, while the multi-tracked vocals on songs like 'If You Tolerate This Your Children Will Be Next' suggested the tone of male voice choirs.

They also opened a path for a host of Welsh indie bands: Catatonia, Stereophonics, Feeder and, particularly, Super Furry Animals and Gorky's Zygotic Mynci. The latter two groups sang in both Welsh and English and, if the Welsh releases sold less well, the fact that they existed at all, and got airplay elsewhere in Britain and abroad, did a great deal to promote international awareness of the language. So too did the inclusion of Welsh songs on twelve-year-old Charlotte Church's million-selling album *Voice of an Angel* (1998).

There was talk by now of Cool Cymru, a local rival to Cool Britannia, and if that was a little overstated, there was certainly – as in Scotland – the sense of a new public perception of Wales. A succession of movies, starting with *Hedd Wyn* (1992), were nominated for best foreign language film in the Oscars, while the actor Rhys Ifans made his name in *Twin Town* (1997), a film set in Swansea and Port Talbot, before becoming an international star. Catherine Zeta-Jones had already made a successful transition from *The Darling Buds of May* to Hollywood, and when she married the actor Michael Douglas in 2000, the media happily reported that the catering included Welsh lamb, Caerphilly cheese and Brains beer.

The image of a modern nation was further projected in sport when the final of the 1999 Rugby World Cup was staged at the newly built Millennium Stadium in Cardiff (Wales were regrettably absent, having been knocked out in the quarter-finals by the eventual victors, Australia). The same year, linking the old and new strands of Welsh culture, the Stereophonics debuted their rugby song 'As Long as We Beat the English (We Don't Care)'.

At a concert held in May 1999 to inaugurate the Assembly, however, the newer acts were conspicuous by their absence. Bassey, Jones, Tyler and Stevens all performed, but the Manic Street Preachers and Catatonia declined an invitation to appear in front of the Queen, while the Stereophonics confined themselves to sending a recorded message. Nonetheless the evening ended with a rendition of Catatonia's song 'International Velvet', with its rousing chorus: 'Every day when I wake up, I thank the Lord I'm Welsh.' (The Welsh language verses were slightly less celebratory. 'Deffrwych Cymru cysglyd,' it opened: 'Wake up, sleepy Wales.') Tony Blair attended the accompanying state banquet, though again his lack of personal commitment was apparent; he said it was 'his greatest conflict of interest in two years', since it meant he was going to miss the Champions League final between Manchester United and Bayern Munich. (Alex Ferguson's team, 1–0 down at 90 minutes, still managed to triumph, with two goals scored during injury time, completing a unique treble-winning season for the club and securing a knighthood for Ferguson himself.)

For those with longer memories, stretching back beyond the first devolution referendum to the investiture of the Prince of Wales in 1969, the progress was impressive. 'In the years since then the Welsh sense of national identity has marvellously revived,' observed the historian and travel writer Jan Morris, three decades on. 'Pride in Welshness is far stronger now, the Welsh language flourishes and is not often resented, the struggling political infant that was Plaid Cymru in 1969 has masterfully established itself as the Party of Wales. Anybody who has lived in this country since the devolution referendum two years ago must have observed the immense change in the national spirit.'

*

The leadership's attempt to influence the Welsh Assembly by blocking the candidature of Rhodri Morgan was repeated in even more naked form in London. When Margaret Thatcher's government had abolished the Greater London Council in the mid-1980s, it was widely seen as an attempt to silence a noisy, awkward, alternative voice, represented by the last leader of the authority, Ken Livingstone. The abolition had also left London, as Livingstone and others never tired of pointing out, as the only major capital city in the western world without a unified political administration. In response the Labour manifesto of 1992 had promised the creation of a Greater London Authority, effectively a new GLC, though one with reduced powers.

There was, however, an alternative proposal, put forward in a Bill in 1990 by Tony Banks, who had been chair of the GLC in Livingstone's time. He suggested the creation of an elected mayor of London, backed up by a city-wide council, and let it be known that he fancied the job himself. He didn't, of course, make any progress at the time, but the idea resurfaced after the election of Tony Blair as Labour leader. Always excited by the thought of making links outside politics, Blair saw the possibility of a non-party figure – he had in mind a businessman like Richard Branson – becoming London mayor in a way that replicated the American model, though with less political muscle. This would, he believed, be the key to reinvigorating local government in Britain.

Accordingly the 1997 manifesto promised 'a new deal for London', based – though few recognised the fact – on Banks's model of a mayor and a Greater London Assembly (GLA), and a referendum was duly held in May 1998, asking the people of London whether they wanted such a system. It was hardly a resounding endorsement, for although 72 per cent agreed with the proposition, turnout was pitifully low at just 31 per cent, meaning that even fewer Londoners than Welsh people were in favour of this devolution of power. Nonetheless, the majority was sufficient for the plan to go ahead. It was at this stage that things became difficult for the government.

The problem was Livingstone. A deeply divisive figure in his GLC days, hated by the Labour leadership and not much liked in the country generally, he was nevertheless very popular in large parts of London. 'Ken Livingstone is a folk hero,' sang Dexys Midnight Runners in 1983, and many expected great things of him when he was first elected to Parliament in 1987. Sadly, nothing much had materialised. 'I think Ken has squandered his talents, which is a great tragedy,' reflected Banks in 1997. 'His attention got diverted, he wasn't willing to start from the bottom again and he never got the chance to build on what he had.'

Newly appointed as sports minister, Banks was now firmly inside the Blairite tent, but Livingstone was still struggling to find a place in Westminster. He had been ostracised by the party hierarchy as soon as he arrived in the Commons, finding that his undoubted gifts were unappreciated. For a year after his arrival he wasn't given a room or a desk, the whips seemingly keen to cut him down to size, and on the rare occasions when he was invited to participate on the margins of the House's activities, nothing went smoothly. 'I was put up for the coypu control committee,' he remembered. 'Then they announced that the coypu was extinct, and the committee disbanded.'

Livingstone was a prophet without honour in his own land, for he looked in retrospect to have been the most influential and significant Labour figure of the 1980s, his contribution doing much to shape the subsequent decade. His espousal of identity politics had been wildly out of step with the times but was now accepted as the norm, whilst his method of campaigning against the abolition of the GLC – using advertising and the media to appeal direct to the public, building coalitions beyond the party, finding common purpose with popular culture – had set a template that Blair was happy to follow. Indeed the fact that the issue had become focused on abolition, rather than on his policies or his conduct in office, was an early triumph for spin, relocating the news story in a way that New Labour never quite matched. Although he was accused of costing the party dear at the ballot box, Labour in London had fared much better in the disaster of the 1983 election than in the country at large.

He was also, though, capable of infuriating those in authority to the extent that they were prepared to do anything to stop his activities. When the GLC took out paid adverts in the press, Thatcher's government responded by passing the 1986 Local Government Act, which prohibited the use of public funds for political advertising. When Livingstone beat Peter Mandelson in the 1997 elections to the NEC, Blair retaliated by changing the rules so that MPs were henceforth not allowed to stand for election in the constituencies section. (Largely unnoticed by the public, this was a significant loss to party democracy, for the constituency representatives had long provided a counterbalance to the leadership, giving a platform to dissenting voices.) And Livingstone equally annoyed many of those with whom he worked and who should have been on his side. Banks wasn't the only one irritated by his actions; the attempt to launch a leadership campaign after John Smith's death 'caused an awful lot of ill will', according to Tony Benn.

Now that there was going to be a mayor, everyone knew that he would be in the running. 'I'd love to be in government,' he'd commented after the NEC election. 'I love running things.' Just one question, therefore, now obsessed the Labour leadership: how to stop the job falling into Livingstone's hands. Blair, who had lived in London in the 1980s, was fearful of bad publicity arising from any association with Labour from that time (he'd already ensured Neil Kinnock's absence from domestic politics by nominating him as a European commissioner), but he claimed that the main objections to the idea of Livingstone being selected as the party's mayoral candidate were raised by Gordon Brown and John Prescott: 'I didn't feel visceral about it, as John and Gordon did.'

The dispute was partly to do with policy. The London Underground was in desperate need of investment, following years of neglect that, in Kenneth Clarke's last budget, had culminated in the cutting of a further £700 million from the system. Livingstone disagreed with the party's plans, devised by Brown and Prescott, to set up a public-private partnership to operate the London Underground; he argued instead that a bond issue could raise the necessary funds. 'It was going to be difficult to have a Labour candidate dedicated to stopping the Labour transport policy,' reflected Blair, though the mistake was perhaps to have devised the policy first without any democratic process, and then to expect the elected mayor to follow it through. In any event, the policy itself was flawed, based on the same model that was already unpopular on the railways: the separation of infrastructure maintenance from the running of the trains. Unsurprisingly, the scheme didn't work out.

Behind this disagreement lay — as ever with New Labour — a personal insecurity that verged on paranoia. Ever since Granita, Brown had been less than supportive of anyone who might one day threaten his succession to the party leadership. His determination to avoid competition had been apparent even in opposition, with the departure of key figures from their roles as economic spokespeople; to give Brown a clear ride as the sole voice on the economy, Robin Cook had been moved from trade and industry, Prescott from employment, and both had been targeted in off-the-record briefings by Charlie Whelan. Now, according to Jonathan Powell, Brown 'saw Ken Livingstone as a rival. In 1999, he told Tony that he knew he was positioning Livingstone as a counterweight to him in the Labour Party.' It seemed unlikely that Livingstone would ever be able to mount a serious challenge to Brown, but he was far and away the best-known politician outside the cabinet and a proven vote-winner with the public; that in itself was enough of a threat.

Seeking to kill two birds with one stone, it was decided that the Labour candidate should instead be Frank Dobson, the bluff, jokey embodiment of non-ideological old Labour, who was currently health secretary but whose presence in the cabinet had never been much desired. 'He was one of the many who considered New Labour a clever wheeze to win,' sniffed Blair. 'He didn't understand it much, and to the extent that he did, he disagreed with it.' If Dobson were chosen as the mayoral candidate, it would remove him from cabinet and dispose of Livingstone at the same time. The only problem was that Dobson lacked the appeal of Livingstone within the party, and stood no chance at all of winning the nomination under the system that had been spelt out as recently as May 1999 by Nick Raynsford, the minister for London: 'the Labour Party will elect its candidate on the basis of one member, one vote.'

So the usual procedure for trying to contain Livingstone was followed: the rules were rewritten. An electoral college was dreamt up, with a third of the votes going to the membership, a third to trade unions and the final third to London MPs, MEPs and GLA candidates. This latter group were denied a secret ballot, while the union section still operated on the long since discredited block vote (just as they had when choosing Alun Michael over Rhodri Morgan).

The result was a humiliatingly narrow victory for Dobson, who beat Livingstone by just 3 per cent despite overwhelming defeats in two of the three sections. Livingstone got the support of 60 per cent of the party membership and 70 per cent of the unions, scoring particularly highly in those unions that actually balloted their members. Had individual votes been counted equally, as originally proposed, Livingstone would have won by a margin of nearly four to one. It was as naked a piece of gerrymandering as British politics had seen for a long time, and it did Dobson no favours at all. 'We had really fucked this from start to finish,' admitted Alastair Campbell, and Jonathan Powell had the same sensation of impending disaster: 'We fucked it up. But we couldn't allow a bozo like Livingstone to win.'

Some had been sceptical all along. 'The trouble is that Ken is cleverer than the people ranged against him, and a much better strategic thinker,' reflected Mo Mowlam; 'he is better at spinning.' Livingstone had learnt how to construct stories that would appeal to the media while Blair and Brown were still waiting to make their maiden speeches in Parliament, and only the arrogance of New Labour prevented the party from recognising that he could be an asset, not a liability. Campbell's sad conclusion, as Livingstone continued to set the agenda – 'He was running rings round us' – inadvertently echoed a 1984 *Daily Mail* headline: THE MAN RUNNING RINGS ROUND MAGGIE.

When the leadership had attempted to stop Livingstone even being put forward to the electoral college, his response had been to start a grassroots campaign demanding his inclusion in the process. Now, cheated of his rightful place as Labour's candidate, he announced that he would run as an independent, and used his body of support to construct an electoral machine. A large proportion of those working for his election were actually members of the Labour Party, working against their official candidate, while many others had already drifted from the party, coming out for one last campaign. Livingstone, it turned out, was still capable of inspiring activists at a time when New Labour didn't seem much interested in their contributions.

He also retained some of that rebel allure that had inspired Dexys Midnight Runners. Blair might have invited Noel Gallagher to a Downing Street reception, but Blur had invited Livingstone to narrate 'Ernold Same' on their 1995 album *The Great Escape*. Now that he was setting himself up in opposition to Blair, he found the remnants of Cool Britannia flocking to his banner. Chris Evans made a big donation to the cause, the likes of Fatboy Slim, Damon Albarn and the Chemical Brothers expressed their support, and the YBAs staged a fund-raising auction. 'I've been waiting all my life for a Labour government and now I've got one, it's shit,' explained Tracey Emin, as she gave her vote to Livingstone: 'Ken's interesting, sexy, dynamic.'

Livingstone was expelled from the party, of course, and a virulent coordinated assault on his integrity was launched, but to no one's great surprise he won the mayoralty with ease, picking up 39 per cent of the first preference votes. Dobson, the fall guy who few blamed personally, narrowly scraped into third place, ahead of the Liberal Democrats. For those who had always resented New Labour's insistence that compromise was the party's only hope, the election provided a sign of hope. As Tony Benn pointed out, 'following Blair is not the only way to win'. For Livingstone, it was a personal vindication; his victory speech started with the words: 'As I was saying before I was so rudely interrupted fourteen years ago . . .' The line was one originally suggested by Tony Banks back in 1991, when nursing his own dream of becoming mayor.

Meanwhile, the contest had been hugely enlivened by the Conservative Party. Seeking a high-profile candidate who might give Livingstone a run for his money, the Tories decided that the novelist Jeffrey Archer was the man for the job. There were some doubts about Archer – he was 'an accident waiting to happen', in the eyes of William Whitelaw – and he hardly distinguished himself in the campaign for the candidacy. Claiming that he approved of modern, multicultural Britain where 'there are the most staggeringly beautiful girls of every nationality', he explained that this was a great improvement on thirty years ago, when 'Your head did not turn if a black woman passed because they were badly dressed, probably overweight and probably had a lousy job.'

There was also a lingering concern about the unpleasantness more than a decade ago, when certain newspapers had alleged that he had paid money to a prostitute. He could, however, reasonably point to his successful claim against the *Daily Star* for libel, so that the story was now behind him.

Except that it wasn't. Archer's case in the libel trial had been grounded in an alibi provided by Ted Francis, a friend of his who had written a letter saying that on the night that Archer was alleged to have visited the prostitute, the two men were actually having dinner together. As far as Francis was concerned, this was just a friend providing cover for his wife: 'It wasn't until the trial started that I realised Jeffrey had manipulated me and intended to use my letter for his defence.' Now, confronted with the possibility that Archer might become mayor of London, Francis admitted that he had lied.

When the story broke, Archer's initial response was that this was just another of those little setbacks he had faced all through his life, another irritant to be overcome. 'I'm pretty confident I can get through this,' he told William Hague, but was soon put in his place: 'Oh no, you can't. You're out, that's final.' Court proceedings were brought against both Archer and Francis and in July 2001, Archer was found guilty of perjury and sentenced to four years in jail, though Francis was acquitted on a charge of perverting the course of justice.

With Archer's withdrawal, the wealthy entrepreneur Ivan Massow was thought briefly to be an alternative. It was just as well, however, that he wasn't chosen, since he left the Tories the following year, denouncing the party under Hague as having become 'less compassionate, more intolerant and frankly just plain nasty'. He would later claim that he had only joined in the first place because, as a gay teenager, he had a love of camp and 'Margaret Thatcher was beyond camp'. Instead Steven Norris – the man whose multiple affairs had provided such entertainment a few years earlier – was selected, though he was profoundly unimpressed by it all. 'People out there will look at the party and think it can't run a fucking whelk stall on an Essex pier,' he commented. Nonetheless, he made the most of a poor hand, and came second with 27 per cent of the first preference votes, a creditable performance in the circumstances.

*

The powers wielded by the new mayor were heavily circumscribed. He had no authority in such fields as health and education, but was charged with creating an integrated transport policy, which – as John Redwood pointed out – raised the intriguing constitutional issue of what would happen if the successful candidate was ideologically opposed to centralised transport planning. Even without that complication, the responsibility wasn't entirely logical; local roads remained within the scope of local authorities, while the mayor took over the bits of trunk roads that lay in London, but not the equivalent sections of motorway. The start of the A1 was therefore within his remit, but not the start of the M1 (which, like the rest of the A1, remained under the purview of the Department of Transport). It was hard to escape the impression that policy was being made up on the hoof.

The same was true of all the piecemeal changes to the constitution introduced in Tony Blair's first term. A bewildering array of voting arrangements were now in place. Elections to the House of Commons and local councils remained unchanged, operating under the first past the post system (the former in single-member constituencies, the latter in multi-member wards), but elsewhere various systems were in use: the Scottish Parliament, the Welsh Assembly and the London Assembly employed one system, the mayor of London (and mayors of any other cities who might follow) another, and the European Parliament yet another.

There was little apparent logic in any of this jigsaw. In places it was progressive – the mix of first past the post and top-up lists in Scotland, Wales and London took a decisive step towards proportional representation – but elsewhere there were signs of Labour's centralising tendency. The European Parliament was to be elected on a closed list system, entitling voters to choose only a party rather than an individual candidate, an arrangement that passed yet more power to the party leaderships. Looked at positively, it suggested that a range of options were being tried, in order to ascertain which might be most effective, but no one expected much further development to take place after the initial flurry of reforms.

In opposition, Blair had flirted with the idea of changing the system by which MPs were elected to the Commons, and the manifesto had promised a referendum on electoral reform. A committee was set up, under Roy Jenkins, to investigate the matter; its report, in late 1998, recommended a complex compromise known as the Alternative Vote Plus. 'This is a day I have looked forward to for half a century,' exulted Paddy Ashdown (which must have made him one of the more electorally sophisticated seven-year-olds in Clement Attlee's Britain), but Blair, who had never been very enthusiastic, knew that on this issue at least he could count on only limited support from his MPs, many of whom would lose their seats. No referendum was staged, the proposal quietly died, and Jenkins's system was implemented nowhere.

All the really difficult issues associated with devolution were similarly shelved. Tam Dalyell's 1978 query — dubbed by Enoch Powell the West Lothian Question — still remained: Why should Scottish MPs sitting in Westminster be able to pass laws that affected people in England but not their own constituents? 'It was a perfectly sensible question,' concluded Blair, 'and an interesting example of a problem in politics to which there is no logical answer.'

There was a logical answer, of course: an English parliament, or even a committee of the House of Commons, comprising all those elected as MPs for constituencies in England, which would be responsible for decisions related specifically and solely to English matters. This would have created two tiers of MP, with a steep reduction in influence for the lower tier; MPs for Scottish constituencies would have even less responsibility than they already did, since so much domestic policy was devolved to the Scottish Parliament. The official government response to the proposal was to reject it because 'at a practical level, there is no room in the precincts large enough to accommodate all 582 members sitting for English seats'. Teresa Gorman voiced an alternative interpretation: 'It doesn't take a genius to work out why the English are denied a referendum and its own parliament; England is where most Conservative voters are to be found.'

Likewise there was no attempt to address the matter of the disproportionately high number of Scottish and Welsh MPs who sat in the House. Nor was there any amendment to the Barnett Formula, the stop-gap system introduced in the 1970s which provided Scotland and Wales with high levels of government spending, and which had remained untouched ever since. David Blunkett did argue for a change in early 2001, but Gordon Brown told him: 'I can't do anything about the Barnett Formula before the election.' Blunkett's response was at least honest: 'No, I don't expect you can. I want to win seats in Scotland and Wales as well.'

Further confusion ensued when changes were made to the House of Lords. The existence of an unelected second chamber with an inbuilt Conservative majority, thanks to the presence of hundreds of hereditary peers, had long been a cause of annoyance on the British left, even if it was difficult to persuade many of those peers to turn up and vote, save in extreme circumstances. Apart from the hereditaries, the House found room for the Archbishop of Canterbury and twenty-five other Anglican bishops, as well as Prince Charles and some of the other royals, but was mostly comprised of life peers, many of them retired or rejected members of the Commons.

When, for example, Lynda Chalker, formerly the minister for overseas development, lost her seat in the 1992 election, she was immediately given a peerage and reappointed to the same job. No one doubted her commitment to the issue of international development, but some were tempted to ask what was the point of elections, if not to remove people from office. Similarly, when Blair's friend Charlie Falconer failed to find himself a safe Labour seat, he was given a peerage as a consolation prize, so that he could be part of the government. The low esteem in which the Lords was held could be seen in Michael Heseltine's suggestion of creating 'a new class of life peers appointed to sit for one parliament only, at the end of which they should have the opportunity to stand for the Commons again'. This off-the-cuff attempt at a constitutional innovation – it wasn't enacted – was conceived solely to keep Chris Patten active in British politics after he lost his Commons seat in 1992.

In short, the Lords was an illogical mishmash of birth, position and patronage, widely perceived on the left to be a block on any radical reform. Its powers were limited to delaying the passage of a Bill, as opposed to stopping it outright, but it was seen to be inherently conservative.

The Labour manifesto's response was to promise to end 'the right of hereditary peers to sit and vote in the House of Lords'. This would be the first phase of reform, to be followed at some unspecified date – possibly in the current parliament, possibly later – by a change to how the membership was chosen and what the chamber should be called. No one could agree on what should replace the Lords, and the suspicion was that the second stage of reform would be delayed indefinitely, with Labour spokespeople seemingly preparing the ground for indecision. 'Better a quango of the living than the dead,' said Jack Straw, before the election. 'Better to have people appointed for their own merit rather than the alleged merit of their forebears.'

As it turned out, even the first phase was far from the clean break that had been promised. In a bid to secure a smooth passage for the reform Bill in 1999, the government put forward a compromise whereby ninety-two hereditary peers, chosen by their fellow hereditaries, would be allowed to remain in place, thus introducing an elected element to the House but one whose electorate was the smallest in the country. This bizarre proposal made even less sense than the system that preceded it, and the situation was scarcely improved by the retention of the Anglican bishops and the creation of new life peerages for ten of those who had previously sat by hereditary right, including Princess Margaret's ex-husband, the Earl of Snowdon. Life peerages were also reported to have been offered to Prince Charles, Prince Andrew and Prince Philip, though they were turned down. (Philip was anyway a firm believer in the hereditary peers: 'I'd rather they were chosen by God than by the prime minister.')

Continuing on its illogical path, the Lords still had not one member elected from outside the House, and was now dominated by life peers, so that those who benefited personally from patronage outnumbered those whose ancestors had been so favoured. It wasn't, however, noticeably more progressive than its earlier incarnation, and the government still had to overrule it when it blocked the passage of legislation to equalise the age of homosexual consent. Meanwhile Tony Blair was so busy promoting people to the Lords that he created more new peers than any other twentieth-century prime minister; by the time he resigned from his position in 2007, nearly half of those in the House would be his appointees. It was not a major democratic advance.

Nonetheless, the changes wrought on the constitution of the country during Blair's first term were substantial. Not all of the demands made by Charter 88 and others had been met, and it was hard not to see the devolution enacted by the Blair government as having a strong vein of self-interest: in one way or another, Labour's control of Scotland, Wales and London was entrenched for a political generation. Even so, there had been a transformation that could be cautiously greeted as allowing the emergence of greater democracy. And if the transition had been managed incompetently at times, perhaps that was inevitable; a party leadership that had no track record whatsoever in administration was attempting to reconstitute the Union on a scale unparalleled in modern British history.

Where New Labour suffered from its lack of experience in government, the Conservative Party had precisely the opposite problem. 'The attractions of opposition are greatly exaggerated by those who have not experienced it,' warned Margaret Thatcher in 1996, and that included virtually the whole of the shadow cabinet; the decreasing age of frontline politicians meant that few had been around in the pre-Thatcher years. It wasn't, however, an entirely unpleasant sensation for some to find that the burden of office had been lifted. John Major made his first speech in the Commons from the opposition back benches in 1998 and was enthused by the freedom it gave him. 'He now sees what a doddle opposition is,' reported Hugo Young, after interviewing the former prime minister. 'So easy to make a speech when you are able to say what you actually think.'

Meanwhile, the new opposition front bench was busily trying to copy New Labour's behaviour and thereby running the risk of making exactly the same mistakes as its rivals. In 1999 the Tories hired Amanda Platell to be head of news and media, though in practice she was, like Alastair Campbell, primarily concerned with building up the leader − in her case William Hague − rather than the party as a whole.

An Australian journalist who had most recently worked for the *Sunday Express*, Platell was clearly intended as the Conservative equivalent of Campbell and, although she was hardly in the same league − just as Hague was no real match for Blair − she did start to get some better coverage than had hitherto been the case. She was also, however, capable of careless blunders, as when she persuaded Ffion Hague to wear a silver pendant in the shape of a pound sign, supposedly a gift from her husband that symbolised his determination to keep Britain out of the euro. The stratagem looked gimmicky and geeky, and backfired completely when the jeweller from whom the piece was bought, annoyed that he hadn't been paid, revealed that it was Platell not Hague who had acquired it. She also set up a notorious interview in *GQ* magazine in 2000 in which Hague bragged of the time he spent, as a teenager, working for his father's drinks company, when he used to consume up to fourteen pints of beer a day. While Hague seemed happy to go along with these silly stunts that were intended to humanise his image, he turned down her one genuine coup, when he refused to interrupt a holiday for a meeting with Rupert Murdoch.

The real problem, however, was the way in which the relationship between Hague and his shadow chancellor, Michael Portillo, appeared to replicate that between Blair and Brown, with all the same tensions, rivalry and bickering. Portillo, like Brown, seemed incapable of accepting that another man had the job he coveted, and he displayed no inclination to accept the authority of his party's elected leader. Repeatedly threatening to resign if he didn't get his way, he fought for every square inch of political turf. In his attempt to assert his power, he threw away the one eye-catching policy he had inherited from Francis Maude, his predecessor as shadow chancellor: a guarantee that, under a Tory government, tax would fall as a share of GDP. The party was already committed, largely through the advocacy of Ann Widdecombe, to matching Labour's spending plans on health and education − emulating New Labour's commitments when in opposition − but still the issue of regaining trust on taxes made political sense. It was Maude too who came up with the phrase 'stealth taxes', to describe Brown's attempts to find other sources of revenue beyond income tax. That slogan was considerably more effective than anything Portillo devised.

Just as Blair and Brown would meet in private, with no advisers present and no minutes taken, so too did Hague and Portillo. The difference was that Portillo acted from a much stronger base than Hague had been capable of building, with a powerful circle of admirers and supporters, both in the party and in the press. The suspicion was that he exerted a greater influence over policy than did his Labour counterpart. And he too seemed determined to remove any potential rivals to the leadership. His arrival in the shadow cabinet, after his by-election victory, was accompanied by the departure of John Redwood, and there were many who saw the two events as being related, that Portillo had demanded the removal of the man who had stood against Major in 1995. That effectively left Widdecombe as the only serious threat when – as was almost certain – the Tories lost the next election and Hague stepped down. The time for dealing with her would surely come.

Again, though, there was little discernible sign of serious policy development. The twin poles of attraction within the shadow cabinet – Portillo on the left and Widdecombe on the right – had very different visions of the future of Conservatism, and Hague looked as though he were torn between them, fluctuating wildly between an inclusive liberalism and a neo-Thatcherism, without much conviction in either case. Little wonder that when private polling was leaked in 2000, it showed that the word used by the public to describe him was 'weak'. And that seemed the worst option of all, to copy Blair's non-ideological chase after public opinion, but to have no control over his own party. As Blair pointed out: 'there's only one thing the public dislike more than a leader in control of his party, and that is a leader not in control of his party.'

While the Tories were mimicking New Labour's feud culture, the constitutional reforms to the country, the most radical and far-reaching changes of the Blair years, passed them by without any serious Conservative critique or contribution. Theirs was the party that had passed the 1867 Reform Act, given women the vote in 1918 (and extended the female franchise in 1928), invented life peerages, allowed hereditary peers to renounce their titles, created the parliamentary select committee system and been the first to publish the ministerial code. It could, in short, boast a more radical history when it came to reforming the constitution than could Labour, yet it now had nothing to say beyond defending the status quo.

When he was Welsh secretary, William Hague had argued that an Assembly would be 'a waste of time, a waste of space and a waste of money'. In opposition, he continued to oppose devolution, but accepted that once it was a fait accompli, the Conservatives would be obliged to accept the changes. 'We cannot unscramble the omelette,' as he put it in 1998.

15
Adventures
'I can't imagine the world without me'

Mine is the first generation able to contemplate the possibility
that we may live our entire lives without going to war or sending
our children to war. That is a prize beyond value.
 Tony Blair (1997)

I felt sick to the stomach to have to order that rescue mission
by the SAS in Sierra Leone. As a father I was so very aware that
the young guys being sent off to fight and perhaps die were
somebody's children.
Tony Blair (2001)

I am not going to be the first prime minister in a hundred years to
lose a war.
Tony Blair (1999)

'**W**e will pursue policies on defence and foreign affairs which will
make Britain a force for good in the world,' read the foreword to
the manifesto of the SDP/Liberal Alliance in 1987, setting a tone for the
aspirations of the left. Ten years later, almost to the day, when Labour took
power, the same phraseology was again to be heard. Robin Cook came to the
Foreign Office promising that Britain would 'once again be a force for good
in the world' and that 'Our foreign policy must have an ethical dimension
and must support the demands of other people for the democratic rights
on which we insist for ourselves.'

Summarised by the department's press officers, that declaration of
intent became a pledge to operate an 'ethical foreign policy'. This wasn't
quite what Cook had said, and it seemed to offer a hostage to fortune,
for foreign affairs were notoriously susceptible to considerations beyond
morality. Nonetheless, the phrase captured something of the faith that
was placed in Cook's ability to uphold the internationalist principles

traditionally espoused by the Labour Party; more than any other figure in the new government, he was the one to whom the liberal left looked for a moral lead. Much was expected of the man who had led the assault on the Conservatives during the Scott Inquiry.

It was not merely the arms-to-Iraq story that lay behind the pledge. The divisions over Europe that had so badly damaged the Conservative Party had a knock-on effect of ensuring that John Major's government had little time or energy left for international engagement. The successful completion of the Kuwaiti War had not been followed by further such commitments overseas, largely for reasons of housekeeping rather than any Little Englander sentiments. Most strikingly this had been apparent in the Yugoslav wars of 1991–5.

The manner of Yugoslavia's collapse as a unified nation was one of the great world tragedies of the decade. Slobodan Milošević had come to power in Serbia, the largest and most powerful of the constituent republics in the country, on a platform of aggressively defending Serbian dominance over the delicately balanced federation, and his policies had prompted several of the other states to assert their independence, starting with Slovenia and Croatia in 1991, followed the next year by Bosnia-Herzegovina. The conflicts that ensued were bewildering in their complexity. Serbia's war with Croatia began with the aim of keeping the latter within Yugoslavia, but soon became a battle to determine borders and to establish authority over areas of the new country that had substantial Serbian populations. In Bosnia too there were large numbers of Serbs, led by Radovan Karadžić, who took up arms against the Bosnian separatists. Meanwhile Franjo Tudjman, the equally nationalist president of Croatia, had allegedly come to an agreement with Milošević over the division of Bosnia, so that the future sovereignty of that state was even further imperilled.

The divisions were ethnic, nationalist and religious. They were also rooted deep in a history of which most in Western Europe were ignorant. The humanitarian consequences of the conflicts, however, were easier to grasp, and within months the world was witnessing on television the sight of hundreds of thousands of refugees fleeing from the Serb forces, while stories were circulating of war crimes and atrocities committed in the name of ethnic cleansing.

Initially the international response to the developing crises centred on an effort to keep Yugoslavia together as a single entity, but in December 1991 the newly reunited Germany announced it was recognising Croatia as an independent nation. It was argued that a basic principle of self-determination was at stake, though Germany's position was perhaps rooted in an instinctive solidarity with the Croatian Catholics in their struggle with the Eastern Orthodox-influenced Serbia, while the presence of large numbers of Croatian migrant workers in Germany also played its part. Whatever the cause, the move was counter to the wishes of the United Nations and of Britain, but once enacted, it set a pattern duly followed by most of the world. A UN peacekeeping force was sent into Croatia in February 1992, but was able to make only a token attempt to help humanitarian aid get through to the refugees.

Britain contributed to the humanitarian effort, though the decision to do even this proved controversial within the cabinet and the Commons, as well as in the country beyond, which remained unconvinced that anything constructive could be done in the chaos of these civil wars. A large-scale commitment of troops would have been unpopular, while diplomacy seemed like a futile endeavour. 'How were negotiators supposed to negotiate when the twisted logic and self-interest of Yugoslav leaders was in favour of bloodshed?' reflected Major.

As the bloodshed continued, however, the calls for some sort of action grew louder on both the left and the right. This was, argued Chris Mullin, analogous to the Spanish Civil War, and there should be international intervention, just as there should have been in the 1930s. 'Those paying the price of George Bush's and John Major's dithering incompetence,' wrote Peter Mandelson, 'are Bosnian Muslims, seeing their homes burned and their women raped by Serbian and Croatian militia alike.' From the other side, Margaret Thatcher – who had been lobbying hard in private for action against Milošević – gave a television interview in 1993 in which she said that massacres were happening 'in the heart of Europe' and that the conflict 'should be in Europe's sphere of conscience'. Britain, and the EU more generally, she said, 'were like an accomplice to massacre'. The defence secretary, Malcolm Rifkind, dismissed her comments as 'emotional nonsense'.

Instead the British government steadfastly refused to become embroiled in the conflict. In international circles, the creation of a force to defend Croatia was proposed, a no-fly zone in Bosnia was suggested, air strikes against Bosnian Serbs were put forward. Britain objected to all, with the foreign secretary, Douglas Hurd, singled out as the stumbling block to further intervention. 'Any time there was a likelihood of effective action,' observed Tadeusz Mazowiecki, the former Polish prime minister and now a UN emissary to Bosnia, 'a particular Western statesman intervened to prevent it.' He didn't need to spell out who he meant.

When he came to write his memoirs, Hurd himself, while conceding that mistakes were made, remained insistent that the policy was right: 'Britain had no substantial commercial or strategic stake in Croatia, Bosnia or the other states which had made up Yugoslavia.' He also rejected an analysis that suggested there was a simple moral division between the various forces, adding that as 'I grow older I become more suspicious of the straightforward, violent solution to international problems'. Others were not of the same mind, seeing the conflict as a war of aggression in which the Serbs were the culpable party. The memory of Britain standing on the sidelines was to play a major part in subsequent actions.

By the time a peace treaty had been drawn up, in the shape of the Dayton Agreement in December 1995, an estimated total of up to 200,000 people had died, and perhaps another two million had been displaced. For all the violence that had gone before, the borders established by that agreement did remain intact.

Hurd's assessment of British interests during the Yugoslav wars — described in American circles as 'hyper-realist' — was very much in the mind of some Labour figures as the party took office and began talking of an ethical foreign policy and the need to be a 'force for good in the world'. Henceforth it would be a matter of principle that evil should not be allowed to go unchecked, wherever it manifested itself.

An opportunity to demonstrate that commitment soon presented itself. The situation in Indonesia, where President Suharto had come to power in a military takeover in 1967, was not one that excited widespread public interest in Britain, but it had been a long-running concern on the left. In particular the invasion and illegal occupation by Indonesian forces of East Timor in 1976 had been condemned, as had Britain's supply of armaments to Suharto. The issue had received some publicity in July 1996 when four women were prosecuted for causing £1.5 million of damage to Hawk jets that were due to be exported to Indonesia; their defence, that their actions were the lesser of two evils, had successfully won over the jury, and the women had been acquitted.

Asked before the election whether he would end arms sales to Indonesia, Robin Cook had declined to offer any such assurance, but it seemed scarcely credible that he could countenance the continuing trade that saw the export of water cannon and tear gas, clearly destined for use in suppressing pro-democracy demonstrations in both Indonesia and East Timor. Shipments of such materials, as well as armoured cars and a further seventeen Hawk jets, were scheduled for export shortly after the election. The ethical dimension, however, did not seem to apply in this case and — apparently on the instructions of Downing Street – the exports went ahead. The argument coming out of the Foreign Office was that the sales had already been agreed and that cancellation would mean that the government was liable for compensation: 'We are not going to pay for the previous administration's mistakes.' Undoubtedly it was a difficult decision to make, but the subtleties of the argument may have been lost on the people of East Timor. And if the practice continued as before, there was at least a new transparency to the process; Cook felt able to boast that Britain 'now had the most open system of arms sales of any country in Europe'.

What proved somewhat easier was the more symbolic practice of issuing apologies for historical wrongs. There had been some high-profile examples in recent years, as when the Catholic Church in 1992 admitted that it had been wrong to persecute Galileo Galilei three and a half centuries earlier for his insistence that the Earth orbited the Sun. Since the Church claimed some sort of authority in matters of the afterlife, there was an internal logic to the posthumous absolution. Less obvious was the campaign by Outrage! and other gay activists to have an official pardon issued to Oscar Wilde in 1995, that being the centenary of his sentencing to two years' hard labour for homosexuality. Quite properly, Michael Howard rejected the demand. Wilde had been tried and sentenced in accordance with the laws of the day, and anyway the idea that redemption for a maverick, anarchist genius might be within the gift of a Conservative government was seen by some as an insult to his memory. Instead the centenary was marked by the unveiling of a stained glass memorial in Westminster Abbey.

The idea of historical apologies being in the air, New Labour took to it with enthusiasm. In June 1997 Tony Blair apologised for the nineteenth-century potato famine in Ireland, blaming it on 'those who governed in London', and later announced that Britain would be donating money to a memorial for the victims. ('If it was just the potatoes that were affected,' observed Alan Partridge, less sympathetically, 'at the end of the day, you will pay the price if you're a fussy eater.') Blair went on to apologise to the US Congress for Britain's burning of the books of the Library of Congress in 1814, and in 2006 the government offered a posthumous pardon to 306 soldiers executed, mostly for cowardice, during the First World War.

A similar impulse lay behind the creation of a Holocaust Memorial Day, first observed on 27 January 2001, the anniversary of the day that the Soviet Red Army liberated Auschwitz in Poland (as opposed to, say, the day that British troops liberated Belsen, or Yom HaShoah, the Jewish day of commemoration). A ceremony in Westminster Central Hall attracted the great and the good, from Prince Charles to the major party leaders, as well as a collection of celebrities including Antony Sher, Emma Thompson, Ian McKellen, Bob Geldof and Trevor McDonald, presumably chosen to represent ethnic and sexual diversity.

To the surprise of some, this gesture was not universally welcomed. Already observance of Yom HaShoah was in decline and there was a debate within British Jewry about whether the continuing focus on the Nazi genocide was proving counter-productive, alienating younger generations with negative images of victimhood. 'Some Jewish people,' explained David Cesarani, a professor of modern Jewish history, 'think it is wrong to concentrate on destruction and death when there is so much that the Jews should celebrate.' Rabbi Jonathan Romain argued that Yom HaShoah itself should be abandoned, subsumed into Tishah B'Av, the annual day of mourning, while Rabbi Yitzchak Y. Schochet called for better education in schools, rather than the addition of a day to the calendar. Stephen Smith, director of the Beth Shalom Holocaust Memorial Centre, was particularly scathing. 'We have created a soundbite society in which we reduce difficult issues to trivial clichés,' he commented, and wondered whether the new commemoration would 'reduce twentieth-century mass slaughter to the status of National No Smoking Day'.

These issues were safely in the past. When it came to wrongdoing for which apology and reparations to the living might be applicable, there was not always such enthusiasm. In 1966 the Labour government of Harold Wilson had leased the British colony of Diego Garcia in the Indian Ocean to America for use as a military base, a move that involved the eviction of the 2,000 inhabitants and their relocation in Mauritius. The status of Diego Garcia had been the subject of questions in Parliament by Robin Cook as far back as 1975 – his concern was the possible development of nuclear facilities on the base – but when the issue returned to public notice in the late 1990s, he appeared less interested in the historic injustice done to the islanders. A court case in 2000 ruled unequivocally that the evictions of what were termed at the time 'a few Tarzans or Men Fridays' had been an 'abject legal failure', yet the islanders' right to return to their home had still not materialised by the time the Labour government left office ten years later.

Slightly more convincing was the apology issued by Ron Davies for the way that £150,000 had been taken – on the authority of an earlier Welsh secretary, George Thomas – from the relief fund for the 1966 Aberfan disaster, in order to pay for clearing up after the catastrophe, even though it had been occasioned by the National Coal Board's negligence. Here, at least, restitution was made and the money returned. 'It was a wrong perpetrated by a previous government, a Labour secretary of state,' admitted Davies. 'I regarded it as an embarrassment. It was a wrong that needed to be righted.' Nonetheless, the repayment of the stolen money made no attempt to adjust for inflation, let alone for interest.

Despite this patchy record, there was progress in various areas of international relations that had long been cherished causes on the left. The ethical dimension to foreign policy also sought to wipe out the memory of the Pergau Dam affair and other dubious examples of overseas aid, with the creation by Labour of a separate Department for International Development, hived off from the Foreign Office and given a seat in cabinet.

The appointment of Clare Short as the secretary of state was widely welcomed, though she was not always surefooted in her early days in office. Aid was provided for the British territory of Montserrat after its devastation by a volcano in 1997, but Short somewhat blotted her copybook with her accompanying comments on the island's leaders. 'Their answer to an emergency is to demand more and more from Britain,' she moaned. 'Their approach is "give them all golden elephants".' She subsequently apologised for that remark, and more generally was regarded as one of the success stories of the first Blair government.

It was also to Britain's credit that it was in the first wave of countries to ratify the Rome Statute of 1998, creating the International Criminal Court that followed on from the International Criminal Tribunal for the former Yugoslavia (itself a UN initiative instigated by Germany). The new court was intended to try cases of alleged genocide, war crimes and crimes against humanity, though its efficacy was inevitably compromised by the list of countries that refused to sign up, a collection of curious bedfellows that included the USA, Iraq, Israel and China.

Perhaps more important, in terms of international law, was the case of Augusto Pinochet, the former dictator of Chile, who visited London in October 1998 for medical treatment and promptly found himself under threat of extradition to Spain, where he was wanted on charges of torture and genocide. 'This is going to be one helluva story,' remarked Jack Straw, on hearing of Pinochet's arrest in Britain. It proved to be an accurate prediction.

There were to start with questions about what business it was of Spain's in the first place, since the alleged crimes had been committed on Chilean soil. Then there was the matter of whether Pinochet was covered by the principle of sovereign immunity that protects heads of state from criminal prosecution. And finally there was an argument made by many on the right, including most notably Margaret Thatcher, that Pinochet had been a good, loyal friend to Britain, particularly during the Falklands War, and that the persecution of a sick 82-year-old displayed a distinct lack of hospitality. There was a suspicion that the whole thing was politically motivated and an act of leftist spite.

This latter accusation contained a grain of truth. The American-backed military coup in Chile in 1973 that had overthrown the socialist government of Salvador Allende and installed Pinochet at the head of a military junta had long been a burning issue on the left, so much so that, for some, it transcended their more recently acquired reformism. Peter Mandelson had been a student at the time of the coup, having only just left the Young Communists, and now greeted the news of the arrest by calling Pinochet 'a brutal dictator' and describing his claim for immunity as 'pretty gut-wrenching stuff'.

The claim of sovereign immunity took its time to work through the British courts, ending up in the House of Lords, which found against it. In the words of one of the Law Lords: 'international law has made plain that certain types of conduct, including torture and hostage-taking, are not acceptable conduct on the part of anyone.' The case returned twice more to the Law Lords, firmly establishing the principle that torture was an international crime and could therefore result in charges in any country that was a signatory to the UN's Convention against Torture, as Britain and Spain — and indeed Chile — were.

Legal hurdles having been cleared, the decision whether to approve the extradition to Spain came down to Jack Straw, who had taken scrupulous care to observe every letter of the law in a case that had the potential to cause major international embarrassment, and who had resisted attempts by prime ministers past and present to intervene. 'There's no Third Way,' he explained. 'I either say Yes or No.' Eventually, after Pinochet had been under house arrest for more than a year, the medical reports proved conclusive: he had suffered such extensive brain damage from several strokes that he was not fit to stand trial. In March 2000, he was allowed to leave the country and return to Chile.

Many on the left were unhappy at the outcome, including Straw himself, who wrote in his memoirs: 'Pinochet was one of the worst dictators of the post-war era and it is an enduring source of enormous frustration that I was not able to lead him to the dock.' Those on the right were equally unhappy at the humiliation heaped upon the man during his protracted stay in Britain. It was perhaps a muddled outcome but, as Straw made clear in his Commons statement after Pinochet's departure, the case 'established, beyond question, the principle that those who commit human rights abuses in one country cannot assume that they are safe elsewhere. That will be its lasting legacy.'

It was an important principle, though again it laid Britain open to a charge of operating double standards when it came to that ethical dimension. For human rights abuses were obviously never going to be the sole criterion on which foreign policy was based. The grubby reality of power meant that when dealing with, say, Jiang Zemin, the president of China, other considerations took precedence, despite that country's less than perfect human rights record and the running sore of the occupation of Tibet. In a meeting with Jiang just before the handing over of Hong Kong, Blair 'slipped in a very brief mention of human rights', though in a subsequent encounter, in London in 1999, not even that token nod was given. 'The press reported that Tony had raised the issue of human rights,' noted Clare Short, 'but I was at the meeting and he had not done so.'

That visit by Jiang to London was marked by what *The Times* called 'zero tolerance towards human rights and Free Tibet demonstrators'. The police uncovered a long-forgotten law prohibiting demonstrations in royal parks and used it to prevent even the display of banners by protestors on The Mall (technically a part of St James's Park) in what was hardly an advert for liberal democracy. *The Economist* linked the occasion to Pinochet's detention, pointing out of the latter that 'His sins were many. But they were fewer than those of Mr Jiang.' On the part of the authorities there was perhaps some residual embarrassment from the state visit of the Emperor Akihito of Japan the previous year, when hundreds of Second World War veterans, proudly wearing their medals, lined The Mall so that they could turn their backs in silent protest as the son of the wartime emperor passed by.

Questions of human rights, historical wrongs and ethics were not, however, what Tony Blair's government would ultimately be remembered for in foreign policy. Rather it was a willingness to engage in armed action overseas, and a determination to stand by America at all costs.

The latter trait had already been seen before the election, when Bill Clinton ordered the bombing of Iraq in 1996, and found ready support not only from John Major's government but also from the opposition. It was evident again in August 1998 when, in retaliation for terrorist attacks on US embassies in Tanzania and Kenya, American forces bombed targets in Afghanistan, where the group al-Qaeda – held responsible for the attacks – was based, and Sudan, where a factory was destroyed. The factory was said to have been producing chemical weapons, but it turned out that the intelligence was flawed, and that it was actually a pharmaceutical plant making antibiotics. 'Everyone knew that what Clinton was doing was wrong,' explained one of Blair's circle, 'but we also knew that supporting him was right.' Robin Cook, at least, was not so impressed and 'refused to go on the *Today* programme' to defend the action.

Faulty intelligence was to prove a contentious issue in the later years of Blair's premiership, much of the controversy centred on the question of weapons of mass destruction. The phrase had been in circulation for some time: 'Who can think without horror of what another widespread war would mean, waged as it would be with all the new weapons of mass destruction?' worried Cosmo Gordon Lang, Archbishop of Canterbury, in 1937. But it had gained greater currency in the years after Hiroshima, referring specifically to nuclear weapons, and then extended to include chemical and biological weapons, though not cluster bombs or massive 'conventional' bombs like the BLU-82 (nicknamed the daisy cutter). The phrase had become particularly associated with Saddam Hussein, whose government boasted of possessing weapons of mass destruction and threatened their use during the Iran–Iraq War in the mid-1980s. 'Some Western military attachés discount the Iraqi claims as propaganda,' it was reported at the time, but mustard gas – a primitive form of chemical weaponry – was used during that conflict and again against Iraqi Kurds in 1988.

The real fear, though, was that Iraq would develop nuclear weapons. Therefore, as part of the conditions imposed upon the country in the wake of the Kuwaiti War, a Security Council resolution authorised UN weapons inspectors to monitor and examine the Iraqi weapons programme. Within a few months of becoming prime minister, Tony Blair was making it publicly clear that he couldn't rule out military strikes against Iraq, and was privately telling Paddy Ashdown that he had seen intelligence reports that were 'pretty scary'; Saddam was, he said, 'very close to some appalling weapons of mass destruction'. Whether that were true was hard to evaluate, for the inspectors were thrown out of the country in November 1998 and, although they were then allowed to return, the decision had already been taken in Washington and London to bomb Baghdad.

This was Blair's first war and it was undertaken, he told his aides, only with 'a heavy heart'. The advice he was given suggested that '2,500 people would die and UK planes and bombs would be responsible for about 250 of them'. The bombing was preceded by discussion in cabinet and by a Commons debate in which a small, and predictable, chorus of voices spoke against the action, including Tony Benn, Edward Heath and Tam Dalyell. The latter dubbed the conflict 'the war of Clinton's penis', suggesting that it was an attempt to divert attention from the sexual scandals then besetting the president. Also speaking against was the eloquent Labour MP George Galloway, who compared the operation to a crusade led not by 'Richard the Lionheart, but Clinton the Liar'. Galloway's moral authority, however, had been somewhat compromised by a visit to Iraq in 1994, when he had been seen on television speaking with the dictator, using words that he was not soon allowed to forget — 'Sir, I salute your courage, your strength and your indefatigability'. The *Daily Mirror* was prompted to denounce him as 'the mother of all idiots'.

The objective in this instance was simply that of punishment. Blair talked of the need to 'degrade the ability of Saddam Hussein to build and use weapons of mass destruction', but since the UN inspectors had been unable to locate sites that were being used for this purpose, it seemed unlikely that those determining the targets of the air strikes would be any more successful. There was also, though, the stated long-term desire to oust the current Iraqi government, even if regime change wasn't currently achievable: 'It's a broad objective of our policy to remove Saddam Hussein,' Blair told the Commons.

The 1998 bombing campaign was primarily an American operation and attracted very little support elsewhere, save in Britain; France was particularly vocal in its disapproval of the action. Nonetheless, in a round of interviews immediately afterwards, Blair pronounced himself satisfied with the results, though he couldn't help exaggerating the truth, as Alastair Campbell noted: 'he said we hit every target, when we hadn't.'

If Saddam remained the ultimate bogeyman, he was briefly rivalled by Slobodan Milošević. The Dayton Agreement had brought peace to the Balkans and was still holding, but it had left Serbia with control of the province of Kosovo, a tiny, landlocked enclave mostly populated by ethnic Albanians, and here there remained problems. During the earlier wars of independence, a separatist movement calling itself the Kosovo Liberation Army (KLA) had engaged in terrorist attacks on Serbian government forces and on Serbs living in the province. With the other conflicts now resolved, the KLA stepped up its campaign and was met with a harsh response by the Serbian government. By the spring of 1998 reports were emerging of gross human rights abuses by the state, and the civil service were suggesting to Blair that he ought to be aware of the issues. 'You'd better give me a note on it,' he replied. 'Starting with: where is it?'

The ignorance was understandable. Few in the West knew anything about Kosovo, let alone of its enormous emotional significance in Serbian history, dating back to the Battle of Blackbird Field in 1389, when Serb forces had fought the might of the Ottoman Empire and sustained heavy losses. Indeed Yugoslavia itself had been largely a closed book until recent years. When Paddy Ashdown had first begun to take an interest in the region – he went on to make it his own specialist subject – he had started by asking a colleague 'to show me maps as I didn't even know where all the countries were'. The media were not much better informed, and focused instead on photogenic images of suffering Kosovars; little attempt was made to explain the complexities of context and history.

Those images were significant, for the war that followed was the first time that the media had been largely responsible for British military action. Through 1998 a massive weight of news reports built up a single message: that this was a straightforward case of good versus evil, with the Serbs cast in the role of bad guy. Privately Blair and Cook were clear that 'the KLA were not much better than the Serbs', but Blair was also conscious of Britain's non-involvement in the Balkans in the early 1990s, and determined that what he saw as a shameful mistake shouldn't be made again. It was, he insisted, 'essentially a moral issue'. By June he was resolved on military intervention, though it was not until March 1999 that he went to the Commons to announce that bombing of Serbia would commence.

A strike against a sovereign nation without United Nations approval was of dubious legality; 'we breached international law and took pre-emptive action in Kosovo without UN sanction,' as David Blunkett later admitted. But UN backing would have been impossible to obtain, since Russia and China were opposed, so that option was simply discounted. Instead the action was carried out under the auspices of NATO, an organisation that was in search of a role in the post-Cold War world. In Kosovo it found a new identity; its function no longer purely defensive, it now became an instrument for controlling domestic policy in non-member countries.

The bombing was expected to last for seventy-two hours, with Milošević rapidly caving in to the demands of NATO and withdrawing Serb forces from Kosovo. There would be no need to put troops on the ground, with all the concomitant risks to British soldiers; the mission would be achieved from the air. That proved to be wishful thinking, and it took seventy-eight days of killing before peace could be declared. Even then it was the result not of the bombing, which had solidified Serbian support for Milošević against an external enemy, but international diplomacy, led by Russia, and – after Blair had talked Clinton into it – the threat of a ground invasion. The government might have done well to listen to the advice of Martin McGuinness, a former IRA leader now turned politician, who knew something about the subject, and who pointed out that '"bombing into submission" isn't always a sensible policy'.

Mistakes were inevitably made during the campaign. A cluster bomb aimed at an airfield instead hit a market and killed sixty civilians; eighty-seven Kosovars were killed in a bomb attack on the village of Koriša; worst of all from a diplomatic point of view, a bomb struck the Chinese embassy in Belgrade (again a case of faulty intelligence). Perhaps most distressing, the original prediction that some 200,000 people might be driven from their homes as a consequence of the war turned out to be a hopeless underestimate; in fact more than a million refugees fled, many of them ending up in the camps on the Macedonian and Albanian borders, which Blair visited himself during the bombing. 'This is obscene,' he argued, with post-hoc reasoning. 'It's criminal. Just criminal. How can anyone think we shouldn't be stopping this?'

The terrible pictures that came out from the camps helped to ensure public support for the war, though as the conflict dragged on, much of this melted away. By June 1999, Philip Gould's focus groups were showing dissatisfaction with the costs of the operation, leaving a petulant Alastair Campbell to 'wonder why we bothered' if the public were going to be so ungrateful, and Gould himself to advise Blair to ignore popular opinion: 'The only important thing is to win.'

In some respects, this was a very different conflict from those that followed and became the defining incident of Blair's premiership, not least because it attracted the support of much of the left. 'This was the liberals' war,' wrote Mark Steel. '"We have to do *something*," they screamed at those of us opposed to it.' A handful of MPs on the old left might have been in opposition, but it was noticeable that Ken Livingstone was in full support. Milošević was seen as a right-wing dictator who had to be fought, a perception only aided by Alan Clark's typically eccentric take on the war: 'Those loathsome, verminous gypsies; and the poor brave Serbs.'

In other ways, however, Kosovo set a pattern that was to be repeated, from the characterisation of the enemy as a new Adolf Hitler (Livingstone, as well as Blair, was amongst those resorting to such lazy imagery), through Gordon Brown's absence from key decision-making and silence in cabinet, to the complete lack of thought about what was to happen if and when the war was won. 'There was no real clarity about an endgame at the moment,' wrote Campbell, as the bombing started, and the failure to prepare what was becoming known as an exit strategy became all too apparent when the Serbian forces did eventually withdraw.

The province was put under UN administration, policed by an

international peacekeeping force, but that didn't stop a further wave of refugees as tens, and possibly hundreds, of thousands of Serbs fled Kosovan reprisals for the safety of Serbia. This was not a stable state but one which, as Clare Short wrote, had been left 'in limbo, with high levels of unemployment which exacerbate ethnic tension'. Chris Patten, now an EU commissioner, visited in 2004, shortly after a major outbreak of violence directed against those Serbs who remained, and concluded that the prospects weren't good: 'the unresolved question of Kosovo's long-term status – the tensions between the majority Albanian and minority Serbian communities, and the hold of organised criminals over much of what there was of commercial life – deterred the inward investment that the territory still needs if it is to have any chance of picking itself up.'

Little of this seemed to concern Tony Blair, who was received as a conquering hero when he visited Kosovo. Having insisted throughout that this was not 'just a military conflict. It is a battle between good and evil; between civilisation and barbarity', he celebrated victory in the same terms: 'war can be necessary to uphold civilisation. Good has triumphed over evil. Justice has overcome barbarism. And the values of civilisation have prevailed.'

Such a frame of mind made it unlikely that lessons would be learned. While the conflict was still continuing, Blair made a significant and influential speech to the Economic Club of Chicago in which he outlined what he called 'a new doctrine of international community', based on the right, indeed the duty, of countries to wage war for moral and humanitarian reasons: 'Intervention to bring down a despotic dictatorial regime could be justified on grounds of the nature of that regime, not merely its immediate threat to our interests.' This was hazardous territory, offering a justification for the invasion of sovereign countries with no external or objective check on whether such action was appropriate. The one existing body that might have served in such a capacity was the UN, but that had already been bypassed in Kosovo, and its place taken by NATO.

Blair believed, he made clear, in 'the enforcement of liberal democracy', which couldn't help but sound like a contradiction in terms. And there were questions too about the practice of his doctrine. He rejected out of hand concerns about the lack of planning carried out with regard to the post-war settlement in Kosovo: 'Success is the only exit strategy I am prepared to consider.' It was a meaningless soundbite at best, downright dangerous at worst.

The key, though, was the set of five tests that Blair argued should be met before action was taken: 'Are we sure of our case?'; 'Have we exhausted all diplomatic options?'; 'Are there military operations we can sensibly and prudently undertake?'; 'Are we prepared for the long term?'; 'Do we have national interests involved?' These were the lessons he had learned from Kosovo, and they were the bases on which his future decisions should be judged.

Blair's doctrine of liberal intervention was to be tested over the next decade. For now, it provoked some discussion and much dissent. Alan Clark, who – for all his oddities and provocative posturing – was a distinguished military historian, wrote that 'a huge change of mood infects society and politics [which] has extended out of touchy-feely Diana-caring into a *correctness* that has become an orthodoxy. So that "human rights" can override all considerations of national sovereignty.' The political philosopher John Laughland elaborated on the same theme: 'Human rights are, by definition, antithetical to the concept of national sovereignty. The idea that there can be such a thing as universal human rights implies that there can be a single global system of civil law with NATO playing the role of world government.' This, he concluded, 'is not moral: it is megalomaniac'.

There was much in these reservations, but the first new engagement for British forces after Blair's speech was a rare case of unqualified success. Sierra Leone had been in a state of civil war since 1991, a terrible conflict in which 50,000 were killed, many more left with amputated limbs and up to two million made homeless, all of it the result of a struggle to control the country's vast diamond wealth. In 1997 the elected government of Ahmed Tejan Kabbah was overthrown by the main rebel group, the Revolutionary United Front (RUF), and although Kabbah was subsequently reinstated, following international intervention, the war continued.

Officially Britain had instituted sanctions that forbade the export of weapons to the country, though a moment of controversy came in April 1998 when it was revealed that arms had indeed been sent to Sierra Leone, for the use of Kabbah's forces, with the tacit support of the Foreign Office. For Robin Cook, who had harried the Tories during the arms-to-Iraq debate, this was deeply awkward, though this time there was less negative publicity, with Blair insisting that the intention 'was to help the democratic regime restore its position from an illegal military coup'. An inquiry into the arms dealing was instituted, but it was never likely to deliver a damning verdict when Blair had already made his position clear, even citing Sierra Leone as a fine example of an ethical foreign policy.

As the position in the country deteriorated, and the capital Freetown came under threat, British troops were sent to the country in May 2000 to support a struggling United Nations mission. The aim, recorded Lance Price, was 'ostensibly to secure the airport and help to evacuate British nationals, but in reality to do all they can to keep the rebels back from the capital'. Further reinforcements were added in what some feared was, in another new term of the decade, mission creep, an 'inexorable slide into ever worsening complications'.

Some military engagements were undertaken, most famously in August 2000 when eleven British soldiers were taken hostage by an armed group referred to in the British media as the West Side Boys (though, being fans of American rap star Tupac Shakur, they preferred to call themselves the West Side Niggaz), who were not part of the RUF but a gang of 'stoned bandits' operating independently. A rescue operation by British paratroopers and members of the SAS was entirely successful, with just one British fatality, in terms of both freeing the hostages and smashing the gang.

More important than any combat, though, was simply the presence of the British troops on the ground, backed by strong political involvement, which halted the progress of the RUF and inspired a more decisive commitment by the UN to work for a ceasefire. The war was officially declared to be at an end in January 2002, with Britain's involvement having proved decisive. There had been no reliance on aerial bombing, no attempt to sideline the UN, no talk of regime change. As an example of liberal intervention, the operation could hardly have been bettered.

During the course of these foreign adventures there was broad public support — as there generally is when British troops are sent into action — but they had no great impact on perceptions of the government or on life in Britain. Certainly they meant little compared to perhaps the single most significant development of the decade: the attempt to bring to an end the low-level war within Britain's own borders in Northern Ireland.

By the time John Major arrived in Downing Street at the end of 1990, the conflict had been raging for two decades and had resulted in the deaths of over three thousand people, mostly in Northern Ireland itself, but also spilling out into the rest of the United Kingdom. In terms of the mainland population's attitude, little had changed since the height of the Troubles in the mid-1970s. Neither the Republicans of the IRA and Sinn Fein, nor the loyalist majority enjoyed significant support, and there was scarcely more than a weary feeling of 'a plague on both their houses'. There was too a sense of distaste about the support in some American circles for republican terrorists, while the revelation in the early 1990s that campaigners had been right all along about the wrongful imprisonment of the Guildford Four and the Birmingham Six merely added the British state to the list of those who had failed.

It was noticeable, though, that those miscarriages of justice were hardly greeted by a wave of outrage in Britain; the film *In the Name of the Father* (1993), based on the account of Gerry Conlon, one of the Guildford Four, was better received in America, where it was nominated for seven Oscars, than at home, where it gained just two BAFTA nominations. Meanwhile the twenty-one people murdered by the IRA in the Birmingham pub bombings of 1974 seemed to have been forgotten; 'we asked for justice, but it never came,' as the Birmingham-born Lawrence sang on a Denim song in 1992.

Perhaps the most remarkable feature of the Troubles was one that attracted virtually no comment: the absence of widespread anti-Irish feeling on the streets of Britain. The far right attempted to stir up hatred, and in 1995 managed to grab headlines by disrupting a football match staged in Dublin between Ireland and England; after just twenty-seven minutes, the game was called off as a hail of missiles descended from the stands housing 2,000 England fans, accompanied by repeated choruses of 'No surrender to the IRA'. More generally, however, the National Front's slogan 'Hang IRA Scum!' found little or no support in a country fatigued by years of random atrocities.

The conflict had become a seemingly inescapable part of British life, a running sore that disfigured the nation with no hope of healing. Yet change was in the air. In 1990 the world had watched Nelson Mandela walk free from jail after twenty-seven years of incarceration, and the expectation was that South Africa was on the brink of abandoning apartheid, just as Eastern Europe had chosen to turn away from communism. If such progress could be made elsewhere, the possibility surely existed too in Northern Ireland.

In early 1991 Major and his Northern Ireland secretary, Peter Brooke, initiated a new series of talks with what were known as the 'constitutional' parties, i.e. those who didn't have an armed wing, but the process was soon derailed by a trivial incident of the kind that had blighted politics in the province so many times. Appearing as a guest on the Irish television programme, *The Late Late Show*, Brooke was prevailed upon by the presenter to deliver a song; with evident reluctance, he attempted a couple of verses of 'My Darling, Clementine', and promptly faced a chorus of calls for him to resign. It was, argued his detractors, in shockingly poor taste to be seen singing on television on the very day that seven people had been murdered by the Provisional Irish Republican Army (IRA), even if he had taken the opportunity of his appearance to denounce the bombing.

Despite this false start, the reality was dawning on all parties that the war had been fought to a standstill. Terrorists on both sides were still fully armed, despite twenty years of a British military presence, and were capable of continuing the fight, but the litany of deaths was bringing a solution no closer, and it was clear that the stalemate was merely delaying any possibility of a settlement. The weariness of the people of Northern Ireland, bludgeoned by the years of violence, was matched by the bemused impatience of those on the mainland, for whom the conflict was largely incomprehensible.

In February 1993 the IRA sent a secret message to the British government: 'The conflict is over but we need your advice on how to bring it to a close.' They pointed out that they couldn't announce a ceasefire publicly, since it would be interpreted as a surrender, but said they were prepared to give a private undertaking to that effect.

Wary of what this development actually meant, but determined to explore the possibilities it promised, Major began another series of talks, concentrating this time on dealing with Albert Reynolds, Taoiseach of the Irish Republic. Together the two men issued in December that year the Downing Street Declaration, which made explicit the right of the people of Northern Ireland to determine their own political future, enshrined the principle of mutual consent between the people of North and South as the only road to a settlement, and paved the way for parties associated with terrorism to become part of negotiations if they renounced violence. Nine months later, in August 1994, the IRA officially and publicly declared a unilateral ceasefire.

It was the most important breakthrough since the start of the Troubles in 1969, though a farcical element was not entirely lacking. The announcement of the ceasefire was broken to viewers of ITV in a banner headline running across the bottom of the screen during a broadcast of the film *Carry On Teacher*; unfortunately it happened to be at the precise moment when a bomb made by pupils in a chemistry class exploded underneath Ted Ray's desk.

The ceasefire was greeted by Tony Blair with a change of Labour policy. For years the party had argued for Ireland to be peacefully unified, but Blair – without consultation, in his usual fashion – overturned this, letting it be known that henceforth Labour would no longer seek to act as a 'persuader' towards unification. The IRA initiative also met with a response from the Combined Loyalist Military Command, the umbrella group of Protestant terrorist groups, who declared their own ceasefire just weeks later.

Unfortunately for John Major, he was by this stage such a damaged figure in the eyes of the public that he reaped no political benefit. The first opinion poll conducted in Britain revealed that people gave most credit for the ceasefire to John Hume, leader of the Social Democratic and Labour Party

(SDLP) in Northern Ireland, to Gerry Adams, leader of the IRA's political wing Sinn Fein, and to Albert Reynolds. Major trailed them in fourth place.

Nonetheless, he threw himself into an attempt to build on the initiative at considerable personal risk, for as a Conservative prime minister, he was undoubtedly a potential target. Over the years it had been the Tories, rather than Labour, who had been marked out for attack by the IRA; the MPs Airey Neave, Anthony Berry and Ian Gow were amongst those who had been murdered, while there had been assassination attempts on Edward Heath, Margaret Thatcher and even Major himself. Yet he seemed to derive pleasure from the task, perhaps finding an escape from the travails of Westminster. 'The cares of the world would fall from his shoulders on our many visits to Ulster,' remembered his press secretary, Christopher Meyer. 'To the consternation of police and security men, he plunged into crowds, Catholic and Protestant, and was greeted warmly by almost all. Here he was the bold statesman and natural-born politician.' There were echoes of Major's 1992 soapbox appearances, as he worked the crowds even on trips to such potentially dangerous places as the border town of Newry.

By authorising talks between British officials and Sinn Fein, he also put himself in considerable political danger. The Conservative Party had long relied on the assistance of the Ulster Unionists in the Westminster Parliament and, at a time when he was hanging on to power with such a meagre minority, Major risked a crucial loss of support by dealing – however remotely – with the likes of Gerry Adams, a man to whom the Unionist MP Ken Maginnis reportedly refused to speak, even some years later: 'I don't talk to fucking murderers.' And indeed Major did pay a price. In 1995 another Unionist MP, John Taylor, announced that his party's informal alliance with the Tories was over: 'It is finished. From here on in the government is in deep trouble.' The Unionists proceeded to oppose the government in a vote on the EU, though the government just survived since the usual Tory rebels (with the notable exception of Norman Lamont) decided this time not to abandon their own leadership.

Progress in the talks was painfully slow at best and faced obstructions from every direction. Major recorded one meeting with Ian Paisley and Peter Robinson of the Democratic Unionist Party (DUP) – an even less cooperative organisation than the Unionists – in which the two men sat chanting over and over in unison: 'The people of Northern Ireland alone. The people of Northern Ireland alone.' In a 1995 radio interview, John Bruton, who had succeeded Reynolds as Taoiseach, expressed his own impatience: 'I'm sick of answering questions about the fucking peace process.'

Nonetheless, the number of deaths fell that year to just nine, the lowest toll since the commencement of the conflict, and John Cole, the Belfast-born former political editor of the BBC, was cautiously optimistic about the government's policy. 'At worst, it has saved lives,' he wrote, 'and made the existences of ordinary people in Northern Ireland more tolerable. At best, peace becomes a habit which it is too difficult for either set of paramilitaries to break.' In February 1996, however, it was broken, when the IRA called off their ceasefire, blaming a lack of progress in the talks. A bomb in Canary Wharf, London, killed two people, and later that year an attack on Manchester, the biggest bomb detonated in mainland Britain since the war, injured over a hundred. In Northern Ireland, meanwhile, the annual march by the Portadown Orange Lodge — the route of which went through Catholic residential areas — descended into serious rioting. Clearly no further advance was likely before the forthcoming general election.

Although Major left office without achieving the settlement for which he had worked, he did leave a legacy on which his successor could build. The prospect of peace existed where it had previously been absent; all sides had — to varying degrees — shown a willingness to work for the future; and the assistance of America, in the shape of Bill Clinton, had been successfully solicited. The principle of consent had been established, and a genuinely bipartisan approach had been adopted by the Tories and Labour. Indeed it was one of the few areas in which Major could find anything positive to say about Tony Blair. 'I could not have asked for more consistent and honest backing,' he wrote, adding that, as prime minister, Blair had the benefit of a fresh start: 'he was also unencumbered by the baggage one collects in years of negotiation, and was therefore better able to show tactical flexibility.'

Blair had other advantages too. On a personal level, he managed to bridge the sectarian divide, with a grandfather who had been a Grand Master of an Orange Order lodge and a wife who was a Liverpudlian Catholic of Irish descent, while politically he was the recipient in Northern Ireland of the same wave of goodwill that had greeted him elsewhere in Britain. Within weeks of his election, the IRA ceasefire had been reinstated and a new body — the awkwardly named Independent International Commission on Decommissioning — had been set up to pursue the goal of putting terrorist weapons beyond use. In October 1997 he went a stage further than Major and met the Sinn Fein MPs Gerry Adams and Martin McGuinness. On a subsequent walkabout in a Protestant area, he was besieged by people waving rubber gloves at him, a symbol intended to suggest that he should have worn protective clothing when shaking hands with men of violence. Like Major, Blair threw himself wholeheartedly into the peace process, taking the risk that he might squander political capital on an enterprise that was far from guaranteed of success. 'I was putting my whole prime ministerial authority on the line for a deal,' he was later to write. Many of the characteristics that distinguished Major – a firm negotiating style combined with a desire to find common ground and an ability to make people feel that he was on their side – were shared by Blair and were nowhere employed more effectively than in Northern Ireland. Equally impressive were the contributions of some of his inner circle: Jonathan Powell proved a reassuring figure for Unionists, while Alastair Campbell's presence kept the local media on board.

And then there was Mo Mowlam, the new Northern Ireland secretary. During the general election campaign, she had faced some abusive reporting that centred on her weight (she was 'losing the battle of the bulge', jibed the *Daily Mail*) and had responded by going public with the fact that she had recently been diagnosed with a brain tumour; the treatment had included a course of steroids – hence the weight gain – and radiotherapy, the resultant hair loss meaning that Mowlam was obliged to wear a wig. The huge wave of public support that naturally followed her revelation carried over into her government appointment, and when she visited Belfast two days after the election, she was already being acclaimed by crowds as the human face of politics.

Her informal style – she would frequently take the wig off during meetings – and her direct language proved particularly successful in her dealings with Sinn Fein. 'I am not in favour of a British prime minister appointing a secretary of state for Northern Ireland,' commented Martin McGuinness, 'but Mo Mowlam must stay. She is really good.' She proved less popular with the Unionists. She was 'awful', said Ken Maginnis, 'she didn't understand'. Indeed it probably wasn't wise to tell Ian Paisley to 'fuck off', but she was articulating a sentiment that many millions of Britons had felt over the decades. Even so, she earned respect for her courage with an early visit to the Maze prison to talk to convicted terrorists from both sides of the divide, an initiative that paid dividends when the prisoners changed their position and came out in support of negotiations.

In April 1998 the various negotiating parties convened at Stormont Castle for what was hoped would be the final push to reach agreement on the future of the province. 'This is no time for soundbites,' Blair told the media, as he arrived. 'But I feel the hand of history on our shoulders.' Even he recognised how ridiculous those comments were, but they weren't entirely mistaken. Out of those talks, over the course of several days and nights, came the Belfast Agreement, signed on Good Friday, which laid out the terms on which Great Britain, Northern Ireland and the Republic of

Ireland would proceed to a lasting settlement, establishing the framework for the creation of a Northern Ireland Assembly and an executive that would be comprised of representatives from both communities. It was an extraordinary moment in British and Irish history, and moved even the most cynical. 'I felt really quite emotional,' Alastair Campbell wrote in his diary. 'I could see in some of the NI hacks too a real deep emotion, and a desire for this to be true. I actually felt like crying.' Many did.

It hadn't been a straightforward process, and absurdities continued to manifest themselves. At the last minute it seemed as though negotiations might break down on the issue of language. Irish Gaelic was to be recognised as an official minority language, but the Unionists then declared that they required equal provision for Ullans, sometimes known as Ulster Scots, a dialect that just 2 per cent of Ulster's population were said to speak. Perhaps it could all be included under the heading of Celtic languages, suggested Alastair Campbell, at which the Unionist leader, David Trimble, was outraged: 'Ullans is not a Celtic tongue.'

The Agreement had also to be ratified by referendums held on both sides of the border in 1998. While it was carried overwhelmingly in the South, some doubt remained about whether the Protestant community in the North would come out in support, particularly since there was dissent in Unionist ranks, with Ian Paisley's DUP refusing to have any part of the deal. Blair again demonstrated just how convincing a campaigner he could be, making several trips to the province, accompanied at various points by John Major and William Hague, that helped swing the vote so that both communities voted in favour.

To celebrate what Mowlam called 'a new period in Northern Ireland history and a new millennium', a concert was staged in the grounds of Stormont Castle by the newly knighted Elton John, New Labour's favourite rock star ever since the funeral of Diana. A crowd of 15,000 people, both Unionists and nationalists, came together in a spirit of hope that normality was returning to the province, though a small demonstration was staged outside by the DUP.

There were also some on the Catholic side who disagreed in principle with any negotiation with the British government, and in August 1998 a splinter group calling themselves the Real IRA exploded a bomb in Omagh that caused the greatest loss of life of any terrorist incident in the history of the Troubles. Twenty-nine people were killed and hundreds more injured, provoking such a wave of revulsion that, inadvertently, the attack actually assisted the peace process; some of the smaller terrorist groups took the opportunity to announce their own ceasefires.

The Omagh bombing also revealed the less statesmanlike side of New Labour. Parliament was hurriedly recalled and sat through the night to pass emergency anti-terrorism legislation that allowed the financial assets of terrorist groups to be seized. Membership of named terrorist organisations, specifically the Real IRA, the Continuity IRA, the Irish National Liberation Army and the Loyalist Volunteer Force, was made punishable by ten years' imprisonment; other terrorist groups, those who had signed up to the peace process, were not included. Some MPs and many in the House of Lords objected to the way that legislation was rushed through, without even any discussion in cabinet, noting that the original proposals had allowed for someone to be convicted of being a member of a prohibited group simply on the word of a senior police officer; this at least was amended in the actual legislation. David Blunkett's conclusion that 'making at least some gesture in respect of the horror of Omagh is politically understandable', merely illustrated the complaint already being widely aired that, for New Labour, legislation often seemed to be more about gestures than reality.

There was, however, a more worryingly illiberal attitude at work as well, which ran counter to the agenda of campaigners in organisations like Charter 88. With the reduced threat of terrorism originating in Northern Ireland, the existing emergency legislation was replaced in the Terrorism Act of 2000 by new permanent laws, which were more draconian than anything that had preceded them. The definition of terrorism was broadened to include damage caused to property 'for the purpose of advancing a political, religious or ideological cause', thereby ensuring that direct action as practised by, say, animal rights campaigners, hunt saboteurs or protestors against genetically modified crops was now officially classed as terrorism. The Act also extended the period of time that a suspect could be held without charge, gave the police substantial new powers to stop and search, and created a new offence of possession of information 'likely to be useful to a person committing or preparing an act of terrorism'. As Tony Benn pointed out: 'we are handing over the most repressive powers ever to a future government, which will say they were introduced by the Labour government.' More such laws were to be passed in the new century.

Meanwhile, Mo Mowlam was removed from her job in October 1999 to facilitate the return to cabinet of Peter Mandelson. He proved to be a strong replacement ('At least when we talk to Mandelson we know we're talking to Blair,' observed a senior Sinn Fein member), but his reappearance just ten months after his enforced resignation seemed a little hasty, and there was considerable disquiet at the whispering campaign against Mowlam that led up to, and continued beyond, her departure from the Northern Ireland office. She had become the most popular politician in the country and, whether rightly or wrongly, some in the Blair camp were believed to be motivated by petty jealousy. A brief attempt was made to parachute her in as Labour's mayoral candidate for London, once it became clear that Frank Dobson was no match for Livingstone, but she resisted the offer; it was 'a shitty job', she explained, and she had no intention of taking it. Instead she was hidden from view as the minister for the cabinet office.

'She is fed up with being bad-mouthed and done over and resents it bitterly,' noted Blunkett. 'She thinks it is because they want to cut her down to size and make sure that she doesn't become any sort of threat, but I think it's because there is a recognition that she is becoming more ill and less reliable by the day.' Even if he were right, Mowlam's treatment left a sour taste after the euphoria of the Good Friday Agreement.

The Agreement was not the end of the peace process by any measure, and the continued existence of IRA weaponry in particular remained a stumbling block to implementation of the deal. Nearly a decade passed before the power-sharing executive finally found a sustainable form, by which time it was headed by the unlikely alliance of Ian Paisley and Martin McGuinness. The divisions between the two communities, notably in the area of education, would take even longer to heal. But it was a remarkable achievement to have got so far at all, and to have created the conditions where normality might return. In 1998 the Nobel Peace Prize was awarded to two key architects of the Agreement, John Hume of the SDLP and David Trimble of the Ulster Unionist Party, for putting aside centuries-old differences. It was also a tribute to John Major and Tony Blair, both of whom could legitimately point to the peace process as their most significant political contribution to the nation. It had brought out the best in both men and each had helped to make history.

Unlike the other exercises in passing power from Westminster, this was embraced in a genuine spirit of decentralisation. It helped, of course, that the major Westminster parties were absent from the province, but more importantly, this was something that really mattered; the turnout in the Northern Ireland referendum was over 80 per cent, considerably higher than it had been in those held in Scotland, Wales or London. There truly was a sense of a new day dawning. 'People did things to each other and to themselves that now we can only look on with a sense of astonishment,' wrote Blair in his memoirs. 'For decades, such barbaric atavism defined Northern Ireland.' To have changed that was the high point of the 1990s.

16
Reality
'What I really really want'

Churchill got his lucky number, but tomorrow there's another.
Blur, 'It Could Be You' (1995)

The consorts, the lovers, the walkers, the alibis, the mistresses,
the toyboys. Famous, or famous for being famous, or famous for
fucking the famous, they were all there.
Terence Blacker, *The Fame Hotel* (1992)

Opinions are like arseholes – everyone's got one.
T-shirt slogan (c. 1991)

Ever since the 1970s, Saturday evening television had been dominated by the family-friendly fare offered by BBC One, and in 1994 the channel secured the rights to broadcast what was hoped would be a major addition to its portfolio: the weekly draw of the National Lottery. In November Noel Edmonds presented the first programme to great national excitement and an audience of nearly twenty-two million viewers. Unfortunately, no one became a millionaire that first week – the jackpot was shared between seven winners – and the viewing figures soon began to slide, largely because it made for very mundane television.

There was another reason why fewer people were watching the programme. The year after its launch, ITV fought back with the quiz show *Who Wants to Be a Millionaire?*, hosted by Chris Tarrant, which became a huge success, reaching a peak audience of nineteen million, leaving the Lottery far behind. Its simple but effective format was exported to dozens of countries, far beyond the usual markets of Europe and the Commonwealth, so that by the early years of the new century it was said to be the most popular television programme right across the Arab world. Perhaps the Lottery show might have done better in the battle for ratings if it had followed the advice of Elizabeth Peacock, the kind of Conservative MP who could teach

Tony Blair a thing or two about being tough on crime. 'Flogging criminals live on television before or after the National Lottery draw will create a great impact,' she argued. 'The punishment should be done in public as a humiliation and to show others what will happen to them, and the National Lottery has a big audience to reach.'

Even without the added attraction of corporal punishment, the Lottery itself was instantly adopted as part of British life. Some two-thirds of adults bought a ticket in any given week, the average weekly spend being £2.05 per head of population, slightly less than half the amount spent on cigarettes. This was despite the absurdly poor odds: 14 million to 1 against scooping the jackpot, 54 to 1 against winning anything at all. 'Someone told me a sobering fact,' remarked a character in Peter Lovesey's crime novel *Upon a Dark Night*. 'No matter who you are, what kind of life you lead, it's more likely you'll drop dead by eight o'clock Saturday night than win the big one. So I don't do it any more.' But Kenneth Baker, the home secretary who had launched the Lottery white paper in 1992, had suggested that it was 'a chance for the government to introduce a little gaiety into British life', and that aspiration at least was realised.

There were those who objected to the creation of the Lottery. Some had a vested interest in other forms of gambling that were bound to suffer, particularly the pools companies; Littlewoods curtailed its donations to the Conservative Party in protest, while Vernons reported an instant fall of 15 per cent in revenue. Others were concerned that charitable giving would be similarly hurt, a charge airily dismissed by the government. However, early findings suggested that discretionary donations to charity fell in 1995 and, although compensation came from the Lottery, so that the average household contribution remained unchanged from the previous year, the impact of having an additional layer of bureaucracy meant that actual spending was delayed. More significant was the existence of that bureaucracy, representing a transfer of power from individuals to the quango of the National Lottery Charities Board. This combined with a trend towards charities receiving cash directly from central and local government; Barnardo's, for example, was by the middle of the decade reliant on the state for around 47 per cent of its income. By the end of the decade, the entire charitable sector had been transformed, almost beyond recognition.

There was a further concern that the state's endorsement of gambling might prove detrimental to society. John Major, a keen enthusiast for the Lottery, argued that this complaint was misplaced and that a little flutter was a quite separate thing from serious betting; with such long odds, the game was 'unlikely to attract the serious gambler'. That, however, somewhat missed the point. The number of people placing bets rose sharply as a result of the game's introduction, and amongst the newcomers were some who became addicted to gambling, particularly after the launch of Lottery scratchcards provided an immediate thrill in the long days between draws.

Research published in 1998 showed that half of all children aged between twelve and fifteen had bought a scratchcard, despite being under the legal age to do so, and one report predicted that 'within ten years gambling will be a bigger youth problem than drugs'. A suggestion by Camelot, the company running the Lottery, that it might have a draw every day was rejected by the regulator on the grounds that this would encourage excessive gambling, but some felt that the damage had already been done. By normalising the idea of betting, the Lottery had instilled in the nation a habit that would inevitably result in increasing numbers of addicts. Meanwhile spread betting was starting to become popular, and the first online casinos were being launched, promising a wild new frontier. By the end of the 1990s, spending on gambling had outstripped that on beer and wine, and nine-tenths of the population were placing bets, even if only occasionally, up from two-thirds at the start of the decade.

A less obvious consequence was remarked upon by Mervyn King, the chief economist of the Bank of England (and later its governor), who claimed in 1995 that the Lottery had 'taken money out of the economy and is one of the reasons for the lack of a "feel-good" factor'. Such a belief was, of necessity, impossible to verify, let alone quantify, but an economist with HSBC Greenwell estimated that 'between £250 million and £750 million worth of lottery spending would appear to have been diverted from retail spending' as a consequence of that first full year of operation.

The defence of the Lottery, its justification as a social enterprise, was the money that it raised for what were always called 'good causes'. When the idea of a lottery had first been floated in the late 1970s, by a royal commission on gambling chaired by Victor Rothschild, it was in response to a financial crisis that was hitting arts spending hard, and the suggestion was that this was the easiest way of raising money for endeavours that required subsidy. By the time the commission's report was published, however, the government of James Callaghan was in its dying days, and its successor was disinclined to follow up the recommendations. Margaret Thatcher did look at the idea of an NHS lottery but rejected it with Methodist distaste: 'I did not think that the government should encourage more gambling.'

With the arrival in office of John Major, the report was dusted off and swiftly put into practice, though the originally proposed recipients of the proceeds were expanded from the arts, heritage and sport to include charities and, an element that no one fully comprehended, a so-called Millennium Fund. These would receive 28 per cent of the money collected by Camelot, shared equally between the five areas of interest.

Since most of this money was to be distributed through various quangos, including the Arts Councils and the National Heritage Memorial Fund (the latter chaired by Jacob Rothschild, son of Victor), it didn't take long to work out that there was a curious transfer of wealth in play here. The guaranteed winners were always going to be the government, which taxed the sale of tickets, and Camelot itself, as the singer Eddi Reader cheekily made clear when she was invited to start the draw: 'It could be you. It's definitely Camelot!' But given the way the 'good causes' were structured, the other winners would now include those cultural institutions much favoured by the great and the good.

'In public spending,' explained David Mellor, when taking the legislation through Parliament, 'one cannot expect the restoration of the Royal Opera House or the construction of a new opera house in Cardiff to take priority over the legitimate demands of the health service, and that is why the lottery was created.' He also admitted that charities had only been included in the list of beneficiaries at a late stage, in an attempt to forestall claims that charitable giving would be hit by the Lottery. No one suggested that the people who actually played the Lottery might be given a say in how the proceeds were to be distributed.

If the recipients of the Lottery's largesse were most likely to be those with sufficiently rarefied tastes in music, art and dance to appreciate the finer things in life, the contributions were disproportionately made by the working class, both in terms of actual amounts spent and, even more markedly, as a share of household income. A greater percentage of those in socio-economic classes C2, D and E bought tickets than those in classes A and B, and they bought more of them. As Julian Critchley summed up the arrangement: 'The working class and the underclass are encouraged to spend in pursuit of unimaginable riches. The money raised is then spent on a series of middle-class good causes.'

This process didn't always run smoothly. The first big purchase from the heritage monies was the acquisition for the nation of Winston Churchill's papers in April 1995. It was supposed to be a populist gesture, evoking the memory of the great wartime leader in the run-up to the VE Day anniversary, but when it was discovered that the Churchill family was being paid £13 million out of the pot for 'good causes', there was a public outcry. It didn't help that one of those cashing in was Churchill's grandson, himself a Tory MP. NEVER HAS SO MUCH BEEN PAID BY SO MANY TO SO FEW was the *Daily Mirror*'s scathing headline, while the *Independent* called it a 'startling redistribution of wealth from ordinary working people to leading Conservatives'. Following on from the £55 million donated to the Royal Opera House – where a ticket to see Luciano Pavarotti that year cost £267 – the publicity was appalling. 'The lottery is our only hope. The working classes need hope,' a Glaswegian woman told Nick Danziger, but she resented the consequences of her weekly flutter. 'I'm not spending me money on lottery when they're giving £58 million to opera, to the fucking toffs. I'll pay for half a ticket, and I begrudge even that.'

Thereafter a major effort was made to improve the presentational side of the Lottery's awards, with a much greater focus on promoting small community projects, even if, in reality, these received only a small proportion of the sums being made available. Further rehabilitation came with the incoming Labour government's pledge to redirect some of the grants towards health and education, which was broadly welcomed by the public, though it was sometimes seen as merely a sticking plaster. Hope Park, the school in the television drama series *Hope and Glory*, had a beautifully equipped music room, thanks to Lottery funding, but no music teacher.

A major factor in the Lottery's continuing success was the enthusiasm with which the tabloid press greeted big winners who agreed to have their names made public. This ready supply of good-luck stories helped to plug a gap that had been growing ever since the arrival on British news-stands of *Hello!* magazine in 1988 had outflanked the established print media, by offering uncritical attention and vast sums of money to those celebrities featured in exchange for exclusive coverage. Such offers were not restricted to international stars; in 1999 it was reported that James Major, son of the former prime minister, had sold to *Hello!* the photographic rights of his wedding to the model Emma Noble for a sum of £400,000. Unable to match such largesse, the tabloids struggled along with celebrities of ever greater triviality: footballers, soap actors, members of boy bands and girl groups, and pretty much anyone who'd been on British television yet wasn't big enough to command a serious fee.

The diminishing returns of this culture were illustrated in 1997 when ITV's show *The Cook Report* decided to investigate corruption in the pop charts, a practice so long established that as far back as 1964 Brian Epstein, the manager of the Beatles, had felt obliged to deny rumours that he'd hyped the group's first single into the top twenty. To illustrate the sharp practices involved, *The Cook Report* set out to make a star of one of its researchers, 22-year-old Debbie Currie, whose mother Edwina was then fighting a doomed campaign to save her South Derbyshire seat. Debbie was given a remake of 'You Can Do Magic' (a 1973 hit for Limmie and the Family Cookin'), with vocals donated by erstwhile pop star Sinitta and production by Mike Stock of the Stock, Aitken and Waterman hit factory, and sent out to sell the record.

As an exercise in investigative journalism it looked a bit excessive — 'the costs were huge,' admitted the programme's producer, David Warren — and was entirely undermined by the fact that awareness of the operation circulated in the music industry from an early stage. As an illustration of the media's desperate desire for off-the-peg celebrities, however, it could hardly have been bettered. Currie was great copy, a Lycra-clad flirt 'boasting of four-in-a-bed romps' and proclaiming her intention of being 'Sexy Spice'. In the days before the single's release, she notched up forty-seven press interviews, twenty-six radio interviews and fifteen television appearances. She was also seen doing spots in sixty-two nightclubs, five festivals and one football match. The record may have sold only 400 copies, and might have stalled at number eighty-six in the charts, but briefly Debbie Currie was indeed a media star.

Almost as unsuccessful was the attempt to turn the supermodel Naomi Campbell into a pop star. In 1994 a novel titled *Swan* was published under her name, though it was doubtful how much she had contributed to the enterprise. (In *Drop the Dead Donkey*, Sally is horrified to find bad language in her own novel: 'I knew I should have read it before it went to the publishers.') To accompany the book came a single, a remake of T. Rex's classic 'Ride a White Swan', which was promoted on *Top of the Pops* but still failed to get any further than number forty, while its accompanying album *Babywoman* (1994) sold just 240 copies in its first week. It seemed that there was a limit to the British public's appetite for shoddy goods, however celebrated the purveyor.

To promote the themed book and single, Campbell took to wearing a dress intended to evoke the natural beauty of a swan. And at a press conference to launch the products, the comedian Paul Kaye, in his guise as Dennis Pennis, put to her one of his finest lines: 'Hey Naomi, how come you're dressed like a duck?'

Kaye's character was designed as an irritant. 'In a country which is largely governed by the celebrity party, I am the voice of opposition,' Pennis explained on his television show, as he went about cheeking anyone he could find at publicity launches and premieres, from Joan Collins at the Venice Film Festival ('You look like a million lire') to Michael Howard ('If you reintroduce capital punishment, will that just affect London?'). He was not the only one purveying this kind of prank television, adapting the format of *Candid Camera* and *Beadle's About* to trick public figures into making fools of themselves. Other comics providing variations on this comedy of dramatic irony included Mark Thomas, Mrs Merton (initially, at least) and, towards the end of the decade, Sacha Baron Cohen, whose characters Ali G, Brüno and Borat all went on to star in their own movies.

The practice began, as did so much else, with *The Day Today*, where Chris Morris would interview, for example, the sometimes pompous Labour MP Paul Boateng and induce him to comment on a fictitious rap star: 'Herman the Tosser is not someone who has invaded my own particular consciousness.' In his own series, *Brass Eye* (1997), Morris took this to extraordinary lengths, persuading dozens of minor celebrities to support made-up campaigns to protect a Sri Lankan village from the effects of heavy electricity, to save an elephant in a German zoo which has its trunk stuck in its rectum, to thunder against a musical based on the Yorkshire Ripper, and to lead a fight against a new drug named 'cake'. On this latter subject, Bernard Manning had the best lines to read ('One young kiddie on cake cried all the water out of his body. Just imagine how his mother felt. It's a fucking disgrace'), while the MP David Amess was prevailed upon to ask a question in the Commons about the fictitious drug.

If ultimately all that the tactic revealed was the willingness of the mildly famous to do absolutely anything that might keep them in the public eye, it did along the way result in some wonderfully absurd imagery, such as the former TV-am weather girl Tania Bryer delivering a nonsensical voice-over as though she understood what she was saying: 'This is footage of the river Euphrates flowing backwards. It looks like it's flowing forwards but only because we've reversed the film. Heavy water deeply confuses river flow systems. Just last month two rivers got completely lost and were found wandering uselessly about the southern oceans.'

The main point of *Brass Eye*, though, was to satirise and deconstruct the clichéd conventions of current affairs shows in the same way that *The Day Today* had tackled television news. A black studio guest would be captioned as 'Representing every single black person in Britain', and Morris would turn portentously to the camera after a film report to announce: 'The situation is clearly grave enough to merit a black-and-white freeze frame.'

Much of the best television comedy of the decade was similarly rooted in playing with the medium itself, from *Drop the Dead Donkey* and Stephen

Fry's investigative journalist in *This Is David Lander*, through Vic Reeves and Bob Mortimer's triumphant parody of a game show in *Shooting Stars*, to the obscure targets of some of *The Fast Show*'s best-known sketches: Country Matters, Jazz Club and Channel 9. Television was also at the heart of much of the era's post-alternative stand-up. 'I tell you what my comedy is,' observed Eddie Izzard. 'It's pop culture stand-up. It's all television. All the stuff I talk about, history, whatever, it's from the History Channel, the Discovery Channel. It's all from television.' For a generation that had never known a home without a television set, had grown up watching the world through a screen in the corner of the room, the media had become the unifying culture.

Much of this comedy was essentially a warm embrace of television, particularly that of the recent past. *Brass Eye*, on the other hand, displayed a rage against the medium that could be genuinely disturbing. The programme's peak came with the 2001 special 'Paedogeddon', which confronted the greatest of all tabloid subjects, and was broadcast at a particularly sensitive time.

In the summer of 2000 an eight-year-old Sussex girl named Sarah Payne had been abducted and murdered and, in response, the *News of the World*, under its editor Rebekah Wade, began a campaign to allow public access to the Sex Offenders Register, so that the identity and whereabouts of paedophiles released from jail could be known. The paper published an initial batch of the names and locations of forty-nine such offenders and announced that it would continue doing so until it had got through the entire list. This was clearly an implausible undertaking – there were 110,000 convicted paedophiles in the country and, at the rate the *News of the World* was going, it would take over forty years to identify them all – but although it was soon abandoned, in the interim the disclosure did considerable damage.

A wave of vigilante attacks took place, particularly on the Paulsgrove estate in Plymouth, and several people who happened to share names with those in the paper were attacked. *Private Eye* ran a cartoon of a man running from a mob, protesting that he was a paediatrician not a paedophile, but fiction was becoming increasingly difficult to separate from fact; the following week a paediatrician in South Wales woke to find that the word 'paedo' had been painted on the front of her house.

With such hysteria fresh in the memory, it wasn't surprising that *Brass Eye*'s treatment of the subject attracted enormous hostility. Morris parodied pop music's longstanding interest in underage sex with a 1970s glitter pop band singing 'Playground Bang-a-Round' and a white rapper, JLB-8, singing 'Little White Butt' (based on the old Tommy Steele song 'Little White Bull').

He mocked campaigners whose definitions of abuse stretched beyond the credible ('Today the number of children having sex with adults is beyond belief; if you define a child as anyone under thirty, the figure is over 86 per cent'). And he pinned the prurience of the media, introducing a case study with the words: 'We believe his story is actually too upsetting to transmit. We only do so tonight with that proviso.' He ended with a reassuring word of advice to the viewer: 'Look, if a child does take your fancy, please remember: leave it a couple of years.'

In response to the broadcast, Channel 4 received bomb threats, Scotland Yard said they were considering an investigation on grounds of obscenity, and politicians queued up to voice their thoughts. Blunkett, now the home secretary, was on holiday and unfortunately missed the show but, having been told about it, decided that he 'did not find it remotely funny'; Home Office minister Beverly Hughes said it was 'unspeakably sick', though it turned out she hadn't seen it either; and culture secretary Tessa Jowell suggested that regulations might be changed to prevent such programmes being repeated.

Press reaction was confused. The *Daily Mail* said it was 'the sickest TV show ever', but still found room in its pages for photographs of the Duchess of York's children, Beatrice (aged thirteen) and Eugenie (eleven), wearing bikinis, while the *Star* put one of its denunciations next to a photograph of fifteen-year-old Charlotte Church, and expressed its admiration of her figure as 'looking chest swell'. Even those who might normally defend Morris were in condemnatory mood. It was 'a deeply unpleasant piece of television that degraded children', editorialised the *Guardian*. And in the midst of the controversy, the public figures duped into taking part were understandably furious, including the MPs Gerald Howarth and Syd Rapson, as well as Phil Collins, Gary Lineker and the radio disc jockey Dr Fox, the latter having proved eager to tell us: 'Genetically paedophiles have more genes in common with crabs than they do with you and me. Now that is scientific fact. There's no real evidence for it but it is scientific fact.'

Nearly a decade on from *The Day Today*, that episode of *Brass Eye* had taken provocation as far as anyone would be permitted in the foreseeable future. It represented the culmination of a style of comedy that had nowhere else left to go. The assault on the media's acquiescence in the cult of celebrity had been relentless, but had proved difficult to sustain. Indeed the blurring of the lines between current affairs and celebrity trivia had arguably been exposed most convincingly not by Chris Morris but by ITN's main news programme, *News at Ten*, which during the 1998 football World Cup, had opened a bulletin with the words: 'The main news tonight is David

Beckham's apology for being sent off against Argentina last night.' It was hard to know quite what satire could add to such a statement.

The need for cut-price celebrities remained, but in the wake of the television pranksters, such figures were now required also to develop a reputation as good sports or for having no sense of dignity. When Neil Hamilton was removed from the House of Commons by his constituents in 1997, he and his wife, Christine, promptly appeared as a double-act on *Have I Got News for You* — where they were handed their fee by Angus Deayton in a brown envelope — and embarked upon a media career that relied entirely on their lack of any discernible sense of shame. Every media appearance seemed to involve the heaping of humiliation upon them, and they cheerfully went along with the game, giving every impression of being a 'macabre pair of attention-seeking mutants', in the words of Andy Hamilton.

There were still plenty of news stories to be wrung from celebrities, but newspapers also required a more reliable source of human interest tales. Which is where the Lottery proved so useful, by suggesting that ordinary folk who had got lucky might be of interest to readers.

There was a precedent for such stories. The acquisition of sudden wealth by members of the working class had long been the stuff of fiction, from Gillian Freeman's 1959 novel *Jack Would Be a Gentleman* to the 1960s American sitcom *The Beverly Hillbillies*. Real life had added the Yorkshire housewife Viv Nicholson, who won the football pools in 1961 and announced that she intended to 'spend, spend, spend', before doing just that and ending up penniless. Now the Lottery promised such human life dramas on a regular, possibly even a weekly, basis. In this context, it was no great surprise that a musical based on Nicholson's life — titled *Spend Spend Spend* and starring Barbara Dickson — proved a hit with critics and audiences alike when it opened in 1998. (The theme of a working-class couple winning the Lottery itself was the subject of John Godber's play *Lucky Sods*, which opened in 1995.)

Around the same time as the Lottery came a quieter development whose impact took longer to become evident. The series *Sylvania Waters*, a co-production by the Australian Broadcasting Corporation and the BBC, debuted on British television in 1993, and depicted the lives of a newly rich couple in the eponymous upmarket suburb of Sydney. Though little more than a cult success, it did suggest that the fly-on-the-wall documentary — which had hitherto been obliged to justify its existence by claiming sociological worthiness — might now be permitted purely as voyeuristic entertainment. A host of other shows followed in the middle of the decade, including most notably *Airport* (1996), *The Cruise* (1997) and *Driving School*

(1997). Each of the three brought tabloid fame to one of their participants. Aeroflot employee Jeremy Spake went on to become a television presenter; cruise singer Jane McDonald achieved a number one album and a presenting career; and inept learner driver Maureen Rees bizarrely managed to have a minor hit single, with a cover of Madness's 'Driving in My Car'. By now such shows had been rebranded as docusoaps, an awkward coinage that nonetheless gave an accurate description of their content.

Alongside them came the genre of makeover shows. Interior decor had become a fashionable subject for magazines in the 1980s, with *Interiors* (later retitled *World of Interiors*) followed by the likes of *Country Homes & Interiors* and *Elle Decoration*, but only when the interest was applied to more humble homes did programme-makers consider it suitable for television. *Changing Rooms* (1996) was the most durable format, making stars of designer Lawrence Llewelyn-Bowen and carpenter 'Handy' Andy Kane as it brought together two couples to redecorate a room in each other's houses. The appeal was partly that of seeing into other people's homes, and partly the joy of the occasional catastrophe, when someone would express their distress about what had been done to their living room. The formula was then applied externally with *Ground Force* (1997), a series based on the improbable notion that a garden could be created in two days, and which introduced television viewers to the braless charms of Charlie Dimmock.

Somewhere in the mix too was the oddity that was *Stars in Their Eyes*, in which members of the public were given the right to appear on television, but only by imitating existing stars. Essentially an evening of tribute bands crossed with a grand karaoke competition, aided by professional make-up and costumes, it became for some a passport to a career. When the group Hot Chocolate needed a replacement for their singer Errol Brown, who had left for a solo career, they recruited Greg Bannis from the show. 'We got him from *Stars in Their Eyes*,' said guitarist Harvey Hinsley. 'He was copying Errol, doing "You Sexy Thing", and he was exactly like Errol.' Perhaps too there was a connection to be made with the rise of the concept that stardom could be taught, with the opening of the Brit School in Croydon – sponsored by the British Record Industry Trust – and then the Liverpool Institute for Performing Arts. The impact of such academies was to become evident in the charts and on television in the following decade, producing artists as diverse as Amy Winehouse, the Kooks and Leona Lewis, as well as a substantial number of cast members in various television soaps.

In a separate, but related, development came the popularisation of the camcorder. The television series *You've Been Framed* (1990) encouraged viewers to send in humorous home videos, and was followed by the likes of *Neighbours from Hell* (1997), which itself span off into other themed shows, including weddings and holidays. The BBC, taking a more high-minded approach, launched *Video Diaries* (1990), in which people were given a camera to record themselves talking about their everyday lives. The format was adopted in other areas, including an advertising campaign for Superdrug in 1996, and a programme in which Amanda Platell documented the Conservatives' 2001 election campaign, displaying little apparent interest in loyalty to the party that employed her. Meanwhile comedians Steve Punt and Hugh Dennis gave us the video diary of Samuel Pepys from 1665. More significant was the trend to include amateur footage in news programmes, a process mocked as 'genutainment' by *The Day Today*. 'Real events shot by chance on amateur cameras are increasingly putting real news crews out of business,' announced Chris Morris, before introducing a segment titled 'It's Your Blood'. By the end of the decade, television channels were actively seeking such material.

All these strands – the docusoap, the makeover show, the video diary – were rooted in the idea that the lives of ordinary people could be made interesting for the public, a belief that led inexorably to reality television. The arrival in the summer of 2000 of *Big Brother*, a format developed in Holland, saw ten previously unknown people – all but one in their twenties – locked up in a house together for sixty-four days and nights, while viewers progressively voted for their eviction, one a week. When just three contestants were left, viewers voted for their favourite, who received a prize of £70,000. They were given tasks to perform, but this was not a game show, more a popularity contest, combined with twenty-four-hour video surveillance. It turned into Channel 4's greatest ratings winner, with a final-night audience of ten million and nearly eight million votes cast, although by that point the best-known contestant, 'Nasty' Nick Bateman, had already been evicted for cheating and lying. The story was covered even in the *Financial Times*.

'It is a shocking truth,' wrote Charles Kennedy; 'more people have voted in recent *Big Brother* polls than voted in the European elections.' That wasn't quite true, since it assumed that every vote cast over the course of the show's nine-week run came from a different person, and the final night's tally was still two million short of the turnout for the 1999 European Parliament election, but something was stirring here, and it demanded attention. As voting in elections declined, the opportunity to be consulted in the field of light entertainment was growing enormously. There was some anguish over what this might mean, particularly when *Big Brother* spawned dozens of sequels and imitators over the next few years.

These reality shows, as they became known, were joined in 2001 by *Popstars* and *Pop Idol*, essentially old-fashioned talent contests which brought at least temporary fame to the group Hear'Say in the former, and to Will Young and Gareth Gates in the latter. Again huge voting figures were recorded, as the public revelled in its chance to choose its own stars even before their careers had started. There was nothing new about the concept, which relied on telephone voting, just as had Bob Monkhouse's *Bob Says Opportunity Knocks* in the 1980s, except for the noise and the hype attached to them. *New Faces* and *Opportunity Knocks* had never been able to command newspaper front pages. Nor had the contestants' life stories mattered in the same way, for now talent was no longer the sole criterion on which they were judged; to be successful on such a show required also a tale of overcoming obstacles and hardship in pursuit of a dream.

And meanwhile there was the steady, inexorable rise of the internet, with its promise of ever greater democracy in culture. 'Whether or not we want it,' wrote the journalist and musician Emer Brizzolara in 1995, 'we are going to have access to the words and music and art of Joe and Janet Average.' These were still early days, when CompuServe, then the leading internet service provider in Britain, was pleased to be registering 1,500 new customers a week, but already the new technology's potential use as a marketing tool was becoming clear. The American record company Capitol had shown the way forward when it set up a site to promote the album *Youthanasia* by Megadeth a month before its release in November 1994. The site attracted a million hits and enabled the album to enter the US charts in the top five, an unusual achievement for a heavy metal band, since the opportunities for exposure in the conventional media were so limited.

Many expressed scepticism about how important this new medium really was, some of them recalling the words of the great American philosopher Henry David Thoreau in the 1850s. 'We are in great haste to construct a magnetic telegraph from Maine to Texas,' he wrote; 'but Maine and Texas, it may be, have nothing important to communicate.' Others, however, were enthusiastic from an early stage. In particular, minorities who felt excluded from mainstream broadcasting found that the internet offered a means of direct communication.

In 1998 the former professional wrestler Jesse 'The Body' Ventura was elected as the governor of Minnesota for the Reform Party, using the net as a major campaigning tool. His victory was not matched by anything comparable in Britain, but there were opportunities to bypass the conventional media. 'The BNP's cyberspace audience is now far larger than the readership of all our printed publications combined,' excitedly reported the British National Party in 1999. 'In terms of reach and impact, our internet operation has already far exceeded the highest hopes with which it was launched three years ago. And the best is undoubtedly yet to come.' By that stage, eight million people in Britain had access to the internet, more than in any other European country.

Perhaps the first British politician to become an advocate for the medium was John Redwood. In April 1995, while still Welsh secretary, he announced plans to connect all primary schools in Wales to the net, recognising that this was the future: 'Our children have no doubt. They are dancing to the tune of cyberspace enthusiastically.' A few months later, Tony Blair unveiled a proposal to do the same for schools throughout the United Kingdom, should Labour be elected. All parties became increasingly keen to lay claim to what was then routinely described as the information superhighway, though — just as the Coronation in 1953 and the marriage of Charles and Diana in 1981 had given huge boosts to television and video recorders respectively — the biggest single spur was again a royal story. The BBC had covered the 1997 election online, but it was with Diana's death that the corporation really became aware of the possibilities; within weeks it had announced that it was setting up a full online news service, which rapidly became the most visited British site.

Part of the appeal for politicians was the dynamic that the internet seemed to offer for the economy, opening a space for entrepreneurs and small businesses to establish themselves, at a time when the tendency was towards ever larger companies. Once, the phrase 'working online' had referred to the production line of a factory; now, in a period of prosperity and affluence, internet start-ups were the new pioneers of capitalism, attracting absurd valuations and inflated share prices on the world's stock markets in what *Private Eye* derided as SouthSeaBubble.com. It was unsustainable and, in March 2000, the bubble duly burst. The internet itself, however, continued to grow, its full impact as yet unknown in the fields of either politics or commerce. It was uncertain, for example, whether Britain would be attracted to the concept of buying goods off a screen; it had taken the American television shopping channel QVC five years to turn a profit after its 1993 launch in the UK, and the short-term prospects of internet shopping were far from rosy. Amazon, one of the genuine successes, was sufficiently realistic that when it launched in 1995 (its British branch followed in 1998), it made clear its expectation that no profit would be recorded for several years.

Instead, as Brizzolara predicted, the real appeal of the net in those earliest days was the chance it gave everyone to have a voice, whether to promote their own work or simply to express their opinions. The latter function had previously been filled primarily by radio phone-in shows, which had started in 1968 with the first BBC local radio stations and had since grown relentlessly, taking a firm hold in the mid-1990s. BBC Radio 5, launched in 1990 as an awkwardly hybrid speech station, offering children's and educational programmes as well as news and sport, was reformatted in 1994 as Radio 5 Live, with a much stronger phone-in element to its daytime magazine shows.

The following year Talk Radio UK, the first commercial national speech station, was launched, promising to bring the American tradition of controversial shock-jock broadcasting to Britain, though the fact that its presenters included Dale Winton and Simon Bates suggested that it wouldn't be quite as confrontational as that implied. For a couple of years it specialised in phone-in shows on current news topics hosted by the likes of Terry Christian, David Starkey, Peter Hitchens and Chris 'Caesar the Geezer' Rogers, before being bought up and rebranded as Talksport in 2000. Meanwhile Radio 4's *Any Answers*, which had previously relied on letters written by listeners in response to what they had heard on *Any Questions*, was changed to become a phone-in show.

'Opinion-making is this country's most virulent growth industry,' the playwright John Osborne raged in 1993. 'Phone-ins proliferate, choked with calls from the semi-literate, bigoted and barmy.' Osborne died the following year, but it's probably safe to assume that he wouldn't have much approved of the internet, which at times resembled a giant phone-in show, without the selection process or the mediation of a host. Frequently ill-informed, inaccurate and intemperate, it nonetheless had a vitality and energy that many found irresistible.

And it was in tune with trends in the media, for in the 1990s the balance seemed to shift decisively towards the first half of C.P. Scott's famous formulation 'comment is free, but facts are sacred'. As novelist Christopher Brookmyre put it: 'The success of popular reporting since the eighties had lain in the practice of massively increasing the ration of column inches to facts. Facts were both expensive and time-consuming to procure, so you had to use them as sparingly as possible.'

There had long been columnists whose stock-in-trade was commentary on events rather than straight reportage, but the slow withering of the print media was accompanied by a rise in the perceived value of star writers. Considered capable of building loyal fan bases, the likes of Richard Littlejohn, Suzanne Moore, Garry Bushell and Tony Parsons were transferred between titles in the manner of professional footballers. Bushell and Parsons had come from the opinionated world of the late-1970s music press, as had Julie Burchill, Parsons's erstwhile wife, who moved, in her own account, 'from enfant terrible to grande dame, with nothing in between'. Her writing epitomised the best and worst of the genre, capable of entertaining and irritating at the same time, and couched in a flashy, gimmicky style that frequently spilled over into self-parody. There was also a tendency to play fast and loose with evidence when an argument needed bolstering, with mixed results. Burchill's denunciation of John Lennon – 'the tosser was at art school in the early '50s' – didn't quite tally with the fact that the future Beatle didn't leave secondary school until 1957, and her suggestion that George Orwell, who died in 1950, was 'working for the CIA all through the '50s' was no more convincing.

The internet was not noticeably more conscientious when it came to checking facts. On the other hand, it had no obligation to be so, and no editors and sub-editors to keep it on the straight and narrow. 'The internet is a subversive, anarchic, individualistic arena,' wrote Ed Vaizey, another future Conservative MP who worked in public relations and journalism before becoming a political adviser. 'It is a fundamentally Tory medium, promoting freedom, individual choice, and reducing the role of state bureaucracy to a minimum.'

That inherent conflict between the net and the state would come to be one of the world's great political issues in the new century, and – as might have been predicted – in Britain it was to start with scares over pornography. 'The internet is effectively the end of censorship,' enthused one entrepreneur in 1998. 'It is impossible to police, because there are millions of sex sites, with probably new ones starting up every few hours.' To which there came the inevitable calls for control. 'We must find a way to regulate it,' demanded Conservative MP Andrew Rowe, warning about the dangers of 'international arms or drug dealers, or those peddling pornography and encouraging paedophile rings'.

When, in 1995, Elizabeth Coldwell had written in *Forum* about the impact of computer technologies on the sex industry, she had focused on CD-ROMs and had concluded that, by comparison, 'the internet is exciting, but it's not particularly sexy'. Just three years later, however, it was being estimated that around three-quarters of all internet searches were in pursuit of pornography. Since most of the sites were located abroad, there was little that British legislators could do, though a start was made with the Criminal Justice Act of 1994 which extended the offence of possessing indecent photographs of children to computer images, including those held on a hard drive after accessing them on the internet. A decade later, this was further extended to include the possession of 'extreme pornographic images' which were 'grossly offensive, disgusting or otherwise of an obscene character'.

Meanwhile, since America was leading the way in cyber-porn, there was a rise in American imagery and a shift in international taste. At the beginning of the 1990s the existence of a British magazine called *Shaven Ravers* indicated the daring novelty of pubic shaving; by the end of the decade, the practice had become the norm in pornography and increasingly commonplace among the general public.

There was, however, a British reaction to the shaved, pneumatic imports. This built on what was known as the white-panty subgenre, a trend towards amateur models evident in magazines such as *New Talent* and *Amateur Video* – the latter came with a videotape cover-mount – which featured the middle-aged ('old and bold') as well as the 'young and fresh'. A spate of magazines such as *40 Plus* similarly focused on older models, while MIA Video gave us the character Ben Dover ('the randy-cam reporter'), who helmed a series of pornographic videos with amateurs.

The internet was the obvious home for such material, the perfect vehicle for specialist tastes. It also allowed the spread of information about the practice of dogging – meeting in laybys for sexual encounters with strangers – which became a heterosexual equivalent to the time-honoured gay customs of cruising and cottaging. It turned out that there were a great many Joes and Janets Average who wished to share more than their 'words and music and art'.

The essence of the internet was its sense of democracy and, in retrospect, the fact that Nick Bateman was the first reality TV villain came to look ever more appropriate to this new world. He was the oldest contestant in the first series of *Big Brother*, and equally distant from the others in terms of class background. An ex-public schoolboy who had attended Gordonstoun at the same time as Prince Edward, he had gone on to work as an insurance claims broker (he put his deceit on the programme down to his time working in the City, where 'people will stitch you up to further their own careers'). He was, in short, posh, and was referred to in the newspapers as 'posh Nick' before the appellation 'Nasty Nick' took root.

The use of the word was revealing. At the start of the decade 'posh' was seen as a slightly dated term, but in the 1990s it enjoyed a huge revival. Some of its popularity was clearly attributable to the existence of Victoria 'Posh Spice' Adams, but even discounting references to her, there was a nearly threefold increase in the word's usage in newspapers like the *Guardian* and *The Times* during the 1990s, as compared to the previous decade. In the tabloids, where anti-elitism and monosyllabic brevity was of the essence, it was more extensively employed still. And the definition of what was actually deemed to be posh widened considerably. The fact that Adams herself was given the nickname, when she came from a comfortable middle-class family and attended a state secondary school, indicated that it was no longer to be restricted to the highest echelons of society.

None of this represented a sudden change. Much of Britain's post-war history had been the story of crumbling privilege, from criticism of the establishment in the 1950s, through the rise of a pop culture aristocracy in the 1960s and the political power of the trade unions in the 1970s, to Margaret Thatcher's assault on the professions in the 1980s. The result was supposed to be the classless society promised by John Major and enthusiastically endorsed by Tony Blair and New Labour, a new meritocracy in which one's origins and family background would count for nothing. Whether that had been achieved was highly questionable when it came to consideration of real power, privilege and money, but certainly there was a cultural embrace of the concept, and the accusation of being posh came to be a damaging criticism, at least in the world of tabloid editors and commissioners of television programmes. Stories began to appear of a reverse discrimination: Ben Fogle, who became a star on an early reality TV show, *Castaway 2000*, was said to have been earlier turned down as a children's television presenter because 'his accent was too posh'.

The taste now was for the everyday, a celebration of normality in a democratisation of culture that was one of the more pronounced features of the decade and one of its key legacies. There seemed something entirely appropriate about the fact that one of Margaret Thatcher's last acts, before handing over the premiership to John Major, was to approve the appointment as the new Archbishop of Canterbury of George Carey, a man who had failed the eleven-plus and had left school at the age of fifteen. While both Major and Carey remained unusual figures as outsiders in senior establishment positions, they did represent, in the modesty of their origins, a culmination of a process that had begun some decades earlier.

At a less elevated level there was the example of Chris Evans, the most talked-about broadcaster of the decade, who moved from playing records on the London radio station, GLR, to presenting *The Big Breakfast* and *Don't Forget Your Toothbrush* on Channel 4, until – at the height of Cool Britannia – he was hosting both *TFI Friday* on television and the Radio 1 breakfast show. His success was based on his sheer ordinariness, his immersion in mass culture, though with fame came complaints that he had lost contact with normality; he was 'the media's playground bully', in Tony Parsons's words, or, as Luke Haines put it, 'a shallow, bullying man-child, a jumped-up kissogram-turned-light-entertainment colossus'.

But, if there was a presiding spirit of this democratic age, it was made flesh in David Beckham. The son of an East End kitchen-fitter, he underwent a remarkable transformation, becoming a figure who commanded innumerable front pages and was capable of displacing world events from the news bulletins. Initially, of course, his success was based on his sporting prowess, but that in itself was never going to propel him to stardom, for he was a talented, rather than a supremely gifted, footballer. Asked once whether Ringo Starr was the best drummer in the world, John Lennon had joked that he wasn't even the best drummer in the Beatles. By the same token, it could be said that Beckham wasn't in the top three of Manchester United's midfield four in the late 1990s; Roy Keane, Ryan Giggs and Paul Scholes were all more highly rated players.

But Beckham was by far the most media-friendly, both on the pitch – where his contributions featured spectacular free kicks that were football's equivalent of the soundbite, tailor-made for news clips – and in interviews, where he came across as an agreeable, if not overly intelligent, young man. It didn't hurt that he was also as photogenic as a pop star and paid sufficient attention to his image that he could make the tabloid front pages by changing his hairstyle or being photographed in a sarong. There was a brief stutter when he became a national hate figure after being sent off in a 1998 World Cup match against Argentina (hence that *News at Ten* headline), a fall from grace which reached its nadir when the *Daily Mirror* unpleasantly printed an image of his face on a dartboard, but the following year he married Victoria Adams and his elevation to superstardom was complete.

Despite his beauty, his athleticism and his wealth, Beckham's appeal lay in the glamour of normality. In keeping with other 1990s British sports stars, he was no kind of a rebel, and seldom caused trouble for the football authorities. He didn't even get into trouble for drinking. Rather he was a dedicated professional, was happily married and proved to be an exemplar as a father. His genius lay in transforming that slightly dull, boy-next-door image into an internationally marketable brand, imbuing it with the trappings of charisma and glamour. It was no coincidence that he became the most famous person in the country soon after the death of Princess Diana, who had achieved much the same trick of combining a common touch with the exoticism of fame.

*

It was faintly incongruous that this democratisation of popular taste was taking place at a time when social mobility was in decline, a development symbolised by the fact that the country was now being governed by the first prime minister for thirty-three years to have been to a public school. 'The class war is over,' Tony Blair told the Labour conference in 1999, echoing the thoughts of his Old Etonian predecessor, Harold Macmillan, forty years earlier in the wake of the 1959 general election: 'This election has shown that the class war is obsolete.' But despite Blair's best efforts, the gulf between a powerful elite and an increasingly proletarian mass culture suggested that this was not the case.

Even in Westminster politics, the issue of class could never quite be driven away. When, in 2000, Betty Boothroyd stepped down as Speaker of the House of Commons, convention suggested that her replacement should be a Conservative MP, since the two main parties traditionally took turns. But Labour MPs had other ideas and Peter Snape, in proposing his colleague, Michael Martin, broke further with tradition, attacking the Tories by making a great deal of Martin's Glasgow background as a sheet-metal worker who had, explained Snape, gone to his first job 'in an old boiler suit and a pair of boots'. The intention was to draw a class distinction between Martin and his chief rival, the Conservative Sir George Young, an Old Etonian sixth baronet. Martin also had a more direct appeal to backbench MPs, pointing out that his career had been as undistinguished as most of theirs: 'I've never stood to be a whip, a frontbench spokesman or a minister. But come to think of it, nobody ever invited me.'

The continuing awareness of class differences was not restricted to the back benches. In May 2000 Gordon Brown was speaking at a trade union conference when he raised the case of Laura Spence, an A-level student from a state school in Tyne and Wear, whose GCSE results and predicted grades were sufficient to get her into almost any university, but who was turned down by Magdalen College, Oxford and instead was intending to go to Harvard. This was the result, said Brown, of 'an interview system more reminiscent of an old boy network and the old school tie than genuine justice for society'. He added: 'It is about time we had an end to the old Britain, where all that matters is the privileges you were born with, rather than the potential you actually have. It is time that these old universities opened their doors to women and people from all backgrounds.'

Unfortunately, Brown had garbled the facts. He referred to Spence's A-level results, when she had yet to sit the exams, and he failed to notice that of the twenty-seven applicants for five places to study medicine at Magdalen, all had comparable GCSE results, while three of the successful applicants were from ethnic minorities and three were women. It wasn't quite so clear a case of an 'old boy network' as it seemed from the initial newspaper reports, which appeared to be the only information from which Brown was working.

The speech generated a huge amount of press coverage. Some of it was encouraging – 'The chancellor really is talking our language,' said the *Sun* – though the broadsheets were far less favourable, criticising Brown's 'harsh and uninformed attack'. There was clearly an issue here. Only 53 per cent of Oxbridge students came from state schools, where 87 per cent of pupils were educated. But that disparity was not necessarily the result of an admissions policy, for applicants to Oxbridge consisted in roughly equal proportions of private and state pupils; in terms of applications, Oxbridge could legitimately claim to give slightly more favourable treatment to those applying from the state sector. It was also the case that the proportion of privately educated students at Oxford had fallen in the post-war years, so that by 1969 the independent schools accounted for just 38 per cent of Oxford students; the numbers only started rising again with the widespread closure of grammar schools, particularly during the period when Margaret Thatcher was education secretary.

Little of that detail was allowed to cloud the ensuing debate, which lasted for several weeks and split essentially along class lines. The chief accusation on the one side was of 'elitism' at the country's top universities, and on the other of underperforming schools in the state sector. The former charge was curious in this context, as *The Economist* pointed out: 'You might as well attack the England football team on the same grounds. Institutions which seek to select and foster the best are inevitably elitist.' The real question, as Brown had correctly identified, was one of access, though he had offered no answers to it. Nonetheless, it was elitism that came to define the episode, with a belief in some quarters that Oxbridge was largely populated by, in the words of Richard Stott in the *News of the World*, 'hordes of upper-class, public school-educated, stinking rich, thick aristocrats with far inferior grades'. The universities, according to Paul Routledge in the *Daily Mirror*, resented the way in which Brown was exposing 'the dirty little secret that they prefer to give places to public school pupils'.

Brown himself was bewildered by the storm he had unleashed. He 'went on and on,' reported Philip Gould, 'about how this could have happened, why it was that a simple sentiment should cause such a blast from the press. He simply did not understand it.' But at a time when the gloss had been rubbed off the government by the passage of time and a series of difficult events, his comments – backed by supportive interventions from

Robin Cook and John Prescott — provided the opportunity for a good old-fashioned political row. A leader in the *Daily Mail* was headlined NEW LABOUR, OLD CLASS ENVY, precisely the kind of coverage that Tony Blair didn't want to see. And some of those around the prime minister couldn't help wondering whether it was entirely coincidental that Brown, a graduate of the University of Edinburgh, should be choosing as his target Oxford University, where Blair had studied.

Nowhere, though, was the issue of class felt more strongly than on the issue of fox hunting, which had been a fashionable cause on the left for many years. Ostensibly this was a question of cruelty to animals, though few believed that to be the true motivation. Even in its radical manifesto of 1983, when Labour had promised to make illegal 'all forms of hunting with dogs', it had hastily added that shooting and fishing would not be affected, giving a fairly clear indication that there were serious cultural limits to the concern for animals. By the time of the 1997 manifesto, which promised merely a free vote in Parliament on hunting with hounds, this reservation was spelt out even more clearly: 'Angling is Britain's most popular sport.' That was as good a reason as any to leave it untouched.

The reality was that hunting, unlike angling, tended not to be popular in those parts of the country where the Labour Party fared well, and even the surprise victories of the 1997 election extended the party's reach only to the suburbs, not to the rural areas where the hunt was an intrinsic part of life. It was seen, from the left, as an upper-class pursuit favoured by toffs, and therefore more than ripe for banning. Indeed, the first attempts to do so had been made back in the days of the Attlee government.

The battle lines weren't quite so fixed as that suggested, however. In the 1940s most of the senior figures in the cabinet — from Aneurin Bevan and Ernest Bevin to Clement Attlee himself — had supported the continuation of the practice. On the Conservative benches of the 1990s, Alan Clark was a passionate anti-hunt campaigner, while Ann Widdecombe lapsed into almost Blairite language to explain her position. 'The scenes of a hunt are splendid,' she said, 'so splendid that they are all over my dining room curtains, but they are colourful scenes of Olde England, and in an Olde England, not in modern Britain, they belong.' In any event, the nature of the hunt had changed, argued Henry Davenport in *Drop the Dead Donkey*: 'Nowadays it's all bloody awful actresses, scrap metal dealers from Essex and jumped-up media types. The fox doesn't run from terror any more, but social embarrassment.'

Blair himself spoke in favour of a ban whilst in opposition, and voted in support of a failed private members' Bill in 1992, but it was not an issue that he cared deeply about, and as the prospect of legislation approached, he started to have his doubts. 'The more I learned, the more uneasy I became,' he wrote in his memoirs, revealing that he really began to regret his commitment to a ban when he met the mistress of a hunt while on holiday and was swung by her arguments: 'From that moment on, I became determined to slip out of this.' But he was sufficiently sensitive to the mood of his party – and perhaps too to the million-pound donation that Labour had received in 1996 from the International Fund for Animal Welfare – that he did not make his opposition widely known.

Instead the government ensured that several attempts to take a Bill through Parliament were thwarted through lack of support and time. A ban would come, was the repeated promise, but not just yet. In January 2001 Blair chose to go on an inessential trip to Northern Ireland in order that he might miss a vote and thereby send a signal 'to show that fox-hunting wasn't high on his list of priorities'. A couple of months later, he was to protest in a television interview, with less than total honesty, that he had voted to ban hunting, but that the measure had been thrown out by the House of Lords.

Meanwhile the threat to hunting had prompted the formation immediately after the 1997 election of the Countryside Alliance, dedicated primarily to resisting any such moves. Its first demonstration in London in July that year drew 100,000 people and was attended by William Hague and Michael Heseltine, though the most powerful speech came from the Labour peer, Ann Mallalieu, a keen huntswoman who argued that the issue was one of freedom and 'the tolerance of minorities'. In comments that were unlikely to make much impact on abolitionists, she declared: 'Hunting is our music, it is our poetry, it is our art, it is our pleasure. It is where many of our best friendships are made, it is our community. It is our whole way of life.'

Even bigger demonstrations were to be called, reaching a peak of some half a million people in 2002. These were extraordinary events, their composition quite unlike other protests staged in London and, although the preservation of hunting was the central cause, they quickly became a focal point for a host of other grievances. 'All country people share in the problems of closures of rural post offices, inadequate public transport, crippling petrol costs, diminishing village stores and high community taxes,' wrote the former defence secretary, John Nott, of the 2002 march. 'That is why five hundred thousand people came, and I doubt if there are a thousand rich among them.'

Hunting was the touchstone for the Countryside Alliance, as it was for what remained of the left. Perhaps, reflected Alastair Campbell, the attempt to ban the practice 'would get blocked in the Lords and we could then put a middle way in the manifesto for the next parliament'. But there was no point of contact between the two sides, no formula that would satisfy opposing groups whose passion on the subject was unequivocal, no Third Way for Blair to latch on to, despite his undoubted wish to seek compromise. The best he could hope for was to delay making a decision, staving off the inevitable day of reckoning.

The parliament ended, as it had begun, with hunting still a perfectly legal pursuit. In March 2001 the Parliamentary Labour Party met to discuss the manifesto for the forthcoming election and, noted Chris Mullin, 'A ban on hunting with hounds was easily the most popular issue.' It was hard not to see in this singular enthusiasm for what was essentially a fairly trivial piece of class posturing a symbol of how far Labour had drifted from its radical roots.

The emergence of the Countryside Alliance articulated a dimension of regional as well as class conflict, illustrating the vast, and still widening, gap between the town and the country. Rural pursuits were now removed from the mainstream, a situation depicted in a 1998 episode of the BBC sitcom *Game On*, when a character whose principal reading matter is *Loaded* picks up a copy of *Country Life* and wonders: 'Is this what posh blokes wank over?' The incomprehension was perhaps equally marked on the other side. Those attacking the hunt saw themselves as fighting decadent privilege; those defending it saw themselves in opposition to metropolitan liberals. The latter was a theme that William Hague took up with some enthusiasm, believing that it offered a way forward for the Tories, a chance to break out from the party's continuing slump in the opinion polls.

After their dreadful drubbing in the 1993 election, the Canadian Conservatives had staged a comeback in the middle of the decade by adopting the slogan 'the common sense revolution', repositioning themselves as the party of low taxation and individual responsibility, fighting the incompetent bureaucracy of government. The policies were largely drawn from the examples of Margaret Thatcher and Ronald Reagan, and resulted in a major victory in the Ontario election of 1995.

Now, having tried out various options including 'kitchen sink Conservatism' and 'compassionate Conservatism', Hague revived the same slogan. By experimenting with the inclusive New Labour model, and accepting the social and cultural changes in the country, he had failed to make any headway, and he felt that something new was needed. The shadow cabinet was still split between the wings represented by Michael Portillo and Ann Widdecombe, and if the former's modernisation programme wasn't connecting with the electorate, perhaps it was time to try the latter's traditionalism. 'If we could get the common sense revolution to stand up and walk around,' declared Hague in 2000, 'it would look like Ann Widdecombe.' He knew he would be accused of 'lurching to the right', but the Countryside Alliance demonstrations made clear that Blair didn't represent the whole nation; there was still a wellspring of opposition to be tapped. And in this campaign, the battleground was, inevitably, law and order.

Unfortunately for Hague, some of his interventions looked simply inept. The publication in 1999 of the Macpherson Report into the murder of Stephen Lawrence saw him articulate a familiar argument. 'The liberal elite have seized on the report as a stick with which to beat the police,' he thundered. 'We will take on and defeat a liberal elite that has always given more consideration to the rights of criminals than the rights of victims.' This alleged distortion of the justice system in favour of wrongdoers was a long-running complaint – despite Michael Howard's promise to deal with it when he was home secretary – though the murder of Stephen Lawrence was hardly the best example. It was the police, rather than liberals, who had so comprehensively failed the victim and his family here.

More convincing, for many, was another case later that year: a 55-year-old Norfolk farmer named Tony Martin, who was charged with murder after he shot dead a sixteen-year-old burglar, Fred Barras, who had broken into his house. Martin lived alone and had been burgled on several occasions, and there was widespread support for his right to defend his property since the police were evidently unable so to do. The case was not quite so clear cut as first presented, however: the shotgun used had been held without a licence, and Barras had been shot in the back whilst trying to flee from the scene. But Martin had publicist Max Clifford working on his behalf, ensuring that much of the press coverage remained favourable. 'It's something people are really angry about,' Clifford argued. 'William Hague, who desperately needs something to improve his image, should get behind this because the support out there is huge.'

Hague did indeed join in the debate, promising that if he were prime minister, householders would have greater rights to defend their property without fear of such prosecution. His comments rattled Blair's inner circle. 'We need to appear more in touch with public opinion than Hague,' worried Lance Price. 'Having the right to take on burglars is a good populist issue.' But even a prime minister keen to win public approval was unable to indulge in such grandstanding when a court case was imminent.

Meanwhile Hague was revelling in the attacks he faced from some quarters for playing to the gallery. 'We've got the whole liberal establishment railing against me,' he exulted. 'It's just what I wanted.' Common sense said that people had a right to protect themselves, using whatever means they had at their disposal; it was only the liberal elite who got hung up on the belief that, in the words of the *Guardian*'s David McKie, 'execution, official or freelance, is not a proper sentence for burglary'. Hague might have paused for further thought when the verdict was returned. Martin was convicted of murder, though this was reduced to manslaughter on appeal, when his defence argued that he suffered from paranoid personality disorder. He didn't make an obvious hero, and public opinion – expressed through the focus group of a jury – was evidently unimpressed.

During the common sense revolution, as so often in recent times, homosexuality returned to the agenda of the Conservative Party. When he first became leader, Hague had made overtures to Torche, the Tory Campaign for Homosexual Equality, thereby arousing the fury of some traditionalists. 'Why do I share a party with those who advocate sodomite marriage?' demanded Norman Tebbit. But Hague had then been still in inclusive phase. Now he seemed to have decided that gay rights were another concern solely of the liberal establishment, and when, in December 1999, the government proposed the repeal of Section 28 of the Local Government Act 1988, he insisted that the shadow cabinet stand united in opposition.

It was a pointless fight. Repeal was inevitable, despite some disquiet in Labour ranks – the chief whip, Ann Taylor, tried unsuccessfully to get a free vote on the issue – but Hague clearly wanted to send signals to the Tory heartlands. It did him little good, and he found himself obliged to sack Shaun Woodward, his spokesperson on London matters, for refusing to go along with the policy, an event that precipitated Woodward's defection to Labour.

Nor did Hague's stand make the slightest difference to the Conservatives' position in the polls, for the reality was by now that few cared much about the subject. Leaders of various faiths continued to insist that this was a key issue – the *Catholic Herald* declared that the attempt to equalise ages of consent represented 'a new low in this country's slide into moral degeneracy' – and there remained a handful who displayed a horrified fascination with homosexuality, but most of the population had quietly decided that they weren't particularly interested. The battle had been fought and won, and Hague only made himself look absurd.

He also ensured that the 'nasty party' image lived on. The Conservative MP David Curry felt that his children, now in their twenties, should be natural Tories, but regrettably they weren't: 'They think the party is totally out of touch. All the stuff about gays is totally incredible to them. Like the British people, they may not think all that much of Labour, but there's no way they'll vote Tory. They think we're a lot of shits.' As one of his erstwhile colleagues, Michael Brown, observed in response to Woodward's sacking: 'Never mind the common sense revolution — just common sense would have done.'

That raised the more philosophical question of what constituted 'common sense'. Twenty years on from Margaret Thatcher's first election victory, there had been a change in the country, and what was now common was an attitude of tolerance. Hague should perhaps have noticed this, for in his own quiet way, he represented some of that change. At his first conference as Conservative leader, he had let it be known — to the horror of Thatcher and others on the traditionalist wing of the party — that he and his fiancée Ffion would be sharing a hotel room. They even lived together without being married. 'The message is,' wrote the Catholic journalist William Oddie, 'that if the Tory party expects William Hague to lead them back to traditional family values, they had better think again.'

Earlier in 1999 the story had emerged of a Tory MEP, Tom Spencer, who was married with two daughters, even though he was gay and his wife was well aware of the fact. 'We discussed my homosexuality long before we got married,' he explained. 'Part of our arrangement was that occasionally it was acknowledged that I would go away for the weekend.' It all seemed perfectly civilised, and no one would have been much concerned one way or another, had it not been for the fact that on returning from one of those weekends, he was stopped by customs officials at Heathrow Airport and fined for possession of cocaine, cannabis and hardcore pornography. His bag was also reported to have contained 'a sexual accessory and a large black leather suit, with waistcoat and hood'.

Despite this wealth of what should have been media-friendly material, however, the story made very little impact. Spencer stood down as a candidate from the forthcoming Euro-election, of course — being caught breaking the law for anything other than driving at a reckless speed was still a matter for resignation — but his tale disappeared from the papers and from public consciousness within a couple of days. And mainly it did so because neither Spencer nor his wife appeared particularly perturbed.

'Of all sexual perversions, chastity is the most peculiar. I am not capable of it,' he shrugged, in a paraphrase of a line from Aldous Huxley. Not even the previously reliable Richard Littlejohn was able to work up much froth of indignation. 'If his missus can live with it, that's up to her,' he wrote, with weary resignation. 'I'd rather not know.' The Conservative Party, it appeared, was not exempt from the changing climate, and the days of sex scandals seemed to be receding.

Equally unshocking was Spencer's other offence of using recreational drugs. Leading up to the 2000 Conservative conference, Ann Widdecombe wanted to announce that £250 million would be spent on an anti-drugs programme, but Michael Portillo, as shadow chancellor, refused to approve any such commitment. Undeterred, Widdecombe made drugs the centre of her conference speech, calling for a hard-line approach that included £100 on-the-spot fines for smoking cannabis: 'It means zero tolerance for possession. No more getting away with just a caution.' She was given a standing ovation in the hall, but few outside were convinced. The police responded by saying that her policies were impractical, Hague began to backtrack almost immediately, and even the *Daily Mail* was unimpressed: 'Is she really serious about criminalising every spotty adolescent who tokes up behind the bicycle sheds?'

Worse was to come. The *Mail on Sunday* rang around members of the shadow cabinet to ask whether they had ever smoked cannabis. Seven said that they had, including some of the brightest hopes of the party – Francis Maude, Oliver Letwin and David Willetts – with Tim Yeo later joining the chorus. The willingness of so many to go on the record as having broken the law was surprising to say the least, and raised the suspicion that it was all a put-up job, that there had been collusion in an attempt to destroy Widdecombe's career by making her a laughing-stock. It was, reported the *Sun*, 'a calculated bid to damage the shadow home secretary's image as a future Tory leader'.

Had such an operation been staged, the one group who stood to gain were those who supported Portillo. Certainly that was how Widdecombe herself saw it. 'It was a spiteful attempt to damage me,' she asserted. 'They saw me as a rival and set out to damage me. They had done the same to others like Liam Fox and John Redwood when they looked like potential rivals to Portillo. I have no doubt about it.' Whether it were with Portillo's approval or not, the leading Tories did seem to be being picked off one by one, in a way that brought the party no short-term benefit.

Some of the change in attitude was the consequence of a concerted campaign against prejudice. The country's governing and media classes, it was alleged, were in the grip of the cult of political correctness, though since the charge was made on such a regular basis by commentators in most of the national newspapers, by members of the royal family and by politicians of both major parties, it was hard sometimes to see quite where political correctness was so entrenched, save perhaps at the BBC. Certainly there was a determination on the part of broadcasters, politicians and press – in varying degrees – to strive to avoid causing deliberate offence to members of groups marginalised in the past, but arguably the underlying motive shared more with traditional values than it did with modish ideology: 'I call it good manners,' wrote Jon Savage, in the *Guardian* in 1994; 'indeed, being socialised: thinking about people other than yourself.'

Nonetheless, tales of 'political correctness gone mad' were commonplace right through the decade (the first sightings of the phrase were in 1993), if frequently exaggerated. A characteristic news story in 1994 claimed that a school in Greenwich had changed the opening lines of John & Yoko's 'Happy Christmas (War Is Over)', so that it now started: 'So this is December, and what have you done?' The assumption was that this was an act of political correctness, done to avoid offending those of other faiths. The school protested that this could hardly be the case since the rest of the lyrics remained the same (the chorus still ran 'And so happy Christmas'); rather it was just an attempt to encourage pupils to reflect on the passing year. But the explanation received less coverage than the original story, and instead John Lennon was cited as an integral part of British culture that was being silenced by the loony left. (Since he had been regularly lambasted by the right for his blasphemy, drug-taking and support for the IRA, he would presumably have relished the irony, had he still been alive to enjoy it.)

Most of those commentators who denounced political correctness were also exercised by the slipping of standards when it came to bad language, though this concern was not consistent across the country. When, for example, the Broadcasting Standards Council conducted a survey in 1994 on people's attitudes to swearing on television, it found marked regional differences: 'bastard' and 'twat' were regarded as strong swearwords by 59 and 44 per cent respectively of people in the North, but by only 35 and 13 per cent in the South. Meanwhile the ITC, which regulated the commercial channels, noted that scheduling changes attracted far more complaints than questions of taste and decency; the biggest source of grievance in 1993 was the cancellation of the Scottish soap opera *Take the High Road*.

In any event, protests about the coarsening of culture, and about the imposition of new taboos, were, for the moment at least, fruitless. The drive for change appeared unstoppable. It was not simply the work of a demonised elite, but a consequence too of the democratisation of the media, as the everyday became visible. People became more tolerant as they saw individuals just like themselves depicted, with all their failings, foibles and follies, on a daily basis, whether on reality television or the internet.

If there was an elite to be fought, it was rather to be found in the new class of politicians emerging on both sides of the party divide, whose only experience of life after university was in the bubble of Westminster think tanks and on the periphery of the media, before becoming political advisers and then MPs. The gap between this remote, self-contained, self-replicating group and a rapidly democratising culture did not augur well for the future. Nor did the fact that the political elite appeared enthralled by the spectacle of riches, at a time when wealth disparity was continuing to increase. For the moment, with a growing economy, that was not yet critical, but it did not look like a sustainable model for society in the longer term.

When comparisons were made between voting numbers on reality television and those in elections, the lesson generally drawn was of the declining state of democracy in the country. Sometimes an accusation was levelled that there was a causal connection between the two phenomena, that a combination of cheap, imported electronic goods and the material consumed via those goods constituted a latter-day bread and circuses. It was equally possible, however, to see the growing interactivity of the media as the first, inchoate stirrings of a new model of politics.

'It may be that the era of pure representative democracy is coming slowly to an end,' reflected Peter Mandelson in a 1998 speech, observing that the political elites that had dominated democracy for so long – including those in the intellectual, trade union and local council spheres – came from 'an age that has passed away'. In the future, he argued, representative institutions would be 'complemented by more direct forms of popular involvement, from the internet to referenda'.

It wasn't an entirely new thought. Earlier in the decade a character in *The Politician's Wife* had made the same point: 'They'll hold referendums the same way. From Strasbourg to the Senate, virtual reality giving virtual power to the people.' What remained to be seen was whether – if this truly was the dawning of an era and if, as the education minister Kim Howells put it, 'the days of the old political class are over' – the new breed of professional politicians would have a role to play in it. For the present, there was merely an uneasy recognition in some quarters that things were changing and that the manifestations of that change were unpredictable.

In particular, it was unclear whether the new democratising spirit of the age was to be matched by a new level of educated opinion. Recognising the rapid growth in the use of computers, the British government had declared 1982 to be the year of 'information technology', and that phrase had become the default description of the emerging new world, gaining even greater prominence with the spread of the internet. The relationship between information and education, however, remained uncertain, and the celebration of 'emotional literacy' that some detected in the response to Diana's death only added to the confusion. There was a suspicion that the elevation of opinion over fact might yet prove damaging. So although an anti-elitism was undoubtedly evident in the country, there was also a danger that the tendency would shade into a distrust of experts of all kinds. A survey of 8,000 adults by the University of Leeds in 1997 found that 83 per cent believed science created more problems than it solved.

The most acute example of the attitude came in 1998, with the publication in *The Lancet* of research suggesting a link between the MMR vaccination (given to small children to immunise them against measles, mumps and rubella) and the incidence of autism and inflammatory bowel disease. 'If I am wrong,' commented the paper's author, Dr Andrew Wakefield, 'I will be a bad person because I will have raised this spectre. But I have to address the questions my patients put to me.' More than a decade later, *The Lancet* retracted the piece, and Wakefield was struck off by the General Medical Council on grounds of serious professional misconduct in his research.

By then, it was too late for some. Reporting of the controversy had adversely affected vaccination rates for several years after Wakefield's piece, despite overwhelming medical opinion and scientific evidence that the MMR triple jab was not only safe but hugely important for public health; it had played a critical role in slashing the number of cases of measles by 95 per cent in the preceding decade. The inevitable consequence was that the incidence of the diseases had risen. The anti-MMR scare was fanned by a feeling that the medical establishment tended to ignore the concerns of ordinary parents, and by reporting in some parts of the media that was ill-informed and often ignorant of basic science.

Much of the coverage centred on whether Tony Blair had allowed his youngest child, Leo, to have the vaccination, a question which he steadfastly refused to answer, insisting that he wished to protect the privacy of his children. (The story of Leo's conception at Balmoral had yet to be released into the public domain.) Since the real issue was one of social responsibility – by not vaccinating one's own children, one helped to spread the risk of dangerous diseases – it might have been more helpful had he made his position a little clearer.

The same reticence was not evident in Blair's other pronouncements. At times he seemed all too eager to comment on passing news stories, particularly if doing so enabled him to appear in touch with popular culture. In April 1998 he added his voice to the tabloid campaigns calling for the release from prison of Deirdre Rachid, who had been jailed after being unwittingly implicated in a fraud case. The fact that she was a fictional character, played by Anne Kirkbride in *Coronation Street*, didn't seem to trouble him in the slightest.

17
Millennium
'Let's all meet up in the year 2000'

What is the Dome for?
Jacques Chirac (1999)

When I look back and reread the papers, reminding myself of the
sheer horror, depth and scale of the crisis, it is a total miracle we
came through it.
Tony Blair (2010)

To all the people who supported Ken Livingstone, all the people
who backed Labour in opposition but would rather snipe from the
sidelines than be tainted by support; all the people who vote Liberal,
Green or Socialist Labour, the time for such luxuries is now over.
John O'Farrell (2000)

'I knew a lot about history before becoming prime minister,' wrote Tony
Blair in his memoirs. Some commentators were less than convinced,
not sure that he quite comprehended the word itself, suspecting that he
too readily confused the idea with the concept of destiny. Blair, claimed
the writers of Rory Bremner's show, saw history as being 'not something
in the past, but something in the future which will judge him favourably'.
Perhaps that was why he seemed so tremendously excited about the fact
that he would become the first prime minister of the twenty-first century,
and the first holder of the office ever to welcome in a millennium.

In his speech to the 1995 Labour Party conference, Blair had talked of the
challenge that would face an incoming government, using terms that were
hyperbolic even by his own standards. There would be, he said, 'a thousand
days to prepare for a thousand years'. That was a slight miscalculation –
there were actually 964 days between the election and 1 January 2000, which
didn't have quite the same ring – but it did allow his detractors to suggest
there was something of a 'thousand year Reich' about his aspiration. It also

prompted John Major to warn that 'A thousand days of Labour government could ditch a thousand years of British history.'

There was, from an early stage, a conflict about the significance of the forthcoming millennium, a dispute about quite what it meant to Britain, a continuation of the argument about heritage and modernity that had dominated so much of the decade. Why it should mean anything at all was not a question that appeared to trouble too many leading politicians; instead there was a determination to mark the occasion on a scale unmatched in most other countries of the world. The Millennium Commission was created to distribute monies from the National Lottery for events up and down Britain, but that was too diffuse to satisfy the political appetite for spectacle, and Michael Heseltine came up with the idea of a national focus, a major exhibition to be staged in Greenwich. 'As a nation,' he later wrote, 'I believed that we should stake our claim to the future with a statement of great confidence and pride in ourselves.' This was to be a showpiece for the country in the same way as the Great Exhibition of 1851 and the Festival of Britain a hundred years later had been.

There was a symbolism to the choice of location, just a couple of miles from the Royal Observatory, home of the prime meridian and of Greenwich Mean Time, but the site chosen was far from straightforward. Formerly occupied by British Gas, its soil was so poisonous that for the first few months of the reclamation work, visitors were warned not even to open their car windows. The costs of decontamination alone were vast. By the time Labour came to power in 1997, upwards of £100 million had already been spent, with nothing yet to show for the investment. 'I should really cancel it, but my gut instinct tells me otherwise,' reflected Blair. He let it be known that he was minded to continue with the exhibition, though he insisted it should pass the 'Euan test', that it should be sufficiently exciting that his thirteen-year-old son would wish to attend. This was the height of Cool Britannia, and the fantasy of placing Britain at the centre of the global celebrations of the millennium was simply irresistible.

Although Blair had to leave early from the cabinet meeting where the future of the project was to be determined, his wishes were amply represented by John Prescott: 'I knew and they knew that Tony was for it, even though most were critical.' There was little desire to thwart the leader's wishes. 'If the PM were here and said we should go ahead,' shrugged Robin Cook, 'we would all accept it.' And so they did, and though they also resolved that no further public money would be allocated to the project, David Blunkett at least was honest enough to admit that 'nobody believed for a moment that this would be the case'. The Millennium Dome, as it became known, was to go ahead. One last chance to change course came with the death of Diana later in the year, but it too was spurned. 'In retrospect,' reflected Jonathan Powell, 'one idea that I wish we had accepted came from the organisers of the Millennium Dome who suggested we scrap the Dome and replace it with a children's hospital dedicated to her.'

Despite the complexities of the construction project, the Dome itself – designed by the recently ennobled architect Richard Rogers – was the more straightforward part of the equation, and proceeded more smoothly than had the Festival of Britain, the construction of which had been beset by strikes. A greater challenge was what to put inside the building and, as time slipped by, it became ever more apparent that there was no consensus on what that might be, even in the broadest of terms. Various consultants were employed, some more successfully than others. Amongst those who fell by the wayside early on was Malcolm McLaren, formerly the manager of the Sex Pistols and Bow Wow Wow, who suggested that, instead of an exhibition, everyone under the age of twenty-six should be give a free air ticket to any destination of their choosing, 'so they can get the hell out of this country for the millennium celebrations'.

More influential, though still controversial, was Terence Conran, who had worked on the Festival of Britain but was best known for founding the furniture shop Habitat. He insisted that it would be 'entirely inappropriate' for the Dome to have a Christian theme because, rather puzzlingly, the millennium 'is not an event that has very much to do with Christianity. It's to do with time.' Ann Widdecombe called for him to be sacked. As it finally materialised, an area of the Dome designated the Faith Zone featured a celebration of all the major religions practised in Britain, in an attempt to appear inclusive; significantly, however, faith was thus hived off to its own corner, rather than permeating the entire event as it had the Festival of Britain. It was an indication of the way that religion had become a cultural sideshow in the last half-century.

Also on the planning team of what Blair called 'ideas merchants and creative forces' were the theatre impresario Cameron Mackintosh and the usual suspects from cinema and television: David Puttnam, Alan Yentob, Michael Grade. The latter was keen to stress that this wouldn't be like Britain's previous forays into such territory: 'In 1851 and 1951 the great and the good created wonderful tableaux, then lifted the curtain and allowed the great unwashed to have a peep. This show is different. The people are in charge.' Gerald Barry, director general of the Festival of Britain, had made a similar claim – that it was to be 'the People's Show, not organised arbitrarily for them to enjoy, but put on by them'. In the case of the Millennium Dome, as with its predecessor, the rhetoric was misleading.

Because, despite such democratic talk, the person actually in charge this time was Peter Mandelson. His grandfather, Herbert Morrison, had overseen the Festival of Britain – amongst the legacies of which was the Royal Festival Hall where New Labour celebrated its election victory on 2 May 1997 – and Mandelson was determined to live up to the family tradition. Unburdened by a government department, he threw himself into what was still being talked about as an exhibition, and his commitment to the project at the time was all-encompassing (even if, in his memoirs, he spared just two of 566 pages to covering the eighteen months he spent working on it). He took to speaking of 'my Dome', while Tony Banks nicknamed him the Dome Secretary. Unfortunately his enthusiasm wasn't matched by others outside his immediate coterie. The *Sport* newspaper denounced the entire thing as 'bollocks', and a poll in the *Daily Telegraph* found that 98 per cent of the public thought the Lottery money should be spent elsewhere.

Even some of those at the heart of the enterprise doubted the wisdom of the decisions being made. David Puttnam regarded the 'Euan test' as 'a slight and demeaning basis for the Dome', while Richard Rogers was unimpressed by the vagueness of what was to be put inside his big tent: 'It was like an orchestra without a conductor,' he concluded. The consultant creative director, Stephen Bayley, who had earlier created the Boilerhouse Project at the Victoria & Albert Museum and – with Terence Conran – the Design Museum, lasted for just six months before resigning in protest at what he saw as Mandelson's limited artistic vision, as demonstrated by a much-publicised trip to Disney World in Florida to pick up some new ideas. The whole thing, now rebranded as the New Millennium Experience, was, said Bayley, 'a project that could have been one of the great international world exhibitions, but is instead going to be a crabby and demoralising theme park'.

A man who, in his words, saw 'typography as far, far more important in the general run of things than politics itself', Bayley was perhaps not best suited to steering what was rapidly becoming a very political project. For both Mandelson and Blair seemed determined to stake their reputations on the Dome. It would be, announced Blair, 'the most exciting day out in the world'. He was also reported to have referred to the Dome as 'the first paragraph of my next election manifesto', though Alastair Campbell furiously denied the authenticity of the quote, calling it 'journalistic fantasy'. Less disputed, though no more accurate as a prediction, was Blair's claim that the Dome would 'see off cynics who despise anything new'.

That denunciation of cynicism was a familiar one, of course, but there was a little more impatience and irritation in Blair's voice now, a sense that he was deliberately stepping up his attacks on those who failed to share his vision of the future. Midway through the parliament, he seemed painfully aware that the reality hadn't thus far matched the rhetoric and that he hadn't yet lived up to his self-image. 'Pushing to get out of me was the desire to be a leader who led and challenged all the way,' he later wrote.

At the 1999 Labour conference, he launched into an attack on all those who he felt were holding back the birth of the New Britain he wished to create. The next century, he declared, would see a battle 'between the forces of progress and the forces of conservatism. They are what hold our nation back. Not just in the Conservative Party, but within us, within our nation.' In terms that could only recall Margaret Thatcher, he railed against 'the cynics, the elites, the establishment' and 'those who will live in decline'. And he ended with a peroration somewhere between the Book of Ecclesiastes and Martin Luther King: 'To every nation a purpose. To every party a cause. And now, at last, party and nation joined in the same cause for the same purpose: to set our people free.'

It was a speech that went down extremely well in the hall, even with those he would happily include in the 'forces of conservatism'. Elsewhere, though, it marked the end of Blair's long honeymoon with the right-wing press. The *Daily Mail* took the speech to be an attack on the values it held dear – as indeed it was – while the *Sun* retaliated by accentuating the positive, 'such as the conservation of good things like the countryside and our heritage'. It provoked the Tories sufficiently that William Hague sounded genuinely fired up in his own conference speech the following week, giving renewed hope to those who distrusted Blair. 'He spoke for Britain,' exulted Richard Littlejohn, a convert to Hague's cause. 'Not the *Guardian*-reading, polenta-munching, euro-loving, history-hating, public-spending, outreach-coordinating, New Labour elite, but ordinary, hard-working, tax-paying, car-owning, home-loving, small-saving, patriotic, family men and women.'

From the perspective of Downing Street, it even seemed as though Blair's speech had similarly riled the heir to the throne. That autumn Prince Charles was particularly visible in the media, making a speech that criticised genetically modified crops, taking his son, William, out hunting, and declining an invitation to attend the Buckingham Palace reception given in honour of Jiang Zemin. Alastair Campbell was convinced that it was all 'a strategy to put himself at the head of the forces of conservatism. The speech had clearly really struck a nerve.'

The impression was of a government picking fights for the sake of it, happiest when it was in conflict, as though it could only define itself in opposition to others. And yet there seemed little need for such confrontation. The country, as it approached the end of the century, was relatively content. Blair might not have delivered on his implied promises, and many would have been happy to see an increase in public spending, some sign of improvement in the 'schools and hospitals' so often invoked by Labour, but he was more secure than any mid-term prime minister in living memory. There was no hankering for a return to a Conservative government, no real crisis. The economy was still growing, the stock market was booming, unemployment was falling, and the majority were enjoying good times.

A handful of doubters pointed out that this was largely being fuelled by easy credit, which would one day have to be repaid, but they were definitely in a minority, and the rapid accumulation of household debt was generally laughed away. Everyone, it seemed, from toddlers to pensioners, was in receipt of a constant stream of letters that, as parodied by Louise Wener, read along the lines of: 'Dear sir, we hear you are very badly in debt and a loser. We would like to offer you one of our platinum cards so that you can plunge yourself still deeper into destitution and penury.' The mockery didn't stop the acquisition of such cards, nor did it hinder the willingness to use them, creating a continuing sense of well-being.

Contentment, though, was not enough for a government that still thought in terms of tomorrow's headlines and required a daily flow of announcements and initiatives. Targets were still being set, new laws still being introduced at a ferocious rate, but the media appetite for such initiatives was diminishing, and now it became increasingly likely that the Millennium Dome would fail to deliver. The tabloids were mostly brought onside – Rupert Murdoch had even been persuaded to become a sponsor of the project, adding his money to that of McDonald's, the Ford Motor Company and arms manufacturer British Aerospace amongst others – but there were plenty still to be heard predicting a disaster.

Indeed disaster was very much in the air. The last time the western world had confronted the dawning of a new millennium, there had been a widespread belief that the world was about to end, with the serving pope, Sylvester II, amongst those who believed that the coming of the Kingdom of Heaven was nigh. This time round, such concerns seemed laughable even in Christian circles, where the accuracy of the calendar had long been accepted as flawed. Instead there was a new terror, more in keeping with science fiction than eschatology. As the century drew to a close, a worldwide panic arose about what became known as the Millennium Bug, a potential problem arising from the way that dates had been stored in computer code. To minimise memory use, the year had been represented by just two digits and there was a concern therefore that if 99 was followed by 00, programs would interpret this as 1900 rather than as 2000.

The consequences were uncertain, but the media were keen to paint a doomsday scenario. 'Your home is suddenly plunged into darkness as power fails and the lights go out,' opened the *Sun*'s account of what might happen on 1 January 2000. 'When power is restored, the washing machine breaks down and the phone is dead. Your credit cards stop working. You lose your job.' From household appliances to life-support machines to the stock markets, nothing was safe. 'Forty thousand companies could go bankrupt.' Nor was the alarmism confined to the tabloids. 'Bank vaults and prison gates have swung open,' was the *Observer*'s version of what might happen, 'so have valves on sewer pipes.' The *Financial Times* talked of 'the worst case scenario, where aircraft fall out of the sky as air-traffic control fails, power stations shut down and hospital equipment does not operate'.

None of this, of course, materialised, possibly because somewhere in excess of $300 billion was spent in remedial work to fix the problem. Or possibly it was because the problem had been overstated in the first instance. For there were those who saw this international scare as little more than a resurgence of the superstitions of the Dark Ages, proof that society might change but human beings remained stubbornly superstitious.

The Dome was scheduled to open on New Year's Eve, with a party for the great and the good. It was not a triumph. Having apparently forgotten the lessons of the Sheffield rally in 1992, the organisers failed to ensure the proper working of the transport laid on for guests. A train broke down, stranding several thousand guests at Stratford, amongst them the senior members of the media, including the director general of the BBC and seven newspaper editors, who were supposed to be covering the launch. As John Prescott put it, 'That pissed them off.' Any lingering chance of positive coverage died on the cold, concrete platforms of an East End station.

The most memorable images of the event itself were of the Queen and Prince Philip looking as though they would prefer to be at home, or indeed anywhere else at all, rather than spending the evening in a South London tent, linking arms with the Blairs for a rendition of 'Auld Lang Syne'. The arrogance of New Labour was revealed in a diary entry by Oona King, who was present, remarking that 'the Queen had both her hands the wrong way round', untroubled by the likelihood that Her Majesty had a better grasp of protocol on such occasions than did a recently elected MP in her early thirties. King added the magnificently patronising comment: 'considering how old she is, she did pretty well.' Meanwhile, outside, tens of thousands had gathered on the banks of the Thames to welcome the millennium and to witness a display of pyrotechnics that, it was promised, would create a breathtaking 'river of fire'. It was no such thing, and not even the television pictures were convincing.

Humiliatingly, it all looked so much more fun in Sydney and Rio, while the world's media chose as their image of the night the superb firework display at the Eiffel Tower. Despite all the emphasis that Labour had placed on looking forward, on the excitement of the new, it was a structure from the nineteenth century that won the front pages.

The Eiffel Tower had been built to accompany the Paris Exposition in 1889, which attracted over thirty million visitors. The Millennium Dome never stood a chance of matching that, but it was confidently predicted that between twelve and fifteen million would attend during 2000. In the event, it managed just 6.5 million, two million fewer even than the main exhibition at the Festival of Britain, which had run for just five months (those attending at least one event in 1951 were estimated at upwards of twenty-five million). Nor was it a great unifying force in the nation; the *Daily Record* was pleased to announce that in the first two months of 2000, just 400 tickets had been bought in Scotland. Although the Dome was Britain's most popular tourist attraction that year, the numbers were disappointing. So too was the fact that repeated injections of cash were required from Lottery funds just to keep it running. It wasn't even as though it were a cheap day out. Adult tickets cost £20 – twice the cost of entry to the London Dungeon or the Blackpool Tower and Circus – but nonetheless each visitor to the Dome was subsidised out of public funds to the tune of £90 a head.

The other big projects of 2000 met with mixed results. The Millennium Wheel, a massive Ferris wheel on the South Bank of the Thames, was scheduled to open on New Year's Eve but, although the ceremony went ahead, it wasn't yet ready to start turning. 'I don't think that really matters for tonight,' said Bob Ayling, chief executive of British Airways, who had paid for the attraction. 'It does if it's called the Millennium Wheel,' rejoined Blair tartly, as he pressed the button to start a firework display that failed to happen. Later known as the London Eye, the wheel came in at three times its original budget – one of the reasons why Ayling subsequently lost his job – but it was a genuine success and, although intended as a temporary structure, it stayed to become a fixture of the London skyline.

Also a hit was the new gallery further down the Thames, Tate Modern.

Converted from a disused power station with £50 million of Lottery money, it exceeded expectations, albeit at a cost to other institutions; its parent gallery, now rebranded Tate Britain, saw visitor numbers fall. Tate Modern was connected to the City of London on the north bank by the Millennium Footbridge, a steel suspension bridge for pedestrians that, like the London Eye, suffered a troubled start. The day it opened, some reported experiencing a swaying motion, and the bridge was promptly taken out of service — for two years — so that engineering work to counter the wobble could be carried out. 'We opened the first new bridge over the river Thames in a hundred years,' boasted culture secretary Chris Smith, at the Labour conference that year, adding: 'Then we closed the first new bridge over the river Thames in a hundred years.'

The popularity of the London Eye and Tate Modern made the Dome look even more forlorn, and the failure to meet its targets became a reliable source of fodder for journalists, the butt of endless jokes and attacks. John O'Farrell was one of the few trying to buck the trend. He hadn't been to the Millennium Experience himself, he wrote, but 'everyone I know who's been along there seemed to enjoy themselves and come away impressed'. Yet this happy news was being quashed because 'Everyone who dislikes this government was determined to hate the Dome with or without going there.' On the other hand, the members of the House of Commons culture committee did go, and came back to report: 'There is no single element to make the visitor gasp in astonishment, to provide the "wow" factor that was originally sought.'

That was a fair assessment of the attractions on offer, a random collection of exhibits that were all slightly inferior to the versions available elsewhere — the interactive technology was bettered by At-Bristol, the main show was less impressive than the Cirque du Soleil — but O'Farrell had a point. Most visitors were relatively satisfied with the show, if not overwhelmed, their attitude summed up in the slightly surprised comments of Tony Benn, who went along with his family: 'It was actually a thoroughly enjoyable day.'

Perhaps unsurprisingly, Benn's approval wasn't enough, and by February 2000 Alastair Campbell had come to the belated realisation that 'Governments shouldn't run tourist attractions.' Blair picked up the theme. 'Hindsight is a wonderful thing,' he mused in September; 'if I had my time again, I would have listened to those who said governments shouldn't try to run big visitor attractions.' Meanwhile William Hague was happily ignoring the Conservative origins of the project and describing it as 'a symbol of New Labour, an empty pointless tent in the middle of nowhere'.

*

Hague's mockery of the Dome was barely more convincing than had been Blair's espousal of it. For he too went into the new century looking unsure of his ground and losing support. The enthusiasm for his 1999 conference speech didn't last amongst commentators; one of his key allies in the Conservative Party, Alan Duncan (a 'ghastly little cunt', according to Nicholas Soames), was privately voicing his concern that his leader had 'lost the plot'; and Margaret Thatcher — now nearly a decade out of office but still wielding an authority in Tory circles — couldn't even pretend that the next election offered any hope. 'We must all work hard to cut down the [Labour] majority as much as possible next time,' she said in December 1999, 'and eliminate it altogether as soon as we can.' Hague's continuing irrelevance to national debate, however, was less significant than Blair's waning authority.

It was by now generally accepted that Thatcher's downfall — however much it might have been triggered by the specific issues of Europe and the poll tax — was largely attributable to the way that she had become distanced from her natural constituency. Her great strength as a politician had always been her instinctive feel for the public (or at least for the section that was likely to vote for her), but it was hard for that instinct to survive the remoteness of office, after what Alan Clark once described as 'a decade of motorcades'. Now it seemed that, just a couple of years into his premiership, Blair was heading in the same direction. 'There's a bit of a feeling about the place that TB is losing touch with ordinary people and what matters to them,' noted Lance Price in January 1999. 'He seems almost bored with all the ordinary stuff and interested only in all the foreign leaders, Clinton, wars, etc.'

Blair himself, of course, acknowledged no such doubts. 'I know I am right,' he insisted in May 2000. 'I am where the country is.' The need to reassure himself on the point was occasioned by Philip Gould's latest set of focus-group findings, which showed the government was perceived as being weak on crime, Europe, asylum, defence and the family. In response Blair had written a personal memo that was duly leaked to the press. 'It is bizarre that any government I lead should be seen as anti-family,' he noted. 'All these things add up to a sense that the government — and this even applies to me — is somehow out of touch with gut British instincts.' He demanded yet more policy initiatives to grab the headlines: 'the government needs something tough with immediate bite which sends a message through the system. Maybe the driving licence penalty for young offenders. But this should be done soon and I personally should be associated with it.'

Chris Mullin observed of that memo: 'It is remarkably shallow and short term. There is an air of panic running through it.' More than that, it displayed no insight into how to remedy the problem. If there was a failing, it was the fact that the government appeared more interested in sending signals than in real action, but Blair's only response was to seek out yet more signals that might be sent.

In the absence of ideology or philosophy, New Labour had promised competence, but there was little of that currently on show. In pursuit of modernity, the government was entranced by technology, commissioning large computer systems such as the one intended to deal with passport applications; introduced in 1999, it promptly built up a backlog of over half a million applications, a failure already experienced in the immigration service and one that was to be repeated elsewhere. Computers were widely believed to be the tool of the future, but getting them to work proved harder than governments of either stripe had imagined. Perhaps that was partly due to a certain technological illiteracy at the top for, despite Blair's boast of being 'a modern man' and 'part of the rock and roll generation', he wasn't entirely sure of himself when it came to a straightforward computing concept like the Millennium Bug: 'David Miliband tried to explain it once, and I honestly didn't have a clue what he was talking about.'

The real difficulties, though, came with much more old-fashioned issues. In January 2000 the NHS was put under huge strain by a particularly bad flu epidemic, and struggled to cope. Amongst the host of horror stories to emerge was the appallingly casual treatment of an elderly woman whose son happened to be Professor Robert Winston, a Labour peer and one of the best-known doctors in the country, thanks to his broadcasting career. In an interview with the *New Statesman*, Winston described the NHS as the worst health service in Europe and said the government had failed to improve it: 'we have made medical care deeply unsatisfactory for many people.'

This hit hard at the heart of Labour, whether old or new, and Tony Blair responded to the criticism by announcing in a television interview that health spending in Britain would be raised to the average level of other EU countries. The declaration hadn't been agreed with Gordon Brown, who made clear that he saw it as 'not a commitment, but an aspiration', but both had revealed themselves to be out of step with the public. So focused had they been on establishing an image of financial rectitude, that they had failed to take into account the people's appetite, after years of rising prosperity, for the increased spending on health and education that they thought they had voted for in 1997 (even if no such pledges had been made). The budget in 2000 promised yet again, this time more credibly, the release of more tax revenue.

The clumsiness remained, however, and the days when a sure-footed New Labour opposition was the master of all the media it surveyed seemed ever more distant. The misreading of the popular mood reached a new low in June 2000 with Blair's very public humiliation at the hands of the Women's Institute.

The occasion was an appearance at the organisation's national conference, over which Blair had agonised for days, turning to some unlikely figures for help in articulating his message, including the right-wing journalist Paul Johnson. The result was a call for a reassertion of traditional values: 'Respect for the old, for what it has still to teach; respect for others, honour, self-discipline, duty obligation, the essential decency of the British character.' Viewed in a low light, it could almost have been mistaken for John Major's exhortation to return to basics, but in the event it was received with even less enthusiasm. There were heckles, boos and slow handclapping, while several members of the audience walked out, leaving Blair on stage looking as though he were returned to his days as Bambi, this time caught in the headlights of an oncoming truck.

'What on earth was all that about?' he asked as he left the stage, thoroughly rattled by the hostile reception. The answer was spelt out to the press by Helen Carey, the WI's national chairman: 'We made the point very clearly that this was not a political platform. We told them that if Mr Blair was political it would backfire because members would not like it. I think they felt their meeting had been hijacked.' As the media revelled in the prime minister's discomfort, even Campbell acknowledged that he couldn't spin his way out of this one: 'there was no way we would win a war of words with the Women's Institute.'

So much of the marketing of New Labour had focused exclusively on Blair himself that the incident reflected disproportionately badly on the whole enterprise. The only answer, he concluded, was that 'we simply had to hold our nerve and have balls of steel'. Seldom had his favourite formulation been more inappropriate, or more revealing of the laddishness of his premiership, than when responding to the Women's Institute.

David Blunkett reflected that the public relations disaster of the speech might prove beneficial, since 'It shook people in the party out of complacency at a time when we had dropped to just a three per cent lead in one opinion poll.' That was overly optimistic, for more unwinnable fights were yet to be picked.

The flu outbreak that had hospitalised Robert Winston's mother contributed to the highest winter death rate amongst the elderly for a decade. But politically the bone of contention for pensioners was the announcement the previous autumn that the basic state pension would rise in 2000 by just 75 pence a week. Pensioners' campaigning groups, led by veteran figures from the Labour movement including the former trade union leader Jack Jones and the former cabinet minister Barbara Castle, had long called for pension increases to be linked to pay rises, but a succession of chancellors – including Gordon Brown – had resisted such expenditure and opted instead for a link with prices. Now, a fall in the rate of inflation had produced what was widely seen as a derisory increase.

Through the years of Conservative government, support for pensioners had been a sacred part of Labour rhetoric. The heartless Tories' treatment of the elderly was regularly cited as an example of how little they cared for the weakest in society, particularly in 1993 when the pension had increased by just 70 pence a week. Now, it seemed, such concerns were no longer a priority. In April 2000 Clive Soley, the chair of the Parliamentary Labour Party, was reported to have spoken of the elderly in disparaging terms to a meeting of party researchers: 'I would not say they are all racist but some have been expressing racist views.' He also implied that politically they were not worth worrying about: 'They are the only age group in Britain where there has been a consistent Tory majority. We are talking about people more than half of whom are bound not to be our supporters.' There were further reports that Peter Mandelson shared that latter position, concluding that there was 'no mileage' to be gained from chasing the pensioner vote.

As the press hunted for further such insults, it was revealed that Charlie Falconer had told a retired dinner lady that he would have no problem living on a state pension. In response Jeff Rooker, the social security minister, back-pedalled as fast as he could, remarking that he certainly wouldn't be able to live on such an income and 'wouldn't even dream of trying'. It was hard to know which was more damaging: the remote arrogance or the truth.

The depiction of older members of society as natural Tories was a self-fulfilling analysis. In July 2000 Labour held a four-point lead in the polls over the Conservatives amongst pensioners; as the controversy grew, and the reality of the 75p rise sank in, that position was more than reversed, with Labour falling ten points behind. In vain did Brown point to the substantial increase in money paid to pensioners; the system of means-tested benefits he had established was so complex it ensured that many simply didn't feel the benefit, and the labyrinthine nature of his tax schemes was never going to compete for headline space with the brevity of 75p. The anger was very real. Tony Blair was horrified to see an old woman with a placard reading

BLAIR, YOU ARE A CUNT. 'I couldn't believe it. I was really shocked,' he recalled. 'She looked like your typical sweet granny.'

In September the Labour conference voted against the measure and called for the restoration of the link between pensions and earnings. Such votes were not binding, but Blair looked suitably chastened, even as he sought to allocate blame to the person who he clearly felt was responsible for the fiasco: 'I tell you now, as Gordon made crystal clear yesterday, we get the message.' He delivered the speech in his shirtsleeves, presumably intending to convey the impression that he was getting down to business, but unfortunately he was wearing a blue shirt and the patches of sweat under his arms made him look both unattractive and flustered. As Michael Dobbs had once observed: 'Prime ministers aren't meant to sweat, to show pressure or exasperation.'

It was announced that the following year the pension rise would be £2 a week, and in November a further concession was made with an increase in the winter fuel allowance for pensioners from £150 to £200. Some cynics noted that the timing of this decision might have been made not with winter in mind, but with spring, when a general election was expected.

The panicked response also reflected a dawning awareness on the part of politicians that, with an ageing population, it was foolish to dismiss pensioners in such a cavalier manner. A change of national atmosphere was evident on television, where *One Foot in the Grave*, *Waiting for God* and *In Sickness and in Health* — as well as other sitcoms including *The Upper Hand* and *As Time Goes By* — depicted an older generation unwilling to accept being written off by society, determined to remain engaged and often angry. 'It'll change,' points out a professor of geriatric medicine in *Waiting for God*. 'As soon as the baby boomers become the wrinkly boomers, then there'll be a whole new set of attitudes appearing.' There were even signs in youth culture of such a change; the first single from Robbie Williams's debut album (following his departure from Take That) reversed the Who's famous maxim to announce: 'I hope I'm old before I die.'

The battles with the Women's Institute and with pensioners helped to erode further the national spirit of optimism engendered by the cultural excitement of the mid-1990s and by Blair's election. In June 2000 Philip Gould revealed that, according to his focus-group studies, people now felt 'that the country has little hope, is going to the dogs, is not a great country any more'. It began to look as though New Labour had failed to study hard enough the example of Major's government and its ability to court unpopularity even with a booming economy.

The conflicts were also clearly taking their toll on the prime minister.

In July 2000 he addressed the conference of the African and Caribbean Evangelical Alliance and sounded unusually weary: 'I know it's only been three years, but sometimes it seems like thirty,' Blair said, echoing — perhaps inadvertently — words from *Jesus Christ Superstar*, the rock opera that had been such a sensation at the time of his brief attempt to make it in the music business. 'Tried for three years, felt like thirty; could you ask as much from any other man?' despairs Jesus in the Garden of Gethsemane.

If there were to be a Gethsemane for Blair in his first term, however, it had yet to come. For the government returned from its summer holidays to find itself embroiled in a far more damaging dispute, perhaps the worst of the parliament.

In 1993, the Conservative government had introduced what was known as the fuel duty escalator, a system designed to ensure that the tax on petrol would rise faster than inflation, with an increase in real terms of at least 3 per cent a year, later rising to 5 per cent. Like the introduction of VAT on domestic fuel, this was billed as a green tax though, as Tony Blair acknowledged, 'no one took that reasoning very seriously'. It was, however, a very useful source of income and so the Labour government kept the policy in place, and increased it to 6 per cent, calculating that a steady year-on-year escalation of prices at the pumps was sustainable. That turned out not to be the case.

Demonstrations against fuel tax in 1999 helped convince Gordon Brown to end the escalator in his budget in November that year, but by then — critics argued — the damage had been done to the competitiveness of British industry. Over 80 per cent of the price of petrol was now accounted for by tax, through a combination of VAT and fuel duty, making Britain the most expensive country in Europe to fill up a car. Or, more pertinently, a lorry. For it was haulage drivers whose patience finally snapped as world oil prices rose sharply. In September 2000, acting in conjunction with farmers' pressure groups, lorry drivers began a series of blockades of oil refineries and distribution depots, effectively shutting off the supply line to petrol stations.

Within a couple of days a genuine crisis emerged. In recent years supermarkets and petrol stations had adopted a 'just in time' supply system, whereby stocks were kept to a minimum at retail points, making them extremely vulnerable to any interruption in deliveries. A fuel shortage thus had an immediate and powerful impact, striking at a fragile food chain. 'We weren't far off a crisis in the basic infrastructure of the nation,' reflected Alastair Campbell, while Jonathan Powell was later to write:

'The public never realised quite how close we had come to shutting the country down on 13 and 14 September 2000. Ford had been about to close its European operations; hospitals were about to shut down for lack of fuel; and cashpoints were about to run out of money.' The Queen was prevailed upon to sign an Emergency Order, allowing a state of emergency to be declared if it was considered necessary.

There was an echo here of the fabled winter of discontent when, in the early months of 1979, the last Labour government had found itself in conflict with various trade unions. The most disruptive element in that dispute had been a transport workers' strike that prevented food and other supplies from being moved around the country. The ensuing chaos had provided the backdrop to Margaret Thatcher's election victory, and the Conservatives had never been shy of reminding the country of those times in subsequent years. Talk of the country being 'held to ransom' by the unions had become an important part of the demonology of the right. It was the lingering effectiveness of that charge, more than anything else, that had persuaded Blair to distance the Labour Party from the union movement.

Now, however, it was not the unions that were at the root of the government's troubles, but the self-employed, the small businessmen and women, the self-reliant, non-unionised, aspirational workers whose votes and support Blair had spent so much time trying to court. It was a point not lost on the unions, as a spokesperson for the GMB observed: 'It is ironic that the country is being brought to a standstill by blockades and pickets conducted by small businessmen and traditional allies of the Conservatives.' The irony didn't end there. 'The life of a nation is being strangled,' thundered John Monks, general secretary of the TUC, using precisely the language associated with the Thatcher government. 'This has gone well beyond democratic protests. It is bullying and intimidation – holding the country to ransom.'

The blockades ('or picket lines as we used to call them', noted David Blunkett) were, at least to start with, generally well supported. The protestors' demand for an immediate and substantial reduction in fuel duty struck a chord with virtually every motorist in the country. The newspapers, although in some cases reluctant to back direct action, were broadly sympathetic, and were scathing towards the government. The most powerful front page came from the normally loyal *Daily Mirror*, which printed pictures of Tony Blair, Gordon Brown and John Prescott, superimposed on petrol pumps, with the headline: EMPTY. The text read: 'These three men run the country. Today the country will run dry. None of them knows quite how to get it going again, but they all agree it's not their fault.'

The Tories benefited from the confusion and their standing rose in the opinion polls, briefly overtaking Labour for the first time in eight years and causing panic in government ranks. The prime minister's anger was directed both at the newspapers for their supposed role in whipping up the crisis – 'I felt that a Tory government would not be treated like this,' he complained, conveniently forgetting the media treatment of John Major – and at the police for not dispersing the protestors: 'if this was Thatcher and the miners, the police would waste no time wading in.'

The action provoked mixed responses on the left. 'Although I don't support this type of action, it is a popular movement – if the word "popular" is used in its proper sense – against a high level of tax,' reflected Tony Benn, in grudging admiration, while for Chris Mullin it merely illustrated the futility of New Labour's electoral strategy: 'After years of creeping and crawling to Middle England, they've abandoned us at the first whiff of grapeshot.'

Perhaps most significantly, the speed with which the protests spread – helped in no small measure by the growing popularity of mobile phones – suggested that the prime minister had drifted out of touch with the public, the very danger he had been warned about the previous year. 'I had messed up big time,' admitted Blair in his memoirs. 'My antennae should have been twitching.' For a man who, according to his adviser David Miliband, was impatient with the details of opinion polls – 'He is much more fingertip sensitive, trusts his instincts not the figures' – there was a shocked realisation at how things had slipped. He hadn't even paid attention to his own domestic focus group: 'I should have realised that for your ordinary motorist, the rising cost of filling the car was a big, not an insignificant one (after all, the children's nanny, Jackie, had been complaining about it for weeks).'

The response, however, once the scale of the problem was grasped, was swift and effective. The police were told to take more decisive action against the blockades, with the threat that the army would be called in should they fail so to do, and a major public relations operation swung into action. The propaganda initiative was seized with briefings about the potential threat to the NHS, a line strengthened when nurses were sent to put their case to the pickets. Meanwhile, Gordon Brown simply refused to cede any ground on the demonstrators' demands, arguing that if he yielded, it would merely encourage further such protests. It was an entirely reasonable attitude, though Peter Mandelson thought 'politically it was tone-deaf'.

The combination of measures brought the immediate crisis to an end and within a couple of days normal service was restored in the country and in politics. The Conservatives' lead in the polls proved short-lived, largely because, at the start of the protests, Michael Portillo had vetoed William Hague's proposal to promise a major cut in petrol tax. By the time he agreed to pledge a more modest reduction, it was too late and the Tories were accused of bandwagon-jumping. Come November the Labour lead was back up to seven points, but the image of a government that was both out of touch and incompetent, the same dangerous combination seen in John Major's administration, lingered on.

Blair's personal rating at the height of the crisis fell to minus 34, the lowest for a Labour leader since Neil Kinnock in 1989. Comparisons with the latter days of Thatcher seemed ever more apposite. 'I don't know why they don't like me,' she had complained of the public in her last months in office. Now Blair was, according to Philip Gould, similarly 'mystified as to why a government that is doing well economically should not be popular'.

Perhaps the most disappointing aspect of the entire affair, though, was that it seemed to prompt no serious thought on the part of the government, despite revealing a precariously poised society, its support system existing in a delicate state of balance which was no more than a few days away from serious breakdown. The perception in Whitehall was that the situation became so serious so quickly because of panic-buying by consumers. 'The instinct to buy was perfectly logical individually but disastrous collectively,' observed Jonathan Powell. To this there was apparently no answer, despite Blair's longstanding promise to rebuild a spirit of community. And when it came to the roles played by the supermarkets and the oil companies, the necessary questions weren't even raised. The underlying issue, however, was much the same: 'just in time' policies maximised profits, but were dangerously anti-social, leaving the country vulnerable to attack. But by now no one really expected this, or any other, government to demand responsibility or morality from major companies.

Whether there was much demand at this point for political action to curb the power of multinational companies was doubtful. A loose coalition of anti-capitalist groups had staged a major protest in November 1999 outside a meeting of the World Trade Organisation in Seattle, but a May Day demonstration in London in 2000 attracted only some 5,000 people. The event turned into a riot during which a McDonald's restaurant was wrecked, several shops looted, the Cenotaph defaced and – in one of the wittier images to come out of a British demonstration for some time – the statue of Winston Churchill in Parliament Square adorned with a strip of turf, giving him a grass Mohican. Unsurprisingly the press weren't amused. The patriotic *Sun* was outraged (RIOT YOBS DESECRATE CHURCHILL MONUMENT) but for once was outdone by the *Daily Mirror*: THIS WAS THEIR VILEST HOUR. The *Sun* was also keen to point out that the demonstration was 'largely organised on the internet'. In response to these disturbances, the police developed the tactic of 'kettling' for the next May Day demonstration, surrounding and containing protestors for long periods of time until weariness replaced anger.

There seemed little prospect that such moments would turn into a coherent movement any time soon, and most of the substantial incidents of social disorder during this parliament (as in Oldham, Burnley and Bradford in 2001) were primarily racial, related to the rise of the British National Party. The virtual disappearance of socialism in Britain and beyond, combined with the absence of leadership – Ken Livingstone was quick to condemn the 'mindless thugs' and 'violent hooligans' seen in London just days before the mayoral elections – meant that anti-capitalism was likely to remain a minority slogan rather than a coherent philosophy for the foreseeable future. The one exception was an irritant left over from the Major government.

The Hatfield rail crash in October 2000 was, by the standards of such incidents, not one of the worst disasters the country had witnessed. Four people were killed, fewer than half the average daily total that year on Britain's roads. But railway privatisation had always been controversial, even in New Labour circles, and the discovery that the cause was faulty maintenance of the track prompted a panic about the state of the rail infrastructure. In what many considered an extreme over-reaction, rail schedules were disrupted for over a year as hundreds of speed restrictions were imposed and track replacement works undertaken. The impact on Railtrack, the company responsible for the rails, was sufficient to send it into administration, at which point its duties were handed over to a new body called Network Rail. Still privately owned, it was at least a not-for-dividend company, which provided some comfort to those on the left who had always objected to privatisation.

There was no such reassurance to be found with the government's response to the news in late 2000 that Richard Desmond, having made his fortune with downmarket pornographic magazines including *Asian Babes*, *40 Plus* and *Women on Top*, and then branched out into celebrity gossip with *OK!* magazine, was now to become a newspaper proprietor, by buying the *Daily Express*, the *Sunday Express* and the *Daily Star*. Such a purchase could have been the subject of an inquiry, but in February 2001 the trade secretary, Stephen Byers, announced that he wouldn't be asking the Competition Commission to stage an investigation. Barely a week later, Desmond made a donation to the Labour Party, much to the horror of some senior ministers, particularly Tessa Jowell and Harriet Harman, who disapproved of the source of his wealth. Desmond's reported comment to Alastair Campbell – 'I'm not happy about these bitches Jowell and Harman' – did nothing to suggest that their estimation of him was far wrong.

Relations between the government and the press continued, however, to deteriorate. Indeed, the media was shortly to claim its greatest scalp. Peter Mandelson, having been obliged to resign once already from the cabinet, found himself again mired in controversy at the start of 2001, the year that was widely expected to see a general election. At issue was the case of two Indian businessmen, the brothers G.P. and S.P. Hinduja, and their effort to acquire British passports. Having applied for passports in 1990, the Hindujas had been turned down by the Conservative government on the grounds that they didn't spend enough time in the country and were being investigated in relation to an alleged financial scandal in India. Charges brought against the two men in 2000 were later thrown out by the High Court in Delhi for lack of evidence, but during the investigation some speculated that part of the reason they wanted British nationality was that they could then establish a bolthole if things got too hot at home. Following the 1997 election, G.P. Hinduja's passport application was approved, as, a little later, was S.P. Hinduja's. Soon after they received this happy news, the brothers agreed to sponsor the Faith Zone in the Millennium Dome, then being overseen by Peter Mandelson.

The story, such as it was, fell dormant until January 2001, when the *Observer* ran an article suggesting that Mandelson had helped the brothers get their passports. He explained that he had indeed been asked by the Hindujas to assist with their application, but – he insisted – that he had very properly refused to do so: 'At no time did I support or endorse this application for citizenship.' That was the story passed to the press by Alastair Campbell and to Parliament. Unfortunately, a Home Office minister named Mike O'Brien had a different tale to tell. He remembered Mandelson himself phoning to discuss the Hindujas' applications. Campbell apologised to the lobby journalists for having misled them, saying that, while Mandelson had no memory of such a phone call, it had clearly been made. Mandelson, on the other hand, continued to deny that he had made any such call and was furious with Campbell for his briefings.

It was a confused, messy and murky tale, in the midst of which the truth seemed likely to be lost. But in the context of a government that had always promoted its personalities, it offered the instant attraction of open conflict between Campbell and Mandelson, Blair's two greatest courtiers and two men who had long had their differences. One was bound to lose. And unfortunately for Mandelson, he had few friends left; he was, said Blair, 'pretty much alone and without support except for me'.

The danger for the government, observed Lance Price, was of 'a perceived cover-up' and, without even the courtesy of an inquiry, Mandelson was forced to resign from the cabinet for a second time in a single parliament. Blair's diary secretary, Anji Hunter, was said to have been reduced to tears: 'It's the end of New Labour. It was all due to Peter, Gordon and me and now Peter is going, it's all over.' But grief was not the primary emotion in Westminster. 'The truth is,' wrote Chris Mullin in his diary, 'that most people on our side are delighted to see the back of him and are doing their best, with varying degrees of success, not to gloat.'

In his briefings to the press, Campbell hinted heavily that this was the end of Mandelson's political ambitions: 'It is an absolute tragedy that his entire career is in tatters.' There was also an implication, reported by the lobby journalists, that Mandelson's behaviour was, like that of Ron Davies, a 'moment of madness'. And this time round, there was no encouragement for Mandelson to be found in the press, which simply revelled in his fall: GOODBYE AND GOOD RIDDANCE (THIS TIME DON'T COME BACK) waved the *Sun*; YOU WERE THE WEAKEST LINK — GOODBYE jeered the *Daily Mirror*. (The latter referred to a newly popular television quiz show hosted by Anne Robinson, though it was some way wide of the mark; Mandelson was far from the weakest link in the New Labour chain.)

Mandelson's resignation statement expressed some of the frustration he had been bottling up for years: 'There must be more to politics than the constant media pressure and exposure that had dogged me over the last five or so years. I want to remove myself from the countless stories of controversies, feuds and divisions.' Those with long political memories could detect an echo here of Richard Nixon's notorious press conference after losing the 1962 gubernatorial election in California: 'you don't have Nixon to kick around any more because, gentlemen, this is my last press conference.' Six years later, of course, Nixon had been elected president, and just five weeks after Mandelson's swansong an official inquiry into the Hinduja affair concluded that his actions had been neither dishonest nor improper. No one was entirely convinced that they could really write off his chances of another return to government.

The loss of Mandelson for a second time gave the lie to New Labour's claims to competence in government. The highest profile resignation from John Major's cabinet had been David Mellor, a confidant of the prime minister, but still no more than the minister for fun. Mandelson, however, had been obliged to step down first from trade and industry, and then from Northern Ireland, the latter at a stage when the future of the peace process still hung in the balance. Even his official positions, let alone his acknowledged role as the founder of New Labour, meant that his departure was of a different order altogether from anything Major had suffered. Although he was no longer a central figure – and hence was deemed expendable ('the need for a Peter Mandelson has withered,' as John O'Farrell put it) – the image of Blair sacrificing his mentor could hardly fail to resonate.

There was a perfectly coherent case to be made – Mandelson made it himself, repeatedly and forcefully – that he had done nothing wrong and had been pushed out with unnecessary haste, given no chance to defend himself. But somehow that only made the government's fitness for office even more questionable, revealing the macho egos and power struggles in Downing Street. There was, however, one consolation for ministers to cling on to, no matter how bad the headlines. As David Blunkett put it in his diary: 'Thank the Lord the Tories are so useless.'

To complete the picture of John Major's government repeating itself, this time as farce, there came in February 2001 the first outbreak of foot-and-mouth disease for twenty years, creating a farming crisis to rival that of BSE. In terms of public health, there was no comparison. The terrifying fear that BSE could be transmitted to humans in the form of vCJD was simply not matched by foot-and-mouth; the last case of a human being infected in Britain by the latter had been in 1966, and such incidents were vanishingly rare – certainly it couldn't be passed on through eating contaminated meat. Nonetheless, the new outbreak inevitably provoked memories that were still fresh in the mind. Indeed there was a suggestion that the two issues were linked, that since the closure of small, local abattoirs during the BSE crisis, animals were being moved far greater distances, thereby facilitating the rapid spread of foot-and-mouth.

The Labour Party had never been noted for its commitment to the rural economy, and the present government was no exception to that rule. Apart from the long and wearisome campaign to ban hunting, its principal contribution thus far had been its decision in 2000 to remove the restrictions introduced by the Attlee government upon the placement of advertising hoardings in fields, but even that had been reversed before its implementation. Now, facing a nationwide epidemic amongst cattle, and with its options restricted by EU regulations, it decided to follow the same path as the Major government and to slaughter any herd that had been infected. That programme expanded into the killing of animals in the vicinity of such a farm, and soon the funeral pyres were blazing again, one of them, Blair noted sardonically, 'situated near the Heathrow flight path, to delight the passengers hoping to spend a few days in rural idyllic Britain'. By April Michael Meacher, the environment minister, was reporting: 'We've slaughtered a million animals, 97 per cent of them healthy. It's animal genocide. Just like the Somme. The prime minister won't opt for vaccination because the farmers object and he won't go against them.'

That judgement was a little unfair. In truth there was little else the government could do. For if the experience of BSE was still a recent memory for the British, so too was it for the rest of the world. As soon as the news broke, the EU banned the export of meat and related animal products from the UK, and the message went out again that British food was unsafe. An outbreak of swine fever in 2000 had already resulted in a temporary ban on pork exports and the slaughter of 12,000 pigs, and for once the tabloid headlines – PLAGUE ON THE LAND, read the *Daily Mirror* – didn't seem exaggerated. There was still scope for panic, of course (NO MEAT LEFT BY END OF THE WEEK, shrieked the *Express*), but farming in Britain did seem to be blighted. If confidence in the industry was ever to be restored, extreme and high-profile measures were necessary.

Apart from anything else, foot-and-mouth is a highly contagious disease and the mass slaughter of animals was only one element of the government's attempt to prevent its spread. The other was the effective isolation of the countryside. Much of the horse-racing calendar was suspended, rambling and recreational riding were discouraged, the National Trust and the RSPB closed many of their properties to the public. The movement of livestock was banned, and that of humans heavily restricted.

If the government's public response, however heavy-handed, was inevitable, it came with all the usual turf wars that had become such a common feature of the New Labour hierarchy. The agriculture minister was Nick Brown, MP for the distinctly non-rural constituency of Newcastle East, and the response to foot-and-mouth should have been primarily his concern. But he was a close ally of his namesake Gordon, which meant that foot-and-mouth became another weapon in the war of Downing Street. Jonathan Powell overheard Gordon Brown on the phone telling Nick to resist Blair's 'presidential style' and to keep hold of the issue: 'We have to stop him taking foot-and-mouth away from you.' From the other side, Nick Brown's position in the Ministry of Agriculture, Fisheries and Food meant that the department was seen as being suspect; Alastair Campbell talked about Downing Street having 'pretty much lost confidence in MAFF'.

Again, there were potential lessons to be learnt about the fragility of society, had the right questions only been asked in the right places. 'All this export of animals for slaughter, the global trade in food and so on, is bringing health hazards,' observed Tony Benn; 'it would be better to have local farmers growing local food and feeding local people from local markets.'

As the story ran on, unvarying in its horror, the media struggled to maintain its interest. In desperation, a story was found of a farm where all the cattle had been given lethal injections and left to die. Some days later, however, a calf was said to have been discovered still alive amidst the carnage, just one day old at the time the death sentence was enacted, and born – happily enough – on Good Friday. Swiftly named Phoenix, the suspiciously photogenic white calf became a tabloid star, with the *Daily Mirror* leading a campaign to have the animal reprieved. As though it made any difference, the order duly went out from Downing Street that Phoenix was to be spared. As Campbell put it, 'we had to play along.'

More significantly, the fact that the countryside was now closed for business meant that the projected general election date was looking increasingly unlikely. A range of opinion-formers, from Dennis Skinner through to the Queen, told Blair that the election would have to be postponed. In truth, there was very little choice; an election long intended for May was put back to 7 June 2001.

The outcome of that election, the colour of the government that would emerge, was never in doubt. To have overcome Labour's parliamentary majority, the Conservatives would have required a huge swing and, apart from that brief aberration during the fuel crisis, they hadn't enjoyed a lead in the opinion polls for nearly nine years. In any event Tony Blair had always been clear that he was seeking two full terms in office and, after eighteen years of Tory government, the country was inclined to give him the benefit of the doubt.

Peter Mandelson had insisted in 1997 that the Labour government could only be properly judged after 'ten years of success in office', but some were prepared to issue an interim report. In 1999 David Miliband itemised what he saw as the legacies put in place thus far: 'independence for the Bank of England, the national minimum wage, devolution, a settlement in Northern Ireland (hopefully) and the Dome.' Blair himself offered a similar list in 2002, though obviously omitting the Dome: 'If I die tomorrow, they would say he was the guy who modernised the Labour Party, made it electable, won two landslides, sorted the economy, improved public services, Bank of England, Kosovo, Northern Ireland.' In December 2000, he had been asked what his greatest achievement had been. 'There's our part in the progress toward peace in Northern Ireland and also in giving Britain a strong voice again in Europe,' he replied. 'I'm also proud of the fact that the New Deal has helped to reduce youth unemployment by 70 per cent.'

That latter claim, in particular, was crucial, for employment was the one issue that most demonstrated continuity with the best traditions of the Labour movement. It had been a long time since leading members of the party had talked of full employment as a realisable aspiration, but progress in that direction was desperately wanted. In March 2001, just in time for the election, the official figures showed that unemployment had fallen to below a million, for the first time since the days of James Callaghan in 1975.

That month Robin Cook was at pains to stress how much Labour had achieved for its working-class base. 'This government has done far, far better than any previous Labour government,' he argued; '800,000 new jobs, the New Deal, long-term unemployment halved. Look also at the minimum wage, trade-union recognition.' David Blunkett was likewise at pains to make a comparison with old Labour: 'I suspect that what will be remembered from our government will be much more substantial than anything from 1964–70 or 1974–79.' And Clare Short insisted that in the first term there were 'many achievements of which Labour people could be proud, most importantly the return to full employment'.

Much depended on those official figures and on whether they could be trusted. In opposition, Labour had been scathing of attempts to manipulate the statistics; now it was understandably more content to accept the good news that came its way, though there were still doubters. Chris Mullin noted that 9,000 people were claiming Jobseekers' Allowance in Sunderland, but that also 'a staggering 38,000 are claiming for sickness, incapacity or disability. None of these are even in the market for work, although many of them must be capable of doing something.' It was alleged by many that right through the 1990s, under governments of both parties, there had been a policy of encouraging the unemployed to register as disabled in order to make the figures look more respectable. There might be fewer than a million signing on, but – it was said – that didn't fully reflect the reality of the job market. Certainly that figure was dwarfed by the number of people of working age who were, to use a phrase that was gaining currency, economically inactive, some four million who didn't show up in the official figures for the unemployed.

Mullin added to his description of the state of Sunderland a warning note: 'Benefit culture is our greatest inheritance from the Thatcher Decade.

It hangs around our neck like a huge albatross.' This was what Frank Field had been drafted into government to address, before it was realised that his prescription was simply too radical. And perhaps his departure from office was inevitable. The welfare state had been created fifty years earlier by the Attlee government, to a blueprint provided by William Beveridge, and had been based on the concept of full employment; without the political will to reinstate that objective, it was unlikely that a genuine return to the principles of Attlee and Beveridge could be achieved.

Perhaps too the statistics were unfair to Blair's administration, if compared with the last Labour government in the 1970s, since they took no account of the rise in the numbers of women in the workforce. There were now three million more people employed in Britain than there had been in the mid-1970s, not all of whom were accounted for by the growth in the population.

In any event, it could safely be said that, since its peak in 1992, official unemployment had fallen by two million, half of that fall being achieved during Tony Blair's first term in office; the downward trend had been maintained. Similarly the annual rise in GDP inherited from John Major had been maintained, interest rates had experienced no abrupt changes and the inflation rate had continued to fall. Taxes as a share of GDP had increased, although in buoyant times, this was comfortably sustainable. More worryingly, job insecurity had continued to grow, wealth inequality had resumed its rise, after the stabilising years under Major, and there were longer-term implications arising from the continuing failure to regulate properly the financial industry, and from the availability of easy credit. But senior politicians of both parties chose not to dwell on such matters. The important thing in the immediate moment was that, unlike most previous Labour governments, this one could go to the polls boasting of economic success. It was a point that Gordon Brown made forcefully to Blair as they laid their plans for the 2001 election. 'The Tories screwed up the economy, and we've given people stability and growth,' he argued. 'It's about time you fucking realised that's all the election is about.'

Implicit in that analysis was a recognition that, even if New Labour had proved economically competent, it had failed to communicate any sense of philosophy or direction. As Alastair Campbell admitted: 'people felt we were better at defining what we weren't than what we were.' After three years of preparation for and four years in office, Labour was able to trumpet few achievements that were specifically of its own making. Even the very modest proposals on the pledge cards issued in 1997 seemed unlikely to be met by the time of voting, a problem for which the spin doctor Lance Price had an answer: 'We will just have to say that the pledges were for a five-year parliament.' It was Price too who admitted the truth of the forthcoming campaign: 'We mustn't let the election slip back to being a referendum on the government's record. Must stick to the Choice.' The strongest card that Labour had to play was that the alternative to Tony Blair was a return to Conservative rule.

Indeed the only real question for the election was how badly the Conservatives would fare. The more optimistic saw William Hague's task as being to reduce Labour's parliamentary majority to double figures, thereby allowing a serious assault to be mounted next time. Not many were so hopeful, and plenty expected still further decline. 'I may not hold this seat and will go down with 60–70 existing Conservative MPs,' worried the Worcestershire MP, Michael Spicer. 'We may even lose our position as the official opposition.'

Even tried and tested Tory policies were looking like vote-losers, as the journalist Boris Johnson – now the Conservative candidate for Michael Heseltine's old, and very safe, seat of Henley – observed. 'Slowly, and barely perceptibly, the phrase "tax cut" has become a little ambiguous, and certainly no longer guaranteed to raise a cheer,' he wrote. 'It is extraordinary. This is the same electorate that mutinied over the cost of petrol.' He was also concerned that the campaign against the single currency, which William Hague had made the central plank of the Tory platform, smacked rather of desperation. 'We are saying that there are seven days to save the pound,' he noted. 'It sounds too much like seven days to save the Tory party.'

The nervousness was evident in a poster that showed Blair at his most smug, captured in a bubble, being approached by a hand bearing a pin. GO ON, BURST HIS BUBBLE, ran the caption, in a damage-limitation exercise, pleading with the public not to give Labour another landslide.

It was, even by comparison with 1997, a dull campaign, almost all the moments of interest being crammed into a single day at the outset. On 16 May the launch of the Labour manifesto was followed by what should have been an unexceptional photo-opportunity for Blair as he visited the Queen Elizabeth Hospital in Birmingham. It turned into a deeply awkward trip when the prime minister was cornered on camera by Sharron Storer, whose husband was being treated for cancer in the hospital, and who was unhappy with the treatment he was receiving. As so often in such cases (Margaret Thatcher being quizzed by Diana Gould in 1983 about the sinking of the *Belgrano*, Gordon Brown being accosted by Gillian Duffy in 2010), outrage was much more effective on television when voiced by a woman. Blair looked bewildered and lost as he attempted to reassure someone who had no apparent appetite for reassurance, just action.

Coverage of Blair's discomfort at least ensured that the news bulletins didn't lead on the sight of Jack Straw being slow-handclapped and heckled at the Police Federation conference. But even Blair himself was driven into second spot by John Prescott who, on a visit to Rhyl in North Wales, was struck on the back of the neck by an egg thrown by a local farmer, Craig Evans. Without pause for thought, Prescott turned and hit out with a straight left that connected perfectly; his years of training as an amateur boxer had clearly not been forgotten. He was later to explain that he hadn't realised it was merely an egg: 'It certainly didn't feel like one, but then I would never have believed an egg crashing into you can feel so powerful.'

There was a moment of panic in the prime minister's circle as they digested the news and tried to work out what the response should be. Clearly the physical assault of voters by members of the cabinet was not to be encouraged, but there was also the fact, as Blair commented, that the incident was 'extraordinarily funny'. There was a split, according to David Blunkett, between 'those who liked it and those who didn't, men on the one hand and women, middle-class women in particular, on the other'. Confirming that division, Prescott received messages of support from the likes of Alex Ferguson and Sean Connery, neither of them men noted for their readiness to turn the other cheek. In the end, it was decided to laugh the whole thing off. Prescott's nickname in the party had long been Thumper and Blair's public comment was a simple shrug: 'John is John.' William Hague echoed the jovial tone, explaining: 'It's not my policy to hit voters during an election.'

The only other moment of excitement came with the issue of those promises of tax cuts by the Conservatives. Hague announced that these would amount to a total of £8 billion, but a report in the *Financial Times* then quoted an anonymous senior Conservative suggesting that somewhere around £20 billion might be achievable. Media enquiries soon uncovered the source of this figure as being Oliver Letwin, a treasury spokesperson, who promptly disappeared from public view in the hope that the story would disappear. The Labour Party, while strongly protesting that it deplored the triviality of the media ('the best I could hope for was that underneath some whizz-bang piece of marketing creativity or twist to a story, we might squeeze some policy,' reflected Blair, piously), produced 'Wanted' posters with Letwin's face on them, while a press officer was dressed up as Sherlock Holmes, posing as though he were on the track of the missing MP. If that was embarrassingly childish on the part of a government, the response of the Conservative Party was simply a mess. Hague restated the £8 billion target, while the shadow chancellor, Michael Portillo, suggested that £20 billion might indeed be right.

Unlike 1997, this was not a time for the Cool Britannia message. The Labour Party's anthem for the campaign was 'Lifted' by the Lighthouse Family, though few noticed, while the stars lining up in support were old faithfuls rather than young fashionistas: Alex Ferguson, Mick Hucknall, 93-year-old John Mills, as well as Michael Cashman and Michelle Collins, formerly of *EastEnders*. The party did, however, adorn its election broadcasts with a couple of actors from the television soap *Hollyoaks* and with former Spice Girl Geri Halliwell, who had apparently transferred her allegiance from Margaret Thatcher.

Labour went into the last week of campaigning with a lead of twenty-three points in the polls and the results of the election came as no surprise. Labour representation in the Commons was down by five seats, the Liberal Democrats under Charles Kennedy had improved by six, and the Conservatives had gained just one MP. This latter figure was seen as a disaster for the Tories, and William Hague immediately resigned as leader.

His tenure had hardly been a success. Clearly he was too young and inexperienced for the role he had accepted, but even beyond those considerations, he was probably the wrong person for the job anyway. In happier times, he would have made a fine second-in-command, but with the absence from Parliament of Michael Portillo, he was promoted too far and too fast. Even so, he had done as well as perhaps anyone could have done. Inheriting a tainted party that was determined to fight an internal, ideological war, he had held it just about together. He had behaved during the last couple of years with dignity and – in public, at any rate – with a degree of humour and resilience that must have been hard to maintain. If he had looked, at the time of his election as leader, as if he might be the Tory Michael Foot, he had ended up more like Neil Kinnock in 1987, ensuring the survival of a party that might have disappeared entirely into history.

That, however, was clutching at Westminster straws. And the real story of the election had nothing to do with Parliament. Spike Milligan had once joked: 'One day the don't knows will get in, and then where will we be?' Now it had happened. For the first time in British electoral history, fewer had voted for the victorious party than had chosen not to vote at all, and the gap between the two figures was enormous. Blair's first electoral success had set a new post-war record for low turnout, with just 71.3 per cent of the electorate casting a vote; this time round, the Labour Party attracted the support of less than a quarter of the electorate, while over 40 per cent stayed at home. More than half of those aged between eighteen and twenty-five absented themselves.

It was the worst turnout since 1918, when the election had been staged barely a month after the end of the First World War. For the Conservative Party, the news was more dire still. With even less support than it had achieved in 1997, it had now lost well over five and a half million voters since 1992, and secured the backing of fewer people than Michael Foot's Labour Party had managed in the disaster of 1983.

Some of this could be attributed to the fact that the result was so obvious from the start. Turnout declines in the face of certainty, so that Thatcher's weakest showing in her three election victories was in 1983, when victory was inevitable. Even so, the fact that an incumbent government could sink so low that it inspired fewer than one in four of the population to cast a supportive vote – and still get re-elected – was unprecedented. And, following the pattern of the last few years, the turnout was noticeably poor in Labour's safest seats, where even the party's share of the vote fell. Chris Mullin's Sunderland South constituency was typical of the Labour heartlands; he had lost nearly 10,000 voters since 1992.

Other individual results proved of minor interest. Peter Mandelson held his safe seat in Hartlepool and celebrated with a wonderfully emotional acceptance speech, proclaiming that 'I'm a fighter not a quitter', while Peter Lilley held on to Hitchin and Harpenden, despite a challenge from Labour's Alan Amos, last seen as a Tory MP on Hampstead Heath. Martin Bell didn't seek re-election in Tatton, leaving it to return to its natural state as a safe Tory seat, thereby providing an easy route into Parliament for one of Hague's closest advisers, George Osborne, while a further new star appeared in the form of David Cameron. He stepped into another true blue constituency, Witney, which had been abandoned by his old boss, the defector Shaun Woodward.

But perhaps the most significant result was the one that seemed to buck the trend and revealed a discontent with Labour's policies. Local politics in the Wyre Forest constituency had been dominated for some time by the closure of the accident and emergency department at Kidderminster Hospital, as part of a restructuring that included the building of a PFI hospital in Worcester. Amongst those campaigning against the plans was Robert Plant, formerly the singer with the group Led Zeppelin, who wrote to Blair and received a reply that seemed desperate to parade the prime minister's rock and roll roots. 'I am certainly a Led Zeppelin fan,' the prime minister gushed. 'I can't tell you how many memories I have of you.' It turned out that no one was much interested in his memories, and the sitting Labour MP in Wyre Forest shed 16,000 votes, to be overtaken by a Kidderminster physician, Richard Taylor, standing on a Health Concern platform, who won 58 per cent of the vote. At a time when political parties were losing support at an unprecedented rate, they could not afford to ignore the spectacular success of a genuine independent.

Nonetheless, the results were largely ignored. 'In a way it is even better than 1997,' wrote John O'Farrell, of the 2001 election, 'because we weren't just voting to get rid of a government; the country made a positive choice of public services over tax cuts.' His self-delusion was far from unique. Two years earlier, Peter Hain had warned about New Labour's tendency to be 'gratuitously offensive to its own natural supporters', but nothing had changed. Membership of the party was falling fast as though, like a malignant parasite, New Labour was gradually killing its host organism, in the same way that Thatcherism looked as though it might have destroyed the Conservative Party.

Neither party really meant a great deal in terms of the everyday social life of the country any more, and the decline was considered an inevitable fact of modern life. There was no reason why this should be so. The rise in Labour Party membership in Blair's early days had demonstrated that there was another way forward, as had − the previous decade − the enormous wave of support that had greeted the creation of the SDP. What was missing now was any sense that hope for change could be realised, any sign of genuine leadership that sought mass participation rather than media representation.

In his first speech to the Conservative conference as leader, Hague had predicted that Blair's government would provoke 'fascination, admiration, disillusion and finally contempt'. That had sounded like whistling in the wind in 1997. By 2001 it seemed more like a diagnosis of the state of modern politics.

William Hague's resignation as leader of the Conservative Party triggered the first election under the new system that he had introduced. Five candidates presented themselves to the MPs, with David Davis and Michael Ancram knocked out in the first two rounds of voting. That meant there was one final round in order to produce the two candidates who would be presented to the party membership for their consideration.

Leading the field were the two heavyweights who were expected to make the run-off − the old bruiser Kenneth Clarke and the young(ish) pretender Michael Portillo − as well as the little-known Iain Duncan Smith. The verdict should have been a foregone conclusion, but Portillo's behaviour since the 1997 defeat, his abandonment of Thatcherite social policies, his perceived arrogance and the factionalism of his followers, had alienated too many of his colleagues, and he failed by one vote to reach the final contest. That missing vote belonged to William Hague, who had cast it instead for Iain Duncan Smith.

Portillo was said not to be overly distressed as he stepped out of the firing line. Whoever became leader faced an unhappy future, with years of struggle over the party's identity almost certain to be followed by a third defeat at the polls. Portillo's argument for a more inclusive vision of Conservatism would subsequently emerge victorious, but he lacked the forces necessary to push it through, for he was out of step with too many others in the party ('I am liberal, and I am a member of the elite,' as he told the shadow cabinet). In his reborn incarnation, he also found that he attracted the fire of those right-wing commentators who had been so opposed to John Major. 'It was not that Tories oppose in principle the toleration of black people and homosexuals,' reflected journalist Simon Heffer, musing on the reception accorded to Portillo by the party conference; 'they just don't expect to be evangelised on the subject by a shadow chancellor.'

As in 1997, the outcome when the membership of the party were invited to cast their votes in the final leadership ballot should have been a foregone conclusion. On the one side there was the popular and successful Clarke, an MP for over thirty years, with a track record as chancellor of the exchequer and as secretary of state successively for health, education and home affairs; on the other, there was Duncan Smith, elected only in 1992, whose principal contribution had been to rebel against his own government on the issue of Europe. But even if the general public knew nothing of him, and even if he had initially attracted just one member of the shadow cabinet to his team, Duncan Smith was an attractive candidate for the faithful.

He was seen as Norman Tebbit's anointed successor as the MP for Chingford; he had the backing of Margaret Thatcher; as a Roman Catholic, he was socially conservative on questions such as homosexuality and abortion; and he had made the most of his recent post as shadow defence spokesperson to remind people that he had served as a Scots Guards officer in Northern Ireland and Rhodesia. He was also more determined and ambitious than many recognised. In 1997 he had run John Redwood's campaign for the leadership, but even then he had his eyes on a higher prize: 'Next time, I'll be running my own campaign.'

More important still, he was a Eurosceptic, and his contest with Clarke became, in the words of Nicholas Soames, 'the physical incarnation of the split that has poisoned our party'. At a hustings in London, pictures were circulated of Clarke sharing a pro-European platform with Tony Blair, accompanied by the ominous slogan: 'Lest We Forget'. At the same meeting Duncan Smith mentioned that he'd voted against the party whip eleven times over the Maastricht Treaty, and received a standing ovation for his confession. The 1997 leadership election had shown that there was no more important issue for Tory MPs than Europe; 2001 confirmed that this was also the case with the dwindling army of activists in the country. Duncan Smith won over 60 per cent of membership votes, more than 155,000 people, and became leader of the Conservative Party.

It was a choice that baffled those members of the wider electorate who bothered to pay attention. The reaction was encapsulated in the announcement by the waxworks museum Madame Tussaud's that Duncan Smith would be the first Tory leader in 130 years of whom they would not make an effigy. 'He is not in the papers very much and you never hear his name,' explained a spokesperson, some months after Duncan Smith's accession. 'We are not sure if our visitors will recognise him, especially as many are from abroad.'

Nor was the selection likely to cause many sleepless nights in Downing Street, save perhaps in relation to the one issue that Duncan Smith had made his own. 'They thought Ken would win the leadership, and then they would have gone gangbusters on the euro,' reflected Duncan Smith, in later years. 'And they believed that the Tory Party would have been wrecked, because it would have had its leader on the same platform as Blair and most of the rest of the party opposed. That would have been the end for us as a party, we would probably have disintegrated.' Instead, with Duncan Smith at the helm, it was at least certain that the entire party would be united in defence of sterling, had Gordon Brown decided that his five tests had been met and permitted Tony Blair to call a referendum. The prospect of Britain joining the single currency receded still further.

That was the one legacy of a leadership seemingly doomed by bad luck from the outset. The schedule for the election called for ballot papers to be returned by 11 September, with the results to be announced at a press conference the following day. Unfortunately that press conference had to be delayed for twenty-four hours when it was realised that no one much was likely to attend. For on 11 September 2001 the terrorist group al-Qaeda launched a coordinated wave of suicide attacks on the USA, killing nearly 3,000 people, most of them in the destruction of the World Trade Center in New York. In the immediate aftermath of that devastation, the choice of who was going to lose the next election for the Tories seemed to be of little significance.

OUTRO
Renewal

'Weren't the nineties great?'

The failure of the Millennium Dome had done nothing to blunt Tony Blair's sense of destiny. 'In retrospect the Millennium marked only a moment in time,' he observed, in his speech to the Labour Party conference in 2001. 'It was the events of September 11 that marked a turning point in history.' He was speaking some three weeks after the al-Qaeda attacks, and some regretted that the person making such bold claims on the part of history continued to display such a shaky grasp of it himself. He'd already been to New York to express his solidarity with the USA as he remembered how his father's generation had endured the Blitz: 'There was one country and one people that stood by us at that time. That country was America, and the people was the American people.' By the time the USA entered the Second World War, of course, the worst of the Blitz had long since passed, while the former dominions and colonies of the British Empire might have felt slighted by being overlooked yet again.

But his comments went down very well with his hosts, and when George Bush mentioned Blair in an address to both Houses of Congress, the assembled politicians turned to give him a standing ovation. Whatever else resulted, the repercussions of those attacks were to change the public perception of Blair's premiership, both at home and abroad. 'The events of September 11,' wrote Clare Short in 2004, 'seemed to electrify Blair. He had been searching for his legacy. After September 11, he seemed to have found his cause.' In that conference speech Blair mentioned public services in passing, but it sounded like – and was – an afterthought. His real focus was on international affairs, and that was to remain the case.

For much of the rest of the New Labour establishment, however, life carried on as normal. After the 2001 general election victory, it was said, Gordon Brown had visited the prime minister and told him to 'fuck off' so that the alleged Granita agreement could be honoured. The terrorist attacks made no difference. 'In the aftermath of 9/11, Tony rang Gordon to ask for his advice,' reported Jonathan Powell. 'Instead of responding,

Gordon used the call to demand to know when Tony was going to resign. Tony slammed the phone down in a rage.'

Even more characteristic was the response of Jo Moore, a press officer in the Department of Transport, who circulated a memo to her colleagues as the al-Qaeda story broke: 'It's now a very good day to get out anything we want to bury. Councillors' expenses?' Those sixteen words seemed to sum up so much that had gone wrong with politics in Britain, from the instinctive response of seeking party advantage in a tragedy, through the appallingly insensitive language ('a very good day . . . bury'), to the bathetic conclusion about a reform to the system of payments to local councillors, revealing a scale of priorities that was breathtaking in its offensiveness and ineptitude.

Moore was no novice in her post. She had worked as a press officer for the Labour Party for years – she had been present in John Smith's flat when he suffered his fatal heart attack – and had served under Blair through his time in opposition. It was not naivety but normality that prompted the memo. Nor was the idea of 'burying bad news' novel. Back in 1995 it had been planned to release the story about Harriet Harman's son going to a selective school on the day that the report of the Scott Inquiry about arms to Iraq was due to be published, although this was scuppered when the news got out ahead of schedule.

When Moore's memo was leaked to the press, it caused outrage and demands for her to be sacked, though no one was much surprised when all that resulted was a brief, scripted apology. Blair 'felt Jo was basically a decent person, very committed and professional, and it was a bit much to destroy her career over one leaked email that she should never have written or sent'. The absence of serious disciplinary action suggested that, despite the transformative effects of al-Qaeda's actions, New Labour planned to continue operating as it had before.

In terms of British politics, the impact of the 11 September attacks was most apparent in relation to Europe. The debate over the single currency was expected to dominate Blair's second term in office. The coins and notes for the euro had been distributed to the banks of the participating nations earlier that same month, and Britain's potential participation seemed to be the most important issue on the domestic agenda. That now disappeared entirely, swallowed up in a rush to war.

The first target was Afghanistan, where al-Qaeda was based and where it ran its training camps. This was expected to be a straightforward operation. 'We thought back then that the equation was relatively simple,' Blair explained in his memoirs: 'knock out the Taliban, give Afghanistan a UN-supervised election, provide billions for development, and surely the outcome is progress.' The next stage was a return to Iraq to complete unfinished business left over from ten years earlier. At a briefing meeting, barely a week after the World Trade Center had been destroyed, Blair was asked about Iraq. His equivocation led Chris Mullin, who was present, to reflect: 'I take that to mean that a second front, against Iraq, is being considered.' Indeed it was, and more than anything else, the invasion of Iraq two years later, in conjunction with America, was to become the defining issue of Blair's time as prime minister.

The British involvements in Afghanistan and, particularly, in Iraq were to split opinion at home, while the shelving of serious debate on Europe merely postponed an issue that would have to be resolved at some point. But in other areas, the period of just over a decade that separated John Major's arrival in Downing Street from Tony Blair's re-election had already settled much.

Ever since the war the country had swung uncertainly between different, conflicting images of itself. 'Great Britain has lost an Empire and has not yet found a role,' the former US secretary of state, Dean Acheson, had famously pronounced in 1962, and although his subject had been the global balance of power, the words also resonated in terms of national identity. The question of what a post-imperial Britain might actually be like had underpinned much of the cultural expression of recent decades as well as much of the political posturing.

Culturally there were three sources of influence from overseas: from Europe, which — so long as it was interpreted to mean Tuscany and Provence — shaped the tastes of the liberal section of the establishment; from America, which attracted the enthusiasm of much of the younger working class, to the despair of the left; and from the Commonwealth, a more diffuse source of inspiration but one which also played its part. The balance between these was affected too by the history of Britain itself, and especially by the parts of that history deemed to be of greatest significance by each of the competing political and cultural interests.

For a long time this meant, way ahead of anything else, the Second World War. The myths of the nation standing alone against Nazism, snatching victory from the jaws of defeat at Dunkirk, enduring the Blitz in a spirit of stoicism to which only Britain could aspire — such things were vital to the morale of a country slipping down the international league table. The Empire might be disintegrating, but at least Britain was confident of its place on the moral high ground.

As decline turned to economic, industrial and political crisis in the 1970s, that evaluation came under strain. Immigration from the countries of what was then known as the New Commonwealth helped shape the left's espousal of anti-racism, which in turn led to an increasingly self-flagellating attitude to the Empire and even to the war. 'The British disease, if there is such a thing,' reflected Peter Shore in 1974, 'is gloom about being British.' Set against this was, for a while, Margaret Thatcher's evocation of the spirit of Winston Churchill, following the Falklands War of 1982, as well as an idealised vision of 1950s suburban Britain, seen as a stable, ordered, decent society.

In the 1990s the war continued to play a role in shaping the nation's thinking about itself, but it found ever more trivial expression, whether it were spam fritter-frying contests or tabloid coverage of football matches with Germany. As the number of survivors dwindled, there were few tangible remains for most of Britain to cling to; in 1998 the last remaining bombsite in the City of London was cleared for development. The war remained a source of fascination, but was becoming irretrievably distant. To commemorate the sixtieth anniversary of the declaration of war in 1939, ITV ran a documentary series, *The Second World War in Colour*, collecting newsreels, official footage and home movies all shot in colour; although startling in its freshness, it wasn't enough to overcome decades of seeing the Europe of the 1930s and '40s in period black-and-white.

The battleground instead became the 1960s, a struggle over the meaning of that decade: whether the liberal reforms and rise of personal liberty had been a disaster for traditional morality and social structures, and should be reversed wherever possible, or whether they had set a desirable course towards a more tolerant, happier society, 'a country at ease with itself', to appropriate John Major's phrase. In this debate, it was noticeable how peripheral politics had become. The rehabilitation of the 1960s by Cool Britannia, and the extension into a new mood of tolerant morality, was achieved by the new left of the 1980s when it seized control of the cultural industries; politicians trailed behind, desperately trying to stay in touch.

In that pursuit, even the most surefooted of politicians sometimes misjudged the moment. In the spring of 1999 a neo-Nazi terrorist, David Copeland, planted a series of nail bombs in London, targeting areas with large ethnic minority populations in Brixton and Brick Lane, and a gay pub, the Admiral Duncan in Soho. The first two bombs injured scores of people, while the latter killed three and injured a further seventy-nine. The prime minister's response was not quite as hard-hitting as it might have been. An article under his name appeared in the *Sunday Times*, but in more than a thousand words, he found room for just one sentence about the murderous attack on the Admiral Duncan.

When the pub reopened two months later, Blair sent a message of support that again seemed reluctant to address the fact that homosexuals were in the firing line for right-wing extremists. It was 'an horrific attack on innocent civilians', he wrote. Some in his own inner circle were distinctly unimpressed. 'At no time did he really address the gay community directly,' regretted Lance Price; 'happy to talk to the majority but even now terrified of speaking to a minority for whom his precious coalition of support has little sympathy. I was genuinely disappointed and even a little surprised.'

The violence of Copeland's short-lived campaign of terror was a reminder that the whole country had yet to be won over to what Blair called 'the tolerant society the overwhelming majority are determined to build'. But Blair was right to say that, despite his own timidity, the majority of the country had ceased to worry too much about what consenting adults did in their spare time.

In 'A Perfectly Simple Explanation', a 1996 episode of *Hamish Macbeth*, we were introduced to Malachai MacBean, an extremist Calvinist minister, the leader of the Church of the Stony Path. 'He could be mad,' shrugs the town's doctor. 'Or then again, he might just be embarked on some kind of Back to Basics campaign. Which would make him mad in my book anyway.' MacBean is counterbalanced by a dope-smoking, BMW-driving, hippy guru named Zoot, with whom we are expected to have more sympathy, until the denouement reveals that MacBean's speaking-in-tongues, fire-and-brimstone act is just a cover to conceal the fact that he and Zoot are deeply in love with each other and having a passionate affair. And life in the picturesque village of Lochdubh continues on its liberal, inclusive way.

That, however, may have distorted the facts on the ground a little. When the repeal of Section 28 of the Local Government Act was up for debate in the Westminster Parliament, a prominent SNP-supporting businessman, Brian Souter, founder of the Stagecoach transport company, ran a privately funded referendum in Scotland in which over a million Scots registered their wish to keep the legislation. The power of the Catholic Church still held more sway north of the border than any church in England. Similarly Northern Ireland – where male homosexuality had only been legalised in 1982 – saw much greater resistance to the liberalising of society.

But even if Tony Blair did lose touch with the public mood, his position remained unassailable thanks to the lingering image of the Conservatives as the nasty party, still refusing to accept that the country had moved on.

In the early days of his leadership, William Hague made strenuous efforts to discard that legacy, espousing 'patriotism without bigotry' and attending the 1997 Gay Pride rally, but as the 2001 election drew closer, and the polls failed to turn his way, he returned to the old themes. 'Talk about Europe and they call you extreme,' he protested in a speech in March 2001. 'Talk about tax and they call you greedy. Talk about crime and they call you reactionary. Talk about asylum and they call you racist. Talk about your nation and they call you Little Englanders.' He went on to suggest that Labour's policies risked turning Britain into 'a foreign land'.

Although his press officers insisted that he was talking about EU encroachments on British sovereignty, and that his speech should in no way be interpreted as being racist or relating to immigration, that was precisely how it was seen. It was difficult to avoid the conclusion that he intended to send such signals, when he was promising to 'clear up Labour's asylum mess'.

A couple of months earlier, the *Guardian* columnist Polly Toynbee, stung by being singled out by name as part of the 'liberal elite', had responded with a withering assault on the modern Conservative Party: 'Hague is marooned in yesteryear with his shrinking blue-rinse party while we are swimming in the sea of pluralism, multiculturalism, complex families, difficult choices, all the muddle born of freedom.' In short, she argued: 'We liberals are closer to the majority.'

She was right. Just as economic liberalism now shaped the policies of all the major parties, so social liberalism began to shape the country more widely. The rise of the economic liberals and the triumph of the free market in the 1980s had been fought, unsuccessfully, by the left and had split the Labour Party. Now there was a matching rearguard action by those on the right who wished to preserve tradition in all but the economic sphere, and who were prepared to tear at the flesh of the Conservative Party in pursuit of that goal. It was equally unsuccessful. There were areas of dispute about how far liberalism was prepared to tolerate dissident thinking and practices, whether it truly respected the civil liberties of those who rejected its metropolitan bias – which was why hunting with hounds became such a contentious issue – but in broad terms, there had been a remarkable transformation in the country, building over the last three decades, that emerged in triumph in the 1990s.

It wasn't simply the changes themselves, but the fact that change itself had become entrenched as a part of the country's identity. Britain had, until recently, cherished its sense of tradition and continuity. It was a country that could look back on its history as the world's first industrialised nation and still believe that the essential character of the country had remained intact, undergoing only minor modifications, eschewing the violent upheavals of revolution and therefore able to take most things in its stride.

Partly in consequence of this, the image of the Englishman, in particular, had become probably the most easily recognised national stereotype in the world. A couple of decades earlier, savage caricatures of the type in *Monty Python's Flying Circus* — John Cleese's bowler-hatted bureaucrat, Graham Chapman's eccentric colonel — had exported remarkably well and had helped parody it out of existence. What remained was more likely to be played for a gentler effect, as when Hugh Grant stammered out his emotions through the medium of a Partridge Family song in *Four Weddings and a Funeral*. Now Britain celebrated both its cultural diversity and, as it began to talk of being the world's first post-industrial nation, its ability to adapt to new circumstances and to reinvent itself. At the start of the decade, there had been a feeling of weariness after a decade of Thatcherite espousal of permanent revolution; now the idea of change had become accepted as the norm.

It was a trend epitomised by Tony Blair himself, a man whose life — Fettes, Oxford, the Bar — was steeped in tradition and the establishment. He'd even been to the same school as both James Bond and the Marvel Comics superhero Captain Britain. Yet his entire appeal as a politician was based on his image as a rootless modern man with no allegiance to the past save for a bit of flag-waving, and even that owed more to the Swinging Sixties than to the Empire.

Blair displayed no respect for tradition or for institutions of any kind, on either a political or a personal level. His doctrine of liberal intervention was launched without consultation with the Foreign Office. He regarded the trade unions, the Labour Party itself, as a block on his vision of progress. Even the armed forces, on whose reputation for efficiency he came to count so heavily, were a source of frustration at times with their allegiance to the past. (Though he was never as crass as Peter Mandelson, who described the Household Division as 'chinless wonders'.)

The same trait was seen in his religious faith. Although Blair didn't officially become a Catholic until after his term in office, he had long been in the habit of receiving communion in a Catholic church until he was told by Cardinal Basil Hume in 1996 that this wasn't appropriate; his tart rejoinder — 'I wonder what Our Lord will make of this' — suggested that he was not yet ready to accept the discipline of Rome. And indeed, when he was eventually received into the Church, there was little sign of humility, as he launched into a criticism of the Pope's teachings on personal morality, particularly on homosexuality and contraception, and suggested that a new generation shouldn't be stuck in the past: 'We need an attitude of mind where rethinking and the concept of evolving attitudes becomes part of the discipline with which you approach your religious faith.'

Blair was entirely serious about the 'modernity' of which he spoke so often, though ironically he was, in the 1990s at least, widely seen as an opportunist. His immense gifts as a political salesman meant that when he attempted to sell his vision – with all the soundbites and slogans, from 'tough on crime' onwards – he conveyed little more than the sincerity and depth of an advertiser, since the substance needed to support the straplines was so rarely in evidence. It was a problem that came in large part from the recent history of the Labour Party, and its disastrous electoral performance; such a premium was placed on winning that little energy was left for thoughts of governing. Bryan Gould's assessment of Peter Mandelson served equally as a summation of Blair: 'He was always disappointing as someone who is said to be a visionary for the Labour Party. He had a vision of how Labour could win an election, but not too much idea of how to change society.'

There was a further irony here. Such vision was lacking partly because New Labour had so deliberately distanced itself from the movement that had given it birth. It was possible to find a way of articulating John Prescott's ambition of 'traditional values in a modern setting', but New Labour hadn't done so, instead choosing the path of least resistance wherever possible. Most noticeably, Blair had trumpeted the need to reform public services, but had signally failed to deliver. The default position of the left – that any change to the status quo was to be resisted – remained in place. Spending rose, the infrastructure was substantially rebuilt and outcomes improved (though not in proportion to the increased funding), but the health and education services continued to produce less impressive results than their continental counterparts, and the moment passed when it would have been possible to revitalise the welfare state at a time of steady economic growth. Instead New Labour took up the Conservative cause of setting targets and passing legislation as though these could achieve change on their own. And when those endeavours proved unsuccessful, Blair's interest seemed to wander away from the home front and onto the world stage.

As it did so, he fell out of step with the public that he had sought to represent. The changes in Britain in the last decades had been profound, so much so that they inevitably left little scope for a true internationalism at this stage. The reinvention of the 1990s was essentially inward-looking, a country putting its own house in order, without a great deal of reference to the outside world. This too was new. Britain's traditional image of itself had been grounded in a moral certainty, a sense of destiny that sought to remake the world in its own image, exporting its own values – including a judicial system, a civil service, a regimental structure, a codified concept of sport – in a belief that it was on a civilising mission. The Second World War, and 1940 in particular, had been so significant because it could be seen as the culmination of that characteristic; in the words of Winston Churchill's 'finest hour' speech, it had been about 'the survival of Christian civilisation' at a time when failure would mean that 'the whole world will sink into the abyss of a new Dark Age'.

Blair's wish to impose liberal democracy on the world's trouble spots was an extension of that faith, but it was either a pale echo of a vanished age or, perhaps, was simply too early a rebirth. The relocation of the nation's creation myth to the 1960s replaced crusading with creativity, and high-minded idealism with a messy democracy. It was enough to be getting on with.

Blair, for all his belief that he was in tune with the zeitgeist, missed much of this. During Cool Britannia's Sixties-revivalism phase, he could participate happily enough, while his class-transcending image allowed him to navigate the wake of Diana's death with impressive confidence. But he missed a crucial development. Underneath his pose as 'a pretty straight guy', he, just as much as William Hague, was still inherently a believer in the power of a liberal elite, of the kind that had led the reforms of the 1960s. He hadn't recognised that liberalism – both economic and social – had brought into being a new movement, demanding equality initially in terms of culture, with the possibility that it might extend into the political sphere.

Blair deluded himself that he was a leader, when actually he was following. When he ceased to do that convincingly, the electorate turned away from him. There was no decisive moment of rejection, as there had been with Major, just a slow waning of attention, as seen in the victory of the don't knows at the 2001 election, a phenomenon that was repeated in 2005, when an even smaller proportion of the electorate gave Labour its support and the gap between the abstentions and the government's vote grew still greater. While the economy was still buoyant, and times were still good, the cracks could be papered over. But there were real tensions building between a political class that sought to gather more powers to itself, and a democratic impulse that was losing faith in politicians altogether.

And still there was the ever-widening gulf between the rich and the rest. Despite all Gordon Brown's tax credit schemes, wage inequality was reported to be at its greatest since records began, which in this instance turned out to be the 1880s. Some feared that Brown's measures even risked entrenching such divisions, that by facilitating low wages with state subsidy (in pursuit of what politicians of both parties liked to call a flexible economy), any hope of progress was being choked off. But there were many more, certainly within the Labour Party, who hoped fervently that the policy would work, clinging to the belief that the socialism-by-stealth of redistribution would lead to a fairer, more equal society. At the time of the 2001 election, after just four years, it was still too early to draw any conclusions about the impact, about whether the social problems grouped together under the umbrella of 'the underclass' were any nearer to being resolved. All that could be said was that, in economic terms, Britain was no closer to being a classless society.

But then this was a government that said it no longer believed in class. In 1998 it announced the creation of a new measure of social classification, replacing the old six-band system with seventeen categories, a move heralded in the press as a recognition that 'We are all middle class now.' But under the more familiar distinctions, where the working class were defined as socio-economic groups C2, D and E, there were around twenty-two million members of this supposedly endangered sector of the population at the end of the 1990s. Even in the exciting new world of technology, most of the jobs created were low-paid and low-skilled; the rise of the call centre merely provided a modern twist on the sweatshop. The reality was still a country deeply divided by class: working hours were longer in Britain than in any of its EU partners, while chief executives' pay was higher. Labour's rhetoric in opposition about fat cats didn't seem to have made much impact.

As the leadership of both major parties became ever more homogenised, vast parts of the electorate were going unrepresented. This was particularly noticeable on the Labour benches. 'Labour has changed, with just 13 per cent of our MPs from skilled manual backgrounds,' noted Ken Jackson, general secretary of the AEEU, in 1999. 'Barristers, academics and doctors have taken their place. Parliament is fast becoming the preserve of the professional.' Unskilled workers were even thinner on the ground.

'We are citizens proud to say that there is such a thing as society and proud to be part of it,' declared Blair in 1999. 'Yet today we feel our social fabric torn.' It was the same tune that he had been playing since his speech on the murder of James Bulger, and the core beliefs it expressed were not very different from those of John Major. Yet what might have been true at the start of the decade was not necessarily the case now. There were still deep, underlying problems – as there always would be – but mostly Britain had come to terms with its new role as a messy, muddled collection of peoples, united only by a lack of unity, by a desire to avoid causing too much offence to anyone else and by a rapidly declining interest in the country's history. If the social fabric remained threadbare, it had at least been patched up. In any event, what was much more striking was that the political fabric was torn.

In 1992 Margaret Thatcher had insisted in an interview that nothing had changed since her departure from office. 'There isn't such a thing as Majorism,' she had said. 'Thatcherism will live. It will live long after Thatcher has died, because we had the courage to restore the great principles and put them into practice.' Thatcherism had indeed transformed much of the nation, but it had left the job unfinished, unable to extend economic liberalism into its social expression. That was completed during the years of Blajorism. But neither John Major nor Tony Blair really made the difference. Both had sought to create a classless society, both had failed, with wealth inequality increasing and social mobility decreasing, and both found themselves ill at ease with the kind of classless culture that emerged instead.

Their vision of classlessness had essentially been – as had Thatcher's – a wish to create a meritocracy. And meritocracy, of course, is merely another form of elitism, albeit one that claims to be based on a supposedly natural, rather than an inherited, hierarchy. The dominant strand of culture that emerged in the 1990s, on the other hand, was very clearly anti-elitist, as expressed through the National Lottery, reality television, the internet and the celebration of Princess Diana and David Beckham.

During Blair's second term, as he busied himself waging war on the peoples of Afghanistan and Iraq, there emerged the figure of Jade Goody, star of the third series of *Big Brother*. A dental nurse from Essex, roundly ridiculed in the press for her ignorance of the world, her stupidity and her vulgarity, she became rich and famous because she represented a huge swathe of British society that had hitherto been denied a voice in the mainstream media. Her death in 2009, at the age of twenty-seven, prompted a change in NHS policy on cervical cancer screening and attracted tributes from the new prime minister (Gordon Brown having finally made it to the job he had craved for so long). Goody's status in the popular consciousness was a direct result of trends in the 1990s that had little or nothing to do with the politicians of the decade.

For in their own ways both John Major and Tony Blair had proved unable to impose themselves on society or to control the forces that were reshaping Britain, as anti-establishment feelings eroded much of the authority and legitimacy they would have wished to claim for themselves. As Norman Lamont might have said, they had between them spent the decade in office, but not in power.

References

Where quotes in the text are derived from interviews or from email correspondence, they are shown here as (pc) to indicate personal communication.

p.v **These should be** – The Wonder Stuff, 'The Size of a Cow' (Universal Music Publishing Ltd, 1991)

p.v **After all, this is the caring nineties** – Andy Hamilton & Guy Jenkin, *Drop the Dead Donkey*, series 2, episode 9: 'Damien Down and Out'

p.v **If you and your New Labour Party** – Peter Flannery, *Our Friends in the North*, episode 9: '1995'

Intro: Nineties

p.4 **There is no such thing** – *Woman's Own* 23 September 1987

p.4 **make changes** – Major, *The Autobiography* p. 193

p.5 **the chance to take forward** – Barnett, *This Time* p. 65

p.5 **I want to see us build** – *Times* 29 November 1990

p.5 **not a society without difference** – Major op. cit. p. 205

p.5 **Although in the 1980s** – Sopel, *Tony Blair* p. 252

p.6 **I am not a Tory** – Richards, *Whatever It Takes* p. 142

p.6 **a truly classless society** – Bower, *Gordon Brown* p. 186

p.6 **The zeitgeist was free** – Blair, *A Journey* p. 132

p.7 **The campaign never really caught** – *Guardian* 13 April 1992

p.9 **people want** – Weight, *Patriots* p. 692

p.9 **Never have I** – Barnett op. cit. p. 131

p.10 **the waning fashions** – www.margaretthatcher.org/document/108011

p.11 **a sham** – *Independent on Sunday* 27 October 1996

p.11 **fucking prelates** – Price, *The Spin Doctor's Diary* p. 15

p.11 **I pray every night** – *Sunday Times* 3 November 1996

p.11 **Never talk about God** – Campbell, *The Blair Years* p. 112

p.11 **no longer appropriate** – *Independent* 19 December 1992

p.12 **a contemporary City entrepreneur** – *Sunday Times* 27 December 1992

p.13 **the most stripped-down** – *Independent* 9 September 1994

p.13 **The menu offers** – *Times* 13 June 1994

p.13 **The cooking is pleasant** – *Times* 20 February 1993

Part One: The Buddha of Suburbia

p.15 **We are not slaying** – Currie, *Diaries*, p. 275

p.15 **It's a great responsibility** – routine at *Hysteria 3* benefit

p.15 **Do you enjoy anything** – Alan Bennett, *The Madness of King George*

1: Enter John Major

p.17 **People forget** – Patrick Marber, Steve Coogan & Armando Iannucci, *Knowing Me, Knowing You with Alan Partridge* episode 1

p.17 **I've always voted** – Lodge, *Therapy* p. 87

p.18 **who'd have thought it?** – Baker, *The Turbulent Years* p. 427

p.18 **he was what happened** – *Independent* 3 May 1997

p.18 **I simply find myself** – Wheatcroft, *The Strange Death of Tory England* p. 185

p.19 **Trying to write jokes** – introduction to *Drop the Dead Donkey* series 2 DVD (Hat Trick International, 2005)

p.19 **least like to see** – *Independent* 24 December 1996

p.19 **a minor Dickens character** – *Independent* 9 November 1996

p.19 **Monsieur Ordinaire** – *Guardian* 4 April 1992

p.20 **very, very competent** – Patten, *Not Quite the Diplomat* p. 78

p.20 **more politically astute** – Cole, *As It Seemed To Me* p. 445

p.20 **The public liked him** – Heseltine, *Life in the Jungle* p. 407

p.20 **I have never** – Benn, *Free at Last* p. 5

p.20 **bowled over** – Campbell, *The Blair Years* p. 104

p.20 **It was very seductive** – Gorman, *The Bastards* p. 154

p.20 **Would you like** – Ashdown, *The Ashdown Diaries* p. 480

p.20 **listed for the amazed assembly** – Diamond, *Snake Oil* p. 111

p.21 **His polling figures** – Young, *The Hugo Young Papers* p. 330

p.21 **to be prime minister** – Major, *The Autobiography* p. 210

p.21 **Most Tory backbenchers** – *Times* 23 November 1990

p.21 **I'm not a Thatcherite** – Currie, *Diaries* p. 247

p.21 **everything I've dreamt of** – Junor, *The Major Enigma* p. 205

p.21 **he has deceived me** – Wyatt, *The Journals of Woodrow Wyatt Volume Two* p. 586

p.22 **If it isn't hurting** – Major op. cit. p. 662

p.22 **He smiles** – Spicer, *The Spicer Diaries* p. 437

p.22 **His whole life** – Currie op. cit. p. 251

p.22 **I love my party** – Young, *This Blessed Plot* p. 413

p.23 **I don't want old style** – Wyatt op. cit. pp. 401–2

p.23 **I want to bring into being** – Major op. cit. p. 205

p.23 **Never has so much** – *Times* 12 October 1991

p.23 **He is terribly lacking** – Young, *The Hugo Young Papers* p. 325

p.24 **an ancient matinée idol** – Brandreth, *Breaking the Code* p. 470

p.24 **It distracted us** – Junor op. cit. p. 215

p.25 **Peter Snow clambered** – Steel, *Reasons to Be Cheerful* p. 213

p.26 **languishing** – Major op. cit. p. 662

p.27 **The politics of the property-owning democracy** – Heseltine, *Life in the Jungle* p. 392

p.27 **Sort out the fucking interest rates** – Campbell, May & Shields, *The Lad Done Bad* p. 78

p.27 **unpleasant and untalented** – Currie op. cit. p. 295

p.27 **I never believed** – Hurd, *Memoirs* p. 427

p.27 **a discontented squirrel** – Radice, *Diaries 1980–2001* p. 331

p.27 **It is nice** – Smith, *I Think the Nurses Are Stealing My Clothes* p. 83

p.27 **Rising unemployment** – *Sunday Times* 19 May 1991

p.27 **This recession** – *Independent* 10 June 1993

p.28 **some of his colleagues** – Gould, *Goodbye to All That* p. 238

p.28 **Kinnock was considered** – Ashdown op. cit. p. 24

p.28 **Kinnock wouldn't** – ibid. p. 81

p.29 **looked and sounded** – Heseltine op. cit. p. 409

p.29 **world of realities** – *Times* 4 October 1990

p.29 **I would rather** – *Times* 27 September 1991

p.29 **Not one of** – Shore, *Leading the Left* p. 171

p.30 **If John Smith** – *Times* 24 April 1992

p.30 **the great gift** – *Guardian* 9 February 1993

p.30 **All the resources** – *Sunday Times* 26 July 1992

p.30 **if there was an election** – Benn op. cit. p. 57

p.31 **Had John moved** – Blair, *A Journey* p. 52

p.31 **so many prawns** – Shephard, *Shephard's Watch* p. 82

p.31 **counter inflationary discipline** – Shore op. cit. p. 183

p.31 **No more ideology** – Cole op. cit. p. 395

p.32 **It is difficult** – Shore op. cit. p. 170

p.32 **Vote Conservative** – *Sunday Times* 19 July 1992

p.32 **Kinnock didn't understand** – Prescott, *Prezza* p. 170

p.32 **come back to us** – Brandreth op. cit. p. 73

p.32 **we are starting** – *Financial Times* 17 March 1992

p.32 **Very clever** – Benn op. cit. p. 86

p.33 **every sub-editor** – Richards, *Preparing for Power* p. 38

p.33 **Most of the comment** – Currie op. cit. p. 307

p.34 **It's pure theatre** – Major op. cit. p. 297

p.34 **I liked the unpredictability** – ibid. p. 290

p.35 **surreal** – Straw, *Last Man Standing* p. 180

p.35 **It's what Johnny Cash** – http://www.youtube.com/watch?v=CmVyNV0FBC4, accessed 25 April 2013

p.36 **There is a fine line** – Baker op. cit. p. 469

p.36 **for just a few seconds** – *Sunday Times* 11 April 1993

p.36 RED KINNOCK – *Guardian* 4 April 1992

p.36 **We were trying** – Gould op. cit. p. 250

p.36 **the clique of spin doctors** – Sopel, *Tony Blair* p. 138

p.37 **it looks to me** – Benn op. cit. p. 88

p.37 **From the very top** – Baker op. cit. p. 471

p.39 **Can Labour ever win?** – Radice op. cit. p. 271

p.39 **We live in a dominant party system** – *Times* 18 May 1992

p.39 **the most able** – *Independent on Sunday* 2 August 1992

p.39 **I had lost** – Major op. cit. p. 305

p.39 **he knows he hasn't** – Young op. cit. p. 436

p.40 **dreadfully badly** – Wyatt op. cit. p. 681

p.40 **a great night** – ibid. p. 691

p.40 **last Labour government** – Thatcher, *Downing Street Years* p. 4

p.40 **heroes of this campaign** – *Financial Times* 14 April 1992

p.41 **majority of its readers** – Patten op. cit. p. 56

p.41 **You imagine** – Campbell op. cit. p. 79

p.41 **What a bloody way** – Richards, *Whatever It Takes* p. 40

p.41 **Neil was** – Major op. cit. p. 307

p.42 **Gordon had not seized** – Blair op. cit. p. 54

p.42 **He chickened out** – Beckett, *Gordon Brown* p. 74

p.42 **I felt I had to be loyal** – Routledge, *Gordon Brown* p. 164

p.42 **the most odious man** – Pearse & Matheson, *Ken Livingstone* p. 29

p.42 **look at restricting** – Gould op. cit. p. 220

p.43 **belief that monetary measures** – ibid. p. 268

p.43 **Like Nigel Lawson** – Major op. cit. p. 661

p.43 **arrogance** – Giles Radice (pc)

p.43 **It always amazed me** – Bryan Gould (pc)

p.43 **A 'safety first' approach** – Brown, *Fighting Talk* p. 211

p.44 **do not trust Labour** – Radice op. cit. p. 281

p.44 **the wavering voters** – ibid. p. 322

p.44 **We were finding** – Sopel op. cit. p. 130

p.44 **Playing safe** – Brown op. cit. p. 207

p.45 **More compassionate** – Gould op. cit. p. 281

p.45 **Our victory** – Major op. cit. p. 311

2: Lads

p.46 **Basically, when all's said** – *Loaded* October 1994

p.46 **The higher up the tree** – Gadney, *Just When We Are Safest* p. 3

p.46 **In a divided and troubled world** – Richard Fegen & Andrew Norris, *The Brittas Empire*, series 1, episode 4: 'Underwater Wedding'

p.46 **For fuck's sake** – Baddiel, *Whatever Love Means* p. 1

p.46 **I think it was at that point** – ibid. p. 2

p.47 **people whose intelligence** – Savage, *Time Travel* p. 397

p.47 **They offered me the office** – The Clash, 'Career Opportunities' (Strummer/Jones, Nineden Ltd, 1977)

p.48 **the world of the new puritans** – O'Farrell, *Things Can Only Get Better* p. 62

p.48 **I've had relations** – Billy Bragg, 'Sexuality' (Bragg/Marr, Warner/Chappell, 1991)

p.49 **You have to tell me** – Planer, *The Right Man* p. 90

p.49 **Men are struggling** – *Times* 31 May 1991

p.49 **a tentatively positive** – *Sunday Times* 2 June 1996

p.50 **Well, that's because** – *Times* 25 March 1995

p.50 **He did not invent** – *Sunday Times* 10 October 1993

p.50 **We're aspiring yobbos** – *Independent* 8 June 1994

p.51 **The characters are conducting** – *Times* 18 July 1996

p.51 **all the good time** – Eric Burdon and the Animals, 'Good Times' (Burdon/Briggs/Weider/Jenkins/McCulloch, Sealark Ent/Slamina Music Inc., 1967)

p.51 **Like most blokes** – Lewisohn, *Radio Times Guide to TV Comedy* p. 431

p.52 **Radio 1's Steve Lamacq** – *Independent* 20 July 2004

p.52 **dedicated to life** – *Loaded* issue 1, May 1994

p.52 **Post-feminism has forced men** – *Sunday Times* 10 October 1993

p.52 **they've got a fanny** – quoted in Campbell, May & Shields, *The Lad Done Bad* p. 122

p.53 **a finite number of readers** – *Independent* 18 August 1998

p.53 **Most of our readers** – *Independent* 8 September 1994

p.54 **I do feel I've created** – *Sunday Times* 2 June 1996

p.54 **if I didn't move on** – *Independent* 5 October 1997

p.54 **I don't read magazines** – *Times* 18 December 1998

p.54 **I can't help feeling** – *Guardian* 16 December 1994

p.54 **accepted what we are** – *Independent* 8 September 1994

p.54 **It was about self-esteem** – *Independent* 9 March 2004

p.56 **Men will be men** – *Independent* 11 October 1996

p.56 **Complete with purple lipstick** – *Times* 17 January 1996

p.57 **unintelligent, promiscuous** – *People* 16 August 1998

p.57 ESSEX GIRLS – quoted in *Guardian* 2 April 2011

p.57 **women are choosing** – *Forum* Vol. 34 No. 5, 2000

p.57 **Under Labour** – *Independent* 3 October 1996

p.57 **Bastards. All of them** – Green, *Straight Talking* p. 2

p.57 **forget about men** – ibid. p. 3

p.57 **Maybe I'm wrong** – ibid. p. 9

p.58 **help meet public concern** – *Independent* 27 November 1996

p.58 **Fwoarrrgh!** – quoted in *Independent on Sunday* 10 March 1995

p.59 **generation's heedless flirtation** – Currie, *A Parliamentary Affair* p. 245

p.59 **The most worrying thing** – *Independent* 5 January 1998

p.60 **We hope we have gone** – Banks & Swift, *The Joke's On Us* p. ix

p.60 **trite, casual sexism** – Raphael, *Never Mind the Bollocks* p. 147

p.60 **These girls want sex** – *Forum* Vol. 28 No. 8, 1995

p.60 **We talk just like them** – Wener, *Different for Girls* p. 198

p.60 **Women, Sex** – Liz Evans, *Women, Sex and Rock 'n' Roll* (Pandora, London, 1994); Karen O'Brien, *Hymn to Her: Women Musicians Talk* (Virago, London, 1995); Lucy O'Brien, *She Bop* (Penguin, London, 1995); Amy Raphael, *Never Mind the Bollocks: Women Rewrite Rock* (Virago, London, 1995)

p.60 **My guitar's not** – *Independent on Sunday* 24 November 1996

p.61 **the first Spice Girl** – *Times* 13 December 1996

p.61 **corporate girlypop** – O'Brien, *She Bop II* p. 465

p.61 **They're the sort of girls** – *Observer* 20 April 1997

p.62 **You can look like a babe** – *Independent on Sunday* 24 November 1996

p.62 **It was only after the media** – *Times* 16 March 1994

p.62 **She wasn't a tits-out** – Anderson & Levene, *Grand Thieves & Tomb Raiders* p. 240

p.62 **The rules at the time** – ibid. p. 239

p.63 **This seems like a demented extension** – *Independent* 2 October 1997

p.63 **This is a small local event** – *Independent* 31 October 1997

p.63 **If there's a meaning** – *Times* 25 October 1997

p.63 **Maybe I'm old-fashioned** – *Total Sport* issue 18, June 1997

p.63 **Boxing is a high-risk sport** – *Independent* 14 February 1998

p.64 **It used to be** – *Times* 26 April 2001

p.64 **mini-skirted women** – *Times* 24 July 1991

p.65 **They say the Chippendales** – *Q* issue 75, December 1992

p.65 **Any normal woman** – *Independent on Sunday* 18 July 1993

p.65 **It's straight sex** – *Sunday Mirror* 1 May 1994

p.65 **no children** – Peter Darvill-Evans (pc)

p.66 **Got any straight sex** – Freeman, *The Undergrowth of Literature* p. 79

p.66 **market research** – *Daily Mirror* 14 July 1993

p.67 **the bulk of them** – *Guardian* 31 July 1997

p.68 **A man is still** – *GQ* issue 100, October 1997

p.68 **all-consuming, irrational** – Pearson, *The Far Corner* p. 48

p.68 **was won by** – Engel & Morrison, *The Sportspages Almanac 1992* p. 9

p.68 **Rugby or association** – *Times* 13 October 1990

p.69 **What, Man Utd *still* haven't** – Campbell, May & Shields op. cit. p. 91

p.70 **Eric likes to do** – Harris, *The Foreign Revolution* p. 141

p.71 **And I want to apologise** – ibid. p. 147

p.71 OOH AHH PRISONA – *Sun* 26 March 1995

p.71 **When the seagulls** – *Daily Mirror* 1 April 1995

p.71 **The British have succeeded** – Harris op. cit. p. 145

p.71 **I'm gobsmacked** – Reynolds, *The Wrong Kind of Shirts '99* p. 21

p.71 **I think we all give the wife** – Reynolds, *The Wrong Kind of Shirts 2* p. 45

p.72 **I like real, modern football** – Harris op. cit. p. 224

p.72 **Bloody hell** – Reynolds op. cit. p. 33

p.73 **He's put me on grilled fish** – Harris op. cit. pp. 233–4

p.73 **It's truly a different world** – Reynolds op. cit. p. 16

p.73 **If all football players** – *Times* 27 December 1999

p.74 **The secret of our success** – Reynolds op. cit. p. 77

p.74 **At that time** – Harris op. cit. p. 155

p.74 **We all know we're being exploited** – *Sun* 16 March 1998

p.74 **Loyalty doesn't seem to be** – *Times* 30 December 1995

p.74 **He's done a brilliant job** – *Times* 27 July 1996

p.75 **quintessentially postmodern** – *Times* 10 October 1992

p.75 **If you don't know** – *Sunday Times* 17 May 1992

p.75 **It was a catastrophe** – Engel & Morrison op. cit. p. 12

p.76 **As if to take the piss** – Steel, *Reasons to Be Cheerful* p. 238

p.76 **The game's identity** – *Times* 10 October 1992

p.77 **There's a cancer** – *Independent* 8 March 1997

p.77 **most of them** – *Daily Mirror* 6 March 1997

p.77 **make his life hell** – *Times* 6 March 1997

p.77 **He crossed the dividing line** – *Daily Mirror* 6 March 1997

p.77 **I don't think you can** – *Times* 6 March 1997

p.77 **You don't even have to** – *GQ*, issue 100, October 1997

p.78 **the new vaudeville** – *Independent on Sunday* 17 July 1994

p.78 **something about the spectacle** – Thompson, *Sunshine on Putty* p. 37

p.78 **If you believe** – *Independent on Sunday* 7 March 1999

3: Events

p.80 **What an ageing patient** – Chris Morris & Armando Iannucci, *The Day Today*, episode 2

p.80 **What should you look for** – Ashdown, *The Ashdown Diaries* p. 259

p.80 **John Smith is** – Laurence Marks & Maurice Gran, 'The Irresistible Rise of Alan B'stard', *The New Statesman* (1992)

p.80 **it can't be any worse** – Kochan, *Ann Widdecombe* p. 139

p.80 **spent the whole evening** – Brandreth, *Breaking the Code* pp. 130–1

p.81 **trapped in the dollar-deutschmark crossfire** – Major, *The Autobiography* p. 314

p.82 **the mother of all mistakes** – Patten, *Things to Come* p. 24

p.82 **catastrophic defeat** – Major op. cit. p. 334

p.82 **nobody's got any confidence** – Oborne, *The Triumph of the Political Class* p. 130

p.82 **My wife said** – *Times* 22 September 1992

p.83 **With it has gone** – Gorman, *The Bastards* p. 80

p.83 **They may hold office** – *Independent* 25 September 1992

p.84 **Very little thought** – Mandelson, *The Third Man* p. 145

p.84 **White for us** – Blunkett, *The Blunkett Tapes* p. 118

p.84 **intellectually liberated** – John Redwood (pc)

p.85 **we had for the moment** – Hurd, *Memoirs* p. 426

p.85 **fool's gold** – Seldon, *How Tory Governments Fall* p. 419

p.85 **It was clear** – Major op. cit. p. 194

p.85 **Both were plainly getting ready** – Clark, *Diaries* p. 377

p.85 **Of those six points** – Williams, *Guilty Men* p. 19

p.86 **I have a bucket load** – *Daily Mail* 16 June 2012

p.86 **David's definition** – Major op. cit. p. 406

p.86 **said he was unable** – *Financial Times* 21 July 1992

p.87 **Having grown** – *Times* 26 September 1992

p.87 **An affair with an actress?** – Major op. cit. p. 552

p.87 **drinking in the** – *Financial Times* 22 December 1989

p.87 **any further measures** – *Guardian* 27 July 1992

p.87 PRESS ON PROBATION – *Times* 10 July 1992

p.87 **This is the man** – this and next two quotes, *Times* 20 July 1992

p.88 **I was glad** – Clifford, *Max Clifford* p. 134

p.89 **The lights would not** – Heseltine, *Life in the Jungle* p. 437

p.89 **We have an enduring obligation** – *Sunday Times* 18 October 1992

p.89 **The trouble with this bloody government** – Junor, *The Major Enigma* p. 274

p.90 **totally unacceptable** – *Daily Mirror* 17 October 1992

p.90 **He looks weak** – *Times* 16 October 1992

p.90 **I have rarely** – Heseltine op. cit. p. 441

p.91 **My feelings were based** – Major op. cit. p. 670

p.92 **We all took our eye** – *Sunday Times* 25 October 1992

p.92 **the biggest tax increase** – Sopel, *Tony Blair* p. 249

p.92 **I have no need** – Major op. cit. p. 676

p.93 **You can never trust** – *Times* 2 September 1993

p.93 **We did the party a favour** – Gorman, *No, Prime Minister!* p. 257

p.93 **The VAT increase** – Major op. cit. p. 686

p.93 **I can't help thinking** – *People* 11 April 1993

p.94 **The case for reform** – *Independent* 21 July 1993

p.95 **I am short** – Kochan op. cit. p. 209

p.95 **a death-watch beetle** – Brandreth op. cit. p. 320

p.95 **She is as hard as nails** – *Daily Mirror* 11 January 1996

p.96 **I was perfectly happy** – Kochan op. cit. p. 192

p.96 **mums-in-chains** – *Daily Mirror* 11 January 1996

p.97 **the growth in family break-up** – *Guardian* 4 March 1992

p.97 **He blatantly misled** – *Independent* 12 May 1994

p.98 **Resignation would be** – *Times* 12 May 1994

p.98 **close to tears** – *Observer* 22 May 1994

p.98 **it would cost** – *Independent on Sunday* 22 May 1994

p.98 **I don't think** – *Times* 2 July 1994

p.98 **Everything we did** – Iain Duncan Smith (pc)

p.98 **The show has an attitude** – *Independent on Sunday* 28 February 1993

p.98 **less loved** – Brandreth op. cit. p. 184

p.99 **John Major has the lowest** – Lodge, *Therapy* p. 259

p.100 **There is something wrong** – *Independent* 10 June 1993

p.100 **Norman's statement** – Brandreth op. cit. p. 187

p.100 **devious he would one day** – Bayley, *Labour Camp* p. 103

p.101 **I am comfortable** – Naughtie, *The Rivals* p. 47

p.101 **Why not?** – Stephens, *Tony Blair* p. 74

p.101 **masterful inactivity** – *Guardian* 19 November 1992

p.101 **the party appears** – ibid.

p.101 **Simply relying** – *Guardian* 14 November 1992

p.101 **demand that** – Benn, *Free at Last* p. 148

p.101 **a target** – *Independent* 24 September 1994

p.102 **A lot of people** – Benn op. cit. p. 201

p.103 **No say, no pay** – Sopel op. cit. p. 135

p.103 **Why can't you get Gordon** – ibid. p. 162

p.104 **There's no doubt** – Brown, *Fighting Talk* pp. 4–5

p.104 **I suspect language** – Smith, *I Think the Nurses Are Stealing My Clothes* p. 256

p.104 **John Prescott** – *Times* 30 September 1993

p.104 **incoherently eloquent** – Radice, *Diaries 1980–2001* p. 304

p.104 **I had to turn it** – Brown op. cit. p. 226

p.104 **I may get the grammar wrong** – Prime minister's questions, 29 March 2006

p.105 **What fools we were** – *Sun* 14 January 1994

p.105 **What a mistake** – Currie, *Diaries Vol II* p. 124

p.105 **Love her or hate her** – *People* 13 March 1994

p.105 **dead in the water** – Wheatcroft, *The Strange Death of Tory England* p. 213

p.105 **transitional short-term figure** – Young, *The Hugo Young Papers* p. 413

p.105 **Open speculation** – Brandreth op. cit. p. 322

p.106 **He won't last** – Gould, *Goodbye to All That* p. 253

p.106 **It's just a fingertip thing** – Brandreth op. cit. p. 174

p.106 **If John dies** – Blair, *A Journey* p. 61

p.106 **Britain's next prime minister** – McSmith, *Faces of Labour* p. 335

p.106 **Until the 1992 election** – Beckett, *Gordon Brown* p. 69

p.106 **rounded on me** – Hain, *Outside In* p. 166

p.106 **He'd have no chance** – Bower, *Gordon Brown* p. 122

p.106 **I have given** – Young op. cit. p. 390

p.107 **his somewhat dour appearance** – Sopel op. cit. p. 180

p.107 **Funnily enough** – Benn op. cit. p. 179

p.107 **looks as if you could not** – ibid. p. 196

p.107 **Very irritating** – ibid. p. 142

p.107 **the thinking man's** – Mandelson op. cit. p. 134

p.107 **He was probably** – Prescott, *Prezza* p. 215

p.107 **apparently I am too ugly** – Ashdown op. cit. p. 263

p.107 **Some feel the party** – Sopel op. cit. p. 136

p.108 **It is difficult indeed** – Shore, *Leading the Left* p. 187

p.108 **southern appeal** – Routledge, *Mandy* p. 157

p.108 **there not just to mourn** – Ashdown op. cit. p. 267

p.109 **He's too like one of those** – Major op. cit. p. 592

p.109 **avoided the trap** – Radice op. cit. p. 320

p.109 **it might have been** – Giles Radice (pc)

p.109 **I now believe** – Mandelson op. cit. p. 173

p.109 **Tony Blair has become** – *Sunday Times* 2 October 1994

4: Cool

p.110 **Tony Blair's speech** – *Guardian* 19 October 1996

p.110 **Britain is now the place** – *GQ* issue 100, October 1997

p.110 **The Britpop movement was wrong** – Randall, *Exit Music* p. 123

p.110 **SUEDE: THE BEST NEW BAND** – *Melody Maker* 25 April 1992

p.110 **genuine teen mayhem** – Haines, *Bad Vibes* p. 31

p.111 **The future of the programme** – *Times* 14 July 1992

p.111 **Pop is dead** – Radiohead, 'Pop Is Dead' (Radiohead, Warner Chappell Music Ltd, 1993)

p.111 **that neo-trampish** – *Sunday Times* 28 June 1992

p.111 **The world had changed** – Middles, *Manic Street Preachers* p. 91

p.112 **We always knew** – *Q* issue 77, February 1993

p.112 **I thought: He's a star** – Barnett, *Suede* p.71

p.113 **Ben Elton thinks** – *Daily Mirror* 13 May 1995

p.113 **I'd had ten years** – *Independent* 14 April 1998

p.113 **We can't blame Mrs Thatcher** – Elton, *Inconceivable* p. 65

p.114 **I was never a big fan** – *Room 101* 26 January 2007

p.114 **We're just your bog-standard** – *Q* issue 90, March 1994

p.114 **Vic Reeves and Paul Merton** – *People* 6 February 1994

p.114 **I'm interested in stylish comedy** – *Daily Mirror* 24 July 1993

p.115 **I know I'm doing a good job** – *Sunday Times* 26 January 1992

p.115 **I think it's time** – *Daily Mirror* 9 December 1995

p.116 **When you and I started** – Monkhouse, *Over the Limit* p. 125

p.116 **that feels about right** – *Independent on Sunday* 17 July 1994

p.116 **Variety's for the working class** – Monkhouse op cit. p. 234

p.117 **We should broaden its appeal** – *Times* 21 July 1993

p.117 **Fourteen-year-old girlies** – *Times* 24 July 1993

p.117 **sassy pop-literate** – Lee, *How I Escaped My Certain Fate* p. 16

p.117 **When Rob Newman flew** – ibid. p. 20

p.118 **that artist who paints** – *Daily Mail* 1 July 2011

p.118 **Everybody in the late 1980s** – Millree Hughes (pc)

p.118 **We had so little** – Luke Haines (pc)

p.119 **a classic pseudo-event** – Bayley, *Labour Camp* p. 92

p.119 **But is it good art** – Luke Haines (pc)

p.119 **Great art is when** – Brown, *The Tony Years* p. 228

p.119 **Hirst is, in any real sense** – ibid. p. 229

p.120 **the dish of the day** – Aslet, *Anyone for England?* p. 77

p.120 **How do you cook a chicken** – *Sun* 19 September 1997

p.120 **eating out has become** – *Times* 14 July 2001

p.121 **When I'm working hard** – *Guardian* 7 May 1999

p.121 **Adidas shell-toes** – *Daily Mirror* 25 August 2000

p.121 **upper-class Oxford** – *Times* 2 February 1989

p.121 **About as working class** – *Daily Mirror* 14 August 2000

p.122 **diet strategy** – *Financial Times* 8 February 1995

p.122 **You could feel** – *Independent on Sunday* 21 January 1996

p.124 **There's been a depoliticisation** – *Times* 6 February 1991

p.124 **Without any doubt** – Steel, *Reasons to Be Cheerful* p. 225

p.124 **I had always known** – O'Farrell, *Things Can Only Get Better* p. 276

p.124 **my political activism** – Hardy, *Jeremy Hardy Speaks to the Nation* p. 104

p.124 **There is a lot of talk** – Wyatt, *The Journals of Woodrow Wyatt Volume Two* p. 556

p.125 **the worst in the western world** – *Times* 19 October 1992

p.125 **a distinguished Frenchman** – *Times* 22 May 1995

p.125 **There will be no cuts** – *Independent* 30 December 1995

p.125 **Part of my job** – *Observer* 19 May 1996

p.126 **I didn't like them much** – *Guardian* 20 March 1996

p.126 **He is breaking** – *News of the World* 24 March 1996

p.126 **It's embarrassing** – *Independent* 28 March 1996

p.127 **Who wants to be** – Harris, *The Last Party* p. 241

p.127 **The screaming at gigs** – James, *A Bit of a Blur* p. 130

p.128 **Part of the reason** – Wener, *Different for Girls* p. 296

p.128 **Once, cool Britannia** – *Guardian* 30 May 1992

p.128 **currently the coolest country** – *Sunday Times* 22 September 1996

p.129 **the coolest English actor** – Weight, *Patriots* p. 711

p.130 **Ron had great humour** – *Times* 30 March 1995

p.130 **They promised a funeral** – *Daily Mirror* 30 March 1995

p.131 **Thirty years of hurt** – Baddiel, Skinner & the Lightning Seeds, 'Three Lions' (Ian Broudie/David Baddiel/Frank Skinner, Chrysalis Music Ltd/Avalon Management Group Ltd, 1996)

p.131 **Britain has won** – *Independent* 12 November 1996

p.131 **Fucking plank!** – *Vanity Fair* March 1997

p.132 **I am a modern man** – Hernon, *The Blair Decade* p. 17

p.132 **The great bands** – Harris op. cit. p. 191

p.132 **British music is back** – *Times* 20 February 1996

p.132 **Bearing in mind** – *Times* 24 February 1996

p.132 **Alan's just been telling me** – Harris op. cit. p. 304

p.133 **It's a bit cheap** – *Independent on Sunday* 3 November 1996

p.133 **What on earth** – Radice, *Diaries 1980–2001* p. 361

p.133 PLEASE NOTE CHANGE – *Independent* 4 October 1996

p.133 **In sport** – *Observer* 2 June 1996

p.134 **The Conran image** – *Sunday Times* 9 February 1997

p.134 **If the Tories** – Green, *Days in the Life* p. vi

p.134 **He's anaesthetising** – *Sunday Times* 3 November 1996

p.134 **I prefer John Major's style** – *Sun* 31 July 1997

p.134 **The Blair image** – Redwood, *The Death of Britain?* pp. 189–90

p.134 **Suffice to say** – *Q* issue 97 October 1994

p.134 **I want us** – *Daily Mirror* 4 October 1995

p.135 **Until video discs** – *Independent* 13 August 1993

p.136 **This game is sick** – *Daily Mirror* 3 December 1997

p.136 **So-called games** – *News of the World* 23 November 1997

p.136 **Max Clifford** – Anderson & Levene, *Grand Thieves & Tomb Raiders* p. 274

p.136 **If only they would return** – Bennett, *Writing Home* p. 147

p.137 **established a mini-city** – *Times* 31 May 1992

p.137 **The travellers bring** – *Guardian* 28 May 1992

p.137 **This is anarchy working** – *Observer* 24 May 1992

p.137 **Most people were as sickened** – *Times* 8 October 1992

p.137 **We have all too many** – *Financial Times* 7 October 1993

p.139 **Wheelie-bins being set on fire** – *Daily Mirror* 14 October 1998

p.139 **Cocaine is the binding agent** – *Independent on Sunday* 21 January 1996

p.140 **the same old pub rock** – *Independent* 12 August 1997

p.140 **follows the *Lock, Stock*** – rogerebert. suntimes.com, retrieved 30 May 2012

p.140 **Lara was becoming** – Anderson & Levene op. cit. p. 249

p.141 **a cross between** – *Sunday Times* 28 February 1988

p.141 **Soho was fizzing** – James op. cit. p. 151

p.141 **not only were we drunk** – Allen, *Grow Up* p. 348

p.141 **the whole country** – *Independent on Sunday* 24 April 1994

5: Bastards

p.142 **I don't know about you** – Simon Nye, *Men Behaving Badly*, series 2, episode 8: 'Rent Boy'

p.142 **Why do our people** – Major, *The Autobiography* p. 605

p.142 **One thing I think** – Armando Iannucci, *The Friday Night Armistice* (1996)

p.143 **a new and decisive** – Young, *This Blessed Plot* p. 389

p.143 **game, set and match** – *Financial Times* 11 December 1991

p.144 **I hate coming** – Spicer, *The Spicer Diaries* p. 178

p.144 **I will not allow** – *Times* 10 October 1991

p.144 **It is not on** – *Financial Times* 9 October 1991

p.144 **pass the buck** – *Times* 12 March 1975

p.144 **bind and fetter** – *Guardian* 12 March 1975

p.144 **the country is being sold** – Spicer op. cit. p. 193

p.145 **two warring armies** – ibid. p. 181

p.145 **the fault-line** – Heseltine, *Life in the Jungle* p. 388

p.146 **Walter Elliott said** – Gorman, *The Bastards* p. 149

p.146 **Four of the 1992 intake** – Major op. cit. p. 347

p.146 **We are all trying** – *Times* 13 May 1992

p.147 **An issue of such vital** – *Have I Got News for You*, 22 May 1992

p.147 **It was Margaret's support** – Major op. cit. pp. 350–1

p.147 **When Britain was forced** – Baker, *The Turbulent Years* p. 444

p.148 **I could have borne** – Major op. cit. p. 338

p.148 **We spent much of our time** – Hurd, *Memoirs* p. 432

p.149 **There wasn't a lot** – Tristan Garel-Jones (pc)

p.149 **The doors were left open** – Giles Radice (pc)

p.149 **procrastinating on principle** – Major op. cit. p. 273

p.149 **I think John Major** – Richards, *Preparing for Power* p. 66

p.149 **since there was a general will** – Young, *The Hugo Young Papers* p. 353

p.150 **inserting itself** – Hurd op. cit. p. 417

p.150 **He went rather quiet** – Wyatt, *The Journals of Woodrow Wyatt Volume Two* p. 637

p.150 **the only man** – Young op. cit. p. 325

p.150 **vulgar, grandstanding** – Brandreth, *Breaking the Code* p. 124

p.150 **I hope, prime minister** – *Times* 7 October 1992

p.151 **Let us decide** – ibid.

p.151 **It is something** – Gorman op. cit. p. 101

p.151 **the best treaty available** – Shore, *Leading the Left* p. 179

p.152 **The electorate has rejected** – Gorman op. cit. pp. 199–200

p.152 **a mad-hatter coalition** – Major op. cit. p. 375

p.152 **In the voting lobbies** – Spicer op. cit. p. 203

p.152 **the biggest bore** – Critchley & Halcrow, *Collapse of Stout Party* p. 162

p.152 **I am the biggest** – Young op. cit. p. 377

p.153 **The Conservative establishment** – *Times* 29 December 1995

p.153 **a populist cause** – Heseltine op. cit. p. 451

p.153 **You're cunts** – Brandreth op. cit. p. 165

p.153 **I was talking** – Bird & Fortune, *The Long Johns* p. 24

p.154 **The awkward-squad** – *Sun* 23 August 1993

p.154 **Did she play** – Iain Duncan Smith (pc)

p.154 **devils on the fringe** – *Sunday Times* 19 September 1993

p.154 **I shall not be** – *Times* 3 January 1991

p.154 **like a sulk** – Pearce, *The Senate of Lilliput* p. 146

p.154 **She can be petty** – Wyatt op. cit. p. 500

p.154 **She was always criticising** – Cole, *As It Seemed To Me* p. 397

p.155 **Isn't she beautiful?** – Brandreth op. cit. p. 109

p.155 **only acolytes** – Currie, *Diaries* p. 231

p.155 **How can it be principled** – Gorman op. cit. pp. 229–30

p.155 **I must admit** – Benn, *Free at Last* p. 192

p.156 **The prime minister's got the party** – Gorman op. cit. p. 210

p.156 **Under the leadership** – *Times* 24 July 1993

p.156 **a party that is still** – Major op. cit. p. 343

p.156 **Loyalty is the Tories' secret weapon** – *Sunday Times* 19 October 2003

p.157 **There is no vacancy** – *Times* 2 May 1994

p.157 **I'm as strong and loyal** – Bird & Fortune op. cit. p. 30

p.157 **I'm going to fucking crucify** – *Sunday Times* 16 January 1994

p.157 **I don't see how** – Brandreth op. cit. p. 201

p.158 **no surrender** – *Independent* 23 March 1994

p.158 **It was a gratuitous** – Major op. cit. p. 590

p.158 **It was a most humiliating retreat** – ibid. p. 589

p.158 **an uproar** – Spicer op. cit. p. 250

p.158 **My right honourable friend** – *Times* 30 March 1994

p.158 **The balance of probability** – *Independent* 30 March 1994

p.158 **There is a limit** – *Times* 30 March 1994

p.159 **So, God's a Tory** – Williams, *Guilty Men* p. 68

p.159 **By lunchtime** – Heseltine op. cit. p. 474

p.160 **The whips capitulated** – Gorman, *No, Prime Minister!* p. 257

p.161 **Sunday shopping** – *Daily Mirror* 28 January 1993

p.161 **It's a cancer** – Lovesey, *Upon a Dark Night* p. 149

p.162 **two hours of animals** – *Independent on Sunday* 16 August 1998

p.162 **It reminds me of films** – *Sunday Times* 27 September 1992

p.163 **It is as unpleasant** – *Independent* 21 January 1993

p.163 **I am appalled** – *Sunday Mirror* 26 July 1992

p.163 **Seen much worse** – *Times* 27 January 1993

p.163 UP YOURS DELORS – *Sun* 1 November 1990

p.163 **According to the commission's media** – *Sunday Times* 3 November 1991

p.164 **It's supposed to last** – *Daily Mirror* 16 March 1993

p.164 **What could possibly** – *Sunday Times* 7 March 1993

p.165 **From what I gather** – *Times* 29 March 1993

p.165 **following the herd** – Blur, 'Girls and Boys' (Albarn/Coxon/James/Rowntree, MCA Music Ltd, 1994)

p.166 **In a moment of anger** – *Times* 31 August 1998

p.167 **the government's reckless disregard** – *Financial Times* 26 March 1996

p.167 WE'VE ALREADY EATEN – *Daily Mirror* 20 March 1996

p.167 MAD COW ALERT OVER KIDS – *Sun* 21 March 1996

p.167 COULD IT BE WORSE THAN AIDS? – Heseltine op. cit. p. 504

p.167 I would not hesitate – Major op. cit. p. 652

p.168 Why the hell – *Sun* 28 March 1996

p.168 For those who believe – Heseltine op. cit. p. 506

p.168 I have never been so worried – Ashdown, *The Ashdown Diaries* p. 417

p.168 MAD COW GERMS – *Daily Mirror* 10 October 1997

p.169 Buy our burgers – *Independent on Sunday* 9 June 1996

p.169 We cannot continue – *Independent* 22 May 1996

p.169 twenty things – *Sun* 22 May 1996

p.170 I reckon I'll just – Monkhouse, *Over the Limit* p. 309

p.170 The problems facing this country – *Financial Times* 13 June 1995

p.170 that, in many ways – Shephard, *Shephard's Watch* p. 47

p.170 burying their ghosts – Tristan Garel-Jones (pc)

p.170 when British ministers spoke – Major op. cit. p. 583

p.171 We can't do it – Patten, *Not Quite the Diplomat* p. 45

p.171 no more than Texas – *Times* 22 September 1962

p.171 the establishment of a confederation – *Manchester Guardian* 8 September 1867

p.171 People are asked – *Independent* 9 June 1993

p.171 We didn't read – *Daily Mail* 4 October 1994

p.171 It was the small print – Spicer op. cit. p. 396

p.171 Nobody out there – *Daily Mirror* 7 October 1992

p.172 overly obsessed – *Hansard* 24 March 1993

p.172 My aims for the community – *Financial Times* 12 March 1991

p.172 I could have played – Junor, *The Major Enigma* p. 294

p.173 it would be better – Young op. cit. p. 449

p.173 The principle of Parliament – Walter Bagehot, *The English Constitution* (1867) chapter V

6: Charters

p.174 The Met has never been cleaner – J.C. Wilshire, *Between the Lines* series 1, episode 13: 'The Chill Factor'

p.174 If this government can't even privatise – Andy Hamilton & Guy Jenkin, *Drop the Dead Donkey* series 4, episode 6: 'Sally in TV Times'

p.174 State schools, I used to joke – Eclair, *Camberwell Beauty* p. 60

p.174 You can put us girls down – Currie, *A Parliamentary Affair* p. 445

p.174 medium-sized idea – Patten, *Things to Come* p. 20

p.174 People who depend – *Sunday Times*, 24 March 1991

p.175 I know that for millions – Major, *The Autobiography* p. 391

p.175 as a young man – ibid. p. 247

p.176 a bad miscarriageway – *Daily Mirror* 6 September 1994

p.177 Chris Woodhead had many qualities – Blunkett, *The Blunkett Tapes* p. 32

p.178 My overriding aim – *Sunday Times* 31 January 1993

p.178 the first tests – Phillips, *All Must Have Prizes* p. 4

p.179 When I asked to speak – Cable, *Free Radical* p. 212

p.179 They are the people – *Independent* 15 October 1994

p.179 I wasn't prepared – Blunkett, *The Blunkett Tapes* p. 109

p.180 a Labour leader – Campbell, *The Blair Years* p. 35

p.180 I am not going to make – *Independent on Sunday* 1 January 1995

p.180 the most unpleasant – *Daily Mirror* 5 October 1995

p.181 For God's sake – *Daily Mirror* 5 October 1995

p.181 Tony has targeted – Mandelson, *The Third Man* p. 191

p.181 fat, pompous bugger – Campbell op. cit. p. 90

p.181 When socialists fall out – *Daily Mirror* 5 October 1995

p.181 Not the most well-liked – Currie, *Diaries Vol II* p. 209

p.181 fishperson – *Sunday Times* 25 July 1993

p.181 I'm not going to defend – Brown, *Fighting Talk* p. 290

p.181 reveal her stepchildren – Campbell op. cit. p. 101

p.181 I suppose Lisanne – Radice, *Diaries 1980–2001* p. 350

p.181 had exactly the same choice – Benn, *Free at Last* p. 353

p.182 I just want to be tough – *Independent* 24 January 1996

p.182 let's not fight the war – *Observer* 29 January 1995

p.182 I'm not going to allow – *Guardian* 25 January 1996

p.182 She is a doughty Commons performer – *Independent* 25 January 1996

p.182 won genuine cheers – *Times* 25 January 1996

p.182 a bloody good hiding – *Times* 9 October 1985

p.182 The comprehensive schools – *Independent* 25 January 1996

p.183 Ten years ago – *Independent on Sunday* 23 April 1995

p.183 I don't criticise – *Guardian* 22 January 1996

p.183 In my heart of hearts – Blair, *A Journey* p. 203

p.184 **It was degrading** – *Independent* 29 January 1997

p.184 **there was an argument** – Prescott, *Prezza* p. 171

p.185 **You buggers have pinched** – ibid. p. 173

p.185 **I used to be** – Lodge, *Therapy* p. 37

p.186 **Privatising the railways** – Patten, *Not Quite the Diplomat* p. 69

p.186 **I had been responsible** – Heseltine, *Life in the Jungle* p. 451

p.186 **The Post Office is part** – Palin, *Hemingway's Chair* p. 57

p.186 **Fight everyone out there** – ibid. pp. 147–8

p.186 **It was more like** – ibid. p. 201

p.186 **The full greeting** – ibid. p. 197

p.187 **No matter what** – Brookmyre, *Quite Ugly One Morning* p. 143

p.188 **amazingly inefficient** – Young, *The Hugo Young Papers* p. 411

p.189 **This approach also means** – Patten, *Things to Come* p. 112

p.189 **a factor in our dismal 1997** – Major op. cit. p. 393

p.189 **fragrant, intelligent** – *Sunday Times* 4 September 1988

p.189 **insufferably patronising** – Currie, *Diaries Vol II* p. 33

p.189 **Margaret Thatcher** – Ed Borrie/ S*M*A*S*H, '(I Want to) Kill Somebody' (Copyright Control, 1994)

p.189 **The only reason** – Hardy, *Jeremy Hardy Speaks to the Nation* p. 27

p.189 **She was the kind** – Williams, *Guilty Men* p. 56

p.190 **search for economies** – *Independent* 16 November 1993

p.190 **The prime minister's policies** – *Sun* 14 June 1996

p.190 **They are overpaid** – Baker, *The Turbulent Years* p. 451

p.190 **The silent majority** – *Independent* 7 October 1993

p.191 **Jack was sensible** – Blair op. cit. p. 204

p.191 **one of our most impressive** – *Sun* 10 November 1998

p.191 **none of us could be part** – Ashdown, *The Ashdown Diaries* p. 559

p.191 **We have literally to reclaim** – *Independent* 5 September 1995

p.191 **It is not acceptable** – *Times* 28 May 1994

p.192 **It is not exactly** – *Times* 14 November 1996

p.192 **if he didn't behave** – Townsend, *Adrian Mole: The Cappuccino Years* p. 206

p.192 **we're against it** – J. Jones, *Labour of Love* pp. 25–6

p.192 **So you're to the left** – Young op. cit. p. 518

p.193 **statement of common purpose** – *Guardian* 21 February 1990

p.194 **That level of obstruction** – *Observer* 14 April 1991

p.194 **It's painful for me** – *Independent* 15 June 1993

p.194 **overplayed** – *Guardian* 17 May 1991

p.194 **arrogant, ungracious** – Dexter, *Death Is Now My Neighbour* p. 250

p.194 **hypotheses, imaginings** – ibid. p. 83

p.195 **Press conference** – ibid. p. 205

p.195 **It was a shame** – *Daily Mirror* 11 May 2000

p.195 **Rebus will be for Edinburgh** – *Daily Mirror* 6 April 2000

p.197 **the man dubbed** – *Daily Mirror* 12 December 1994

p.197 **extreme sexual personality** – *Independent* 15 September 1994

p.197 **I do not understand** – *Independent on Sunday* 18 September 1994

p.198 **a blatant attempt** – *Independent* 15 September 1994

p.198 **My life has been ruined** – *Sunday Times* 18 September 1994

p.198 **I hope that now** – *Daily Mirror* 15 September 1994

p.199 **MURDERERS** – *Daily Mail* 14 February 1997

p.199 **internalised** – *Times* 22 February 1999

p.199 **It can be seen** – *Independent* 23 February 1999

p.199 **The loony left** – *Independent* 25 February 1999

p.199 **making sweeping assumptions** – *Times* 26 January 1999

p.200 **the NHS was riddled** – Blunkett, *The Blunkett Tapes* p. 113

p.200 **We have recognised** – *Independent* 26 February 1999

p.200 **Sixty-seven of the seventy** – Straw, *Last Man Standing* p. 248

p.200 **most police officers** – *Guardian* 9 February 1999

p.200 **shooting niggers** – *Independent* 25 April 1995

p.201 **the undermining of institutions** – Patten op. cit. p. 52

p.202 **at a higher risk of arson** – *Guardian* 25 July 2000

p.202 **I can't remember** – Mullin, *A View from the Foothills* p. 34

p.202 **a cosmetic public relations exercise** – *Financial Times* 20 July 1991

p.203 **We don't want a leader** – Brandreth, *Breaking the Code* p. 122

p.203 **Maastricht, Mellor** – ibid. p. 147

7: Basics

p.204 **The spectacle of a cabinet minister** – Currie, *A Parliamentary Affair* p. 400

p.204 **The great moral issue** – Peter Flannery, *Our Friends in the North*, episode 2: '1966' (1996)

p.204 **Too many Conservative MPs** – *Sun* 6 January 1997

p.204 **we pulled down** – johnmajor.co.uk

p.205 **Within seconds** – Parris, *Great Parliamentary Scandals* p. 324

p.205 **was intent on rolling back** – *Guardian* 17 January 1994

p.206 **trend in some places** – Williams, *Guilty Men* p. 47

p.206 **To me there is** – *Independent* 7 January 1994

p.206 **Conservatives do make** – *Independent* 7 January 1994

p.206 **This is our chance** – Brandreth, *Breaking the Code* p. 232

p.207 **dreadful, but brilliant** – Ashdown, *The Ashdown Diaries* p. 141

p.207 **discarded condoms** – *Guardian* 18 April 1992

p.207 GAY SEX SHAME – *Guardian* 11 March 1992

p.207 **wandering at dusk** – Parris op. cit. p. 298

p.207 **childish and stupid** – *Times* 13 March 1992

p.207 **in the best interests** – *Times* 10 March 1992

p.207 **Yet another victory** – *Guardian* 10 March 1992

p.207 **gay and proud** – *Times* 13 March 1992

p.208 **Mere infidelity** – West, *Murder in the Commons* p. 160

p.208 **As Mrs Bottomley speaks** – *Guardian* 11 July 1992

p.208 **My expectation was** – Short, *An Honourable Deception?* p. 53

p.209 **admitted totally fabricating** – *Times* 1 December 1992

p.209 **a last resort** – *Times* 20 October 1992

p.210 ANOTHER BACK TO BASICS – *Sunday Mirror* 13 February 1994

p.210 **a three-in-a-bed romp** – *People* 9 April 1995

p.210 **her husband found them** – *Observer* 2 June 1996

p.210 **a frilly garter** – *News of the World* 14 January 1996

p.210 **the bloody 'Back to Basics'** – Currie, *Diaries Vol II* p. 91

p.210 **They apply one standard** – *People* 16 January 1994

p.210 **I will be a figure of fun** – Clark, *The Last Diaries* p. 90

p.210 **I still think** – *Times* 8 June 1993

p.210 **Quite frankly** – *Sunday Times* 29 May 1994

p.211 **friendship with another man** – *Sunday Times* 9 January 1994

p.211 **I have got to keep** – *Daily Mirror* 11 January 1994

p.211 **queenie** – *Independent* 29 November 1995

p.211 **poofter** – *Independent* 28 November 1995

p.211 **It is the usual** – *Independent on Sunday* 10 March 1996

p.211 **They're a bunch of shits** – Parris op. cit. p. 349

p.212 **the press who wildly throw** – ibid. p. 392

p.213 **Sleaze-baiting** – *Independent* 26 June 1993

p.213 **It was perceived** – Major, *The Autobiography* pp. 692–3

p.213 **Is the Labour Party** – Clark, *The Tories* p. 510

p.213 **I would like to be** – Brandreth op. cit. p. 237

p.214 **Bad not just** – Radice, *Diaries 1980–2001* p. 313

p.214 WOULD THE LAST DECENT PERSON – *Daily Mirror* 9 February 1994

p.214 **a desperate personal tragedy** – *Independent* 10 February 1994

p.214 **Stephen was neither miserable** – *Times* 11 February 1994

p.214 **Stephen was gloriously happy** – Brandreth op. cit. p. 240

p.214 **Personally, I hope** – *Independent on Sunday* 13 February 1994

p.214 **How do you feel** – *Independent* 11 March 1994

p.215 **suggestions that officers** – *Times* 11 March 1994

p.215 **The first indications** – *Daily Mirror* 8 February 1994

p.215 **another chance to show** – *Sunday Telegraph* 20 September 1992

p.216 **What Mrs Currie is seeking** – *Independent* 22 February 1994

p.216 **Sodomy is unhygienic** – *Sunday Times* 10 March 1991

p.216 **a matter of equality** – *Independent* 18 February 1994

p.216 **a humdinger** – Currie op. cit. p. 95

p.216 **We need to protect** – *Guardian* 22 February 1994

p.217 **The British soldier** – *Sun* 5 March 1996

p.217 **People are entitled** – *Guardian* 22 February 1994

p.218 **quite a serious impact** – *Times* 30 September 1998

p.218 **How can a law** – *Times* 31 January 1994

p.218 **I said they should change** – *Times* 11 December 1996

p.218 **a bisexual man** – Barnett, *Suede* p. 102

p.219 **I'm more homosexual** – Harris, *The Last Party* p. 163

p.219 **I first had gay sex** – *Daily Mirror* 6 January 1994

p.219 **the stereotypical dyke** – *Daily Mirror* 1 December 1993

p.219 **I'd play a lesbian** – *Times* 22 January 1993

p.219 **Any form of ostentatious behaviour** – *Guardian* 22 July 1967

p.220 **I think it was charming** – youtube.com, retrieved 8 May 2012

p.220 **vice squad officers** – *Independent* 30 March 1996

p.220 **a 250-year-old law** – *Guardian* 26 October 1996

p.221 **I am the Billy Graham** – *Independent on Sunday* 27 August 1995

p.221 **Amongst great British institutions** – *Q* issue 76, January 1993

p.222 GLITTER LIKED ME – *Sun* 10 November 1999

p.222 **highly reprehehsible** – *Guardian* 12 November 1999

p.222 **This is not a witch-hunt** – *Times* 20 December 1990

p.223 **it's really no worse** – *Independent* 22 March 1995 p.223 **Consensual sadomasochism** – *Times* 2 December 1992

p.223 **silly and naughty** – *Sunday Times* 27 April 1997

p.223 **there must be some limitation** – *Forum* Vol. 2 No. 11, 1996

p.223 **sexual activity between** – ibid.

p.224 **an extraordinary programme** – Benn, *Free at Last* p. 458

p.224 **poked fun at** – Elizabeth Coldwell (pc)

p.224 **Radical Marxist Sex Kitten** – *Financial Times* 22 August 1991

p.225 **I'm not really** – *Daily Mirror* 8 January 1972

p.225 **I always wanted to be** – *Independent on Sunday* 4 June 1995

p.225 **I've enjoyed the evening** – *Daily Mirror* 13 December 1993

p.225 **Aren't the gays** – *Sunday Times* 26 December 1993

p.225 **It's an activity** – Clary, *A Young Man's Passage* p. 305

p.226 **witty, well-acted** – *People* 28 February 1999

p.226 **which proves we can make** – *Sun* 24 March 1999

p.226 **If Stuart had taken Nathan** – *Sunday Times* 7 February 1999

p.227 **Even a 'madam'** – *Times* 15 June 1999

p.228 **The result was** – Blair, *A Journey* p. 219

p.228 **Brown confessed** – *Guardian* 16 November 1998

p.228 ARE WE BEING RUN – *Sun* 9 November 1998

p.228 **the government's determination** – *Sun* 10 November 1998

p.228 **a camp icon** – *Times* 10 November 1998

p.229 **Chris Smith is openly** – *Daily Mirror* 28 October 1998

p.229 **I know he's that way** – Naughtie, *The Rivals* p. 35

p.229 **From the conversation** – *Financial Times* 12 November 1998

p.229 **From now on the *Sun*** – *Guardian* 12 November 1998

p.229 **The trouble with Blair** – Oborne & Walters, *Alastair Campbell* p. 166

p.230 **Odious is too polite** – *Sun* 29 December 1997

p.230 **British homosexuals** – *Sunday Times* 19 March 2000

p.230 **Hain is taking it calmly** – Campbell, *The Blair Years* p. 448

p.230 **a classic Christ-type figure** – *Independent* 16 April 2001

p.230 **Are you trying** – *Observer* 11 November 2001

p.230 **As soon as Blair got in** – *New Statesman* 11 February 2012

8: Resignation

p.231 **There are at least two oppositions** – *Times* 2 May 1994

p.231 **After the defeat** – Young, *The Hugo Young Papers* p. 405

p.231 **terrorism is unpleasant** – *Hansard*, 22 June 1995 col. 472

p.232 **I am no longer prepared** – Major, *The Autobiography* p. 626

p.232 **He just wants an answer** – *Times* 26 June 1995

p.233 **Sometimes I feel** – *Independent* 14 October 1994

p.233 **Running a country** – *Independent* 15 October 1994

p.233 **It was a terrible meeting** – Iain Duncan Smith (pc)

p.233 **They were very rude** – Young op. cit. p. 453

p.233 **lie down in a dark room** – *Sunday Times* 25 June 1995

p.234 **I'm ready to stand** – Brandreth, *Breaking the Code* p. 339

p.234 **He preened** – *Sunday Times* 13 March 1994

p.234 **he attracts the same kind** – Sopel, *Tony Blair* p. 248

p.234 **eyes of an assassin** – *Observer* 27 November 1994

p.234 **Skip a generation** – Spicer, *The Spicer Diaries* p. 195

p.235 **We must listen** – *Independent* 23 April 1994

p.235 **a Jew overcompensating** – Young op. cit. p. 437

p.235 **privately courteous** – *Independent* 11 August 1994

p.235 **Portillo struck me** – Young op. cit. p. 414

p.236 **There's nothing worse** – quoted in *Independent on Sunday* 14 August 1994

p.236 **Choke on your champagne** – *Independent* 3 December 1994

p.236 **I could tell** – Brandreth op. cit. p. 297

p.236 **It was horrible** – *Times* 9 September 1999

p.236 **He's an orgasmatron** – *Independent on Sunday* 4 December 1994

p.236 **a man who speaks** – Critchley & Halcrow, *Collapse of Stout Party* p. 63

p.237 **the cabinet's most junior member** – *Financial Times* 15 December 1993

p.237 **he had heard gossip** – Major op. cit. p. 621

p.238 **infiltrators from a strange** – *Times* 26 October 1989

p.238 **an improved version** – *Times* 17 May 1994

p.238 **John has never been exposed** – Critchley & Halcrow op. cit. p. 57

p.238 **The key to Redwood** – Williams, *Guilty Men* p. 23

p.238 **He's nice and everyone likes him** – *Times* 27 June 1995

p.238 **Daddy Woodentop** – Brandreth op. cit. p. 340

p.238 **beatable, Eurosceptic** – Major op. cit. p. 633

p.239 **decisive disaster** – John Redwood (pc)

p.239 **a nice guy, but a loser** – *Guardian* 23 June 1995

p.239 **would have looked good** – Major op. cit. p. 634

p.240 **will back Portillo** – Spicer op. cit. p. 254

p.240 **Today good Conservatives** – *Times* 4 July 1995

p.240 **appeasement** – see, for example, Conservative MPs William Cash and John Wilkinson in *Times* 14 March 1994 and 29 November 1994 respectively

p.241 **It was not really enough** – Major op. cit. p. 645

p.241 **least worst option** – *Independent* 5 July 1995

p.241 **The election has been decided** – Critchley & Halcrow op. cit. p. 65

p.241 **It is healthy** – *Daily Telegraph* 5 July 1995

p.241 **Yesterday Conservative MPs** – *Times* 5 July 1995

p.241 CHICKENS HAND IT TO BLAIR – *Sun* 5 July 1995

p.241 **That's perfect** – Campbell, *The Blair Years* p. 70

p.241 **None of us** – Mandelson, *The Third Man* p. 192

p.241 **It was a rather brilliant tactic** – Blair, *A Journey* p. 100

p.242 **My re-election ended the frenzy** – Major op. cit. p. 646

p.242 **I don't think it settled** – Iain Duncan Smith (pc)

p.242 **slightly loopy** – Clark, *The Last Diaries* p. 194

p.242 **some kind of Faustian bargain** – Meyer, *DC Confidential* p. 18

p.243 **misrepresented their origins** – *Daily Mail* 8 March 1990

p.243 **You need to rent an MP** – *Observer* 23 October 1994

p.243 **Every month we got a bill** – *Times* 20 October 1994

p.244 **He was a man** – Heseltine, *Life in the Jungle* p. 462

p.244 **If it falls to me** – *Financial Times* 11 April 1995

p.244 **the Tories these days** – *Daily Telegraph* 10 October 1994

p.245 **The more I looked** – Heseltine op. cit. p. 446

p.245 **couldn't see an apple-cart** – Wheatcroft, *The Strange Death of Tory England* p. 199

p.245 **despite guidelines** – Critchley & Halcrow op. cit. p. 93

p.245 **economical with** – *Times* 5 November 1992

p.245 **How can they believe this** – Ashdown, *The Ashdown Diaries* p. 257

p.246 **I can't be expected** – *People* 23 January 1994

p.246 **He came out** – Radice, *Diaries 1980–2001* p. 313

p.246 **the extremely emotional way** – Barnett, *This Time* p. 234

p.246 **I accept the genuineness** – *Financial Times* 16 February 1996

p.246 **designedly** – Cohen, *Pretty Straight Guys* p. 172

p.246 **we could find ourselves** – Critchley & Halcrow op. cit. p. 90

p.246 **There was no conspiracy** – *Independent* 16 February 1996

p.246 **It will be hairy** – Barnett op. cit. p. 53

p.247 **Answers given** – ibid. p. 242

p.247 **an arrogant government** – *Daily Mirror* 27 February 1996

p.247 **one of the most startling speeches** – Ashdown op. cit. p. 405

p.247 **the luxuries of** – *Times* 12 November 1992

p.247 **grubby and wheedling** – Ashdown op. cit. p. 406

p.247 **economical with the truth** – *Guardian* 19 November 1986

p.247 **being conservative** – Hawkins, *The Anarchist* p. 21

p.247 **much of the public anxiety** – Major op. cit. p. 574

p.248 **We in this House** – *Financial Times* 19 May 1995

p.248 **I deeply resent** – *Independent* 19 May 1995

p.248 **What is really sleazy** – *Independent on Sunday* 24 January 1993

p.248 **fat cats** – *Times* 28 June 1991

p.249 **You're doing the same job** – Hill, *On Beulah Height* p. 262

p.249 **We are unearthing** – *Independent on Sunday* 17 January 1993

p.249 **the number one** – *Daily Mirror* 1 March 1995

p.249 **Government was powerless** – Heseltine op. cit. p. 468

p.250 **a light-hearted gesture** – Parris, *Great Parliamentary Scandals* p. 320

p.250 **This is truly tragic news** – *Times* 6 November 1991

p.251 **The problem with John** – Thatcher, *The Path to Power* p. 483

p.251 **an irrelevance** – *Times* 22 May 1995

p.251 **We are all Eurosceptics** – *Independent* 11 October 1995

p.251 **His own intellectual analysis** – Hurd, *Memoirs* p. 511

p.251 **The truth is** – Brandreth op. cit. p. 479

p.251 **new chancellor** – *Times* 6 December 1996

p.251 **Hughie, get your tanks** – *Independent* 28 January 2004

p.251 **class-ridden, prejudiced** – *Independent on Sunday* 14 January 1996

p.252 **What I hope** – Clark, *The Last Diaries* p. 204

p.252 **There are bad moments** – Currie, *Diaries Vol II* p. 234

p.252 **harmonise uniforms** – *Times* 11 October 1995

p.252 **for Britain** – *Financial Times* 11 October 1995

p.253 **Cheap and nasty** – *Daily Mirror* 11 October 1995

p.253 **grown newspapermen** – *Independent* 11 October 1995

p.253 **deplorable . . . grotesque** – *Independent* 12 October 1995 p.253 **rabble-rousing** – *Times* 13 October 1995

p.253 **He has damaged** – ibid.

p.253 **He knows he went too far** – Brandreth op. cit. p. 353

p.254 **he is rash, amusing** – *Times* 10 February 1997

p.254 **has predicted twelve** – Johnson, *Friends, Voters, Countrymen* p. 157

p.254 **the recovery took place** – Redwood, *The Death of Britain?* p. 15

p.254 **Unemployment rose** – Major op. cit. p. 663

p.255 **for political reasons** – Campbell, *The Blair Years* p. 124

p.255 **a wholly unprecedented sense** – Dexter, *Death Is Now My Neighbour* p. 282

p.255 **mildly depressed** – Young op. cit. p. 480

p.255 **If there's going to be** – *Independent* 15 March 1997

p.255 **As I look around me** – Iannucci, *Facts and Fancies* p. 99

9: Election

p.256 **A tidal wave** – on BBC's *Election '97*, quoted in N. Jones, *Campaign 1997* p. 260

p.256 **It is a great rising up** – Fielding, *Bridget Jones: The Edge of Reason* p. 203

p.256 **Because I haven't always** – Brandreth, *Breaking the Code* p. 518

p.257 **half a generation** – *Sunday Times* 23 August 1992

p.257 **that things are going to be** – *Observer* 8 November 1992

p.258 **the Third Way** – Meyer, *DC Confidential* p. 95

p.258 **All the ideas from Clinton** – Brown, *Fighting Talk* p. 273

p.258 **We don't need** – Mandelson, *The Third Man* p. 151

p.258 **said that for the first time** – Ashdown, *The Ashdown Diaries* p. 260

p.258 **doesn't mention the Labour Party** – Benn, *Free at Last* p. 177

p.259 **John was making the party** – Richards, *Preparing for Power* p. 30

p.259 **Labour is not against wealth** – *Times* 18 August 1993

p.259 **he was not going to add** – Cole, *As It Seemed To Me* p. 423

p.259 **I was middle class** – Blair, *A Journey* p. 26

p.259 **more European than the Tories** – McSmith, *Faces of Labour* p. 336

p.260 **one of the most explicit** – Straw, *Last Man Standing* p. 186

p.260 **The changing character** – Shore, *Leading the Left* pp. 72–3

p.261 **Tony Blair yesterday** – *Times* 5 October 1994

p.261 **was in raptures** – Campbell, *The Blair Years* p. 21

p.261 **She said *Tatler*** – ibid. p. 27

p.262 **That began making me feel** – Benn op. cit. p. 315

p.262 **Yesterday the loony left** – *Sunday Times* 30 April 1995

p.262 **I was surprised** – Seldon, *Blair* p. 221

p.263 **there was no room** – Blair op. cit. p. 94

p.263 **the recognition** – Hutton, *The State We're In* p. 326

p.263 **The old answers** – *Times* 17 July 1993

p.264 **The lessons which the British left** – Seldon op. cit. p. 133

p.264 **He trusts his own judgement** – Young, *The Hugo Young Papers* p. 675

p.264 **a daily mandate** – Stephens, *Tony Blair* p. 188

p.264 **had balls** – Blair op. cit. p. 98

p.264 **clanking great balls** – ibid. p. 80 and Campbell op. cit. p. 64

p.264 **balls of steel** – N. Jones op. cit. p. 15

p.264 **brass nerve** – Blair op. cit. p. 98

p.264 **tough choices** – *Sunday Times* 17 July 1994

p.265 **wealth for the many** – *Times* 12 October 1996

p.265 **a hand up** – *Sunday Times* 3 July 1994

p.265 **Our Conservatism** – *Financial Times* 28 June 1991

p.265 **with opportunity** – Seldon, *Blair* p. 125

p.265 **our policies are based** – http://www.johnmajor.co.uk/page1153.html retrieved 17 December 2012

p.265 **a modern relationship** – Blair op. cit. p. 231

p.265 **Some people tend** – *Times* 12 March 1991

p.265 **The language of New Labour** – Major, *The Autobiography* p. 214

p.265 **We paid inordinate attention** – Oborne, *The Triumph of the Political Class* p. 234

p.265 **hand to hand fighting** – N. Jones op. cit. p. 10

p.266 **Journalists are inherently lazy** – ibid. p. 22

p.267 **in a fair tax system** – *Daily Mirror* 15 April 1996

p.267 **fucked up** – Campbell op. cit. p. 117

p.267 **That woman** – ibid.

p.267 **We won't win** – N. Jones op. cit. p. 115

p.267 **people who live** – Richards op. cit. p. 26

p.267 **How can I be off-message** – Williams, *Guilty Men* p. 144

p.267 **Mandelson project** – Gould, *Goodbye to All That* p. 226

p.267 **the Kinnockite project** – McSmith op. cit. p. 336

p.267 **Our new economic approach** – ibid. p. 340

p.267 **It's not Brown's** – *Independent on Sunday* 16 October 1994

p.268 **the fastest-growing** – Richards op. cit. p. 16

p.268 **That woman fucking killed** – Campbell op. cit. p. 78

p.268 **They all loathe Blair** – Benn op. cit. p. 339

p.268 **At times his competence** – Parris, *Off-Message* p. 2

p.268 **If only I could speak** – Blair op. cit. p. 36
p.268 **I thought I told him** – McSmith op. cit. p. 351
p.268 **One of his skills** – Junor, *The Major Enigma* p. 201
p.269 **Tony has a habit** – Prescott, *Prezza* p. 188
p.269 **Standing together** – *Sun* 13 November 1998
p.269 **The buck stops here** – *Independent* 2 October 1996
p.269 **I have spent sixteen years** – *Times* 4 October 1995
p.269 **My ambition is clear** – *GQ* issue 100, October 1997
p.269 **Power without principle** – Hernon, *The Blair Decade* p. 5
p.270 **From my experience** – Ashdown op. cit. p. 324
p.270 **a vampire** – *Times* 17 May 1994
p.270 **The greatest con job** – Young op. cit. p. 470
p.270 **a mistake to try** – ibid. p. 430
p.271 **Tony Blair is a practising Christian** – N. Jones op. cit. p. 143
p.271 **drew on the public's** – *Guardian* 10 January 1997
p.272 **flattened his bouffant hairstyle** – *Financial Times* 6 November 1996
p.272 **worried enough** – *Times* 21 October 1992
p.272 **If I really were dyeing** – Major op. cit. p. 360
p.272 **It was a black day** – Campbell op. cit. p. 138
p.272 **Political coverage** – Mullin, *A View from the Foothills* p. 15
p.272 **Labour has stolen our ground** – Ashdown op. cit. p. 324
p.273 **there's real danger** – *Sunday Times* 4 May 1997
p.273 **We should now dispose** – Patten, *Things to Come* p. 15
p.273 **a light-hearted interview** – *Independent* 5 March 1997
p.273 **appalling** – *Sun* 5 March 1997
p.273 **the prissy ideologues** – Barnett, *This Time* p. 39
p.274 **I've been here** – Brandreth op. cit. p. 397
p.275 **in a very threatening manner** – *Independent* 7 February 1995
p.275 **a series of homosexual encounters** – Brandreth op. cit. p. 501
p.275 **piggybacking** – McSmith op. cit. p. 237
p.277 **My thought process** – N. Jones op. cit. p. 128
p.277 **made a mockery** – Heseltine, *Life in the Jungle* p. 525
p.277 **He sounds tough** – Radice, *Diaries 1980–2001* p. 379
p.277 **I will not take** – Barnett op. cit. p. 37
p.277 **his most dramatic** – *Daily Mail* 17 April 1997
p.277 **What they thought** – Iain Duncan Smith (pc)

p.277 **This is a single-issue** – *Times* 25 October 1995
p.278 **I would not go that far** – *Sun* 25 April 1996
p.278 **He is in part an anarchist** – Young op. cit. p. 495
p.278 **Ken Clarke's ventriloquist's dummy** – Critchley & Halcrow, *Collapse of Stout Party* p. 112
p.278 **pitiful piece of publicity** – N. Jones op. cit. p. 230
p.278 **This was not a Eurosceptic concept** – Heseltine op. cit. p. 527
p.279 **I know you're bored** – Barnett op. cit. p. 108
p.279 **clinging to his magic soapbox** – Critchley & Halcrow op. cit. p. 122
p.279 **papered house** – Clark, *The Last Diaries* p. 280
p.279 **There's none of the bitterness** – quoted in *Sunday Times* 4 May 1997
p.279 **He was sitting** – Iain Duncan Smith (pc)
p.280 **the devil we know . . . however reluctantly** – N. Jones op. cit. p. 258
p.280 **the long night** – Routledge, *Gordon Brown* p. 276
p.280 **I discovered not just admiration** – N. Jones op. cit. p. 264
p.280 **I touched him** – ibid. p. 265
p.280 **the *Mirror* is merely** – *Guardian* 25 April 1997
p.281 **None of these farces** – *Evening Standard* 29 April 1997
p.281 **There is widespread umbrage** – Critchley & Halcrow op. cit. p. 147
p.281 **What the fuck's going on?** – Wheatcroft, *The Strange Death of Tory England* p. 230
p.283 **revolution** – Critchley & Halcrow op. cit. p. 8
p.283 **a bourgeois revolution** – Williams op. cit. p. 183
p.283 **Nothing prepared me** – Cathcart, *Were You Still Up for Portillo?* p. 18
p.284 **Up and down the country** – Kochan, *Ann Widdecombe* p. 205
p.285 **The scale of the defeat** – Shephard, *Shephard's Watch* p. 172
p.285 **This was what it was** – Shepherd, *Enoch Powell* p. 487
p.285 **a glorious new dawn** – Townsend, *Adrian Mole: The Cappuccino Years* pp. 65–6
p.285 **We're having a Tony** – Fielding op. cit. p. 207
p.286 **Out, out, out** – Prescott, *Prezza* p. 213
p.286 **It's marvellous** – *Independent* 25 March 1996
p.286 **It was the defining moment** – Steel, *Reasons to Be Cheerful* p. 248
p.286 **It was so relentlessly bad** – Brandreth op. cit. pp. 516–17
p.286 **cheering and shouting** – J. Jones, *Labour of Love* p. 56
p.287 **One thing alone** – Cathcart op. cit. p. 117

p.287 **I believed we had stretched** — Major op. cit. p. 309

p.287 **You can ask the people** — *Sunday Times* 5 May 1996

p.287 **If I had stood unopposed** — *Observer* 13 February 2000

p.287 **This is a time to be magnanimous** — Cathcart op. cit. p. 38

p.287 **it was disgraceful to resign** — Young, *The Hugo Young Papers* p. 574

p.287 **When the curtain falls** — *Financial Times* 3 May 1997

p.287 **It's a great job** — Major op. cit. p. 726

p.288 **the recession I inherited** — ibid. p. 689

p.288 **These are fantastically good** — Bower, *Gordon Brown* p. 207

p.288 **Margaret Thatcher buried** — Tristan Garel-Jones (pc)

p.289 **I felt it was beyond** — Iain Duncan Smith (pc)

p.289 **could break the Tory Party** — Weight, *Patriots* p. 330

p.289 **Majorism** — Cole op. cit. p. 433

p.289 **There's no banter** — N. Jones op. cit. pp. 115–16

p.290 **I was warmed** — Major op. cit. p. 632

p.290 **You had a rough decision** — ibid. p. 727

Intermission: Patriotism

p.291 **You cannot suppress** — speech to European Policy Forum 27 July 1994 (johnmajor.co.uk)

p.291 **England is obsessed** — Patten, *Not Quite the Diplomat* p. 40

p.291 **We are forging** — *Sunday Times* 29 March 1998

p.293 **I think an essential** — *Independent on Sunday* 17 September 1995

p.293 **If there is a desire** — *Sunday Times* 28 February 1993

p.294 **the joie de vivre** — *Sunday Times* 16 February 1992

p.294 **John Major would call it** — *Sunday Times* 21 April 1991

p.294 **The prime minister seems** — *Sunday Times* 7 February 1993

p.295 **Fifty years from now** — Major, *The Autobiography* p. 376

p.295 **a caricature** — ibid.

p.295 **too easily caricatured** — John Redwood (pc)

p.296 **WHAT A LOT OF TOSH** — *Independent on Sunday* 25 April 1993

p.296 **We desperately need** — *Sunday Times* 16 May 1993

p.296 **our strongest export sector** — *Independent* 8 September 1997

p.297 **socialist** — *Daily Mirror* 9 October 1992

p.297 **If it's going to get up** — *Times* 6 October 1992

p.298 **From time to time** — *Independent on Sunday* 22 March 1998

p.298 **soap operas which had the quality** — *Independent* 17 March 1998

p.298 **The target of Tony Blair's Cool Britannia** — *Sunday Times* 15 March 1998

p.298 **In those days foreigners** — *Independent* 17 March 1998

p.298 **I'm old enough to remember** — Lodge, *Therapy* p. 35

p.299 **the best generation** — Parsons, *Big Mouth Strikes Again* p. 205

p.299 **His youth might** — Parsons, *Man and Boy* p. 95

p.299 **I'm happy to be a bloke** — Hornby, *High Fidelity* p. 103

p.299 **I mused that if Dad** — O'Farrell, *The Best a Man Can Get* p. 205

p.299 **I don't know what it** — Izzard, *Dress to Kill* p. 86

p.299 **a man's legs** — Planer, *The Right Man* p. 118

p.299 **My father has carried** — Eclair, *Camberwell Beauty* p. 342

p.300 **Due to Mr Blair's obvious hatred** — Townsend, *Adrian Mole: The Cappuccino Years* p. 305

p.301 **We beat them in 1945** — Engel & Morrison, *The Sportspages Almanac 1991* p. 8

p.301 ACHTUNG! SURRENDER — *Daily Mirror* 24 June 1996

p.301 TEN NASTIES — *Daily Mirror* 20 June 1996

p.301 **If Germany beat us** — Patten, *Not Quite the Diplomat* p. 49

p.302 **He looked like a Greek god** — Lodge op. cit. p. 90

p.302 **It was a time of hope** — ibid. p. 91

p.302 **We'll have spam** — *Daily Mirror* 21 April 1994

p.302 **celebrations and commemorations** — *Independent* 19 April 1994

p.302 **festivities and public relations stunts** — *Times* 18 April 1994

p.303 **They have their history** — *Daily Mirror* 19 April 1994

p.303 **trivial light entertainment** — *Sunday Times* 17 April 1994

p.303 **carnival atmosphere** — *Daily Mirror* 21 April 1994

p.303 **It's a bit like saying** — *People* 24 April 1994

p.303 If someone wants — ibid.

p.303 **The debacle and retreat** — *Independent* 22 April 1994.

p.303 **The D-Day anniversary** — *Times* 21 April 1994

p.304 **The most potent** — Williams, *Guilty Men* p. 8a **seductive, subterranean** — *Observer* 7 May 1995

p.304 THEN AS NOW — *Private Eye* 871, 5 May 1995

p.304 **deliberately backward-looking** — *Independent* 10 May 1995

p.304 **Looking around** — Thompson, *Sunshine on Putty* p. 25

p.305 **Is it possible to have kitsch** — Fielding, *Bridget Jones's Diary* p. 123

p.305 **We are the last** — Morrissey/Alain Whyte, 'We'll Let You Know' (Copyright Control/MCA Music Ltd, 1992) p.305 **Has Morrissey gone** – *New Musical Express* 22 August 1992

p.305 **I like the flag** – *Observer*, 6 December 1992

p.305 **When I see reports** – *Q* issue 72 September 1992

p.306 **a strange swell of pride** – Engel & Morrison, op. cit. p. 15

p.306 **flirting with fascist imagery** – Maconie, *3862 Days* p. 149

p.306 **It's the greatest flag** – Harris, *The Last Party* p. 130

p.307 **No wonder the English** – Parsons, *Man and Boy* p. 299

p.307 **individualism, pragmatism** – Paxman, *The English* p. 264

p.307 **It was a matter shut up** – Rudyard Kipling, *Stalky & Co*, chapter 6: 'The Flag of Their Country'

p.307 **a monopoly of patriotism** – *Financial Times* 21 May 1987

p.307 **When you see** – ibid.

p.307 **It is no good waving** – *Daily Mirror* 4 October 1995

p.308 **discreetly woven** – *Financial Times* 1 October 1991

p.308 **Let us say it with pride** – *Times* 4 October 1995

p.308 **I am proud** – Kampfner, *Blair's Wars* p. 4

p.308 **felt a tug** – Blair, *A Journey* p. 126

p.308 **become a wheezing caricature** – Aslet, *Anyone for England?* p. 33

p.308 **It was the National Front** – Benn, *Free at Last* p. 285

p.309 **We have reclaimed** – *Times* 6 February 1998

p.309 **Union Jack election** – *Independent* 4 October 1994

p.309 **People haven't got a clue** – *Sunday Times* 4 May 1997

p.309 **This coming election** – *Daily Mirror* 4 October 1995

p.309 **Economics are the method** – Hewison, *Culture and Consensus* p. 212

p.309 **Wherever you go** – *Independent* 19 February 1993

p.309 **Very effectively** – Blair op. cit. p. 57

p.310 **If we do not learn** – *Times* 22 February 1993

p.310 **crusade against crime** – *Times* 22 February 1993

p.310 **We should condemn** – *Times* 24 February 1993

p.310 **We are the party** – Sopel, *Tony Blair* p. 141

p.310 **The two of them** – *Independent* 23 February 1993

p.311 **the toughest-ever** – *Times* 13 April 1993

p.311 **Violence is not a knife** – *Times* 13 December 1995

p.311 **the government and those who shape society** – *Times* 27 December 1995

p.311 **to show everyone** – philiplawrenceawards. net, retrieved 24 May 2012

p.312 **I don't believe** – *Independent* 25 September 1996

p.312 **flaws** – *Times* 19 March 1996

p.312 **unworkable** – *Financial Times* 19 March 1996

p.312 **a thorny area** – *Independent* 19 March 1996

p.312 **she's wasting her time** – *Sun* 19 March 1996

p.312 **This generation** – *Independent* 14 October 1995

p.313 **I think that if we win** – *Sunday Times* 3 November 1996

p.313 **complains that we haven't** – Radice, *Diaries 1980–2001* p. 401

p.313 **We made a very big mistake** – Blair op. cit. p. 126

p.314 **changes just as exciting** – *Guardian* 10 April 1964

p.314 **to build a new** – *Times* 4 October 1995

p.314 **One-nation Labour** – *Times* 7 October 1995

p.314 **a party for everyone** – Wheatcroft, *The Strange Death of Tory England* p. 249

p.314 **good at being a man** – Young, *The Hugo Young Papers* p. 479

p.314 **He is clearly going** – Radice op. cit. p. 73

p.314 **I had always been fortunate** – Blair op. cit. p. 663

p.315 **Sin isn't a word** – Wilson, *The Vicar of Sorrows* pp. 193–4

p.315 **jollier forms** – ibid. p. 202

p.315 **A married man** – ibid. p. 30

p.315 **The great *Who's Who*** – ibid. pp. 350–1

p.316 **unlikely to cause** – *Times* 25 May 1994

p.316 **Diesel's advertising** – *Evening Standard* 3 March 1998

p.316 **nuns as sexual beings** – *Times* 12 August 1998

p.316 **The Bible is clear** – *Times* 29 March 2000

p.317 **Three of them** – *Daily Mirror* 16 April 1993

p.317 **to warm up food** – *Independent* 13 December 1994

p.318 **Immigration, an issue** – *Independent* 10 September 1995

p.319 **I understand Britishness** – *Guardian* 12 November 1998

p.319 **I do not accept** – *Times* 20 April 2001

p.319 **Chicken tikka masala** – *Evening Standard* 19 April 2001

p.319 **a 'catastrophic intervention'** – Campbell, *The Blair Years* p. 522

Part Two: New Angels of Promise

p.321 **If there's such a thing** – *Sun* 26 September 1996

p.321 **What we want to know** – *Sunday Telegraph* 1 March 1998

p.321 **The strangest Tory** – *The Economist*, 30 April 1998

10: Enter Tony Blair

p.323 **A media-friendly** – *The Election Night Armistice*

p.323 **The Blair government** – Radice, *Diaries 1980–2001* p. 422

p.323 **I think the Party** – Clark, *The Last Diaries* p. 285

p.324 **torture** – *Observer* 3 April 1960

p.324 **listening to twenty-two** – *Times* 31 May 1969

p.324 **Each year you say** – *Sun* 29 April 1997

p.324 **Britain proudly took** – *Daily Mirror* 5 May 1997

p.324 **We are delighted** – *Independent* 5 May 1997

p.324 **It's been a long time** – *Daily Mirror* 5 May 1997

p.325 **If Blair succeeds** – *Times* 1 May 1997

p.325 **the Labour Party is the one** – *Sun* 3 May 1997

p.325 **I have no doubt at all** – *Times* 31 May 1995

p.325 **If Robin Cook went** – Critchley & Halcrow, *Collapse of Stout Party* p. 220

p.325 **This was our Velvet Revolution** – *Guardian* 3 May 1997

p.325 **There was an almost tangible sense** – Blunkett, *The Blunkett Tapes* p. 7

p.325 **It was a joy** – Hain, *Outside In* p. 186

p.325 **A great sigh of relief** – Ashdown, *The Ashdown Diaries* p. 561

p.325 **I am sure we will all** – Richards, *Whatever It Takes* pp. 98–9

p.326 **The corridors of Broadcasting House** – 'Drive', Radio 5 Live, 10 May 2007

p.326 **the journey's end** – Blair, *A Journey* p. 4

p.326 **What will Tony's success** – Radice op. cit. p. 397

p.326 **When Tony Blair came to power** – Bremner et al. *You Are Here* p. 7

p.326 **Hey listen** – Hislop, *The Private Eye Annual 1997* p. 68

p.327 **I have always been** – Sopel, *Tony Blair* p. 22

p.327 **We were rather tragic** – ibid. p. 26

p.327 **reedy** – C. Blair, *Speaking for Myself* p. 185

p.328 **a civilised, middle class pedigree** – *Guardian* 10 May 1982

p.328 **I developed a theory** – Blair op. cit. p. 79

p.328 **He could be one of us** – Brandreth, *Breaking the Code* p. 178

p.329 **Tony Blair is the first** – Fielding, *Bridget Jones: The Edge of Reason* p. 206

p.330 **sterile, disease-ridden** – *Independent* 10 April 1997

p.330 **Bent Ben** – *Times* 10 April 1997

p.330 **schoolchildren would be** – Cathcart, *Were You Still Up for Portillo?* p. 135

p.330 **a European who can speak** – *Financial Times* 2 May 1997

p.330 **the Stepford Wives** – *Times* 7 February 1998

p.330 **Tony was wise enough** – Powell, *The New Machiavelli* p. 95

p.331 **a new dawn** – *Daily Mirror* 3 May 1997

p.331 **We will govern** – *Times* 2 April 1992

p.331 **They didn't always** – Seldon, *Blair* p. 114

p.331 **I'll have to tell them** – Campbell, *The Blair Years* p. 95

p.331 **They're a farce** – J. Jones, *Labour of Love* p. 260

p.331 **how little real influence** – Price, *The Spin Doctor's Diary* p. 156

p.332 **The cabinet is a rather** – Mandelson & Liddle, *The Blair Revolution* p. 245

p.332 **bilateral and ad hoc** – ibid. p. 244

p.332 **No prizes for guessing** – Routledge, *Mandy* p. 173

p.332 **If he's game** – *People* 13 September 1992

p.332 **Writing was never his strong point** – Oborne & Walters, *Alastair Campbell* p. 113

p.332 **The level of hatred** – Routledge op. cit. p. 172

p.332 **They dare not attack** – *Observer* 12 July 1998

p.333 **they do not like to be reminded** – Johnson, *Best Seat in the House* p. 179

p.333 **The public views him** – Clifford, *Max Clifford* p. 183

p.333 **He was indispensable** – Blair op. cit. p. 7

p.333 **When you heard** – Oborne & Walters op. cit. p. 159

p.333 **They're bullies** – Naughtie, *The Rivals* p. 242

p.333 **It seems that either** – Clifford op. cit. p. 183

p.333 **less than completely open** – *Sun* 3 May 1996

p.334 **He went off** – Campbell op. cit. p. 46

p.334 **If 'spin' means** – Blunkett op. cit. p. 51

p.334 **to create the truth** – Rawnsley, *Servants of the People* p. 103

p.334 **he couldn't stand her** – Blair op. cit. p. 24

p.334 **a rift gradually opened** – Blunkett op. cit. p. 229

p.334 **one of the most bitter feuds** – N. Jones, *Campaign 1997* p. 104

p.334 **they don't trust him** – Young, *The Hugo Young Papers* p. 542

p.334 **We can't go on carving** – Richards, *Preparing for Power* p. 28

p.334 **We found that some of them** – Naughtie, *The Rivals* p. 79

p.334 **Pushmi-pullyu** – McSmith, *Faces of Labour* p. 327

p.335 **The truth is** – Blair op. cit. p. 70

p.335 **There is but a cigarette paper** – *Independent* 24 January 1996

p.336 **You can't go on** – Mandelson, *The Third Man* p. 188

p.336 **John is hopelessly insecure** – Mullin, *A View from the Foothills* p. 14

p.336 **Our main role** – ibid. p. 25

p.336 **I certainly think** – Radice op. cit. p. 409

p.336 **He would have full charge** – *Independent* 10 January 1998

p.336 **deliberately reopening** – *Times* 10 January 1998

p.337 **screaming abuse** – Campbell op. cit. p. 271

p.337 **someone who has an extremely good claim** – *Observer* 18 January 1998

p.337 **That was an understatement** – Oborne & Walters op. cit. p. 186

p.337 **the finest mind** – Radice op. cit. p. 422

p.337 **suffers from a kind of** — *Sunday Times* 10 September 2006

p.337 **We can't have** — Richards, *Whatever It Takes* p. 127

p.337 **as a fact** — Naughtie, *The Rivals* p. 251

p.337 **People want to know** — *Independent on Sunday* 3 March 1996

p.337 **If Gordon Brown** — *Independent* 12 March 1996

p.338 **I told Gordon** — Bower, *Gordon Brown* p. 128

p.338 **I don't try to be** — ibid. p. 162

p.338 **It's nonsense** — *Sun* 13 January 1997

p.338 **not packed** — C. Blair op. cit. p. 284

p.339 **I needed that love** — Blair, *A Journey* p. 65

p.339 **The whole issue** — C. Blair op. cit. p. 287

p.339 **froth of politics** — *Daily Mirror* 20 January 1998

p.339 **'Blair'** — Campbell op. cit. p. 144

p.339 **In retrospect** — Powell op. cit. p. 120

p.339 **His way of managing** — ibid. p. 108

p.339 **I disliked this proposal** — Major, *The Autobiography* p. 675

p.340 **Don't think** — *Daily Telegraph* 9 January 1990

p.340 **more accountable** — Barnett, *This Time* p. 27

p.340 **very good political reasons** — Blair op. cit. p. 113

p.340 **You'll be pleased to hear** — Naughtie op. cit. p. 99

p.340 **Who elected Eddie George?** — Benn, *Free at Last* p. 413

p.341 **what is the point** — Bryan Gould (pc)

p.341 **the decision to give** — Blunkett op. cit. p. 42

p.341 **a policy that** — Cable, *Free Radical* p. 245

p.342 **Tory boom and bust** — *Daily Mail* 18 March 1998

p.342 **This Chancellor does not want** — *Times* 18 May 1994

p.342 **no return** — *Financial Times* 27 November 1995

p.342 **We gave the Bank** — Richards op. cit. p. 113

p.342 **We will make it a priority** — Sopel op. cit. p. 213

p.343 **I'm going to be a lot more radical** — Rawnsley op. cit. p. 6

p.343 **the people's lottery, the people's priorities** — *Sun* 24 April 1997

p.343 **the people's lottery** — *Times* 19 November 1994

p.343 **passionate defence** — *Financial Times* 1 October 1991

p.343 **He was off on one** — Campbell op. cit. p. 274

p.344 **the major beneficiaries** — Short, *An Honourable Deception?* p. 68

p.344 **This is the tax bombshell** — *Guardian* 3 July 1997

p.344 **to milk the middle class** — Richards op. cit. p. 118

p.344 **In the longer term** — Short op. cit. p. 72

p.344 **When he arrived** — Shephard, *Shephard's Watch* p. 208

p.345 **when we came out** — Clark op. cit. p. 306

p.346 **something of the night** — *Sunday Times* 11 May 1997

p.346 **Machiavellian talent** — N. Jones op. cit. p. 66

p.346 **the cabinet's Geoffrey Boycott** — ibid. p. 71

p.346 **We demean our high office** — Kochan, *Ann Widdecombe* p. 216

p.347 **The British people** — Critchley & Halcrow op. cit. p. 224

p.347 **I suppose it will be William** — Nadler, *William Hague* p. 6

p.348 **This is, I think** — Williams, *Guilty Men* p. 219

p.348 **the Conservative Party** — *Guardian* 19 June 1997

p.348 **Is this another Hitler-Stalin** — Critchley & Halcrow op. cit. p. 261

p.348 **he was doomed to fall** — Heseltine, *Life in the Jungle* p. 530

p.348 **You don't need to worry** — Sampson, *The Changing Anatomy of Britain* p. 79

p.349 **It's not the job** — *GQ* issue 100, October 1997

p.349 **roll back the frontiers** — Nadler op. cit. p. 72

p.349 **a juvenile lead** — Critchley & Halcrow op. cit. p. 8

p.349 **elected a foetus** — *Guardian* 2 October 1997

p.350 **I like women** — *Independent* 10 October 1997

p.350 **The Tories are a waste** — *Sun* 24 February 1998

p.350 **a man with a well-founded fear** — Johnson op. cit. p. 175

p.350 **shifty little bureaucrat** — Clark op. cit. p. 288

p.351 **It's getting older** — Currie, *Diaries Vol II* p. 236

p.351 **without them** — ibid. p. 168

p.351 **We couldn't get candidates** — Radice op. cit. p. 340

p.351 **Thus was the new branch** — Spicer, *The Spicer Diaries* p. 261

p.351 **it looks as though Labour** — Cathcart op. cit. p. 159

p.351 LYING SLEAZEBAG — *Sun* 4 July 1997

p.351 **Our current organisation** — Shephard op. cit. p. 191

p.352 **internal democracy** — Richards, *Preparing for Power* p. 23

p.352 **The selection of a candidate** — N. Jones op. cit. p. 181

p.353 **William? Oh, William** — J. Jones, *Labour of Love* p. 93

p.353 **something he really fears** — Price op. cit. p. 102

p.353 **The free and prosperous society** — Nadler op. cit. p. 29

p.353 **I truly believed** — Shephard op. cit. p. 205

p.353 **There are millions** — *Daily Telegraph* 19 May 2006

p.354 **You made it** — Blair op. cit. p. 8

p.354 **In a sense** – ibid. p. 43

p.354 **Forget the past** – *Sun* 2 October 1996

p.354 **Was John Major** – Williams op. cit. p. 234

11: Royalty

p.355 **I've never discussed** – *Independent on Sunday* 1 January 1995

p.355 **I sometimes sense** – *Independent* 9 October 1997

p.355 **Diana's power** – *Express on Sunday* 19 April 1998

p.356 **The heart of the nation** – *Sunday Times* 22 November 1992

p.356 **With the greatest respect** – *Sunday Mirror* 22 November 1992

p.356 **We must have got it wrong** – Aslet, *Anyone for England?* p. 231

p.356 **The suggestion that** – *Sunday Times* 22 November 1992

p.356 H.M. THE TAX DODGER – *Daily Mirror* 12 February 1993

p.357 **not a year** – *Times* 25 November 1992

p.357 **nature has blessed** – Wilson, *The Rise and Fall of the House of Windsor* p. 80

p.357 **Have you ever stopped** – *Independent on Sunday* 13 December 1992

p.358 **I can *hear* my wife** – Wilson op. cit. p. 37

p.358 **the story of her transformation** – quoted in *Times* 25 June 1992

p.359 **Bloody hell!** – *Daily Mirror* 24 August 1992

p.359 **Mother Teresa act** – Wilson op. cit. p. 38

p.359 **I understand people's suffering** – *Sun* 25 August 1992

p.359 **I need you** – Junor, *Charles* p. 169

p.359 **Papa doesn't embarrass me** – ibid. p. 248

p.360 **We're worried that we are** – *Times* 14 January 1993

p.360 **because we are** – *Independent* 22 January 1993

p.360 **I do not want to help** – *Times* 14 January 1993

p.360 **the Prince and Princess** – *Guardian* 12 January 1993

p.360 **I've sent someone** – Junor op. cit. p. 164

p.360 **Do you seriously expect** – quoted in *Observer* 23 October 1994

p.360 **He looks *magnifique*** – *Independent on Sunday* 1 January 1995

p.361 **the Butter Mountain** – Gorman, *The Bastards* p. 194

p.362 **advanced stage of paranoia** – *Independent* 21 November 1995

p.362 **I've never been** – Richard Lindley, *Panorama* p. 368

p.362 **He lay flat** – Pasternak, *Princess in Love* pp. 62–3

p.362 **A terribly, terribly bad book** – *Times* 4 October 1994

p.362 **horse manure** – *Independent* 5 October 1994

p.362 **Grubby and worthless** – this and following quotes in the paragraph, *Independent* 4 October 1994

p.363 **I wouldn't have** – *Daily Mirror* 4 October 1994

p.363 **strip down to his Union flag** – *Independent on Sunday* 23 October 1994

p.363 **The Duchess of York** – Wyatt, *The Journals of Woodrow Wyatt Volume Two* p. 651

p.364 **How much shrapnel** – *Independent* 21 August 1992

p.364 JUST HOW MUCH – *Independent on Sunday* 23 August 1992

p.364 **If she cannot be photographed** – *Independent on Sunday* 23 August 1992

p.364 **What has to be** – *Guardian* 14 December 1994

p.364 **The story went global** – *News of the World* 31 March 1996

p.365 **the girls' talk** – Osborne, *Damn You, England* p. 201

p.365 **never slept together again** – ibid. p. 202

p.365 **She wouldn't do oral sex** – Brandreth, *Breaking the Code* p. 394

p.365 **Princess Diana threw herself** – *Independent on Sunday* 23 August 1992

p.365 **It has turned** – *Times* 24 December 1991

p.365 **The most serious threat** – *Daily Telegraph* 19 December 1992

p.366 **Before they came along** – Barnett, *This Time* p. 128

p.366 **How squalid he looks** – Townsend, *The Queen and I* p. 121

p.366 **What he did work out** – ibid. p. 169

p.367 **There is no republican movement** – *Sunday Times* 19 January 1992

p.367 **eighteenth-century institutions** – *Independent on Sunday* 24 January 1993

p.367 **What I think** – *Times* 19 January 1993

p.367 **Britain could never make** – *New Statesman* 11 December 1992

p.368 **I feel the same obligation** – *Times* 26 December 1991

p.368 **I happen to believe** – *Times* 4 April 1992

p.368 **He spends his time** – *Sun* 2 March 1996

p.369 **My comments** – *Independent* 2 March 1996

p.369 **I have to wonder** – *Mail on Sunday* 5 February 1995

p.369 **the apex of a class system** – *Daily Mirror* 10 December 1992

p.369 **President of the Republic** – McSmith, *Faces of Labour* p. 361

p.370 **effortlessly relegated** – *Independent on Sunday* 18 May 1997

p.370 **the leader of the party** – *Sun* 15 May 1997

p.370 **They think Tony Blair** – Barnett op. cit. p. 90

p.370 **In temperament and time** – Blair, *A Journey* pp. 132–3

p.370 **near-teenage** – Mandelson, *The Third Man* p. 232

p.370 **She had perfect skin** – Campbell, *The Blair Years* p. 59

p.370 **She thinks Tony Blair** – Young, *The Hugo Young Papers* p. 477

p.371 **hopeless** – *Independent* 27 August 1997

p.371 **Many will question** – *Sun* 14 July 1997

p.371 **It's a pity Gucci** – *News of the World* 31 August 1997

p.371 **the inane Sloane-ish inarticulacy** – *Independent on Sunday* 31 August 1997

p.371 **a woman who** – *Observer* 31 August 1997

p.371 **She seems to relish** – *Express on Sunday* 31 August 1997

p.371 **this one is hot** – *Sunday Mirror* 31 August 1997

p.372 **You might not believe this** – *Independent* 1 September 1997

p.373 **We apologise** – Colebatch, *Blair's Britain* p. 95

p.373 **Rosie preferred** – Townsend, *Adrian Mole: The Cappuccino Years* p. 193

p.373 **I hope by this time** – Benn, *Free at Last* p. 434

p.373 **It was also** – Radice, *Diaries 1980–2001* p. 394

p.373 **They're all going** – Junor, *Charles* p. 19

p.373 **I also knew** – Blair op. cit. p. 136

p.373 **Anything before that** – Campbell op. cit. p. 232

p.373 **She was the people's** – *Independent* 1 September 1997

p.374 **Duchess of York** – *Sunday Times* 17 September 1989

p.374 **Princess Anne** – *Times* 17 October 1989

p.374 **most recently** – *Daily Mirror* 19 June 1996

p.374 **Julie Burchill** – *Sunday Times* 26 November 1995

p.374 **James Whitaker** – *Daily Mirror* 23 December 1992

p.374 **THE PEOPLE'S PRINCESS** – *Daily Mirror* 8 November 1993

p.374 **utterly devastated** – *Independent* 1 September 1997

p.374 **he obviously feels** – Powell, *The New Machiavelli* p. 39

p.374 **that this was a moment** – Blair op. cit. p. 143

p.374 **We have to be careful** – Campbell op. cit. p. 235

p.374 **You cannot be** – Colebatch op. cit. p. 90

p.375 **comparison could be made** – *Evening Standard* 6 September 1997

p.375 **I am reminded** – *Daily Mail* 6 September 1997

p.375 **real and charismatic** – *Independent* 8 September 1997

p.375 **We therefore crucified her** – *Independent* 1 September 1997

p.375 **Princess Diana's cleaning bill** – Townsend op. cit. p. 153

p.375 **In time of national crisis** – Iannucci, *Facts and Fancies* p. 94

p.375 **CHARLES WEEPS BITTER TEARS OF GUILT** – *Daily Mail* 2 September 1997

p.375 **There has been** – *Sun* 3 September 1997

p.375 **The mood was really** – Campbell op. cit. p. 240

p.376 **WHERE IS OUR QUEEN** – *Sun* 4 September 1997

p.376 **What upset people** – *Daily Mirror* 15 September 1997

p.376 **The mere presence** – *Times* 4 September 1997

p.376 **THE QUEEN BOWS** – *Independent* 5 September 1997

p.376 **ARE WE HAPPY NOW?** – *Sport* 5 September 1997

p.377 **I didn't want to speak** – *Sunday Sport* 7 September 1997

p.377 **in common with all** – Hislop, *The Private Eye Annual 1997* p. 94

p.377 **I did it for Britain** – *Daily Telegraph* 11 September 1997

p.377 **the most remarkable** – *Daily Telegraph* 6 September 1997

p.378 **near perfect** – Blair op. cit. p. 147

p.378 **clipped, formal** – Clark, *The Last Diaries* p. 297

p.378 **She looked like** – Smith, *I Think the Nurses Are Stealing My Clothes* p. 138

p.379 **Protocol changed forever** – *Daily Mirror* 8 September 1997

p.379 **that speech is worth** – Benn op. cit. p. 437

p.379 **Everyone here had come** – *Forum* Vol. 32 No. 8 1998

p.379 **That single event** – *Financial Times* 20 September 1997

p.379 **Latin American** – Wheatcroft, *The Strange Death of Tory England* p. 241

p.379 **I walked through** – *Sunday Telegraph* 7 September 1997

p.380 **Their dignity** – *Daily Mirror* 15 September 1997

p.380 **his obvious flair** – Townsend, *The Queen and I* p. 191

p.380 **that his own instincts** – Rawnsley, *Servants of the People* p. 62

p.381 **I couldn't work out** – Campbell, *The Blair Years* p. 239

p.381 **Those weeping crowds** – Smith op. cit. p. 138

p.381 **a real feeling** – Bayley, *Labour Camp* p. 24

p.381 **Taking on the establishment** – Steel, *Reasons to Be Cheerful* p. 251

p.382 **hundred greatest Britons** – *News of the World* 20 December 1998

p.382 **Everyone is entitled** – *Independent* 19 December 1997

p.383 **it wasn't her** – Baddiel, *Whatever Love Means* pp. 16–17

p.383 **H.M. Bateman** – ibid. p. 35

p.383 **she would find** – ibid. p. 36

12: Government

p.384 **Take it from me** – Firth, *All Quiet on the Preston Front*, series 1, episode 3: 'Eric's Job'

p.384 **We'll sell you** – Mansun, 'Taxloss' (Paul Draper, PolyGram Music Publishing, 1997)

p.384 **I think you'd prefer** – Parris, *Off-Message* p. 201

p.384 **None of them know** – J. Jones, *Labour of Love* p. 261

p.385 **It is fundamental** – Oborne & Walters, *Alastair Campbell* p. 294

p.386 **I know it's the end** – King, *House Music* p. 115

p.386 **genuinely damaging** – Campbell, *The Blair Years* p. 452

p.386 **like the schoolboy** – Oborne & Walters op. cit. p. 258

p.386 **no respect** – Young, *The Hugo Young Papers* p. 660

p.386 **there is a barely concealed** – Mullin, *A View from the Foothills* p. 58

p.386 **Of course we want** – quoted in *Spectator* 15 January 2000

p.387 **if he is going to say something** – Spicer, *The Spicer Diaries* p. 131

p.387 **task was to be** – Critchley & Halcrow, *Collapse of Stout Party* p. 138

p.387 **Landslides, on the whole** – Turner, *Rejoice! Rejoice!* p. 127

p.387 **Current contempt** – Barnett, *This Time* p. 297

p.388 **Those who are called** – Short, *An Honourable Deception?* pp. 73–4

p.388 **like the old Soviet Union** – Brown, *Fighting Talk* p. 315

p.388 **couldn't find anyone** – Aslet, *Anyone for England?* p. 208

p.389 **Tony's cronies** – *Guardian* 9 April 1997

p.389 **These are jobs** – *Times* 10 April 1997

p.389 **the little shit** – Campbell op. cit. p. 208

p.389 **a control freak** – *Sunday Times* 3 November 1996

p.389 **Diversity must become** – *Guardian* 13 February 2001

p.389 **for parties to be able** – Short op. cit. p. 69

p.390 **Opposition is meant to be** – Young op. cit. p. 359

p.390 **We are asked to think** – *Observer* 12 January 1997

p.390 **We have an approach** – Richards, *Preparing for Power* p. 59

p.390 **What's wrong with managerialism?** – Cohen, *Pretty Straight Guys* p. 254

p.391 **all forms of tobacco** – *Financial Times* 20 May 1997

p.391 **after long negotiations** – *Times* 5 November 1997

p.391 **Europe was looking** – Blair, *A Journey* p. 129

p.392 **Cor, fuck me!** – Campbell op. cit. p. 258

p.392 **to avoid any possible** – *Daily Mirror* 14 November 1997

p.392 **Who the hell** – ibid. p. 259

p.393 **at the beginning** – *Hansard* 12 November 1997 column 899

p.393 **The prime minister** – *Sunday Telegraph* 12 October 2008

p.393 **Have we slain** – *Sun* 13 November 1997

p.393 **hypocrisy on a grand scale** – Rawnsley, *Servants of the People* p. 99

p.393 **I think most people** – *Daily Mirror* 17 November 1997

p.394 **We are intensely relaxed** – Mandelson, *The Third Man* p. 265

p.394 **I saw what others** – ibid. p. 278

p.394 **he is very interested** – Young op. cit. p. 549

p.394 **Most of the people** – Beckett, *Gordon Brown* p. 125

p.394 **Peter goes gaga** – Mullin op. cit. p. 160

p.394 **so craven** – Rawnsley op. cit. p. 155

p.394 **I snuck onto the plane** – *Sun* 19 December 1996

p.394 **He made it only** – *Times* 20 December 1996

p.395 **excruciating** – Straw, *Last Man Standing* p. 220

p.395 **garish demonstration** – Bayley, *Labour Camp* p. 78

p.395 **The residence is quite beautiful** – *Sunday Times* 23 November 1997

p.395 **I'm ashamed of Derry** – J. Jones op. cit. p. 186

p.395 **He has behaved** – ibid. p. 189

p.396 **They think we got rid** – Campbell op. cit. p. 283

p.396 **They say a man** – *Sun* 11 December 1997

p.396 **For the first time** – Short op. cit. p. 66

p.396 **This way for the cuts** – Rawnsley op. cit. p. 115

p.396 **reticent to ask questions** – Spicer, *The Spicer Diaries* p. 379

p.397 **A quarter of all mothers** – Patten, *Things to Come* p. 147

p.397 **The fact that we had enabled** – Blunkett, *The Blunkett Tapes* p. 70

p.397 **make a mockery** – *Sunday Telegraph* 21 December 1997

p.397 **It is no use** – *Sunday Times* 18 January 1998

p.398 **go the full monty** – *Sunday Times* 18 January 1998

p.398 **Who's Harriet Harman?** – J. Jones op. cit. p. 150

p.398 **booted out of the young Tories** – *Guardian* 3 July 2010

p.398 **a good man** – *Independent* 6 February 1993

p.399 **For fifteen years** – *Sunday Times* 14 August 1994

p.399 **We are leapfrogging over** – *Guardian* 3 October 1994

p.399 **thinking the unthinkable** – *Sun* 6 May 1997

p.399 **she wanted Frank** – Mandelson op. cit. p. 247

p.399 **Some are made** – Blair op. cit. p. 217

p.400 **It barely read like** – Campbell op. cit. p. 230

p.400 **The upper-crust daughter** – *News of the World* 1 February 1998

p.400 **we will see** – *Times* 22 November 1997

p.400 **Labour will do everything** – *Independent on Sunday* 6 April 1997

p.400 **There is no great principle** – Mullin op. cit. p. 50

p.401 **I am, all said and done** – Blair op. cit. p. 116

p.401 **Our strategic aim** – Powell, *The New Machiavelli* p. 26

p.401 **essentially middle class** – Blair op. cit. p. 272

p.401 **we need to be** – Price, *The Spin Doctor's Diary* p. 44

p.401 **their essential direction** – Blair op. cit. p. 262

p.402 **a campaign to make** – *News of the World* 14 March 1999

p.402 **all the usual razzmatazz** – Blunkett op. cit. p. 162

p.403 **To bridge the gap** – Blair op. cit. p. 211

p.403 **Tony was seduced** – Mandelson op. cit. p. 252

p.403 **the otter has secured** – *Times* 8 June 1998

p.403 **We are getting a reputation** – Mullin op. cit. p. 26

p.404 **to set targets** – Heseltine, *Life in the Jungle* p. 401

p.404 **God knows who invented** – Blunkett op. cit. p. 198

p.404 **It's the signals** – J. Jones op. cit. p. 201

p.404 **the whole terminology** – Blair op. cit. p. 283

p.404 **Keith Hill and I** – Mullin op. cit. p. 61

p.405 **result in the public** – *Observer* 12 July 1998

p.405 **the biggest decision** – Young op. cit. p. 514

p.405 **important that our choice** – McSmith, *Faces of Labour* p. 317

p.405 **it is economics** – Campbell op. cit. p. 249

p.405 **single currency will not** – Spicer op. cit. p. 270

p.405 **I still retain** – Ashdown, *The Ashdown Diaries* p. 476

p.406 **EMU is and was always** – Scott, *Off Whitehall* p. 33

p.406 **the wretched referendum** – Blunkett op. cit. p. 45

p.406 **The real obstacle** – Radice, *Diaries 1980–2001* p. 400

p.406 IS THIS THE MOST DANGEROUS – *Sun* 24 June 1998

p.406 BROWN RULES OUT – *Times* 18 October 1997

p.406 LABOUR SPINS – these headlines 20 October 1997

p.407 **making a decision** – *Sunday Telegraph* 31 October 2004

p.407 **For the first time** – Spicer op. cit. p. 375

p.407 **an appropriate note** – *Observer* 5 July 1998

p.408 **Our intention is clear** – *Financial Times* 24 February 1999

p.408 **One of the problems** – *Financial Times* 5 June 2007

p.408 **Blair is mad** – Radice op. cit. p. 437

p.409 **Now I could understand it** – *Independent* 7 October 1998

p.410 **He notes the fact** – Young op. cit. p. 685

p.410 **a grabbing and inhumane** – *Sun* 10 October 1997

p.410 **tolerance is part** – *Times* 10 October 1997

p.410 **We admire** – *Financial Times* 10 October 1997

p.410 **If the people want me** – *Times* 13 December 1996

p.410 **Is he really** – *Express* 13 September 1999

p.410 **a sort of Ann Widdecombe** – *Sunday Times* 26 September 1999

p.411 **to discuss whether** – *Times* 9 September 1999

p.411 **There was this louche community** – *News of the World* 12 September 1999

p.411 **We live in a world** – *Sun* 13 September 1999

p.411 **We now know** – *Daily Mail* 24 September 1999

p.412 **there is real animosity** – Ashdown, *The Ashdown Diaries* p. 231

p.412 **the importance of party** – Young op. cit. p. 379

p.412 **believes there is** – Ashdown op. cit. p. 242

p.412 **I have more in common** – ibid. p. 419

p.412 **Except on law and order** – Blair op. cit. p. 266

p.413 **No way, I'm not going** – Price op. cit. p. 53

p.413 **a Conservative defeat** – Ashdown op. cit. p. 386

p.413 **I still wish** – Naughtie, *The Rivals* p. 157

p.413 **a very attractive personality** – Campbell op. cit. p. 367

p.413 **All that talent** – Rawnsley op. cit. p. 195

p.414 **Terribly sorry** – Spicer op. cit. p. 440

p.414 **Do you mind** – Rawnsley op. cit. p. 359

p.414 **Mind you, does it** – Price op. cit. p. 116

p.414 **a culture of contentment** – Rawnsley op. cit. p. 291

p.415 **The fact that 83 per cent** – *Guardian* 25 April 2000

p.415 **I was sure** – Blair op. cit. p. 528

p.415 **We have had three elections** – Sopel, *Tony Blair* pp. 226–7

p.415 **There are five people** – *Financial Times* 8 May 1999

p.415 **I can't see** – Manic Street Preachers, 'Socialist Serenade' (Nick Jones/James Dean Bradfield/Sean Moore, Sony Music Publishing, 1999)

p.416 **an empty shell** – Sopel op. cit. pp. 278–9

p.416 **A number of us** – Ashdown op. cit. p. 422

p.416 **when we started mentioning** – ibid. p. 423

p.416 **the disappearance** – Benn, *Free at Last* p. 134

p.416 **I joined the party** – *Guardian* 25 April 2000

p.416 **More anti-European** – Patten, *Not Quite the Diplomat* p. 82

p.417 **The nice people** – Currie, *Diaries Vol II* p. 161

p.417 **These people are stupid** – Campbell op. cit. p. 71

p.417 **What amazed me** – Prescott, *Prezza* p. 193

p.417 **I still had the feeling** – ibid. p. 185

p.418 **I'd be frank with them** – N. Jones, *Campaign 1997* p. 118

p.418 **Blair's a piece of cake** – Spicer op. cit. p. 333

p.418 **It isn't that Dennis** – Benn op. cit. p. 502

p.418 **I am very strongly** – Elliott & Atkinson, *The Age of Insecurity* p. 142

p.418 **It seems that** – Ashton, *Red Rose Blues* p. 355

p.418 **close to unbeatable** – Blair op. cit. p. 99

p.419 **Peter Mandelson had** – ibid. p. 219

p.419 **private rather than secret** – Mandelson op. cit. p. 271

p.419 **it all feels wrong** – Blunkett op. cit. p. 104

p.419 **it was a political** – Blair op. cit. p. 220

p.419 **You have been the victim** – Mandelson op. cit. p. 276

p.419 **Mandelson's acute judgement** – McSmith op. cit. p. 279

p.419 **vanity and arrogance** – Campbell op. cit. p. 350

p.419 **How many times** – ibid. p. 353

p.420 **a star-fucker** – Routledge, *Mandy* p. 206

p.420 **stupid cunt** – Rawnsley op. cit. p. 223

p.420 **Tony had never liked** – Mandelson op. cit. p. 239

p.420 **We've briefed that Peter** – Price op. cit. p. 67

p.420 **GOODBYE . . . FOR NOW** – *Guardian* 24 December 1998

p.420 **a sense of doom** – Blair op. cit. p. 220

p.420 **I think it is the end** – Benn op. cit. p. 520

13: Generations

p.421 **You do get this feeling** – Benn, *Free at Last* p. 78

p.421 **'We're the lost generation!'** – Williams, *East of Wimbledon* p. 31

p.421 **Politics isn't showbiz** – *Guardian* 17 October 1994

p.421 **With such rebels** – *Guardian* 29 September 1975

p.422 **Oh, Dad** – Benn op. cit. p. 162

p.422 **His death** – *Independent* 24 May 1994

p.422 **People will look back** – Stephens, *Tony Blair* p. 101

p.423 **Maastricht, and most of** – Gorman, *The Bastards* p. 48

p.423 **against the EU** – Radice, *Diaries 1980–2001* p. 411

p.423 **progressive forces** – Livingstone, *Livingstone's Labour* p. 237

p.424 **It was the first time** – Benn, *The End of an Era* p. 569

p.424 **the Labour movement** – Straw, *Last Man Standing* p. 178

p.424 **By driving out communism** – *Sunday Times* 23 August 1992

p.425 **a Labour voter** – *Independent* 3 April 1999

p.427 **concerned as much** – *Times* 12 February 1993

p.427 **Ten years ago** – Cohn, *Yes We Have No* p. 71

p.427 **Some people may show up** – ibid. p. 76

p.427 **an England where** – Forster, *Maurice* p. 221

p.427 **Stonehenge was** – Hawkins, *The Anarchist* p. 147

p.427 **Suburbia celebrates** – ibid. p. 272

p.428 **The justification** – ibid. p. 217

p.428 **the nation's favourite** – *Independent* 1 February 1997

p.428 **We are living** – *Independent* 9 October 1996

p.429 **In 1980 it was worth** – Danziger, *Danziger's Britain* p. 73

p.429 **The great quality** – Cohen, *Pretty Straight Guys* p. 4

p.429 **Liverpool is still awful** – Currie, *Diaries Vol II* p. 154

p.429 **We're living** – Cohn op. cit. p. 113

p.429 **There's been about six billion** – ibid. p. 114

p.429 **I work with children** – Parsons, *Big Mouth Strikes Again* p. 223

p.430 **her primary objective** – Danziger op. cit. p. 200

p.430 **as the British government** – ibid. p. 8

p.430 **having worked** – Dalrymple, *If Symptoms Persist* p. v

p.430 **Libraries gave us power** – Manic Street Preachers, 'A Design for Life' (Nicky Wire/ James Dean Bradfield/Sean Moore, Sony Music Publishing, 1996)

p.430 **my old days** – Prescott, *Prezza* p. 182

p.430 **We no longer work** – Danziger op. cit. p. 3

p.430 **the unskilled** – *Guardian* 27 September 1988

p.430 **the socially excluded** – *Guardian* 12 January 2000

p.431 **20 per cent of all households** – Young, *The Hugo Young Papers* p. 499

p.431 **The cause is twofold** – Junor, *The Major Enigma* p. 306

p.431 **ugly face** – *Guardian* 3 October 1984

p.431 **teenage temptress** – *People* 6 February 1994

p.432 **There are more adolescents** – Elton, *Inconceivable* p. 143

p.432 **The other kids** – Mullin, *A View from the Foothills* p. 124

p.433 **You'll never get it right** – Pulp, 'Common People' (Jarvis Cocker/Pulp, Island Music Ltd, 1995)

p.433 **With a lack of any great vision** – *Independent* 17 November 1997

p.434 **a respectable working-class family** – *Independent* 9 October 1993

p.434 **because he single-handedly** – *Times* 12 July 1994

p.435 **colleges of crime** – *Independent* 3 March 1993

p.435 **We would welcome** – *Independent* 17 May 1997

p.435 **To lose one prisoner** – *Daily Mirror* 12 April 1993

p.435 **A thug might think** – *Guardian* 1 July 2000

p.436 **Punishing people** – ibid.

p.436 **just another** – ibid.

p.436 **It was a great piece** – Blair, *A Journey* p. 279

p.436 **People knock ASBOs** – Smith, *I Think the Nurses Are Stealing My Clothes* p. 242

p.436 **multitudes of men** – *Times* 3 September 1816

p.436 **the almost unchecked parading** – *Times* 24 May 1828

p.436 **They were accustomed** – Paxman, *The English* p. 251

p.437 **In the days before** – Pearson, *The Far Corner* p. 179

p.437 **they weren't a huge cause** – Blair op. cit. p. 280

p.437 **I must say** – Williams op. cit. p. 6

p.437 **a squalid little place** – ibid. p. 205

p.438 **A Sunday night show** – *Independent* 21 March 1996

p.438 **He'd joined the police** – *Independent on Sunday* 17 March 1996

p.438 **We got to adolescence** – Hornby, *High Fidelity* p. 127

p.439 **what really matters** – ibid. p. 99

p.439 **It is as hard for me** – ibid. pp. 134–5

p.439 **they have smart jobs** – ibid. p. 164

p.439 **I flicked through** – O'Farrell, *The Best a Man Can Get* p. 187

p.439 **this culture of middle youth** – Smith op. cit. p. 296

p.439 **chief British iconographer** – *Sunday Times* 16 April 1995

p.440 **Fiona meant it** – Hornby, *About a Boy* p. 97

p.440 **he put a Pet Shop Boys CD on** – ibid. p. 98

p.440 **A peculiarly contemporary** – ibid. p. 119

p.440 **knew nothing about** – ibid. p. 113

p.440 **I bloody hate** – ibid. p. 286

p.441 **the self-destructive sickness** – *Independent* 15 January 1994

p.441 **British self-irony** – Young op. cit. p. 395

p.441 **all-pervading cynicism** – *Times* 5 May 1994

p.441 **Bugger my career** – *Independent on Sunday* 3 November 1996

p.441 **Ennui is over** – Oborne & Walters, *Alastair Campbell* p. 223

p.441 **They are turning out** – *Sunday Times* 18 January 1998

p.441 **There is a very grave danger** – *Independent on Sunday* 15 February 1998

p.441 **The most gruesome aspect** – *Independent* 14 April 1998

p.442 BETRAYED – *NME* 14 March 1998

p.442 **I'm not ashamed** – *Daily Mirror* 20 March 1998

p.442 **I lashed out** – Prescott op. cit. p. 251

p.442 **Someone's having** – *Times* 14 November 1998

p.442 **Here is a person** – Harris, *The Last Party* p. xvi

p.442 **favourite singles** – *Sun* 18 December 1996

p.442 **little more than** – *Financial Times* 5 June 2009

p.443 **We enjoy music** – *Sunday Times* 20 July 1997

p.443 **I was very suspicious** – *Sun* 15 February 1997

p.443 **We met Tony Blair** – *Times* 13 December 1996

p.443 **I felt, in art** – Blair op. cit. p. 91

p.443 **never, ever** – Fielding, *Bridget Jones: The Edge of Reason* p. 56

p.444 **Where are the people?** – Naughtie, *The Rivals* p. 120

p.444 **The men remain** – *Guardian* 6 August 1998

p.444 **militaristic, macho** – *Times* 9 March 1999

p.444 **I believed I was elected** – *Guardian* 20 June 2001

p.445 **confined to those** – quoted in Oborne, *The Triumph of the Political Class* p. 208

p.445 **not notable** – Baker, *The Turbulent Years* p. 469

p.445 **The brat pack hits back** – *Times* 11 April 1992

p.445 **No one reminds me** – *Times* 1 April 1997

p.445 **He is undoubtedly** – *Observer* 9 February 1997

p.445 **a suave Old Etonian** – *Guardian* 2 April 1992

p.445 **one of the brightest** – *Times* 30 March 1992

p.446 **the most powerful man** – *Guardian* 16 July 1994

p.446 **the all-party trend** – *Guardian* 9 March 1996

p.446 **identikit young men** – Currie, *Diaries Vol II* p. 245

p.447 **Some of us have** – Brown, *Fighting Talk* p. 207

p.447 **They may be young** – *Guardian* 3 October 1994

p.447 **This generation exudes** – *Times* 17 July 1993

p.447 **I do. They are called** – Heseltine, *Life in the Jungle* p. 379

p.448 **For nearly two decades** – Richards, *Whatever It Takes* p. 4

p.449 **only purpose of being** – Rawnsley, *Servants of the People* p. 3

p.449 **Britain under Tony Blair** – *Observer* 12 July 1998

14: Power

p.450 **Too much power** – Shore, *Leading the Left* p. 183

p.450 **Democracy is all very well** – Chris Langham, *Look at the State We're In!*, 'Local Government'

p.450 **Honk if you hate** – *Sunday Times* 21 August 1994

p.451 **It is now the turn** – *Sunday Times* 4 December 1988

p.452 **those few words** – Straw, *Last Man Standing* p. 275

p.452 **suffered a death** – O'Farrell, *Global Village Idiot* p. 147

p.452 **You idiot** – Blair, *A Journey* p. 516

p.453 **The United Kingdom** – Major, *The Autobiography* p. 424

p.453 **undermine the unity** – *Times* 21 February 1997

p.454 **The tactic was obvious** – Blair op. cit. p. 252

p.454 **It's Gordon's passion** – Naughtie, *The Rivals* p. 158

p.454 **Devolution seemed** – Johnes, *Wales Since 1939* p. 413

p.454 **I am particularly pleased** – Routledge, *Gordon Brown* p. 153

p.454 **People should not underestimate** – Young, *The Hugo Young Papers* p. 482

p.454 **in Scotland** – *Independent* 27 January 1999

p.455 **It speaks volumes** – Weight, *Patriots* p. 670

p.455 **Once the powers** – *Times* 4 April 1997

p.455 **Walking in the Scottish highlands** – *Sunday Times* 29 December 1996

p.455 **they view us** – Campbell, *The Blair Years* p. 49

p.455 **unreconstructed wankers** – Oborne & Walters, *Alastair Campbell* p. 141

p.456 **similar to the Militant** – *Sun* 30 June 1998

p.457 **pure Australian shite** – Weight op. cit. p. 700

p.457 **terrific** – Routledge, *Mandy* p. 6

p.458 **We don't kill people** – West, *Murder in the Commons* p. 209

p.459 **The people of Wales** – Johnes op. cit. p. 335

p.459 **was almost single-handedly** – Hain, *Outside In* p. 194

p.459 **This is a loyalty vote** – ibid. p. 201

p.459 **a bulwark against** – Rhodri Morgan (pc)

p.459 **We voted Labour** – Johnes op. cit. p. 331

p.460 **short, fat, slimy** – *Times* 21 December 1994

p.460 **Are you a minicab driver** – Price, *The Spin Doctor's Diary* p. 46

p.460 **the talismanic Rhodri** – Hain op. cit. p. 192

p.461 **What sort of election** – Johnes op. cit. p. 418

p.461 **Fucking Welsh** – *Guardian* 19 September 2005

p.462 **Every day when I wake up** – Powell/Richards/Jones/Matthews/Roberts, 'International Velvet' (Sony/ATV Music Publishing Ltd, 1998)

p.462 **his greatest conflict** – Blunkett, *The Blunkett Tapes* p. 125

p.462 **In the years since then** – *Independent* 27 May 1999

p.463 **Ken Livingstone is a folk hero** – Dexys Midnight Runners, 'Reminisce (Part 1)' (Rowland, EMI Music Publishing Ltd, 1983)

p.463 **I think Ken** – *Independent on Sunday* 24 August 1997

p.464 **I was put up** – *Times* 24 April 1992

p.464 **caused an awful lot** – Benn, *Free at Last* p. 250

p.465 **I'd love to be** – Routledge, *Mandy* p. 230

p.465 **I didn't feel visceral** – Blair op. cit. p. 267

p.465 **It was going to be difficult** – ibid. p. 267

p.465 **saw Ken Livingstone** – Powell, *The New Machiavelli* p. 130

p.466 **He was one of the many** – Blair op. cit. p. 263

p.466 **the Labour Party will elect** – Naughtie op. cit. p. 297

p.466 **We had really fucked this** – Campbell op. cit. p. 428

p.466 **We fucked it up** – Mullin, *A View from the Foothills* p. 80

p.466 **The trouble is** – Young op. cit. p. 641

p.466 **He was running rings** – Campbell op. cit. p. 443

p.466 **THE MAN RUNNING RINGS** – *Daily Mail* 16 May 1984

p.467 **I've been waiting** – *Guardian* 5 April 2000

p.467 **following Blair** – Benn op. cit. p. 602

p.467 **As I was saying** – *Daily Mirror* 6 May 2000, *Financial Times* 5 July 1991

p.467 **an accident waiting** – Wheatcroft, *The Strange Death of Tory England* p. 209

p.468 **there are the most** – *Financial Times* 10 August 1999

p.468 **It wasn't until** – Clifford, *Max Clifford* p. 187

p.468 **I'm pretty confident** – Walters, *Tory Wars* p. 51

p.468 **less compassionate** – *Daily Mirror* 2 August 2000

p.468 **Margaret Thatcher was** – *Daily Mirror* 9 February 2002

p.469 **People out there** – Nadler, *William Hague* p. 227

p.469 **This is a day** – Rawnsley, *Servants of the People* p. 206

p.470 **It was a perfectly** – Blair op. cit. p. 251

p.470 **at a practical level** – Shephard, *Shephard's Watch* p. 253

p.470 **It doesn't take a genius** – Gorman, *No, Prime Minister!* p. 321

p.470 **I can't do anything** – Blunkett op. cit. p. 252

p.471 **a new class of life peers** – Heseltine, *Life in the Jungle* p. 418

p.471 **Better a quango** – Richards, *Preparing for Power* p. 58

p.472 **I'd rather they were chosen** – Jones op. cit. p. 145

p.472 **The attractions of opposition** – *Independent* 12 January 1996

p.472 **He now sees** – Young op. cit. p. 547

p.474 **there's only** – Rawnsley op. cit. p. 363

p.474 **a waste of time** – Nadler op. cit. p. 166

p.474 **We cannot unscramble** – Critchley & Halcrow, *Collapse of Stout Party* p. 191

15: Adventures

p.475 **Mine is the first** – Bremner, *You Are Here* p. 39

p.475 **I felt sick** – *People* 20 May 2001

p.475 **I am not going to be** – Rawnsley, *Servants of the People* p. 159

p.475 **We will pursue policies** – *Financial Times* 19 May 1987

p.475 **once again be a force** – *Financial Times* 13 May 1997

p.475 **Our foreign policy** – *Independent on Sunday* 1 June 1997 p.477   **How were negotiators** – Major, *The Autobiography* p. 546

p.477   **Those paying the price** – *People* 23 August 1992

p.477   **in the heart of Europe** – *Times* 14 April 1993

p.477   **Any time there was** – Nick Cohen, *What's Left?* p. 140

p.478   **Britain had no** – Hurd, *Memoirs* p. 444

p.478   **I grow older** – ibid. p. 476

p.478   **hyper-realist** – Kampfner, *Blair's Wars* p. 38

p.478   **force for good** – *Times* 1 September 1997

p.479   **We are not going to pay** – *Independent* 23 May 1997

p.479   **now had the most open** – Young, *The Hugo Young Papers* p. 703

p.479   **those who governed** – *Independent* 2 June 1997

p.479   **Some Jewish people** – *Times* 19 October 1999

p.479   **We have created** – *Independent* 27 January 2000

p.480   **a few Tarzans** – *Guardian* 4 November 2000

p.480   **It was a wrong** – http://news.bbc.co.uk/1/hi/wales/983056.stm retrieved 28 July 2011

p.481   **Their answer** – *Independent on Sunday* 24 August 1997

p.481   **This is going to be** – Rawnsley op. cit. p. 185

p.482   **a brutal dictator** – *Financial Times* 19 October 1998

p.482   **international law** – Straw, *Last Man Standing* p. 255

p.482   **There's no Third Way** – Rawnsley op. cit. p. 189

p.482   **Pinochet was one** – Straw op. cit. p. 266

p.482   **established, beyond question** – *Guardian* 3 March 2000

p.483   **slipped in** – Campbell, *The Blair Years* p. 219

p.483   **The press reported** – Short, *An Honourable Deception?* p. 70

p.483   **zero tolerance** – *Times* 20 October 1999

p.483   **His sins were many** – *Economist* 23 October 1999

p.484   **Everyone knew** – Kampfner op. cit. p. 28

p.484   **refused to go** – Price, *The Spin Doctor's Diary* p. 28

p.484   **Who can think** – *Manchester Guardian* 28 December 1937

p.484   **Some Western** – *Financial Times* 9 June 1984

p.484   **pretty scary** – Kampfner op. cit. p. 22

p.484   **a heavy heart** – Price op. cit. p. 62

p.484   **2,500 people would die** – Campbell op. cit. pp. 331–2

p.484   **the war of Clinton's penis** – ibid. p. 273

p.485   **Richard the Lionheart** – *Financial Times* 18 December 1998

p.485   **Sir, I salute** – *Independent* 20 January 1994

p.485   **the mother of all idiots** – *Daily Mirror* 20 January 1994

p.485   **degrade the ability** – *Financial Times* 18 December 1998

p.485   **It's a broad objective** – ibid.

p.485   **he said we hit** – Campbell op. cit. p. 347

p.485   **You'd better give** – Mandelson, *The Third Man* p. 281

p.486   **to show me maps** – Ashdown, *The Ashdown Diaries* p. 117

p.486   **the KLA were not** – Campbell op. cit. p. 362

p.486   **essentially a moral issue** – Blair, *A Journey* p. 228

p.486   **we breached** – Blunkett, *The Blunkett Tapes* p. 122

p.487   **'bombing into submission'** – Campbell op. cit. p. 372

p.487   **This is obscene** – Rawnsley op. cit. p. 276

p.487   **wonder why** – Campbell op. cit. p. 408

p.487   **The only important thing** – Rawnsley op. cit. p. 281

p.487   **This was the liberals' war** – Steel, *Reasons to Be Cheerful* p. 262

p.487   **Those loathsome** – Clark, *The Last Diaries* p. 389

p.487   **There was no real** – Campbell op. cit. p. 371

p.488   **in limbo** – Short op. cit. p. 96

p.488   **the unresolved question** – Patten, *Not Quite the Diplomat* p. 168

p.488   **just a military conflict** – *Sunday Telegraph* 4 April 1999

p.488   **war can be necessary** – Rawnsley op. cit. p. 288

p.488   **a new doctrine** – Kampfner op. cit. p. 52

p.488   **Intervention to bring down** – Blair op. cit. p. 248

p.488   **enforcement of** – ibid. p. 225

p.488   **Success is the only exit** – Kampfner op. cit. p. 52

p.489   **a huge change of mood** – Clark op. cit. p. 390

p.489   **Human rights are** – *Times* 22 April 1999

p.489   **was to help** – Rawnsley op. cit. p. 180

p.490   **ostensibly to secure** – Price op. cit. p. 219

p.490   **inexorable slide** – *Times* 27 September 1994

p.490   **stoned bandits** – *Guardian* 12 March 2005

p.491   **we asked for justice** – Denim, 'The Osmonds' (Lawrence, Boys Own Recordings, 1992)

p.492   **The conflict is over** – Major op. cit. p. 431

p.493   **The cares of the world** – Meyer, *DC Confidential* p. 19

p.493   **I don't talk** – Rawnsley op. cit. p. 129

p.493   **It is finished** – *Financial Times* 2 March 1995

p.493   **The people of Northern Ireland** – Major op. cit. p. 457

p.493   **I'm sick of answering** – *People* 23 April 1995

p.494   **At worst, it has** – Cole, *As It Seemed To Me* p. 418

p.494   **I could not have asked** – Major op. cit. p. 493

p.495   **I was putting** – Blair op. cit. p. 171

p.495 **losing the battle** – *Independent on Sunday* 13 April 1997

p.495 **I am not in favour** – Benn, *Free at Last* p. 550

p.495 **awful** – Campbell op. cit. p. 375

p.495 **fuck off** – Rawnsley op. cit. p. 125

p.495 **This is no time** – Blair op. cit. p. 166

p.496 **I felt really** – Campbell op. cit. p. 298

p.496 **Ullans is not** – ibid. p. 298

p.496 **a new period** – *Daily Mirror* 28 May 1998

p.497 **making at least** – Blunkett op. cit. p. 92

p.497 **we are handing over** – Benn op. cit. p. 592

p.497 **At least when we talk** – ibid. p. 568

p.498 **a shitty job** – Rawnsley op. cit. p. 347

p.498 **She is fed up** – Blunkett op. cit. p. 161

p.498 **People did things** – Blair op. cit. p. 156

16: Reality

p.499 **Churchill got his lucky number** – Blur, 'It Could Be You' (Albarn/Coxon/James/ Rowntree, MCA Music Ltd, 1995)

p.499 **The consorts, the lovers** – Blacker, *The Fame Hotel* p. 46

p.500 **Flogging criminals** – *Daily Mirror* 20 March 1995

p.500 **Someone told me** – Lovesey, *Upon a Dark Night* p. 155

p.500 **a chance for the government** – Baker, *The Turbulent Years* p. 462

p.501 **unlikely to attract** – Major, *The Autobiography* p. 408

p.501 **within ten years** – *Independent* 26 May 1998

p.501 **taken money out** – Radice, *Diaries 1980–2001* p. 344

p.501 **between £250 million** – *Financial Times* 15 April 1996

p.501 **I did not think** – Thatcher, *The Downing Street Years* p. 610

p.502 **It could be you** – Kibble-White & Williams, *The Encyclopaedia of Classic Saturday Night Telly* p. 227

p.502 **In public spending** – Adonis & Pollard, *A Class Act* p. 266

p.502 **The working class** – Critchley & Halcrow, *Collapse of Stout Party* p. 147

p.503 NEVER HAS SO MUCH – *Daily Mirror* 27 April 1995

p.503 **startling redistribution** – *Independent* 27 April 1995

p.503 **The lottery is our only hope** – Danziger, *Danziger's Britain* p. 119

p.504 **the costs were huge** – *Independent* 2 June 1997

p.504 **boasting of four-in-a-bed romps** – *Sun* 29 May 1997

p.506 **I tell you what** – Izzard, *Dress to Kill* p. 127

p.507 **did not find it** – *Daily Mail* 30 July 2001

p.507 **unspeakably sick** – *Sunday Telegraph* 29 June 2001

p.507 **sickest TV show ever** – *Daily Mail* 28 June 2001

p.507 **looking chest swell** – *Observer* 5 August 2001

p.507 **a deeply unpleasant piece** – *Guardian* 31 July 2001

p.507 **The main news tonight** – *Sunday Times* 27 December 1998

p.508 **macabre pair** – Smith, *I Think the Nurses Are Stealing My Clothes* p. 316

p.509 **We got him** – Harvey Hinsley (pc)

p.510 **It is a shocking truth** – *Independent* 18 September 2000

p.511 **Whether or not** – *ikon* issue 1, September 1995

p.511 **We are in great haste** – Henry David Thoreau, *Walden*, chapter 1: 'Economy' (1854)

p.511 **The BNP's cyberspace audience** – *Spearhead* April 1999

p.512 **Our children have no doubt** – *Times* 3 April 1995

p.513 **Opinion-making** – Osborne, *Damn You, England* p. 199

p.513 **The success of popular reporting** – Brookmyre, *Quite Ugly One Morning* p. 38

p.514 **from enfant terrible** – Burchill, *The Guardian Columns* p. 49

p.514 **the tosser was at art school** – ibid. p. 298

p.514 **working for the CIA** – ibid. p. 183

p.514 **The internet is a subversive** – *Guardian* 12 August 1999

p.514 **The internet is effectively** – *Daily Mail* 18 May 1998

p.514 **We must find a way** – *Sunday Mirror* 21 June 1998

p.514 **the internet is exciting** – *Forum* Vol. 28 No. 8 1995

p.515 **people will stitch you up** – *Financial Times* 19 August 2000

p.516 **his accent was too posh** – *Evening Standard* 14 December 2000

p.517 **the media's playground bully** – Parsons, *Big Mouth Strikes Again* p. 243

p.517 **a shallow, bullying man-child** – Haines, *Bad Vibes* p. 182

p.518 **The class war** – *Daily Mail* 29 September 1999

p.518 **This election has shown** – *Times* 10 October 1959

p.518 **in an old boiler suit** – *Daily Telegraph* 24 October 2000

p.518 **I've never stood** – *Independent* 24 October 2000

p.518 **an interview system** – Beckett, *Gordon Brown* p. 133

p.519 **The chancellor really is** – *Sun* 26 May 2000

p.519 **harsh and uninformed** – *Times* 27 May 2000

p.519 **You might as well** – *Economist* 3 June 2000

p.519 **hordes of upper-class** – *News of the World* 28 May 2000

p.519 **the dirty little secret** – *Daily Mirror* 9 June 2000 p.519 went on and on — Young, *The Hugo Young Papers* p. 676

p.520 NEW LABOUR, OLD CLASS ENVY — *Daily Mail* 27 May 2000

p.520 The scenes of a hunt — Kochan, *Ann Widdecombe* p. 249

p.521 The more I learned — Blair, *A Journey* p. 306

p.521 to show that fox-hunting — Price, *The Spin Doctor's Diary* p. 288

p.521 the tolerance of minorities — *Times* 11 July 1997

p.521 All country people — Nott, *Mr Wonderful Takes a Cruise* p. 139

p.522 would get blocked — Campbell, *The Blair Years* p. 488

p.522 A ban on hunting — Mullin, *A View from the Foothills* p. 186

p.523 If we could get — *Times* 1 April 2000

p.523 The liberal elite — Walters, *Tory Wars* p. 107

p.523 It's something — *Times* 17 September 1999

p.523 We need to appear — Price op. cit. p. 214

p.524 We've got the whole — Walters op. cit. p. 56

p.524 execution, official or freelance — *Guardian* 27 April 2000

p.524 Why do I share — *Financial Times* 10 October 1997

p.524 a new low — *Daily Telegraph* 27 June 1998

p.525 They think the party — Young op. cit. p. 667

p.525 Never mind — *Independent* 4 December 1999

p.525 The message is — *Sun* 26 September 1997

p.525 We discussed — *Independent* 2 February 1999

p.525 a sexual accessory — *Observer* 31 January 1999

p.526 Of all sexual perversions — *Independent* 1 February 1999

p.526 If his missus — *Sun* 2 February 1999

p.526 It means zero tolerance — *Daily Mail* 5 October 2000

p.526 Is she really serious — *Daily Mail* 5 October 2000

p.526 a calculated bid — *Sun* 9 October 2000

p.526 It was a spiteful attempt — Walters op. cit. p. 82

p.527 I call it good manners — Savage, *Time Travel* p. 390

p.527 'bastard' and 'twat' — *Independent* 8 December 1994

p.528 It may be that the era — *Times* 20 March 1998

p.528 complemented by more — *Times* 23 March 1998

p.528 the days of the old — *Times* 20 March 1998

p.529 If I am wrong — *Independent* 3 March 1998

17: Millennium

p.531 What is the Dome for? — Cohen, *Pretty Straight Guys* p. 138

p.531 When I look back — Blair, *A Journey* p. 312

p.531 To all the people — O'Farrell, *Global Village Idiot* p. 200

p.531 I knew a lot — Blair op. cit. p. 224

p.531 not something — Bremner et al, *You Are Here* p. 43

p.532 A thousand days of Labour — Barnett, *This Time* p. 29

p.532 As a nation — Heseltine, *Life in the Jungle* p. 509

p.532 I should really cancel it — Routledge, *Mandy* p. 183

p.532 Euan test — *Daily Mirror* 20 June 1997

p.532 I knew and they knew — Prescott, *Prezza* p. 236

p.532 If the PM were here — Cohen op. cit. p. 141

p.532 nobody believed — Blunkett, *The Blunkett Tapes* p. 24

p.533 In retrospect — Powell, *The New Machiavelli* p. 40

p.533 everyone under the age — Strange, *Strange* p. 244

p.533 entirely inappropriate — *Times* 13 January 1998

p.533 ideas merchants — *Times* 21 June 1997

p.533 In 1851 and 1951 — Cohen op. cit. p. 142

p.533 the People's Show — Weight, *Patriots* p. 195

p.534 my Dome — *Independent on Sunday* 18 January 1998

p.534 bollocks — Routledge op. cit. p. 196

p.534 a slight and demeaning — Young, *The Hugo Young Papers* p. 548

p.534 It was like an orchestra — Rawnsley, *Servants of the People* p. 327

p.534 a project that could — Bayley, *Labour Camp* p. 59

p.534 typography — ibid. p. 63

p.534 the most exciting — *Mail on Sunday* 1 March 1998

p.534 the first paragraph — *Financial Times* 21 February 2000

p.534 journalistic fantasy — *Financial Times* 28 February 2000

p.534 see off cynics — *Independent* 18 December 1999

p.535 Pushing to get out — Blair op. cit. p. 254

p.535 between the forces — *Guardian* 29 September 1999

p.535 such as the conservation — *Sun* 30 September 1999

p.535 He spoke for Britain — *Sun* 8 October 1999

p.535 a strategy to put himself — Campbell, *The Blair Years* p. 426

p.536 Dear sir — Wener, *Goodnight Steve McQueen* p. 130

p.537 Your home is suddenly — *Sun* 30 January 1998

p.537 Bank vaults — *Observer* 13 December 1998

p.537 the worst case scenario — *Financial Times* 29 August 1998

p.537 That pissed them off — Prescott op. cit. p. 236

p.537 the Queen had both — King, *House Music* p. 136

p.538 **I don't think** – Blair op. cit. p. 258

p.539 **everyone I know** – O'Farrell op. cit. p. 162

p.539 **There is no single** – *Sunday Times* 6 August 2000

p.539 **It was actually** – Benn, *Free at Last* p. 585

p.539 **Governments shouldn't run** – Campbell op. cit. p. 441

p.539 **Hindsight is** – *Guardian* 27 September 2000

p.539 **a symbol of New Labour** – *Times* 7 September 2000

p.540 **ghastly little cunt** – Price, *The Spin Doctor's Diary* p. 280

p.540 **lost the plot** – Spicer, *The Spicer Diaries* p. 411

p.540 **We must all work** – ibid. p. 431

p.540 **a decade of motorcades** – Clark, *The Tories* p. 494

p.540 **There's a bit** – Price op. cit. p. 69

p.540 **I know I am right** – Campbell op. cit. p. 454

p.540 **It is bizarre** – *Guardian* 17 July 2000

p.540 **It is remarkably shallow** – Mullin, *A View from the Foothills* p. 117

p.541 **a modern man** – Hernon, *The Blair Decade* p. 17

p.541 **David Miliband tried** – Blair op. cit. p. 255

p.541 **we have made medical care** – *New Statesman* 14 January 2000

p.541 **not a commitment** – Rawnsley op. cit. p. 339

p.542 **Respect for the old** – *Times* 8 June 2000

p.542 **What on earth** – Rawnsley op. cit. p. 372

p.542 **We made the point** – *Express* 8 June 2000

p.542 **there was no way** – Campbell op. cit. p. 458

p.542 **we simply had to hold** – ibid. p. 459

p.542 **It shook people** – Blunkett op. cit. p. 186

p.543 **I would not say** – *Express* 17 April 2000

p.543 **no mileage** – *Times* 17 April 2000

p.543 **wouldn't even dream** – *Times* 17 April 2000

p.544 **BLAIR, YOU ARE A CUNT** – Blair op. cit. p. 299

p.544 **I tell you now** – *Financial Times* 27 September 2000

p.544 **Prime ministers aren't meant** – Dobbs, *The Final Cut* p. 317

p.544 **that the country** – Young op. cit. p. 653

p.545 **I know it's only been** – *Independent* 7 July 2000

p.545 **Tried for three years** – Tim Rice & Andrew Lloyd p.545 Webber, 'Gethsemane' (Leeds Music, 1971)

p.545 **no one took** – Blair op. cit. p. 292

p.545 **We weren't far off** – Campbell, *The Blair Years* p. 471

p.546 **The public never realised** – Powell, *The New Machiavelli* p. 44

p.546 **It is ironic** – *Times* 12 September 2000

p.546 **The life of a nation** – *Times* 14 September 2000

p.546 **or picket lines** – Blunkett op. cit. p. 204

p.546 **These three men** – *Daily Mirror* 13 September 2000

p.547 **I felt that a Tory** – Blair op. cit. p. 294

p.547 **if this was Thatcher** – Campbell op. cit. p. 469

p.547 **Although I don't support** – Benn, *Free at Last* pp. 625–6

p.547 **After years of creeping** – Mullin, *A View from the Foothills* p. 127

p.547 **I had messed up** – Blair op. cit. p. 293

p.547 **He is much more** – Young op. cit. p. 705

p.547 **I should have realised** – Blair op. cit. p. 293

p.547 **politically it was tone-deaf** – Mandelson, *The Third Man* p. 305

p.548 **I don't know why** – Wyatt, *Journals Volume 2* pp. 76–7

p.548 **mystified as to why** – Young op. cit. p. 673

p.548 **The instinct to buy** – Powell op. cit. p. 43

p.548 **RIOT YOBS** – *Sun* 2 May 2000

p.548 **THIS WAS** – *Daily Mirror* 2 May 2000

p.549 **mindless thugs** – *Independent* 2 May 2000

p.550 **I'm not happy** – Oborne & Walters, *Alastair Campbell* p. 208

p.550 **politically motivated** – Routledge op. cit. p. 267

p.550 **At no time** – Cohen op. cit. p. 169

p.551 **pretty much alone** – Blair op. cit. p. 308

p.551 **a perceived cover-up** – Price op. cit. p. 291

p.551 **It's the end** – Oborne & Walters op. cit. p. 263

p.551 **The truth is** – Mullin op. cit. p. 157

p.551 **I spot Geoffrey Robinson** – Radice, *Diaries 1980–2001* p. 479

p.551 **It is an absolute tragedy** – Oborne & Walters op. cit. p. 265

p.551 **GOODBYE** – *Sun* 25 January 2001

p.551 **YOU WERE THE WEAKEST LINK** – *Daily Mirror* 25 January 2001

p.551 **There must be more** – Mandelson op. cit. p. 313

p.552 **the need for a Peter** – O'Farrell op. cit. p. 272

p.552 **Thank the Lord** – Blunkett op. cit. p. 20

p.553 **situated near** – Blair op. cit. p. 310

p.553 **We've slaughtered** – Mullin op. cit. p. 191

p.553 **PLAGUE** – *Daily Mirror* 22 February 2001

p.553 **NO MEAT** – *Express* 24 February 2001

p.553 **presidential style** – Blair op. cit. p. 311

p.553 **We have to stop him** – Powell op. cit. p. 117

p.553 **pretty much lost confidence** – Campbell op. cit. p. 514

p.554 **All this export** – Benn, *Free at Last* p. 658

p.554 **we had to play along** – ibid. p. 520

p.554 **ten years of success** – Routledge op. cit. p. 227

p.554 **independence for the Bank** – Price op. cit. p. 118

p.554 **If I die tomorrow** – Campbell op. cit. p. 606

p.555 **There's our part** – *Independent* 13 December 2000

p.555 **This government has done** – Young op. cit. pp. 648–9

p.555 **I suspect that what will** – Blunkett op. cit. p. 202

p.555 **many achievements** – Short, *An Honourable Deception?* p. 65

p.555 **a staggering 38,000** – Mullin op. cit. p. 230

p.556 **The Tories screwed up** – Mandelson op. cit. p. 306

p.556 **people felt** – Campbell op. cit. p. 453

p.557 **We will just** – Price op. cit. p. 285

p.557 **We mustn't let** – ibid. p. 343

p.557 **I may not hold** – Spicer op. cit. p. 451

p.557 **Slowly, and barely perceptibly** – Johnson, *Friends, Voters, Countrymen* p. 217

p.557 **We are saying** – ibid. p. 206

p.558 **It certainly didn't feel** – Prescott op. cit. p. 246

p.558 **extraordinarily funny** – Blair op. cit. p. 323

p.558 **those who liked it** – Blunkett op. cit. p. 261

p.558 **It's not my policy** – Walters, *Tory Wars* p. 196

p.558 **the best I could hope for** – Blair op. cit. p. 315

p.559 **One day the don't knows** – Shephard, *Shephard's Watch* p. 111

p.560 **I'm a fighter** – *Daily Mirror* 9 June 2001

p.560 **I am certainly** – Bremner op. cit. p. 32

p.561 **In a way it is** – O'Farrell op. cit. p. 338

p.561 **gratuitously offensive** – Rawnsley op. cit. p. 299

p.561 **fascination, admiration** – Nadler, *William Hague* p. 230

p.562 **I am liberal** – Walters op. cit. p. 109

p.562 **It was not that Tories** – *Sunday Telegraph* 15 April 2001

p.562 **Next time, I'll be running** – Williams, *Guilty Men* p. 225

p.562 **the physical incarnation** – Wheatcroft, *The Strange Death of Tory England* p. 253

p.563 **He is not in the papers** – *Daily Mail* 8 February 2002

p.563 **They thought Ken** – Iain Duncan Smith (pc)

Outro: Renewal

p.564 **In retrospect** – *Daily Telegraph* 3 October 2001

p.564 **There was one country** – *Guardian* 21 September 2001

p.564 **The events of September 11** – Short, *An Honourable Deception?* p. 107

p.564 **fuck off** – Oborne & Walters, *Alastair Campbell* p. 269

p.564 **In the aftermath** – Powell, *The New Machiavelli* p. 124

p.565 **It's now a very good day** – *Independent* 9 October 2001

p.565 **felt Jo was basically** – Campbell, *The Blair Years* p. 578

p.565 **We thought back then** – Blair, *A Journey* pp. 349–50

p.566 **I take that to mean** – Mullin, *A View from the Foothills* p. 224

p.567 **The British disease** – *Observer* 28 July 1974

p.567 **an horrific attack** – *Times* 3 July 1993

p.568 **At no time** – Price, *The Spin Doctor's Diary* p. 102

p.568 **the tolerant society** – *Sunday Times* 2 May 1999

p.568 **patriotism without bigotry** – Barnett, *This Time* p. 48

p.569 **Talk about Europe** – *Financial Times* 5 March 2001

p.569 **clear up Labour's asylum mess** – *Daily Mail* 5 March 2001

p.569 **Hague is marooned** – *Guardian* 15 December 2000

p.570 **chinless wonders** – *People* 12 March 2000

p.570 **I wonder what Our Lord** – Campbell op. cit. p. 126

p.571 **We need an attitude** – *Times* 8 April 2009

p.571 **He was always disappointing** – Routledge, *Mandy* p. 279

p.573 **We are all middle class** – *Sunday Times* 13 September 1998

p.573 **Labour has changed** – *Independent on Sunday* 6 September 1999

p.573 **We are citizens** – *Guardian* 29 September 1999

p.574 **There isn't such a thing** – Evans, *Thatcherism and British Politics* p. 165

Bibliography

Much of the material included in this book, as will be apparent from the references, is drawn from the newspapers and magazines of the time. The following works have also been consulted.

Non-Fiction

Note: Where a paperback or revised edition is shown, it indicates that any page references are to that edition.

Andrew Adonis & Stephen Pollard, *A Class Act: The Myth of Britain's Classless Society* (Hamish Hamilton, London, 1997 – pbk edn: Penguin, London, 1998)

Keith Allen, *Grow Up: An Autobiography* (Ebury Press, London, 2007 – pbk edn: 2008)

Magnus Anderson & Rebecca Levene, *Grand Thieves & Tomb Raiders: How British Video Games Conquered the World* (Aurum, London, 2012)

Paddy Ashdown, *The Ashdown Diaries: The Ashdown Diaries Volume I: 1988–1997* (Allen Lane, London, 2000 – pbk edn: Penguin, London, 2000)

Joe Ashton, *Red Rose Blues: The Story of a Good Labour Man* (Macmillan, London, 2000)

Clive Aslet, *Anyone for England? A Search for British Identity* (Little, Brown, London, 1997)

Kenneth Baker, *The Turbulent Years: My Life in Politics* (Faber & Faber, London, 1993)

Morwenna Banks & Amanda Swift, *The Joke's On Us: Women in Comedy from Music Hall to the Present Day* (Pandora, London, 1987)

Anthony Barnett, *This Time: Our Constitutional Revolution* (Vintage, London, 1997)

David Barnett, *Suede – Love and Poison: the Authorised Biography* (André Deutsch, London, 2003 – pbk edn: 2004)

Stephen Bayley, *Labour Camp: The Failure of Style Over Substance* (Pan Books, London, 1999)

Francis Beckett, *Gordon Brown: Past, Present and Future* (Haus, London, 2007)

Tony Benn (ed. Ruth Winstone), *The End of an Era: Diaries 1980–90* (Hutchinson, London, 1992 – pbk edn: Arrow, London, 1994)

Tony Benn (ed. Ruth Winstone), *Free at Last: Diaries 1991–2001* (Hutchinson, London, 2002 – pbk edn: Arrow, London, 2003)

Alan Bennett, *Writing Home* (Faber & Faber, London, 1994 – pbk edn: 1995)

Cherie Blair, *Speaking for Myself* (Little, Brown, London, 2008)

Tony Blair, *A Journey* (Hutchinson, London, 2010)

David Blunkett, *The Blunkett Tapes: My Life in the Bear Pit* (Bloomsbury, London, 2006)

Tom Bower, *Gordon Brown* (HarperCollins, London, 2004 – revised pbk edn: *Gordon Brown, Prime Minister*, Harper Perennial, 2007)

Duncan Brack & Iain Dale (eds), *Prime Minister Portillo . . . and Other Things that Never Happened* (Politico's, London, 2003)

Gyles Brandreth, *Breaking the Code: Westminster Diaries* (Weidenfeld & Nicolson, London, 1999 – pbk edn: Phoenix, London, 2000)

Rory Bremner, John Bird & John Fortune with Geoff Atkinson, *You Are Here: A Dossier* (Weidenfeld

& Nicolson, London, 2004)

Colin Brown, *Fighting Talk: The Biography of John Prescott* (Simon & Schuster, London, 1997)

Craig Brown, *The Tony Years* (Ebury Press, London, 2006)

Julie Burchill, *The Guardian Columns 1998–2000* (Orion, London, 2001)

Vince Cable, *Free Radical: A Memoir* (Atlantic, London, 2009 – pbk edn: 2010)

Alastair Campbell (ed. Richard Stott), *The Blair Years: Extracts from the Alastair Campbell Diaries* (Hutchinson, London, 2007)

Beatrix Campbell, *Diana, Princess of Wales: How Sexual Politics Shook the Monarchy* (Women's Press, London, 1998)

Denis Campbell, Pete May & Andrew Shields, *The Lad Done Bad: Sex, Sleaze and Scandal in English Football* (Penguin, London, 1996)

Brian Cathcart, *Were You Still Up for Portillo?* (Penguin, London, 1997)

Alan Clark, *Diaries* (Weidenfeld & Nicolson, London, 1993 – pbk edn: Orion, London, 1994)

Alan Clark, *The Tories: Conservatives and the Nation State 1922–1997* (Weidenfeld & Nicolson, London, 1998 – pbk edn: Phoenix, London, 1999)

Alan Clark (ed. Ion Trewin), *The Last Diaries: In and Out of the Wilderness* (Weidenfeld & Nicolson, London, 2002 – pbk edn: Phoenix, London, 2003)

Julian Clary, *A Young Man's Passage* (Ebury Press, London, 2005 – pbk edn: 2006)

Max Clifford & Angela Levin, *Max Clifford: Read All About It* (Virgin, London, 2006)

Nick Cohen, *Pretty Straight Guys* (Faber & Faber, London, 2003)

Nick Cohen, *What's Left: How the Left Lost Its Way* (Fourth Estate, London, 2007 – pbk edn: Harper Perennial, London, 2007)

Nik Cohn, *Yes We Have No: Adventures in Other England* (Secker & Warburg, London, 1999)

John Cole, *As It Seemed To Me: Political Memoirs* (Weidenfeld & Nicolson, London, 1995 – revised pbk edn: Phoenix, London, 1996)

Hal Colebatch, *Blair's Britain: British Culture Wars and New Labour* (Claridge Press, London, 1999)

Julian Critchley & Morrison Halcrow, *Collapse of Stout Party: The Decline and Fall of the Tories* (Victor Gollancz, London, 1997 – Indigo, London, 1998)

Edwina Currie, *Diaries 1987–1992* (Little Brown, London, 2002 – pbk edn: Time Warner, London, 2003)

Edwina Currie, *Diaries Volume II: 1992–1997* (Biteback Publishing, London, 2012)

Iain Dale, *The Unofficial Book of Political Lists* (Robson Books, London, 1997)

Theodore Dalrymple, *If Symptoms Persist* (André Deutsch, London, 1994)

Nick Danziger, *Danziger's Britain: A Journey to the Edge* (HarperCollins, London, 1996)

John Diamond, *Snake Oil and Other Preoccupations* (Vintage, London, 2001)

G.M.F. Drower, *Neil Kinnock: The Path to Leadership* (Weidenfeld & Nicolson, London, 1984)

Niall Edworthy, *The Second Most Important Job in the Country* (Virgin, London, 2000)

Larry Elliott & Dan Atkinson, *The Age of Insecurity* (Verso, London, 1998)

Matthew Engel & Ian Morrison, *The Sportspages Almanac 1991: The Complete Sporting Factbook* (Simon & Schuster, London, 1990)

Matthew Engel & Ian Morrison, *The Sportspages Almanac 1992: The Complete Sporting Factbook* (Simon & Schuster, London, 1991)

Brendan Evans, *Thatcherism and British Politics 1975–1999* (Sutton Publishing, Gloucestershire, 1999)

Nigel Farage, *Flying Free* (Biteback Publishing, London, 2010)

Gillian Freeman, *The Undergrowth of Literature* (Thomas Nelson & Sons, London, 1967 – pbk edn: Panther, London, 1969)

Teresa Gorman with Heather Kirby, *The Bastards: Dirty Tricks and the Challenge to Europe* (Pan, London, 1993)

Teresa Gorman, *No, Prime Minister!* (John Blake, London, 2001)

Bryan Gould, *Goodbye to All That* (Macmillan, London, 1995)

Jonathan Green, *Days in the Life: Voices from the English Underground 1961–1971* (William Heinemann, London, 1988 – pbk edn: Pimlico, London, 1998)

Peter Hain, *Outside In* (Biteback, London, 2012)

Luke Haines, *Bad Vibes: Britpop and My Part in Its Downfall* (William Heinemann, London, 2009)

John Harris, *The Last Party: Britpop, Blair and the Demise of English Rock* (Fourth Estate, London, 2003 – pbk edn: Harper Perennial, London, 2004)

Nick Harris, *The Foreign Revolution: How Overseas Footballers Changed the English Game* (Aurum, London, 2006 – originally published as *England Their England*, Pitch, London, 2003)

Stephen Haseler, *The End of the House of Windsor* (I.B. Tauris, London, 1993)

Ian Hernon, *The Blair Decade* (Politico's, London, 2007)

Michael Heseltine, *Life in the Jungle: My Autobiography* (Hodder & Stoughton, London, 2000)

Robert Hewison, *Culture and Consensus: England, Art and Politics since 1940* (Methuen, London, 1995 – rev pbk edn: 1997)

Douglas Hurd, *Memoirs* (Little, Brown, London, 2003)

Will Hutton, *The State We're In* (Jonathan Cape, London, 1995 – rev pbk edn: Vintage, London, 1996)

Armando Iannucci, *Facts and Fancies* (Michael Joseph, London, 1997)

Eddie Izzard with David Quantick & Steve Double, *Dress to Kill* (Virgin, London, 1998 – pbk edn: 2000)

Alex James, *A Bit of a Blur: The Autobiography* (Little, Brown, London, 2007)

Stuart Jeffries, *Mrs Slocombe's Pussy: Growing Up in Front of the Telly* (Flamingo, London, 2000 – pbk edn: 2001)

Simon Jenkins, *Thatcher and Sons: A Revolution in Three Acts* (Allen Lane, London, 2006 – rev pbk edn: Penguin, London, 2007

Martin Johnes, *Wales Since 1939* (Manchester University Press, Manchester, 2012)

Boris Johnson, *Friends, Voters, Countrymen: Jottings on the Stump* (HarperCollins, London, 2001)

Frank Johnson (ed. Virginia Fraser), *Best Seat in the House: The Wit and Parliamentary Chronicles of Frank Johnson* (JR Books, London, 2009)

Janet Jones, *Labour of Love: The 'Partly-Political' Diary of a Cabinet Minister's Wife* (Politico's, London, 1999)

Nicholas Jones, *Campaign 1997: How the General Election Was Won and Lost* (Indigo, London, 1997)

Penny Junor, *The Major Enigma* (Michael Joseph, London, 1993)

Penny Junor, *Charles: Victim or Villain?* (HarperCollins, London, 1998)

John Kampfner, *Blair's Wars* (Free Press, London, 2003 – pbk edn: 2004)

Jack Kibble-White & Steve Williams, *The Encyclopaedia of Classic Saturday Night Telly* (Allison & Busby, 2007 – pbk edn: 2008)

Oona King, *House Music: The Oona King Diaries* (Bloomsbury, London, 2007)

Nicholas Kochan, *Ann Widdecombe: Right from the Beginning* (Politico's, London, 2000)

Stewart Lee, *How I Escaped My Certain Fate: The Life and Deaths of a Stand-Up Comedian* (Faber & Faber, London, 2010)

Mark Lewisohn, *Radio Times Guide to TV Comedy* (BBC Worldwide, London, 1998)

Richard Lindley, *Panorama: Fifty Years of Pride and Paranoia* (Politico's, London, 2002)

Ken Livingstone, *Livingstone's Labour: A Programme for the Nineties* (Unwin Hyman, London, 1989)

Donald MacIntyre, *Mandelson: The Biography* (HarperCollins, London, 1999)

David McKittrick & David McVea, *Making Sense of the Troubles* (Blackstaff Press, Belfast, 2000 – revised edn: Penguin, London, 2001)

Andy McSmith, *Faces of Labour: The Inside Story* (Verso, London, 1996)

Stuart Maconie, *3862 Days* (Virgin, London, 1999)

John Major, *The Autobiography* (HarperCollins, London, 1999 – pbk edn: 2000)

Peter Mandelson, *The Third Man: Life at the Heart of New Labour* (Harper Press, London, 2010)

Peter Mandelson & Roger Liddle, *The Blair Revolution* (Faber & Faber, London, 1996)

Christopher Meyer, *DC Confidential: The Controversial Memoirs of Britain's Ambassador to the U.S. at the Time of 9/11 and the Iraq War* (Weidenfeld & Nicolson, London, 2005)

Mick Middles, *Manic Street Preachers: A Biography* (Omnibus, London, 1999)

Bob Monkhouse, *Over the Limit: My Secret Diaries 1993–8* (Century, London, 1998)

Gregor Muir, *Lucky Kunst: The Rise and Fall of Young British Art* (Aurum, London, 2009 – pbk edn: 2010)

Chris Mullin (ed. Ruth Winstone), *A View from the Foothills: The Diaries of Chris Mullin* (Profile, London, 2009 – pbk edn: 2010)

Jo-Anne Nadler, *William Hague: In His Own Right* (Politico's, London, 2000)

James Naughtie, *The Rivals: The Intimate Story of a Political Marriage* (Fourth Estate, London, 2001 – rev pbk edn: 2002)

John Nott, *Mr Wonderful Takes a Cruise: The Adventures of an Old Age Pensioner* (Ebury Press, London, 2004)

Lucy O'Brien, *She Bop II* (originally published as *She Bop*, Penguin, London, 1995 – new edn: Continuum, London, 2002)

John O'Farrell, *Things Can Only Get Better: Eighteen Miserable Years in the Life of a Labour Supporter* (Doubleday, London, 1998 – pbk edn: Black Swan, London, 1999)

John O'Farrell, *Global Village Idiot: Dispatches from the Turn of a Century* (Doubleday, London, 2001 – pbk edn: Black Swan, London, 2002)

Peter Oborne, *The Triumph of the Political Class* (Simon & Schuster, London, 2007 – pbk edn: Pocket Books, London, 2008)

Peter Oborne & Simon Walters, *Alastair Campbell* (Aurum, London, 2004)

John Osborne, *Damn You, England: Collected Prose* (Faber & Faber, London, 1994 – pbk edn: 1999)

Matthew Parris, *Great Parliamentary Scandals: Four Centuries of Calumny, Smear and Innuendo* (Robson Books, London, 1995 – rev pbk edn: 1997)

Matthew Parris, *Off-Message: New Labour, New Sketches* (Robson, London, 2001)

Tony Parsons, *Big Mouth Strikes Again: A Further Collection of Two-Fisted Journalism* (André Deutsch, London, 1998 – pbk edn: 1999)

Anna Pasternak, *Princess in Love* (Bloomsbury, London, 1994)

Chris Patten, *Not Quite the Diplomat: Home Truths about World Affairs* (Allen Lane, London, 2005 – pbk edn: Penguin, London, 2006)

John Patten, *Things to Come: The Tories in the 21st Century* (Sinclair-Stevenson, London, 1995)

Jeremy Paxman, *The English: A Portrait of a People* (Michael Joseph, London, 1998 – pbk edn: Penguin, London, 1999)

Edward Pearce, *The Senate of Lilliput* (Faber & Faber, London, 1983)

Peter Gerard Pearse & Nigel Matheson, *Ken Livingstone, or The End of Civilization as We Know It: A Selection of Quotes, Quips and Quirks* (Proteus Books, London, 1982)

Harry Pearson, *The Far Corner: A Mazy Dribble through North-East Football* (Little, Brown, London, 1994 – pbk edn: Warner, London, 1996)

Melanie Phillips, *All Must Have Prizes* (Little, Brown, London, 1996 – rev pbk edn: Warner, London, 1998)

Jonathan Powell, *The New Machiavelli: How to Wield Power in the Modern World* (Bodley Head, London, 2010 – pbk edn: Vintage, London, 2011)

John Prescott with Hunter Davies, *Prezza: My Story* (Headline Review, London, 2008 – pbk edn: *Docks to Downing Street: My Story*, 2009)

Lance Price, *The Spin Doctor's Diary: Inside Number 10 with New Labour* (Hodder & Stoughton, London, 2005)

Sonia Purnell, *Just Boris: The Irresistible Rise of a Political Celebrity* (Aurum, London, 2011)

Giles Radice, *Diaries 1980–2001: From Political Disaster to Election Triumph* (Weidenfeld & Nicolson, London, 2004)

Mac Randall, *Exit Music: The Radiohead Story* (Omnibus, London, 2000)

Amy Raphael, *Never Mind the Bollocks: Women Rewrite Rock* (Virago, London, 1995)

Andrew Rawnsley, *Servants of the People: The Inside Story of New Labour* (Hamish Hamilton, London, 2000)

John Redwood, *The Death of Britain? The UK's Constitutional Crisis* (Macmillan, London, 1999)

Mark Reynolds (compiler), *The Wrong Kind of Shirts 2: More Curious Quips and Wild Accusations from the Soccer World* (Fourth Estate, London, 1997)

Mark Reynolds (compiler), *The Wrong Kind of Shirts '99* (Fourth Estate, London, 1999)

Steve Richards (ed.), *Preparing for Power: New Statesman Interviews 1996–1997* (New Statesman Books, London 1997)

Steve Richards, *Whatever It Takes: The Real Story of Gordon Brown and New Labour* (Fourth Estate, London, 2010)

Paul Routledge, *Gordon Brown: The Biography* (Simon & Schuster, London, 1998 – rev pbk edn: Pocket Books, London, 1998)

Paul Routledge, *Mandy: The Unauthorised Biography of Peter Mandelson* (Simon & Schuster, London, 1999)

Anthony Sampson, *The Changing Anatomy of Britain* (Hodder & Stoughton, London, 1982)

Jon Savage, *Time Travel – From the Sex Pistols to Nirvana: Pop, Media and Sexuality, 1977–96* (Chatto & Windus, London, 1996 – pbk edn: Vintage, London, 1997)

Derek Scott, *Off Whitehall: A View from Downing Street by Tony Blair's Adviser* (I.B. Tauris, London, 2004)

Anthony Seldon (ed.), *How Tory Governments Fall: The Tory Party in Power since 1783* (Fontana Press, London, 1996)

Anthony Seldon with Chris Ballinger, Daniel Collings & Peter Snowdon, *Blair* (Free Press, London, 2004 – pbk edn: 2005)

Gillian Shephard, *Shephard's Watch: Illusions of Power in British Politics* (Politico's, London, 2000)

Robert Shepherd, *Enoch Powell: A Biography* (Hutchinson, London, 1996 – pbk edn: Pimlico, London, 1997)

Peter Shore, *Leading the Left* (Weidenfeld & Nicolson, London, 1993)

Clare Short, *An Honourable Deception? New Labour, Iraq and the Misuse of Power* (Free Press, London, 2004)

Linda Smith (ed. Warren Lakin & Ian Parsons), *I Think the Nurses Are Stealing My Clothes: The Very Best of Linda Smith* (Hodder & Stoughton, London, 2006)

Jon Sopel, *Tony Blair: The Moderniser* (Michael Joseph, London, 1995)

Michael Spicer, *The Spicer Diaries* (Biteback, London, 2012)

Mark Steel, *Reasons to Be Cheerful: From Punk to New Labour through the Eyes of a Dedicated Troublemaker* (Scribner, London, 2001 – pbk edn: 2002)

Philip Stephens, *Tony Blair: The Price of Leadership* (Penguin, New York, 2004 – rev pbk edn: Politico's, London, 2004)

Richard Strange, *Strange: Punks and Drunks and Flicks and Kicks – the Memoirs of Richard Strange* (André Deutsch, London, 2002)

Jack Straw, *Last Man Standing: Memoirs of a Political Survivor* (Macmillan, London, 2012)

Mark Stuart, *Douglas Hurd: The Public Servant* (Mainstream, Edinburgh, 1998)

John Sutherland, *Offensive Literature: Decensorship in Britain 1960–1982* (Junction Books, London, 1982)

John Sutherland, *Reading the Decades: Fifty Years of the Nation's Bestselling Books* (BBC Worldwide, London, 2002)

Norman Tebbit, *Upwardly Mobile* (Weidenfeld & Nicolson, London, 1988)

Margaret Thatcher, *The Downing Street Years* (HarperCollins, London, 1993)

Margaret Thatcher, *The Path to Power* (HarperCollins, London, 1995)

Ben Thompson, *Sunshine on Putty: The Golden Age of British Comedy from Vic Reeves to The Office* (Fourth Estate, London, 2004 – pbk edn: HarperCollins, London, 2004)

Alwyn W. Turner, *Rejoice! Rejoice! Britain in the 1980s* (Aurum Press, London, 2010)

Simon Walters, *Tory Wars: conservatives in crisis* (Politico's, London, 2001)

Richard Weight, *Patriots: National Identity in Britain 1940–2000* (Macmillan, London, 2002 – rev pbk edn: Pan, London, 2003)

Louise Wener, *Different for Girls: My True-Life Adventures in Pop* (Ebury, London, 2010)

Geoffrey Wheatcroft, *The Strange Death of Tory England* (Allen Lane, London, 2005 – pbk edn: Penguin, London, 2005)

Hywel Williams, *Guilty Men: Conservative Decline and Fall 1992–1997* (Aurum, London, 1998)

A.N. Wilson, *The Rise and Fall of the House of Windsor* (Sinclair-Stevenson, London, 1993)

Woodrow Wyatt (ed. Sarah Curtis), *The Journals of Woodrow Wyatt Volume Two* (Macmillan, London, 1999)

Hugo Young, *This Blessed Plot: Britain and Europe from Churchill to Blair* (Macmillan, London, 1998)

Hugo Young (ed. Ion Trewin), *The Hugo Young Papers: Thirty Years of British Politics – Off the Record* (Allen Lane, London, 2008)

Fiction

Note: Where a paperback edition is shown, it indicates that any page references are to that edition.

David Baddiel, *Time for Bed* (Little, Brown, London, 1996)

David Baddiel, *Whatever Loves Means* (Little, Brown, London, 2000)

John Bird & John Fortune, *The Long Johns* (Hutchinson, London, 1996)

Terence Blacker, *The Fame Hotel* (Bloomsbury, London, 1992 – pbk edn: Black Swan, London, 1993)

Christopher Brookmyre, *Quite Ugly One Morning* (Little, Brown, London, 1996 – pbk edn: Abacus, London, 1997)

Edwina Currie, *A Parliamentary Affair* (Hodder & Stoughton, London, 1994 – pbk edn: 1994)

Colin Dexter, *Death Is Now My Neighbour* (Macmillan, London, 1996 – pbk edn: Pan, London, 1997)

Michael Dobbs, *The Final Cut* (HarperCollins, London, 1995)

Jenny Eclair, *Camberwell Beauty* (Little, Brown, London, 2000 – pbk edn: Warner, London, 2001)

Ben Elton, *Inconceivable* (Bantam Press, London, 1999 – pbk edn: Black Swan, London, 2000)

Helen Fielding, *Bridget Jones's Diary* (Picador, London, 1996 – pbk edn: 1997)

Helen Fielding, *Bridget Jones: The Edge of Reason* (Picador, London, 1999)

E.M. Forster, *Maurice* (Edward Arnold, London, 1971 – pbk edn: Penguin, Harmondsworth, 1972)

Reg Gadney, *Just When We Are Safest* (Faber & Faber, London, 1995)

Jane Green, *Straight Talking* (Mandarin, London, 1997)

Jeremy Hardy, *Jeremy Hardy Speaks to the Nation* (Methuen, London, 1993)

Tristan Hawkins, *The Anarchist* (Flamingo, London, 1996)

Reginald Hill, *On Beulah Height* (HarperCollins, London, 1998 – pbk edn: 1999)

Susan Hill, *Breaking Glass* (Star, London, 1980)

Ian Hislop (ed.), *The Private Eye Annual 1997* (Private Eye, London, 1997)

Nick Hornby, *High Fidelity* (Victor Gollancz, London, 1995 – pbk edn: Indigo, London, 2000)

Nick Hornby, *About a Boy* (Victor Gollancz, London, 1998 – pbk edn: Indigo, London, 1999)

David Lodge, *Therapy* (Martin Secker & Warburg, London, 1995)

Peter Lovesey, *Upon a Dark Night* (Little, Brown, London, 1997 – pbk edn: Time Warner, London, 2003)

John O'Farrell, *The Best a Man Can Get* (Doubleday, London, 2000)

Michael Palin, *Hemingway's Chair* (Methuen, London, 1995 – pbk edn: Arrow, London, 1996)

Tony Parsons, *Man and Boy* (HarperCollins, London, 1999 – pbk edn: 2000)

Nigel Planer, *The Right Man* (Hutchinson, London, 1998)

Stephen Rawlings, *Jane and Her Master* (Silver Moon, London, 1996)

Sue Townsend, *The Queen and I* (Methuen, London, 1992 – pbk edn: Mandarin, London, 1993)

Sue Townsend, *Adrian Mole: The Cappuccino Years* (Michael Joseph, London, 1999 – pbk edn: Penguin, London, 2000)

Louise Wener, *Goodnight Steve McQueen* (Hodder & Stoughton, London, 2002 – pbk edn: 2003)

Nigel West, *Murder in the Commons* (Macmillan, London, 1992 – pbk edn: Headline, London, 1993)

Nigel Williams, *East of Wimbledon* (Faber & Faber, London, 1993 – pbk edn: 1994)

A.N. Wilson, *The Vicar of Sorrows* (Sinclair-Stevenson, London, 1993)

Films and Television Programmes

Note: Films are listed by director. TV programmes are credited to their creators, though other writers may also have been involved in the series.

Caroline Aherne, *The Mrs Merton Show* (Granada Television, 1994–8)

Michael Aitkens, *Waiting for God* (BBC Television, 1990–4)

Kevin Allen, *Twin Town* (Polygram Filmed Entertainment, 1997)

Alexander Armstrong & Ben Miller, *Armstrong and Miller* (Absolutely Productions, 1997–2001)

David Attwood, *Wild West* (Channel 4 Films, 1992)

Richard Bates, *The Darling Buds of May* (Yorkshire Television, 1991–3)

M.C. Beaton, *Hamish Macbeth* (BBC Scotland, 1995–7)

Antonia Bird, *Face* (BBC Films, 1997)

Danny Boyle, *Shallow Grave* (Channel 4 Films, 1994)

Danny Boyle, *Trainspotting* (PolyGram, 1996)

Jo Brand, *Through the Cakehole* (Channel 4 Television, 1993–6)

Craig Brown, *Norman Ormal: A Very Political Turtle* (Tiger Aspect Productions, 1998)

Peter Cattaneo, *The Full Monty* (Channel 4 Films, 1997)
Gurinder Chadha, *Bhaji on the Beach* (Channel 4 Films, 1993)
Ted Childs, *Kavanagh QC* (1995–2001)
Roy Clarke, *Last of the Summer Wine* (BBC Television, 1973–2010)
Roy Clarke, *Keeping Up Appearances* (BBC Television, 1990–5)
Stephen Daldry, *Billy Elliot* (BBC Films/Tiger Aspect, 2000)
Andrew Davies & Bernadette Davies, *Game On* (Hat Trick Productions, 1995–8)
Jack Dee, *The Jack Dee Show* (Open Mike Productions, 1992–4)
Jack Dee, *Jack Dee Live at the Duke of York's Theatre* (Open Mike Productions, 1992)
Colin Dexter, *Inspector Morse* (Zenith Productions, 1987–2000)
Brian Eastman & Stuart Doughty, *Bugs* (Carnival Films, 1995–9)
Richard Fegen & Andrew Norris, *The Brittas Empire* (BBC Television, 1991–7)
Tim Firth, *All Quiet on the Preston Front* (BBC Television, 1994–7)
Peter Flannery, *Our Friends in the North* (BBC Television, 1996)
Lucy Gannon, *Hope and Glory* (BBC Television, 1999–2000)
Mel Gibson, *Braveheart* (Icon Productions, 1995)
Caroline Graham, *Midsomer Murders* (ITV, 1997–)
Andy Hamilton & Guy Jenkin, *Drop the Dead Donkey* (Channel 4 Television, 1990–8)
Charlie Hanson, *Harry Hill: First Class Scamp* (1998)
Have I Got News for You (Hat Trick Productions, 1990–)
Mark Herman, *Brassed Off* (Channel 4 Films/Miramax, 1996)
Nicholas Hytner, *The Madness of King George* (Channel 4 Films, 1994)
Armando Iannucci, *The Saturday Night Armistice* (BBC Television, 1995), *The Friday Night Armistice*
   (1996–8), *The Election Night Armistice* (1997)
Armando Iannucci, *The Armando Iannucci Shows* (Talkback Productions, 2001)
Amy Jenkins, *This Life* (World Productions, 1996–7)
Shekhar Kapur, *Elizabeth* (Working Title, 1998)
Peter Kay, *That Peter Kay Thing* (Open Mike Productions, 1999)
Paul Kaye, *Anyone for Pennis?* (BBC Television, 1995), *Very Important Pennis* (1996–7), *Dennis Pennis RIP*
   (1997)
Patrick Keiller, *London* (BFI, 1992)
Chris Langham, Guy Jenkin, Sean Hardie & John Cleese, *Look at the State We're In!* (Video Arts/
   Sisyphus, 1995)
Linda La Plante, *Prime Suspect* (Granada Television, 1991–2006)
Mike Leigh, *Naked* (Thin Man Films, 1993)
Ken Loach, *Ladybird, Ladybird* (Channel 4 Films, 1994)
Ken Loach, *My Name Is Joe* (Channel 4 Films, 1998)
Jimmy McGovern, *Cracker* (Granada Television, 1993–6)
Patrick Marber, Steve Coogan & Armando Iannucci, *Knowing Me, Knowing You with Alan Partridge*
   (Talkback Productions, 1994)
Tony Marchant, *Holding On* (BBC Television, 1997)
Laurence Marks & Maurice Gran, *The New Statesman* (Yorkshire Television, 1987–94)
Laurence Marks & Maurice Gran, *Goodnight Sweetheart* (BBC Television, 1993–9)
Paula Milne, *The Politician's Wife* (Producers Films, 1995)
Peter Moffat, *North Square* (Channel 4 Television, 2000–1)
Chris Morris, *Brass Eye* (Channel 4 Television, 1997–2001)
Chris Morris & Armando Iannucci, *The Day Today* (BBC Television, 1994)
John Morton, *People Like Us* (BBC Television, 1999–2000)
Mike Newell, *Four Weddings and a Funeral* (PolyGram Filmed Entertainment, 1994)
G.F. Newman, *Judge John Deed* (BBC Television, 2001–7)
Andrew Norriss & Richard Fegen, *The Brittas Empire* (BBC Television, 1993–2001)
Simon Nye, *Men Behaving Badly* (Hartswood Films, 1992–8)
Damien O'Donnell, *East Is East* (Channel 4 Films, 1999)

Gary Oldman, *Nil by Mouth* (Europa, 1997)

Andrew Payne, *Pie in the Sky* (BBC Television, 1994–7)

David Renwick, *One Foot in the Grave* (BBC Television, 1990–2000)

David Renwick, *Jonathan Creek* (BBC Television, 1997–)

Tony Robinson, *Maid Marian and Her Merry Men* (BBC Television, 1989–94)

Jennifer Saunders, *Absolutely Fabulous* (BBC Television, 1992–)

Paul Whitehouse & Charlie Higson, *The Fast Show* (BBC Television, 1994–2000)

J.C. Wilsher, *Between the Lines* (World Productions, 1992–4)

R.D. Wingfield, *A Touch of Frost* (Yorkshire Television, 1992–2010)

Victoria Wood, *Dinnerladies* (BBC Television, 1998–2000)

Acknowledgements

Primarily my thanks go to those who were kind enough to speak with me about the period and to help on this project, including Dan Atkinson, Bill Cash, Edwina Currie, Elizabeth Coldwell, Peter Darvill-Evans, Iain Duncan Smith, John Flaxman, Hugo Frey, Tristan Garel-Jones, Bryan Gould, Luke Haines, Harvey Hinsley, Martin Johnes, Millree Hughes, Rebecca Levene, Rhodri Morgan, Felicity Page, Giles Radice, John Redwood and Norman Tebbit, as well as those who asked not to be mentioned by name.

I'm enormously grateful to Aurum for their continuing support and encouragement. Amongst those who have been involved are Jessica Axe, Graham Coster, David Graham, Sam Shone, Melissa Smith and Lucy Warburton.

Chris Shamwana designed a beautiful jacket, Steve Gove was a terrific text editor and, above all, Sam Harrison has been the best editor I've worked with: he's not entirely responsible for everything here, but I blame him for quite a lot of it.

As ever, my thanks go to Thamasin Marsh for putting up with this over a protracted period of time. The next one will be shorter, I promise.

This book is dedicated to Brian Freeborn and Richard Pain, who separately provided me with gainful employment during the 1990s and who remain friends.

Chapter Titles

The quotes that form part of the chapter titles come from the following songs: Manic Street Preachers, 'From Despair to Where'; Jesus Jones, 'The Devil You Know'; Saint Etienne, 'You're in a Bad Way'; Denim, 'Here Is My Song for Europe'; Oasis, 'Cigarettes and Alcohol'; Suede, 'New Generation'; Supergrass, 'Caught by the Fuzz'; Radiohead, 'Creep'; Chumbawamba, 'Tubthumping'; D:Ream, 'Things Can Only Get Better'; Blur, 'Sunday, Sunday'; Gene, 'As Good as It Gets'; Placebo, 'Nancy Boy'; Catatonia, 'Storm the Palace'; Supernaturals, 'Smile'; Teenage Fanclub, 'I Don't Want Control of You'; Echobelly, 'I Can't Imagine the World Without Me'; Spice Girls, 'Wannabe'; Pulp, 'Disco 2000'; Auteurs, 'The Rubettes'.

The section titles are, as ever, taken from songs by David Bowie.

Index